DATE DUE

FE 4 '08			
JE 2 '09			

DEMCO 38-296

Women in Modern American Politics

Women in Modern American Politics

A Bibliography 1900–1995

Elizabeth M. Cox

Congressional Quarterly Inc.
Washington, D.C.

To Georgette Castelle VanSickle

Library of Congress Cataloging-in-Publication Data

Cox, Elizabeth, 1939–
    Women in modern American politics : a bibliography, 1900–1995 / Elizabeth M. Cox
        p.   cm.
    ISBN 1-56802-133-X
    1. Women in politics — United States — History — 20th century — Bibliography.   I. Title
    Z7963.P64C69   1996
    [HQ1236.5.U6]
    016.30542 — dc20   96-38898

Contents

Contents

Contents

Contents

Contents

Foreword

As the twentieth century comes to a close and we assess the changes that it has brought, the status of women occupies a prominent place. At the end of the last century politics was a particularly masculine domain. Women had equal suffrage with men in only four of the forty-five states and partial suffrage in another twenty-six. Women were just beginning to be elected to public office, usually to school boards and sometimes to municipal offices in small towns. The first three women elected to a state legislature were in Colorado in 1894. Within the political parties, women found warmer welcome in insurgent parties—populist, prohibitionist, socialist—but they were also digging toeholds in the major parties, which found women to be particularly effective canvassers. Three women attended the Republican National Convention as alternates in 1892; each of the major parties had one woman delegate in 1900. Throughout the 1890s, even in states where they could not vote, women organized political clubs—some of which survived the campaign season. They also spoke and wrote campaign literature, urging men and the occasional voting woman to support their candidates.

By 1996 women held 20 percent of all state legislative offices, 10 percent of congressional seats, and 25 percent of statewide elective offices. The Democratic party requires that half of all national party bodies and convention delegations be women; the Republican party requires equal division only on convention committees, and females average about one-third of the convention delegates. Most state parties require equal division on some party committees, and almost half require it on all. Minor parties are not as important as they were a century ago, but women play more prominent roles within them. Women comprise 53 percent of registered voters and usually vote at slightly higher rates than men. The "gender gap" in voting patterns has forced politicians of both sexes and both major parties to pay attention to women in ways only dreamed of a century ago. While women are a long way from possessing equal political power, they are no longer on the outside looking in.

The nearly 6,000 listings in this bibliography document some, though not all, of this progress. They also tell their own story, a parallel account to that of women's entries into politics throughout this century. Women's gains are incremental most of the time, but during periods of social turmoil, especially when women are organizing to improve their status, they make great advances. If one plots the entries in this bibliography by year, allowing for some anomalies, the early 1920s show greatly increased interest in women and politics. After universal suffrage was granted, women wanted to do more than just vote for good men. Everyone wondered what women would do with their vote and how they would fare in electoral politics. Articles were especially frequent during election years. By the late 1920s, just as the woman's vote was increasing, interest in women and politics was decreasing; annual entries in this bibliography declined significantly and stayed down for almost forty years. When the contemporary feminist movement emerged in the late 1960s, it stimulated interest and political activity by women. Women's advances in political office increased sharply from about 1970 on; the articles on women and politics reflect these gains. These articles cover not just what contemporary women are doing but also what their foremothers did decades ago. Women's political history, which was buried and ignored for so long, is at last beginning to be explored and inscribed. Thus this bibliography on women and politics is just a beginning; there is much more for women to do in politics and there are many gaps in women's history to be filled in by future scholars. Use this bibliography to find out not only what is known but also what is lacking.

Jo Freeman

Preface

This bibliography is the result of a lengthy process. In 1994 Jeanne Ferris, an acquisitions editor at Congressional Quarterly Books, asked me to compile a bibliography on women in modern politics in the United States. She, in turn, had been urged to do the same by Dr. Jo Freeman, who had been researching and writing on the subject since the late 1960s. Although I had not yet completed my book on the history of women state legislators, I agreed to take on what became a massive project, with Dr. Freeman as editorial advisor.

The initial entries—about one-third of the 5,985 listings—came from Dr. Freeman's bibliography on women and politics, my own research on women voters, and my eight years of work identifying 6,000 women state legislators. Most of the rest came from many months of intensive research at the Library of Congress; the libraries of George Washington University, Howard University, and American University; and the Martin Luther King, Jr., Memorial Public Library in Washington, D.C.

The Internet opened the gates of libraries across the country so that I could surf for additional sources. My son, Benjamin Lee Cox, surveyed a wide range of gophers and home pages and advised me as I launched my own searches. I subscribed to the H-Women network and followed international scholars' queries and answers on the subject of U.S. women in history. Dr. Freeman monitored several bulletin boards and forwarded new items uncovered in her current research project on women and political parties. I used the electronic resources available at the Library of Congress, accessing World Cat, UREKA, and a variety of materials on CD-ROM—especially Dissertation Abstracts and American History and Life.

Many other people helped me along the way. Fenton Martin, librarian at the Political Science Research Collection at Indiana University, graciously answered my questions, offered helpful suggestions, and provided superb assistance in preparation of the subject index. Doris Baker, a freelance copyeditor for Congressional Quarterly Books, helped me create a more uniform and useful document. Dave Goldman of Research Software Design answered numerous questions and helped me use his PAPYRUS program to create this book. I am most appreciative for the patience, wise counsel, and recommendations of Jo Freeman. Thanks also to Dave Tarr and Talia Greenberg of Congressional Quarterly Books for their assistance and persistence in producing a book from the manuscript.

Two projects for the seventy-fifth anniversary of woman suffrage identified some exciting new sources; I am grateful to Lynda Robb, director of the Center for Legislative Archives at the National Archives, and Ruth Pollack, producer of the *One Woman, One Vote* film of the Education Film Center, for sharing them with me. Suzanne Marilley, author of *Woman Suffrage and the Origin of Liberal Feminism in the United States, 1820–1920*, and Kristi Andersen, author of *After Suffrage: Women in Partisan and Electoral Politics Before the New Deal*, sent me the bibliographies of their forthcoming books. Liette Gidlow of Cornell University and Diane Michele of the University of New Mexico, Albuquerque, shared their working dissertation bibliographies with me. Others who helped with research suggestions and bibliographical lists include Amelia Fry, Mary Beth Koechlin, Mary Martha Thomas, Ilene Cornwell, and Suzanne O'Day Schenken.

I owe much to my friends and colleagues—especially Georgette Castelle VanSickle—for their parts in my own education and learning experiences, and to my family, especially my uncle Charles David Williams, who began reading to his young niece her favorite story by insisting that he start at the *beginning* of the book because the title page was *very important*. I still feel guilty if I neglect to follow his advice. I hope that everyone else will read these first pages, for they are essential parts of a book. Thanks also to my husband, Dave, who generously gave his time, technical assistance, and advice.

Scope

This book begins with selections from magazines, journals, and books in 1900, the first year of the twentieth century. Writings, both popular and scholarly, introduced the "new woman" and the "year of the woman" so frequently that we will have to coin new descriptive terms in the twenty-first century. I have included political activities of women in their homes, churches, workplaces, and social and political movements—as well as in electoral and partisan politics.

Entries are listed only once, by most recent edition. Previous editions are included in parentheses. Listings are from magazines; journals; books; theses; and papers delivered at professional conferences, including the American Political Science Association (APSA) and Southern Association of Women Historians (SAWHC). No newspaper articles have been included.

Although I tried to validate all entries and code them in appropriate categories, there may be mistakes and omissions for which I apologize and about which I would appreciate being informed.

Resources

After surveying several publications of this century, I chose to follow two publications: the *Woman's Journal*, from 1900 to 1931, and *Independent Woman*, from 1919 to 1995. These journals, more than any others, published articles about women in politics, and between them spanned the ninety-five years covered in this book. The *Woman's Journal* merged with four other suffrage journals to become the *Woman's Citizen* in 1917; it became the *Woman's Journal* again in 1928, until it ceased publication in 1931.

The *Independent Woman* began publication in 1919 as the magazine of the newly formed National Federation of Business and Professional Women (BPW). It took a new title in 1957 and became the *National Business Woman*. These journals are available on microfilm at many libraries. I spent many pleasurable hours at the small library BPW maintains in Washington, D.C., where librarian Danuta Kuhl provided considerable assistance.

Democratic women produced a national magazine for more than three decades. Different groups of Republican women published a variety of magazines and newsletters at the national level and in several states for much shorter periods of time.

Government publications are not included in this book. There is a recent and excellent annotated bibliography, *U.S. Government Documents on Women, 1890–1990*, by Mary Ellen Huls. Government departments and agencies can be accessed electronically for recent publications.

The Future

One-third—or two thousand—of the entries in this book were published in the past fifteen years, possibly indicating a significant increase in the participation of women as well as interest in the effect of the increase. Women constituted only a few thousand voters in the 1900 presidential election, but we dominated the most recent presidential election in 1996. If our participation was a sidebar in 1900, it is the main story in 1996.

Elizabeth M. Cox

I. Movement and Advocacy

Introduction

1. Anthony, Susan B. "Fifty Years of Work for Woman." *The Independent* 52 (15 February 1900): 414–417.

2. ———. "Outlook for Woman Suffrage." *Cosmopolitan* 28 (April 1900): 621–623.

3. Catt, Carrie Chapman. "Women in Politics." *Colliers* 26 (20 October 1900): 18. Reprinted in *Woman's Journal*, 27 October 1900: 337–338.

4. Dunne, F. P. "Mr. Dooley on Marriage and Politics." *Harper's Weekly* 44 (26 May 1900): 493.

5. Meredith, Ellis. "The Feminine Factor: Woman and the Industrial Problem." *Arena* 23 (August 1900): 438–442.

6. Williams, Fannie Barrier. "The Club Movement among Colored Women of America." In *A New Negro for a New Century*, edited by Booker T. Washington, Norman B. Wood, and Fannie Barrier Williams, 378–428. Chicago: American Publishing House, 1900. Reprint. New York: Arno Press, 1969.

7. "Working-Girls' Clubs." *Current Literature* 29 (August 1900): 195.

General

8. Beckwith, Karen. "The Public-Private Distinction and Why Women Can't Be Citizens." Paper presented at the annual conference of the Midwest Political Science Association, Cincinnati, 1981.

9. Bell, Raley Husted. *Woman from Bondage to Freedom*. New York: The Critic and Guide Company, 1921.

10. Berkin, Carol Ruth, and Mary Beth Norton. *Women of America: A History*. Boston: Houghton Mifflin, 1979.

11. Blackwell, Alice Stone. "Woman's Seventy-Five Year Fight." *The Nation* 117 (18 July 1923): 53–54.

12. Boles, Janet K. "Systematic Factors Underlying Legislative Responses to Woman Suffrage and the Equal Rights Amendment." *Women and Politics* 2, no. 1–2 (Spring–Summer 1982): 5–22.

13. Breckinridge, Sophonisba P. *Women in the Twentieth Century: A Study of Their Political, Social and Economic Activities*. New York: McGraw-Hill, 1933. Reprint. New York: Arno Press, 1972.

14. Buechler, Steven M. *Women's Movements in the United States: Woman Suffrage, Equal Rights, and Beyond.*

1

New Brunswick NJ: Rutgers University, 1990.

15. Carson, Gerald. "Woman Movement: After One Hundred Years." *Scribner's Magazine* 88 (September 1930): 263–269.

16. "Centennial of Women's Rights Initiation." *Monthly Labor Review* 26 (April 1948): 112.

17. Chafetz, Janet Saltzman, and Anthony Gary Dworkin. *Female Revolt: Women's Movements in World and Historical Perspective.* Lanham, MD: Rowman and Littlefield, 1986.

18. Clemens, Elsabeth S. "Organizational Repertoires and Institutional Change: Women's Groups and the Transformation of U.S. Politics, 1890–1920." *American Journal of Sociology* 98, no. 4 (January 1993): 755–978.

19. Cott, Nancy F., ed. *History of Women in the United States: Historical Articles on Women's Lives and Activities.* 28 vols. New York: K. G. Saur, 1992.

20. Davis, Allen F. *American Heroine: The Life and Legend of Jane Addams.* New York: Oxford University Press, 1973.

21. Davis, Julia. "Victorians Thought Her a Down-Right Scandal: As She Was." *Smithsonian* 8, no. 7 (October 1977): 131–141.

22. Deutrich, Mabel E., and Virginia C. Purdy, eds. *Clio Was a Woman: Studies in the History of American Women.* Washington, DC: Howard University Press, 1980.

23. DuBois, Ellen Carol, ed. *The Elizabeth Cady Stanton–Susan B. Anthony Reader.* Boston: Northeastern University Press, 1992.

24. DuBois, Ellen Carol, and Vicki L. Ruiz, eds. *Unequal Sisters: A Multicultural Reader in U.S. Women's History.* New York: Routledge, 1990.

25. Freedman, Estelle B. "Separatism as Strategy: Female Institution Building and American Feminism, 1870–1930." *Feminist Studies* 5, no. 3 (Fall 1979): 512–552.

26. George, Carol V. R. *'Remember the Ladies': New Perspectives on Women in American History.* Syracuse: Syracuse University Press, 1920.

27. Hewitt, Nancy A., and Suzanne Lebsock, eds. *Visible Women: New Essays on American Activism.* Urbana: University of Illinois Press, 1993.

28. Kraditor, Aileen S. *Up from the Pedestal: Selected Writings in the History of American Feminism.* Chicago: Quadrangle, 1968.

29. Lerner, Gerda. *The Woman in American History.* Reading, MA: Addison-Wesley, 1971.

30. ———, ed. *Black Women in White America: A Documentary History.* New York: Random House, 1973.

31. Lightbody, W. M. "Feminism in Politics." *Westways* 170 (October 1908): 409–415.

32. Massey, Mary Elizabeth. "The Making of a Feminist." *Journal of Social History* 39 (February 1973): 3–22.

33. Mathews, Glenna. *The Rise of Public Woman: Woman's Power and Woman's Place in the United States, 1630–1970.* New York: Oxford University Press, 1992.

34. Mathews, Shaler, ed. *The Woman Citizen's Library*. 12 vols. Chicago: The Civics Society, 1913.

35. McGlen, Nancy E., and Karen O'Connor. *Women's Rights: The Struggle for Equality in the 19th and 20th Centuries*. New York: Praeger, 1983.

36. Menchken, Henry Louis. *In Defense of Women*. 2d rev. ed. New York: Knopf, 1928.

37. O'Neill, William L. *Everyone Was Brave: The Rise and Fall of Feminism in America*. Chicago: Quadrangle, 1969.

38. Schneider, Dorothy, and Carl J. Schneider. *American Women in the Progressive Era, 1900–1920*. New York: Facts on File, 1993.

39. Scott, Anne Firor. *Natural Allies: Women's Associations in American History*. Urbana: University of Illnois Press, 1991.

40. Sinclair, Andrew. *The Emancipation of the American Woman*. New York: Harper and Row, 1966.

41. Sochen, June. *Movers and Shakers: American Women Thinkers and Activists, 1900–1970*. New York: Quadrangle, 1973.

42. Spencer, Anna Garlin. *The Council Idea and May Wright Sewall*. New York: J. Heidingsfeld Company, 1930.

43. Spendor, Dale. *There's Always Been a Woman's Movement in This Century*. Boston: Pandora Press, 1982.

44. Stephen, C. E. "Representation of Women: A Consultative Chamber of Women." *19th Century* 64 (December 1908): 1018–1024.

45. Tarbell, Ida M. "The American Woman: Her First Declaration of Independence." *American Magazine of Civics* 69, no. 4 (February 1910): 468–481.

46. Thompson, Dorothy. "Century of Women's Progress." *Ladies Home Journal* 65 (August 1948): 11–12.

47. Walker, Alice. *In Search of Our Mothers' Gardens*. New York: Harcourt Brace Jovanovich, 1983.

48. "The Woman Movement: The Struggle for Equal Rights." In *Women in American Life: Selected Readings*, edited by Anne Firor Scott. Part II. New York: Houghton Mifflin, 1970.

National Suffrage

History

49. Antell, Joan B. "The Suffrage Movement." *Current History* (May 1976): 203–205, 231–232.

50. Buhle, Mari Jo, and Paul Buhle, eds. *The Concise History of Woman Suffrage, Selections from the Classic Work of Stanton, Anthony, Gage and Harper*. Urbana: University of Illinois Press, 1978.

51. Campbell, Karlyn Kohrs. *Man Cannot Speak for Her*. 2 vols. New York: Praeger, 1989.

52. Catt, Carrie Chapman, and Nettie Rogers Shuler. *Woman Suffrage and Politics, The Inner Story of the Suffrage Movement*. New York: Charles Scribner's Sons, 1923. Reprint. University of Washington Press, 1970.

53. Collidge, Olivia. *Woman's Right: The Suffrage Movement in America, 1848–1920.* New York: E. P. Dutton, 1966.

54. Faber, Doris. *Petticoat Politics: How American Women Won the Right to Vote.* New York: Lothrop, Lee and Shephard, 1967.

55. Flexner, Eleanor. *Century of Struggle: The Women's Rights Movement in the United States.* Cambridge: Belknap Press of Harvard University Press, 1959.

56. Florey, Kenneth. "Artifacts of the Woman Suffrage Movement." *Bookman's Weekly* (1 March 1989).

57. Giele, Janet Zollinger. *Two Paths to Women's Equality: Temperance, Suffrage, and the Origins of Modern Feminism.* New York: Twayne, 1995.

58. Graham, Sara Sally Hunter. "The Suffrage Renaissance: A New Image for a New Century, 1896–1910." In *One Woman, One Vote, Rediscovering the Woman Suffrage Movement,* edited by Marjorie Spruill Wheeler, 157–178. Troutdale, OR: NewSage Press, 1995.

59. Irwin, Inez Haynes. *Angels and Amazons: A Hundred Years of American Women.* Garden City, NY: Doubleday, Doran, 1933.

60. Kraditor, Aileen S. *The Ideas of the Woman Suffrage Movement, 1890–1920.* New York: Columbia University Press, 1965.

61. Marilley, Suzanne M. "Why the Vote?: Woman Suffrage and the Politics of Democratic Development in the United States." Ph.D. dissertation, Harvard University, Cambridge, 1985.

62. ———. *Women Suffrage and the Origins of Liberal Feminism in the United States, 1820–1920.* Cambridge: Harvard University Press, 1995.

63. McDonagh, Eileen Lorenzi. "Issues and Constituencies in the Progressive Era: House Roll Call Voting on the Nineteenth Amendment, 1913–1919." *Journal of Politics* 51, no. 1 (1989): 119–136.

64. ———. "The Significance of the Nineteenth Amendment: A New Look at Civil Rights, Social Welfare, and Woman Suffrage Alignments in the Progressive Era." *Women and Politics* 10, no. 2 (1990): 59–94.

65. McDonagh, Eileen Lorenzi, and H. Douglas Price. "Woman Suffrage in the Progressive Era: Patterns of Opposition and Support in Referenda Voting 1910–1918." *American Political Science Review* 79, no. 2 (June 1985): 415–435.

66. Morrison, Mary Foulke. "Votes for Women, Story of the Fight for Equal Suffrage." *Woman's Home Companion* 67 (November 1940): 8, 122, 125.

67. Murphy, Cliona. *The Women's Suffrage Movement and Irish Society in the Early Twentieth Century.* Philadelphia: Temple University Press, 1989.

68. National American Woman Suffrage Association. *Victory: How Women Won It, A Centennial Symposium 1840–1940.* New York: H. W. Wilson, 1940.

69. O'Neill, William L. "Feminism in America, 1848–1986: The Fight for Suffrage." *Wilson Quarterly* 10 (Autumn 1986): 99–109.

70. Papachristou, Judith. "Woman's Suffrage Movement: New Research and New Perspectives." *The Organization of American Historian's Newsletter* 14, no. 3 (1986): 6–8.

71. Pascoe, Peggy. *Relations of Rescue: The Search for Female Moral Authority in the American West, 1874–1939.* New York: Oxford University Press, 1990.

72. Pugh, Martin D. *Electoral Reform in War and Peace, 1906–18.* Boston: Routledge and Kegan Paul, 1976.

73. Ray, P. Orman. "The World Wide Woman Suffrage Movement." *Journal of Comparative Legislation and International Law* 1, no.3 (1919): 220–238.

74. Scott, Anne Firor, and Andrew M. Scott. *One Half the People: The Fight for Woman Suffrage.* Philadelphia: Lippincott, 1975.

75. Severn, Williams. *Free but Not Equal: How Women Won the Right to Vote.* New York: Julian Messner, 1967.

76. Spencer, Anna Garlin. "Woman and the State." *Forum* 48 (July 1912): 394–408.

77. Stanton, Elizabeth Cady, Susan B. Anthony, and Matilda J. Gage, eds. *History of Woman Suffrage.* Vols. 1–3. Rochester, NY: Fowler and Wells, 1881–1886. Vol. 4, Susan B. Anthony and Ida Husted Harper, eds., Indianapolis: Hollenbeck Press, 1902. Vols. 5–6, Ida Husted Harper, ed. New York: National American Woman Suffrage Association, 1922. Reprint. New York: Arno Press, 1969, 6 vols.

78. Story, Douglas. "Woman in Politics." *Munsey's* 29 (1903): 256.

79. Wheeler, Marjorie Spruill, ed. *One Woman, One Vote, Rediscovering the Woman Suffrage Movement.* Troutdale, OR: NewSage Press, 1995.

Leaders and Activists

80. Anthony, Katherine. *Susan B. Anthony: Her Personal History and Her Era.* New York: Doubleday, 1954.

81. Blake, Katherine Deveraux, and Margaret Louise Wallace. *Champion of Women: The Life of Lillie Deveraux Blake.* New York: Fleming H. Revell, 1943.

82. Bland, Sidney R. "Never Quite As Committed As We'd Like: The Suffrage Militancy of Lucy Burns." *Journal of Long Island History* 17, no. 2 (Summer 1981): 4–23.

83. Brown, Olympia. *Acquaintances Old and New among Reformers.* Milwaukee, WI: S. E. Tate, 1911.

84. Brown, Victoria Bissell. "Jane Addams, Progressivism, and Woman Suffrage: An Introduction to 'Why Women Should Vote'." In *One Woman, One Vote, Rediscovering the Woman Suffrage Movement,* edited by Marjorie Spruill Wheeler, 179–201. Troutdale, OR: NewSage Press, 1995.

85. Campbell, Barbara. *The 'Liberated Woman' of 1914: Prominent Women in the Progressive Era.* Ann Arbor: University of Michigan Institute Research Press, 1979.

86. Cheney, Lynne. "How Alice Paul Became the Most Militant Feminist of Them All." *Smithsonian* 3, no. 8 (November 1972): 94–100.

87. Cooley, Winifred Harper. "The Younger Suffragists." *Harper's Weekly* 57 (27 September 1913): 7–8.

88. Dobkin, Marjorie Houspian. *The Making of a Feminist: Early Journals and Letters of M. Carey Thomas.* Kent, OH: Kent State University, 1979.

89. Dorr, Rheta Childe. *Susan B. Anthony: The Woman Who Changed the Mind of a Nation.* New York: F. A. Stokes, 1928. Reprint. New York: Arno Press, 1970.

90. Dow, Bonnie J. "The 'Womanhood' Rationale in the Woman Suffrage Rhetoric of Francis E. Willard." *Southern Communication Journal* 56, no. 4 (Summer 1991): 298–307.

91. Duster, Alfreda, ed. *Crusade for Justice: The Autobiography of Ida B. Wells.* Chicago: University of Illinois Press, 1970.

92. Fonn, Barbara R. "Anna Howard Shaw and Women's Work." *Frontiers* 4, no. 3 (1979): 21–25.

93. Fowler, Robert Booth. *Carrie Catt: Feminist Politician.* Boston: Northeastern University Press, 1986.

94. ———. "Carrie Chapman Catt, Strategist." In *One Woman, One Vote, Rediscovering the Woman Suffrage Movement,* edited by Marjorie Spruill Wheeler, 295–314. Troutdale, OR: NewSage Press, 1995.

95. Fry, Amelia R. "The Two Searches for Alice Paul." *Frontiers* 7, no. 1 (1983): 21–24.

96. Geidel, Peter. "Alva E. Belmont: A Forgotten Feminist." Ph.D. dissertation, Columbia University, New York, 1993.

97. Griffith, Elizabeth. *In Her Own Right, The Life of Elizabeth Cady Stanton.* New York: Oxford, 1984.

98. Gurovitz, Judy. "Suffragists Still Going Strong." *Ms.* 2, no. 1 (July 1973): 7–53.

99. Hall, Florence Howe. *Julia Ward Howe and the Woman Suffrage Movement.* New York: Arno Press, 1969.

100. Harper, Ida Husted. *Life and Work of Susan B. Anthony.* 3 vols. Indianapolis: Bowen-Merrilly, 1899.

101. Horner, Patricia Voeller. "May Arkwright Hutton: Suffragist and Politician." In *Women in Pacific Northwest History: An Anthology.* Seattle: University of Washington, 1988.

102. Hurwitz, Edith. "Carrie C. Catt's 'Suffrage in the Gilded Age'." *The Historian* 42 (February 1978): 225–243.

103. Jones, Beverly Washington, ed. *Quest for Equality: The Life and Writings of Mary Eliza Church Terrell, 1863–1954.* Vol. 13 of *Black Women in United States History,* edited by Darlene Clark Hine. 16 vols. Brooklyn, NY: Carlson, 1990.

104. Keeler, Rebecca T. "Alva Belmont: Exacting Benefactor for Women's Suffrage." *Alabama Review* 41 (April 1988): 132–145.

105. Kerr, Andrea. *Lucy Stone: Speaking Out for Equality.* New Brunswick, NJ: Rutgers University Press, 1992.

106. Kinkaid, Mary Holland. "The Feminine Charms of the Woman Militant." *Good Housekeeping* 54 (February 1912): 146–155.

107. Louis, James P. "Sue Shelton White and the Woman Suffrage Movement, 1913–1920." *Tennessee Historical Quarterly* 22, no. 2 (June 1963): 170–190.

108. Lutz, Alma. *Created Equal: A Biography of Elizabeth Cady Stanton, 1815–1902.* New York: John Day, 1940.

109. Montgomery, James. *Liberated Women, A Life of May Arkwright Hutton.* Spokane, WA: Gingko House, 1974.

110. Peck, Mary Gray. *Carrie Chapman Catt: A Biography.* New York: H.W. Wilson, 1944.

111. Scharf, Lois. "Eleanor Roosevelt and Feminism." In *Without Precedent,* edited by Joan Hoff-Wilson, 226–253. Bloomington: Indiana University Press, 1984.

112. Shaw, Anna Howard. *The Story of a Pioneer.* New York: Harper and Brothers, 1915.

113. Sherr, Lynn, ed. *Failure Is Impossible: Susan B. Anthony in Her Own Words.* New York: Random House, 1995.

114. Spencer, Ralph W. "Anna Howard Shaw." *Methodist History* 13, no. 2 (1975): 33–51.

115. Terrell, Mary Church. *A Colored Woman in a White World.* Salem, NH: Ayer Co., 1940. Reprint. Washington, DC: Randsdell, 1986.

Organizations

116. Anthony, Susan B., and Ida Husted Harper. "National Organizations of Women." Vol. 4 of *History of Woman Suffrage,* edited by Susan B. Anthony and Ida Husted Harper, 1042–73. Indianapolis: Hollenbeck Press, 1902. Reprint. New York: Arno Press, 1969.

117. Baker, Abby Scott. "Woman's Party." *Outlook* 113 (23 August 1916): 1002–1004.

118. Beard, Charles A. "The Woman's Party." *The New Republic* 7 (29 July 1916): 329–331.

119. Bland, Sidney R. "Mad Women of the Cause: The National Woman's Party in the South." *Furman Studies* 26 (December 1980): 82–91.

120. Boyd, Mary Sumner. *The Woman Citizen: A General Handbook of Civics, with Special Consideration of Women's Citizenship.* New York: Frederick A. Stokes Co., 1918.

121. Fry, Amelia R. "Along the Suffrage Trail: From West to East for Freedom Now!" *American West* 6, no. 1 (January 1969): 16–25.

122. Hume, Leslie Parker. *The National Union of Women's Suffrage Society, 1897–1914.* New York: Garland, 1982.

123. Irwin, Inez Haynes. *Up Hill with Banner Flying: The Story of the National Woman's Party.* New York: Harcourt Brace, 1921. Reprints. Penobscot Traversity, 1964; New York: Karus, 1971.

124. Lewenson, Sandra. "'Of Logical Necessity...They Hang Together,' Nursing and the Women's Movement, 1901–1912." *Nursing History Review* 2 (1994): 99–113.

125. Lunardini, Christine A. *From Equal Suffrage to Equal Rights: Alice*

Paul and the National Woman's Party, 1910–1928. New York: New York University Press, 1986.

126. National American Woman Suffrage Association. *Proceedings of Annual Conventions 1900–1920.* New York: National American Woman Suffrage Association, 1920.

127. Nelson, Marjory. "Ladies in the Streets: A Sociological Analysis of the National Woman's Party, 1910–1930." Ph.D. dissertation, State University of New York, Buffalo, 1976.

128. Paul, Alice. *Conversations with Alice Paul: Woman Suffrage and the Equal Rights Amendment.* Berkeley: University of California, 1975. Interview by Amelia Fry for the Suffragists Oral History Project, the Bancroft Library Oral History Program.

129. "A Portfolio of the Sometimes Violent Struggle for Feminine Rights." *Smithsonian* 1 (July 1970): 28–31.

130. Robinson, Helen Ring. "What About the Woman's Party ?" *The Independent* 87 (11 September 1916): 381–383.

131. *The Suffragists: From Tea–Parties to Prison.* Berkeley: University of California, 1975. Interviews of Sylvie Thygeson, Jessie Haver Butler, Miriam Allen DeFord, Laura Ellsworth Seiler, Ernestine Kettler for the Suffragists Oral History Project, the Bancroft Library Oral History Program.

132. Vernon, Mabel. *The Suffrage Campaign, Peace and International Relations.* Berkeley: University of California, 1975. Interview by Amelia Fry for the Suffragists Oral History Project, the Bancroft Library Oral History Program.

133. Zimmerman, Loretta Ellen. "Alice Paul and the National Woman's Party, 1912–1920." Ph.D. dissertation, Tulane University, New Orleans, 1964.

Women of Color

134. Alexander, Adele Logan. "How I Discovered My Grandmother ... And the Truth about Black Women and the Suffrage Movement." *Ms.* 12, no. 5 (November 1983): 29–37.

135. DuBois, W. E. B. "Votes for Women: A Symposium of Leading Thinkers of Colored America." *The Crisis* 8 (August 1914): 176–192.

136. Duster, Alfreda. "Seeking the Negro Vote." In *Crusade for Justice: The Autobiography of Ida B. Wells,* edited by Alfreda Duster, 345–353. Chicago: University of Illinois, 1970.

137. Grimke, Francis J. "'Votes for Women': Symposium of Leading Thinkers of Colored America." *The Crisis* 4 (September 1912): 240–247.

138. Gruening, Martha. "Two Suffrage Movements." *The Crisis* 4 (September 1912): 245–247.

139. Higginbotham, Evelyn Brooks. *Righteous Discontent: The Women's Movement in the Black Baptist Church, 1880–1920.* Cambridge: Harvard University Press, 1993.

140. "An Indian Woman's Victory: Miss Ida B. Allison." *The Woman's Journal* 41 (6 August 1910): 130.

141. Logan, Adella Hunt. "Woman Suffrage." *Colored American Magazine* (9 September 1905): 487–489.

142. Neverdon-Morton, Cynthia. "The Black Woman's Struggle for Equality in the South, 1895–1925." In *The Afro-American Woman: Struggles and Images,* edited by Sharon Harley and Rosalyn Terborg-Penn, 43–57. Port Washington, NY: Kennikat Press, 1978.

143. "Suffering Suffragettes." *The Crisis* 4 (June 1912): 77–78.

144. Terborg-Penn, Rosalyn. "Afro-Americans in the Struggle for Woman Suffrage." Ph.D. dissertation, Howard University, Washington, DC, 1978.

145. ———. "Discontented Black Feminism: Prelude and Postscript to the Passage of the Nineteenth Amendment." In *Decades of Discontent: The Women's Movement 1920–1940,* edited by Lois Scharf and Joan M. Jensen, 261–278. Westport, CT: Greenwood, 1983. Reprinted in *Black Women in United States History,* Vol. 4, edited by Darlene Clark Hine, 1159–1176. Brooklyn, NY: Carlson, 1990.

146. ———. "African-American Women and the Woman Suffrage Movement." In *One Woman, One Vote, Rediscovering the Woman Suffrage Movement,* edited by Marjorie Spruill Wheeler, 134–155. Troutdale, OR: NewSage Press, 1995.

147. Terrell, Mary Church. "The Justice of Woman Suffrage." *The Crisis* 4 (September 1912): 243–245. Reprint. 90 (June 1984): 6.

148. Williams, Katherine E. "The Alpha Suffrage Club." *The Half Century Magazine* (September 1916): 12+.

Strategy

149. Beard, Charles A. "Woman Suffrage and Strategy." *The New Republic* 1 (12 December 1914): 22–23.

150. Bland, Sidney R. "Techniques of Persuasion: The National Woman's Party and Woman Suffrage, 1913–1919." Ph.D. dissertation, George Washington University, Washington, DC, 1972.

151. Brown, Gertrude Foster. "The Opposition Breaks." In *Victory: How Women Won It, a Centennial Symposium 1840–1940,* edited by National American Woman Suffrage Association. New York: H. W. Wilson, 1940.

152. Buenker, John D. "The Urban Political Machine and Woman Suffrage: A Study in Political Adaptability." *The Historian* 33, no. 2 (February 1971): 264–279.

153. Caird, Mona "Militant Tactics and Woman's Suffrage." *Westways* 170 (November 1908): 525–530.

154. Catt, Carrie Chapman. *Woman Suffrage by Federal Constitutional Amendment.* New York: National Woman Suffrage Publishing Co., 1917.

155. ———. "Why We Did Not Picket the White House." *Good Housekeeping* 66 (March 1918): 32, 109.

156. Cushman, Robert E. "Woman Suffrage on the Installment Plan."

Nation 105 (6 December 1917): 633–634.

157. "Feminine Political Strategy." *Literary Digest* 53 (23 September 1916): 730.

158. Ford, Linda G. *Iron Jawed Angels: The Suffrage Militancy of the National Women's Party, 1912–1920.* Lanham, MD: University Press of America, 1991.

159. ———. "Alice Paul and the Triumph of Militancy." In *One Woman, One Vote, Rediscovering the Woman Suffrage Movement,* edited by Marjorie Spruill Wheeler, 277–294. Troutdale, OR: NewSage Press, 1995.

160. "Is It Politics?" *The Woman's Journal* 42 (11 March 1911): 73.

161. Morgan, David. *Suffragists and Democrats: The Politics of Woman Suffrage in America.* East Lansing: Michigan State University Press, 1972.

162. Osborne, Duffield. "Xanthippe on Woman Suffrage." *Yale Review* 4 (April 1915): 590–607.

163. "Suffragist and the G. O. P." *Harper's Weekly* 52 (4 July 1908): 16.

164. "Tactics of Woman Suffrage." *The Independent* 64 (23 April 1908): 930–932.

165. Tucker, Henry St. George. *Woman's Suffrage by Constitutional Amendment.* New Haven, CT: Yale University Press, 1916.

166. Van Kleeck, Mary. *Suffragist and Industrial Democracy.* New York: National Woman Suffrage Publishing Co., 1919.

167. Wells, Mrs. B. B. "Militant Movement for Woman Suffrage." *The Inde-pendent* 64 (November 1908): 525–530.

168. Wiley, Anna Kelton. "Why We Did Picket the White House." *Good Housekeeping* 66 (February 1918): 29, 124–125.

Campaign

169. Addams, Jane. "Why Women Should Vote." *Ladies Home Journal* 27 (January 1910): 21–22.

170. ———. "The Larger Aspects of the Woman's Suffrage Movement." *Annals of the American Academy of Political and Social Science* 56 (November 1914): 1–8.

171. ———. "Women, War and Suffrage." *The Survey* 35 (6 November 1915): 148.

172. Anthony, Susan B., and Ida Husted Harper. "Suffrage Work in Political and Other Conventions." Chap. 23 in *History of Woman Suffrage.* Vol. 4, edited by Susan B. Anthony and Ida Husted Harper, 434–449. Indianapolis: Hollenbeck Press, 1902. Reprint. New York: Arno Press, 1969.

173. Belmont, Alva. "Woman's Right to Govern Herself." *North American Review* 190 (November 1909): 664–674.

174. Bjorkman, Frances M., and Annie G. Porritt. *Woman Suffrage: Arguments and Results, 1910–1911.* New York: National American Woman Suffrage Association, 1911. Reprint 1971.

175. Bland, Sidney R. "New Life in an Old Movement: Alice Paul and the

Great Suffrage Parade of 1913 in Washington, D.C." *Records of the Columbia Historical Society* (1971–72): 657–678.

176. Breckinridge, Sophonisba P. "Woman Suffrage." In *Cyclopedia of American Government,* 3d ed., edited by Andrew C. McLaughlin and Albert Bushnell Hart, 694–698. New York: D. Appleton, 1914.

177. Dodge, Mrs. Arthur M. "Woman Suffrager Opposed to Woman's Rights." *Annals of the American Academy of Political and Social Science* 56 (November 1914): 99–104.

178. Evans, Jennifer. "Organizing for Visibility: A Legacy of the Campaign for Women Suffrage." *Sojourner, Massachusetts Institute of Technology* 20, no. 12 (August 1995): 1, 12–13.

179. Gluck, Sherna, ed. *From Parlor to Prison: Five American Suffragists Talk about Their Lives.* New York: Random House, 1976.

180. Graham, Sara Sally Hunter. "Woodrow Wilson, Alice Paul, and the Woman Suffrage Movement." *Political Science Quarterly* 98 (Winter 1983): 665–679.

181. Havemeyer, Louisine. "The Suffrage Torch: Memories of a Militant." Parts 1, 2. *Scribner's Magazine* (May, June 1922): 528–539, 661–676.

182. Hirshfield, Claire. "The Actresses' Franchise League and the Campaign for Women's Suffrage, 1908–1914." *Theatre Research International* 10 (Summer 1985): 129–153.

183. Hitchcock, Nevada Davis. "Mobilization of Women." *Annals of the American Academy of Political and Social Science* 78 (July 1918): 24–31.

184. Howe, Julia Ward. "The Case for Woman Suffrage." *Outlook* 91 (3 April 1909): 780.

185. Hutchinson, Emilie J. "Socializing Influence of the Ballot Upon Women." *Annals of the American Academy of Political and Social Science* 56 (November 1914): 105–110.

186. Lape, Esther Everett. "When Are Equal Suffragists Equal ?" *Ladies Home Journal* 37 (July 1920): 35.

187. Matthews, Shailer. "Woman Suffrage" Vol. 7 of *Women Citizen's Library.* 20 vols. New York: National American Woman's Suffrage Association, 1914.

188. Owen, Robert L. "Discussion of Equal Suffrage for Women." *Annals of the American Academy of Political and Social Science* 35, Supplement (May 1910): 6–9.

189. Park, Maud Wood. *Front Door Lobby.* Boston: Beacon, 1960.

190. Parsons, Frank. "Shall Our Mothers, Wives and Sisters Be Our Equals or Our Subjects?" *Arena* 40 (July 1908): 92–94.

191. Peck, Mary Gray. *The Rise of the Woman Suffrage Party.* Chicago: Myra Strawn Hartshorn, 1911.

192. Potter, Frances Boardman. *Women, Economics, and the Ballot.* Youngstown, OH: Vindicator Press, 1909.

193. Pugh, Evelyn L. "Suffragetts Prisoners at the Occoquon Workhouse." *Northern Virginia Heritage* 1 (1972): 9.

194. Schirmacker, Kathe. *The Modern Woman's Rights Movement: A Historical Survey.* New York: Macmillan, 1912.

195. Shaw, Anna Howard. "Equal Suffrage—A Problem of Political Justice." *Annals of the American Academy of Political and Social Science* 56 (November 1914): 93–98.

196. Spencer, Anna Garlin. "The Logical Basis of Woman Suffrage." *Annals of the American Academy of Political and Social Science* 35, Supplement (May 1910): 10–15.

197. Squire, Belle. *The Woman Movement in America: A Short Account of the Struggle for Equal Rights.* Chicago: A. C. McClurg & Co., 1911.

198. Stapler, Martha G., ed. *The Woman Suffrage Year Book.* New York: National Woman Suffrage Publishing Company, 1917.

199. Stevens, Doris. *Jailed for Freedom.* New York: Boni and Liveright, 1920. Reprint. New York: Shocken Books, 1976.

200. "The Suffragists Fight over Equality." *Literary Digest* 89 (12 July 1920): 10–11.

201. Trecker, Janice Law. "The Suffrage Prisoners." *The American Scholar* 40, no. 3 (Summer 1972): 409–423.

202. "War Breaking Down the Barriers to Prohibition and Woman Suffrage." *Current Opinion* 64 (February 1918): 82–84.

203. "Watch Out, Mr. Congressman, Miss Younger Has Your Number." *Literary Digest* 60 (29 March 1919): 82–84.

204. "Western Women's Drive on Democracy." *Literary Digest* 53, no. 9 (26 August 1916): 444–445.

205. "Woman's Part in the Election." *Literary Digest* 66 (7 August 1920): 22–23.

206. "Women Legislators and Ratification." *The Woman Citizen* 4 (21 February 1920): 898.

207. Younger, Maud. "Revelations of a Woman Lobbyist." *McCalls* 47 (September 1919): 7, 32–33; (October 1919): 12, 38–41; (November 1919): 14, 41, 46, 50–51.

Presidential Politics

208. Beveridge, Albert J. "To the Women of America." *Colliers* 65 (12 June 1920): 8, 38, 40, 42, 44.

209. Bryan, William Jennings. "To the Women of America." *Colliers* 65 (12 June 1920): 9, 46, 48, 50.

210. Cleveland, Grover. "Would Woman Suffrage Be Unwise?" *Ladies Home Journal* 22 (October 1905): 7–8.

211. Halliday, E. M. "Theodore Roosevelt, Feminist." *American Heritage* 30 (December 1978): 106–107.

212. Harper, Ida Husted. "President and the Suffragists." *The Independent* 68 (28 April 1910): 902–904.

213. Lunardini, Christine A., and Thomas J. Knock. "Woodrow Wilson and Woman Suffrage: A New Look." *Political Science Quarterly* 95, no. 4 (Winter 1980–81): 655–671.

214. McFarland, Charles, and Nevin Neal. "The Reluctant Reformer: Woodrow Wilson and Woman's Suffrage." *Rocky Mountain Social Science Journal* 11, no. 2 (April 1974): 33–43.

215. "Mr. Hughes New Suffrage Plank." *Literary Digest* 53 (12 August 1916): 337–338.

216. "President and the Suffragists." *Literary Digest* 47 (20 December 1913): 1209–1211.

217. Roosevelt, Theodore. "Women's Rights and Duties of Both Men and Women." In *The Works of Theodore Roosevelt*. National ed., 208–09. Vol. 16. New York: Charles Scribner's Sons, 1926. Reprint. *Outlook* 100 (3 February 1912): 302–304.

218. Silverman, Elaine M. "Reform as a Means of Social Control: Theodore Roosevelt and Women's Suffrage." *Atlantis (Canada)* 2, no. 1 (1976): 22–26.

219. Stanton, Elizabeth Cady. "Mrs. Stanton to President Roosevelt." *The Independent* 54, no. 6 (November 1902): 2621–2622.

220. "Theodore Roosevelt and Elihu Root on Woman's Suffrage." *Outlook* 90 (19 December 1908): 848–849.

221. "Wilson, Women and Weather." *Sunset* 37 (November 1916): 35.

Media

222. Bennion, Sherilyn Cox. "Woman Suffrage Papers of the West, 1869–1914." *American Journalism* 3 (1986): 129–141.

223. Cheney, Lynne V. "Mrs. Frank Leslie's Illustrated Newspaper: Running the Leslie Publishing Empire." *American Heritage* 26 (October 1975): 42–48, 90–91.

224. Cooper, Anne Messerly. "Suffrage as News: Ten Dailies' Coverage of the Nineteenth Amendment." *American Journalism* 1 (1983): 75–91.

225. Dunne, F. P. "Mr. Dooley on Woman's Suffrage." *American Magazine of Civics* 68 (June 1909): 198–200.

226. Masel-Walters, Lynne. "A Burning Cloud By Day: The History and Content of the 'Women's Journal'." *Journalism History* 3, no. 4 (1976–77): 103–110.

227. ———. "To Hustle with the Rowdies: The Organization and Functions of the American Woman Suffrage Press." *Journal of American Culture* 3 (Spring 1980): 167–183.

228. Sheppard, Alice. *Cartooning for Suffrage*. Albuquerque: University of New Mexico Press, 1994.

229. Sloan, Kay. "Sexual Warfare in the Silent Cinema: Comedies and Melodrama of Woman Suffragism." *American Quarterly* 33 (Fall 1981): 412–436.

230. Solomon, Martha M., ed. *A Voice of Their Own: The Woman Suffrage Press, 1840–1910*. Tuscaloosa: University of Alabama Press, 1991.

231. Stern, Madeleine B. *Purple Passage: The Life of Mrs. Frank Leslie*. Norman: University of Oklahoma Press, 1953.

Men

232. Berman, David R. "Male Support for Woman Suffrage: An Analysis of Voting Patterns in the Mountain West." *Social Science History* 11 (Fall 1987): 281–294.

233. Foner, Philip S. *Frederick Douglass on Women's Rights.* New York: Da Capo, 1992.

234. Kimmel, Michael S., and Thomas Mosmiller. *Against the Tide: Pro-Feminist Men in the United States. 1776–1990.* Boston: Beacon, 1992.

235. Ryan, Thomas G. "Male Opponents and Supporters of Woman Suffrage: Iowa in 1916." *Annals of Iowa* 45, no. 7 (Winter 1981): 537–550.

236. Villard, Fanny Garrison. "Garrison and Woman's Suffrage." *The Crisis* 4 (September 1912): 240–244.

237. White, Kevin F. "Men Supporting Women: A Study of Men Associated with the Woman Suffrage Movement in Britian and America, 1909–1920." *The Maryland Historian* 18, no. 1 (Spring–Summer 1987): 45–59.

238. Yellin, Jean Fagan. "DuBois' Crisis and Women's Suffrage." *Massachusetts Review* 14, no. 2 (1973): 365–375.

Racism

239. Allen, Robert L., and Pamela P. Allen. "Woman Suffrage: Feminism and White Supremacy." In *Reluctant Reformers: Racism and Social Reform Movements in the United States,* 127–172. Garden City, NY: Anchor Books, 1975.

240. Hendricks, Wanda Ann. "The Politics of Race: Black Women in Illinois, 1890–1920." Ph.D. dissertation, Purdue University, 1990.

241. McGoldrick, Neale. "Women's Suffrage and the Question of Color." *Social Education* 59, no. 5 (September 1995): 270–273.

242. Sneider, Alison. "The Impact of Empire on the North American Woman Suffrage Movement: Suffrage Racism in an Imperial Context." *UCLA Historical Journal* 14 (August 1995): 14–32.

243. Terborg-Penn, Rosalyn. "Discrimination against Afro-American Women in the Woman's Movement, 1830–1920." In *The Afro-American Woman: Struggles and Images,* edited by Sharon Harley and Rosalyn Terborg-Penn, 17–27. Port Washington, NY: National University Publications, 1978.

Religion

244. Fishburn, Janet Forsythe. "The Methodist Social Gospel and Woman Suffrage." *Drew Gateway* 54, no. 2–3 (1984): 85–104.

245. Greene, Dana, ed. *Suffrage and Religious Principle: Speeches and Writings of Olympia Brown.* Metuchen, NJ: Scarecrow Press, 1983.

246. Iversen, Joan. "The Mormon-Suffrage Relationship: Personal and Political Quandaries." *Frontiers* 11, no. 2–3 (1990): 8–16.

247. Kirkley, Evelyn A. "'This Work Is God's Cause': Religion in the Southern Woman Suffrage Movement, 1880–1920." *Church History* 59, no. 4 (December 1990): 507–522.

248. Nutt, Rick. "Robert Lewis Dabney: Presbyterians and Women's Suffrage." *Journal of Presbyterian History* 62 (Winter 1984): 339–353.

249. "Pope on Equal Suffrage." *Harper's Weekly* 53 (1 May 1909): 5.

250. Summers, Bill. "Southern Baptists and Women's Right to Vote, 1910–1920." *Baptist History and Heritage* 12, no. 1 (1977): 45–51.

Victory

251. "The American Woman Voter Arrives." *Literary Digest* 66, no. 9 (28 August 1920): 9–11.

252. Catt, Carrie Chapman. "On the Inside." *The Woman Citizen* 4 (6 March 1920): 947–948.

253. Curry, Margaret. "The Victory Convention." *Life and Labor* 10 (March 1920): 70–72.

254. Harper, Ida Husted. "The American Woman Gets the Vote." *Review of Reviews* 44 (1920): 384.

255. Toombs, Elizabeth O. "The Suffrage Jubilee." *Good Housekeeping* 70 (May 1920): 78–79, 118, 121–122, 125.

256. "The Triumph of Woman Suffrage." *Current History* 13 (October 1920).

Nations and Tribes

257. Bernstein, Alison. "A Mixed Record: The Political Enfranchisement of American Indian Women during the Indian New Deal." *Journal of the West* 23 (July 1984): 13–20.

258. "Hopi Prototypes of the 'Suffragettes'." *Indian's Friend* 21, no. 8 (1909): 10.

259. "Indian Suffragettes." *Indian's Friend* 25, no. 6 (1913): 11.

260. Kasee, Cynthia R. "Let Your Women Hear Our Words: The Rights of Cherokee Women before the 19th Amendment." Paper, Department of Sociology and Anthropology, Miami University, Oxford, OH, 1989.

261. Landsman, Gail H. "Images of Indians in the Woman Suffrage Movement." *Ethnohistory* 39, no. 3 (Summer 1992): 247–284.

262. Taber, Ronald W. "Sacagawea and the Suffragettes." *Pacific Northwest Quarterly* 58, no. 1 (1967): 7–13.

In the Regions

North

263. "Both Sides Encouraged by the Suffrage Defeat." *Literary Digest* 51 (November 1915): 1065–1067.

264. "The Eastern Suffrage Campaigns." *American Review* 52 (November 1915): 518–520.

Midwest

265. Jensen, Richard. *The Winning of the Midwest.* Chicago: University of Chicago Press, 1971.

South

266. Johnson, Kenneth R. "Kate Gordon and the Woman Suffrage Movement in the South." *Journal of South-*

ern History 37, no. 3 (August 1972): 365–392.

267. Kraditor, Aileen S. "Tactical Problems of the Woman Suffrage Movement in the South." *Louisiana Studies* 5, no. 4 (Winter 1966): 289–307.

268. Turner, Elizabeth Hayes. "Southern Suffragists and the Progressive Period." Paper presented at the annual meeting of the Organization of American Historians, 1991.

269. Wheeler, Marjorie Spruill. *New Women of the New South: The Leaders of the Woman Suffrage Movement in the Southern States.* New York: Oxford University Press, 1993.

West

270. Duniway, Abigail Scott. *Path Breaking: An Autobiographical History of the Equal Suffrage Movement in the Pacific Coast States.* New York: Schocken Books, 1971. Originally published 1917.

271. Grimes, Alan P. *The Puritan Ethic and Woman Suffrage.* New York: Oxford University Press, 1967.

272. Larson, T. A. "Woman Suffrage in Western America." *Utah Historical Quarterly* 38, no. 1 (Winter 1970): 7–19.

273. ———. "Emancipating the West's Dolls, Vassals and Hopeless Drudges." In *Essays in Western History in Honor of T. A. Larson,* edited by R. Daniels, 1–58. Vol. 37. Laramie: University of Wyoming Press, 1971.

274. ———. "Dolls, Vassals, and Drudges—Pioneer Women in the

West." *Western Historical Quarterly* 3, no. 1 (1972): 5–16.

275. Moynihan, Ruth Barnes. "Of Women's Rights and Freedom: Abigail Scott Duniway." In *Women in Pacific Northwest History: An Anthology,* edited by Karen J. Blair. Seattle: University of Washington, 1988.

276. Pearce, S. E. "Suffrage Pacific North West." *Pacific Northwest Quarterly* 3 (1912): 23.

In the States

Alabama

277. Allen, Lee Norcross. "The Woman Suffrage Movement in Alabama." *Alabama Review* 11, no. 2 (April 1958): 83–99.

278. Goodrich, Gillian. "Romance and Reality: The Birmingham Suffragists 1892–1920." *Journal of the Birmingham Historical Society* 5 (January 1978): 5–20.

279. Hidreth, Ellen Stephens. "Alabama." In *History of Woman Suffrage,* edited by Susan B. Anthony and Ida Husted Harper, 465–469. Vol. 4. Indianapolis: Hollenbeck Press, 1902. Reprint. New York: Arno Press, 1969.

280. Hundley, Mrs. Oscar R. "Woman Suffrage and the Alabama State Legislature." *Birmingham Magazine* (October 1915): 28–29, 52–54.

281. Jacobs, Mrs. Pattie Ruffner, and Helen J. Benners. "Alabama." In *History of Woman Suffrage,* edited by Ida Husted Harper, 1–9. Vol. 6. New York: National American Woman Suffrage Association, 1922. Reprint. New York: Arno Press, 1969.

282. Jemison, Marie Stokes. "Ladies Become Voters: Pattie Furrner Jacobs and Women's Suffrage in Alabama." *Southern Exposure* 7, no. 1 (Spring 1979): 48–59.

283. Thomas, Mary Martha. "The 'New Woman' in Alabama: 1890–1920." *Alabama Review* 43, no. 3 (July 1990): 164–175.

284. ———. *The New Woman in Alabama: Social Reforms and Suffrage, 1890–1920.* Tuscaloosa: University of Alabama Press, 1992.

Arizona

285. Hughes, Mrs. L. C. "Arizona." In *History of Woman Suffrage,* edited by Susan B. Anthony and Ida Husted Harper, 470–474. Vol. 4. Indianapolis: Hollenbeck Press, 1902. Reprint. New York: Arno Press, 1969.

286. Munds, Frances Willard "Arizona." In *History of Woman Suffrage,* edited by Ida Husted Harper, 10–15. Vol. 6. New York: National American Woman Suffrage Association, 1922. Reprint. New York: Arno Press, 1969.

287. Snapp, Meredith A. "Defeat the Democrats: The Congressional Union for Woman Suffrage in Arizona, 1914 and 1916." *Journal of the West* 14, no. 4 (October 1975): 131–139.

Arkansas

288. Campbell, Catherine. "Arkansas." In *History of Woman Suffrage,* edited by Susan B. Anthony and Ida

Husted Harper, 475–477. Vol. 4. Indianapolis: Hollenbeck Press, 1902. Reprint. New York: Arno Press, 1969.

289. Ellington, Mrs. O. F., and Mrs. T. T. Cotname. "Arkansas." In *History of Woman Suffrage,* edited by Ida Husted Harper, 16–26. Vol. 6. New York: National American Woman Suffrage Association, 1922. Reprint. New York: Arno Press, 1969.

290. Jones, Dorcey D. "Catherine Campbell Cunningham, Advocate for Equal Rights for Women." *Arkansas Historical Quarterly* 12 (Summer 1953): 85–90.

291. Taylor, A. Elizabeth. "The Woman Suffrage Movement in Arkansas." *Arkansas Historical Quarterly* 15 (Spring 1956): 17–52.

California

292. Ames, K. "Woman Suffrage Movement in California." *Overland* 51 (June 1908): 513–514.

293. Chandler, Robert J. "In the Van: Spiritualists as Catalysts for the California Women's Suffrage Movement." *California History* 73 (Fall 1994): 188–201.

294. Deering, Mabel Craft. "Women's Demonstration: How They Won and Used the Vote in California." *Colliers* 48 (6 January 1912): 17–18.

295. Englander, Susan. *Class Conflict and Coalition in the California Woman Suffrage Movement, 1907–1912: The San Francisco Wage Earners' Suffrage League.* San Francisco: Mellen Research University Press, 1992.

17

296. Jensen, Joan M., and Gloria Ricci Lothrop. *California Women: A History.* San Francisco: Boyd and Fraser, 1987.

297. Katz, Sherry J. "A Politics of Coalition: Socialist Women and the California Suffrage Movement, 1900–1911." In *One Woman, One Vote, Rediscovering the Woman Suffrage Movement,* edited by Marjorie Spruill Wheeler, 245–262. Troutdale, OR: NewSage Press, 1995.

298. Keith, Mary McHenry, Lillian Harris Coffin, M. Frances Wills, and Adelia D. Wade. "California." In *History of Woman Suffrage,* edited by Ida Husted Harper, 27–58. Vol. 6. New York: National American Woman Suffrage Association, 1922. Reprint. New York: Arno Press, 1969.

299. Kneeland, Marilyn. "The Modern Boston Tea Party: The San Diego Suffrage Campaign of 1911." *Journal of San Diego History* 23 (Fall 1977): 35–42.

300. Loewy, Jean. "Katherine Phillips Edson and the California Suffragette Movement, 1919–1920." *California Historical Society Quarterly* 47, no. 4 (December 1968): 343–350.

301. Sarent, Ellen Clark, Carrie A. Whelan, and Alice Moore McComas. "California." In *History of Woman Suffrage,* edited by Susan B. Anthony and Ida Husted Harper, 478–508. Vol. 4. Indianapolis: Hollenbeck Press, 1902. Reprint. New York: Arno Press, 1969.

302. Schaffer, Ronald. "The Problem of Consciousness in the Woman Suffrage Movement: A California Perspective." *Pacific Historical Review* 45, no. 4 (Nov 1976): 469–493.

303. Stewart, J. A. "Winning of California." *Journal of Education* 74 (9 November 1911): 480–481.

304. Wall, Louise Herrick. "Moving to Amend, Campaign of the College Equal Suffrage League in California." *Sunset* 27, no. 4 (October 1911): 377–384.

Colorado

305. Fetter, Rosemary, and Marcia T. Goldstein, eds. *1893–1993, Colorado Suffrage Centennial.* Aurora, CO: Auraria Reprographics, 1993. Colorado Committee for Women's History.

306. Hosmer, Katherine Tipton. "Colorado." In *History of Woman Suffrage,* edited by Ida Husted Harper, 59–67. Vol. 6. New York: National American Woman Suffrage Association, 1922. Reprint. New York: Arno Press, 1969.

307. Kelley, Florence. "Colorado Beeters and Woman Suffrage." *The Survey* 36 (1 July 1916): 372.

308. Meredith, Emily, and Ellis Meredith. "Colorado." In *History of Woman Suffrage,* edited by Susan B. Anthony and Ida Husted Harper, 509–534. Vol. 4. Indianapolis: Hollenbeck Press, 1902. Reprint. New York: Arno Press, 1969.

Connecticut

309. Bacon, Elizabeth D. "Connecticut." In *History of Woman Suffrage,* edited by Susan B. Anthony and Ida Husted Harper, 535–542. Vol. 4. Indianapolis: Hollenbeck Press, 1902. Reprint. New York: Arno Press, 1969.

310. Connecticut Woman Suffrage Association, ed. *Memorial of the Connecticut Woman Suffrage Association to the Constitutional Convention Assembled in Hartford, Connecticut, January 1, 1902.* Hartford: Plimpton Mfg. Co., 1902.

311. Farnam, Anne. "Isabella Beecher Hooker, 'Shall Women Be Allowed to Vote Upon the Sale of Liquor and in School Matters?'" *Connecticut Historical Society Bulletin* 36 (April 1971): 41–51.

312. Forsyth, Anne. "Campaigning for the Vote: Touring Connecticut for Suffrage." Parts 1, 2. *Colliers* 50 (28 September 1912): 20–21, 26; (5 October 1912): 16–17, 35–36.

313. Porritt, Annie G. "Connecticut." In *History of Woman Suffrage,* edited by Ida Husted Harper, 68–95. Vol. 6. New York: National American Woman Suffrage Association, 1922. Reprint. New York: Arno Press, 1969.

314. Wilson, Tracey Morgan. "Beyond the Ballot Box: The Connecticut Woman Suffrage Movement, 1911–1920." Master's thesis, Trinity College, 1984.

Delaware

315. Cranston, Martha S. "Delaware." In *History of Woman Suffrage,* edited by Susan B. Anthony and Ida Husted Harper, 563–566. Vol. 4. Indianapolis: Hollenbeck Press, 1902. Reprint. New York: Arno Press, 1969.

316. de Vou, Mary R. "Delaware." In *History of Woman Suffrage,* edited by Ida Husted Harper, 96–103. Vol. 6. New York: National American Woman Suffrage Association, 1922. Reprint. New York: Arno Press, 1969.

317. ———. "The Woman Suffrage Movement in Delaware." Chap. 15 in *Delaware, A History of the First State,* edited by Henry Clay Reed and Marion Bjornson Reed, 349–370. Vol. 1. New York: Lewis Historical Publishing Company, 1947.

318. Hoffecker, Carol E. "Delaware's Woman Suffrage Campaign." *Delaware History* 20, no. 3 (1983): 149–167.

Florida

319. Burnett-Haney, Mrs. C. S. "Florida." In *History of Woman Suffrage,* edited by Susan B. Anthony and Ida Husted Harper, 577–580. Vol. 4. Indianapolis: Hollenbeck Press, 1902. Reprint. New York: Arno Press, 1969.

320. Johnson, Kenneth R. "The Woman Suffrage Movement in Florida." Ph.D. dissertation, Florida State University, Tallahassee, 1966.

321. ———. "Florida Women Get the Vote." *Florida Historical Quarterly* 48, no. 3 (January 1970): 299–312.

322. Kollock, Alice G. "Florida." In *History of Woman Suffrage,* edited by Ida Husted Harper, 113–120. Vol. 6. New York: National American Woman Suffrage Association, 1922. Reprint. New York: Arno Press, 1969.

323. Taylor, A. Elizabeth. "The Woman Suffrage Movement in Florida." *Florida Historical Quarterly* 36 (July 1957): 42–60.

Georgia

324. Floyd, Josephine Bonem. "Rebecca Latimer Felton: Champion of Women's Rights." *Georgia Historical Quarterly* 30 (June 1946): 81–104.

325. Gidlund, Lenora. "Georgia Feminists Before and After the Franchise." In *Proceedings of the Georgia Association of History,* 29–35. Atlanta: Georgia Association of History, 1983.

326. McLendon, Mary Latimer. "Georgia." In *History of Woman Suffrage,* edited by Susan B. Anthony and Ida Husted Harper, 581–588. Vol. 4. Indianapolis: Hollenbeck Press, 1902. Reprint. New York: Arno Press, 1969.

327. ———. "Georgia." In *History of Woman Suffrage,* edited by Ida Husted Harper, 121–142. Vol. 6. New York: National American Woman Suffrage Association, 1922. Reprint. New York: Arno Press, 1969.

328. Taylor, A. Elizabeth. "The Origin of the Woman Suffrage Movement in Georgia." *Georgia Historical Quarterly* 28 (June 1944): 63–79.

329. ———. "Revival and Development of the Woman Suffrage Movement in Georgia." *Georgia Historical Quarterly* 42 (December 1958): 339–354.

330. ———. "The Last Phase of the Woman Suffrage Movement in Georgia." *Georgia Historical Quarterly* 43 (March 1959): 11–28.

331. ———. "Woman Suffrage Activities in Atlanta." *Atlanta History Journal* (Winter 1980): 45–54.

Idaho

332. Balderston, William, and Eunice Pon Athey. "Idaho." In *History of Woman Suffrage,* edited by Susan B. Anthony and Ida Husted Harper, 589–597. Vol. 4. Indianapolis: Hollenbeck Press, 1902. Reprint. New York: Arno Press, 1969.

333. Larson, T. A. "Woman's Rights in Idaho." *Idaho Yesterdays* 16 (Spring 1972): 2–15, 18–19.

334. ———. "Idaho's Role in America's Woman Suffrage Crusade." *Idaho Yesterdays* 18, no. 1 (1974): 2–15.

335. Roberts, Margaret S. "Idaho." In *History of Woman Suffrage,* edited by Ida Husted Harper, 143–144. Vol. 6. New York: National American Woman Suffrage Association, 1922. Reprint. New York: Arno Press, 1969.

Illinois

336. Beldon, Gertrude May. "A History of the Woman Suffrage Movement in Illinois." Master's thesis, University of Chicago, 1913.

337. Buechler, Steven M. *The Transformation of the Woman Suffrage Movement: The Case of Illinois, 1850–1920.* New Brunswick, NJ: Rutgers University Press, 1986.

338. Fitch, George. "The Noiseless Suffragette: She Painlessly Extracted Suffrage from the Illinois Legislature." *Colliers* 51 (9 August 1913): 5–9.

339. Hendricks, Wanda Ann. "Ida B. Wells-Barnett and the Alpha Suffrage Club of Chicago." In *One Woman, One Vote, Rediscovering the Woman Suffrage Movement,* edited by Marjorie Spruill Wheeler, 263–275. Troutdale, OR: NewSage Press, 1995.

340. Hill, Caroline M. "Woman's Battle for the Ballot in Chicago." *Colliers* 43 (3 April 1909): 26–27.

341. Holmes, Mary E. "Illinois." In *History of Woman Suffrage,* edited by Susan B. Anthony and Ida Husted Harper, 598–613. Vol. 4. Indianapolis: Hollenbeck Press, 1902. Reprint. New York: Arno Press, 1969.

342. McGraw, Mrs. J. W., and Grace Wilbur Trout. "Illinois." In *History of Woman Suffrage,* edited by Ida Husted Harper, 145–165. Vol. 6. New York: National American Woman Suffrage Association, 1922. Reprint. New York: Arno Press, 1969.

343. Todd, Helen M. "Getting Out the Vote: Week's Automobile Campaign by Women Suffragists." *American Magazine of Civics* 72 (September 1911): 611–619.

344. Trout, Grace Wilbur. "Sidelights on Illinois Suffrage History." *Illinois State Historical Journal* 13, no. 2 (July 1920): 145–179.

345. Wheeler, Adade Mitchell. "Conflict in the Illinois Suffrage Movement of 1913." *Journal of Illinois State Historical Society* 76, no. 2 (Summer 1983): 95–115.

Indiana

346. Clarke, Alice Judah. "Indiana." In *History of Woman Suffrage,* edited by Susan B. Anthony and Ida Husted Harper, 614–627. Vol. 4. Indianapolis: Hollenbeck Press, 1902. Reprint. New York: Arno Press, 1969.

347. Noland, Anna Dunn, and Lenore Hanna Cox. "Indiana." In *History of Woman Suffrage,* edited by Ida Husted Harper, 166–180. Vol. 6. New York: National American Woman Suffrage Association, 1922. Reprint. New York: Arno Press, 1969.

348. Sayler, Oliver M. "Indiana's Double Somersault into Both Suffrage and Prohibition Columns." *New Republic* 10 (17 March 1917): 192–194.

349. Sloan, L. Alene. "Some Aspects of the Woman Suffrage Movement in Indiana." Ph.D. dissertation, Ball State University, 1982.

350. Stephens, Jane. "May Wright Sewall: An Indiana Reformer." *Indiana Magazine of History* 78 (December 1982): 273–295.

Iowa

351. Dunlap, Flora. "Iowa." In *History of Woman Suffrage,* edited by Ida Husted Harper, 181–192. Vol. 6. New York: National American Woman Suffrage Association, 1922. Reprint. New York: Arno Press, 1969.

352. Fuller, Steven J., and Alsatia Mellecker. "Behind the Yellow Banner: Anna B. Lawther and the Winning of Suffrage for Iowa Women."

Palimpsest 65 (May–June 1984): 106–116.

353. Haselmayer, Louis A. "Belle A. Mansfield." *Women Lawyers Journal* 55, no. 1 (Winter 1969): 46–54.

354. Noun, Louise R. *Strong Minded Women: The Emergence of the Woman Suffrage Movement in Iowa.* Ames: Iowa State University Press, 1969.

355. Richey, Clara M. "Iowa." In *History of Woman Suffrage,* edited by Susan B. Anthony and Ida Husted Harper, 628–637. Vol. 4. Indianapolis: Hollenbeck Press, 1902. Reprint. New York: Arno Press, 1969.

Kansas

356. Caldwell, Martha B. "The Woman Suffrage Campaign of 1912." *Kansas Historical Quarterly* 12, no. 3 (August 1943): 300–318.

357. Diggs, Annie L. "Kansas." In *History of Woman Suffrage,* edited by Susan B. Anthony and Ida Husted Harper, 638–664. Vol. 4. Indianapolis: Hollenbeck Press, 1902. Reprint. New York: Arno Press, 1969.

358. Grant, Philip A., Jr. "Kansas and the Woman Suffrage Amendment, 1917–1919." *Heritage of the Great Plains* 19 (Fall 1986): 1–8.

359. Johnston, Lucy B. "Kansas." In *History of Woman Suffrage,* edited by Ida Husted Harper, 193–206. Vol. 6. New York: National American Woman Suffrage Association, 1922. Reprint. New York: Arno Press, 1969.

360. Smith, Wilda M. "A Half Century of Struggle: Gaining Woman Suffrage in Kansas." *Kansas History* 4 (Summer 1981): 74–95.

Kentucky

361. Breckinridge, Sophonisba P. *Madeline McDowell Breckinridge: A Leader in the New South.* Chicago: University of Chicago Press, 1921.

362. Clay, Laura. "Kentucky." In *History of Woman Suffrage,* edited by Susan B. Anthony and Ida Husted Harper, 665–677. Vol. 4. Indianapolis: Hollenbeck Press, 1902. Reprint. New York: Arno Press, 1969.

363. Fuller, Paul E. *Laura Clay and the Women's Rights Movement.* Lexington: University of Kentucky Press, 1975.

364. Guethlein, Carol. "Women in Louisville Moving toward Equal Rights." *Filson Club Historical Quarterly* 55, no. 2 (1981): 151–178.

365. Knott, Claudia. "The Woman Suffrage Movement in Kentucky, 1879–1920." Ph.D. dissertation, University of Kentucky, 1989.

366. McDowell, Madeline. "Kentucky." In *History of Woman Suffrage,* edited by Ida Husted Harper, 207–215. Vol. 6. New York: National American Woman Suffrage Association, 1922. Reprint. New York: Arno Press, 1969.

367. Porter, Melba Dean. "Madeline McDowell Breckinridge: Her Role in the Kentucky Woman Suffrage Movement, 1908–1920." *Register of the Kentucky Historical Society* 72, no. 4 (Oct. 1974): 342–363.

Louisiana

368. Gilley, B. H. "Kate Gordon and Louisiana Woman Suffrage." *Louisiana History* 24 (Summer 1983): 289–306.

369. Gordon, Kate M. "Louisiana." In *History of Woman Suffrage,* edited by Susan B. Anthony and Ida Husted Harper, 678–688. Vol. 4. Indianapolis: Hollenbeck Press, 1902. Reprint. New York: Arno Press, 1969.

370. Gordon, Kate M., and Ethel Hutson. "Louisiana." In *History of Woman Suffrage,* edited by Ida Husted Harper, 216–235. Vol. 6. New York: National American Woman Suffrage Association, 1922. Reprint. New York: Arno Press, 1969.

371. Lindig, Carmen. *The Path from the Parlor: Louisiana Women 1879–1920.* Lafayette, LA: Center for Louisiana Studies, University of Southwestern Louisiana, 1986.

372. Spiers, Patricia L. "The Woman Suffrage Movement in New Orleans." Master's thesis, Southeastern Louisiana College, 1965.

Maine

373. Colvin, Caroline, Helen N. Batu, and Mabel Connor. "Maine." In *History of Woman Suffrage,* edited by Ida Husted Harper, 236–247. Vol. 6. New York: National American Woman Suffrage Association, 1922. Reprint. New York: Arno Press, 1969.

374. Day, Lucy Hobart. "Maine." In *History of Woman Suffrage,* edited by Susan B. Anthony and Ida Husted Harper, 689–694. Vol. 4. Indianapolis: Hollenbeck Press, 1902. Reprint. New York: Arno Press, 1969.

375. Des Cognets, Marian B. "Woman Suffrage: Ally or Enemy for Maine's Franco-Americans, 1917–1920." Master's thesis, University of Maine, Orono, 1988.

Maryland

376. Funck, Emma Maddox. "Maryland." In *History of Woman Suffrage,* edited by Ida Husted Harper, 248–266. Vol. 6. New York: National American Woman Suffrage Association, 1922. Reprint. New York: Arno Press, 1969.

377. Son, Mal Hee. "The Woman Suffrage Movement in Maryland from 1870–1920." Master's thesis, University of Maryland, College Park, 1962.

378. Thomas, Mary Bentley. "Maryland." In *History of Woman Suffrage,* edited by Susan B. Anthony and Ida Husted Harper, 695–700. Vol. 4. Indianapolis: Hollenbeck Press, 1902. Reprint. New York: Arno Press, 1969.

379. Weaver, Diane E. "Maryland Women and the Transformation of Politics, 1890's-1930." Ph.D. dissertation, University of Maryland, College Park, 1992.

Massachusetts

380. Blackwell, Alice Stone. "Massachusetts." In *History of Woman Suffrage,* edited by Susan B. Anthony and Ida Husted Harper, 701–750. Vol. 4. Indianapolis: Hollenbeck Press,

1902. Reprint. New York: Arno Press, 1969.

381. Blackwell, Alice Stone, and Teresa A. Crowley. "Massachusetts." In *History of Woman Suffrage,* edited by Ida Husted Harper, 267–302. Vol. 6. New York: National American Woman Suffrage Association, 1922. Reprint. New York: Arno Press, 1969.

382. Grandfield, Robert S. "The Massachusetts Suffrage Referendum of 1915." *Historical Journal of Western Massachusetts* 7 (January 1979): 46–57.

383. Kenneally, James J. "Catholicism and Woman Suffrage in Massachusetts." *Catholic Historical Review* 53, no. 1 (April 1967): 43–57.

384. ———. *Blanche Ames and Woman Suffrage, the Story of the Fight for Passage of the Woman Suffrage Amendment in the Town of Easton and the State of Massachusetts, 1915–1920.* Boston: Friends of Borland, 1993.

385. Merk, Lois Bannister. "Massachusetts in the Woman Suffrage Movement." Ph.D. dissertation, Radcliff, Harvard University, Cambridge, 1956.

386. Strom, Sharon Hartman. "Leadership and Tactics in the American Woman Suffrage Movement: A New Perspective from Massachusetts." *Journal of American History* 62, no. 2 (September 1975): 296–315.

Michigan

387. Arthur, Clara B., and Belle Brotherton. "Michigan." In *History of Woman Suffrage,* edited by Ida Husted

Harper, 303–316. Vol. 6. New York: National American Woman Suffrage Association, 1922. Reprint. New York: Arno Press, 1969.

388. Caruso, Virginia Ann Paganelli. "A History of Woman Suffrage in Michigan." Ph.D. dissertation, Michigan State University, 1986.

389. Doe, Mary L., and May Stocking. "Michigan." In *History of Woman Suffrage,* edited by Susan B. Anthony and Ida Husted Harper, 755–771. Vol. 4. Indianapolis: Hollenbeck Press, 1902. Reprint. New York: Arno Press, 1969.

390. *Michigan Women's Suffrage: A Political History.* Lansing: Michigan Political Society and Michigan Women's Studies Association, 1995.

391. Sleeman, Allison Mook. "The Michigan Woman Suffrage Movement, 1912–1919." Ph.D. dissertation, Eastern Michigan University, 1983.

Minnesota

392. Nelson, Julia B., Cora Smith Eaton, and Emod E. Hurd. "Minnesota." In *History of Woman Suffrage,* edited by Susan B. Anthony and Ida Husted Harper, 772–782. Vol. 4. Indianapolis: Hollenbeck Press, 1902. Reprint. New York: Arno Press, 1969.

393. Stockwell, Maud C. "Minnesota." In *History of Woman Suffrage,* edited by Ida Husted Harper, 317–325. Vol. 6. New York: National American Woman Suffrage Association, 1922. Reprint. New York: Arno Press, 1969.

394. Stuhler, Barbara. "Organizing for the Vote: Leaders of Minnesota's Woman Suffrage Movement." *Minnesota History* 54, no. 7 (Fall 1995): 290–303.

395. ———. *Gentle Warriors: Clara Ueland and the Minnesota Struggle for Woman Suffrage.* Minneapolis: Minnesota Historical Society Press, 1995.

396. Ziebarth, Marilyn. "Woman's Rights Movement." *Minnesota History* 42, no. 6 (1971): 225–230.

Mississippi

397. Belt, Mrs. Hala Hammond. "Mississippi." In *History of Woman Suffrage,* edited by Susan B. Anthony and Ida Husted Harper, 783–789. Vol. 4. Indianapolis: Hollenbeck Press, 1902. Reprint. New York: Arno Press, 1969.

398. Kearney, Belle. "The Making of a Woman Suffragist." *Southern Exposure* 12 (May–June 1984): 64.

399. Meredith, Mary Louise. "The Mississippi Woman's Rights Movement, 1889–1923: The Leadership of Nellie Nugent Somerville and Greenville in Suffrage Reform." Master's thesis, Delta State University, Cleveland, MS, 1974.

400. Prince, Vinton M. "Woman Behind the Woman Voter." *Journal of Mississippi History* 44, no. 2 (May 1987): 115–129.

401. Taylor, A. Elizabeth. "The Woman Suffrage Movement in Mississippi, 1890–1920." *Journal of Mississippi History* 30, no. 1 (February 1968): 1–34.

402. Thompson, Lily Wilkinson. "Mississippi." In *History of Woman Suffrage,* edited by Ida Husted Harper, 326–341. Vol. 6. New York: National American Woman Suffrage Association, 1922. Reprint. New York: Arno Press, 1969.

Missouri

403. Garesche, Marie R. "Missouri." In *History of Woman Suffrage,* edited by Ida Husted Harper, 342–359. Vol. 6. New York: National American Woman Suffrage Association, 1922. Reprint. New York: Arno Press, 1969.

404. Johnson, Addie. "Missouri." In *History of Woman Suffrage,* edited by Susan B. Anthony and Ida Husted Harper, 790–795. Vol. 4. Indianapolis: Hollenbeck Press, 1902. Reprint. New York: Arno Press, 1969.

405. Morris, Monia Cook. "The History of Woman Suffrage in Missouri, 1867–1901." *Missouri Historical Review* 25, no. 1 (October 1930): 67–82.

406. Scott, Mary Semple. "History of the Woman Suffrage Movement in Missouri." *Missouri Historical Review* 14, no. 3–4 (April–July 1920): 281–385.

407. Young, Dina M. "The Silent Search for a Voice: The St. Louis Equal Suffrage League and the Dilemma of Elite Reform, 1910–1920." *Gateway Heritage* 8 (Spring 1988): 2–19.

Montana

408. Anderson, Mary Long. "Montana." In *History of Woman Suffrage,* edited by Susan B. Anthony and Ida Husted Harper, 796–801. Vol. 4. Indianapolis: Hollenbeck Press, 1902. Reprint. New York: Arno Press, 1969.

409. Cole, Judith K. "A Wide Field for Usefulness: Women's Civil Status and the Evolution of Women's Suffrage on the Montana Frontier, 1864–1914." *American Journal of Legal History* 34, no. 3 (1990): 262–294.

410. Larson, T. A. "Montana Women and the Battle of the Ballot." *Montana, The Magazine of Western History* 23 (Winter 1973): 24–41.

411. Schaffer, Ronald. "The Montana Woman Suffrage Campaign, 1911–1914." *Pacific Northwest Quarterly* 55 (January 1964): 9–15.

412. Topping, Lucile Dyas. "Montana." In *History of Woman Suffrage,* edited by Ida Husted Harper, 360–367. Vol. 6. New York: National American Woman Suffrage Association, 1922. Reprint. New York: Arno Press, 1969.

Nebraska

413. Abbott, Othman. "Struggle for Woman's Rights in Nebraska." *Nebraska History* 11 (July–September 1928): 150–170.

414. Coulter, Thomas Chalmer. "History of Woman Suffrage in Nebraska, 1856–1920." Ed.D. dissertation, Ohio State University, 1967.

415. Fus, Daniel Anthony. "Persuasion on the Plains: The Woman Suffrage Movement in Nebraska." Ph.D. dissertation, Indiana University, 1972.

416. Hayward, Mary Smith. "Nebraska." In *History of Woman Suffrage,* edited by Susan B. Anthony and Ida Husted Harper, 802–809. Vol. 4. Indianapolis: Hollenbeck Press, 1902. Reprint. New York: Arno Press, 1969.

417. Potter, James E. "Barkley Vs. Pool: Woman Suffrage and the Nebraska Referendum Law." *Nebraska History* 69, no. 1 (1988): 11–18.

418. Wheeler, Grace M., and Mary H. Williams. "Nebraska." In *History of Woman Suffrage,* edited by Ida Husted Harper, 368–383. Vol. 6. New York: National American Woman Suffrage Association, 1922. Reprint. New York: Arno Press, 1969.

419. Wilhite, Ann L. Wiegman. "Sixty-Five Years Till Victory: A History of Woman Suffrage in Nebraska." *Nebraska History* 49, no. 2 (Summer 1968): 149–163.

Nevada

420. Mark, Mrs. O. H. "Nevada." In *History of Woman Suffrage,* edited by Ida Husted Harper, 384–399. Vol. 6. New York: National American Woman Suffrage Association, 1922. Reprint. New York: Arno Press, 1969.

421. Smith, Ann Warren. "Anne Martin and a History of Woman Suffrage in Nevada, 1869–1914." Ph.D. dissertation, University of Nevada, Reno, 1975.

422. Totton, Kathryn Dunn. "Hannah Keziah Clapp: The Life and Career of a Pioneer Nevada Educator." *Nevada Historical Society Quarterly* 20, no. 3 (1977): 167–183.

423. Williamson, Frances A. "Nevada." In *History of Woman Suffrage,* edited by Susan B. Anthony and Ida Husted Harper, 810–814. Vol. 4. Indianapolis: Hollenbeck Press, 1902. Reprint. New York: Arno Press, 1969.

424. Winter, Jill M. "Woman Suffrage in Nevada during the Progressive Era." *The Organization of American Historian's Newsletter* 16, no. 1 (1988): 8, 18.

New Hampshire

425. Abbott, Frances M. "New Hampshire." In *History of Woman Suffrage,* edited by Ida Husted Harper, 400–411. Vol. 6. New York: National American Woman Suffrage Association, 1922. Reprint. New York: Arno Press, 1969.

426. Harder, Ida Husted. "New Hampshire." In *History of Woman Suffrage,* edited by Susan B. Anthony and Ida Husted Harper, 815–819. Vol. 4. Indianapolis: Hollenbeck Press, 1902. Reprint. New York: Arno Press, 1969.

427. Hunton, Clara L. "Claremont Equal Suffrage Association." *Granite Monthly* 47 (1915): 75–77.

428. "New Hampshire and Woman Suffrage." *Outlook* 73 (21 February 1903): 418.

429. Pillsbury, Hobart. "Woman Suffrage in New Hampshire." *Granite Monthly* 58 (1926): 260–268.

430. Ricker, Marilla M. "Woman Suffrage." *Granite Monthly* (January 1907): 16–22.

431. ———. "A Plea for Equal Suffrage." *Granite Monthly* (January 1909): 53–56.

432. "Woman Suffrage Defeated in New Hampshire." *Chautauquan* 37 (July 1903): 334–335.

New Jersey

433. Hall, Florence Howe, and Mary D. Hussey. "New Jersey." In *History of Woman Suffrage,* edited by Susan B. Anthony and Ida Husted Harper, 820–834. Vol. 4. Indianapolis: Hollenbeck Press, 1902. Reprint. New York: Arno Press, 1969.

434. Hussey, Mary D. "New Jersey." In *History of Woman Suffrage,* edited by Ida Husted Harper, 412–433. Vol. 6. New York: National American Woman Suffrage Association, 1922. Reprint. New York: Arno Press, 1969.

435. Mahoney, Joseph F. "Woman Suffrage and the Urban Masses." *New Jersey History* 87, no. 3 (Autumn 1969): 151–172.

436. McNeal, Margaret. *Reclaiming Lost Ground: The Struggle for Woman Suffrage in New Jersey.* Ridgewood, NJ: Woman's Project of New Jersey, 1993.

437. Reynolds, Minnie J. "Why Suffrage Failed in New Jersey." *The New Republic* 5 (13 November 1915): 43–44.

438. Strauss, Sylvia. "The Passage of Woman Suffrage in New Jersey, 1911–1920." *New Jersey History* 111, no. 3–4 (Winter 1993): 19–40.

New Mexico

439. Furman, Necah Stewart. "Women's Campaign for Equality: A National and State Perspective." *New Mexico Historical Review* 53 (October 1978): 365–374.

440. Jensen, Joan M. "Disfranchisement Is a Disgrace: Women and Politics in New Mexico, 1900–1940." In *New Mexico Women: Intercultural Perspectives,* edited by Joan M. Jensen and Darlis A. Miller, 301–332. Albuquerque: University of New Mexico Press, 1986. *New Mexico Historical Review* 56, no. 1 (January 1981): 5–35.

441. Lindsey, Deane H. "New Mexico." In *History of Woman Suffrage,* edited by Ida Husted Harper, 434–439. Vol. 6. New York: National American Woman Suffrage Association, 1922. Reprint. New York: Arno Press, 1969.

442. Wallace, Catherine P. "New Mexico." In *History of Woman Suffrage,* edited by Susan B. Anthony and Ida Husted Harper, 835–838. Vol. 4. Indianapolis: Hollenbeck Press, 1902. Reprint. New York: Arno Press, 1969.

443. Whaley, Charlotte. *Nina Otero-Warren of Santa Fe.* Albuquerque: University of New Mexico Press, 1995.

New York

444. Blatch, Harriet Stanton. "Woman Suffrage in New York." *National Monthly* 6 (1914): 80.

445. Blatch, Harriet Stanton, and Alma Lutz. *Challenging Years, The Memoirs of Harriet Stanton Blatch.* New York: G. P. Putnam's Sons, 1940.

446. Carter, Patricia A. "Becoming the 'New Women': The Equal Rights Campaigns of New York City Schoolteachers, 1900–1920." In *Teacher's Voice: A Social History of Teaching in Twentieth Century America,* edited by Richard J. Altenbaugh, 40–58. London: Falmer Press, 1991.

447. Chapman, Mariana Wright, and Jean Brooks. "New York." In *History of Woman Suffrage,* edited by Susan B. Anthony and Ida Husted Harper, 839–873. Vol. 4. Indianapolis: Hollenbeck Press, 1902. Reprint. New York: Arno Press, 1969.

448. Crossett, Ella Hawley. "New York." In *History of Woman Suffrage,* edited by Ida Husted Harper, 440–489. Vol. 6. New York: National American Woman Suffrage Association, 1922. Reprint. New York: Arno Press, 1969.

449. Daniels, Doris. "Building a Winning Coalition: The Suffrage Fight in New York State." *New York History* 60 (January 1979): 59–80.

450. DuBois, Ellen Carol. "Working Women, Class Relations, and Suffrage Militance, Harriet Stanton Blatch and the New York Woman Suffrage Movement, 1894–1909." *Journal of American History* 74 (June 1987): 34–58. Reprinted in *One Woman, One Vote, Rediscovering the Woman Suffrage Movement,* edited by Marjorie Spruill Wheeler, 221–244. Troutdale, OR: NewSage Press, 1995.

451. Huff, Robert A. "Anne Miller and the Geneva Political Equality Club, 1897–1912." *New York History* 65 (October 1984): 324–348.

452. "Indemnities to the Suffragists." *Life and Labor* 8 (December 1918): 258–260.

453. Lerner, Elinor. "Jewish Involvement in the New York City Woman Suffrage Movement." *American Jewish History* 70, no. 4 (June 1981): 442–461.

454. Mathews, Jane. "The Woman Suffrage Movement in Suffolk County, New York: 1911–1917. A Case Study of the Tactical Differences Between Two Prominent Long Island Suffragists: Mrs. Ida Bunce Sammis and Miss Rosalie Jones." Master's thesis, Adelphi University, 1987.

455. McDonald, David Kevin. "Organizing Womanhood: Women's Culture and the Politics of Woman Suffrage in New York State, 1865–1917." Ph.D. dissertation, State University of New York, Stony Brook, 1987.

456. Roosevelt, Theodore. "Women and the New York Constitutional Convention." *Outlook* 107, no. 14 (1 August 1914): 796–798.

457. Schaffer, Ronald. "The New York City Woman Suffrage Party, 1909–1919." *New York History* 43 (July 1962): 269–287.

458. Simkovitch, Mary K. "Casual Reflections on the Election." *The Survey* 39 (17 September 1917): 160–161.

459. Wesser, Robert F. "Women Suffrage, Prohibition, and the New York Experience in the Progressive ERA." In *An American Historian: Essays to Honor Selig Adler,* edited by Milton Plesur, 140–148. Buffalo: State University of New York, 1983.

460. "Woman Suffrage and the New York Convention." *Outlook* 110 (2 June 1915): 243.

North Carolina

461. Burd, Clara Booth. "North Carolina." In *History of Woman Suffrage,* edited by Ida Husted Harper, 490–500. Vol. 6. New York: National American Woman Suffrage Association, 1922. Reprint. New York: Arno Press, 1969.

462. Gilmore, Glenda Elizabeth. "Gender and Jim Crow: Women and the Politics of White Supremacy in North Carolina, 1896–1920." Ph.D. dissertation, University of North Carolina, Chapel Hill, 1992.

463. Russell, Sarah A. "North Carolina." In *History of Woman Suffrage,* edited by Susan B. Anthony and Ida Husted Harper, 874–876. Vol. 4. Indianapolis: Hollenbeck Press, 1902. Reprint. New York: Arno Press, 1969.

464. Taylor, A. Elizabeth. "The Woman Suffrage Movement in North Carolina, Part I." *North Carolina Historical Review* 38 (January 1961): 45–62.

465. ———. "The Woman Suffrage Movement in North Carolina, Part II." *North Carolina Historical Review* 38 (April 1961): 173–189.

North Dakota

466. Knox, Janette Hill. "North Dakota." In *History of Woman Suffrage,* edited by Susan B. Anthony and Ida Husted Harper, 544–552. Vol. 4. Indianapolis: Hollenbeck Press, 1902. Reprint. New York: Arno Press, 1969.

467. Marcella, Andre. "They Won the Right to Vote … But Little More." *Red River Valley Historian* (Summer 1975): 9.

468. Pierce, Emma S. "North Dakota." In *History of Woman Suffrage*, edited by Ida Husted Harper, 501–507. Vol. 6. New York: National American Woman Suffrage Association, 1922. Reprint. New York: Arno Press, 1969.

Ohio

469. Ohio Woman Suffrage Association. *Year Book of the Ohio Woman Suffrage Association, 1914.* Warren, OH: Ohio Woman Suffrage Association, 1915.

470. "Ohio Women Win." *The Independent* 89 (26 February 1917): 345.

471. Rausch, Eileen Regina. "'Let Ohio Women Vote': The Years of Victory, 1900–1920." Ph.D. dissertation, Notre Dame University, 1985.

472. Upton, Harriet Taylor. "Ohio." In *History of Woman Suffrage*, edited by Susan B. Anthony and Ida Husted Harper, 877–885. Vol. 4. Indianapolis: Hollenbeck Press, 1902. Reprint. New York: Arno Press, 1969.

473. ———. "Ohio." In *History of Woman Suffrage*, edited by Ida Husted Harper, 508–519. Vol. 6. New York: National American Woman Suffrage Association, 1922. Reprint. New York: Arno Press, 1969.

Oklahoma

474. James, Louise Boyd. "The Woman Suffrage Issue in the Oklahoma Constitutional Convention, 1906." *Chronicles of Oklahoma* 56 (Winter 1979): 379–392.

475. ———. "Woman's Suffrage, Oklahoma Style, 1890–1918." In *Women in Oklahoma, A Century of Change*, edited by Melvena K. Thurman, 182–197. Oklahoma City: Oklahoma Historical Society, 1986.

476. Mullinax, Ira D. "Woman Suffrage in Oklahoma." *Strum's Oklahoma Magazine* 11, no. 3 (November 1910): 59–63.

477. Rhode, Margaret Olive. "Oklahoma." In *History of Woman Suffrage*, edited by Susan B. Anthony and Ida Husted Harper, 886–890. Vol. 4. Indianapolis: Hollenbeck Press, 1902. Reprint. New York: Arno Press, 1969.

478. Stephens, Adelia C., and Katherine Pierce. "Oklahoma." In *History of Woman Suffrage*, edited by Ida Husted Harper, 520–537. Vol. 6. New York: National American Woman Suffrage Association, 1922. Reprint. New York: Arno Press, 1969.

479. Women Suffrage Association of Oklahoma, ed. *Memorial of the Women of Oklahoma and Indian Territory to the Oklahoma Constitutional Convention.* Guthrie: Women Suffrage Association of Oklahoma, 1906.

480. Wright, James R., Jr. "The Assiduous Wedge: Woman Suffrage and the Oklahoma Constitutional Conventions." *Chronicles of Oklahoma* 51, no. 4 (Winter 1973–74): 421–443.

Oregon

481. Blackwell, Alice Stone. "Object Lesson in Oregon." *The Independent* 61 (26 July 1906): 198–199.

482. Chittenden, Elizabeth F. "'By No Means Excluding Women': Abigail Scott Duniway, Western Pioneer in the Struggle for Equal Voting Rights." *American West* 12, no. 2 (1975): 24–27.

483. Duniway, Abigail Scott. "Oregon." In *History of Woman Suffrage,* edited by Susan B. Anthony and Ida Husted Harper, 891–897. Vol. 4. Indianapolis: Hollenbeck Press, 1902. Reprint. New York: Arno Press, 1969.

484. Evans, Sarah A. "Oregon." In *History of Woman Suffrage,* edited by Ida Husted Harper, 538–549. Vol. 6. New York: National American Woman Suffrage Association, 1922. Reprint. New York: Arno Press, 1969.

485. Kelley, Florence. "Campaign for the Enfranchisement of Women in Oregon." *Outlook* 83 (21 July 1906): 675–676.

486. Kessler, Lauren. "The Ideas of Women Suffragists and the *Portland Oregonian.*" *Journalism Quarterly* 57, no. 4 (1980): 597–605.

487. ———. "The Ideas of Woman Suffrage and the Mainstream Press." *Oregon Historical Quarterly* 84 (Fall 1983): 257–276.

488. ———. "A Siege of the Citadels: Search for a Public Forum for the Ideas of Oregon Woman Suffrage." *Oregon Historical Quarterly* 84 (Summer 1983): 116–149.

489. ———. "The Fight for Woman Suffrage and the Oregon Press." In *Women in Pacific Northwest History: An Anthology,* edited by Karen J. Blair, 43–59. Seattle: University of Washington, 1988.

490. Moynihan, Ruth Barnes. "Abigail Scott Duniway of Oregon: Woman and Suffragist of the American Frontier." Ph.D. dissertation, Yale University, New Haven, 1979.

491. Websdale, Neil. "Female Suffrage, Male Violence, and Law Enforcement in Lane County, Oregon, 1853 to 1960." *Social Justice* (Fall 1992): 82–107.

Pennsylvania

492. Hubbs, Harriet L. "Pennsylvania." In *History of Woman Suffrage,* edited by Ida Husted Harper, 551–564. Vol. 6. New York: National American Woman Suffrage Association, 1922. Reprint. New York: Arno Press, 1969.

493. Johnson, Emily S. "Discovering Pennsylvania." *The Survey* 35 (9 October 1915): 39–42.

494. Katzenstein, Caroline. *Lifting the Curtain: The State and National Woman Suffrage Campaigns in Pennsylvania as I Saw Them.* Philadelphia: Dorrance, 1955.

495. Krone, Henrietta Louise. "Dauntless Women: The Story of the Woman Suffrage Movement in Pennsylvania, 1910–20." Ph.D. dissertation, University of Pennsylvania, Philadelphia, 1946.

496. Leach, Roberts. "Jennie Bradley Roessing and the Fight for Woman Suffrage in Pennsylvania." *Western Pennsylvania History Magazine* 67, no. 3 (1984): 189–211.

497. Longshore, Lucretia. "Pennsylvania." In *History of Woman Suffrage,* edited by Susan B. Anthony and Ida Husted Harper, 898–906. Vol. 4. Indianapolis: Hollenbeck Press, 1902. Reprint. New York: Arno Press, 1969.

498. McKenzie, Edna B. "Daisy Lampkin: A Life of Love and Service." *Pennsylvania Heritage* 9, no. 3 (1983): 9–12.

499. Preston, L. E. "Speakers for Women's Rights in Pennsylvania." *Western Pennsylvania Historical Magazine* 54, no. 3 (July 1971): 245–264.

500. Roessing, Jennie Bradley. "The Equal Suffrage Campaign in Pennsylvania." *Annals of the American Academy of Political and Social Science* 56 (November 1914): 153–160.

501. Winsor, Mary. "The Militant Suffrage Movement." *Annals of the American Academy of Political and Social Science* 56 (November 1914): 134–142.

Rhode Island

502. Algeo, Sara M. *The Story of a Sub-Pioneer.* Providence: Snow and Farnham, 1925.

503. Garlin, Anna. "Rhode Island." In *History of Woman Suffrage,* edited by Susan B. Anthony and Ida Husted Harper, 907–921. Vol. 4. Indianapolis: Hollenbeck Press, 1902. Reprint. New York: Arno Press, 1969.

504. Harper, Ida Husted. "What Do the Newport Suffrage Meetings Mean?" *The Independent* 67 (9 September 1909): 575–595.

505. Rae, John B. "The Great Suffrage Parade." *Rhode Island Historical Journal* 1, no. 3 (July 1942): 90–95.

506. Stevens, Elizabeth Cooke. "From Generation to Generation: The Mother and Daughter Activisim of Elizabeth Buffum Chace and Lillie Chace Wyman." Ph.D. dissertation, Brown University, Providence, 1993.

507. Yates, Elizabeth Upham. "Rhode Island." In *History of Woman Suffrage,* edited by Ida Husted Harper, 565–578. Vol. 6. New York: National American Woman Suffrage Association, 1922. Reprint. New York: Arno Press, 1969.

South Carolina

508. Bland, Sidney R. "Fighting the Odds: Militant Suffragists in South Carolina." *South Carolina Historical Magazine* 82, no. 1 (January 1981): 32–43.

509. Cathcart, Mrs W. C. "South Carolina." In *History of Woman Suffrage,* edited by Ida Husted Harper, 579–584. Vol. 6. New York: National American Woman Suffrage Association, 1922. Reprint. New York: Arno Press, 1969.

510. Smedley, Katherine. "Martha Schofield and the Rights of Women." *South Carolina Historical Magazine* 85, no. 3 (1984): 195–210.

511. Taylor, A. Elizabeth. "South Carolina and the Enfranchisement of

Women: The Early Years." *South Carolina Historical Magazine* (April 1976): 115–125.

512. Young, Virginia D. "South Carolina." In *History of Woman Suffrage,* edited by Susan B. Anthony and Ida Husted Harper, 922–925. Vol. 4. Indianapolis: Hollenbeck Press, 1902. Reprint. New York: Arno Press, 1969.

South Dakota

513. Easton, Patricia O'Keefe. "Woman Suffrage in South Dakota: The Final Decade, 1911–1920." *South Dakota History* 13 (Fall 1983): 206–226.

514. Hipple, Ruth B. "South Dakota." In *History of Woman Suffrage,* edited by Ida Husted Harper, 585–595. Vol. 6. New York: National American Woman Suffrage Association, 1922. Reprint. New York: Arno Press, 1969.

515. Pickler, Alice M. A. "South Dakota." In *History of Woman Suffrage,* edited by Susan B. Anthony and Ida Husted Harper, 552–562. Vol. 4. Indianapolis: Hollenbeck Press, 1902. Reprint. New York: Arno Press, 1969.

516. Riessen-Reed, Dorinda. *The Woman Suffrage Movement in South Dakota.* 2d ed. South Dakota Commission on the Status of Women, 1975. Governmental Research Bureau, State University of South Dakota, Report No. 41, 1958.

Tennessee

517. Ambrose, Andrew M. "Sister Reforms: An Examination of the Relationship between the Tennessee Women Temperance Union and State Women Suffrage Movement, 1890–1920." Master's thesis, University of Tennessee, Knoxville, 1979.

518. Arendale, Marirose. "Tennessee and Womens' Rights." *Tennessee Historical Quarterly* 39, no. 1 (Spring 1980): 62–78.

519. Berkeley, Kathleen Christine. " 'An Advocate for Her Sex': Feminism and Conservatism in the Post–Civil War South." *Tennessee Historical Quarterly* 43, no. 4 (Winter 1984): 390–407.

520. Kenny, Mrs. John, and Margaret Ervin Ford. "Tennessee." In *History of Woman Suffrage,* edited by Ida Husted Harper, 598–625. Vol. 6. New York: National American Woman Suffrage Association, 1922. Reprint. New York: Arno Press, 1969.

521. Meriwether, Lida A. "Tennessee." In *History of Woman Suffrage,* edited by Susan B. Anthony and Ida Husted Harper, 926–930. Vol. 4. Indianapolis: Hollenbeck Press, 1902. Reprint. New York: Arno Press, 1969.

522. Prescott, Grace Elizabeth. "The Woman Suffrage Movement in Memphis: Its Place in the State Sectional and National Movements." *West Tennessee Historical Society Papers* 18 (1964): 87–106.

523. Sims, Anastastia. " 'Powers That Pray' and 'Powers That Prey': Tennessee and the Fight for Woman Suffrage." *Tennessee Historical Quarterly* 50 (Winter 1991): 203–225.

524. ———. "Armageddon in Tennessee: The Final Battle Over the Nineteenth Amendment." In *One*

Woman, One Vote, Rediscovering the Woman Suffrage Movement, edited by Marjorie Spruill Wheeler, 333–352. Troutdale, OR: NewSage Press, 1995.

525. Taylor, A. Elizabeth. "A Short History of the Woman Suffrage Movement in Tennessee." *Tennessee Historical Quarterly* 2 (1943): 195–215.

526. ——. *The Woman Suffrage Movement in Tennessee.* New York: Bookman, 1957.

527. ——. "Sue Shelton White and the Women Suffrage Movement." *Tennessee Historical Quarterly* 22 (June 1963): 179–190.

528. Wheeler, Marjorie Spruill. *Votes for Women! The Woman Suffrage Movement in Tennessee, the South, and the Nation.* Nashville: University of Tennessee Press, 1995.

529. Yellin, Carol Lynn. "Countdown in Tennessee, 1920." *American Heritage* 30, no. 1 (1978): 12–35.

Texas

530. Eudy, John Carroll. "The Vote and Lone Star Women: Minnie Fisher Cunningham and the Texas Equal Suffrage Association." *East Texas Historical Journal* 14, no. 2 (Fall 1976): 52–59.

531. Graham, Sara Sally Hunter. "Woman Suffrage and the New Democracy." Ph.D. dissertation, University of Texas, Austin, 1988.

532. Marilley, Suzanne M. "Democrats Divided: Why the Texas Legislature Gave Women Primary Suffrage in 1918." Paper presented at the annual meeting of the SAWHC, 1991.

533. McArthur, Judith N. "Minnie Fisher Cunningham's Back Door Lobby in Texas: Political Maneuvering in a One-Party State." In *One Woman, One Vote, Rediscovering the Woman Suffrage Movement,* edited by Marjorie Spruill Wheeler, 315–332. Troutdale, OR: NewSage Press, 1995.

534. McArthur, Judith N., Ruthe Winegarten, and A. Elizabeth Taylor, eds. *Citizens at Last: The Women Suffrage Movement in Texas.* Austin: E. C. Temple, 1987.

535. McCallum, Jane Y. "Texas." In *History of Woman Suffrage,* edited by Ida Husted Harper, 626–643. Vol. 6. New York: National American Woman Suffrage Association, 1922. Reprint. New York: Arno Press, 1969.

536. ——. *A Texas Suffragist: Diaries and Writings of Jane Y. McCallum.* Edited by Janet G. Humphrey. Austin: E. C. Temple, 1988.

537. Scott, Janelle D. "Local Leadership in the Woman Suffrage Movement: Houston's Campaign for the Vote 1917–1918." *Houston Review* 12, no. 1 (1990): 3–22.

538. Stoddard, Helen M. "Texas." In *History of Woman Suffrage,* edited by Susan B. Anthony and Ida Husted Harper, 931–935. Vol. 4. Indianapolis: Hollenbeck Press, 1902. Reprint. New York: Arno Press, 1969.

539. Taylor, A. Elizabeth. "The Woman Suffrage Movement in Texas." *Journal of Southern History* 17 (May 1951): 194–215.

540. Turner, Elizabeth Hayes. "Women Progressives and the Origins of Local Suffrage Societies in

Texas." Paper presented at the annual meeting of the Southern Historian Association, 1991.

541. ———. "'White Gloved Ladies' and 'New Women' in the Texas Woman Suffrage Movement." In *Southern Women: Histories and Identities,* edited by Virginia Bernhard, 129–156. Columbia: University of Missouri, 1992.

542. Wygant, Larry J. "'A Municipal Broom': The Woman Suffrage Campaign in Galveston, Texas." *Houston Review* 3 (1984): 117–134.

Utah

543. Beeton, Beverly. "'I Am an American Woman': Charlotte Ives Cobb Godbe Kirby." *Journal of the West* 27, no. 2 (1988): 13–19.

544. Gates, Susa Young. "Utah." In *History of Woman Suffrage,* edited by Ida Husted Harper, 644–650. Vol. 6. New York: National American Woman Suffrage Association, 1922. Reprint. New York: Arno Press, 1969.

545. Madsen, Carol Cornwall. "Emmeline B. Wells: 'Am I Not A Woman and a Sister?'" *Brigham Young University Studies* 22, no. 2 (1982): 161–178.

546. Wells, Emmeline B. "Utah." In *History of Woman Suffrage,* edited by Susan B. Anthony and Ida Husted Harper, 936–956. Vol. 4. Indianapolis: Hollenbeck Press, 1902. Reprint. New York: Arno Press, 1969.

547. White, William Griffin. "The Feminist Campaign for the Exclusion of Brigham Henry Roberts from the Fifty-Sixth Congress." *Journal of the West* 17, no. 1 (1978): 45–52.

Vermont

548. Clifford, Deborah P. "The Drive for Woman's Municipal Suffrage in Vermont, 1883–1917." *Vermont History* 47, no. 3 (Summer 1979): 173–190.

549. Moore, Laura. "Vermont." In *History of Woman Suffrage,* edited by Susan B. Anthony and Ida Husted Harper, 957–963. Vol. 4. Indianapolis: Hollenbeck Press, 1902. Reprint. New York: Arno Press, 1969.

550. Parmelee, Annette W. "Vermont." In *History of Woman Suffrage,* edited by Ida Husted Harper, 651–664. Vol. 6. New York: National American Woman Suffrage Association, 1922. Reprint. New York: Arno Press, 1969.

Virginia

551. Clare, Carol Jean. "The Woman Suffrage Movement in Virginia: Its Nature, Rationale, and Tactics." Master's thesis, University of Virginia, Charlottesville, 1968.

552. Coleman, Elizabeth Dabney. "Genteel Crusader: Lila Meads Valentine Fought the Good Fight for Woman's Rights but the Fruits of Victory Were Denied Her." *Virginia Cavalcade* 4, no. 2 (Autumn 1954): 29–32.

553. ———. "Penwoman of Virginia's Feminists." *Virginia Cavalcade* 6 (Winter 1956): 8–11.

554. Cowles, Edith Clark, Adele Clark, and Ida Mae Thompson. "Virginia." In *History of Woman Suffrage,* edited by Ida Husted Harper, 665–672. Vol. 6. New York: National American Woman Suffrage Association, 1922. Reprint. New York: Arno Press, 1969.

555. Graham, Sara Sally Hunter. "Woman Suffrage in Virginia: The Equal Suffrage League and Press-Group Politics, 1909–1920." *Virginia Magazine of History and Biography* 101, no. 2 (April 1993): 227–250.

556. Harper, Ida Husted. "Virginia." In *History of Woman Suffrage,* edited by Susan B. Anthony and Ida Husted Harper, 964–966. Vol. 4. Indianapolis: Hollenbeck Press, 1902. Reprint. New York: Arno Press, 1969.

557. Scura, Dorothy. "Ellen Glasgow and Women's Suffrage." *Research in Action* 6 (Spring 1982): 12–15.

558. Shelton, Charlotte Jean. "Woman Suffrage and Virginia Politics, 1909–1920." Master's thesis, University of Virginia, Charlottesville, 1969.

559. Wheeler, Marjorie Spruill. "Mary Johnston, Suffragist." *Virginia Magazine of History and Biography* 100 (January 1992): 99–118.

Washington

560. Bjorkman, Frances M. "Women's Political Methods." *Colliers* 45 (20 August 1910): 22–24.

561. Harper, Ida Husted. "New State for Woman Suffrage: Washington." *Harper's Bazaar* 45 (January 1911): 38.

562. King, Cora Smith, Smith DeVoe, Mrs. Horner M. Hill, and Sarah A. Kendall. "Washington." In *History of Woman Suffrage,* edited by Ida Husted Harper, 673–686. Vol. 6. New York: National American Woman Suffrage Association, 1922. Reprint. New York: Arno Press, 1969.

563. Larson, T. A. "The Woman Suffrage Movement in Washington." *Pacific Northwest Quarterly* 67, no. 2 (1976): 49–62.

564. Pike, Martha E. "Washington." In *History of Woman Suffrage,* edited by Susan B. Anthony and Ida Husted Harper, 967–979. Vol. 4. Indianapolis: Hollenbeck Press, 1902. Reprint. New York: Arno Press, 1969.

565. "Woman's Victory in Washington." *Colliers* 46 (7 January 1911): 25, 28.

West Virginia

566. Caldwell, Annie. "West Virginia." In *History of Woman Suffrage,* edited by Susan B. Anthony and Ida Husted Harper, 980–984. Vol. 4. Indianapolis: Hollenbeck Press, 1902. Reprint. New York: Arno Press, 1969.

567. Effland, Anne Wallace. "Exciting Battle and Dramatic Finish: The West Virginia Woman Suffrage Movement, Part I, 1867–1916." *West Virginia History* 46, no. 1 (1985): 137–158.

568. ———. "Exciting Battle and Dramatic Finish: West Virginia's Ratification of the Nineteenth Amendment." *West Virginia History* 48 (1989): 61–92.

569. ———. "A Profile of Political Activity: Women of the West Virginia Woman Suffrage Movement." *West Virginia History* 49 (1990): 103–114.

570. Jones, Harriet B., and Lenna Lowe. "West Virginia." In *History of Woman Suffrage,* edited by Ida Husted Harper, 687–698. Vol. 6. New York: National American Woman Suffrage Association, 1922. Reprint. New York: Arno Press, 1969.

571. Melosh, Barbara. "Recovery and Revision: Women's History and West Virginia." *West Virginia History* 49 (1990): 3–6.

572. Spindel, Donna J. "Women's Legal Rights in West Virginia, 1863–1984." *West Virginia History* 51 (1992): 29–43.

Wisconsin

573. Brown, Olympia. "Wisconsin." In *History of Woman Suffrage,* edited by Susan B. Anthony and Ida Husted Harper, 985–993. Vol. 4. Indianapolis: Hollenbeck Press, 1902. Reprint. New York: Arno Press, 1969.

574. Duckett, Kenneth W. "Suffragettes on the Stump: Letter from the Political Equality League of Wisconsin, 1912." *Wisconsin Magazine of History* 38 (Autumn 1954): 32.

575. Freeman, Lucy, Sherry LaFollette, and George A. Zabriskie. *Belle: The Biography of Belle Case la Follette.* New York: Beaufort Books, 1985.

576. Grant, Marilyn. "The 1912 Suffrage Referendum: An Exercise in Political Action." *Wisconsin Magazine*

of History 64 (Winter 1980–81): 107–118.

577. Graves, Lawrence L. "The Wisconsin Woman Suffrage Movement, 1846–1920." Ph.D. dissertation, University of Wisconsin, 1954.

578. Kennedy, Kathleen. "Loyalty and Citizenship in the Wisconsin Women's Suffrage Association, 1917–1919." *Mid-America* 76 (Spring 1994): 109–132.

579. McBride, Genevieve G. "Theodora Winton Youmans and the Wisconsin Woman Movement." *Wisconsin Magazine of History* 71, no. 4 (1988): 243–275.

580. ———. *On Wisconsin Women: Working for Their Rights from Settlement to Suffrage.* Madison: University of Wisconsin Press, 1993.

581. Neu, Charles E. "Olympia Brown and the Woman's Suffrage Movement." *Wisconsin Magazine of History* 43 (Summer 1960): 277–287.

582. Vaughn, Stephen. "An Arena for Debate: Woman Suffrage, the Brewing Industry, and the Press, Wisconsin, 1910–1919." Ph.D. dissertation, University of Wisconsin, Madison, 1995.

583. Willis, Gwendolen B. "Olympia Brown." *Universalist Historical Society Journal* 4, no. 1 (1963): 1–76.

584. Wisconsin Woman's Suffrage Association, ed. *Social Forces, a Topical Outline, with Bibliography.* Madison: Wisconsin Woman's Suffrage Association, 1913.

585. Youmans, Theodora W. "Wisconsin." In *History of Woman Suffrage,* edited by Ida Husted Harper, 699–708. Vol. 6. New York: National American Woman Suffrage Association, 1922. Reprint. New York: Arno Press, 1969.

Wyoming

586. Chapman, Miriam. "The Story of Woman Suffrage in Wyoming, 1869–1990." Master's thesis, University of Wyoming, 1952.

587. Hebard, Grace Raymond. "Wyoming." In *History of Woman Suffrage,* edited by Ida Husted Harper, 709–713. Vol. 6. New York: National American Woman Suffrage Association, 1922. Reprint. New York: Arno Press, 1969.

588. Larson, T. A. "Wyoming's Contribution to the Regional and National Woman's Rights Movement." *Annals of Wyoming* 52, no. 1 (1980): 2–15.

589. Morris, Robert C. "Wyoming." In *History of Woman Suffrage,* edited by Susan B. Anthony and Ida Husted Harper, 994–1011. Vol. 4. Indianapolis: Hollenbeck Press, 1902. Reprint. New York: Arno Press, 1969.

In the Territories and District

Alaska

590. Clark, Jeannette Drury. "Alaska." In *History of Woman Suffrage,* edited by Ida Husted Harper, 713–715. Vol. 6. New York: National American Woman Suffrage Association, 1922. Reprint. New York: Arno Press, 1969.

591. Hall, Robert F. "Women Have Been Voting Ever Since." *Adirondack Life* 2, no. 1 (1971): 46–49.

District of Columbia

592. Chase, Florence Adele. "District of Columbia." In *History of Woman Suffrage,* edited by Susan B. Anthony and Ida Husted Harper, 567–576. Vol. 4. Indianapolis: Hollenbeck Press, 1902. Reprint. New York: Arno Press, 1969.

593. O'Toole, Mary. "District of Columbia." In *History of Woman Suffrage,* edited by Ida Husted Harper, 104–112. Vol. 6. New York: National American Woman Suffrage Association, 1922. Reprint. New York: Arno Press, 1969.

Hawaii

594. Clark, Jeannette Drury. "Hawaii." In *History of Woman Suffrage,* edited by Ida Husted Harper, 715–719. Vol. 6. New York: National American Woman Suffrage Association, 1922. Reprint. New York: Arno Press, 1969.

Philippine Islands

595. Clark, Jeannette Drury. "Philippines." In *History of Woman Suffrage,* edited by Ida Husted Harper, 719–721. Vol. 6. New York: National American Woman Suffrage Association, 1922. Reprint. New York: Arno Press, 1969.

596. Fisher, Miriam L. "Portia of the Philippines." *Independent Woman* 29 (January 1950): 7–8.

597. "Votes for Women." *Time* 29 (10 May 1937): 18.

598. Wood, Margaret Mary. "The Independent Filipina." *Independent Woman* 24 (October 1945): 276–279.

Puerto Rico

599. Azize-Vargas, Yamila. "The Roots of Puerto Rican Feminism: The Struggle for Universal Suffrage." *Radical America* 21, no. 1 (1990): 71–80.

600. Clark, Jeannette Drury. "Porto Rico." In *History of Woman Suffrage,* edited by Ida Husted Harper, 722–724. Vol. 6. New York: National American Woman Suffrage Association, 1922. Reprint. New York: Arno Press, 1969.

601. Jimenez-Munoz, Gladys M. "'A Storm Dressed in Skirts': Ambivalence in the Debate on Women's Suffrage in Puerto Rico, 1927–1929." Ph.D. dissertation, State University of New York, Binghampton, 1994.

602. "More Votes for Women: Porto Rico." *The Nation* 128 (26 June 1929): 755–756.

603. "Woman Suffrage in Porto Rico." *The Woman Citizen* 11 (May 1927): 31.

Social Reform

General

604. Addams, Jane. *Twenty Years at Hull House.* New York: Macmillan, 1911.

605. ———. *The Second Twenty Years at Hull House.* New York: Macmillan, 1930.

606. "America and the Immigrant, A Suffragist Strikes the Balance." *The Woman Citizen* 1 (2 June 1917): 13, 18.

607. Bosell, Helen V. "Promoting Americanization." *Annals of the American Academy of Political and Social Science* 64 (March 1916): 204–209.

608. Cantarow, Ellen, Susan O'Malley, and Sharon Hartman Strom. *Moving the Mountain: Women Working for Social Change.* Old Westbury, NY: Feminist Press, 1980.

609. Clark, Walter. "Woman Suffrage as a Labor Movement." *American Federationist* 26 (May 1919): 389–392.

610. Davis, Allen F. "The Campaign for the Industrial Relations Commission, 1911–1913." *Mid-America* 45, no. 4 (1963): 211–228.

611. Frankel, Noralee, and Nancy Schrom Dye, eds. *Gender, Class, Race and Reform in the Progressive Era.* Lexington: University Press of Kentucky, 1991.

612. Kelley, Florence. "Women and Social Legislation in the United States." *Annals of the American Academy of Political and Social Science* 56 (November 1914): 62–71.

613. Lebsock, Suzanne. "Women and American Politics, 1880–1920." In *Women, Politics and Change,* edited by Louise A. Tilly and Patricia Gurin, 35–62. New York: Russell Sage, 1990.

614. Muncy, Robyn. *Creating a Female Dominion in American Reform,*

1890–1935. New York: Oxford University Press, 1991.

615. Nathan, Mrs. Frederick. "Woman Suffrage, an Aid to Social Reform." *Annals of the American Academy of Political and Social Science* 35, Supplement (May 1910): 33–35.

616. Sage, Olivia Slocum. "Opportunities and Responsibilities of Leisured Women." *North American Review* 181 (November 1905): 712–721.

617. Salem, Dorothy C. *To Better Our World: Black Women in Organized Reform, 1890–1920.* Brooklyn, NY: Carlson, 1990.

618. Wolfson, Theresa. "Trade Union Activities of Women." *Annals of the American Academy of Political and Social Science* 143, no. 2 (May 1929): 120–131.

Leaders and Activists

619. Addams, Jane. "Julia Lathrop at Hull House: Women and the Art of Government." *Survey Graphic* 24 (September 1935): 434–438, 457.

620. ———. *My Friend, Julia Lathrop.* New York: Macmillan, 1935.

621. Blumberg, Dorothy Rose. *Florence Kelley: The Making of a Social Pioneer.* New York: A. M. Kelley, 1966.

622. Bowie, Walter Russell. *Sunrise in the South: The Life of Mary Cooke Branch Munford.* Richmond, VA: William Byrd Press, 1942.

623. Conway, Jill K. "Women Reformers and American Culture, 1870–1930." *Journal of Social History* 72, no. 5 (1971): 164–177.

624. Cook, Blanche Wiesen. "Female Support Networks and Political Activism: Lillian Wald, Crystal Eastman, Emma Goldman." *Chrysalis: A Magazine of Women's Culture* 3 (1977): 43–61.

625. Costin, Lela B. *Two Sisters for Social Justice: A Biography of Grace and Edith Abbott.* Urbana: University of Illinois Press, 1983.

626. Dreier, Mary E. *Margaret Drier Robins, Her Life, Letters and Work.* New York: Island Press Cooperative, 1950.

627. Fitzpatrick, Ellen. *Endless Crusade: Women Social Scientists and Progressive Reform.* New York: Oxford University Press, 1990.

628. Gilman, Charlotte Perkins. *The Living of Charlotte Perkins Gilman, An Autobiography.* New York: D. Appleton-Century, 1935.

629. Hareven, Tamara K. "Eleanor Roosevelt and Reform." In *Without Precedent,* edited by Joan Hoff-Wilson, 201–213. Bloomington: Indiana University Press, 1984.

630. Jensen, Richard. "Family, Career and Reform: Women Leaders of the Progressive Era." In *The American Family in Social-Historical Perspective,* 267–280. New York: St. Martin's Press, 1973.

631. Katz, Sherry J. "Frances Nacke Noel and 'Sister Movements': Socialism, Feminism and Trade Unionism in Los Angeles, 1909–1916." *California History* 67, no. 3 (1988): 180–189.

632. O'Farrell, M. Brigid, and Lydia Kleiner. "Anna Sullivan: Trade Union Organizer." *Frontiers* 2, no. 2 (1977): 29–36.

633. Philips, J. O. C. "The Education of Jane Addams." *History of Education Quarterly* 14, no. 1 (1974): 49–67.

634. Reid, Bill G. "Elizabeth Preston Anderson and the Politics of Reform." In *The North Dakota Political Tradition,* edited by Thomas Howard, 189–202. North Dakota Centennial Heritage Series. Vol. 1. Ames: Iowa State University Press, 1981.

635. Rouse, Jacqueline Anne. *Lugenia Burns Hope, Black Southern Reformer.* Athens: University of Georgia Press, 1989.

636. Schechter, Patricia Ann. "'To Tell the Truth Freely': Ida B. Wells and the Politics of Race, Gender, and Reform in America, 1880–1913." Ph.D. dissertation, Princeton University, 1994.

637. Scott, Anne Firor. "Jane Addams and the City." *Virginia Quarterly Review* 43, no. 1 (1967): 53–62.

638. Sklar, Kathryn Kish. *Florence Kelley and the Nation's Work: The Rise of Women's Political Culture, 1830–1900.* New Haven, CT: Yale University Press, 1995.

639. Travis, Anthony R. "Sophonisba Breckinridge, Militant Feminist." *Midwest Journal of Political Science* 58, no. 2 (1976): 111–118.

Organizations

National Consumers' League

640. Dorr, Rheta Childe. *Women's Demand for Humane Treatment of Women Workers in Shop and Factory.* New York: Consumer's League of New York City, 1909.

641. Keyserling, Mary Dublin. "The First National Consumer Organization: The National Consumers League." In *Consumer Activists: They Made a Difference, A History of Consumer Action Related by Leaders in the Consumer Movement,* 343–365. Mount Vernon, NY: Consumers Union Foundation, 1982.

642. Levine, Susan. "Workers' Wives: Gender, Class and Consumerism in the 1920s United States." *Gender and History* 3, no. 1 (1991): 45–64.

643. National Consumers' League. *Roots of the Consumer Movement, A Chronicle of Consumer History in the Twentieth Century.* Washington, DC: National Consumers' League, 1979.

644. Wolfe, Allis Rosenberg. "Women, Consumerism, and the National Consumers' League in the Progressive Era, 1900–1923." *Labor History* 16 (1975): 378–392.

National Women's Trade Union League

645. Amsterdam, Susan. "The National Women's Trade Union League." *Social Service Review* 56, no. 2 (1982): 259–272.

646. Chappell, Winifred L. "The National Women's Trade Union League." *The Woman Citizen* 9 (16 May 1925): 12, 28.

647. Conn, Sandra. "Three Talents: Robins, Nestor, and Anderson of the Chicago Women's Trade Union

League." *Chicago History* 9, no. 4 (1980–81): 234–247.

648. Davis, Allen F. "The Women's Trade Union League: Origins and Organization." *Labor History* 5 (Winter 1964): 3–17.

649. Delzell, Ruth. *The Early History of Women's Trade Unionists of America.* Chicago: National Women's Trade Union League, 1914.

650. Dye, Nancy Schrom. "Feminism or Unionism? The New York Women's Trade Union League." *Feminist Studies* 3, no. 1–2 (Fall 1975): 111–125.

651. ———. *As Equals and As Sisters: Feminism, The Women's Trade Union League of New York.* Columbia: University of Missouri Press, 1980.

652. Henry, Alice. *The Trade Union Woman.* New York: D. Appleton, 1915.

653. Jacoby, Robin Miller. "The Women's Trade Union League and American Feminism." *Feminist Studies* 3, no. 1–2 (Fall 1975): 126–140.

654. Nathan, Maud. *The Story of an Epoch-Making Movement.* New York: Doubleday, Page, 1926.

655. Payne, Elizabeth Anne. *Reform, Labor and Feminism: Margaret Dreier Robins and the Women's Trade Union League.* Urbana: University of Illinois, 1988.

National Association of Colored Women

656. Jones, Beverly Washington. "Mary Church Terrell and the National Association of Colored Women, 1896–1901." *Journal of Negro History* 67, no. 1 (1982): 20–33.

657. Kendrick, Ruby M. "They Also Serve: The National Association of Colored Women, 1895–1954." *Negro History Bulletin* 17 (May 1954): 171–175. Reprinted in *Black Women in United States History*, Vol. 3, edited by Darlene Clark Hine, 817–825. Brooklyn, NY: Carlson, 1990,

658. Salem, Dorothy C.. "National Movements and Issues: Women, Race, and the National Association of Colored Women, 1890–1910." In *To Better Our World: Black Women in Organized Reform, 1890–1920,* 29–64. Brooklyn, NY: Carlson, 1990.

659. Shaw, Stephanie F. "Black Club Women and the Creation of the National Association of Colored Women." *Journal of American History* 78, no. 2 (September 1991): 559–590. Reprint. *"We Specialize in the Wholly Impossible": A Reader in Black Women's History,* Darlene Clark Hine, Wilma King, and Linda Reed, eds., 443–448. Brooklyn, NY: Carlson, 1995.

Young Women's Christian Association

660. Cochrane, Sharlene Voogd. "'And the Pressure Never Let Up': Black Women, White Women, and the Boston YWCA, 1918–1948." In *Women in the Civil Rights Movement: Trailblazers and Torchbearers,* edited by Vicki L. Crawford, Jacqueline Anne Rouse, and Barbara Woods, 259–270. Vol. 16 of *Black Women in United States History,* edited by Darlene Clark Hine. Brooklyn, NY: Carlson, 1990.

661. Hook, Alice P. "The YWCA in Cincinnati: A Century of Service, 1868–1968." *Cincinnati Historical Society Bulletin* 26, no. 2 (1968): 119–136.

662. Sims, Mary S. *The Natural History of a Social Institution: The Young Woman's Christian Association.* New York: Woman's Press, 1936.

Child Labor

663. Chambers, Clarke A. "The Crusade for Children." In *Seedtime of Reform: American Social Service and Social Action, 1918–1933,* 27–58. Minneapolis: University of Minnesota Press, 1963.

664. Gordon, Lynn. "Women and the Anti-Child Labor Movement in Illinois, 1890–1920." *Social Services Review* 51, no. 2 (1977): 228–248.

665. McArthur, Judith N. "Saving the Children: The Women's Crusade against Child Labor, 1902–1918." In *Women and Texas History,* edited by Fane Downs and Nancy Baker Jones, 57–71. Austin: Texas State Historical Association, 1993.

666. McFarland, Charles K. "Crusade for Child Laborers: 'Mother' Jones and the March of the Mill Children." *Pennsylvania History* 38 (July 1971): 283–296.

667. Trattner, Walter I. *Crusade for the Children: A History of the National Child Labor Committee and Child Labor Reform in America.* New York: Quadrangle, 1970.

Consumers

668. Frank, Dana. "Housewives, Socialists, and the Politics of Food: The 1917 New York Cost-of-Living Protests." *Feminist Studies* 11 (Summer 1985): 255–286.

669. Heath, Mrs. Juhan. "The Housewife's Fight Is the Nation's." *Good Housekeeping* 55, no. 4 (1912): 511–512.

670. Hyman, Paule E. "Immigrant Women and Consumer Protest: The New York City Kosher Meat Boycott of 1902." *American Jewish History* 70 (September 1980): 91–105.

Lynching

671. Aptheker, Bettina. "Woman Suffrage and the Crusade Against Lynching." In *Woman's Legacy: Essays on Race, Sex, and Class in American History,* edited by Bettina Aptheker, 53–76. Amherst: University of Massachusetts Press, 1982.

672. Dudley, Julius Wayne. "A History of the Association of Southern Women for the Prevention of Lynching, 1930–1942." Ph.D. dissertation, Harvard University, Cambridge, 1979.

673. Hall, Jacquelyn Dowd. "Women and Lynching." *Southern Exposure* 4, no. 4 (Winter 1977): 53–54.

674. ———. *Revolt against Chivalry: Jessie Daniel Ames and the Women's Campaign against Lynching.* New York: Columbia University Press, 1979.

675. Miller, Kathleen Atkinson. "The Ladies and the Lynchers: A Look at the Association of Southern Women for the Prevention of Lynching." *Southern Studies* 17, no. 3 (1978): 221–240.

676. Well-Barnett, Ida. *On Lynching.* Reprint. New York: Arno Press, 1969.

Minimum Wage

677. Breckinridge, Sophonisba P. "Political Equality for Women and Women's Wages." *Annals of the American Academy of Political and Social Science* 56 (November 1914): 122–133.

678. Hart, Vivien. "Feminism and Bureaucracy: The Minimum Wage Experiment in the District of Columbia." *Journal of American Studies (Great Britain)* 26, no. 1 (1992): 1–22.

679. Ingalls, Robert P. "New York and the Minimum-Wage Movement, 1933–1937." *Labor History* 15, no. 2 (1974): 179–198.

680. Johnson, Ethel M. "The Drive for Minimum Wage." *Current History* 38 (September 1933): 688–694.

681. Patterson, James T. "Mary Dewson and the American Minimum Wage Movement." *Labor History* 5 (Spring 1964): 134–152.

Protective Legislation

682. Beyer, Clara Mortenson. "What Is Equality?" *The Nation* 116 (31 January 1923): 116.

683. Blatch, Harriet Stanton, and Clara M. Beyer. "Do Women Want Protection? Wrapping Women in Cotton Wool." *The Nation* 116 (31 January 1923): 115–116.

684. Brandeis, Elizabeth. "Organized Labor and Protective Labor Legislation." In *Labor and the New Deal,* edited by Milton Derber and Edwin Young, 197. Madison: University of Wisconsin, 1957.

685. Creel, George. "The 'Protected Sex' in Industry." *Harper's Weekly* 60 (8 May 1915): 443, 446.

686. Englander, Susan. "The Science of Protection: Gender-Based Legal Arguments for the Ten-Hour Work Day." *UCLA Historical Journal* 14 (August 1995).

687. Hamilton, Alice. "The 'Blanket' Amendment: Protection for Women Workers." *Forum* 72 (August 1924): 152–160.

688. Johnsen, Julia, ed. *Special Legislation for Women.* New York: H. W. Wilson, 1926.

689. Kelley, Florence. "Blanket Equality Bill." *Woman's Home Companion* 49 (August 1922): 4.

690. ———. "Should Women Be Treated Identically with Men by the Law?" *American Review* 3 (May–June 1923): 276–284.

691. Lehrer, Susan. *Origins of Protective Labor Legislation for Women: 1905–1925.* Albany: SUNY Press, 1987.

692. Lemons, J. Stanley. "Social Feminism in the 1920s: Progressive Women and Industrial Legislation." *Labor History* 14 (Winter 1973): 83–91.

693. "Suffragist Fight Over Industrial Equality." *Literary Digest* 89 (12 June 1926): 10–11.

Prostitution

694. Feldman, Egal. "Prostitution, the Alien Woman and the Progressive Imagination, 1910–15." *American Quarterly* 19, no. 2 (1967): 192–206.

695. Hobson, Barbara M. *The Politics of Prostitution and the American Reform Tradition.* New York: Basic Books, 1987.

Prisons

696. Butler, Anne M. "Women's Work in Prisons of the American West, 1865–1920." *Western Legal History* 7 (Summer–Fall 1994): 201–221.

697. Freedman, Estelle B. *Their Sisters' Keepers: Women's Prison Reform in America, 1830–1930.* Ann Arbor: University of Michigan Press, 1981.

698. Lucko, Paul M. "The Next 'Big Job': Women Prison Reformers in Texas, 1918–1930." In *Women and Texas History,* edited by Fane Downs and Nancy Baker Jones, 72–87. Austin: Texas State Historical Association, 1993.

699. Rafter, Nicole Hahn. "Gender, Prisons, and Prison History." *Social Science History* 9, no. 3 (1985): 233–248.

Social Welfare

700. Gordon, Linda. "Black and White Visions of Welfare: Women's Welfare Activism, 1890–1945." *Journal of American History* 78, no. 2 (September 1991): 559–590. Reprint. *'We Specialize in the Wholly Impossible', A Reader in Black Women's History.* Darlene Clark Hine, Wilma King, and Linda Reed, eds., 449–486. Brooklyn, NY: Carlson, 1995

701. Hertz, Susan H. "The Politics of the Welfare Mothers Movement: A Case Study." *Signs* 3, no. 2 (1977): 600–611.

702. ———. *The Welfare Mothers Movement: A Decade of Change for Poor Women?* Washington, DC: University Press, 1981.

703. Kotz, Nick, and Mary Lynn Kotz. "Welfare Mothers and the Civil Rights Movement." *Civil Liberties Review* 4, no. 4 (1977): 74–83.

704. Ladd-Taylor, Mary Madeleine. "Mother-Work: Ideology, Public Policy, and the Mothers' Movement, 1890–1930." Ph.D. dissertation, University of Maryland, College Park, 1988.

705. Ladd-Taylor, Mary Madeleine, and Molly Taylor. "'My Work Came Out of Agony and Grief': Mothers and the Making of the Sheppard-Towner Act." In *Mothers of a New World: Maternalist Politics and the Origins of Welfare States,* edited by Seth Koven and Sonya Michel, 321–342. New York: Routledge, 1988.

706. Pope, Jacqueline. *Biting the Hand That Feeds Them: Organizing Women at the Grass Roots Level.* New York: Praeger, 1989.

707. Sklar, Kathryn Kish. "Historical Foundations of Women's Power in the Creation of the American Welfare State, 1830–1930." In *Mothers of a New World: Maternalist Politics and the Origins of Welfare States,* edited by Seth Koven and Sonya Michel, 43–93. New York: Routledge, 1993.

708. Skocpol, Theda, Marjorie Abend-Wein, Christopher Howard, and Susan Goodrich Lehmann. "Women's Associations and the Enactment of Mothers' Pension in the United States." *American Political Science Review* 87, no. 3 (1993): 686–701.

709. Stehno, Sandra M. "Public Responsibility for Dependent Black Children: The Advocacy of Edith Abbott and Sophonisba Breckinridge." *Social Service Review* 62, no. 3 (September 1988): 485–503.

710. Tarantino, Thomas Howard, and Dismas Becker, eds. *Welfare Mothers Speak Out: We Ain't Gonna Shuffle Anymore.* New York: Norton, 1972.

711. West, Guida. *The National Welfare Rights Movement: The Social Protest of Poor Women.* New York: Praeger, 1981.

Working Women

General

712. Beard, Mary R. "The Legislative Influence of Unenfranchised Women." *Annals of the American Academy of Political and Social Science* 56 (November 1914): 54–62.

713. Buhle, Mari Jo. "Socialist Women and the 'Girl Strikers,' Chicago, 1910." *Signs* 1 (Summer 1976): 1039–1052.

714. Cobble, Dorothy Sue. "Rethinking Troubled Relations between Women and Unions: Craft Unionism and Female Activism." *Feminist Studies* 16, no. 3 (Fall 1990): 519–548.

715. ———, ed. *Women and Unions: Forging a Partnership.* Ithaca, NY: ILR Press, 1993.

716. ———. "Recapturing Working-Class Feminism, Union Women in the Postwar Era." In *Not June Cleaver,* edited by Joanne Meyerowitz, 57–83. Philadelphia: Temple University, 1994.

717. DiGirolamo, Vincent. "The Women of Wheatland: Female Consciousness and the 1913 Wheatland Hop Strike." *Labor History* 34, no. 2–3 (1993): 236–255.

718. Dimos, Helen. "The 33 Million Secretaries, Salesclerks, Factory Workers, Hairdressers, Service Workers—Low Pay, Low Status, High Hopes." *Ms.* 8, no. 11 (May 1980): 44–49.

719. Murolo, Priscilla. "Working Girls' Clubs, 1884–1928: Class and Gender on the 'Common Ground of Womanhood'." Ph.D. dissertation, Yale University, 1992.

720. Roydhouse, Marian. "The 'Universal Sisterhood of Women': Women and Labor Reform in North Carolina, 1900–1932." Ph.D. dissertation, Duke University, Durham, 1980.

History

721. Balser, Diane. *Sisterhood and Solidarity: Feminism and Labor in Modern Times.* Boston: South End Press, 1987.

722. Blewett, Mary H. *Men, Women, and Work: Class, Gender, and Protest in the New England Shoe Industry, 1780–1910*. Champaign: University of Illinois Press, 1988.

723. Cameron, Ardis. *Radicals of the Worst Sort: Laboring Women in Lawrence, Massachusetts, 1860–1912*. Urbana: University of Illinois, 1994.

724. Dorr, Rheta Childe. *What Eight Million Women Want*. Boston: Small, Maynard and Company, 1910.

725. Fitzpatrick, Tara Kathryn. "Women's Work: Self-Sacrifice, Republicanism, and the Character of American Women, 1682–1920." Ph.D. dissertation, Yale University, 1992.

726. Johnstone, Elizabeth. "Women in Economic Life: Rights and Opportunities." *Annals of the American Academy of Political and Social Science* 375 (January 1968): 102–114.

727. Kreps, Juanita Morris. *Sex in the Marketplace: American Women at Work*. Baltimore: Johns Hopkins Press, 1971.

728. McCourt, Kathleen. *Working Class Women and Grass Roots Politics*. Bloomington: Indiana University Press, 1977.

729. McGlashan, Zena Beth. "Club 'Ladies' and Working 'Girls': Rheta Childe Dorr and the *New York Evening Post*." *Journalism History* 8, no. 1 (1981): 7–13.

730. O'Sullivan, Judith. *Workers and Allies: Female Participation in the American Trade Union Movement, 1824–1976*. Washington, DC: Smithsonian Institution Press, 1975.

Leaders and Activists

731. Atkinson, Linda. *Mother Jones, the Most Dangerous Woman in America*. New York: Crown, 1978.

732. Buss, Fran Leeper, ed. *Forged Under the Sun—Foriada Bajo el Sol: The Life of Maria Elena Lucas*. Ann Arbor: University of Michigan, 1993.

733. de la Cruz, Jessie Lopez, and Ellen Cantarow. "My Life." *Radical America* 12, no. 6 (1978): 23–40.

734. Garcia, Richard A. "Dolores Huerta: Woman, Organizer, Symbol." *California History* 72, no. 1 (Spring 1993): 56–72.

735. Larralde, Carlos. "Emma Tenayuca: La Pasionaria." In *Mexican American: Movements and Leaders*, 159–167. Los Alamitos, CA: Hwong, 1976.

736. Nestor, Agnes. *Woman's Labor Leaders: An Autobiography*. Rockford, IL: Bellevue Books, 1954.

737. Reverby, Susan. "From Aide to Organizer: The Oral History of Lillian Roberts." In *Women of America: A History*, edited by Carol Ruth Berkin and Mary Beth Norton, 289–317. Boston: Houghton Mifflin, 1979.

738. Salmond, John A. *Miss Lucy of the CIO: The Life and Times of Lucy Randolph Mason, 1882–1959*. Athens: University of Georgia, 1988.

739. Scholten, Pat Creech. "The Old Mother and Her Army: The Agitative Strategies of Mary Harris Jones." *West Virginia History* 40, no. 4 (1979): 365–374.

740. Steel, Edward M. "Mother Jones and the Fairmont Field, 1902." *Journal of American History* 57 (September 1970): 290–307.

741. Yancy, Dorothy Cowser. "Dorothy Bolden, Organizer of Domestic Workers: She Was Born Poor But She Would Not Bow Down." *Sage* 3, no. 1 (1986): 53–55.

Organizations

742. Klotzburger, Kay. "Political Action by Academic Women." In *Academic Women on the Move*, edited by Alice Rossi, 359–391. New York: Russell Sage, 1973.

743. MacLean, Annie Marion. "A Progressive Club of Working Women." *The Survey* 15 (2 December 1905): 299–302.

744. Nelson, Barbara J. "The Women's Caucus for Political Science: Five Views of Its Significance Today." *PS* 23, no. 3 (1990): 439–444.

745. Schofield, Ann. "An 'Army of Amazons': The Language of Protest in a Kansas Mining Community, 1921–22." *American Quarterly* 37 (Winter 1985): 686–701.

746. Seifer, Nancy, and Barbara M. Wertheimer. "New Approaches to Collective Power: Four Working Women's Organizations." In *Women Organizing: An Anthology*, edited by Bernice Cummings and Victoria Schuck, 133–183. Metuchen, NJ: Scarecrow Press, 1979.

747. Sexton, Patricia Mayo. "Workers (Female) Arise!: On Founding the Coalition of Labor Union Women." *Dissent* 21 (Summer 1974): 380–395.

748. Walker, Samuel. "The Rise and Fall of the Police Women's Movement, 1905–1975." In *Law and Order in American History*, edited by Joseph M. Hawed, 101–111. Port Washington, NY: Kennikat Press, 1979.

749. Weiss, Chris. "Appalachian Women Fight Back: Organizational Approaches to Non-traditional Job Advocacy." In *Fighting Back in Appalachia: Traditions of Resistance and Change*, edited by Steven Fisher. Philadelphia: Temple University Press, 1992.

Women of Color

750. Coburn, Judith. "People: Dolores Huerta—La Pasionaria of the Farmworkers." *Ms.* 5, no. 5 (November 1976): 11–18.

751. Coyle, Laurie, Gail Hershatter, and Emily Honig. "Women at Farah: An Unfinished Story." In *Mexican Women in the United States: Struggles Past and Present*, edited by Magdalena Mora and Adelaida R. DelCastillo, 117–142. Los Angeles: University of California Chicano Studies Research Center, 1980.

752. Duron, Clementina. "Mexican Women and Labor Conflict in Los Angeles: The ILGWU Dressmakers' Strike of 1933." *Azlan* 15, no. 1 (1984): 145–161.

753. Fernandez-Kelly, M. Patricia, and Alma M. Garcia. "Power Surrendered, Power Restored: The Politics of Work and Family Among Hispanic

Garment Workers in California and Florida." In *Women, Politics and Change,* edited by Louise A. Tilly and Patricia Gurin, 130–152. New York: Russell Sage, 1990.

754. Garcia, Mario T. "The Chicano in American History: The Mexican Women of El Paso, 1880–1920: A Case Study." *Pacific Historical Review* 49, no. 2 (May 1980): 315–337.

755. Harley, Sharon. "When Your Work Is Not Who You Are: The Development of a Working-Class Consciousness among Afro-American Women." In *Gender, Class, Race, and Reform in the Progressive Era,* edited by Noralee Frankel and Nancy S. Dye, 25–38. Lexington: University Press of Kentucky, 1991. Reprint. *"We Specialize in the Wholly Impossible": A Reader in Black Women's History,* Darlene Clark Hine, Wilma King, and Linda Reed, eds., 521–542. Brooklyn, NY: Carlson, 1995.

756. Hield, Melissa. "'Union Minded': Women in the Texas ILGWU, 1933–1950." *Frontiers* 4, no. 2 (1979): 59–70.

757. Hine, Darlene Clark. *Black Women in White: Racial Conflict and Cooperation in the Nursing Profession, 1890–1950.* Bloomington: Indiana University Press, 1989.

758. Janiewski, Dolores. "Sisters Under Their Skins: Southern Working Women, 1880–1950." In *Black Women in United States History,* Vol. 3, edited by Darlene Clark Hines, 779–804. Brooklyn, NY: Carlson, 1990.

759. Laslett, John H. M. "Gender, Class, or Ethno-Cultural Struggle? The Problematic Relationship between Rose Pesotta and the ILGWU." *California History* 72, no. 1 (Spring 1993): 20–39.

760. Ledesma, Irene. "The Newspapers and Chicana Worker's Activism, 1919–1974." *Western Historical Quarterly* 26, no. 3 (Autumn 1995): 309–332.

761. Lee, Patricia. "Asian Immigrant Women and HERE Local 2." *Labor Research Review* 11 (1988): 29–38.

762. Marquez, Benjamin. "Organizing Mexican-American Women in the Garment Industry: La Mujer Obrera." *Women and Politics* 15, no. 1 (1995): 65–87.

763. Monroy, Dugleas. "La Costura en Los Angeles, 1933–1939: The ILGWU and the Politics of Domination." In *Mexican Women in the United States: Struggles Past and Present,* edited by Magdalena Mora and Adelaida R. DelCastillo, 171–178. Los Angeles: University of California Chicano Studies Research Center, 1980.

764. Riccucci, Norma M. *Women, Minorities and Unions in the Public Sector.* Westport, CT: Greenwood, 1990.

765. Rose, Margaret Eleanor. "Women in the United Farm Workers: A Study of Chicana and Mexicana Participation in a Labor Union, 1950–1980." Ph.D. dissertation, University of California, 1988.

766. ———. "Traditional and Nontraditional Patterns of Female Activism in the United Farm Workers of America, 1962 to 1980." *Frontiers* 11, no. 1 (1990): 26–32.

767. Rozek, Barbara J. "The Entry of Mexican Women into Urban Based Industries: Experiences in Texas During the Twentieth Century." In *Women and Texas History,* edited by Fane Downs and Nancy Baker Jones. Austin: Texas State Historical Association, 1993.

768. Ruiz, Vicki L. *Cannery Women, Cannery Lives: Mexican Women, Unionization, and the California Food Processing Industry, 1930–1950.* Albuquerque: University of New Mexico Press, 1987.

769. Schlein, Lisa. "Los Angeles Garment District Sews a Cloak of Shame." In *Mexican Women in the United States: Struggles Past and Present,* edited by Magdalena Mora and Adelaida R. DelCastillo, 113–116. Los Angeles: University of California Chicano Studies Research Center, 1980.

770. Vazquez, Mario F. "The Election Day Immigration Raid at Lilli Diamond Originals and the Response of the ILGWU." In *Mexican Women in the United States: Struggles Past and Present,* edited by Magdalena Mora and Adelaida R. DelCastillo, 145–148. Los Angeles: University of California Chicano Studies Research Center, 1980.

771. Zavella, Patricia. "The Politics of Race and Gender: Organizing Chicana Cannery Workers in Northern California." In *Women and the Politics of Empowerment,* edited by Ann Bookman and Sandra Morgen, 202–226. Philadelphia: Temple University Press, 1988.

772. ———. *Women's Work and Chicano Families: Cannery Workers of the Santa Clara Valley.* Ithaca, NY: Cornell University Press, 1987.

Unions

773. Argersinger, Jo Ann E. "'Struggle Without Triumph': Women Workers and the 1932 Garment Strike." Paper presented at the annual Southern Labor History Conference, Atlanta, 1980.

774. Baden, Naomi. "Developing an Agenda: Expanding the Role of Women in Unions." *Labor Studies Journal* 10 (1986): 229–249.

775. Bailey, Cheryl. "Changing Woman's 9 to 5 Lives, a Baltimore Organization's History of Local Success." *National Business Woman* 67, no. 3 (June–July 1985): 22–25.

776. Barton, Joan Keller. "Dilemmas of Organizing Women Office Workers." *Gender and Society* 1, no. 4 (1987): 432–446.

777. Bookman, Ann. "The Process of Political Socialization among Women and Immigrant Workers: A Case Study of Unionization in the Electronic Industry." Ph.D. dissertation, Harvard University, Cambridge, 1977.

778. Cobble, Dorothy Sue. *Dishing It Out: Waitresses and Their Unions in the Twentieth Century.* Urbana: University of Illinois Press, 1991.

779. Cook, Alice H. "Women and American Trade Unions." *Annals of the American Academy of Political and Social Science* 375 (January 1968): 125–132.

780. Costello, Cynthia B. "'WEA're Worth It!': Work Culture and Conflict at the Wisconsin Education Insurance Trust." *Feminist Studies* 11, no. 3 (1985): 497–515.

781. Dickason, Gladys. "Women in Labor Unions." *Annals of the American Academy of Political and Social Science* 251 (May 1947): 70–78.

782. Dubin, Marshall Frank. "'1199: The Bread and Roses Union'." Ph.D. dissertation, Columbia University, 1988.

783. DuRivage, Virginia. *Working at the Margins: Part–Time and Temporary Workers in the United States.* Cleveland, OH: 9 to 5, National Association of Working Women, 1986.

784. Faue, Elizabeth. "'The Dynamo of Change': Gender and Solidarity in the American Labor Movement of the 1930s." *Gender and History* 1 (Summer 1989): 138–158.

785. Feldberg, Roslyn. "'Union Fever': Organizing Among Clerical Workers, 1900–1930." *Radical America* 14 (May–June 1980): 53–67.

786. Gabin, Nancy F. *Feminism in the Labor Movement: Women and the United Auto Workers 1935–1975.* Ithaca, NY: Cornell University Press, 1991.

787. Gain, Nancy. "'They Have Placed a Penalty on Womanhood': Women Auto Workers in the Detroit-Area UAW Locals, 1945–1947." *Feminist Studies* 8, no. 2 (1982): 373–398.

788. Goldberg, Roberta. *Organizing Women Office Workers: Dissatisfaction, Consciousness, and Action.* New York: Praeger, 1983.

789. Goldstein, Mark L. "Blue-Collar Women and American Labor Unions." *Industrial and Labor Relations Forum* 7 (October 1971): 1–35.

790. Hoyman, Michele. "Working Women: The Potential of Unionization and Collective Action in the United States." *Women's Studies International Forum* 12, no. 1 (1989): 51–58.

791. Jameson, Elizabeth. "Imperfect Unions: Class and Gender in Cripple Creek, 1894–1904." *Frontiers* 1 (Spring 1976): 79–119. Reprint. *Class, Sex, and the Woman Worker,* Milton Cantor and Bruce Laurie, eds., 166–202. Westport, CT: Greenwood, 1977.

792. Janiewski, Dolores. "Seeking 'A New Day and a New Way': Black Women and Unions in the Southern Tobacco Industry." In *Black Women in United States History,* Vol. 3., edited by Darlene Clark Hines, 761–778. Brooklyn, NY: Carlson, 1990.

793. Kates, Carol. "Working Class Feminism and Feminist Unions: Title VII, the UAW and NOW." *Labor Studies Journal* 14 (Summer 1989): 28–45.

794. Kenneally, James J. "Women and Trade Unions, 1870–1920: The Quandary of the Reformer." *Labor History* 14 (Winter 1973): 42–55.

795. Kessler-Harris, Alice. "Where Are the Organized Women Workers?" *Feminist Studies* 3, no. 1–2 (1975): 92–110.

796. ———. "Problems of Coalition-Building: Women and Trade Unions in the 1920s." In *Women, Work and Protest: A Century of U.W. Women's*

Labor History, edited by Ruth Milkman, 110–138. Boston: Routledge and Kegan Paul, 1985.

797. King, Sarah. "Feminists in Teaching: The National Union of Women Teachers, 1920–1945." In *Teachers: The Culture and Politics of Work*, edited by Martin Lawn and Gerald Grace, 311–349. New York: Falmer Press, 1987.

798. Kingsolver, Barbara. *Holding the Line: Women in the Great Arizona Mine Strike of 1983*. Ithaca NY: ILR Press, 1989.

799. McCreesh, Carolyn D. *Women in the Campaign to Organize Garment Workers, 1880–1917*. New York: Garland, 1985.

800. Melcher, Dale, Jennifer L. Eichstedt, Shelley Eriksen, and Dan Clawson. "Women's Participation in Local Union Leadership: The Massachusetts Experience." *Industrial and Labor Relations Review* 45, no. 2 (1992): 267–280.

801. Milkman, Ruth. *Women, Work and Protest: A Century of U.W. Women's Labor History*. Boston: Routledge and Kegan Paul, 1985.

802. Nelson, Anne H. "Women in Unions." In *American Woman, 1987–88,* edited by Sara E. Ries and Anne J. Stone, 232–238. New York: Norton, 1987.

803. Newman, Joseph W. "A History of the Atlanta Public School Teachers' Association, Local 89 of the American Federation of Teachers, 1919–1956." Ph.D. dissertation, Georgia State University, 1978.

804. Noble, Linda. "My Struggle to Fight Harassment, 9 to 5 Assists in Maine." *Glamour* 92 (May 1994): 139.

805. O'Connell, Lucille. "The Lawrence Textile Strike of 1912: The Testimony of Two Polish Women." *Polish American Studies* 36, no. 2 (1979): 44–62.

806. O'Neill, Colleen. "Domesticity Deployed: Gender, Race and the Construction of Class Struggle in the Bisbee Deportation." *Labor History* 31, no. 2–3 (1993): 256–273.

807. Sacks, Karen. *Caring by the Hour: Women, Work and Organizing at Duke Medical Center.* Urbana: University of Illinois Press, 1988.

808. Sansbury, Gail Gregory. "'Now, Girls, What's the Matter with You Girls?': Clerical Workers Organize." *Radical America* 14, no. 6 (1980): 67–75.

809. Schofield, Ann. "Rebel Girls and Union Maids: The Woman Question in the Journals of the AFL and IWW, 1905–1920." *Feminist Studies* 9 (Summer 1983): 335–358.

810. Shelton, Brenda K. "Organized Mother Love: The Buffalo Women's Educational and Industrial Union, 1885–1915." *New York History* 67, no. 2 (April 1986): 155–176.

811. Snyder, Robert E. "Women, Wobblies, and Worker's Rights: The 1912 Textile Strike in Little Falls, New York." *New York History* 60, no. 1 (1979): 29–57.

812. Stern, Majorie. "An Insider's View of the Teachers Union and Women's Rights." *Urban Review* 5–6 (1973): 46–49.

813. Thomas, William B., and Kevin J. Moran. "Women Teacher Militancy in the Workplace, 1910–1922." *Paedagogica Historica* (*Belgium*) 27, no. 1 (1991): 35–53.

814. Van Raaphorst, Donna L. *Union Maids Not Wanted, Organizing Domestic Workers.* New York: Praeger, 1988.

815. Wertheimer, Barbara M., and Anne H. Nelson. *Trade Union Women: A Study of Their Participation in New York City Locals.* New York: Praeger, 1975.

Civil Rights

General

816. Black, Allida M. "A Reluctant but Persistent Warrior: Eleanor Roosevelt and the Early Civil Rights Movement." In *Women in the Civil Rights Movement: Trailblazers and Torchbearers,* edited by Vicki L. Crawford, Jacqueline Anne Rouse, and Barbara Wood, 233–250. Vol. 16. of *Black Women in United States History,* edited by Darlene Clark Hine. Brooklyn, NY: Carlson, 1990.

817. Duke, Lois Lovelace. "Virginia Foster Durr: An Analysis of One Woman's Contribution to the Civil Rights Movement in the South." In *Women in Politics: Outsiders or Insiders? A Collection of Readings,* edited by Lois Lovelace Duke, 267–287. Englewood Cliffs, NJ: Prentice Hall, 1993.

818. Greene, Christina. "'We'll Take Our Stand': Race, Class, and Gender in the Southern Student Organizing Committee, 1964–1969." In *Hidden Histories of Women in the New South,* edited by Virginia Bernhard, Elizabeth Fox-Genovese, and Theda Perdue, 173–203. Columbia: University of Missouri Press, 1994.

819. Hayden, Casey, and Mary King. "Sex and Caste: A Kind of Memo." Parts I, II. *Liberation* 9, no. 2 (April 1966): 35–36; 9, no. 9 (December 1966): 26–33.

820. King, Mary. *Freedom Song; A Personal Story of the 1960s Civil Rights Movement.* New York: William Morrow, 1987.

821. Rothschild, Mary Aickin. "White Women Volunteers in the Freedom Summers: Their Life and Work in a Movement for Social Change." *Feminist Studies* 5, no. 3 (1979): 466–495.

822. Sosna, Morton. "Race and Gender in the South: The Case of Georgia's Lillian Smith." *Georgia Historical Quarterly* 71, no. 3 (1987): 427–437.

African American

823. Albrier, Frances Mary. *Determined Advocate for Racial Equality.* Berkeley: University of California, 1979. The Bancroft Library Oral History Interview.

824. Barnett, Bernice McNair. "Black Women's Collectivist Movement Organizations: Their Struggles During the 'Doldrums'." In *Feminist Organizations: Harvest of the New Women's Movement,* edited by Myra Marx Ferree and Patricia Yancey Martin, 199–222. Philadelphia: Temple University Press, 1995.

825. Bates, Daisy. *The Long Shadow of Little Rock: Memoir.* New York: David McKay, 1962.

826. Burks, Mary Fair. "Trailblazers: Women in the Montgomery Bus Boycott." In *Women in the Civil Rights Movement: Trailblazers and Torchbearers,* edited by Vicki L. Crawford, Jacqueline Anne Rouse, and Barbara Wood, 71–84. Vol. 16 of *Black Women in United States History,* edited by Darlene Clark Hine. Brooklyn, NY: Carlson, 1990.

827. Clark, Septima Poinsette. *Echo in My Soul.* New York: E. P. Dutton, 1962.

828. ———. *Ready from Within, Septima Clark and the Civil Rights Movement.* Navarro, CA: Wild Tress, 1986.

829. Coleman, Willie Mae. "Black Women and Segregated Public Transportation: Ninety Years of Resistance." In *Black Women in United States History,* Vol. 5, edited by Darlene Clark Hine, 296–298. Brooklyn, NY: Carlson, 1990.

830. Crawford, Vicki L. "We Shall Not Be Moved: Black Female Activists in the Mississippi Civil Rights Movement, 1960–1965." Ph.D. dissertation, Emory University, Atlanta, 1987.

831. ———. "Beyond the Human Self: Grassroots Activists in the Mississippi Civil Rights Movement." In *Women in the Civil Rights Movement: Trailblazers and Torchbearers,* edited by Vicki L. Crawford, Jacqueline Anne Rouse, and Barbara Wood, 13–26. Vol. 16 of *Black Women in United States History,* edited by Darlene Clark Hine. Brooklyn, NY: Carlson, 1990.

832. Crawford, Vicki L., Jacqueline Anne Rouse, and Barbara A. Woods, eds. *Women in the Civil Rights Movement: Trailblazers and Torchbearers.* Vol. 16 of *Black Women in United States History,* edited by Darlene Clark Hine. Brooklyn, NY: Carlson, 1990.

833. Davis, Angela Yvonne. *Women, Culture, and Politics.* New York: Random House, 1989.

834. Davis, Elizabeth Lindsay. *Lifting as They Climb.* Washington, DC: National Association of Colored Women, 1937.

835. Fleming, Cynthia Griggs. "'More Than a Lady': Ruby Doris Smith Robinson and Black Women's Leadership in the Student Nonviolent Coordinating Committee." In *Hidden Histories of Women in the New South,* edited by Virginia Bernhard, Elizabeth Fox-Genovese, and Theda Perdue, 204–223. Columbia: University of Missouri Press, 1994.

836. Garrow, David J., ed. *The Montgomery Bus Boycott and the Women Who Started It: The Memoir of Jo Ann Gibson Robinson.* Knoxville: University of Tennessee, 1987.

837. Giddings, Paula. *When and Where I Enter: The Impact of Black Women on Race and Sex in America.* New York: William Morrow, 1984.

838. Grant, Jacquelyn. "Civil Rights Women: A Source for Doing Womanist Theology." In *Women in the Civil Rights Movement: Trailblazers and Torchbearers,* edited by Vicki L. Crawford, Jacqueline Anne Rouse, and Barbara Wood, 39–50. Vol. 16 of *Black Women in United States History,* edited by Darlene Clark Hine. Brooklyn, NY: Carlson, 1990.

839. Harley, Sharon, and Rosalyn Terborg-Penn, eds. *The Afro-American Woman: Struggles and Images.* Port Washington, NY: Kennikat, 1978.

840. Hine, Darlene Clark, ed. *Black Women in United States History.* 16 vols. Brooklyn, NY: Carlson, 1990.

841. Hine, Darlene Clark, Wilma King, and Linda Reed, eds. *'We Specialize in the Wholly Impossible', A Reader in Black Women's History.* Brooklyn, NY: Carlson, 1995.

842. Langston, Donna. "The Women of Highlander." In *Women in the Civil Rights Movement: Trailblazers and Torchbearers,* edited by Vicki L. Crawford, Jacqueline Anne Rouse, and Barbara Wood, 145–168. Vol. 16 of *Black Women in United States History,* edited by Darlene Clark Hine. Brooklyn, NY: Carlson, 1990.

843. Locke, Mamie E. "The Role of African-American Women in the Civil Rights Movements in Hinds County and Sunflower County, Mississippi." *Journal of Mississippi History* 53, no. 3 (1991): 229–239.

844. Matthews, Mark D. "'Our Women and What They Think', Amy Jacques Garvey and the Negro World." *The Black Scholar* 10 (May–June 1979): 2–13.

845. Matthews, Tracye. "'No One Ever Asks What a Man's Place in the Revolution Is ...': Gender Construction in the Black Panther Party, 1966–1971." *Voices of the African Diaspora: The Caas Research Review* 8, no. 3 (Spring 1993): 3–10.

846. McFadden, Grace Jordan. "Septima P. Clark and the Struggle for Human Rights." In *Women in the Civil Rights Movement: Trailblazers and Torchbearers,* edited by Vicki L. Crawford, Jacqueline Anne Rouse, and Barbara Wood, 85–98. Vol. 16 of *Black Women in United States History,* edited by Darlene Clark Hine. Brooklyn, NY: Carlson, 1990.

847. Mills, Kay. *This Little Light of Mine: The Life of Fannie Lou Hamer.* New York: E. P. Dutton, 1993.

848. Moody, Anne. *Coming of Age in Mississippi.* New York: Dial, 1968.

849. Mueller, Carol M. "Ella Baker and the Origins of 'Participatory Democracy'." In *Women in the Civil Rights Movement: Trailblazers and Torchbearers,* edited by Vicki L. Crawford, Jacqueline Anne Rouse, and Barbara Wood, 51–70. Vol. 16 of *Black Women in United States History,* edited by Darlene Clark Hine. Brooklyn, NY: Carlson, 1990.

850. Nasstrom, Kathryn L. "Women, the Civil Rights Movement, and the Politics of Historical Memory in Atlanta, 1946–1973." Ph.D. dissertation, University of North Carolina, Chapel Hill, 1993.

851. O'Dell, J. H. "Life in Mississippi: An Interview with Fannie Lou Hamer." In *Black Women in United States History,* Vol. 3, edited by Darlene Clark Hines, 951–962. Brooklyn, NY: Carlson, 1990.

852. Oldendorf, Sandra B. "The South Carolina Sea Island Citizenship Schools, 1957–1961." In *Women in the Civil Rights Movement: Trailblaz-*

ers and Torchbearers, edited by Vicki L. Crawford, Jacqueline Anne Rouse, and Barbara Wood, 169–182. Vol. 16 of *Black Women in United States History,* edited by Darlene Clark Hine. Brooklyn, NY: Carlson, 1990.

853. Payne, Charles. "Ella Baker and Models of Social Change." *Signs* 14 (1989): 885–899.

854. ———. "Men Led, But Women Organized: Movement Participation of Women in the Mississippi Delta." In *Women in the Civil Rights Movement: Trailblazers and Torchbearers,* edited by Vicki L. Crawford, Jacqueline Ann Rouse, and Barbara Wood, 1–12. Vol. 16 of *Black Women in United States History,* edited by Darlene Clark Hine. Brooklyn, NY: Carlson, 1990.

855. Perlez, Jane. "Margaret Bush Wilson: NAACP's New Head." *The Crisis* 82, no. 3 (1975): 80–82.

856. Powledge, Fred. *The Montgomery Bus Boycott and the Women Who Started It.* Knoxville: University of Tennessee Press, 1991.

857. Pruitt, Mary Christine. "Racial Justice in Minnesota: The Activism of Mary Toliver Jones and Josie Robinson Johnson." In *Black Women in America,* edited by Kim Marie Vaz, 71–80. Vol. 2. Thousand Oaks, CA: Sage, 1995.

858. Robnett, Belinda. "African-American Women in Southern-Based Civil Rights Movement Organizations, 1954–1965: Gender, Grass Roots Leadership and Resource Mobilization Theory." Ph.D. dissertation, University of Michigan, 1991.

859. Salem, Dorothy C. "Black Women and the NAACP: Evolution of an Interracial Protest Organization." In *To Better Our World: Black Women in Organized Reform, 1890–1920,* 145–180. Brooklyn, NY: Carlson, 1990.

860. ———. "Response to Urbanization: Black Women and the National Urban League." In *To Better Our World: Black Women in Organized Reform, 1890–1920,* 181–200. Brooklyn, NY: Carlson, 1990.

861. ———. "Black Women and the NAACP, 1909–1922: An Encounter with Race, Class, and Gender." In *Black Women in America,* edited by Kim Marie Vaz, 54–70. Vol. 2. Thousand Oaks, CA: Sage, 1995.

862. Scales-Trent, Judy. "Black Women and the Constitution: Finding Our Place, Asserting Our Rights." In *Black Women in United States History,* Vol. 10, edited by Darlene Clark Hine, 539–574. Brooklyn, NY: Carlson, 1990.

863. Standley, Anne. "The Role of Black Women in the Civil Rights Movement." In *Women in the Civil Rights Movement: Trailblazers and Torchbearers,* edited by Vicki L. Crawford, Jacqueline Anne Rouse, and Barbara Wood, 183–202. Vol. 16 of *Black Women in United States History,* edited by Darlene Clark Hine. Brooklyn, NY: Carlson, 1990.

864. Travis, Toni-Michelle. "Black Women in the Continuing Struggle for Equality." In *Race, Sex and Policy Problems,* edited by Marian Lief Palley and Michael B. Preston, 27–37. Lexington, MA: Lexington Books, 1979.

865. Turque, Bill. "Within the Struggle, Women and the NAACP." *Newsweek* 124 (5 September 1994): 35–36.

866. Woods, Barbara A. "Modjeska Simkins and the South Carolina Conference of the NAACP, 1939–1957." In *Women in the Civil Rights Movement: Trailblazers and Torchbearers,* edited by Vicki L. Crawford, Jacqueline Anne Rouse, and Barbara Wood. Vol. 16 of *Black Women in United States History,* edited by Darlene Clark Hine. Brooklyn, NY: Carlson, 1990.

Asian American

867. Chair, Alice Yun. "The Struggle of Asian and Asian American Women toward a Total Liberation." In *Spirituality and Social Responsibility,* edited by Rosemary Skinner Keller, 249–263. Nashville, TN: Abington, 1993.

868. Chetin, Helen. *Angel Island Prisoner 1922.* Berkeley, CA: New Seed Press, 1982.

869. Chow, Esther Ngan-Ling. "Acculturation Experience of the Asian American Woman." In *Beyond Sex Roles,* 2d ed., edited by Alice Sargent, 238–251. St. Paul, MN: West, 1985.

870. Chu, Judy. "Asian Pacific American Women in Mainstream Politics." In *Making Waves: An Anthology of Writings By and For Asian American Women,* edited by Asian Women United of California, 405–421. Boston: Beacon, 1989.

871. Toy, Fran. "Cutting through the Double Bind." *Daughters of Sara* 15, no. 2 (March–April 1989): 18–19.

Latina American

872. Chavez, Jennie V. "Women of the Mexican American Movement." *Mademoiselle* (April 1972): 82, 150–152.

873. Cordova, Teresa, Norma Cantu, Gilberto Cardenas, Juan Garcia, and Christine Marie Sierra, eds. *Chicana Voices: Intersections of Class, Race and Gender.* Austin: Center for Mexican American Studies, University of Texas, 1986.

874. DeValdez, Theresa A. "Organizing as a Political Tool for the Chicana." *Frontiers* 5, no. 2 (1980): 7–13.

875. Hernandez, Patricia. "Lives of Chicana Activists: The Chicano Student Movement." In *Mexican Women in the United States: Struggles Past and Present,* edited by Magdalena Mora and Adelaida R. DelCastillo, 17–25. Los Angeles: University of California Chicano Studies Research Center, 1980.

876. Lopez, Sonia A. "The Role of the Chicana Within the Student Movement." In *Essays on La Mujer,* edited by Rosa Ura Sanchez and Rosa Martinez Cruz, 16–30. Los Angeles: University of California Chicano Studies Research Center, 1977.

877. Melville, Margarita B., ed. *Twice a Minority: Mexican American Women.* St. Louis, MO: C. V. Mosby Company, 1980.

878. Mora, Magdalena, and Adelaida R. DelCastillo, eds. *Mexican Women in the United States: Struggles Past and Present.* Los Angeles: University of California Chicano Studies Research Center, 1980.

879. Orozco, Cynthia E. "Women in the Mexican American Civil Rights Movement." *National Women's Studies Association Journal* 1 (1988): 163–164.

880. ———. "The Origins of the League of United Latin American Citizens (LULAC) and the Mexican American Civil Rights Movement in Texas with an Analysis of Women's Political Participation in a Gendered Context, 1910–1929." Ph.D. dissertation, University of California, Los Angeles, 1992.

881. Zamora, Emilio. "Sara Estela Ramirez: Unia Rosa Roja En El Movimiento." In *Mexican Women in the United States: Struggles Past and Present,* edited by Magdalena Mora and Adelaida R. DelCastillo, 163–169. Los Angeles: University of California Chicano Studies Research Center, 1980.

Native American

882. Baird-Olson, Karren. "Reflections of an AIM Activist: Has It All Been Worth It ?" *American Indian Culture and Research Journal* 18, no. 4 (1994): 233–252.

883. Berman, Susan. "Working for My People: Thorpe's Daughter Indian Activist." *Akwesasne Notes* 3 (March 1971): 27.

884. Chato, Genevieve, and Christine Conte. "The Legal Rights of American Indian Women." In *Western Women: Their Land, Their Lives,* edited by Lillian Schlissel, Vicki L. Ruiz, and

Janice Monk, 227–258. Albuquerque: University of New Mexico, 1988.

885. Christoffarson, Carla. "Tribal Courts Failure to Protect Native American Woman: A Reevaluation of the Indian Civil Rights Act." *Yale Journal of Law and Feminism* 101 (October 1981): 100–105.

886. Crow Dog, Mary. *Lakota Woman.* New York: Harper, 1991.

887. Green, Rayna. "The Pocahontas Perplex: The Image of Indian Women in American Culture." *Massachusetts Review* 16, no. 4 (Autumn 1975): 698–714.

888. ———. "Review Essay: Native American Women." *Signs* 6, no. 2 (Winter 1980): 248–267.

889. Hauptman, Laurence M. "Alice Lee Jemison: Seneca Political Activist." *The Indian Historian* 12 (1974): 15–40.

890. ———. "The Only Good Indian Bureau Is a Dead Indian Bureau: Alice Lee Jemison, Seneca Political Activist." In *The Iroquois and the New Deal.* Syracuse, NY: Syracuse University Press, 1981.

891. Indian Rights Association. "Special Issue on Native Women." *Indian Truth* 239 (May–June 1981).

892. Jaimes, M. Annette, and Theresa Halsey. "American Indian Women: At the Center of Indigenous Resistance in North America." In *Native America: Genocide, Colonization, and Resistance,* edited by M. Annette Jaimes. Boston: South End Press, 1992.

893. Johnson, David L., and Raymond Wilson. "Gertrude Simmons

Bonnin, 1876–1938: 'Americanize the First Americans'." *American Indian Quarterly* 12 (Winter 1988): 27–40.

894. La Duke, Winona. "Interview with Roberta Blackgoat, Dine' Elder." *Woman of Power: A Magazine of Feminism, Spirituality, and Politics* 4 (Fall 1986): 29–31.

895. Lurie, Nancy O. "Indian Women: A Legacy of Freedom." In *Look to the Mountain,* edited by Robert L. Iacopi, 29–36. San Jose: Gousha Publications, 1972.

896. McClintock, Laura V. "A Critical Analysis of Women in the American Indian Movement." B.S. thesis, James Madison University, 1994.

897. Olguin, Rocky. "Listening to Native American Women." *Heresies* 13, no. 4–1 (1981): 17–21.

898. Starr, M. L. "She Did Not Lead a Movement." *American History Illustrated* 15 (August 1980): 44–47.

899. Welch, Deborah. "An American Indian Leader: The Story of Gertrude Bonnin, 1876–1939." Ph.D. dissertation, University of Wyoming, Laramie, 1985.

900. Witt, Shirley Hill. "Native Women Today: Sexism and the Indian Woman." *Civil Rights Digest* 6 (Spring 1974): 29–35.

901. ———. "The Brave-Hearted Women: The Struggle at Wounded Knee." *Akwesasne Notes* 8, no. 2 (1976): 16–17.

902. "A Woman's Ways: An Interview with Judy Swamp, Maintaining Traditional Values in the Context of Con-

temporary Conflict." *Parabola* 5, no. 4 (1980): 52–61.

Equal Rights Amendment

History

903. Becker, Susan D. *The Origins of the Equal Rights Amendment: American Feminism between the Wars.* Westport, CT: Greenwood, 1981.

904. Berry, Mary Frances. *Why ERA Failed: Politics, Women's Rights and the Amending Process of the Constitution.* Bloomington: Indiana University Press, 1986.

905. Catt, Carrie Chapman. "Con: The Equal Rights Amendment." *Congressional Digest* 22 (April 1943): 118–128.

906. Chambers, Clarke A. "The Campaign for Women's Rights." Chap. 3 in *Seedtime of Reform: American Social Service and Social Action 1918–1933,* 59–84. Minneapolis: University of Minnesota Press, 1963.

907. Cott, Nancy F. "Historical Perspective: The Equal Rights Amendment Conflict in the 1920s." In *Conflict in Feminism,* edited by Eleanor Hirsch and Elizabeth Fox-Keller, 44–59. New York: Routledge, 1990.

908. DeHart, Jane Sherron. "Oral Sources and Contemporary History: Dispelling Old Assumptions." *Journal of American History* 80 (September 1992): 582–595.

909. Farley, Jennie. "Women's Magazines and the ERA: Friend or Foe?"

Journal of Communication 28, no. 1 (1978): 187–193.

910. Geidel, Peter. "The National Woman's Party and the Origins of the Equal Rights Amendment." Master's thesis, Columbia University, New York, 1977.

911. Hoff-Wilson, Joan, ed. *Rights of Passage: The Past and Future of the ERA.* Bloomington: Indiana University Press, 1986.

912. Kelley, Florence. "Why Other Women's Groups Oppose It." *Good Housekeeping* 78 (March 1924): 19, 162–165.

913. Kenton, Edna. "Ladies' Next Step: The Case for the Equal Rights Amendment." *Harper's Weekly* 152 (February 1926): 366–374.

914. Kimball, Alice Mary, and Wanda Weiner. "Fair Ways to Freedom: World's Fairs and Centennials as Battle Ground in American Women's Struggle for Equal Rights." *Independent Woman* 17 (November 1938): 343, 360–362.

915. Lutz, Alma. "Only One Choice." *Independent Woman* 26 (July 1947): 199–205.

916. Mathews, Jane DeHart, Donald G. Mathews, and Roxie Nicholson-Guard. "Women in the Contemporary South: The Symbolic Politics of ERA." *Furman Studies* 26 (December 1980): 6–18.

917. Mayo, Edith P. "The Battle's Not Over: ERA, 1923–1982." *Keynoter* 82, no. 3 (1982): 18–25.

918. Murrell, Ethel Ernest. "Full Citizenship for Women: An Equal Rights Amendment, 1923–1951." *American Bar Association Journal* 38 (January 1952): 47–49.

919. "Next Step in the Emancipation of Women—An Equal Rights Amendment?" *Graduate Woman* 31 (April 1938): 160–164.

920. Paul, Alice. "PRO: Should Congress Approve the Proposed Equal Rights Amendment to the Constitution?" *Congressional Digest* 22 (April 1943): 107–117.

921. Rawalt, Marguerite. "The Equal Rights Amendment." In *Women in Washington,* edited by Irene Tinker, 49–78. Beverly Hills, CA: Sage, 1983.

922. Schulman, Donna L. "Social Sciences—Social Science: Sex, Gender, and the Politics of the ERA." *Library Journal* 115, no. 14 (September 1990): 245.

923. Sealander, Judith. "Feminist against Feminist: The First Phase of the Equal Rights Amendment Debate, 1923–1963." *South Atlantic Quarterly* 81, no. 2 (Spring 1982): 147–161.

924. Ware, Susan. "ERA and Democratic Politics: Women in the Postsuffrage Era." In *Without Precedent: The Life and Career of Eleanor Roosevelt,* edited by Joan Hoff-Wilson and Marjorie Lightman, 46–60. Bloomington: Indiana University Press, 1984.

925. Whitney, Sharon. *The Equal Rights Amendment: The History and the Movement.* New York: F. Watts, 1984.

926. "Wisconsin, Where Women Are People." *Literary Digest* 70 (30 July 1921): 10.

Leaders and Activists

927. Anderson, Kathryn. "Anne Martin and the Dream of Political Equality for Women." *Journal of the West* 27, no. 2 (April 1988): 28–34.

928. "Fighting First Lady: Betty Ford's Support for the Equal Rights Amendment." *Time* 105 (3 March 1975): 20.

929. Fry, Amelia R. "Alice Paul and the ERA." *Social Education* 59, no. 5 (September 1995): 285–290.

930. Patterson, Judith. *A Biography of Marguerite Rawalt.* Austin, TX: Eakin Press, 1986.

931. Pinckney, Elise. "Anita Pollitzer: She Found a Career in Her Belief of Equal Rights for Women." *South Carolina Magazine* 8, no.3 (March 1954): 12–13.

932. Sargent, Ruth. *Gail Laughlin, ERA's Advocate.* Portland, ME: House of Falmouth, 1979.

933. Williams, Roger M. "Women Against Women —The Clamor over Equal Rights." *Saturday Review* 4 (1977): 7–13, 46.

National Women's Party

934. Belmont, Mrs. O. H. P. "Women As Dictators." *Ladies Home Journal* 39 (September 1922): 7.

935. Cott, Nancy F. "Feminist Politics in the 1920s: The National Woman's Party." *Journal of American History* 71 (June 1984): 43–68.

936. Danzig, Myrna. "Alice Paul and the World Woman's Party." Paper presented at the New School Conference on Women and Political Change in the 20th Century, New York, 1990.

937. Eastman, Crystal. "Alice Paul's Convention." *The Liberator* 4 (April 1921): 9–10.

938. Geidel, Peter. "The National Woman's Party and the Origins of the Equal Rights Amendment, 1920–1923." *The Historian* 42 (August 1980): 555–582.

939. Irwin, Inez Haynes. "Why the Woman's Party Is for It." *Good Housekeeping* 78 (March 1924): 18, 158–161.

940. Kelley, Florence. "The New Woman's Party." *The Survey* 45 (5 March 1921): 827.

941. Kirchwey, Freda. "Alice Paul Pulls the Strings." *The Nation* 112 (2 March 1921): 332–333.

942. Martin, Anne. "Equality Laws Vs. Women in Government." *The Nation* 115 (16 August 1922): 165–166.

943. ———. "Feminists and Future Political Action." *The Nation* 120 (18 February 1925): 185–186.

944. Patterson, Cynthia M. "New Directions in the Political History of Women: A Case Study of the National Women's Party's Campaign for the Equal Rights Amendment, 1920–1927." *Women's Studies* 5, no. 6 (1982): 585–598.

945. Rupp, Leila J. "The Women's Community in the National Woman's Party, 1945 to the 1960s." *Signs* 10, no. 4 (Summer 1985): 715–740.

946. "White Woman's Burden: Letters of Members of the National Advisory Committee of the National Woman's Party." *The Nation* 112 (16 February 1921): 257–258.

947. "The Woman's Party and Mr. Hoover." *The Nation* 127 (3 October 1928): 312.

Women of Color

948. Cotera, Marta. "ERA: The Latina Challenge." *Nuestro* 5, no. 8 (1981): 47–48.

949. Murray, Pauli. "The Negro Woman's Stake in the Equal Rights Amendment." *Harvard Civil Rights–Civil Liberties Law Review* 6 (March 1971): 253–259.

Congress

950. Conroy, Sarah Booth. "Set Stage for New Equal Rights Battle." *McCalls* 98 (May 1971): 37.

951. East, Catherine. "The First Stage: ERA in Washington, 1961–1972." *Women's Political Times* (September 1982): 1.

952. "Equal Rights Amendment." *Congressional Quarterly Almanac* 2 (1946): 540–541.

953. "Equal Rights Amendment." *Congressional Quarterly Almanac* 6 (1950): 419–422.

954. "Equal Rights Amendment." *Congressional Quarterly Weekly Report* (15 January 1954): 51.

955. "Equal Rights for Women." *Congressional Quarterly Weekly Report* (18 September 1964): 2184.

956. "Equal Rights for Women? Things May Never Be the Same." *U.S. News and World Report* 69 (24 August 1970): 29–30.

957. Helmes, Winifred Gertrude. "Equal Rights, Where Do We Stand?" *Graduate Woman* 46 (March 1953): 165.

958. Kuhne, Catherine. "Responsibility Is the Word She Lives By: Equal Rights Amendment Before New Congress." *Independent Woman* 34 (March 1955): 91, 118.

959. Randall, Susan Louise. "A Legislative History of the Equal Rights Amendment." Ph.D. dissertation, University of Utah, Salt Lake, 1979.

960. Temple, Majorie L. "What Do Our Congressmen Think about the Equal Rights Amendment?" *Independent Woman* 32 (April 1953): 129–138, 142.

Strategy

961. Berlow, Albert. "Constitutional Law Experts Disagree Over Extension of ERA Approval Deadline." *Congressional Quarterly Weekly Report* 35 (26 November 1977): 2493–2496.

962. Boles, Janet K.. "Building Support for the ERA; A Case of 'Too Much, Too Late'." *PS* 15 (Fall 1982): 572–577.

963. Carroll, Bernice. "Direct Action and Constitutional Rights: The Case of the ERA." In *Rights of Passage: The*

Past and Future of the ERA, edited by Joan Hoff-Wilson, 63–75. Bloomington: Indiana University Press, 1986.

964. "Feminism in the Federal Constitution." *World's Work* 45 (November 1922): 20–21.

965. Freeman, Jo. "The Quest for Equality: The ERA vs. 'Other Means'." In *Ethnicity and Women,* edited by Winston A. Horne, 46–78. Milwaukee: University of Wisconsin System American Ethnic Studies Coordinating Committee, 1986.

966. Joyner, Nancy Douglas. "Coalition Politics: A Case Study of an Organization's Approach to a Single Issue." *Women and Politics* 2, no. 1–2 (Spring–Summer 1982): 57–70.

967. Machlean, Joan. "Women Fight Back: ERA Extension." *Progressive* 43 (February 1979): 38–40.

968. Winkler, Karen J. "Scholars Examine Failures of Strategy and Interpretation in Explaining Defeat of the Equal Rights Amendment." *Chronicle of Higher Education* 33, no. 14 (December 1986): 7, 10.

Ratification in the States

969. Arrington, Theodore S., and Patricia A. Kyle. "Equal Rights Amendment Activists in North Carolina." *Journal of Women in Culture and Society* 3 (Spring 1978): 666–680.

970. Boles, Janet K.. *The Politics of the Equal Rights Amendment—Conflict and the Decision Process.* New York: Longman, 1979.

971. ———. "Feminists as Agents of Social Change: Lobbying for the Equal Rights Amendment." *Peace and Change* 6, no. 3 (1980): 1–9.

972. "Campaign Headquarters Opened to Work for the Equal Rights Amendment." *Independent Woman* 26 (April 1947): 112.

973. Carpenter, Liz. "But We're Getting Smart." In *Women Organizing— An Anthology,* edited by Bernice Cummings and Victoria Schuck, 321–328. Metuchen, NJ: Scarecrow Press, 1979.

974. Carter, Judy Langford. "The Reagan I Love, Friendship and Campaigning for ERA with Maurine Reagan." *Redbook* 156 (March 1981): 21–22, 60.

975. Carver, Joan S. "The Equal Rights Amendment and the Florida Legislature." *Florida Historical Quarterly* 60 (1982): 455–481.

976. Ginsburg, Ruth Bader. "Ratification of the Equal Rights Amendment: A Question of Time." *Texas Law Review* (1979): 919–920.

977. Goodman, Patricia W. "The ERA in Virginia: A Power Playground." *Southern Exposure* 6, no. 3 (1978): 59–62.

978. McGovern, James R. "Helen Hunt West: Florida's Pioneer for E.R.A." *Florida Historical Quarterly* 57, no. 1 (1978): 39–53.

979. Huber, Joan, Cynthia Rexroat, and Glenna Spitze. "A Crucible of Opinion on Women's Status: ERA in Illinois." *Social Forces* 57 (December 1978): 549–565.

980. Jones, Judson H. "The Effect of the Pro- and Anti-ERA Campaign Contributions on the ERA Voting Behavior of Eightieth Illinois House of Representatives." *Women and Politics* 2, no. 1–2 (Spring–Summer 1982): 71–86.

981. Keerdoja, Eileen, and Jane Whitmore. "LBJ's Daughter Stumps for ERA: L. B. J. Robb." *Newsweek* 94 (17 December 1979): 15.

982. Lilie, Joyce R., Roger Handberg, Jr., and Wanda Lowery. "Women State Legislators and the ERA: Dimensions of Support and Opposition." *Women and Politics* 2, no. 1–2 (Spring–Summer 1982): 23–38.

983. Mansbridge, Jane. *Why We Lost the ERA*. Chicago: University of Chicago Press, 1986.

984. ———. "Organizing for the ERA: Cracks in the Facade of Unity." In *Women, Politics and Change*, edited by Louise A. Tilly and Patricia Gurin, 323–339. New York: Russell Sage, 1990.

985. Mathews, Donald G., and Jane Sherron DeHart. *Sex, Gender and the Politics of ERA: A State and the Nation.* New York: Oxford University Press, 1990.

986. Meyer, Howard N. "Women, 'Big Fourteen' and Equal Rights." *New Politics* 10 (Fall 1972): 50–60.

987. Mueller, Carol M. "Oppositional Consciousness and ERA Activist in Three States." Paper presented at the American Sociological Association, San Francisco, 1980.

988. Ross, Charlotte Guinn. "Federal Equal Rights Amendment as an Issue in the Texas Legislature, 1971–1975." Master's thesis, Texas Woman's University, Denton, 1979.

989. Sargent, Mary Lee. "Women Rising in Resistance: A Direct Action Network." *Women's Studies International Forum* 12, no. 1 (1989): 113–118.

990. Shear, S. Sue. "The 27th in Missouri." *Focus* 9 (December 1973): 632–644.

991. Shiflet, Katherine Hancock. "Politicians' Attitudes toward the Equal Rights Amendment: A Study of the West Vrginia and Virginia State Legislatures." Master's thesis, Virginia Polytechnic Institute, 1979.

992. Slavin, Sarah, ed. *The Equal Rights Amendment: The Politics and Process of Ratification of the 27th Amendment to the U.S. Constitution.* New York: Haworth Press, 1982.

993. Steiner, Gilbert Y. *Constitutional Inequality: The Political Fortunes of the Equal Rights Amendment.* Washington, DC: Brookings Institution, 1985.

994. Wohl, Lisa Cronin. "White Gloves and Combat Boots: The Fight for ERA." *Civil Liberties Review* 1, no. 4 (Fall 1974): 77–86.

Religion

995. Allured, Janet. "Arkansas Baptists and Methodist and the Equal Rights Amendment." *Arkansas Historical Quarterly* 43 (Spring 1984): 55–66.

996. Kenneally, James J. "Women Divided: The Catholic Struggle for an Equal Rights Amendment, 1923–

1945." *Catholic Historical Review* 75 (April 1989): 249–263.

997. Tedin, Kent L., David W. Brady, Mary E. Buston, Barbara M. Gorman, and Judy L. Thompson. "Religious Preference and Pro-Anti Activism on the Equal Rights Amendment Issue." *Pacific Sociological Review* 21 (1978): 55–66.

Law

998. Brown, Barbara A., Thomas I. Emerson, Gail Falk, and Anne E. Freedman. "The Equal Rights Amendment: A Constitutional Basis for Equal Rights for Women." *Yale Law Journal* 80 (April 1971): 871–985.

999. Ginsburg, Ruth Bader. "The Need for the Equal Rights Amendment." *American Bar Association Journal* 59, no. 9 (1973): 1013–1019.

1000. Kanowitz, Leo. *Equal Rights: The Male Stake.* Albuquerque: University of New Mexico, 1981.

1001. Law, Sylvia A. "Rethinking Sex and the Constitution." *University of Pennsylvania Law Review* 132 (June 1983): 955–1040.

1002. Lee, Rex E. *A Lawyer Looks at the Equal Rights Amendment.* Provo, UT: Brigham Young University Press, 1980.

1003. Littleton, Christine. "Reconstructing Sexual Equality." *California Law Review* 75 (1987): 1279.

1004. Motley, Constance Baker. "Constitution: Key to Freedom." *Ebony* 18 (September 1963): 221–222.

1005. Puller, Edwin S. "When Equal Rights Are Unequal." *Virginia Law Review* 13 (June 1927): 619–630.

Post-1983

1006. Basch, Norma. "Equality of Rights and Feminist Politics." *Law and Society Review* 21 (1988): 783–787.

1007. Battistoni, Richard M. "Feminist Voices, Equality and the U.S. Constitution." Paper presented at the annual meeting of the American Political Science Association, Washington, DC, 1988.

1008. Daniels, Mark, and Robert Darcy. "As Time Goes By: The Arrested Diffusion of the Equal Rights Amendment." *Publius* 15 (Fall 1985): 51–60.

1009. Daniels, Mark, Robert Darcy, and Joseph W. Westphal. "The ERA Won——At Least in the Opinion Polls." In *Women Leaders in American Politics,* edited by James David Barber and Barbara Kellerman, 41–46. Englewood Cliffs, NJ: Prentice Hall, 1986. First printed in *PS* (Fall 1982): 578–584.

1010. Eisler, Riane, and Allie C. Hixson. *The Equal Rights Amendment Facts and Action Guide.* Washington, DC: National Women's Conference Center, 1986.

1011. Jones, Arthur. "Politics for the Post-ERA Era." *Progressive* 46 (October 1982): 15–16.

1012. Mansbridge, Jane. "Post ERA: Should Every Flower Bloom?" *Ms.* 15, no. 1 (July 1986): 46, 84.

1013. ———. "Not NOW, Renewed Campaign for the ERA." *The Nation* 244 (10 January 1987): 5.

1014. Marilley, Suzanne M. "Towards a New Strategy for the ERA: Some Lessons from the American Woman Suffrage Movement." *Women and Politics* 9, no. 4 (1989): 23–42.

1015. Pleck, Elizabeth. "The ERA Defeat: An Historian's Perspective." *The Organization of American Historian's Newsletter* (August 1982): 1.

1016. Smeal, Eleanor. "The ERA: Should We Eat Our Words?" *Ms.* 16, no. 1–2 (July–August 1987): 170, 218.

1017. Williams, Wendy W., and Judith L. Lichtman. "Closing the Law's Gender Gap." *The Nation* 239 (29 September 1984): 281–284.

Feminism, 1920–1965

1018. Andersen, Kristi. "Working Women and Political Participation, 1952–1972." *American Journal of Political Science* 19, no. 3 (August 1975): 439–453.

1019. Beard, Mary R. "After Equality—What?" *Independent Woman* 11 (June 1930): 227–228, 258.

1020. Brown, Dorothy M. *Setting a Course: American Women in the 1920s.* Boston: Twayne, 1986.

1021. Bugbee, Emma. "The Woman's Centennial Congress." *Independent Woman* 20 (January 1941): 19, 20.

1022. Carroll, Mary. "Wanted—A New Feminism: An Interview with Emily Newell Blair." *Independent Woman* 11 (December 1930): 499, 544.

1023. Freeman, Jo. "Feminist Organizations and Activities from Suffrage to Women's Liberation." In *Women: A Feminist Perspective,* 4th ed., edited by Jo Freeman, 541–555. Mayfield, CA: Mountain View, 1989.

1024. ———. "From Suffrage to Women's Liberation: Feminism in Twentieth-Century America." In *Women: A Feminist Perspective,* 5th ed., edited by Jo Freeman, 509–528. Mountain View, CA: Mayfield, 1995.

1025. Gatlin, Rochelle. *American Women Since 1945.* Jackson: University Press of Mississippi, 1987.

1026. Gluck, Sherna. "Socialist Feminism between the Two World Wars: Insights from Oral History." In *Decades of Discontent—The Women's Movement 1920–1940,* edited by Lois Scharf and Joan M. Jensen, 279–297. Westport, CT: Greenwood, 1983.

1027. Hartmann, Susan M. *The Home Front and Beyond: American Women in the 1940s.* Boston: Twayne, 1982.

1028. ———. *From Margin to Mainstream: American Woman and Politics Since 1960.* Philadelphia: Temple University Press, 1989.

1029. Jensen, Joan M. "All Pink Sisters: The War Department and the Feminist Movement in the 1920s." In *Decades of Discontent—The Women's Movement 1920–1940,* edited by Lois Scharf and Joan M. Jensen, 199–221. Westport, CT: Greenwood, 1983.

1030. Kaledin, Eugenia. *Mothers and More: American Women in the 1950s.* Boston: Twayne, 1984.

1031. Lemons, J. Stanley. *The Woman Citizen: Social Feminism in the 1920s.* Urbana: University of Illinois Press, 1973.

1032. Lynn, Susan. *Progressive Women in Conservative Times, Racial Justice, Peace, and Feminism, 1945 to the 1960's.* New Brunswick, NJ: Rutgers University Press, 1992.

1033. Mauel, Frances. "Accent Is on Political Action." *Independent Woman* 26 (August 1947): 120–124.

1034. Meyerowitz, Joanne, ed. *Not June Cleaver, Women and Gender in Postwar America, 1945–1960.* Philadelphia: Temple University Press, 1994.

1035. Orleck, Annelise. "'We Are That Mythical Thing Called the Public': Militant Housewives during the Great Depression." *Feminist Studies* 19, no. 1 (1993): 147–160.

1036. Park, Maud Wood. "The Woman's Movement in Review." *Independent Woman* 11 (June 1930): 236–237, 256–258.

1037. Rupp, Leila J. "The Survival of American Feminism: The Women's Movement in the Post War Period." In *Reshaping America Society and Institutions, 1945–1960,* edited by Robert H. Bremner and Gary W. Reichard, 33–66. Columbus: Ohio State University Press, 1982.

1038. ———. "Women's Culture and the Continuity of the Women's Movement." In *Moving On: New Perspectives on the Women's Movement,* edited by Tayo Andreasen. Aarhus, Denmark: Aarhus University Press, 1991.

1039. Rupp, Leila J., and Verta Taylor. *Survival in the Doldrums: The American Women's Rights Movement, 1945 to 1960s.* New York: Oxford University Press, 1987.

1040. Scharf, Lois. "The Forgotten Woman: Working Women, the New Deal, and Women's Organizations." In *Decades of Discontent: The Women's Movement, 1920–1940,* edited by Lois Scharf and Joan M. Jensen, 243–259. Westport, CT: Greenwood, 1983.

1041. Scharf, Lois, and Joan M. Jensen, eds. *Decades of Discontent: The Women's Movement, 1920–1940.* Westport, CT: Greenwood, 1983.

1042. Scott, Anne Firor. "After Suffrage: Southern Women in the Twenties." *Journal of Southern History* 30 (August 1964): 298–318.

1043. ———. *The Southern Lady: From Pedestal to Politics, 1830–1930.* Chicago: University of Chicago Press, 1970.

1044. Showalter, Elaine. *These Modern Women: Autobiographical Essays from the Twenties.* New York: Feminist Press, 1978.

1045. ———. "Feminism's Awkward Age: The Deflated Rebels of the 1920s." *Ms.* 7, no. 7 (January 1979): 64–65, 70, 72.

1046. Stone, Kathryn H. "Women as Citizens." *Annals of the American Academy of Political and Social Science* 251 (May 1947): 79–86.

1047. Swain, Martha H. "The Public Role of Southern Women." In *Sex,*

Race, and the Role of Women in the South, edited by Joanne V. Hawks and Sheila Skemp. Jackson: University Press of Mississippi, 1983.

1048. Taylor, Verta. "Social Movement Continuity: The Women's Movement in Abeyance." *American Sociological Review* 54 (1989): 761–775.

1049. Walls, Patricia Carol. "Defending Their Liberties: Women's Organizations During the McCarthy Era." Ph.D. dissertation, University of Maryland, College Park, 1994.

1050. Ware, Susan. *Beyond Suffrage: Women in the New Deal.* Cambridge: Harvard University Press, 1981.

1051. ———. *Holding Their Own: American Women in the 1930s.* Boston: Twayne, 1982.

1052. ———. "American Women in the 1950s: Nonpartisan Politics and Women's Politicization." In *Women, Politics and Change,* edited by Louise A. Tilly and Patricia Gurin, 281–299. New York: Russell Sage, 1990.

1053. Young, Louise M. *Understanding Politics: A Practical Guide for Women.* New York: Pellegrini and Cudahy, 1950.

New Feminism

General

1054. Cassell, Joan. *A Group Called Women: Sisterhood and Symbolism in the Feminist Movement.* New York: McKay, 1977.

1055. Deckard, Barbara Sinclair. *The Women's Movement: Political, Socioeconomic and Psychological Issues.* New York: Harper and Row, 1983 (1975).

1056. Hole, Judith, and Ellen Levine. *Rebirth of Feminism.* New York: Quadrangle, 1971.

1057. Katzenstein, Mary Fainsod. "Feminism Within American Institutions: Unobtrusive Mobilization in the 1980s." *Signs* 16 (1990): 27–54.

1058. Rossi, Alice S. *Feminists in Politics: A Panel Analysis of the First National Women's Conference.* New York: Academic Press, 1982.

1059. Sapiro, Virginia. "Feminism: A Generation Later." *Annals of the American Academy of Political and Social Science* 515 (May 1991): 10–22.

1060. Steinem, Gloria. "The First National Women's Conference." In *Women Leaders in American Politics,* edited by James David Barber and Barbara Kellerman, 166–173. Englewood Cliffs, NJ: Prentice Hall, 1986.

About the Movement

1061. Backhouse, Constance, and David H. Flaherty, eds. *Challenging Times: The Women's Movement in Canada and the United States.* Montreal, Canada: McGill-Queens' University Press, 1992.

1062. Carden, Maren Lockwood. *The New Feminist Movement.* New York: Russell Sage, 1974.

1063. Castro, Ginette. *American Feminism: A Contemporary History.* New York: New York University Press, 1990.

1064. Davis, Flora. *Moving the Mountain: The Women's Movement in America Since 1960.* New York: Simon and Schuster, 1991.

1065. Echols, Alice. *Daring to Be Bad: Radical Feminism in America 1967–1975.* Minneapolis: University of Minnesota, 1989.

1066. Evans, Sara M. *Personal Politics: The Roots of Women's Liberation in the Civil Rights Movement and the New Left.* New York: Vintage, 1980.

1067. Ferree, Myra Marx, and Beth Hess. *Controversy and Coalition: The New Feminist Movement.* Boston: Twayne, 1985.

1068. Freeman, Jo. "The Women's Liberation Front." *Moderator* (November 1968): 42.

1069. ———. "The New Feminists." *The Nation* 208, no. 8 (24 February 1969): 239.

1070. ———. "The Revolution Is Happening in Our Minds." *College and University Business* 48, no. 2 (February 1970): 63.

1071. ———. "The Women's Liberation Movement: It's Origin, Structure and Ideas." In *Recent Sociology No. 4: Family, Marriage and the Struggle of the Sexes,* edited by Hans Peter Dreitzel, 201–216. New York: Macmillan, 1972. Reprint. *Politic U.S.A.,* Andrew M. Scott and Earle Wallace, eds., 468–479. New York: Macmillan, 1974.

1072. ———. "The Origins of the Women's Liberation Movement." *American Journal of Sociology* 78, no. 4 (January 1973): 792–811. Reprint. *Changing Women in a Changing Society,* Joan Huber, ed. Chicago: University of Chicago Press, 1973.

1073. ———. *The Politics of Women's Liberation.* New York: McKay, 1975.

1074. ———. "The Women's Liberation Movement: Its Origins, Organizations, Activities and Ideas." In *Women: A Feminist Perspective,* 2d ed., edited by Jo Freeman, 543–556. Palo Alto, CA: Mayfield, 1979.

1075. Fritz, Leah. *Dreamers and Dealers: An Intimate Appraisal of the Women's Movement.* Boston: Beacon, 1979.

1076. Lear, Martha Weinman. "Second Feminist Wave." *The New York Times Magazine* (10 March 1968): 24–25, 50–58, 60, 62.

1077. Lerner, Gerda. "Women's Rights and American Feminism." *The American Scholar* 40 (Spring 1971): 235–248.

1078. Mandle, Joan. "Women's Liberation: Humanizing Rather Than Polarizing." *Annals of the American Academy of Political and Social Science* 397 (September 1971): 118–128.

1079. McDowell, Margaret B. "Reflections on the New Feminism." *Midwest Quarterly* 12 (April 1971): 309–333.

1080. O'Neill, William L. *The Woman Movement: Feminism in the United States.* Chicago: Quadrangle, 1971.

1081. Pruitt, Mary Christine. "'Women Unite!' The Modern Women's Movement in Minnesota." Ph.D. dissertation, University of Minnesota, 1988.

1082. Romer, Karen T., and Cynthia Secor. "The Time Is Here for

Women's Liberation." *Annals of the American Academy of Political and Social Science* 397 (September 1971): 129–139.

1083. Ryan, Barbara. "Ideological Purity and Feminism: The U.S. Women's Movement from 1966 to 1975." *Gender and Society* 3, no. 2 (June 1989): 238–257.

1084. Salper, Roberta. "The Development of the American Women's Liberation Movement, 1967–1971." In *Female Liberation: History and Current Politics,* edited by Roberta Salper, 169–184. New York: Knopf, 1972.

1085. Sochen, June, ed. *The New Feminism in Twentieth Century America.* Lexington, MA: D. C. Heath, 1971.

1086. Taylor, Verta, and Nancy E.Whittier. "The New Feminist Movement." In *Feminist Frontiers: Rethinking Sex, Gender and Society,* 3d ed., edited by Laurel Richardson and Verta Taylor, 533–548. Reading, MA: Addison-Wesley, 1993.

1087. Wandersee, Winifred D. *On the Move: American Women in the 1970s.* Boston: Twayne, 1988.

1088. Ware, Cellestine. *Woman Power: The Movement for Women's Liberation.* New York: Tower Publications, 1970.

By the Movement

1089. Friedan, Betty. "N.O.W. How It Began." *Woman Speaking* (April 1967).

1090. ———. *It Changed My Life: Writings on the Women's Movement.* New York: Random House, 1976.

1091. Fund for a Feminist Majority. *The Feminization of Power, 50–50 by the Year 2000.* Washington, DC: Fund for a Feminist Majority, 1992.

1092. Gornick, Vivian, and Barbara K. Moran. *Women in Sexistsociety, Studies in Power and Powerlessness.* New York: Ace Books, 1971.

1093. Koedt, Anne, Ellen Rapone, and Anita Levine. *Radical Feminism.* Chicago: Quadrangle, 1973.

1094. *Liberation Now! Writings From the Women's Liberation Movement.* New York: Ace Books, 1971.

1095. Morgan, Robin, ed. *Sisterhood Is Powerful.* New York: Random House, 1970.

1096. National Organization for Women. *And Justice for All.* Chicago: National Organization for Women, 1972.

1097. Popkin, Ann Hunter. "The Personal Is Political: The Women's Liberation Movement." In *They Should Have Served That Cup of Coffee,* edited by Dick Custer, 181–222. Boston: South End Press, 1979.

1098. Redstockings, ed. *Feminist Revolution.* New York: Random House, 1978.

1099. Schneir, Miriam, ed. *Feminism in Our Time: The Essential Writings from World War II to the Present.* New York: Vintage, 1994.

1100. Stambler, Sookie, ed. *Women's Liberation: Blueprint for the Future.* New York: Ace Books, 1970.

1101. Tanner, Leslie B., ed. *Voices from Women's Liberation.* New York: Signet, 1970.

1102. Thompson, Mary Lou. *Voices of the New Feminism.* Boston: Beacon Press, 1970.

Leaders and Activists

1103. Christopher, S. M. "Women, USA, Bella Abzug, Founder." *Redbook* 151 (October 1979): 52, 54.

1104. Cohen, Marcia. *The Sisterhood: The True Story of the Women Who Changed the World.* New York: Simon and Schuster, 1988.

1105. Frappallo, Elizabeth. "At 91 Jeanette Rankin Is the Feminists' New Heroine." *Life* 72 (3 March 1972): 65.

1106. Gedert, Sam. "Movers and Shakers: Harriet Woods." *Campaigns and Elections* 14, no. 5 (October 1993): 63.

1107. Haney, Eleanor Humes. *A Feminist Legacy: The Ethics of Wilma Scott Heide and Company.* Buffalo, NY: Margaretdaughters, Inc., 1985.

1108. Morgan, Robin. *Going Too Far: The Personal Chronicle of a Feminist.* New York: Random House, 1977.

1109. Murray, Pauli. *Pauli Murray: The Autobiography of a Black Activist, Feminist, Lawyer, Priest, and Poet.* Knoxville: University of Tennessee Press, 1989.

1110. Steinem, Gloria. *Outrageous Acts and Everyday Rebellions.* New York: Holt, Rinehart and Winston, 1983.

Organizations

General

1111. Acker, Joan. "Feminist Goals and Organizing Processes." In *Feminist Organizations: Harvest of the New Women's Movement,* edited by Myra Marx Ferree and Patricia Yancey Martin, 137–144. Philadelphia: Temple University Press, 1995.

1112. Ferree, Myra Marx, and Patricia Yancey Martin. "Doing the Work of the Movement: Feminist Organizations." In *Feminist Organizations: Harvest of the New Women's Movement,* edited by Myra Marx Ferree and Patricia Yancey Martin, 3–26. Philadelphia: Temple University Press, 1995.

1113. ———, eds. *Feminist Organizations: Harvest of the New Women's Movement.* Philadelphia: Temple University Press, 1995.

1114. Freeman, Jo. "Political Organization in the Feminist Movement." *Acta Sociologica* 18, no. 2–3 (1975): 222–224.

1115. Gelb, Joyce. "Feminist Organization Success and the Politics of Engagement." In *Feminist Organizations: Harvest of the New Women's Movement,* edited by Myra Marx Ferree and Patricia Yancey Martin, 128–136. Philadelphia: Temple University Press, 1995.

1116. Leidner, Robin. "Stretching the Boundaries of Liberalism: Democratic Innovation in a Feminist Organization." *Signs* 16 (Winter 1991): 263–289.

National Organization for Women

1117. Florer, John Harmon. "NOW: The Formative Years, the National Effort to Acquire Federal Action on Equal Employment Rights for Women in the 1960s." Ph.D. dissertation, Syracuse University, 1972.

1118. Hammel, Lisa. "NOW Organized." In *The New Feminism in Twentieth Century America*, edited by June Sochen, 173–178. Lexington, MA: D. C. Heath, 1971.

1119. Ireland, Patricia. *What Women Want*. New York: E. P. Dutton, 1995.

1120. Langer, Howard J. "The Women's Movement: What N.O.W.?" *Social Education* 47, no. 2 (1983): 112–121.

1121. Mano, D. Keith. "Lib on the Rocks: Meeting at Town Hall." *National Review* 26 (15 March 1974): 326.

1122. McMurran, Kristin. "Septuagenarian Molly Yard May Not Be Unsinkable, But She's Just the Thing for NOW." *People's Weekly* 28 (12 October 1987): 38–39.

1123. "A New Battlefield for NOW's Fearless Leader." *Newsweek* 110 (20 July 1987): 30–31.

1124. Wandersee, Winifred D. "Into the Mainstream: The National Organization for Women and Its National Constituency." In *On the Move: American Women in the 1970s*, 36–54. Boston: Twayne, 1988.

National Women's Political Caucus

1125. Burrell, Barbara C. "A New Dimension on Political Participation: The Women's Political Caucus." In *A Portrait of Marginality: The Political Behavior of American Women*, edited by Marianne Githens and Jewell Prestage, 241–258. New York: McKay, 1977.

1126. Engel, Margaret. "Wanted: Young Activists to Fight for Women's Rights." *Glamour* 86, no. 2 (February 1988): 95–96.

1127. Feit, Rona F. "Organizing for Political Power: The National Women's Political Caucus." In *Women Organizing: An Anthology*, edited by Bernice Cummings and Victoria Schuck, 184–208. Metuchen, NJ: Scarecrow Press, 1979.

1128. Jaquith, Cindy. "Where Is the Women's Political Caucus Going?" *International Socialist Review* 33, no. 5 (1972): 4–7.

1129. Rogers, Mary Beth. *How to Be Effective: A Manual for Leaders of the National Women's Political Caucus*. Washington, DC: National Women's Political Caucus, 1979.

1130. "Women's Movement Under Siege." *Time* 110 (26 September 1977): 64.

1131. "Women's Political Caucus." *U.S. News and World Report* 71 (16 August 1971): 67–68.

Other Organizations

1132. Dade, Julie E. "Redividing the Political Pie." *Focus* 13, no. 6 (6 July 1985): 8.

1133. Daniels, Arlene. "W.E.A.L.: The Growth of a Feminist Organization." In *Women Organizing: An An-*

thology, edited by Bernice Cummings and Victoria Schuck, 133–151. Metuchen, NJ: Scarecrow Press, 1979.

1134. Hansen, Karen V. "The Women's Unions and the Search for a Political Identity." *Socialist Review* 16 (March–April 1986): 67–95.

1135. Moses, Wilson Jeremiah. "Black Bourgeois Feminism versus Peasant Values: Origins and Purposes of the National Federation of Afro-American Women." In *The Golden Age of Black Nationalism,* edited by Wilson Jeremiah Moses, 301–331. Hamden, CT: Shoe String Press, 1978.

1136. Popkin, Ann Hunter. "Bread and Roses: An Early Moment in the Development of Socialist-Feminism." Ph.D. dissertation, Brandeis University, 1978.

1137. Riger, Stephanie. "Vehicles for Empowerment: The Case of Feminist Movement Organizations." *Prevention in Human Services* 3 (1984): 99–117. Reprint. *Studies of Empowerment,* Julian Rappaport, Carolyn Smith, and Robert Hess, eds. New York: Haworth Press.

1138. Rothstein, Vivian, and Naomi Weisstein. "Chicago Women's Liberation Union." *Women: A Journal of Liberation* 2, no. 4 (1972): 5.

1139. Stroebel, Margaret. "Women's Liberation Unions." In *Encyclopedia of the New Left,* edited by Mari Jo Buhle, Paul Buhle, and Dan Georgakas, 841–842. New York: Garland, 1990.

1140. ———. "Consciousness and Action: Historical Agency in the Chicago Women's Liberation Union." In *Provoking Agents: Gender and Agency in Theory and Practice,* edited by Judith Kegan Gardiner, 52–68. Urbana: University of Illinois Press, 1995.

1141. ———. "Organizational Learning in the Chicago Women's Liberation Union." In *Feminist Organizations: Harvest of the New Women's Movement,* edited by Myra Marx Ferree and Patricia Yancey Martin, 145–164. Philadelphia: Temple University Press, 1995.

1142. Teasley, Regina Lorraine. "The Structure and Groups Within a Local Social Movement: A Case Study of the Women's Movement in Ann Arbor from 1969–1973." Master's thesis, Michigan State University, Ann Arbor, 1976.

Women of Color

General

1143. Almquist, Elizabeth M. "The Experiences of Minority Women in the United States: Intersections of Race, Gender, and Class." In *Women: A Feminist Perspective,* 5th ed., edited by Jo Freeman, 573–606. Mountain View, CA: Mayfield, 1995.

1144. Caraway, Nancie. *Segregated Sisterhood: Racism and the Politics of American Feminism.* Knoxville: University of Tennessee Press, 1991.

1145. Moraga, Cherrie, and Gloria Anzaldua, eds. *The Bridge Called My Back: Writings by Radical Women of Color.* Watertown, MA: Persephone Press, 1981.

1146. Willis, Ellen. "Sisters Under the Skin? Confronting Race and

Sex." *Village Voice Literary Supplement* 8 (June 1982): 12.

African American

1147. Chisholm, Shirley. "Race, Revolution and Women." *The Black Scholar* 3 (7 December 1971): 17–21.

1148. "Combahee River Collective Statement." In *Homegirls,* edited by Barbara Smith, 272–282. New York: Kitchen Table Women of Color Press, 1983.

1149. Gabriel, Peter M. "Conservative Women Flex Their Political Muscles." *National Minority Politics* 6, no. 8 (August 1994): 24.

1150. Gilkes, Cheryl Townsend. " 'If It Wasn't for the Woman ...': African American Women, Community Work, and Social Change." In *Women of Color in U. S. Society,* edited by Maxine Baca Zinn and Bonnie Thornton Dill, 229–246. Philadelphia: Temple University, 1994.

1151. Gilliam, Dorothy. "Political Clout and How to Get It." *Essence* 16 (May 1985): 112–115.

1152. ———. "Shirley Chisholm to Head Black Woman's Congress." *Jet* 68 (24 June 1985): 6.

1153. Guseiler, Mert. "Black Woman and the Women's Liberation Movement." *Sepia* 19 (October 1970): 63–65.

1154. Hemmons, Willie Mae. "The Women's Liberation Movement: Understanding Black Women's Attitudes." In *The Black Woman,* edited by LaFrances Rodgers-Rose. Beverly Hills, CA: Sage, 1980.

1155. Hood, Elizabeth F. "Black Women, White Women: Separate Paths to Liberation." *The Black Scholar* 9, no. 7 (1978): 45–56.

1156. Hooks, Bell. *Ain't I a Woman: Black Women and Feminism.* Boston: South End Press, 1981.

1157. King, Helen H. "Black Woman and Women's Lib." *Ebony* 26 (March 1971): 68–70, 74–76.

1158. Koontz, Elizabeth Duncan. "Women as a Minority Group." In *Voices of the New Feminism,* edited by Mary Lou Thompson, 77–86. Boston: Beacon, 1970.

1159. LaRue, Linda J. "Black Movement and Women's Liberation." *The Black Scholar* 1 (May 1970): 36–42.

1160. Marshall, Thelma E. "Women in the United States." *The Black Scholar* 9, no. 8–9 (1978): 29–34.

1161. Morrison, Toni. "What the Black Woman Thinks about Women's Lib." *The New York Times Magazine* (22 August 1971): 63–64, 66, 214–215.

1162. Murray, Pauli. "The Liberation of Black Women." In *Voices of the New Feminism,* edited by Mary L. Thompson, 87–102. Boston: Beacon, 1970. Reprint. *Women: A Feminist Perspective,* Jo Freeman, ed., 351–363. Mountain View, CA: Mayfield, 1975.

1163. Polatnick, M. Rivka. "Poor Black Sisters Decided for Themselves: A Case Study of 1960s Women's Liberation Activism." In *Black Women in America,* edited by Kim Marie Vaz, 110–130. Vol. 2. Thousand Oaks, CA: Sage, 1995.

1164. Solomon, Irvin D. *Feminism and Black Activism in Contemporary America.* New York: Greenwood, 1989.

1165. Terrelonge, Pauline. "Feminist Consciousness and Black Women." In *Women: A Feminist Perspective.* 5th ed., edited by Jo Freeman, 607–616. Palo Alto, CA: Mayfield, 1995.

1166. Wilcox, Clyde. "Black Women and Feminism." *Women and Politics* 10, no. 3 (1990): 65–84.

1167. Williams, Maxine, and Pamela Newman. *Black Women's Liberation.* New York: Pathfinder Press, 1972.

Asian American

1168. Asian Women United of California. *Making Waves: An Anthology of Writings By and About Asian American Women.* Boston: Beacon, 1989.

1169. Chair, Alice Yun. "Global Feminism and Hawaiian Feminist Politics." Paper presented at the Conference on Exploration in Feminist Ethics: Theory and Practice, University of Minnesota, Duluth, 1988.

1170. Chow, Esther Ngan-Ling. "The Development of Feminist Consciousness Among Asian American Women." *Gender and Society* 1 (September 1987): 238–251.

1171. ———. "The Feminist Movement: Where Are All the Asian American Women?" In *Making Waves: An Anthology of Writings By and About Asian American Women,* edited by Asian Women United of California, 363–377. Boston: Beacon Press, 1989.

1172. Hohri, Sasha. "Are You a Liberated Woman?: Feminism, Revolution, and Asian American Women." In *All American Women: Lines That Divide, Ties That Bind,* edited by Johnnetta B. Cole, 420–426. New York: Free Press, 1986.

1173. Ling, Susie. "The Mountain Movers: Asian American Women's Movement in Los Angeles." *Ameriasia Journal* 15 (1989): 51–67.

1174. Loo, Chalsa, and Paul Ong. "Slaying Demons with a Sewing Needle: Feminist Issues for Chinatown's Women." *Berkeley Journal of Sociology* 27 (1982): 77–88.

Latina American

1175. Aragon de Valdez, Theresa. "Organizing as a Political Tool for the Chicana." *Frontiers* 5 (1980): 7–13.

1176. Barrios, Mary. "The Chicana Experience and the Current Feminist Movement." Paper presented at the annual meeting of the Southern Social Science Association, Atlanta, 1993.

1177. Cortera, Marta. *The Chicana Feminist.* Austin, TX: Information Systems Development, 1977.

1178. ———. "Feminism: The Chicana and the Anglo Version." In *Twice a Minority: Mexican American Women,* edited by Margarita B. Melville, 217–234. St. Louis, MO: C. V. Mosby Company, 1980.

1179. Garcia, Alma M.. "The Development of Chicana Feminist Discourse, 1970–1980." *Gender and Society* 3, no. 2 (June 1989): 217–238.

1180. Gonzales, Sylvia. "The White Feminist Movement: The Chicana Perspective." *Social Science Journal* 14, no. 2 (April 1977): 67–76.

1181. Nieto, Consuelo. "The Chicana and the Women's Rights Movement: A Perspective." *Civil Rights Digest* 6 (1974): 36–42.

1182. Pesquera, Beatriz M., and Denise A. Segura. "'There Is No Going Back': Chicanas and Feminism." In *Chicana Critical Issues: Mujeres Activas en Letras y Cambio Social,* 95–115. Berkeley, CA: Third Woman Press, 1993.

1183. Segura, Denise A., and Beatriz M. Pesquera. "Chicana Feminisms: Their Political Context and Contemporary Expressions." In *Women: A Feminist Perspective,* 5th ed., edited by Jo Freeman, 617–631. Mountain View, CA: Mayfield, 1995.

1184. Vidal, Mirta. *Chicanas Speak Out, Women: New Voice of La Raza.* New York: Pathfinder Press, 1971.

1185. Zavella, Patricia. "Reconciling 'Difference' in the Feminist Movement: A Latina Perspective." Paper presented at the Conference on Perspectives on Feminism: Past, Present and Future, National Women and the Law Association, Washington, DC, 1986.

Native American

1186. Allen, Paula Gunn. "Angry Women Are Building: Issues and Struggles Facing Native American Women." In *All American Women, Lines That Divide, Ties That Bind,* edited by Johnnetta B. Cole, 407–410. New York: Free Press, 1986.

1187. Davis, Ann. "Ceilia Fire Thunder: She Inspires Her People." In *Experiencing Race, Class and Gender in the United States,* edited by Virginia Cyrus, 437–440. Mountain View, CA: Mayfield, 1993.

1188. Green, Rayna. "Honoring the Vision of Changing Woman: A Decade of American Feminism." In *Sisterhood Is Global,* edited by Robin Morgan, 705–713. New York: Doubleday, 1983.

1189. ———. "Diary of a Native American Feminist." *Ms.* 11 (July–August 1982): 170–172.

1190. Wittstock, Laura Waterman. "Native American Women in the Feminist Milieu." In *Contemporary Native American Address,* edited by John Maestas, 373–376. Salt Lake City, UT: Brigham Young University, 1976.

Diversity

1191. Cook, Elizabeth Adell. "The Generations of Feminism." In *Women in Politics: Outsiders or Insiders?: A Collection of Readings,* edited by Lois Lovelace Duke, 55–66. New York: Prentice Hall, 1993.

1192. Freeman, Jo. "Women's Liberation and Its Impact on the Campus." *Liberal Education* 57 (December 1971): 468–478.

1193. Glazer, Ilsa M. "A Cloak of Many Colors: Jewish Feminism and Feminist Jews in America." In *Women:*

A Feminist Perspective, 5th ed., edited by Jo Freeman, 632–640. Mountain View, CA: Mayfield, 1995.

1194. Kamen, Paula. *Feminist Fatale: Voices from the 'Twentysomething' Generation Explore the Future of the Women's Movement.* New York: Donald I. Fine, 1991.

1195. Schneider, Beth. "Political Generations in the Contemporary Women's Movement." *Sociological Inquiry* 58 (1988): 4–21.

1196. Sigel, Roberta, and John V. Reynolds. "Generational Differences and the Women's Movement." *Political Science Quarterly* 94 (Winter 1979): 635–648.

1197. Weitz, Rose. "What Price Independence? Social Reactions to Lesbians, Spinsters, Widows, and Nuns." In *Women: A Feminist Perspective,* 5th ed., edited by Jo Freeman, 448–457. Mountain View, CA: Mayfield, 1995.

1198. Whittier, Nancy E. *Feminist Generations: The Persistence of the Radical Women's Movement.* Philadelphia: Temple University Press, 1995.

1199. ———. "Personnel Change in the Columbus, Ohio, Women's Movement, 1969–1984." In *Feminist Organizations: Harvest of the New Women's Movement,* edited by Myra Marx Ferree and Patricia Yancey Martin, 180–198. Philadelphia: Temple University Press, 1995.

Impact

1200. Bonafede, Dom. "Women's Movement Broadens the Scope of Its Role in American Politics." *National Journal* 14 (11 December 1982): 2108–2111.

1201. ———. "Still a Long Way to Go: The Women's Movement in the United States Finds Itself at a Crossroads." *National Journal,* 18, no. 1 (13 September 1986): 2175–2179.

1202. DeHart, Jane Sherron. "Rights and Representation: Women, Politics, and Power in the Contemporary United States." In *U.S. History as Women's History,* edited by Linda K. Kerber, Alice Kessler-Harris, and Kathryn Kish Sklar, 214–244. Chapel Hill: University of North Carolina Press, 1995.

1203. Ehrenreich, Barbara. "The Women's Movements: Feminist and Anti-Feminist." *Radical America* 15 (Spring 1981): 98–104.

1204. Faludi, Susan. *Backlash: The Undeclared War Against American Women.* New York: Crown, 1991.

1205. Ferree, Myra Marx. "Equality and Autonomy: Feminist Politics in the United States and West Germany." In *The Women's Movements of the United States and Western Europe: Consciousness, Political Opportunity and Public Policy,* edited by Mary F. Katzenstein and Carol M. Mueller, 172–195. Philadelphia: Temple University Press, 1987.

1206. Friedan, Betty. "Twenty Years after *The Feminine Mystique.*" *The New York Times Magazine* (27 February 1983): VI, 34–36, 42, 54–55.

1207. Harder, Sarah. "Flourishing in the Mainstream: The U.S. Women's Movement Today." In *The American Woman, 1990–91: A Status Report,* edited by Sara E. Ries and Anne J. Stone, 273–286. New York: Norton, 1990.

1208. Harrison, Cynthia E. "A Richer Life: A Reflection on the Women's Movement." In *American Woman, 1987–88,* edited by Paula Ries and Anne J. Stone, 53–77. New York: Norton, 1988.

1209. Henry, Sherrye. *The Deep Divide: Why American Women Resist Equality.* New York: Macmillan, 1994.

1210. Hyde, Cheryl. "Feminist Social Movement Organizations Survive the New Right." In *Feminist Organizations: Harvest of the New Women's Movement,* edited by Myra Marx Ferree and Patricia Yancey Martin, 306–322. Philadelphia: Temple University Press, 1995.

1211. Kaminer, Wendy. "Put the Blame on Mame: Backlash: The Undeclared War against American Women by Susan Faludi." *Atlantic Monthly* 268, no. 6 (December 1991): 123–126.

1212. Katzenstein, Mary Fainsod, and Carol M. Mueller, eds. *The Women's Movements of the United States and Western Europe: Consciousness, Political Opportunity and Public Policy.* Philadelphia: Temple University Press, 1987.

1213. Kimmel, Michael S. "Misogynists, Masculinist Mentors, and Male Supporters: Men's Responses to Feminism." In *Women: A Feminist Perspective,* 5th ed., edited by Jo Freeman, 561–672. Mountain View, CA: Mayfield, 1995.

1214. Paterson, Ann, Karen Ruchs, Carol Giesen, and Betsy Hobbs. "Status Report on the Women's Movement." In *Toward the Second Decade:* *The Impact of the Women's Movement on American Institutions,* edited by Renate Pore and Betty Justice, 189–223. Westport, CT: Greenwood, 1981.

1215. Taylor, Verta. "The Future of Feminism in the 1980s: A Social Movement Analysis." In *Feminist Frontiers: Rethinking Sex, Gender and Society,* 3d rev. ed., edited by Laurel Richardson and Verta Taylor. Reading, MA: Addison-Wesley, 1989 (1986, 1983).

1216. "The Woman's Movement: Moving Ahead." *Ladies Home Journal* 96, no. 10 (October 1979): 185. Special issue, Women in the 80's.

Strategy

1217. Chisholm, Shirley. "Women Must Rebel." In *Voices of the New Feminism,* edited by Mary Lou Thompson, 207–216. Boston: Beacon, 1970.

1218. Freeman, Jo. "Structure and Strategy in the Women's Liberation Movement." *Urban and Social Change Review* 5, no. 2 (Spring 1972): 71–75.

1219. Friedan, Betty. "How to Get the Women's Movement Moving Again." *The New York Times Magazine* (3 November 1985): VI, 26–29, 66–67, 84–85, 89, 98, 106–107.

1220. Hirsch, Marianne, and Elizabeth Fox-Keller, eds. *Conflicts in Feminism.* New York: Routledge, 1990.

1221. Nelson, Barbara J., and Nancy J. Johnson. "Political Structures and Movement Tactics: The Women's Policy Agenda in the United States in the 1990s." Paper presented at the Fourth International Interdisciplinary Congress on Women, New York, June 6, 1990.

1222. Ryan, Barbara. *Feminism and the Women's Movement: Dynamics of Change in Social Movement Ideology and Activism.* New York: Routledge, Chapman and Hall, 1992.

1223. Smeal, Eleanor. "Why I Support a New Party." *Ms.* 2 (January–February 1991): 72–73.

1224. Spalter-Roth, Roberta. "Outside Issues and Insider Tactics: Strategic Tensions in the Women's Policy Network during the 1980s." In *Feminist Organizations: Harvest of the New Women's Movement,* edited by Myra Marx Ferree and Patricia Yancey Martin, 105–127. Philadelphia: Temple University Press, 1995.

1225. Udovitch, Mim. "Women in Action, A New Generation Takes to the Street." *Harper's Bazaar* 125 (November 1992): 164.

1226. Wohl, Lisa Cronin. "Toward a Mass Feminist Movement." *International Socialist Review* 32 (1971): 19–23, 57–66.

Media

1227. Beasley, Baurine, and Sheila Silver, eds. *Women in Media: A Documentary Source Book.* New York: Women's Institute for Freedom of the Press, 1977.

1228. Bonk, Kathy. "The Selling of the 'Gender Gap': The Role of Organized Feminism." In *The Politics of the Gender Gap: The Social Construction of Political Influence,* edited by Carol M.

Mueller, 82–101. Beverly Hills, CA: Sage, 1988.

1229. Butler, Matilda, and William Paisley. "Magazine Coverage of Women's Rights." *Journal of Communication* 28, no. 1 (1978): 183–186.

1230. Farrell, Amy. " 'Like a Tarantula on a Banana Boat': Ms. Magazine, 1972–1989." In *Feminist Organizations: Harvest of the New Women's Movement,* edited by Myra Marx Ferree and Patricia Yancey Martin, 53–68. Philadelphia: Temple University Press, 1995.

1231. Harrison, Cynthia E. *Women's Movement Media.* New York: Bowker, 1975.

1232. Martin, Joanna. "Confessions of a Non-Bra Burner." *Journalism Review* 4 (July 1971): 11–15.

1233. Mather, Anne. "A History of Feminist Periodicals." *Journalism History* 1, no. 3 (Autumn 1974): 82–85; 1, no. 4 (Winter 1974–75): 108–111; 2, no. 1 (Spring 1975): 19–23, 31.

1234. Morris, Monica B. "Newspapers and the New Feminists: Black Out as Social Control?" *Journalism Quarterly* 50 (Spring 1973): 37–42.

1235. North, Sandie. "Reporting the Movement." *Atlantic Monthly* 225, no. 3 (March 1970): 71–126.

1236. Sackett, Victori. "Color Me Political: Changing Fashions in Women's Magazines." *Public Opinion Quarterly* 7 (August-September 1984): 12–25.

1237. Sanders, Marlene. "Kathy Bonk: The Great Communicator." *Ms.* 2 (March–April 1991): 90.

1238. Wandersee, Winifred D. "'You've Come a Long Way, Baby': The Media and Women's Liberation." In *On the Move: American Women in the 1970s*, 150–174. Boston: Twayne, 1988.

Religion

1239. Hutchens, Trudy. "NOW Members Attack Religion." *Family Voice* (March 1992): 26–27.

1240. Johnson, Sonia. *Going Out of Our Minds: The Metaphysics of Liberation*. Freedom, CA: Crossing Press, 1987.

1241. Katzenstein, Mary Fainsod. "Discursive Politics and Feminist Activism in the Catholic Church." In *Feminist Organizations: Harvest of the New Women's Movement*, edited by Myra Marx Ferree and Patricia Yancey Martin, 35–52. Philadelphia: Temple University Press, 1995.

Sexual Liberation

1242. Burstyn, Varda, ed. *Women against Censorship*. Vancouver: Douglas and McIntyre, 1985.

1243. Cowan, Gloria. "Pornography: Conflict among Feminist." In *Women: A Feminist Perspective*, 5th ed., edited by Jo Freeman, 347–364. Mountain View, CA: Mayfield, 1995.

1244. Echols, Alice. "Cultural Feminism and the Anti-Pornography Movement." *Social Text* 7 (1983): 34–53.

1245. ———. "The New Feminism of Yin and Yang." In *Powers of Desire: The Politics of Sexuality*, edited by Ann Snitow, Christine Stansell, and Sharon Thompson, 439–459. New York: Monthly Review Press, 1983.

1246. ———. "The Taming of the Id: Feminist Sexual Politics, 1968–83." In *Pleasure and Danger: Exploring Female Sexuality*, edited by Carol Vance, 50–72. Boston: Routledge and Kegan Paul, 1984.

1247. Leidholdt, Corchen, and Janice Raymond, eds. *The Sexual Liberals and the Attack on Feminism*. New York: Pergamon, 1990.

Lesbian Rights

1248. Abbott, Sidney, and Barbara Love. *Sappho Was a Right On Woman: A Liberated View of Lesbianism*. Briarcliff Manor, NY: Stein and Day Publishers, 1972.

1249. Abdulahad, Tania, Gwendolyn Rogers, Barbara Smith, and Jameelah Waheed. "Black Lesbian-Feminist Organizing: A Conversation." In *Home-girls*, edited by Barbara Smith, 293–319. New York: Kitchen Table Women of Color Press, 1983.

1250. Adam, Barry D. *The Rise of a Gay and Lesbian Movement*. Boston: Tawyne, 1987.

1251. Atkinson, Ti-Grace. "Lesbianism and Feminism." In *Amazon Expedition: A Lesbian Feminist Anthology*, edited by Phyllis Birkby, 11–14. New York: Times Change Press, 1973.

1252. ———. *Amazon Odyssey*. New York: Links Books, 1974.

1253. Baker, Andrea. "The Problem of Authority in Radical Movement Groups: A Case Study of Lesbian-Feminist Organization." In *Leaders and Followers: Challenges for the Future*, edited by Louise A. Zurcher, 135–155. Greenwich, CT: JAI Press, 1986.

1254. Birkby, Phyllis, ed. *Amazon Expedition: A Lesbian Feminist Anthology*. New York: Times Change Press, 1973.

1255. Cavin, Susan. "The Invisible Army of Women: Lesbian Social Protests, 1969–88." In *Women and Social Protest*, edited by Guida West and Rhoda Blumberg, 321–332. New York: Oxford University Press, 1990.

1256. Echols, Alice. "Justifying Our Love? The Evolution of Lesbianism through Feminism and Gay Male Politics." *Advocate* (26 March 1991): 48–53.

1257. Franzen, Patricia. "Spinsters and Lesbians: Autonomous Women and the Institution of Heterosexuality, 1890–1920 and 1940–1980." Ph.D. dissertation, University of New Mexico, 1990.

1258. H., Pamela. "Asian American Lesbians: An Emerging Voice in the Asian American Community." In *Making Waves: An Anthology of Writings By and For Asian American Women*, edited by Asian Women United of California, 282–290. Boston: Beacon, 1994.

1259. Johnston, Jill. *Lesbian Nation: The Feminist Solution*. New York: Simon & Schuster, 1973.

1260. Katzenstein, Mary Fainsod. "The Spectacle as Political Resistance: Feminist and Gay-Lesbian Politics in the Military." *Ms.* 4 (Spring 1993): 1–16.

1261. Knopp, Lawrence. "Social Theory, Social Movements and Public Policy: Recent Accomplishments of the Gay and Lesbian Movements in Minneapolis, Minnesota." *International Journal of Urban and Regional Research* 11, no. 2 (1987): 243–261.

1262. Myron, Nancy, and Charlotte Bunch. *Lesbianism and the Women's Movement*. Baltimore: Diana Press, 1975.

1263. Pharr, Suzanne. *Homophobia: A Weapon of Sexism*. Inverness. CA: Chardon Press, 1988.

1264. Phelan, Shane. *Identity Politics: Lesbian Feminism and the Limits of Community*. Philadelphia: Temple University Press, 1989.

1265. Ransdell, Lisa. "Lesbian Feminism and the Feminist Movement." In *Women: A Feminist Perspective*, 5th ed., edited by Jo Freeman, 641–654. Mountain View, CA: Mayfield, 1995.

1266. Smith, Elizabeth A. "Bitches, Femmes and Feminist: The Politics of Lesbian Sexuality." *NWSA Journal* 1, no. 3 (1989): 398–421.

1267. Taylor, Verta, and Nancy E. Whittier. "Collective Identity and Lesbian Feminist Mobilization." In *Frontiers of Social Movement Theory*, edited by Aldon Morris and Carol M. Mueller, 104–130. New Haven, CT: Yale University Press, 1992.

1268. Trujillo, Carla. *Chicana Lesbians: The Girls Our Mothers Warned Us About*. Berkeley, CA: Third Woman Press, 1991.

Reproductive Rights

1269. "Abortion: Right, Left." *Economist* 312 (5 August 1988): 29–30.

1270. Alvarez, Luz. "The Latina Reproductive Rights Movement." *National Lawyers Guild Practitioner* 50 (Winter 1993): 4–8.

1271. Baehr, Ninia. *Abortion Without Apology: A Radical History for the 1990s.* Boston: South End Press, 1990. Pamphlet No. 80.

1272. Bart, Pauline B. "Seizing the Means of Reproduction: An Illegal Feminist Abortion Collective —How and Why It Worked." In *Women, Health and Reproduction,* edited by Helen Robert, 109–128. Boston: Routledge and Kegan Paul, 1981.

1273. Bart, Pauline B., and Melinda Bart Schlesinger. "Collective Work and Self-Identity: The Effect of Working in a Feminist Illegal Abortion Collective." In *Workplace Democracy and Social Change,* edited by Frank Lindenfeld and Joyce Rothschild White, 139–153. Boston: Porter Sargen, 1981.

1274. Blakely, Mary Kay. "Remembering Jane." *The New York Times Magazine* (23 September 1990): 26.

1275. Carmen, Arlene, and Howard Moody. *Abortion Counseling and Social Change from Illegal Act to Medical Practice: The Story of the Clergy Consultation Service on Abortion.* Valley Forge, PA: Judson Press, 1973.

1276. Chesler, Ellen. *Woman of Valor: Margaret Sanger and the Birth Control Movement.* New York: Simon and Schuster, 1992.

1277. Cisler, Lucinda. "Unfinished Business: Birth Control and Women's Liberation." In *Sisterhood Is Powerful: An Anthology of Writings from the Women's Liberation Movement,* edited by Robin Morgan, 245–288. New York: Vintage, 1970.

1278. Condit, Celeste. *Decoding Abortion Rhetoric.* Urbana: University of Illinois Press, 1990.

1279. Donovan, Beth. "Early Campaigning Test Abortion Foes' Muscle." *Congressional Quarterly Weekly Report* 48 (10 March 1990): 765–775.

1280. Douglas, Emily Taft. *Margaret Sanger: Pioneer of the Future.* New York: Holt, Rinehart and Winston, 1970.

1281. Falik, Marilyn. *Ideology and Abortion Policy Politics.* New York: Praeger, 1983.

1282. Ginsburg, Faye D. *Experience of Fargo, North Dakota Since 1987.* Berkeley: University of California Press, 1989.

1283. Goggi, Malcolm, ed. *Understanding the New Politics of Abortion.* Thousand Oaks, CA: Sage, 1994.

1284. Gordon, Linda. "Voluntary Motherhood: The Beginnings of Feminist Birth Control Ideas in the United States." In *Clio's Consciousness Raised,* edited by Mary Hartman and Lois W. Banner, 54–72. New York: Harper and Row, 1976.

1285. ———. *Women's Body, Women's Right: A Social History of Birth Control.* New York: Penguin, 1983.

1286. Harrison, Beverly Wildung. *Our Right to Choose: Toward a New Ethic of Abortion.* Boston: Beacon, 1983.

1287. Hutta, Jane, and Alice Kirkman. *Report on Clinic Violence.* Washington, DC: National Abortion Federation, 1990.

1288. Kaplan, Laura. *The Story of Jane.* New York: Pantheon, 1995.

1289. Lader, Lawrence. *Abortion II: Making the Revolution.* Boston: Beacon, 1973.

1290. Lopez, Ann F. "Latinas and Reproductive Rights, Silent No More." *Ms.* 2 (March–April 1991): 91.

1291. Luker, Kristin. *Motherhood and the Politics of Abortion.* Berkeley: University of California Press, 1984.

1292. ———. "The War Between the Women." *Family Planning Perspectives* 16 (May–June 1984): 105–110.

1293. National Women's Health Network. *Abortion Then and Now, Creative Responses to Restricted Access.* Washington, DC: National Women's Health Network, 1989.

1294. O'Neill, Jane. *Barbara Ferraro and Particia Hussey, No Turning Back: Two Nuns' Battle with the Vatican over Women's Right to Choose.* New York: Poseidon, 1990.

1295. Rodriguez-Trias, Helen. "Women Are Organizing: Environmental and Population Policies Will Never Be the Same." *American Journal of Public Health* 84 (September 1994): 1379–1382.

1296. Rodrique, Jessie M. "The Black Community and the Birth-Control Movement." In *Unequal Sisters: A Multicultural Reader in U.S. Women's History,* edited by Ellen DuBois and Vicki L. Ruiz, 333–344. New York: Routledge, 1990.

1297. Roosenquist, Valerie. "NARAL's New Way: Women in Politics." *Southern Exposure* 12 (February 1984): 26–31.

1298. Roosevelt, Theodore. "Birth Reform, from the Positive Not the Negative Side." In *The Foes of Our Own Household,* by Theodore Roosevelt, 250–272. New York: George H. Donan Co., 1926.

1299. Sanger, Margaret. *My Fight for Birth Control.* New York: Farrar, Reinhart, 1931.

1300. ———. "Women and Birth Control, 1929." *North American Review* 272 (September 1987): 86–89.

1301. Simonds, Wendy. *Current Research on Occupations and Professions, At an Impasse: Inside an Abortion Clinic.* Vol. 6. Greenwich, CT: JAI Press, 1991.

1302. ———. "Feminism on the Job: Confronting Opposition in Abortion Work." In *Feminist Organizations: Harvest of the New Women's Movement,* edited by Myra Marx Ferree and Patricia Yancey Martin, 248–262. Philadelphia: Temple University Press, 1995.

1303. Skerry, Peter. "The Class Conflict over Abortion." *The Public Interest* 52 (Summer 1978): 69–84.

1304. Solinger, Rickie. "The Girl Nobody Loved: Pregnancy in the Pre-*Roe v. Wade* Era, 1945–1965." *Frontiers* 11, no. 2–3 (1990): 45–54.

1305. Staggenborg, Suzanne. "Coalition Work in the Pro-Choice Movement: Organizational and Environmental Opportunities and Obstacles." *Social Problems* 33, no. 5 (June 1986): 374–390.

1306. ———. "The Consequences of Professionalization and Formalization in the Pro-Choice Movement." *American Sociological Review* 53 (1988): 585–606.

1307. ———. *The Pro-Choice Movement: Organization and Activism in the Abortion Conflict.* New York: Oxford University Press, 1991.

1308. Tillet, Rebecca. *Empower America: Your Campaign and Abortion Rights.* Washington, DC: National Women's Political Caucus, 1989.

1309. Van Gelder, Lindsey. "The Jane Collective: Seizing Control." *Ms.* 3 (September–October 1991): 83–85.

1310. Wilcox, Clyde. "Political Action Committees and Abortion: A Longitudinal Analysis." *Women and Politics* 9, no. 1 (1989): 1–19.

1311. Women Organized for Reproductive Choice. *The New Right vs. Women's Rights.* New York: Women Organized for Reproductive Choice, 1980.

Other Movements

General

1312. Bartow, Beverly. "Isabel Bevier at the University of Illinois and the Home Economic Movement." *Journal of Illinois State Historical Society* 72, no. 1 (1979): 21–38.

1313. Dillow, Gordon L. "Thank You for Not Smoking, Lucy Page Gaston,

1860–1924." *American Heritage* 32, no. 2 (1981): 94–107.

1314. Dodson, Jualynne E. "Power and Surrogate Leadership: Black Women and Organized Religion." *Sage* 5, no. 2 (1988): 37–42.

1315. Jeffreys, S. "'Free from All Uninvited Touch of Men': Women's Campaigns Around Sexuality, 1880–1914." *Women's Studies International Forum* 5 (1982): 629–645.

1316. Kuzmack, Linda G. "The Emergence of the Jewish Women's Movement in England and the United States, 1881–1933: A Comparative Study." Ph.D. dissertation, George Washington University, Washington DC, 1986.

1317. "Mother's against Pornography: Enough Is Enough." *U.S. News and World Report* 113 (30 November 1992): 18.

Age

1318. Bernard, Jessie. "Age, Sex and Feminism." *Annals of the American Academy of Political and Social Science* 415 (September 1974): 120–137.

1319. Brown, Camie Lou. "Agism and the Women's Movement." In *Women on the Move: A Feminist Perspective,* edited by Jean Ramage Leppaluoto, Joan Acker, Claudeen Naffziger, Karla Brown, Catherine M. Porter, Barbara A. Mitchell, and Roberta Hanna, 225–227. Pittsburgh, PA: Know, 1973.

1320. Huckle, Patricia. *Tish Sommers, Activist: The Founding of the Older*

Women's League. Nashville: University of Tennessee, 1991.

1321. Kuhn, Maggie. "Grass-roots Gray Power." In *The Older Woman: Lavender Rose or Gray Panther,* edited by Marie Marschall Fuller and Cora Ann Martin, 223–237. Springfield, IL: Charles C. Thomas, 1980.

1322. Martin, Cora A. "Lavender Rose or Gray Panther?" In *The Older Woman: Lavender Rose or Gray Panther,* edited by Marie Marschall Fuller and Cora Ann Martin, 55–58. Springfield, IL: Charles C. Thomas, 1980.

1323. Older Woman's League. *Call to Action to End Violence against Midlife and Older Women.* Washington, DC: Older Woman's League, 1994.

Violence Against Women

1324. Ahrens, Lois. "Battered Women's Refuges: Feminism Cooperatives v. Social Service Institutions." *Radical America* 14, no. 3 (1980): 41–47.

1325. Arnold, Gretchen. "Dilemmas of Feminist Coalitions: Collective Identity and Strategic Effectiveness in the Battered Women's Movement." In *Feminist Organizations: Harvest of the New Women's Movement,* edited by Myra Marx Ferree and Patricia Yancey Martin, 323–338. Philadelphia: Temple University Press, 1995.

1326. Gornick, Janet. "Structure and Activities of Rape Crisis Centers in the Early 1980s." *Crime and Delinquency* 31 (1985): 247–268.

1327. Gornick, Janet, Martha R. Burt, and Karen J. Pittman. *Community Relations and Public Image in Rape Crisis Centers.* Washington, DC: The Urban Institute, 1983.

1328. Johnson, John. "Program Enterprise and Official Cooptation in the Battered Women's Movement." *American Behavioral Scientist* 24, no. 6 (1981): 827–842.

1329. Largen, Mary Ann. "Grass-roots Centers and National Task Forces: A History of the Anti-Rape Movement." *Aegis: Magazine on Ending Violence Against Women* (Summer 1981): 46–52.

1330. Matthews, Nancy A. *Confronting Rape: The Feminist Anti-Rape Movement and the State.* New York: Routledge, 1994.

1331. Reinelt, Claire. "Moving Onto the Terrain of the State: The Battered Women's Movement and the Politics of Engagement." In *Feminist Organizations: Harvest of the New Women's Movement,* edited by Myra Marx Ferree and Patricia Yancey Martin, 84–104. Philadelphia: Temple University Press, 1995.

1332. Schechter, Susan. "Speaking to the Battered Women's Movement." *Aegis: Magazine on Ending Violence Against Women* (Autumn 1981): 41–45.

1333. ———. *Women and Male Violence: The Visions and Struggles of the Battered Women's Movement.* Boston: South End Press, 1982.

1334. Simon, Barbara Levy. "In Defense of Institutionalization: Rape Crisis Center as a Case Study." *Journal of Sociology and Social Welfare* 9 (September 1982): 485–502.

1335. Tierney, Kathleen. "The Battered Women Movement and the Creation of the Wife Beating Problem." *Social Problems* 23, no. 3 (February 1982): 207–220.

Environment and Ecofeminism

1336. Blend, Benary. "Mary Austin and the Western Conservation Movement." *Journal of the Southwest* 30, no. 1 (1988): 12–34.

1337. Bomberry, Victoria. "Navajo Organizer Leads Fight against Uranium." *Native Self-Sufficiency* 6 (1981): 16–17.

1338. Cable, Sherry. "Women's Social Movement Involvement: The Role of Structural Availability in Recruitment and Participation Processes." *The Sociological Quarterly* 33, no. 1 (1992): 33–50.

1339. Clarke, Robert. *Ellen Swallow: The Woman Who Founded Ecology.* Chicago: Follett, 1973.

1340. Diamond, Irene, and Gloria Feman Orenstein, eds. *Reweaving the World: The Emergence of Ecofeminism.* San Francisco, CA: Sierra Club Books, 1990.

1341. Merchant, Carolyn. "Women of the Progressive Conservation Movement: 1900–16." *Environmental Review* 8, no. 1 (1984): 57–85.

1342. Todd, Judith. "Opposing the Rape of Mother Earth." In *All American Women: Lines That Divide, Ties That Bind,* edited by Johnnetta B. Cole, 315–323. New York: Free Press, 1986.

1343. Wolf, Hazel. "The Founding Mothers of Environmentalism." *Earth Island Journal* 9, no. 1 (Winter 1993): 36–37.

Health

1344. Morgen, Sandra. "The Dynamics of Cooptation in a Feminist Health Clinic." *Social Science and Medicine* 23, no. 2 (1986): 201–210.

1345. ———. "The Dream of Diversity, the Dilemma of Difference: Race and Class Contradictions in a Feminist Health Clinic." In *Anthropology for the Nineties,* edited by Johnnetta B. Cole. New York: Free Press, 1988.

1346. ———. "Contradictions in Feminist Practice: Individualism and Collectivism in a Feminist Health Center." *Comparative Social Research* 1 (Supplement 1990): 9–59.

1347. ———. "Into Our Own Hands: The Women's Health Movement in the U.S.: 1970–1990." In *Feminist Organizations: Harvest of the New Women's Movement,* edited by Myra Marx Ferree and Patricia Yancey Martin, 234–247. Philadelphia: Temple University Press, 1995.

1348. Ruzek, Sheryl. *The Women's Health Movement.* New York: Praeger, 1978.

Jury

1349. Azar, Robert. "The Liberation of Georgia Women for Jury Service." *Atlanta History Journal* (Fall 1980): 21–26.

1350. Hughes, Sarah T. "Now I Can Throw Away That Speech." *Independent Woman* 34 (February 1955): 63–64.

1351. "Massachusetts Rules against Women Jurors." *Women Lawyers Journal* 19 (Fall 1931): 6–7.

1352. Rawalt, Marguerite. "The Right to Serve." *National Business Woman* 45, no. 4 (April 1966): 5–8.

1353. Rudolph, Wallace M. "Women on Juries: Voluntary or Compulsory?" *Journal of the American Judicature Society* 44 (April 1961): 206–210.

1354. Scheber, Claudine A. "But Some Were Less Equal ... The Fight for Women Jurors." In *Women Organizing: An Anthology*, edited by Bernice Cummings and Victoria Schuck, 329–344. Metuchen, NJ: Scarecrow Press, 1979.

1355. Shankman, Arnold. "A Jury of Her Peers: The South Carolina Woman and Her Campaign for Jury Service." *South Carolina Historical Magazine* 81, no. 2 (1980): 102–121.

1356. Troth, Anise. "How We Won Jury Service in Georgia." *Independent Woman* 33 (February 1954): 77–78.

1357. "Women on the Jury." *National Business Woman* 51, no. 9 (December 1970): 8, 10.

Peace

1358. Addams, Jane. *Newer Ideals of Peace.* New York: Macmillan, 1907.

1359. Alonso, Harriet Hyman. "Suffragists for Peace during the Interwar Years, 1919–1941." *Peace and Change* 14, no. 3 (July 1989): 243–262.

1360. ———. *The Women's Peace Union and the Outlawry of War, 1921–1942.* Knoxville: University of Tennessee Press, 1989.

1361. ———. *Peace as a Women's Issue: A History of the U.S. Movement for World Peace and Women's Rights.* Syracuse, NY: Syracuse University Press, 1993.

1362. Arrington, Leonard J. "Modern Lysistratas: Mormon Women in the International Peace Movement 1899–1939." *Journal of Mormon History* 15 (1989): 88–104.

1363. Boals, Kay. "Some Reflections on Women and Peace." *Peace and Change* 1 (Spring 1973): 56–59.

1364. Boulding, Elise. "Focus On: The Gender Gap." *Journal of Peace Research* 21, no. 1 (1984): 1–3.

1365. Brown, Jenny. "Women for Peace or Women's Liberation? Signposts from the Feminist Archives." *Vietnam Generation* 3–4 (1989): 246–260.

1366. Buehler, Jan. "The Puget Sound Women's Peace Camp: Education as an Alternative Strategy." *Frontiers* 8, no. 2 (1985): 40–44.

1367. Bumpers, Betty. "For Any Parent, Peace Is the Ultimate Issue: It's Up to Women to Sensitize the Nation." *Glamour* 80 (October 1982): 88.

1368. Bussey, Gertrude, and Margaret Tims. *Pioneers for Peace: The Women's International League for Peace and Freedom, 1915–1965.* Oxford: Alden, 1980.

1369. Cagan, Leslie. "Women and the Anti-Draft Movement." *Radical America* 14, no. 5 (1980): 9–11.

1370. Cannon, Kate. "The Separate Spheres of the State: Mobilization Rhetoric and Public Policy Objectives During World War II." *UCLA Historical Journal* 14 (August 1995): 101–127.

1371. Cashdan, Laurie. "Anti-War Feminism: New Directions, New Dualities—A Marxist-Humanist Perspective." *Women's Studies International Forum* 12, no. 1 (1989): 81–85.

1372. Catt, Carrie Chapman. "The Outlawry of War." *Annals of the American Academy of Political and Social Science* 227 (July 1928): 157–163.

1373. Clark, Cal, and Janet M. Clark. "Wyoming Women's Attitudes toward the MX: The 'Old' Vs. 'New' Gender Gap." *Journal of Political Science* 17, no. 1–2 (1989): 127–140.

1374. Craig, John M. "Redbaiting, Pacifism, and Free Speech: Lucia Ames Mead and Her 1926 Tour in Atlanta and the Southeast." *Georgia Historical Quarterly* 71 (Winter 1987): 601–622.

1375. Decter, Midge. "The Peace Ladies." In *The New Feminism in Twentieth Century America,* edited by June Sochen, 120–132. Lexington, MA: D. C. Heath, 1971.

1376. Degen, Marie L. *The History of the Women's Peace Party.* Baltimore: Johns Hopkins University Press, 1939. Reprint. New York: Burt Franklin, 1974.

1377. Elshtain, Jean Bethke. *Women and War.* New York: Basic Books, 1987.

1378. Garrison, Dee. "'Our Skirts Gave Them Courage:' The Civil Defense Protest Movement in New York City, 1955–1961." In *Not June Cleaver: Women and Gender in Postwar America, 1945–1960,* edited by Joanne Meyerowitz, 201–229. Philadelphia: Temple University Press, 1994.

1379. Harris, Adrienne, and Ynestra King, eds. *Rocking the Ship of State.* Boulder, CO: Westview Press, 1989.

1380. Jensen, Joan M. "When Women Worked: Helen Marston and the California Peace Movement, 1915–1945." *California History* 67, no. 2 (1988): 118–131.

1381. Lynn, Susan. "Women and Peace Activsm in Cold War America." In *Progressive Women in Conservative Times, Racial Justice, Peace, and Feminism, 1945 to the 1960's,* 94–110. New Brunswick, NJ: Rutgers University, 1992.

1382. McGuinness, Kate. "Women and the Peace Movement." In *The American Woman, 1990–91: A Status Report,* edited by Sara E. Rix and Anne J. Stone, 301–314. New York: Norton, 1990.

1383. Poise, Anne Marie. "The Politics of Organizing for Change: The United States Section of the Women's International League for Peace and Freedom, 1919–1939." Ph.D. dissertation, University of Colorado, 1988.

1384. Schott, Linda Kay. "The Woman's Peace Party and the Moral

Basis for Women's Pacifism." *Frontiers* 8, no. 2 (1985): 18–25.

1385. ———. "Women against War: Pacifism, Feminism and Social Justice in the United States, 1914–1941." Ph.D. dissertation, Stanford University, Palo Alto, 1985.

1386. Sochen, June. "Henrietta Rodman and the Feminist Alliance: 1914–1917." *Journal of Popular Culture* 4 (Summer 1970): 57–65.

1387. Solomon, Barbara Miller. "Dilemmas of Pacifist Women, Quakers and Others in World Wars I and II." In *Witnesses for Change: Quaker Women over Three Centuries,* edited by Elisabeth Potts Brown and Susan Mosher Stuart, 123–148. New Brunswick, NJ: Rutgers University Press, 1989.

1388. Steinson, Barbara. "'The Mother Half of Humanity': American Women in the Peace and Preparedness Movements in World War I." In *Women, War, and Revolution,* edited by Carol R. Berkin and Clara M. Lovett. New York: Holmes and Meier, 1980.

1389. Swerdlow, Amy. *Women Strike for Peace: Traditional Motherhood and Radical Politics in the 1960's.* Chicago: University of Chicago Press, 1993.

1390. "Woman against War." *Scribner's Magazine* 11 (November 1941): 27–30.

1391. "Woman's Part in the Washington Conference." *Literary Digest* 71 (26 November 1921): 48–53.

1392. "Women for Peace: The Organization of the First Woman's Peace Party." *The Independent* 81 (25 January 1915): 120.

1393. Woolf, S. J. "Mrs. Catt, at Eighty, Calls Women to War on War." *The New York Times Magazine* (8 January 1939): 10.

1394. Zeiger, Susan. "Finding a Cure for War: Women's Politics and the Peace Movement in the 1920's." *Journal of Social History* 24 (Fall 1990): 69–86.

Race

1395. Blee, Kathleen M. "Women in the 1920's Ku Klux Klan Movement." *Feminist Studies* 17 (Spring 1991): 55–77.

1396. ———. *Women of the Klan: Racism and Gender in the 1920s.* Berkeley: University of California Press, 1991.

1397. MacLean, Nancy. "White Women and Klan Violence in the 1920s: Agency, Noncomplicity and the Politics of Women's History." *Gender and History* 3, no. 3 (1991): 285–303.

1398. Young, Mary E. "Women, Civilization, and the Indian Question." In *Clio Was a Woman: Studies in the History of American Women,* edited by Mabel E. Deutrich and Virginia C. Purdy, 98–112. Washington, DC: Howard University Press, 1980.

Repeal Prohibition

1399. Kyvig, David Edward. "Women against Prohibition." *American Quarterly* 28 (1976): 464–482.

1400. Nicoll, Ione. "Should Women Vote Wet ?" *North American Review* 229 (May 1930): 561–565.

1401. Root, Grace C. *Women and Repeal: The Story of the Women's Organization for National Prohibition Reform.* New York: Harper and Brothers, 1934.

1402. Rose, Kenneth David. *American Women and the Repeal of Prohibition.* New York: New York University Press, 1996.

1403. "Wets On Warpath." *The New Republic* 70 (30 March 1932): 180–181.

Temperance

1404. Armstrong, Fanny L. *To the Noon Rest: The Life, Work and Addresses of Mrs. Helen M. Stoddard.* Butler, IN: L. H. Higley, 1909.

1405. Blocker, Jack S., Jr. "Separate Paths: Suffragists and the Women's Temperance Crusade." *Signs* 10, no. 3 (Spring 1985): 460–476.

1406. Bordin, Ruth Birgitta Anderson. *Woman and Temperance: The Quest for Power and Liberty, 1873–1900.* Philadelphia: Temple University Press, 1981.

1407. Caldwell, Dorothy J. "Carry Nation, A Missouri Woman, Won Fame in Kansas." *Missouri Historical Review* 63, no. 4 (1969): 461–488.

1408. Dillon, Mary Earhart. *Frances Willard: From Prayers to Politics.* Chicago: University of Illinois Press, 1944.

1409. Fitzgerald, Louis. "Carry Nation in Iowa, 1901." *Annals of Iowa* 39, no. 1 (1967): 62–74.

1410. Friedrich, Otto. "Mothers against Drunk Drivers: Candy Lightner." *Time* 125 (7 January 1985): 41.

1411. Garner, Nancy Gail. "For God and Home and Native Land: The Kansas Woman's Christian Temperance Union, 1878–1938." Ph.D. dissertation, University of Kansas, 1994.

1412. George, Paul S. "A Cyclone Hits Miami: Carry Nation's Visit to 'The Wicked City'." *Florida Historical Quarterly* 58, no. 2 (1979): 150–159.

1413. Gilmore, Glenda Elizabeth. "'A Melting Time': Black Women, White Women and the WCTU in North Carolina, 1880–1900." In *Hidden Histories of Women in the New South*, edited by Virginia Bernhard, Elizabeth Fox-Genovese, and Theda Perdue, 153–172. Columbia: University of Missouri Press, 1994.

1414. Harris, Katherine. "Feminism and Temperance Reform in the Boulder WCTU." *Frontiers* 4, no. 2 (1979): 19–24.

1415. Hohner, Robert A. "Prohibition Comes to Virginia: The Referendum of 1914." *Virginia Magazine of History and Biography* 75, no. 4 (1967): 473–488.

1416. Ironmonger, Elizabeth. *History of the Woman's Christian Temperance Union of Virginia and a Glimpse of Seventy-five Years, 1883–1958.* VA: Cavalier, 1958.

1417. Knight, Virginia C. "Women and the Temperance Movement." *Current History* (May 1976): 201–204.

1418. Leonard, Priscilla. "Temperance and Woman Suffrage." *Harper's Bazaar* 44 (April 1910): 289.

1419. McMullen, Frances Drewry. "The W. C. T. U." *The Woman Citizen* 10 (27 June 1925): 13, 27.

1420. Morton, Marian J. "Temperance, Benevolence and the City: The Cleveland Non-Partisan Woman's Christian Temperance Union, 1874–1900." *Ohio History* 91 (1982): 58–73.

1421. Nation, Carry A. *The Use and Need of the Life of Carry A. Nation.* Topeka, KS: F. M. Steves and Sons, 1904.

1422. "Organization and Accomplishments of the W.C.T.U. in Illinois, Massachusetts, New York, North Dakota, Ohio and Virginia: Symposium." *Annals of the American Academy of Political and Social Science* 32 (November 1908): 513–530.

1423. Paulson, Ross Evans. *Women's Suffrage and Prohibition, A Comparative Study of Equality and Social Control.* Glenview, IL: Scott, Foresman, 1973.

1424. "Repeal Is Not the Answer." *The Woman's Journal* 16 (May 1931): 22.

1425. Ross, Irwin. "Carry Nation—Saloon's Nemesis." *American History Illustrated* 2, no. 10 (1968): 13–17.

1426. Sims, Anastatia. "'The Sword of the Spirit': The W.C.T.U. and Moral Reform in North Carolina, 1883–1933." *North Carolina Historical Review* 64, no. 4 (1987): 395–415.

1427. Stewart, Ella Seass. "Woman Suffrage and the Liquor Traffic." *Annals of the American Academy of Political and Social Science* 56 (November 1914): 143–152.

1428. Timberlake, James H. *Prohibition and the Progressive Movement: 1900–1920.* Cambridge: Harvard University Press, 1963.

1429. Tyler, Helen E. *Where Prayer and Purpose Meet: The W.C.T.U. Story, 1874–1949.* Evanston, IL: Signal Press, 1949.

1430. Wasserman, Ira M. "Status Politics and the Economic Class Interest: The 1918 Prohibition Referendum in California." *Social Science Quarterly* 31, no. 3 (1990): 475–484.

War

1431. Anderson, Karen. *Wartime Women: Sex Roles, Family Relations, and the Status of Women during World War II.* Westport, CT: Greenwood, 1981.

1432. Blatch, Harriet Stanton. *Mobilizing Woman Power.* New York: The Woman's Press, 1918.

1433. Boris, Eileen. "Tenement Homework on Army Uniforms: The Gendering of Industrial Democracy during WWI." *Labor History* 32 (Spring 1991): 231–252.

1434. Breen, William J. "Black Women and the Great War: Mobilization and Reform in the South." In *Black Women in United States History,* Vol. 5, edited by Darlene Clark Hine, 133–152. Brooklyn, NY: Carlson, 1990.

1435. Byles, Joan Montgomery. "Women's Experience of World War One: Suffragists, Pacifists and Poets." *Women's Studies International Forum* 8, no. 5, (1985): 473–487.

1436. Hartmann, Susan M. "Women's Organizations during World War II: The Interaction of Class, Race and Feminism." In *Woman's Being,*

Women's Place: Female Identity and Vocation in American History, edited by Mary Kelley, 313–328. Boston: G. K. Hall, 1979.

1437. Honey, Maureen. *Creating Rosie the Riveter: Class, Gender, and Propaganda During World War II.* Amherst: University of Massachusetts, 1984.

1438. Kunin, Madeleine May. "In Times of War, It's a Man's World." *Glamour* 89, no. 4 (April 1991): 200.

1439. Maffett, Minnie L. "Mobilizing Womanpower, An Open Letter to the Manpower Commission." *Independent Woman* 21 (December 1942): 356, 380.

1440. Martelet, Penny. "The Woman's Land Army, World War I." In *Clio Was a Woman: Studies in the History of American Women,* edited by Mabel E. Deutrich and Virginia C. Purdy, 136–146. Washington, DC: Howard University Press, 1980.

1441. Purnell, Idella. "The Woman's Land Army." *Westways* 72, no. 10 (1980): 38–41, 80.

1442. Rupp, Leila J. *Mobilizing Women for War: German and American Propaganda, 1939–1945.* Princeton, NJ: Princeton University Press, 1978.

Anti Movements

Anti Suffrage

1443. Abbott, Lyman. "The Assault on Womanhood." *Outlook* 91 (3 April 1909): 784–788.

1444. ———. "Answer to the Arguments in Support of Woman Suffrage." *Annals of the American Academy of Political and Social Science* 35, Supplement (May 1910): 28–32.

1445. Amhi, Jane Jerome. "Women Against Women: Anti-suffragism, 1880–1920." Ph.D. dissertation, Tufts University, Medford, 1991.

1446. "Antis, West and Machines Win Elections." *The Survey* 35 (13 November 1915): 158–159.

1447. Apostol, Jane. "Why Women Should Not Have the Vote: Anti-Suffrage Views in the Southland in 1911." *Southern California Quarterly* 70 (Spring 1988): 29–42.

1448. Benjamin, Anne Myra Goodman. *A History of the Anti–Suffrage Movement in the United States From 1895 to 1920: Women against Equality.* Lewiston, ME: Edwin Mellen Press, 1991.

1449. Bernbaum, Ernest, ed. *Anti-Suffrage Essays by Massachusetts Women.* Boston: Forum Publications, 1916.

1450. Blackwell, Alice Stone. *Liquor against Suffrage.* Boston: Brimes, 1915.

1451. Camhi, Jane Jerome. *Women against Women: American Anti-Suffragism, 1880–1920.* Brooklyn, NY: Carlson, 1994.

1452. Corbin, Caroline F. *Woman's Rights in America: A Retrospect of Sixty Years, 1848–1908.* Chicago: The Illinois Association Opposed to Woman Suffrage, 1908.

1453. Goodwin, Grace Duffield. "The Non-Militant Defenders of the Home." *Good Housekeeping* 55, no. 1 (July 1912): 75–80.

1454. ————. *Anti-Suffrage: Ten Good Reasons.* New York: Duffield, 1913.

1455. Green, Elna C. "Those Opposed: The Antisuffragists in North Carolina, 1900–1920." *North Carolina Historical Review* 67, no. 3 (July 1990): 316–333.

1456. ————. "'Ideal of Government, of Home, and of Women': The Ideology of Southern White Antisuffragism." In *Hidden Histories of Women in the New South,* edited by Virginia Bernhard, Elizabeth Fox-Genovese, and Theda Perdue, 96–113. Columbia: University of Missouri Press, 1994.

1457. Hagan, Martha Ann. "The Rheteroic of the American Anti Suffrage Movement, 1867–1920." Ph.D. dissertation, Washington State University, 1993.

1458. Harvey, George. "The Working of Equal Suffrage." *North American Review* 199, no. 3 (March 1914): 338–343.

1459. Howard, Jeanne. "Our Own Worst Enemies: Women Opposed to Woman Suffrage." *Journal of Sociology and Social Welfare* 9 (September 1982): 463–474.

1460. "In the Name of Southern (White) Womanhood." *New South* 17 (November–December 1962): 16–18.

1461. Jablonsky, Thomas J. "Duty, Nature and Stability: The Female Anti-Suffragists in the United States, 1894–1920." Ph.D. dissertation, University of California at Los Angeles, 1978.

1462. ————. *The Home, Heaven, and Mother Party: Female Anti–Suffragists in the United States, 1868–1920.* Brooklyn, NY: Carlson, 1994.

1463. Jensen, Billie Barnes. "'In the Weird and Wooly West: Anti Suffrage Women, Gender Issues, and Woman Suffrage in the West." *Journal of the West* 32, no. 3 (1993): 41–51.

1464. Johnson, Kenneth R. "White Racial Attitudes as a Factor in the Arguments against the Nineteenth Amendment." *Phylon* 31 (Spring 1970): 31–37.

1465. Jones, Mrs. Gilbert E. "Position of the Anti-Suffragists." *Annals of the American Academy of Political and Social Science* 35, Supplement (May 1910): 16–22.

1466. Leonard, Priscilla. "Working-Woman and Anti-Suffrage." *Harper's Bazaar* 43 (November 1909): 1169–1170.

1467. Lewis, Leonard Lawrence. "How Woman Suffrage Works in Colorado." *Outlook* 82 (27 January 1906): 167–175.

1468. Littell, P. "Circular against Woman Suffrage of the Men's Patriotic Association." *The New Republic* 21 (11 February 1920): 319.

1469. Mambretti, Catherine Cole. "'The Burden of the Ballot', The Woman's Anti-Suffrage Movement." *American Heritage* 30, no. 1 (1978): 24–25.

1470. ————. "The Battle against the Ballot: Illinois Women Anti-Suffragists." *Chicago History* 9, no. 3 (Fall 1980): 168–177.

1471. Marshall, Susan E. "In Defense of Separate Spheres: Class and Status Politics in the Antisuffrage Movement." *Social Forces* 65, no. 2 (1986): 327–351.

1472. Martin, I. T. "Concerning Some of the Anti-Suffrage Leaders." *Good Housekeeping* 55, no. 1 (July 1912): 80–82.

1473. Mayo, Mara. "Fears and Fantasies of the Anti-Suffragists." *Connecticut Review* 7, no. 2 (April 1974): 64–74.

1474. Norman, C. H. "Economic Criticism of Woman Suffrage." *Westways* 175 (January 1911): 91–103.

1475. Parkhurst, Charles H. "The Inadvisability of Woman Suffrage." *Annals of the American Academy of Political and Social Science* 35, Supplement (May 1910): 36–40.

1476. Pier, Florida. "The Delightfully Quaint Anti's." *Harper's Weekly* 53 (11 December 1909): 34.

1477. Seawell, Molly Elliot. "The Ladies' Battle." *Atlantic Monthly* 106 (September 1910): 289–303.

1478. ———. "Two Suffrage Mistakes." *North American Review* 199, no. 3 (March 1914): 366–382.

1479. Stevenson, Louise L. "Women Anti-Suffragists in the 1915 Massachusetts Campaign." *The New England Quarterly* 52, no. 1 (March 1979): 80–93.

1480. Swift, M. E. "Suffrage for Women a Handicap in Civic Work." *New Jersey Bulletin* 1 (Oct 1916): 3.

1481. Thurner, Manuela. "'Better Citizens Without the Ballot': American Antisuffrage Women and Their Rationale during the Progressive Era." *Journal of Women's History* 5, no. 1 (Spring 1993): 33–60. Reprint. *One Woman, One Vote, Rediscovering the Woman Suffrage Movement,* Marjorie Spruill Wheeler, ed., 203–220. Troutdale, OR: NewSage Press, 1995.

1482. Women's Anti-suffrage Association. *Pamphlets Printed and Distributed by the Women's Anti-suffrage Association of the Third Judicial District of the State of New York.* Littleton, CO: F. B. Rothman, 1990.

Anti Equal Rights Amendment

1483. Beck, Roy H. "Washington's Profamily Activists, Concerned Women of America." *Christianity Today* 36 (9 November 1992): 20–23, 26.

1484. Brady, David W., and Kent L. Tedin. "Ladies in Pink: Religion and Political Ideology in the Anti-ERA Movement." *Social Science Quarterly* 56, no. 4 (March 1976): 564–575.

1485. Burris, Val. "Who Opposed the ERA? An Analysis of the Social Basis of Antifeminism." *Social Science Quarterly* 64 (1983): 305–317.

1486. Dunlap, Mary. "Resistance to the Women's Movement in the United States: The ERA Controversy as Prototype." In *Toward the Second Decade: The Impact of the Women's Movement on American Institutions,* edited by Betty Justice and Renate Pore, 163–169. Westport, CT: Greenwood, 1981.

1487. Felsenthal, Carol. *The Sweetheart of the Silent Majority: The Biography of Phyllis Schlafly.* New York: Doubleday, 1981.

1488. Frenier, Mirian Darce. "American Anti-Feminist Women: Comparing the Rhetoric of Opponents of the Equal Rights Amendment with the Opponents of Women's Suffrage." *Women's Studies International Forum* 7, no. 6 (1984): 455–465.

1489. Freund, Paul. "The Equal Rights Amendment Is Not the Way." *Harvard Civil Rights–Civil Liberties Law Review* 6 (March 1971): 234–242.

1490. Mathews, Jane DeHart, Donald G. Mathews, and Roxie Nicholson-Guard. *The Other Women's Movement: Opponents of ERA in North Carolina and the United States.* New York: Oxford University Press, 1980.

1491. Schlafly, Phyllis. "The Case against the ERA." *Radcliffe Quarterly* 68 (March 1982): 18–20.

1492. Solomon, Martha M. "The Rhetoric of STOP ERA: Fatalistic Reaffirmation." *Southern Speech Communication Journal* 44, no. 1 (1978): 442–459.

1493. White, O. Kendall. "Mormonism and the Equal Rights Amendment." *Journal of Church and State* 31 (Spring 1989): 249–267.

1494. Wohl, Lisa Cronin. "Phyllis Schlafly: The Sweetheart of the Silent Majority." *Ms.* 2 (March 1974): 55–57, 85–89.

Anti Reproductive Rights

1495. Bell, Tina. "Operation Rescue." *The Human Life Review* 14, no. 3 (Summer 1988): 37–52.

1496. Blakey, G. Robert. "The RICO Racket." *National Review* 46, no. 9 (16 May 1994): 61–62.

1497. Blanchard, Dallas A. *The Anti–Abortion Movement and the Rise of the Religious Right: From Polite to Fiery Protest.* New York: Maxwell, 1994.

1498. Byrnes, Timothy A., and Mary C. Segers. *The Catholic Church and the Politics of Abortion: A View From the States.* Boulder, CO: Westview Press, 1992.

1499. Cavanaugh, Machale A. "The Case of the Right-To-Life Movement: Secularization and the Politics of Traditionalism." *Sociological Forum* 12, no. 1 (1986).

1500. Conover, Pamela Johnston. "The Mobilization of the New Right: A Test of Various Explanations." *Western Political Quarterly* 632 (1983): 36.

1501. Faludi, Susan. "Where Did Randy Go Wrong?" *Mother Jones* 14, no. 9 (November 1989): 22–28.

1502. Hairston, Julie. "Killing Kittens, Bombing Clinics." *Southern Exposure* 18, no. 2 (Summer 1990): 14–19.

1503. Hertel, Bradley R., and Michael Hughes. "Religious Affiliation, Attendance and Support for the 'Pro-Family' Issues in the United States." *Social Forces* 65, no. 3 (March 1987): 858–882.

1504. Hutchison, Sue, and James N. Baker. "The Right-To-Life Shock Troops." *Newsweek* 114 (1 May 1989): 32.

1505. Jelen, Ted G. "Respect for Life, Sexual Morality, and Opposition to Abortion." *Review of Religious Research* 25 (1984): 220–231.

1506. ———. "Opposition to Abortion: Changes in the Attitudinal Correlates." In *Religion and Politics: Is the Relationship Changing?*, edited by T. E. Scism, 99–109. Charleston, IL: Eastern Illinois University Press, 1987.

1507. ———. "Changes in the Attitudinal Correlates of Opposition to Abortion." *Journal for the Scientific Study of Religion* 27 (June 1988): 211–228.

1508. Markson, Stephen L. "The Roots of Contemporary Anti-Abortion Activism." In *Perspectives on Abortion,* edited by Paul Sachdev, 33–43. Metuchen, NJ: Scarecrow Press, 1985.

1509. McKeegan, Michele. *Abortion Politics: Mutiny in the Ranks of the Right.* New York: Free Press, 1992.

1510. Merton, Andrew H. *Enemies of Choice.* Boston: Beacon, 1981.

1511. Nathanson, Bernard N., and Richard N. Ostling. *Aborting, America.* Garden City, NY: Doubleday, 1979.

1512. Paige, Connie. *The Right to Lifers: Who They Are, How They Operate, Where They Get Their Money.* New York: Summit Books, 1983.

1513. ———. "Watch on the Rights, The Amazing Rise of Beverly La-Haye." *Ms.* 15, no. 8 (February 1987): 24–28.

1514. Scheidler, Joseph M. *Closed: 99 Ways to Stop Abortion.* Westchester, IL: Crossway Books, 1985.

1515. Spitzer, Robert J. *The Right to Life Movement and Third Party Politics.* Westport, CT: Greenwood, 1987.

1516. Terry, Randall. *Operation Rescue.* Springdale, PA: Whitaker House, 1988.

1517. Wilkinson, Francis. "The Gospel According to Randall Terry." *Rolling Stone* 5 (October 1989): 85–86.

1518. Wills, Gary. "Evangels of Abortion." *New York Review of Books* (15 June 1989): 36:10.

1519. ———. "Save the Babies: Operation Rescue, A Case Study On Galvanizing the Antiabortion Movement." *Time* 135 (1 May 1989): 26, 28.

Anti Feminism

1520. Abramovitz, M. "The Conservative Program Is a Woman's Issue." *Journal of Sociology and Social Welfare* 9 (1982): 399–424.

1521. Chafetz, Janet Saltzman, and Anthony Gary Dworkin. "In the Face of Threat: Organized Antifeminism in Comparative Perspective." *Gender and Society* 1 (1987): 33–60.

1522. Chisholm, Shirley. "Racism and Anti-Feminism." *The Black Scholar* 1 (January–February 1970): 40–45.

1523. Conover, Pamela Johnston, and Virginia Gray. *Feminism and the*

New Right—Conflict Over the American Family. New York: Praeger, 1983.

1524. Eisenstein, Zillah. "Antifeminism in the Politics and Election of 1980." *Feminist Studies* 7, no. 2 (Summer 1981): 187–205.

1525. Fowler, Robert Booth. "The Feminist and Antifeminist Debate within Evangelical Protestantism." *Women and Politics* 5, no. 2–3 (1986): 7–39.

1526. Freeman, Bonnie Cook. "Antifeminists and Women's Liberation: A Case Study of a Paradox." *Women and Politics* 3, no. 1 (1983): 21–38.

1527. Gibbs, Nancy. "The War against Feminism." *Time* 139 (9 March 1992): 50–55.

1528. Himmelstein, Jerome L. "The Social Basis of Antifeminism, Religious Networks and Culture." *Journal for the Scientific Study of Religion* 25, no. 1 (1986): 1–15.

1529. Marshall, Susan E. "Ladies against Women: Mobilization Dilemmas of Anti-Feminist Movements." *Social Problems* 32, no. 4 (1985): 348–362.

1530. ———. "Who Speaks for American Women? The Future of Antifeminism." *Annals of the American Academy of Political and Social Science* 515 (1991): 50–62.

1531. ———. "Confrontation and Co-optation in Antifeminist Organizations." In *Feminist Organizations: Harvest of the New Women's Movement,* edited by Myra Marx Ferree and Patricia Yancey Martin, 323–338. Philadelphia: Temple University Press, 1995.

1532. ———. "Keep Us on the Pedestal: Women against Feminism in Twentieth-Century America." In *Women: A Feminist Perspective,* 5th ed., edited by Jo Freeman, 547–560. Mountain View, CA: Mayfield, 1995.

1533. Petchesky, Rosalind Pollack. "Anti-Abortion, Anti-Feminism and the Rise of the New Right." *Feminist Studies* 7 (Summer 1981): 206–246.

1534. Wheeler, Marjorie Spruill. "Feminism and Antifeminism in the South." In *Encyclopedia of Southern Culture,* edited by Charles Reagan Wilson and William B. Ferris, 1543–1545. Chapel Hill: University of North Carolina Press, 1989.

1535. Wilcox, Clyde. "Religious Attitudes and Anti-Feminism: An Analysis of the Ohio Moral Majority." *Women and Politics* 7, no. 2 (1987): 59–87.

1536. ———. "Feminism and Anti-Feminism among White Evangelical Women." *Western Political Quarterly* 42 (1989): 147–160.

New Right

1537. Bashevkin, Sylvia. "Facing a Renewed Right: American Feminism and the Reagan-Bush Challenge." *Canadian Journal of Political Science* 27, no. 2 (December 1994): 669–698.

1538. Bradley, Martha S. "The Women of Fundamentalism: Short Creek, Arizona, 1953." *Dialogue* 23, no. 2 (1990): 15–37.

1539. Bruce, Steve. *The Rise and Fall of the New Christian Right.* New York: Oxford, 1988.

1540. DeHart, Jane Sherron. "Gender on the Right: Meanings behind the Existential Scream." *Gender and History* 3 (1991): 246–267.

1541. Detweiler, John S. "The Religious Right's Battle Plan in the 'Civil War of Values'." *Public Relations Review* 18 (Fall 1992): 247–255.

1542. Diamond, Sara. *The Politics of the Christian Right, Spiritual Warfare.* Boston: South End Press, 1989.

1543. Klatch, Rebecca E. *Women of the New Right.* Philadelphia: Temple University Press, 1987.

1544. ———. "Coalition and Conflict among Women of the New Right." *Signs* 13, no. 4 (Summer 1988): 671–694.

1545. ———. "The New Right and Its Women." *Society* 25 (March–April 1988): 30–38.

1546. ———. "The Two Worlds of Women of the New Right." In *Politics and Change,* edited by Louise A. Tilly and Patricia Gurin, 529–552. New York: Russell Sage, 1990.

1547. Petchesky, Rosalind Pollack. "Antiabortion, Antifeminism, and the Rise of the New Right." *Feminist Studies* 7, no. 2 (1981): 206–246.

1548. Pohli, Carol. "Church Closets and Back Doors: A Feminist View of Moral Majority Women." *Feminist Studies* 9 (Fall 1983): 529–558.

1549. Wilcox, Clyde. "The Christian Right in the Twentieth Century: Continuity and Change." *Review of Politics* 50 (1988): 659–681.

II. Mass Behavior: Participation and Voting

History

1550. Baker, Paula. "The Domestication of Politics: Women and American Political Society, 1780–1920." *American Historical Review* 89, no. 3 (June 1984): 620–647. Reprinted in *Unequal Sisters: A Multicultural Reader in U. S. Women's History,* Ellen Carol Dubois and Vicki L. Ruiz, eds. New York: Routledge, 1990.

1551. Boneparth, Ellen. "Women and Politics: Introduction." *Western Political Quarterly* 34 (March 1981): 3–4.

1552. Chafe, William H. *The American Woman: Her Changing Social, Economic, and Political Roles, 1920–1970.* New York: Oxford University Press, 1972.

1553. Cott, Nancy F. *The Grounding of Modern Feminism.* New Haven, CT: Yale University Press, 1987.

1554. ———. "Across the Great Divide: Women in Politics before and after 1920." In *Women, Politics and Change,* edited by Louise A. Tilly and Patricia Gurin, 153–176. New York: Russell Sage, 1990. Revised and reprinted in *One Woman, One Vote, Rediscovering the Woman Suffrage Movement,* Marjorie Spruill Wheeler, ed., 253–373. Troutdale, OR: NewSage Press, 1995.

1555. Duverger, Maurice. *The Political Role of Women.* New York: UNESCO, 1955.

1556. Flanagan, Maureen A. "Women's Political Power before and after Suffrage in the U.S.: A Local, Two-Generational Perspective." Paper presented at the annual meeting of the Social Science History Association, Illinois, 1992.

1557. Gruberg, Martin. *Women in American Politics: An Assessment and Sourcebook.* Oshkosh, WI: Academia Press, 1968.

1558. Klein, Ethel. *Gender Politics: From Consciousness to Mass Politics.* Cambridge: Harvard University Press, 1984.

1559. Matthews, Glenna. *The Rise of Public Woman: Woman's Power and Woman's Place in the United States 1630–1970.* New York: Oxford University Press, 1992.

1560. Schuck, Victoria. "A Hundred Years of Women and Politics." *Mt. Holyoke Alumnae Quarterly* 32 (November 1948): 117–119.

1561. Young, Louise M. "Women's Place in American Politics: The Historical Perspective." *Annals of the American Academy of Political and Social Science* 251 (1941): 295–335.

1562. ———. "Women's Place in American Politics: The Historical Perspective." *Journal of Politics* 38 (August 1976): 300–320.

Assessments After National Suffrage

1563. Abbott, Grace. "What Have They Done ?" *The Independent* 115 (24 October 1925): 475–476.

1564. Adams, Mildred. "Did They Know What They Wanted?" *Outlook* 147 (28 December 1927): 528–530.

1565. Allen, Florence E. "The First Ten Years." *The Woman's Journal* 15 (August 1930): 5–7, 30–32.

1566. Blair, Emily Newell. "Are Women a Failure in Politics?" *Harper's Weekly* 151 (October 1925): 513–522.

1567. ———. "Why I Am Discouraged About Women in Politics." *The Woman's Journal* 16 (January 1931): 20–22, 44–45.

1568. Butler, Sarah Schuyler. "After Ten Years." *The Woman's Journal* 14 (April 1929): 10–11.

1569. Catt, Carrie Chapman. "Are Women Disappointed in Politics?" *The Woman Citizen* 8 (3 November 1923): 14–15.

1570. ———. "The Cave Man Complex Vs. Woman Suffrage." *The Woman Citizen* 8 (5 April 1924): 16–17.

1571. ———. "What Women Have Done with the Vote." *The Independent* 115 (17 October 1925): 447–448, 456.

1572. ———. "Woman Suffrage: The First Ten Years." *The New York Times Magazine* (24 August 1930): V, 3, 16.

1573. "Celebrating Suffrage: 75 Years Ago U.S. Women Got the Vote." *Ms.* 6 (July–August 1995): 30–39.

1574. Chenery, William L. "Ten Years of Woman Suffrage." *Colliers* 83 (17 May 1930): 94.

1575. "Congress Commemorates 41st Anniversary of Women's Right to Vote." *National Business Woman* 40 (October 1961): 13, 28.

1576. Crocco, Margaret Smith. "The Road to the Vote." *Social Education* 59, no. 5 (September 1995): 257–265.

1577. Eastman, Elizabeth. "Twenty Years After." *Independent Woman* 20 (January 1941): 13–14.

1578. Gilman, Charlotte Perkins. "Women's Achievements since the Franchise." *Current History* 27 (1927): 7–14.

1579. Hardesty, Carolyn. "The Woman Question Today, 1987." *North American Review* 272, special issue (September 1987): 26–93.

1580. Harvey, Anna L. "The Legacy of Disfranchisement: Women in Electoral Politics, 1920–1932." Ph.D. dissertation, Princeton University, Princeton, 1995.

1581. "Is Woman Suffrage Failing? A Symposium." *The Woman Citizen* 8 (19 April 1924): 14–19. William G. Shepherd, Zona Gale, Mary P. Scully, Florence E. Allen, Edythe Rochelle, Jane Addams, Samuel Gompers, Alice Stone Blackwell, Samuel M. Ralston.

1582. Kenton, Edna. "Four Years of Equal Suffrage." *Forum* 72 (July 1924): 37–44.

1583. Kimball, Alice Mary. "What Now." *Independent Woman* 19 (July 1940): 203, 218.

1584. Lippmann, Walter. "Lady Politicians: How the Old-Fashioned Illusion That Women Would Redeem Politics Has Been Destroyed." *Vanity Fair* 29 (January 1928): 43, 104.

1585. Livermore, Mrs. Arthur L. "What Ten Years of Suffrage Has Accomplished." *The Republican Woman* 8, no. 7 (January 1931): 4, 8.

1586. McGowan, Josephine. "A Decade of Equal Rights." *Commonweal* 13 (11 February 1931): 401–403.

1587. McKee, Oliver, Jr. "Ten Years of Woman Suffrage." *Commonwealth* 12 (July 1930): 298–300.

1588. Park, Maud Wood. "Ten Years of Suffrage." *Independent Woman* 11 (August 1930): 316–317, 340–341.

1589. Peak, Mayme Ober. "Women in Politics." *Outlook* 136 (23 January 1924): 147–150.

1590. Perry, Elisabeth Israels. "Why Suffrage for American Women Was Not Enough." *History Today* 43 (September 1993): 36–41.

1591. Russell, Charles Edward. "Is Woman Suffrage a Failure?" *Century* 107 (March 1924): 724–730.

1592. Selden, Charles A. "Four Years of the Nineteenth Amendment." *Ladies Home Journal* 41 (June 1924): 27, 138, 140.

1593. Stevens, Doris. "Suffrage Does Not Give Equality." *Forum* 72 (August 1924): 145–152.

1594. Tarbell, Ida M. "Is Woman's Suffrage a Failure?" *Good Housekeeping* 79 (October 1924): 18–19, 237–239.

1595. "Ten Years of Suffrage." *The Survey* 63 (15 January 1930): 454.

1596. "Ten Years of Woman Suffrage." *Literary Digest* 105 (26 April 1930): 11.

1597. Thompson, C. Mildred. "Decade of Women's Suffrage." *Current History* 33 (October 1930): 13–17.

1598. Wells, Marguerite M. "Some Effects of Woman Suffrage." *Annals of the American Academy of Political and Social Science* 143 (May 1929): 207–216.

1599. "What Have Women Done with the Vote?" *The Woman Citizen* 8 (September 1923): 7–11, 23. Reprinted in *Literary Digest* 78 (22 September 1923): 50, 52.

1600. Wilson, Margaret Woodrow. "Where Women in Politics Fail." *Ladies Home Journal* 38 (September 1921): 10, 70.

1601. "Woman Suffrage Declared a Failure." *Literary Digest* 81 (12 April 1924): 12–13.

1602. "Women Voters' Views on Woman's Suffrage." *Outlook* 97 (28 January 1911): 143–144.

Elections

Campaigns

1603. Boneparth, Ellen. "Women in Campaigns: From Lickin' and Stickin' to Strategy." *American Politics Quarterly* 5, no. 3 (1977): 289–300.

1604. "Cincinnati Women Ring Doorbells—Or How One Woman Got into Local Politics." *National Municipal Review* 42 (March 1953): 147–148.

1605. Declercq, Eugene R., James G. Benze, and Elisa Ritchie. "Macha Women and Macho Men: The Role of Gender in Campaigns Involving Women." Paper presented at the annual meeting of the American Political Science Association, Chicago, September, 1983.

1606. Eliaser, Ann. *From Grassroots Politics to the Top Dollar: Fundraising for Candidates and Non-Profit Agencies.* Berkeley: University of California, 1983. The Bancroft Library Oral History Interview.

1607. Garbett, Arlene. "Jobs Behind the Scenes in Politics." *Glamour* 76 (October 1978): 134, 136.

1608. Greene, Mrs. Frederick Stuart. "They Got Their Man." *The Woman Citizen* 7 (18 November 1922): 12, 27.

1609. Guiterman, A. "Women of the Campaign in 1912." *Woman's Home Companion* 39 (November 1912): 22.

1610. Hickey, Margaret. "What Women Did in Gary, Women Can Get Results." *Ladies Home Journal* 68 (October 1951): 51, 109–111.

1611. Holtzman, Abraham. "Campaign Politics: A New Role for Women." *Southwestern Social Science Quarterly* 40 (March 1960): 314–320.

1612. Monoson, S. Sara. "The Lady and the Tiger: Women's Electoral Activism in New York City before Suffrage." *Journal of Women's History* 2, no. 2 (Fall 1990): 100–134.

1613. Reynolds, Minnie J. "Recollections of a Woman Campaigner." *Delineator* 74 (October 1909): 299, 350–351.

1614. Sanders, Marion K. "Issues Girls, Club Ladies, Camp Followers." *The New York Times Magazine* (1 December 1963): VI, 38, 63, 65–66.

1615. Scott, Mary Semple. "They Fought Their Senator." *The Woman Citizen* 7 (2 December 1922): 11, 25–26.

1616. Spring, Andrea L. "Seventy-Four Women Who Are Changing American Politics: A Special Report." *Campaigns and Elections* 14, no. 2 (June 1993): 16–21.

1617. Villard, Oswald Garrison. "Women in New York Municipal Campaign." *The Woman's Journal* 33 (8 March 1902): 78.

Consultants and Staff

1618. Arnold, Margaret. "Politics, Profession for Women." *American As-*

sociation of University Women 14, no. 2 (November 1920): 34–39.

1619. Faucheux, Ron. "Movers and Shakers: Teresa Vilmain—On Track." *Campaigns and Elections* 14, no. 4 (September 1993): 50.

1620. Glenney, Daryl. "Women in Politics: On the Rise." *Campaigns and Elections* 2, no. 4 (Winter 1982): 18–24.

1621. Hewitt, Bill, and Jane Sims Podesta. "Undivided Loyalty, Mary Matalin." *People's Weekly* 37 (1 June 1992): 57–58, 59.

1622. "Inside Dukakis Headquarters: Susan Estrich." *Campaigns and Elections* 9, no. 3 (August–September 1988): 39–41.

1623. Kurtz, Howard A. "Capitol Gains, Pollster Celinda Lake." *Working Woman* 17 (February 1992): 66–69.

1624. Lake, Celinda C. "Political Consultants: Opening Up a New System of Political Power." *PS* 22, no. 1 (1989): 26–29.

1625. Lerner, Michael A. "Out of the Boiler Room: Nancy Sinnott and Ann Lewis." *Newsweek* 100 (1 November 1982): 29.

1626. Mayer, Jane. "Hail, Mary." *Vogue* 182 (August 1992): 236–237.

1627. Neilson, Melany. *Even Mississippi.* Tuscaloosa: University of Alabama Press, 1989.

1628. Pike, Emily. *Republican Party Campaign Organizer: From Volunteer to Professional.* Berkeley: University of California, 1983. The Bancroft Library Oral History Interview.

1629. Reed, Julia. "Party Girl." *Vogue* 182, no. 8 (August 1992): 238–242.

1630. Siegel, Alexandra. "And on the Right ... Pollster Linda Divall." *Working Woman* 17 (February 1992): 69.

1631. Smith, Chris S. "The Player, Mandy Grunwald." *New York* 25 (13 July 1992): 50–55.

1632. Stewart, Morgan. "Movers and Shakers: Huda Jones—Training to Win." *Campaigns and Elections* 14, no. 4 (September 1993): 48.

1633. Ward, Betsy. "Oh, You've Got to Have Friends, Pamela Lippe." *Working Woman* 16 (February 1991): 84–86.

National Campaigns, by Year

1634. "Mrs. J. Ellen Foster in Utah." *The Woman's Journal* 31 (3 November 1900): 352.

1635. "The Western Woman Voter." *The Woman's Journal* 31 (3 November 1900): 345.

1636. "Republican Women for Taft." *The Woman's Journal* 39 (19 September 1908): 151.

1637. Trattner, Walter I. "Theodore Roosevelt, Social Workers, and the Election of 1912: A Note." *Mid-America* 50, no. 1 (1912): 64–69.

1638. "Women in Politics in the Presidential Campaign." *Harper's Weekly* 56 (9 November 1912): 12.

1639. "Women's Work in the Campaign." *Literary Digest* 45 (31 August 1912): 324–326.

1640. Daggett, Mabel Potter. "The New Chapter in Woman's Progress." *Good Housekeeping* 56 (February 1913): 148–155.

1641. Bates, J. Leonard, and Vanette M. Schwartz. "The Golden Special Campaign Train: Republican Women Campaign for Charles Evans Hughes for President in 1916." *Montana, The Magazine of Western History* 37 (Summer 1987): 26–35.

1642. Women's Committee, National Hughes Campaign, ed. *Women in National Politics.* New York: Women's Committee, National Hughes Campaign, 1916.

1643. Kellor, Frances A. "Women in the Campaign." *Yale Review* 6 (January 1917): 233–243.

1644. "G.O.P. Women Plan Campaign." *The Woman Citizen* 3 (21 December 1918): 616.

1645. Jordan, Elizabeth. "Women in the Presidential Campaign." *Ladies Home Journal* 37 (October 1920): 3–4, 138, 140.

1646. "Democratic Campaign Summary." *The Woman Citizen* 9 (1 November 1924): 15.

1647. "Democratic Party, the Friend of Women." *The Woman Citizen* 9 (6 September 1924): 10.

1648. Hert, Mrs. Alvin T. "Why I Am for Coolidge and Dawes." *The Woman Citizen* 9 (4 October 1924): 14.

1649. Keating, Margaret. "The Progressives and Peace." *The Woman Citizen* 9 (1 November 1924): 14.

1650. Kendig, Isabelle. "Woman's Opportunity in the Progressive Move-

ment." *The Woman Citizen* 9 (4 October 1924): 544. Reprinted in *The Nation* (19 November 1924): 544.

1651. Warburton, Mrs. Barclay. "Coolidge or Chaos." *The Woman Citizen* 9 (1 November 1924): 13.

1652. Wilson, Mrs. Halsey W. "Victory Vote Drive." *The Woman Citizen* 9 (4 October 1924): 15.

1653. "Women Campaigners." *The Woman Citizen* 10 (4 October 1924): 22.

1654. Cunningham, Minnie Fisher. "Red Herrings." *The Woman Citizen* 11 (October 1926): 25.

1655. Hert, Mrs. Alvin T. "National Housekeeping." *The Woman Citizen* 11 (October 1926): 24, 37.

1656. ———. "The Tariff and Your Prosperity." *The Woman Citizen* 11 (September 1926): 21, 38.

1657. Barnard, Eunice Fuller. "Women in the Campaign." *The Woman's Journal* 13, no. 12 (December 1928): 7–9, 44–45.

1658. Blair, Emily Newell. "The Campaign." *Democratic Bulletin* 3, no. 3 (March 1928): 8–9, 14–15.

1659. "Equality of Effort in National Campaign." *The Republican Woman of Illinois* 6, no. 3 (October 1928): 3.

1660. Hert, Mrs. Alvin T. "Herbert Hoover and World Peace." *The Woman's Journal* 13 (September 1928): 19.

1661. ———. "Woman's Work for Herbert Hoover." *The Woman's Journal* 13 (November 1928): 21.

1662. Morrison, Glenda Eileen. "Women's Participation in the 1928 Presidential Campaign." Ph.D. dissertation, University of Kansas, Lawrence, 1978.

1663. Ross, Nellie Tayloe. "Why a Woman 'Dry' Supports Governor Smith." *The Woman's Journal* 13 (September 1928): 18.

1664. Tarbell, Ida M. "A Woman Looks at Smith." *Colliers* 81 (19 May 1928): 19, 46–47.

1665. Coleman, McAlister. "Socialism—1930." *The Woman's Journal* 15 (October 1930): 11, 36.

1666. Dodson, Louise M. "The Tariff as Social Justice." *The Woman's Journal* 15 (September 1930): 8.

1667. Ross, Nellie Tayloe. "The Elections and Excessive Expenditures." *The Woman's Journal* 15 (November 1930): 22, 43.

1668. ———. "A More Honorable Record." *The Woman's Journal* 15 (September 1930): 9.

1669. ———. "Wanted: A Change in Congress." *The Woman's Journal* 15 (October 1930): 13, 36.

1670. Yost, Lenna Lowe. "President and People Govern Together." *The Woman's Journal* 15 (November 1930): 23, 34.

1671. ———. "Women and Political Realities." *The Woman's Journal* 15 (October 1930): 12, 36.

1672. Yost, Lenna Lowe, and Nellie Tayloe Ross. "Should Women Support the Administration's Policies?" *Congressional Digest* 9 (October 1930): 245–246.

1673. Ross, Nellie Tayloe. "What Are Women Going to Do?" *Democratic Bulletin* 7, no. 1 (January 1932): 18–19.

1674. Dewson, Mary W. "Our Part in the Campaign of 1936." *Democratic Digest* 13, no. 12 (December 1936): 5–6.

1675. "Mary Chamberlain, Creator of 83,000,000 Rainbow Flyers." *Democratic Digest* 13, no. 12 (December 1936): 7.

1676. Morgenthau, Mrs. Henry, Jr. "Votes by Wireless." *Democratic Digest* 13, no. 12 (December 1936): 6.

1677. Wilkie, Wendell. *Wendell Wilkie Speaks to Women.* Washington, DC: Republican National Committee, 1940. Address before the Annual Convention of National Federation of Women's Republican Clubs.

1678. Woolf, S. J. "Dewey's Right Hand Woman." *The New York Times Magazine* (18 February 1940): VII, 10.

1679. Tillet, Gladys Avery. "It's Going to Be a Woman's Campaign." *Democratic Digest* 19, no. 6 (June 1942): 3, 14.

1680. "Women Draw Big Supporting Roles in Election-Year Political Drama." *Newsweek* 23 (19 June 1944): 45–46, 48.

1681. McGranery, Regina. "Women Speakers in 1948 Campaign." *Democratic Digest* 25–26, no. 12–1 (December 1948–January 1949): 21–22.

1682. "Enter, the Political Ladies." *The New York Times Magazine* (19 October 1952): VI, 1, 12–13.

1683. Adkins, Bertha. "Vote Republican." *Independent Woman* 35 (October 1956): 3, 34.

1684. Louchheim, Katie. "Vote Democratic." *Independent Woman* 35 (October 1956): 2–5, 35.

1685. Steinem, Gloria. "Coming of Age with McGovern: Notes from a Political Diary." *Ms.* 3, no. 4 (October 1974): 39.

1686. Ford, Gerald, and Jimmy Carter. "Exclusive! Ford and Carter Answer BPW Questions." *National Business Woman* 57, no. 8 (October 1976): 4–7.

1687. Anderson, Linda, and Catherine East. *Straight Talk: A Response to the Administration's 'Talking Points on Issues of Interest to Women'*. Washington, DC: National Women's Political Caucus, 1984.

1688. Simpson, Peggy. "All the Candidate's Women." *Ms.* 17, no. 4 (October 1988): 74–80.

1689. Castor, Laura. "Did She or Didn't She?: The Discourse of Scandal in the 1988 U. S. Presidential Campaign." *Genders* 12 (1991): 62–76.

Surrogates for Candidates

1690. Burden, Barry C., and Anthony Mughan. "The Candidates' Wives." In *Democracy's Feast: Elections in America,* edited by Herbert F. Weisberg, 136–152. Chatham, NJ: Chatham House, 1995.

1691. Grimes, Ann. *Running Mates: The Making of a First Lady: A Penetrat-* *ing Look at Private Woman in the Public Eye.* New York: William Morrow, 1990.

1692. Jackson, Mrs. Jesse L. "I'd Make a Great First Lady." *Ebony* 39 (July 1984): 25–27, 31.

1693. Jacobbi, Marianne. "What Did Happen to Kitty Dukakis?" *Good Housekeeping* 208 (June 1989): 52–55.

1694. Muskie, Jane, and Mary Finch Hoyt. "What I Learned in 1968 About Women, Politics, and My Husband." *McCalls* 96 (April 1969): 92–93, 170–174.

1695. Simon, Jean C. Hurley. *Codename Scarlet: Life on the Campaign Trail by the Wife of a Presidential Candidate.* New York: Continuum, 1989.

Lobbying

1696. Ames, Marie. "Lady Lobbyist." *The Woman's Journal* 15 (November 1930): 12–13.

1697. Becker, Nancy. *Lobbying in New Jersey.* New Brunswick, NJ: Center for the American Woman and Politics, Rutgers University, 1978.

1698. Breckinridge, Sophonisba P. "The Women's Bloc." Chap. 16 in *Women in the Twentieth Century: A Study of Their Political, Social and Economic Activities,* 257–274. New York: McGraw-Hill, 1933.

1699. "Brickerettes: Vigilant Women for the Bricker Amendment." *Reporter* 10 (2 March 1954): 2.

1700. Burris, Carol. "The Woman's Lobby." *Public Welfare* 36, no. 1 (1978): 28–31.

1701. Cirksena, M. Kathryn. "Access, Competence, and Gender in Political Persuading, 1964–1984." Ph.D. dissertation, Stanford University, 1992.

1702. Costain, Anne N. "The Struggle for a National Womens' Lobby: Organizing a Diffuse Interest." *Western Political Quarterly* 33, no. 4 (1980): 476–491.

1703. ———. "Representing Women: The Transition from Social Movement to Interest Group." *Western Political Quarterly* 34, no. 1 (1981): 100–113. Reprinted in *Women, Power and Policy: Toward the Year 2000,* 2d ed., Ellen Boneparth and Emily Stoper, eds., 26–48. New York: Pergamon, 1989.

1704. ———. "Women's Claims as a Special Interest." In *The Politics of the Gender Gap: The Social Construction of Political Influence,* edited by Carol M. Mueller, 150–172. Women's Policy Studies, 12. Beverly Hills, CA: Sage, 1988.

1705. Costain, Anne N., and W. Douglas Costain. "The Women's Lobby: Impact of a Movement on Congress." In *Interest Group Politics,* edited by Allan J. Cigler and Burdett A. Coomis, 191–216. Washington, DC: CQ Press, 1983.

1706. Deardorff, Neva R. "Women in Municipal Activities." *Annals of the American Academy of Political and Social Science* 56 (November 1914): 71–77.

1707. Dubrow, Evelyn. *Oral History Interview with Evelyn Dubrow.* 1978. Interviews by the Institute of Labor and Industrial Relations. Detroit: University of Michigan and Wayne State University.

1708. Eastman, Elizabeth. "Front Door Lobby." *The Woman's Journal* 16 (February 1931): 20–21, 40.

1709. Frazer, Elizabeth. "A Political Forecast." *Good Housekeeping* 75 (September 1922): 49, 157–161.

1710. Freyss, Siegrun Fox. "Women, Power, and the Third Sector: Exploring the Service Delivery Potential of Liberal Interest Groups." Paper presented at the annual meeting of the American Political Science Association, Chicago, 1995.

1711. Gelb, Joyce, and Marian Lief Palley. "Women and Interest Group Politics: A Comparative Analysis of Federal Decision-Making." *Journal of Politics* 41 (May 1979): 362–392.

1712. Goldsmith, Judy B. "How to Win Friends and Influence Legislators." *Ms.* 2 (July–August 1990): 90.

1713. Grenfell, Helen L. "Influence of Woman's Organization on Public Education." *Journal of Education* 66 (25 July 1907): 127.

1714. Hackett, Catherine I. "The Lady Who Made Lobbying Respectable." *The Woman Citizen* 8 (19 April 1924): 12–13.

1715. Hamos, Julie E. *State Domestic Violence Laws and How to Pass Them: A Manual for Lobbyists.* Rockville, MD: National Clearinghouse on Domestic Violence, 1980.

1716. Hefner, Loretta L. "The National Women's Relief Society and the U.S. Sheppard-Towner Act." *Utah*

Historical Quarterly 50, no. 3 (1982): 255–267.

1717. Johnson, Dorothy Elizabeth. "Organized Women and National Legislation, 1920–1941." Ph.D. dissertation, Western Reserve University, 1960.

1718. ———. "Organized Women As Lobbyists in the 1920's." *Capitol Studies* 1 (Spring 1972): 41–58.

1719. Laidlaw, Harriet Burton. "Whose Representative ?" *The Woman Citizen* 10 (30 May 1925): 13.

1720. "Lobbyist in the Winter, Farmer in the Summer." *Successful Farming* 87 (January 1989): 39.

1721. Lore, Helen. "The New Girls Network." *Working Women* (May 1995): 1–2.

1722. Martin, George Madden. "American Woman and Representative Government." *Atlantic Monthly* 135 (March 1925): 363–371.

1723. Mattison, Georgia, and Sandra Storey, eds. *Women in Citizen Advocacy: Stories of 28 Shapers of Public Policy.* Jefferson, NC: McFarland, 1992.

1724. Melosh, Barbara, and Christina Simmons. "From Martha Washington to Alice Paul in Our Nation's Capital." *Radical History Review* 25 (October 1981): 100–113.

1725. Park, Maud Wood. "Women's Joint Congressional Committee." *Independent Woman* 6 (May 1925): 14–15.

1726. Peer, Elizabeth. "Starting Up An Ole Girls' Network." *Newsweek* 101 (18 April 1983): 88–89.

1727. "The Public-Spirited Woman, What She Can Do and How She Can Do It: Women and the Schools." *Pictorial Review* 11, no. 5 (February 1910): 27.

1728. "The Public-Spirited Woman, What She Can Do and How She Can Do It: How to Improve Your Own Town." *Pictorial Review* 11, no. 6 (March 1910): 5.

1729. Reilly, Ann. "Women Lobbyists." *Fortune* 111 (18 February 1985): 119–120.

1730. Richardson, Eudora Ramsay. "Ladies of the Lobby." *North American Review* 227 (June 1929): 648–655.

1731. Schlozman, Kay Lehman. "Representing Women in Washington: Sisterhood and Pressure Politics." In *Women, Politics and Change,* edited by Louise A. Tilly and Patricia Gurin. New York: Russell Sage, 1990.

1732. Selden, Charles A. "Most Powerful Lobby in Washington: The Public Welfare Lobby Backed by Seven Million Organized American Women." *Ladies Home Journal* 39 (April 1922): 5.

1733. Simpson, Peggy. "D.C. Lobby: Who's Minding the Store?" *Ms.* 2 (May–June 1991): 88–89.

1734. Siwolop, Sana. "Fairy Godmother, Mary Lasker." *Business Week* (14 July 1986): 67.

1735. Slavin, Sarah. "An NAACP for Women: The Intersection of Race, Gender, and Ethnicity in Women's Issue Groups That Lobby." Paper, APSA, 1995.

1736. Smith, Ethel M. "Are We a Menace?" _The Woman Citizen_ 10 (13 June 1925): 15, 24.

1737. Stewart, Anne Bigony. "When Women Lobby." _The Woman Citizen_ 2 (1 December 1917): 14.

1738. Strolovitch, Dara. "Representing Women's Interests: The Case of Health Care Reform." Paper presented at the annual meeting of the American Political Science Association, 1995.

1739. Thompson, Joan Hulse. "The Women's Rights Lobby in the Gender Gap Congress, 1983–1984." _Commonwealth_ 2 (1988): 19–35.

1740. Weatherford, J. McIver. "Amazons on the Potomac." In _Tribes on the Hill_, 249–253. New York: Rawson, Wade, 1981.

1741. Willard, William. "Gertrude Bonnin and Indian Policy Reform 1911–1938." In _Indian Leadership_, edited by Walter Williams, 70–75. Manhattan, KS: Sunflower University Press, 1984.

1742. Williams, Nancy Anite. "Lawyer in the Lobby." _Essence_ 18 (July 1987): 113, 130.

1743. Woodward, Helen. _The Lady Persuaders_. Stamford, CT: Astor-Honor, 1960.

1744. Wright, Harriet G. R. "How to Assist Legislation." In _The Woman Citizen's Library_, Vol. 7, Women and the Law, 2098–2106. Chicago: The Civics Society, 1913.

1745. Zimmerman, Jonathan. "'The Queen of the Lobby': Mary Hunt, Scientific Temperance, and the Dilemma of Democratic Education in America." _History of Education Quarterly_ 32, no. 1 (1992): 1–30.

Litigation

1746. Berger, Margaret A. _Litigation on Behalf of Women: A Review for the Ford Foundation_. New York: Ford Foundation, 1980.

1747. Cahn, Naomi R. "Defining Feminist Litigation." _Harvard Women's Law Journal_ 14 (Spring 1991): 1–20.

1748. Cole, David. "Strategies of Difference: Litigating for Women's Rights in a Man's World." _Law and Inequality: A Journal of Theory and Practice_ 2 (February 1984): 33–96.

1749. Cowan, Ruth. "Women's Rights through Litigation: An Examination of the American Civil Liberties Union Women's Rights Project, 1971–76." _Columbia Human Rights Law Review_ 8 (Spring–Summer 1976): 373–412.

1750. George, Tracey E., and Lee Epstein. "Women's Rights Litigation in the 1980's: More of the Same?" _Judicature_ 74, no. 6 (April–May 1991): 314–321.

1751. Sedey, Mary Anne, and Lisa S. VanAmburg. "Practice Before the Supreme Court: Two Lawyers' Experience." _St. Louis Bar Journal_ 35, no. 4 (Spring 1989): 42–49.

1752. Stoddard, Cynthia. _Sex Discrimination in Education and Employment: Legal Strategies and Alternatives._

Holmes Beach, FL: Learning Publications, 1981.

Participation

General

1753. Adams, Mildred. *The Right to be People.* Philadelphia: Lippincott, 1967.

1754. Alpern, Sara, and Dale Baum. "Female Ballots: The Impact of the Nineteenth Amendment." *Journal of Interdisciplinary History* 16 (Summer 1985): 43–67.

1755. Amundsen, Kirsten. *The Silenced Majority: Women and American Democracy.* Englewood Cliffs, NJ: Prentice Hall, 1971.

1756. Beckwith, Karen. *American Women and Political Participation: The Impacts of Work, Generation, and Feminism.* New York: Greenwood, 1986.

1757. Bellush, Jewel. "Women and Political Power: It's About Time." *National Civic Review* 66, no. 4 (1977): 186–188.

1758. Berger, Reva. "Where Women Succeed in Politics." *Working Woman* 3 (March 1978): 52–55.

1759. Bettelheim, Bruno. "Women: Emancipation Is Still to Come." *The New Republic* 155, no. 19 (7 November 1964): 48–53.

1760. Blair, Emily Newell. "Men in Politics as a Woman Sees Them." *Harper's Weekly* 152 (May 1926): 703–709.

1761. Conway, Jill K., Susan C. Bourque, and Joan W. Scott, eds. *Learning about Women: Gender, Politics and Power.* Ann Arbor: University of Michigan Press, 1989.

1762. "Creeping Progress for Women." *Progressive* 59 (October 1995): 8–9.

1763. Davie, Mary. "Women and Politics." *Woman's Home Companion* 67 (October 1940): 13, 38–39.

1764. Douglas, Susan Jeanne. "Snide Celebrations." *Progressive* 59 (October 1995): 17.

1765. Egan, J. "Up with Women in Politics." *McCalls* 98 (September 1971): 47.

1766. Fleming, G. James. "Why Women in Politics." *Vital Speeches* 26 (1 January 1960): 172–173.

1767. Githens, Marianne, and Jewell Prestage, eds. *A Portrait of Marginality: The Political Behavior of American Women.* New York: McKay, 1977.

1768. Graham, Lee. "Who's in Charge Here? Not Women!" *The New York Magazine* (2 September 1962): 8.

1769. Gruenebaum, Jane. "Women in Politics." *Annals of the American Academy of Political and Social Science* 34, no. 2 (1981): 104–120.

1770. Hanhn, Harlan. "Women and American Politics." *American Politics Quarterly* 5, no. 3 (July 1977): 259–260.

1771. Hedblom, Milda K. W. *Women and Power in American Politics.* Washington, DC: American Political Science Association, 1988.

1772. Hickey, Margaret. "Politics without Malice." *Ladies Home Journal* 81 (April 1964): 80, 115–116.

1773. Jaquette, Jane S., ed. *Woman and Politics: A Sourcebook.* New York: Wiley, 1974.

1774. Johnson, Geraldine W. "Women's Good Sense Is Needed in Politics." *Ladies Home Journal* 75 (November 1958): 20, 23.

1775. Karl, Marilee. *Women and Empowerment: Participation and Decision Making.* Atlantic Highlands, NJ: Zed Books, 1995.

1776. Kuhn, Irene Corbally. "Women Don't Belong in Politics." *American Mercury* (August 1953): 5–6.

1777. Levitt, Morris. "Political Role of American Women." *Journal of Human Relations* 15, no. 1 (1967): 23–35.

1778. Lynn, Naomi B. "Women in American Politics: An Overview." In *Women: A Feminist Perspective,* edited by Jo Freeman, 364–385. Palo Alto, CA: Mayfield, 1975.

1779. ———. "Women and Politics: The Real Majority." In *Women: A Feminist Perspective,* 3d ed., edited by Jo Freeman, 402–423. Palo Alto, CA: Mayfield, 1984.

1780. ———. "Women in American Politics: An Overview." In *Women: A Feminist Perspective,* 4th ed., edited by Jo Freeman, 404–442. Palo Alto, CA: Mayfield, 1989.

1781. Mandel, Ruth B. "A Generation of Change for Women in Politics." In *Women, A Feminist Perspective,* 5th ed., edited by Jo Freeman, 405–429. Mountain View, CA: Mayfield, 1995.

1782. McDonagh, Eileen Lorenzi. "Gender Politics and Political Changes." In *New Perspective on American Politics,* edited by Lawrence C. Dodd and Calvin Jillson, 58–74. Washington, DC: CQ Press, 1994.

1783. McGlen, Nancy E., and Karen O'Connor. *Women, Politics and American Society.* Englewood Cliffs, NJ: Prentice Hall, 1995.

1784. Mead, Margaret. "Must Women Be Bored with Politics?" *Redbook* 123 (October 1964): 20, 22.

1785. ———. "Women and Politics." *Redbook* 136 (November 1970): 50–55.

1786. Palley, Marian Lief. "The Women's Movement in Recent American Politics." In *American Woman, 1987–88,* edited by Sara E. Rix and Anne J. Stone, 33–66. New York: Norton, 1987.

1787. Perlez, Jane. "Women, Power, and Politics." *The New York Times Magazine* (24 June 1984): VI, 23–28, 30–31, 72, 76.

1788. Randall, Vicky. *Women and Politics,* 2d ed. Chicago: University of Chicago Press, 1989 (1982).

1789. Ries, Paula, and Anne J. Stone, eds. *The American Woman: 1992–1993.* New York: Norton, 1993.

1790. Romney, Ronna, and Beppie Harrison. *Momentum: Women in American Politics Now.* New York: Crown, 1988.

1791. Roosevelt, Eleanor, and Lorena A. Hickok. *Ladies of Courage.* New York: G.P. Putnam's Sons, 1954.

1792. Roosevelt, Governor Franklin D., and Dorothy Dunbar Bromley. "A Challenge to Women." *Good Housekeeping* 93 (October 1931): 22–23, 175–176, 179–180, 182, 186, 194.

1793. "Salute to Women in Politics." *Independent Woman* 34 (March 1955): 104.

1794. Schlozman, Kay Lehman, Nancy Elizabeth Burns, Sidney Verba, and Jesse Donahue. "Gender and Citizen Participation: Is There a Different Voice?" *American Journal of Political Science* 39, no. 2 (May 1995): 267–293.

1795. Shibrock, C. S. J., Sister Ann Regis, and Brother Gerald J. "Women in Politics." *Social Order* 3 (October 1953): 361–366.

1796. Steuernagel, Gertrude A. "Reflections on Women and Political Participation." *Women and Politics* 7 (Winter 1987): 3–13.

1797. "Symposium on Women and Politics." *Journal of Politics* 41 (May 1979): 361–524.

1798. Thompson, Clara Belle, and Margaret Luken Wise. "Have the Women Any Say?" *Ladies Home Journal* 59 (October 1942): 152–153.

1799. Tilly, Louise A., and Patricia Gurin. "Introduction: Women, Politics and Change." In *Women, Politics and Change,* edited by Louise A. Tilly and Patricia Gurin, 3–32. New York: Russell Sage, 1990.

1800. Tolchin, Susan, and Martin Tolchin. *Clout: Womanpower and Politics.* New York: Coward, McCann and Geoghagan, 1974.

1801. ———. "Women in Politics." *Vogue* 170 (September 1980): 462–465.

1802. Tronto, Joan C. "Changing Goals and Changing Strategies: Varieties of Women's Political Activities." *Feminist Studies* 17 (1991): 85–104.

1803. Weil, Marie. "Women, Community and Organizing." In *Feminist Visions for Social Work,* edited by Nan Van Den Bergh and Lynn B. Cooper, 187–210. Silver Spring, MD: National Association of Social Work, 1986.

1804. "Woman Voters Have Made Our Politics Very, Very Different." *Saturday Evening Post* 233 (27 August 1960): 10.

1805. "Women's Homework." *Life* 35 (23 November 1953): 169–170.

Impact

1806. Bourque, Susan C., and Jean Grossholtz. "Politics as Unnatural Practice: Political Science Looks at Female Participation." *Politics and Society* 4 (Winter 1974): 225–266.

1807. Christy, Carol A. "Economic Development and Sex Differences in Political Participation." *Women and Politics* 4 (Spring 1984): 7–34.

1808. Clark, Cal, and Janet M. Clark. "Models of Gender and Political Participation in the United States." *Women and Politics* 6 (Spring 1986): 5–25.

1809. Conway, M. Margaret. "Women as Voluntary Political Activists: A Review of Recent Empirical Research." In *Women Organizing: An Anthology,* edited by Bernice Cummings and Victoria Schuck, 298–303. Metuchen, NJ: Scarecrow Press, 1979.

1810. Githens, Marianne. "The Elusive Paradigm—Gender Politics and Political Behavior: The State of the Art." In *Political Science: The State of the Discipline,* edited by Ada Finifter, 471–499. Washington, DC: American Political Science Association, 1983.

1811. Jennings, M. Kent. "Another Look at Life Cycle and Political Participation." *American Journal of Political Science* 23 (November 1979): 755–771.

1812. Kathlene, Lyn. "Uncovering the Political Impacts of Gender: An Exploratory Study." *Western Political Science Quarterly* 42, no. 2 (June 1989): 397–421.

1813. Kelly, Rita Mae, Mary Boutilier, and Vincent P. Kelly. "Types of Female Political Participation." In *The Making of Political Women, A Study of Socialization and Role Conflict,* edited by Rita Mae Kelly and Mary Boutilier, 85–170. Chicago: Nelson-Hall, 1978.

1814. Krause, Wilma R. "Political Implications of Gender Roles: A Review of the Literature." *American Political Science Review* 68 (December 1974): 1706–1723.

1815. Lipman-Blumen, Jean. "Role De-differentiation as a System Response to Crisis: Occupational and Political Roles of Women." *Sociological Inquiry* 43 (1973): 105–129.

1816. McDonagh, Eileen Lorenzi. "To Work or Not to Work: The Differential Impact of Achieved and Derived Status Upon the Political Participation of Women, 1956–1976." *American Journal of Political Science* 26, no. 2 (1982): 280–297.

1817. Powell, Lynda W., Clifford W. Brown, and Roman B. Hedges. "Male and Female Differences in Elite Political Participation: An Examination of the Effects of Socioeconomic and Familial Variables." *Western Political Quarterly* 34 (March 1981): 31–45.

1818. Sapiro, Virginia. *Women, Political Action and Political Participation.* Washington, DC: American Political Science Association, 1988.

1819. Welch, Susan. "Women as Political Animals? A Test of Some Explanations for Male-Female Political Participation Differences." *American Journal of Political Science* 21, no. 4 (November 1977): 711–730.

1820. Welch, Susan, and Philip E. Secret. "Sex, Race and Political Participation." *Western Political Quarterly* 34, no. 1 (March 1981): 5–16.

Political Women

1821. Addams, Jane. "Why I Went into Politics." *Ladies Home Journal* 30 (January 1913): 25.

1822. "American Woman: Why Can't She Be Politically Effective?" *Life* 21 (21 October 1946): 36.

1823. Barber, James David, and Barbara Kellerman, eds. *Women Leaders in American Politics.* Englewood Cliffs, NJ: Prentice Hall, 1986.

1824. Blair, Emily Newell. "Job of Being a Feminist, Small Town Style." *Outlook* 151 (24 April 1929): 643–646.

1825. Catt, Carrie Chapman. "The Protected Sex in Politics." *Harper's Weekly* 60 (8 May 1915): 433.

1826. ———. "A Tempest in a Teapot." *The Woman Citizen* 5 (5 February 1921): 950–951, 958–959.

1827. Chisholm, Shirley. "The 51% Majority." In *Black Women in White America,* edited by Gerda Lerner, 352–357. New York: Vintage, 1973.

1828. Clarke, Ida Clyde. *Uncle Sam Needs a Wife.* Philadelphia: The John C. Winston Company, 1925.

1829. Cortland, Ethel Wadsworth. "Kitchen Statesmen: What Is Mother's Destiny in Our Political Life?" *Outlook* 142 (17 March 1926): 21.

1830. Davis, Clare Ogden. "Politicians, Female." *North American Review* 1930, no. 229 (June 1930): 749–756.

1831. Friedan, Betty. "Up from the Kitchen Floor." *The New York Magazine* (4 March 1973): 8.

1832. Garland, Anne Witte. *Women Activists: Challenging the Abuse of Power.* New York: The Feminist Press at the City University of New York, 1988.

1833. Graham, Abbie. *Ladies in Revolt.* New York: The Woman's Press, 1934.

1834. Harris, Corra. "Practical Politics for Gentlewomen." *Ladies Home Journal* 38 (September 1921): 16, 155.

1835. "Have Women Political Power?" *The Republican Woman of Illinois* 8, no. 6 (January 1931): 5, 8.

1836. Holtzman, Elizabeth. "Women Lawyers in the Political Arena." *Women's Rights Law Reporter* 14 (Winter 1992): 1–7.

1837. Holtzman, Elizabeth, and Shirley Williams. "Women in the Political World: Observations." *Daedalus* 116 (Fall 1987): 25–34.

1838. Huffman, Deborah J. "Women in Educational Politics: An Oral History Study from 1987–1991 Culminating with Mary Hatwood Futrell." Ph.D. dissertation, Claremont Graduate School, 1992.

1839. "Is the Female Politician as Deadly as the Male? Reply to E. Green." *The New Republic* 43 (10 June 1925): 76.

1840. Janeway, Elizabeth. "Why Politics Must Begin at Home." *Redbook* 139 (October 1972): 103, 187, 189–190.

1841. Newell, Margaretta. "Must Women Fight in Politics?" *The Woman's Journal* 15 (January 1930): 10–11, 34–35.

1842. Nolan, W. A. "What Can Women Do? Opportunities for Assuming Political Roles." *Social Order* 3 (September 1953): 301–304.

1843. Parish, Audrey. "Political Role of Women in America." *Phi Delta Delta* 35, no. 2 (June 1957): 12.

1844. Richardson, Anna Steese. "Your Home Enters Politics." *Woman's Home Companion* 59 (March 1929): 34.

1845. Richardson, Eudora Ramsay. "A Suffragist Takes a Challenge." *Commonwealth* 5 (May 1938): 24–26.

1846. Robinson, Grace. "Cutting Sex Out of Politics." *Liberty Magazine* (31 March 1928): 23–29.

1847. Roosevelt, Eleanor. "Women in Politics, What Women Should Do." *Good Housekeeping* 110 (April 1940): 45, 201–203.

1848. Saure, Mrs. R. "Homemaker as a Citizen." *Home Economics* 39 (September 1947): 391–395.

1849. Smith, Margaret Chase. "Woman, the Key Individual of Our Democracy." *Vital Speeches* 19 (15 August 1953): 657–659.

1850. Sutherland, Rosamond. "The Appeal of Politics to Woman." *North American Review* 191 (January 1910): 82, 85.

1851. Weir, Ernest T. "Can You Afford to Stay Out of Politics?" *Independent Woman* 31 (February 1952): 33–34.

1852. White, William S. "Public Women." *Harper's Weekly* 220 (January 1960): 86–88.

New Women

1853. Collins, Frederick L. "The New Woman: What She Wanted and What She Got." *Woman's Home Companion* 56 (June 1929): 12, 70.

1854. Gilman, Charlotte Perkins. "The New Generation of Women." *Current History* 18 (August 1923): 731–736.

1855. Harriman, Mrs. J. Borden. "The New Woman in the New World." *Redbook* 49, no. 1 (May 1927): 48, 53, 102, 104, 106, 108.

1856. Hay, Mary Garrett. "Ideals of American Womanhood, the Political Women." *Harper's Weekly* 47 (6 June 1903): 933.

1857. Jordan, Elizabeth. "New Women Leaders in Politics." *Ladies Home Journal* 37 (December 1920): 6–7, 192–193.

1858. Kathlene, Lyn. "Studying the New Voice of Women in Politics." *Chronicle of Higher Education* 39 (18 November 1992): B1-B2.

1859. "The New Woman." *Time* 99 (20 March 1972): 25–103. Special issue.

1860. Scott, Anne Firor. "The 'New Woman' in the New South." *South Atlantic Quarterly* 65 (Autumn 1962): 471–483.

1861. Shreve, Anita, and John Clemans. "New Wave of Women Politicians." *The New York Times Magazine* (19 October 1980): 28–31, 106–110.

1862. Stuart, Mrs. Robert J. "New Political Power of Women." *Ladies Home Journal* 81 (September 1964): 68.

1863. Upton, Harriet Taylor "Woman's View of Practical Politics." *Woman's Home Companion* 48 (1 August 1921): 4.

Women of Color

African American

1864. Berry, Mary Frances. "Increasing Women's Influence in Government and Politics: The Inclusion of Women of Color." *Proteus* 3 (Fall 1986): 1–48.

1865. "Black Women First." *Ebony* 49, no. 5 (March 1994): 44–50.

1866. Clayton, Edward T. "The Woman in Politics." In *The Negro Politician: His Success and Failure,* 122–148. Chicago: Johnson Publishing Company, 1964.

1867. "Fifty Most Important Women in the Last Fifty Years." *Ebony* 50, no. 5 (March 1995): 107–121.

1868. Harper, Marieta L. "Black Women and the Development of Black Politics." *Journal of Afro-American Issues* 5, no. 3 (Summer 1977): 276–284.

1869. King, Mae C. "Oppression and Power: The Unique Status of the Black Woman in the American Political System." *Social Science Quarterly* 56 (June 1975): 116–128.

1870. "New Black Women's Network Strives to Channel Anger into Political Clout." *Black Issues in Higher Education* 12, no. 12 (August 1995): 10–15. National Network for African American Women and the Law.

1871. Prestage, Jewell. "Political Behavior of Black American Women: An Overview." In *Black Woman,* edited by La Frances Rodgers-Rose, 233–250. Beverly Hills, CA: Sage, 1980.

1872. Shaw, Esther Popel. "Challenge to Negro Womanhood." *The Women's Voice* 1, no. 9 (January 1940): 6–7, 18.

1873. "Women Helping Women." *National Business Woman* 43 (January 1964): 14.

Asian American

1874. Lott, Juanita Tamayo. "A Portrait of Asian and Pacific American Women." In *The American Woman 1990–91: A Status Report,* edited by Sara E. Rix and Anne J. Stone, 258–264. New York: Norton, 1990.

1875. Trask, Haunani-Kay. "Coalition Building between Natives and Non Natives, Hawaii." *Stanford Law Review* 43, no. 6 (July 1981): 1197–1213.

Latina American

1876. Bonilla-Santiago, Gloria. "A Portrait of Hispanic Women in the United States." In *The American Woman 1990–91: A Status Report,* edited by Sara E. Rix and Anne J. Stone, 249–257. New York: Norton, 1990.

1877. Chapa, Every, and Armando Guiterrez. "Chicanas in Politics: An Overview and a Case Study." In *Perspectivas en Chicano Studies, I,* edited by Reynaldo Flores Macias. Vol. 1. Los Angeles, CA: National Association of Chicano Social Scientists, 1974.

1878. Hondagneu-Sotelo, Pierrette. "New Perspectives on Latina Women." *Feminist Studies* 19 (Spring 1993): 193–207.

1879. MacManus, Susan A. "A Longitudinal Explanation of Political Participation Rates of Mexican American Females." *Social Science Quarterly* 67 (September 1986): 604–612.

1880. Pardo, Mary. "Mexican American Women Grassroots Community Activists: 'Mothers of East Los Angeles'." *Frontiers* 11, no. 1 (1990): 1–7.

1881. ———. "Doing It for the Kids: Mexican American Community Activists, Border Feminists?" In *Feminist Organizations: Harvest of the New Women's Movement,* edited by Myra Marx Ferree and Patricia Yancey Martin, 323–338. Philadelphia: Temple University Press, 1995.

1882. Saavedra-Vela, Pilar. "Hispanic Women in Double Jeopardy." *Agenda* 7 (1977): 4–7.

1883. Schechter, Hope Mendoza. *Activist in the Labor Movement, the Democratic Party, and the Mexican-American Community.* Berkeley: University of California, 1980. The Bancroft Library Oral History Interview.

1884. Whiteford, Linda. "Mexican American Women as Innovators." In *Twice a Minority: Mexican American Women,* edited by Margarita B. Melville, 109–126. St. Louis, MO: C.V. Mosby Company, 1980.

1885. Zambrana, Ruth E. "Latinas in the United States." In *American Woman, 1987–88,* edited by Sara E. Rix and Anne J. Stone, 262–266. New York: Norton, 1987.

Native American

1886. Allen, Paula Gunn. "Sky Woman and Her Sisters." *Ms.* 4 (September–October 1992): 22–26.

1887. Babcock, Barbara A. "At Home, No Women Are Storytellers: Potteries, Stories, and Politics in Cochiti Pueblo." *Journal of the Southwest* 30 (Autumn 1988): 256–389.

1888. Bermar, Amy. "Speaking for Endangered Species." *We Alaskans Magazine* (24 July 1983): 1–4.

1889. Deer, Ada, and R. E. Simon, Jr. *Speaking Out.* Chicago: Children's Press Open Door Books, 1970.

1890. Fanlund, Lari. "Indians in Wisconsin: A Conversation with Ada Deer." *Wisconsin Trails: The Magazine of Life in Wisconsin* 24 (March–April 1983): 8–21.

1891. Fiske, Jo-Anne. "Native Women in Reserve Politics: Strategies and Struggles." *Journal of Legal Pluralism and Unofficial Law Annual* 1991, no. 303–331 (1991): 121–137.

1892. Klein, Laura F. "Tlingit Women and Town Politics." Ph.D. dissertation, New York University, New York, 1975.

1893. Klein, Laura F., and Lillian A. Ackerman, eds. *Women and Power in Native North America.* Norman: University of Oklahoma Press, 1995.

1894. Knack, Martha C. "Contemporary Southern Paiute Women and the Measurement of Women's Economic and Political Status." *Ethnology* 28 (July 1989): 233–248.

1895. Koester, Susan H., and Emma Widmark. "'By the Words of the

Mouth Let Thee Be Judged': The Alaska Native Sisterhood Speaks." *Journal of the West* 27, no. 2 (April 1988): 35–44.

1896. Lynch, Rob N. "Women in Northern Paiute Politics." *Signs* 11, no. 2 (1986): 352–366.

1897. Mathes, Valerie Sherer. "Susan LaFlesche Picotte: Nebraska's Indian Physician, 1865–1915." *Nebraska History* 63 (Winter 1982): 502–530.

1898. Miller, Liselen M. "Native Women of Alaska." *Pacific Monthly* (February 1902).

1899. Morris, Terry. "LaDonna Harris: A Woman Who Gives a Damn." *Redbook* 140 (February 1970): 75, 115, 117–118.

1900. Paul, Sonya, and Robert Perkinson. "Winona LaDuke." *Progressive* 59 (October 1995): 36–39.

1901. Smith, Andy. "Beyond the Pow-Wow." *Off Our Backs* 19 (July 1989).

1902. "Special Issue on Native American Women." *Off Our Backs* 2 (February 1981).

1903. Thorpe, Dagmar. "Native Political Organizing in Nevada: A Woman's Perspective." *Native Self-Sufficiency* 6 (1981): 14–15.

Women in Washington

1904. Blair, Emily Newell. "Who's Who of Women in Washington." *Good Housekeeping* 102 (January 1936): 38–39, 166–168.

1905. Evans, Ernestine. "Women in the Washington Scene." *Century* 106 (August 1923): 507–517.

1906. Harriman, Mrs. J. Borden. "Women in Washington." *Forum* 72 (July 1924): 45–50.

1907. Hornaday, Mary. "Ladies Behind the Congress: Ladies of the Senate and the Congressional Club." *Christian Science Monitor Magazine* (11 May 1938): 6.

1908. Keyes, Frances Parkinson. "Seven Successful Women in Washington Political Life." *Delineator* 113 (July 1928): 16, 82, 84.

1909. Longworth, Alice Roosevelt. *Crowded Hours*. New York: Charles Scribner's Sons, 1933.

1910. Neuberger, Maurine. "Let's Stop the Ladies from Joining the Ladies." *McCalls* 88 (September 1961): 110–111, 166–167.

1911. Smith, Margaret Chase, and H. Paul Jeffers. *Gallant Women*. New York: McGraw-Hill, 1968.

1912. Wilson, Flora. "Women in National Politics." *Lippincott's Magazine* 98 (April 1915): 81–85.

Organizations

General

1913. Albrecht, Lisa, and Rose Brewer, eds. *Bridges of Power: Women's Multicultural Alliances*. Philadelphia: New Society Publishers, 1990.

1914. Arond, M. Iriam. "At the Center of the Storm: Jewish Women in Politics." *Lilith* 14, no. 4 (Fall 1989): 8–13.

1915. Beeman, Alice L., and Shirley McCune. "Changing Styles: Women's Groups in the Seventies." *American*

Association of University Women 64 (November 1970): 24–26.

1916. Bernays, Edward L. "A Challenge to Women's Clubs." *Delineator* 113 (November 1928): 14, 83–84.

1917. Boyd, Rosamonde Ramsay. "Women and Politics in the United States and Canada." *Annals of the American Academy of Political and Social Science* 375 (January 1968): 52–57.

1918. Cummings, Bernice, and Victoria Schuck, eds. *Women Organizing: An Anthology.* Metuchen, NJ: Scarecrow Press, 1979. Women in Politics Symposium, Adelphia University, 1975.

1919. Horvitz, Eleanor F. "The Jewish Woman Liberated: A History of the Ladies' Hebrew Free Loan Association." *Rhode Island Jewish Historical Notes* 7, no. 4 (1978): 501–512.

1920. Kleiman, Carol. "Political and Labor Networks." In *Women's Networks: The Complete Guide to Getting a Better Job, Advancing Your Career, and Feeling Great as a Woman through Networking,* 84–105. New York: Lippincott and Crowell, 1980.

1921. Knoke, David. "The Mobilization of Members in Women's Associations." In *Women, Politics and Change,* edited by Louise A. Tilly and Patricia Gurin, 383–410. New York: Sage, 1990.

1922. Mandel, Ruth. "Networks of Women in Politics." *Networks, National Identification Program for the Advancement of Women in Higher Education Administration* (Winter–Spring 1981–82). American Council on Education.

1923. Margolis, Diane Tothbard. *Women's Organizations in the Public Service: Toward Agenda Setting.* Washington, DC: U.S. Department of Housing and Urban Development, GPO, 1980. Vol. 2 of *Women in Public Service.* 3 vols. Prepared by Center for the American Woman and Politics. Report Number HUD-PDR-555-2.

1924. ———. "Bargaining, Negotiating and Their Social Contexts: The Case of Organizations of Women in the Public Service." In *Women and Politics: Activism, Attitudes, and Officeholding,* edited by Gwen Moore and Glenna Spitze, 267–281. Greenwich, CT: JAI Press, 1986.

1925. Minnis, Myra S. "Cleavage in Women's Organizations: A Reflection of the Social Structure of a City." *American Sociological Review* 18 (February 1953): 47–53.

1926. ———. "The Patterns of Women's Organizations: Significance, Types, Social Prestige Rank, and Activities." In *Community Structure and Analysis,* edited by Marvin B. Susman, 269–287. New York: Thomas Crowell, 1959.

1927. Pierce, Bessie Louise. "Political Pattern of Some Women's Organizations." *Annals of the American Academy of Political and Social Science* 179 (May 1935): 50–58.

1928. "The Work of Women's Organization." *Social Forces* 1 (November 1922): 50–55.

American Association of University Women

1929. Adams, Mildred. "The A. A. U. W.'s Personality." *The Woman Citizen* 9 (7 March 1925): 11–12, 24.

1930. Talbot, Marion, and Lois Kimball M. Rosenberry. *The History of the American Association of University Women, 1881–1931.* Boston: Houghton Mifflin, 1931.

1931. Tryon, Ruth W. *American Association of University Women: 1881–1949.* Washington, DC: American Association of University Women, 1950.

Business and Professional Women

1932. Allen, Charlotte. *A History of the National Federation of Business and Professional Women's Clubs, Inc.* New York: n.p., 1944.

1933. Banner, Winifred. "I'm Interested in Politics." *Independent Woman* 13 (July 1932): 234–244.

1934. Kenworthy, Jeane. "You in Politics." *National Business Woman* 39 (July 1960): 20, 28.

1935. McMullen, Frances Drewry. "Better Business Women in a Better Business World." *The Woman Citizen* 9 (21 March 1925): 13, 26, 27.

1936. National Federation of Business and Professional Women's Clubs. *A History of the National Federation of Business and Professional Women's Clubs, Inc., 1919–1944.* New York: National Federation of Business and Professional Women's Clubs, 1944.

1937. Rawalt, Marguerite. *A History of the National Federation of Business and Professional Women's Clubs, Inc., 1944–1960.* Washington, DC: National Federation of Business and Professional Women's Clubs, 1969.

League of Women Voters

1938. Black, Naomi. "The Politics of the League of Women Voters." *International Social Science Journal* 35, no. 4 (1983): 585–603.

1939. Bowen, Catherine Drinker. "Salute to Our Women Crusaders, Especially the League of Women Voters." *Smithsonian* 1 (July 1970): 24–27.

1940. Brumbaugh, Sara B. "Democratic Experience and Education in the League of Women Voters." Ph.D. dissertation, Columbia University, New York, 1946.

1941. Cain, Becky. "The League of Women Voters." *Social Education* 59, no. 5 (September 1995): 290–292.

1942. Clusen, Ruth. "The League of Women Voters and Political Power." In *Women Organizing: An Anthology,* edited by Bernice Cummings and Victoria Schuck, 112–132. Metuchen, NJ: Scarecrow Press, 1979.

1943. Decker, Warren D. "The League of Women Voters: Sponsorship, Promotion and Definition of Public Political Debate." Paper presented at the annual meeting of the Speech Communication Association, Anaheim, CA, 1981.

1944. Knapp, Betty, and Mary Ann Guyol. "Learning by Doing with the

LWV." *Journal of Social Issues* 16, no. 1 (1960): 57–65.

1945. Park, Maud Wood. *A Record of Four Years in the National League of Women Voters, 1920–1924.* Washington, DC: League of Women Voters, 1924.

1946. Perry, Elisabeth Israels. *Women in Action, Rebels and Reformers, 1920–1980.* Washington, DC: League of Women Voters Education Fund, 1995.

1947. Shanley, Robert A. "A Study of Pressure Politics in the Public Interest; The League of Women Voters." Ph.D. dissertation, Georgetown University, Washington, DC, 1955.

1948. *A Study of the League of Women Voters of the United States.* 5 vols. Ann Arbor: University of Michigan Institute for Social Research, Survey Research Center, 1956–1958.

1949. Watrous, Hilda R. *In League with Eleanor: Eleanor Roosevelt and the League of Women Voters, 1921–1962.* New York: Foundation for Citizen Education, 1984.

1950. Young, Louise M. *In the Public Interest: The League of Women Voters, 1920–1970.* New York: Greenwood, 1989.

National Council of Negro Women

1951. Collier-Thomas, Bettye. *National Council of Negro Women, 1935–1980.* Washington, DC: Bethune Musuem Archives, 1981.

1952. Fleming, Lethia C. "Bright Horizons Beckon." *The Women's Voice* 1, no. 1 (May 1939): 9, 21–23.

1953. Height, Dorothy. "Speech Delivered at the First African-American Summit." *Vital Issues* 2 (1992): 42–45.

1954. Mueller, Ruth Caston. "The National Council of Negro Women." *Negro History Bulletin* 18 (November 1954): 27–31.

Women's Clubs

1955. Blair, Karen J. *The Clubwoman as Feminist: True Womanhood Redefined, 1868–1914.* New York: Holmes and Meier Publishers, 1980.

1956. "Congress of American Women: Women's Club or Agent?" *Newsweek* 35 (16 January 1950): 21–22.

1957. Decker, Sarah S. Platt. "Meaning of the Woman's Club Movement." *Annals of the American Academy of Political and Social Science* 28, no. 2 (September 1906): 1–6.

1958. Granger, Mrs. A. O. "Effect of Club Work in the South." *Annals of the American Academy of Political and Social Science* 28, no. 2 (September 1906): 50–58.

1959. McCarthy, Kathleen D. *Lady Bountiful Revisited: Women, Philanthropy, and Power.* New Brunswick, NJ: Rutgers University, 1990.

1960. McCracken, Elizabeth. "The Women of America—Fifth Paper—The Woman in Her Club." *Outlook* 76 (13 February 1904): 419–426.

1961. Pierce, Grace Adele. "The Mother of Women's Clubs." *Pictorial Review* 11, no. 1 (October 1909): 42–43.

1962. Shephard, Mrs. Charles E. *History of the New England Conference State Federations of Women's Clubs, 1909–1970.* Warren, MA: New England Conference State Federations of Women's Clubs, 1971.

1963. Sherman, Mrs. John Dickinson. "Women's Clubs in the Middle-Western States." *Annals of the American Academy of Political and Social Science* 28, no. 2 (September 1906): 29–49.

1964. "Thirty-Five Years of Federation." *The Woman Citizen* 10 (30 May 1925): 8–9, 27–28.

1965. Ward, Mary Alden. "Influence of Women's Clubs in New England and in the Middle-Eastern States." *Annals of the American Academy of Political and Social Science* 28, no. 2 (September 1906): 7–28.

1966. Wells, Mildred White. *Unity in Diversity: The History of the General Federation of Women's Clubs.* Washington, DC: General Federation of Women's Clubs, 1953.

1967. Winslow, Helen M. "Club Women and Civics." *Delineator* 67 (February 1906): 374–375.

1968. ———. "The Modern Club Woman." *Delineator* 79 (April 1912): 136–137.

1969. ———. "The Modern Club Woman: How Women First Began to Organize." *Delineator* 80 (November 1912): 370–371.

1970. ———. "The Modern Club Woman: Our Clearing-House for Women's Clubs." *Delineator* 80 (September 1912): 178–193.

1971. ———. "The Modern Club Woman: The Story of Organized Womanhood." *Delineator* 80 (December 1912): 473.

1972. ———. "Where the Modern Club Woman Has 'Won Out'." *Delineator* 80 (October 1912): 262.

1973. ———. "Some Real Worth in Civics." *Delineator* 84 (April 1914): 46.

1974. Wood, Mary I. "Civic Activities of Women's Clubs." *Annals of the American Academy of Political and Social Science* 56 (November 1914): 78–87.

Women of Color, Women's Clubs

1975. Dickson, Lynda F. "Toward a Broader Angle of Vision Uncovering Women's History: Black Women's Clubs Revisited, 1920–1925." *Frontiers* 9, no. 2 (1987): 62–68. Reprinted in *Black Women in United States History,* Vol. 9, edited by Darlene Clark Hine, 103–120. Brooklyn, NY: Carlson, 1990.

1976. Easter, Opal V. "Burroughs: Club Woman and Political Activist." In *Nannie Helen Burroughs,* 97–114. New York: Garland, 1995.

1977. Giddings, Paula. *In Search of Sisterhood: Delta Sigma Theta and the Challenge of the Black Sorority Movement.* New York: William Morrow, 1988.

1978. Lerner, Gerda. "Early Community Work of Black Club Women." *Journal of Negro History* 59 (April 1974): 158–167.

1979. Parker, Marjorie. *Alpha Kappa Alpha: 1908–1958.* Washington, DC: Alpha Kappa Alpha, 1958.

1980. Scott, Anne Firor. "Most Invisible of All: Black Women's Voluntary Associations." *Journal of Southern History* 56 (February 1990): 3–22.

1981. Washington, Mrs. Booker T. "Club Work among Negro Women." In *Progress of a Race*, edited by J. L. Nichols and William H. Crogman, 177–209. Naperville, IL: J. L. Nichols, 1920.

Other Organizations

1982. Kocol, Cleo. "The Women of the CWA [Concerned Women of America]." *The Humanist* 49, no. 2 (March–April 1989): 33–35.

1983. LaGanke, Lucille Evelyn. "The National Society of the Daughters of the American Revolution: Its History, Politics, and Influences, 1890–1949." Ph.D. dissertation, Western Reserve University, 1951.

1984. McLaughlin, M. "Women Who Help Their Neighbors: National Congress of Neighborhood Women." *McCalls* 105 (May 1978): 51.

1985. Miller, Holly G. "Concerned Women for America: Soft Voices with Clout." *Saturday Evening Post* 257 (October 1985): 70–74.

1986. Rich, Winifred Lancashire. "The National Council of Jewish Women." *The Woman Citizen* 10 (11 July 1925): 13, 29.

1987. Strickland, Charles E. "Juliette Low, the Girl Scouts, and the Role of American Women." In *Woman's Being, Woman's Place: Female Identity and Vocation in American History*, edited by

Mary Kelley, 252–264. Boston: G. K. Hall, 1979.

Education

1988. Clifford, Geraldine J. "Lady Teachers and Politics in the United States of America, 1850–1930." In *Teacher: The Culture and Politics of Work*, edited by Martin Law and Gerald Grace, 3–30. Philadelphia: Taylor and Francis, 1987.

1989. Estler, Suzanne E. "Women as Leaders in Public Education." *Signs* 1 (Winter 1975): 336–356.

1990. "If the Women of America: Participation in Public Affairs." *National Education Association Journal* 33 (September 1944): 149.

1991. Lawrence, I. "Women Teachers in Politics." *Education Review* 76 (October 1928): 183–185.

1992. White, Bourk. "Getting After the School Board." *Country Life in America* 23 (April 1913): 60–61.

Training

1993. Garrette, Eve. *A Political Handbook for Women*. New York: Doubleday, 1944.

1994. Hackett, Catherine I. "Summer Politics." *The Woman's Journal* 13 (September 1928): 12–13, 44–45.

1995. Richardson, Anna Steese. "The Good Citizenship Bureau." *Woman's Home Companion* 49 (November 1922): 33–34.

1996. Robinson, Helen Ring. *Preparing Women for Citizenship.* New York: Macmillan Company, 1918.

1997. Winter, Alice Ames. "The Club Citizenship Program." *Ladies Home Journal* 38 (December 1921): 28, 125, 156.

Government

1998. Allen, Florence E. "Participation of Women in Government." *Annals of the American Academy of Political and Social Science* 251 (May 1947): 94–103.

1999. Blunt, Katharine. "How about Women? Their Part in Public Service." *American Association of University Women* 32, no. 1 (October 1938): 17–20.

2000. Grafton, Samuel. "Women in Politics: The Coming Breakthrough." *McCalls* 89 (September 1962): 102–103.

2001. Grinnell, Katherine. *Woman's Place in Government.* New York: Bickerdike and Winegard, 1917.

2002. Kelber, Miriam, ed. *Women and Government: New Ways to Political Power.* Westport, CT: Praeger, 1994. A Woman USA Fund study.

2003. Radin, Beryl A., ed. *Women in Public Life: Report of a Conference Co-Sponsored by the Lyndon Baines Johnson Library and the Lyndon B. Johnson School of Public Affairs.* Austin: Lyndon B. Johnson School of Public Affairs, 1976.

Rural and Urban

2004. Ackelsburg, Martha A. "Women's Collaborative Activities and City Life: Politics and Policy." In *Political Woman: Current Roles in State and Local Government,* edited by Janet A. Flammang, 242–259. Women's Policy Studies, 8. Beverly Hills, CA: Sage, 1984.

2005. Bennett, Helen Christine. *American Women in Civic Work.* New York: Dodd, Mead, 1915.

2006. Bokemeier, Janet L., and John L. Tait. "Women as Power Actors: A Comparative Study of Rural Communities." *Rural Sociology* 45, no. 2 (1980): 238–255.

2007. Cranz, Galen. "Women in Urban Parks." *Signs* 5, no. 3 (1980): 79–95. Supplement.

2008. Dabrowski, Irene. "Working-Class Women and Civic Action: A Case Study of an Innovative Community Role." *Policy Studies Journal* 11 (March 1983): 427–435.

2009. Fincher, Ruth, and Jacinta McQuillen. "Women in Urban Social Movements." *Urban Geography* 10, no. 6 (1989): 604–613.

2010. "Four Women Lead State Leagues of Municipalities." *American City* 70 (April 1955): 134.

2011. Friedberg, Mark. "Women Advocates in the Farm Crisis of the 1980's." *Agricultural History* 67, no. 2 (Spring 1993): 224–234.

2012. Furer, Howard B. "The American City: A Catalyst for the Women's Rights Movement." *Wisconsin Maga-*

zine of History 52, no. 4 (1969): 285–305.

2013. Gittell, Marilyn, and Teresa Shtob. "Changing Women's Roles in Political Volunteerism and Reform of the City." *Signs* 5, no. 3 (1980): 67–78. Supplement.

2014. Gottlieb, Agnes. "Women Journalists and the Municipal Housekeeping Movement." Ph.D. dissertation, University of Maryland, College Park, 1992.

2015. Hallowell, Ann. "Women on the Threshold: An Analysis of Rural Women in Local Politics, 1921–1941." *Rural Sociology* 52 (Winter 1987): 510–521.

2016. Harper, Ida Husted. "Woman's Broom in Municipal Housekeeping." *Delineator* 73 (February 1909): 213–216.

2017. Jellison, Katherine K. *Entitled to Power: Farm Women and Technology, 1913–1963*. Chapel Hill: University of North Carolina, 1993.

2018. Leavitt, Jacqueline. "Women Under Fire: Public Housing Activism in Los Angeles." *Frontiers* 13, no. 2 (1993): 109–126.

2019. Lee, Marcia Manning. "The Participation of Women in Suburban Politics: A Study of the Influence of Women as Compared to Men in Suburban Governmental Decision-Making." Ph.D. dissertation, Tufts University, Medford, MA, 1973.

2020. Marti, Donald B. *Women of the Grange: Mutuality and Sisterhood in Rural America, 1866–1920*. New York: Greenwood, 1991.

2021. Miller, Lorna Clancy, and Mary Neth. "Farm Women in the Political Arena." In *Women and Farming: Changing Roles, Changing Structures,* edited by Wava G. Haney and Jane B. Knowles, 357–381. Boulder, CO: Westview Press, 1988.

2022. Morgen, Sandra. "'Its the Whole Power of the City against Us!' The Development of Political Consciousness in a Woman's Health Care Coalition." In *Women and the Politics of Empowerment,* edited by Ann Bookman and Sandra Morgen, 97–115. Philadelphia: Temple University Press, 1988.

2023. Pratt, William C. "Women and the Farm Revolt of the 1930's." *Agricultural History* 67, no. 2 (Spring 1993): 214–234.

2024. Towne, Ruth Warner. "Marie Turner Harvey and the Rural Life Movement." *Missouri Historical Review* 84 (July 1990): 384–403.

2025. Winsor, Mary. "Practical Workings of Woman Suffrage in Colorado Municipalities." *Conference of City Government* (1910): 317–327.

2026. Woodruff, Clinton Rodgers. "Women and Civics." *National Municipal Review* 3, no. 4 (October 1914): 713–719.

Future

2027. Aburdene, Patricia, and John Naisbitt. *Megatrends for Women.* New York: Villard Books, 1992.

2028. East, Catherine. *American Women: 1963, 1983, 2003.* Washington, DC: National Federation of Business and Professional Women's Clubs, 1983.

2029. Evans, Judith. "The Good Society? Implications of a Greater Participation by Women in Public Life." *Political Studies* 32 (December 1984): 618–626.

2030. Flora, Cornelia Butler. "Working-Class Women's Political Participation: Its Potential in Developed Countries." In *A Portrait of Marginality: The Political Behavior of American Women,* edited by Marianne Githens and Jewell Prestage, 75–95. New York: McKay, 1977.

2031. Milk, Leslie. "2000, Here We Come." *Washingtonian* 29, no. 9 (June 1994): 12–13.

2032. Oberndorf, Meyera E. "The Changing Role of Women in the 21st Century." *Vital Speeches of the Day* 58, no. 24 (1 October 1992): 751–754.

2033. Rossi, Alice S. "Beyond the Gender Gap: Women's Bid for Political Power." *Social Science Quarterly* 64 (December 1983): 718–733.

In the States

Alabama

2034. Alexander, Adele Logan. "Adella Hunt Logan and the Tuskeegee Woman's Club, Building a Foundation for Suffrage." In *Stepping Out of the Shadows, Alabama Women 1819–1990,* edited by Mary Martha Thomas, 96–113. Tuscaloosa: University of Alabama, 1995.

2035. Craighead, Lura Harris. *History of the Alabama Federation of Women's Clubs, 1895–1917.* Vol. 1. Montgomery, AL: Paragon Press, 1936.

2036. Rieff, Lynne A. "'Go Ahead and Do All You Can': Southern Progressives and Alabama Home Demonstration Clubs, 1914–1940." In *Hidden Histories of Women in the New South,* edited by Virginia Bernhard, Elizabeth Fox-Genovese, and Theda Perdue, 134–152. Columbia: University of Missouri Press, 1994.

2037. Swenson, Mary E. "To Uplift a Nation: The Formative Years of the Alabama League of Women Voters, 1920–1921." *Alabama Historical Quarterly* 37 (Summer 1975): 115–135.

2038. Thomas, Mary Martha. *Stepping Out of the Shadow, 1819–1990.* Tuscaloosa: University of Alabama Press, 1995.

2039. Washington, Mrs. Booker T. "The Tuskegee Woman's Club." *The Southern Workman* (August 1920): 365–369.

2040. Wells, Mildred White. *History of the Alabama Federation of Women's Clubs, 1917–1968.* Vol. 2. Montgomery, AL: Paragon Press, 1968.

Arizona

2041. Aulette, Judy, and Trudy Mills. "Something Old, Something New, Auxiliary Work in the 1983–1986 Copper Strike." *Feminist Studies* 14, no. 2 (1988): 251–268.

2042. Campbell, Julie A. "Madres Y Esposas: Tucson's Spanish-American Mothers and Wives Association." *Jour-*

nal of Arizona History 31 (Summer 1990): 161–182.

Arkansas

2043. Evins, Janie Synatzke. "Arkansas Women: Their Contributions to Society, Politics, and Business, 1865–1900." *Arkansas Historical Quarterly* 44, no. 2 (1985): 118–133.

2044. Hanger, Frances Marion Harrow. *History of the Arkansas Federation of Womens' Clubs, 1897–1934.* Van Buren: Arkansas Federation of Womens' Clubs, 1935.

California

2045. Cox, Odessa. *Challenging the Status Quo: The Twenty–Seven Year Campaign for Southwest Junior College.* Berkeley: University of California, 1979. The Bancroft Library Oral History Interview.

2046. Crawford, Evelyn. "The Woman and the Club in California." *Overland Monthly and Out West Magazine* 53 (February 1909): 120–125.

2047. Davis, Reda. *California Women: A Guide to Their Politics, 1885–1911.* San Francisco: California Scene, 1968.

2048. Gardener, Helen H. "The First All-Woman Jury." *The Woman Citizen* 4 (7 February 1920): 810.

2049. Gerberding, Elizabeth. "Woman's Fight against Graft in San Francisco." *Delineator* 76 (October 1910): 245–246, 322–323.

2050. Gibson, Mary S. *A Record of Twenty–five Years of the California Federation of Women's Clubs, 1900–1925.* California Federation of Women's Clubs, 1927.

2051. Gullett, Gayle. "City Mothers, City Daughters, and the Dance Hall Girls: The Limits of Female Political Power in San Francisco, 1913." In *Women and the Structure of Society,* edited by Barbara J. Harris and Jo Ann McNamara, 145–159. Durham, NC: Duke University Press, 1984.

2052. ———. "Women Progressives and the Politics of Americanization in California, 1915–1920." *Pacific Historical Review* 64 (February 1995): 71–94.

2053. Katz, Sherry J. "Dual Commitments: Feminism, Socialism, and Women's Political Activism in California, 1890–1920." Ph.D. dissertation, University of California, Los Angeles, 1991.

2054. Madyun, Gail. "'In The Midst of Things': Rebecca Craft and the Women's Civic League." *Journal of San Diego History* 34, no. 1 (1988): 29–37.

2055. McLean, Hulda Hoover. *A Conservative's Crusades for Good Government.* Berkeley: University of California, 1977. The Bancroft Library Oral History Interview.

2056. Moore, Dorothea. "Work of the Women's Clubs in California." *Annals of the American Academy of Political and Social Science* 28, no. 2 (September 1906): 59–62.

2057. ———. "The Work of the Women's Clubs in California." *Annals of the American Academy of Political and Social Science* 28 (September 1909): 257–260.

2058. Rose, Margaret Eleanor. "Gender and Civic Activism in Mexican American Barrios in California, The Community Service Organization, 1947–1962." In *Not June Cleaver,* edited by Joanne Meyerowitz, 177–200. Philadelphia: Temple University Press, 1994.

2059. Wagner, Eleanor. *Independent Political Coalitions: Electoral Legislative, and Community.* Berkeley: University of California, 1977. The Bancroft Library Oral History Interview.

2060. Ward, Karen. "From Executive to Feminist: The Business Women's Legislative Council of Los Angeles, 1927–1932." *Essays in Economic and Business History* 7 (1989): 60–75.

2061. Younger, Mildred. *Indside and Outside Government and Politics, 1929–1980.* Berkeley: University of California, 1983. Interview by Malca Chall for the Bancroft Library Oral History Interview.

Colorado

2062. Dixon, Lynda. "The Early Club Movement among Black Women in Denver, 1890–1925." *Essays in Colorado History* 13 (1992). Condensed Ph.D. dissertation, University of Colorado, 1982.

2063. Lindsey, Benjamin B. "Voice of Colorado." *Harper's Weekly* 60 (8 May 1915): 450.

2064. Melville, Mildred McClellan. "Colorado's Pioneer Women, The Stories of 'First Women' Who Made a Path for Others." *American Association of University Women* 32, no. 2 (January 1939): 77–81.

2065. Meredith, Ellis. "Women's Political Work in Colorado." *The Woman's Journal* 31 (14 April 1900): 111–112.

2066. Smith, Eudochia Bell. "Women." In *Colorado and Its People,* edited by LeRoy Hafen, 557–570. 2 vols. New York: Lewis Historical Publishing Co., 1948.

2067. Stone, Wilbur Fisk. "What Suffrage Has Accomplished." Chap. 35 in *History of Colorado,* Vol. 1, edited by Wilbur Fisk Stone, 688–720. Chicago: S. J. Clarke Publishing, 1918.

2068. Vaile, Anna Wolcott, and Ellis Meredith. "Woman's Contribution." In *History of Colorado,* Vol. 3, 1927 ed., edited by LeRoy Hafen and James H. Baker, 1075–1147. Denver: Lewis Historical, 1927.

Connecticut

2069. Finley, Ruth E. "Laying Politics Bare." *Good Housekeeping* 73 (October 1921): 69, 101–105.

2070. Hirsche, Adelaide Morgan. *We've Come a Long Way: A History of the League of Women Voters of Connecticut, 1921–1953.* New Haven, CT: John J. Corbett, 1953.

2071. Nichols, Carole. *Votes and More for Women: Suffrage and After in Connecticut.* New York: Haworth Press, 1983.

2072. Nichols, Carole, and Joyce Pendery. "Pro Bono Publico: Voices of Connecticut's Political Women, 1915–1945." *Oral History Review* 11 (1983): 49–74.

2073. Ware, Susan. "Katharine Hepburn: Her Mother's Daughter." *History Today* 40 (April 1990): 47–53.

Delaware

2074. Downs, Dorothy Gardner. *101 Years of Volunteerism.* Smyrna: Delaware State Federation of Womens Clubs, 1990.

2075. Stanislow, Gail. "Domestic Feminism in Wilmington: The New Century Club, 1889–1917." *Delaware History* 22, no. 3 (1987): 158–185.

2076. Taggart, Robert J. "Etta J. Wilson, 1883–1970, a Delaware Reformer." *Delaware History* 24, no. 1 (1990): 33–52.

Florida

2077. Carver, Joan S. "First League of Women Voters in Florida: Its Troubled History." *Florida Historical Quarterly* 63 (April 1985): 406–422.

2078. Hewitt, Nancy A. "Varieties of Voluntarism: Class, Ethnicity, and Women's Activism in Tampa." In *Women, Politics and Change,* edited by Louise A. Tilly and Patricia Gurin, 63–86. New York: Russell Sage, 1990.

Georgia

2079. Felton, Rebecca Ann. *My Memoirs of Georgia Politics.* Atlanta: Index Printing Co., 1911.

2080. ———. *The Romantic Story of Georgia's Women.* Atlanta, GA: Atlanta Georgian and Sunday American, 1930.

2081. Muntz, Leonora Ferguson. "The Reading Club of 1906 Becomes the Women's Club of 1913." *Georgia Life* 4, no. 4 (1978): 44–45.

2082. Rouse, Jacqueline Anne. "The Legacy of Community Organizing, Lugenia Burns Hope and the Neighborhood Union." *Journal of Negro History* 69, no. 3–4 (1984): 114–133.

2083. Saxton, Martha. "The Best Girl Scout of Them All." *American Heritage* 33, no. 4 (June–July 1982): 38–47.

2084. Talmadge, John E. *Rebecca Latimer Felton: Nine Stormy Decades.* Athens: University of Georgia Press, 1960.

Hawaii

2085. Allen, Germfread. "Shaping the 49th State." *Independent Woman* 29 (October 1950): 305–306, 324.

2086. Chair, Alice Yun, and Ho'oipo M. DeCambra. "Evolution of Global Feminism through Hawaiian Feminist Politics: The Case of Wai'Anae Women's Support Group." *Women's Studies International Forum* 12, no. 1 (1989): 59–64.

2087. Watts, Margit Misangyi. *High Tea at Halekulani: Feminist Theory and American Clubwomen.* New York: Carlson, 1993.

Idaho

2088. French, Hiram T. "Women of Idaho, Equal Suffrage, the Columbian Club, Women's Clubs." In Vol. 1 of *History of Idaho,* edited by Hiram T. French, 515–545. Chicago: Lewis Pub. Co., 1914.

2089. Waite, Robert G. "The Woman's Club Movement in Idaho: A Document on the Early Years." *Idaho Yesterdays* 36, no. 2 (1993): 19–23.

Illinois

2090. Davis, Elizabeth Lindsay. *The Story of the Illinois Federation of Colored Women's Clubs.* Chicago: Illinois Federation of Colored Women's Clubs, 1922.

2091. Flanagan, Maureen A. "Gender and Urban Political Reform: The City Club and the Woman's City Club of Chicago in the Progressive Era." *American Historical Review* 95 (October 1990): 1032–1050.

2092. Getis, Victoria. "Doing the Work of Government: The Chicago Woman's Club and Progressive Reform." Paper, Social Science History Association, Baltimore, 1993.

2093. Leonard, Henry B. "Protective League of Chicago, 1908–1921." *Journal of Illinois State Historical Society* 66, no. 3 (1973): 271–284.

2094. Mason, Karen Malinda. "Testing the Boundaries: Women, Politics, and Gender Roles in Chicago, 1890–1930." Ph.D. dissertation, University of Michigan, 1991.

2095. Merriam, Charles Edward. "The Chicago Citizenship School." *Journal of Social Forces* 1, no. 5 (September 1923): 600–601.

2096. Munro, Petra. "Educators as Activists: Five Women from Chicago." *Social Education* 59, no. 5 (September 1995): 274–278.

2097. Robertson, Mary Helen. "Constitutional Revision in Illinois: The League of Women Voters Role." *National Civic Review* 60 (September 1971): 438–443.

Indiana

2098. Cornell, E. T. "Women Run the Rascals Out of Gary." *American Magazine of Civics* 149 (May 1950): 36–37.

2099. Ferguson, Earline Rae. "The Woman's Improvement Club of Indianapolis: Black Women Pioneers in Tuberculosis Work, 1903–1938." *Indiana Magazine of History* 84, no. 3 (September 1988): 237–261. Reprinted, in *Black Women in United States History*, Vol. 5, edited by Darlene Clark Hine, 339–364. Brooklyn, NY: Carlson, 1990.

2100. Hine, Darlene Clark, ed. *When the Truth Is Told: A History of Black Women's Culture and Community in Indiana, 1875–1950.* Indianapolis: National Council of Negro Women, 1981.

2101. Hoover, Dwight W. "Daisy Douglas Barr: From Quaker to Klan 'Kluckeress'." *Indiana Magazine of History* 87 (June 1991): 171–195.

2102. Springer, Barbara Anne. "Ladylike Reformers: Indiana Women and Progressive Reformers 1900–1920." Ph.D. dissertation, Indiana University, 1958.

2103. Stetson, Erlene. "Black Feminism in Indiana, 1893–1930." *Phylon* 44, no. 4 (December 1983): 292–298. Reprinted in *Black Women in United States History*, Vol. 4, edited by Darlene Clark Hine, 139–146. Brooklyn, NY: Carlson, 1990.

Iowa

2104. Noun, Louise R. *More Strong-Minded Women*. Ames: Iowa State University Press, 1992.

2105. Swaim, Ginalie. "Cora Bussey Hillis: Woman of Vision." *Palimpsest* 60, no. 6 (1979): 162–177.

2106. Taylor, Leslie A. "Femininity as Strategy: A Gendered Perspective on the Farmer's Holiday." *Annals of Iowa* 67, no. 2 (Spring 1992): 252–277.

Kansas

2107. Brady, Marilyn Dell. "Kansas Federation of Colored Women's Clubs, 1900–1930." *Kansas History* 9, no. 1 (Spring 1986): 19–30. Reprinted in *Black Women in United States History*, Vol. 5, edited by Darlene Clark Hine, 95–120. Brooklyn, NY: Carlson, 1990

2108. Schofield, Ann. "The Women's March: Miners, Family, and Community in Pittsburg, Kansas, 1921–22." *Kansas History* 7, no. 2 (1984): 159–168.

2109. Underwood, June. "Civilizing Kansas: Women's Organizations, 1880–1920." *Kansas History* 7 (Winter 1984): 291–306.

Kentucky

2110. Forderhase, Nancy K. "'The Clear Call of Thoroughbred Women': The Kentucky Federation of Women's Clubs and the Crusade for Educational Reform 1903–1909." *The Register of the Kentucky Historical Society* 83, no. 1 (1985): 19–35.

2111. Hay, Melba Porter. "The Lexington Civic League: Agent of Reform, 1900–1910." *Filson Club Historical Quarterly* 62, no. 3 (1988): 336–355.

2112. Maggard, Sally Ward. "Women's Participation in the Brookside Coal Strike: Militance, Class and Gender in Appalachia." *Frontiers* 9, no. 3 (1987): 16–21.

Louisiana

2113. Kemp, Kathryn W. "Jean and Kate Gordon: New Orleans Social Reformers, 1898–1933." *Louisiana History* 24 (1983): 389–401.

2114. Wernet, Mary Linn. "Louisiana Federation of Women's Clubs' Conservation Chairman Lee Craig Ragan Levy and the Multiple Conservation Concerns during the 1960s." *North Louisiana Historical Association Journal* 18, no. 2–3 (1987): 71–81.

Maine

2115. Derost, Lilliam Mills, and Grace E. Fitz. *A History of the Federation of Business and Professional Women's Clubs of Maine*. Federation of Business and Professional Women's Clubs of Maine, 1944.

2116. Klein, Elsa. *The Story of the State Maine Division of AAUW in Its First Five Years*. Maine: American Association of University Women, 1952.

2117. Oliver, Velma K. *A History, State of Maine Division of AAUW, 1946–*

1974. American Association of University Women, 1974.

2118. Porter, Georgia Pulsifer. *Maine Federation of Women's Clubs: Historical Sketches, 1892–1924.* Lewiston, ME: Lewiston Journal Printshop, 1925.

Maryland

2119. Cohen, Jane Whitehouse. "Women's Political Power in Maryland, 1920–1964." Ph.D. dissertation, Catholic University of America, Washington, DC, 1993.

Massachusetts

2120. Bomeisler, E. "Women's Work for Women: The Boston Women's Educational and Industrial Union." *New England Medicine* 48 (October 1912): 367–371.

2121. Deutsch, Sarah. "Learning to Talk More Like a Man: Boston Women's Class-Bridging Organizations, 1870–1940." *American Historical Review* (April 1992): 379–404.

2122. Farley, Ena L. "Caring and Sharing Since World War I: The League of Women for Community Services: A Black Volunteer Organization in Boston." *Umoja* 1, no. 2 (1977): 1–12.

2123. Hardy-Fanta, Carol. *Latina Politics: Gender, Culture and Political Participation in Boston.* Philadelphia: Temple University Press, 1993.

2124. Kaufman, Polly Adams Welts. *Boston Women and City School Politics, 1872–1905.* New York: Garland, 1995.

2125. Massachusetts State Federation of Women's Clubs. *Progress and Achievement: A History of the Massachusetts State Federation of Women's Clubs, 1893–1962.* Lexington: Massachusetts State Federation of Women's Clubs, 1962.

2126. Merk, Lois Bannister. "Boston's Historic Public School Crisis." *The New England Quarterly* 31 (1958): 172–199.

2127. Norwood, Stephen H. "From 'White Slave' to Labor Activist: The Agony and Triumph of a Boston Brahmin Woman in the 1910's." *The New England Quarterly* 65 (March 1992): 61–92.

2128. Worrell, Dorothy. *The Woman's Municipal League of Boston: 1908–1943.* Boston: self, 1943.

Michigan

2129. Brown, Alan S. "Caroline Bartlett Crane and Urban Reform." *Michigan History* 56, no. 4 (1972): 287–301.

2130. Fryer, Sarah Beebee. "Fitzgerald's New Women: Harbingers of Change, 1919–1940." Ph.D. dissertation, Michigan State University, 1988.

2131. Marti, Donald B. "Woman's Work in the Grange: Mary Ann Mayo of Michigan, 1882–1903." *Agricultural History* 56, no. 2 (1982): 439–452.

Minnesota

2132. Borchardt, Lena. "The Militant Mothers of Rutabaga County." In *The People Together,* edited by Meridel LeSueur, 17–19. Minneapolis: People's Centennial Book Committee of Minnesota, 1958.

2133. Koch, Raymond L. "Politics and Relief in Minneapolis during the 1930's." *Minnesota History,* no. 41 (1968): 153–170.

Mississippi

2134. Candler, Martha. "Women Scour the Town." *The Woman's Journal* 14 (February 1929): 12–14.

2135. Prince, Vinton M. "Women, Politics, and the Press: The Mississippi Woman Voter." *Southern Studies* 19, no. 4 (1980): 365–372.

2136. Swain, Martha H. "Politics and Public Affairs: Twentieth Century Mississippi Women Activists." *Journal of Mississippi History* 53, no. 3 (1991): 175–183.

Missouri

2137. Carlson, Mrs. Harry. "The First Decade of the St. Louis League of Women Voters." *Missouri Bulletin* (October 1969).

2138. Davidson, Clarissa Start. "Women's Role in Missouri History, 1821–1971." *Missouri Official Manual* 1971–1972 (1972): 20–32.

2139. Toombs, Elizabeth O. "Missouri Shows Us." *Good Housekeeping* 70 (June 1920): 46, 92, 95–97.

Nebraska

2140. Donovan, Ruth Godfrey. "The Nebraska League of Women Voters." *Nebraska History* 52 (Fall 1971): 311–328.

New Hampshire

2141. Harriman, Alice Stratton. *A History of the New Hampshire Federation of Women's Clubs, 1895–1940.* Bristol, NH: Musgrove Printing House, 1941.

2142. Shuler, Marjorie. "Citizenship Schools." *The Woman Citizen* 4 (August 1919): 310, 314.

New Jersey

2143. Gordon, Felice Dosik. *After Winning: The Legacy of the New Jersey Suffragists, 1920–1947.* New Brunswick, NJ: Rutgers University Press, 1986.

New Mexico

2144. Gonzales, Phillip B. "Spanish Heritage and Ethnic Protest in New Mexico: The Anti-Fraternity Bill of 1933." *New Mexico Historical Review* 61, no. 4 (October 1986): 281–300.

2145. Jensen, Joan M. "The Campaign for Women's Community Property Rights in New Mexico, 1940–1960." In *New Mexico Women: Intercultural Perspectives,* edited by Joan M. Jensen and Darlis A. Miller, 333–356. Albuquerque: University of New Mexico Press, 1986.

2146. ———. "'I've Worked, I'm Not Afraid of Work': Farm Women in New Mexico, 1920–1940." *New Mexico Historical Review* 61, no. 1 (January 1986): 27–52.

New York

2147. Baker, Paula. *The Moral Frameworks of Public Life: Gender, Politics and* *the State in Rural New York, 1870–1930.* New York: Oxford, 1991.

2148. Brightman, Carol. "The Women of Williamsburg." *Working Papers for a New Society* 6, no. 1 (1978): 50–57.

2149. Cook, Blanche Wiesen. *Eleanor Roosevelt.* Vol. 1, 1884–1933. New York: Viking, 1992.

2150. Fitzgerald, Maureen. "Irish-Catholic Nuns and the Development of New York City's Welfare System, 1840–1900." Ph.D. dissertation, University of Wisconsin, Madison, 1992.

2151. Lape, Esther Everett. "Teaching the Woman Voter Politics." *Forum* 64 (September 1920): 198–208.

2152. Perry, Elisabeth Israels. "Training for Public Life: ER and Women's Political Networks in the 1920s." In *Without Precedent: The Life and Career of Eleanor Roosevelt,* edited by Joan Hoff-Wilson and Marjorie Lightman, 28–45. Bloomington: Indiana University Press, 1984.

2153. ———. *Belle Moskowitz: Feminine Politics and the Exercise of Power in the Age of Alfred E. Smith.* New York: Oxford University Press, 1987.

2154. ———. "Women Political Choices after Suffrage: The Women's City Club of New York, 1915–1990." *New York History* 62, no. 4 (October 1990): 417–434.

2155. Rosenthal, Naomi. "Social Movement and Network Analysis: A Case Study of Nineteenth Century Women's Reform in New York State, 1840–1914." *American Journal of Sociology* 90, no. 5 (1985): 1022–1054.

2156. Williams, Lillian S. "And Still I Rise: Black Women and Reform, Buffalo, New York, 1900–1940." *Afro-Americans in New York Life and History* 14, no. 2 (1990): 7–33. Reprinted in '*We Specialize in the Wholly Impossible*', *A Reader in Black Women's History,* Darlene Clark Hine, Wilma King, and Linda Reed, eds., 521–542. Brooklyn, NY: Carlson, 1995.

North Carolina

2157. Cotton, Sallie Southall. *History of North Carolina Federation of Woman's Clubs 1901–1925.* Raleigh: Edwards and Broughton Printing Co., 1925.

2158. Leloudis, James L. "School Reform in the New South: The Women's Association for the Betterment of Public School Houses in North Carolina, 1902–1919." *Journal of American History* 69, no. 4 (1983): 886–909.

2159. Nasstrom, Kathryn L. "'More Was Expected of Us': North Carolina League of Women Voters and the Feminist Movement in the 1920s." *North Carolina Historical Review* 68, no. 3 (1991): 307–319.

2160. Wilkerson-Freeman, Sarah. "From Clubs to Parties: North Carolina Women in the Advancement of the New Deal." *North Carolina Historical Review* 68, no. 3 (July 1991).

Ohio

2161. Kornbluh, Andrea Tuttle. *Lighting the Way … The Woman's City Club of Cincinnati 1915–1965.* Cincinnati, OH: Young and Klein, 1986.

2162. Laws, Annie. *History of Ohio Federation of Women's Clubs, 1894–1924.* Cincinnati, OH: Ebbert and Richardson, 1924.

Oklahoma

2163. Allen, Susan L. "Progressive Spirit: The Oklahoma and Indian Territory Federation of Women's Clubs." *Chronicles of Oklahoma* 66, no. 1 (1988): 4–21.

2164. Hoder-Salmon, Marilyn. "Myrtle Archer McDougal: Leader of Oklahoma's 'Timid Sisters'." *Chronicles of Oklahoma* 60, no. 3 (1982): 332–343.

Oregon

2165. Krieger, Nancy. "Queen of the Bolsheviks: The Hidden History of Dr. Marie Equi." *Radical America* 17, no. 5 (1983): 55–73.

Pennsylvania

2166. Pinchot, Gifford. "The Influence of Women in Politics." *Ladies Home Journal* 39 (September 1922): 13.

South Dakota

2167. Alexander, Ruth Ann. "South Dakota Women Stake a Claim: A Feminist Memoir, 1964–1989." *South Dakota History* 19, no. 4 (1989): 538–555.

2168. "The First Ladies of South Dakota." *South Dakota History* 3, no. 2 (1973): 156–168.

Tennessee

2169. Wedell, Marhsha M. "Memphis Women and Social Reform, 1875–1919." Ph.D. dissertation, Memphis State University, 1988.

Texas

2170. Cunningham, Mary S. *The Woman's Club of El Paso.* El Paso: Texas Western Press, 1978.

2171. Cunningham, Minnie Fisher. "Too Gallant a Walk." *The Woman's Journal* 14 (January 1929): 12–13.

2172. Enstam, Elizabeth York. "They Called It 'Motherhood': Dallas Women and Public Life, 1895–1918." In *Hidden Histories of Women in the New South,* edited by Virginia Bernhard, Elizabeth Fox-Genovese, and Theda Perdue, 71–95. Columbia: University of Missouri Press, 1994.

2173. Gammage, Judie K. "Pressure Group Techniques: The Texas Equal Rights Amendment." *Great Plains Journal* 16, no. 1 (Fall 1976): 45–65.

2174. ———. "Quest for Equality: An Historical Overview of Women's Rights Activism in Texas 1890–1973." Ph.D. dissertation, North Texas State University, Denton, 1983.

2175. Hill, Patricia Evridge. "Women's Groups and the Extension of City Services in Early Twentieth-Century Dallas." *East Texas Historical Journal* 30, no. 1 (1992): 3–10.

2176. Jackson, Emma L. Mayer. "Petticoat Politics: Political Activism among Texas Women in the 1920s." Ph.D. dissertation, University of Texas, Austin, 1980.

2177. McArthur, Judith N. "Motherhood and Reform in the New South: Texas Women's Political Culture in the Progressive Era." Ph.D. dissertation, University of Texas, Austin, 1992.

2178. McCallum, Jane Y. "Activities of Women in Texas Politics, 1937." In *Citizens at Last: The Woman Suffrage Movement in Texas*, edited by Elizabeth A. Taylor, 221–230. Austin, TX: Ellen C. Temple, 1987. Reprinted from *Texas Democracy: A Centennial History of Politics and Personalities of the Democratic Party 1836–1936*, Vol. 1, Frank Adams, ed. Austin: Democratic Historical Association, 1937.

2179. Romero, Yolanda Garcia. "From Rebels to Immigrants to Chicanas: Hispanic Women in Lubbock County." Master's thesis, Texas Tech University, Lubbock, 1986.

2180. Seaholm, Megan. "Earnest Women: The White Woman's Club Movement in Progressive Era Texas, 1880–1920." Ph.D. dissertation, Rice University, Houston, 1988.

2181. Turner, Elizabeth Hayes. "Women's Culture and Community: Religion and Reform in Galveston, 1880–1920." Ph.D. dissertation, Rice University, 1991.

Utah

2182. Bentley, Amy L. "Confronting the Motherless Children: The Alice Louise Reynolds Women's Forum." *Dialogue* 23, no. 3 (1990): 39–61.

2183. Carroll, Lavon B. "Melba Judge Lehner and the Child Care in the State of Utah." *Utah Historical Quarterly* 61 (Winter 1993): 40–62.

2184. Howard, Mary W. "An Example of Women in Politics." *Utah Historical Quarterly* 38 (Winter 1970): 61–64.

2185. Madsen, Carol Cornwall. "'At Their Peril': Utah Law and the Case of Plural Wives, 1850–1900." *Western Historical Quarterly* 21, no. 4 (1990): 425–443.

2186. Thatcher, Linda. "'I Care Nothing for Politics': Ruth May Fox, Forgotten Suffragist." *Utah Historical Quarterly* 49, no. 3 (Summer 1981): 239–253.

2187. Winter, Alice Ames. "The Salt Lake City Council." *Good Housekeeping* 73 (September 1921): 73, 114–117.

Vermont

2188. Ashton, Mrs. Oliver C. "Vermont Federation of Women's Clubs." *Vermonter* 15 (May 1910): 137–142.

2189. ———. "The Vermont Federation of Women's Clubs." *Vermonter* 20 (March–April 1915): 38–43.

2190. Clark, Susan E. "History of the Vermont Federation of Women's Clubs." *Vermonter* 10 (March 1905): 245–246.

2191. Clifford, Deborah P. "The Women's War against Rum." *Vermont History* 52, no. 3 (1984): 141–160.

2192. Davis, Gertrude S. "Vermont Federation of Women's Clubs." *Vermonter* 7 (December 1901): 413–417.

2193. Moore, Madeline. "Vermont Women's Town Meeting." In *History* of Women in Vermont, edited by Constance Kite, Elizabeth Dow, and Lenore McNeer. Montpelier: Governor's Commission on the Status of Women, n.d.

Virginia

2194. Allen, Charlotte. *A Record of Twenty–five Years: An Interpretation, Virginia Federation of Business and Professional Women, 1919–1944.* Richmond: n.p., 1946.

2195. Brown, Elsa Barkley. "Womanist Consciousness: Maggie Lena Walker and the Independent Order of Saint Luke." *Signs* 14, no. 3 (Spring 1989): 610–615, 630–633.

2196. Taylor, Lloyd C., Jr. "Lila Meade Valentine: The FFV as Reformer." *Virginia Magazine of History and Biography* 70 (October 1962): 471–487.

Washington

2197. Poppy, John. "Politics on the Split-Level Frontier: Jocelyn Marchisio from Seattle." *Look* 31 (16 May 1967): 94, 96, 98.

2198. Watkins, Marilyn P. "Political Culture and Gender in Rural Community Life: Agrarian Activism in Lewis County, Washington, 1890–1925." Ph.D. dissertation, University of Michigan, 1991.

2199. ———. "Political Activism and Community-Building among Alliance and Range Women in Western Washington, 1892–1925." *Agricultural History* 67, no. 2 (Spring 1993): 197–213.

West Virginia

2200. Howe, Barbara J. "West Virginia Women's Organizations, 1880s-1930 or 'Unsexed Termagants ... Help the World Along'." *West Virginia History* 49 (1990): 81–102.

Wisconsin

2201. Dombeck, J. M. "The Women's Coalition of Milwaukee, 1972–1987: Feminist Activism at the Local Level." Master's thesis, University of Wisconsin, Milwaukee, 1987.

2202. Hochstein, Irma. *A Progressive Primer.* Madison: Wisconsin Women's Progressive Association, 1922.

2203. Laberge, Marie Anne. "'Seeking a Place to Stand': Political Power and Activism among Wisconsin Women, 1945–1963." Ph.D. dissertation, University of Wisconsin, Madison, 1995.

In the Territories and District

District of Columbia

2204. Harley, Sharon. "Beyond the Classroom: Organizational Lives of Black Female Educators in the District of Columbia, 1890–1930." *Journal of Negro Education* 51, no. 3 (1982): 254–265. Reprinted in *Black Women in United States History,* Vol. 5, edited by Darlene Clark Hine, 487–506. Brooklyn, NY: Carlson, 1990.

2205. Trigg, Eula S. "Washington, D.C. Chapter—Links, Incorporated: Friendship and Service." In *Black*

Women in United States History, Vol. 4, edited by Darlene Clark Hine, 1177–1186. Brookyn NY: Carlson, 1990.

Puerto Rico

2206. Azize-Vargas, Yamila. "At the Crossroads: Colonialism and Feminism in Puerto Rico." In *Women and Politics World Wide*, edited by Barbara J. Nelson and Najma Chowdhury, 625–638. New Haven, CT: Yale University Press, 1994.

2207. Carr, Irene Campos. "Proyecto La Mujer: Latina Women Shaping Consciousness." *Women's Studies International Forum* 12, no. 1 (1989): 45–49.

Voting

General

2208. Bailey, Robert W. "Sexual Identity in Bi-Racial Coalitions: The Lesbian and Gay Vote in the 1993 New York and Los Angeles Mayoral Elections." Paper presented at the annual meeting of the American Political Science Association, Chicago, 1995.

2209. Baxter, Sandra. *Women and Politics: The Invisible Majority*. Ann Arbor: University of Michigan Press, 1980.

2210. Baxter, Sandra, and Marjorie Lansing. *Women and Politics: The Visible Majority*. 2d ed. Ann Arbor: University of Michigan Press, 1983.

2211. Campbell, Angus, Philip E. Converse, Warren E. Miller, and Donald E. Stokes. "Sex." In *The American Voter*, 483–493. New York: Wiley, 1960.

2212. Evans, Judith. "Women and Politics: A Re-Appraisal, Voting Behavior and Political Orientation, United States and Great Britain." *Political Studies* 28 (June 1980): 210–221.

2213. Falvey, Major Catherine E. "The Voting Privilege at Home and Abroad." *Democratic Digest* 23, no. 9 (September 1946): 13, 17.

2214. "Fooling the Women in Politics." *Ladies Home Journal* 40 (September 1923): 29, 159–160.

2215. Goot, Murray, and Elizabeth Reid. *Women and Voting Studies: Mindless Matrons or Sexist Scientism*. Beverly Hills, CA: Sage, 1975.

2216. Gosnell, Harold Foote. "Women Go to the Polls." Chap. 4 in *Democracy: The Threshold of Freedom*, 50–77. New York: Ronald Press, 1948.

2217. "How the Other Half Votes." *The Nation* (18 May 1992): 254–260.

2218. Kent, Frank R. "Effect of Women on Machine Strength." Chap. 27 in *The Great Game of Politics*, edited by Frank R. Kent, 168–173. New York: Doubleday, 1923.

2219. Lansing, Marjorie. "The American Woman: Voter and Activist." In *Woman and Politics*, edited by Jane S. Jaquette, 5–24. New York: Wiley, 1974.

2220. League of Women Voters Education Fund. *The Women's Vote: Beyond the Nineteenth Amendment*. Washington, DC: League of Women Voters Education Fund, 1983.

2221. Mandel, Ruth. "The Power of the Women's Vote." *Working Woman* 8 (April 1983): 107–111.

2222. Matlak, Carol. "Women at the Polls." *National Journal* 19 (December 1987): 3208–3215.

2223. Stucker, John J. "Women as Voters: Their Maturation as Political Persons in American Society." In *Women in Politics,* edited by Marianne Githens and Jewell Prestage, 264–283. New York: McKay, 1977.

2224. Vinovskis, Maris A. "Abortion and the Presidential Election of 1976: A Multivariate Analysis of Voting Behavior." In *The Law and Politics of Abortion,* edited by Carl E. Schneider and Maris A. Vinovskis, 184–205. Lexington, MA: D. C. Heath, 1980.

Gender Gap

2225. Abzug, Bella S., and Miriam Kelber. *The Gender Gap: Bella Abzug's Guide to Political Power for American Women.* Boston: Houghton Mifflin, 1984.

2226. Barnes, James A. "Why the Gender Pitch Has Its Limits." *National Journal* 27, no. 13 (April 1995): 827.

2227. Bolce, Louis. "The Role of Gender in Recent Presidential Elections: Reagan and the Reverse Gender Gap." *Presidential Studies Quarterly* 15 (Spring 1985): 372–385.

2228. Borquez, Julio, Edie N. Goldenberg, and Kim Fridkin Kahn.

"Press Portrayals of the Gender Gap." In *The Politics of the Gender Gap: The Social Construction of Political Influence,* edited by Carol M. Mueller, 124–148. Women's Policy Studies, 12. Beverly Hills, CA: Sage, 1988.

2229. Brown, Courtney. *Ballots of Tumult: A Portrait of Volatility in American Voting.* Ann Arbor: University of Michigan Press, 1991.

2230. Brown, Kirk. *The Gender Gap: Differences Between Men and Women in Political Attitudes and Voting Behavior.* Washington, DC: Congressional Research Service, 1983. Report No. 83–633 GOV.

2231. Carroll, Susan J. "Women's Autonomy and the Gender Gap: 1980 and 1982." In *The Politics of the Gender Gap: The Social Construction of Political Influence,* edited by Carol M. Mueller, 158–236. Women's Policy Studies, 12. Beverly Hills, CA: Sage, 1988.

2232. Clark, Janet M., and Cal Clark. "The Gender Gap in 1988: Compassion, Pacifism, and Indirect Feminism." In *Women in Politics: Outsiders or Insiders? A Collection of Readings,* edited by Lois Lovelace Duke, 32–45. Englewood Cliffs, NJ: Prentice Hall, 1993.

2233. Conover, Pamela Johnston. "Feminism and the Gender Gap." *Journal of Politics* 50, no. 4 (November 1988): 985–1010.

2234. Cook, Elizabeth Adell, and Clyde Wilcox. "Feminism and the Gender Gap: A Second Look." *Journal of Politics* 53 (August 1991): 1111–1122.

2235. Cook, Rhodes. "Democratic Clout Is Growing as the Gender Gap Widens." *Congressional Quarterly Weekly Report* 50 (17 October 1992): 3265–3268.

2236. Cox, Elizabeth M., Carol Tucker Foreman, Nikki Heidepriem, and Celinda C. Lake. *The Women's Vote Analysis.* Washington, DC: Women's Voices, 1986.

2237. Dunham, Richard S. "Can the GOP Bridge the Gender Gap?" *Business Week* (19 December 1994): 105–108.

2238. Engel, Margaret. "What Is the Republican Party Doing About the Gender Gap?" *Glamour* 81 (August 1983): 150, 155.

2239. Evans, M. Stanton. "The Gender Gap Revisited." *National Review* 40, no. 18 (16 September 1988): 41, 60.

2240. Farah, Barbara G., and Ethel Klein. "The Return of the Gender Gap." *Polling Report* 4, no. 12 (1988): 1.

2241. ———. "Public Opinion Trends." In *The Election of 1988: Reports and Interpretations,* edited by Gerald Pomper, 103–126. Chatham, NJ: Chatham House, 1989.

2242. Fishman, Joelle. "'Gender Gap': A Big Hurdle for Reaganism." *Political Affairs* 63 (April 1984): 2–8.

2243. Fitzpatrick, Kellyanne. "Gender Gap Politics, the Republican Warning." *Campaigns and Elections* 16, no. 10 (October–November 1995): 24–25, 59.

2244. Frankovic, Kathleen A. "Sex and Politics: New Alignments, Old Issues." *PS* 15, no. 3 (1982): 439–448.

2245. "The Gap Grows." *National Business Woman* 64 (February–March 1983): 32–34.

2246. Garland, Susan B. "Clinton Has Woman Problem, No Its Not What You Think." *Business Week* (1 May 1995): 49.

2247. "The Gender Gap at the State Level." *Public Perspective* 4 (January–February 1993): 100–101.

2248. Gilens, Martin. "Gender and Support for Reagan: A Comprehensive Model of Presidential Approval." *American Journal of Political Science* 32 (1988): 19–49.

2249. Hamick, Joann, and Tony Quinn. "Why the GOP Worries about Bridging the Gender Gap." *California Journal* 14 (July 1983): 251–253.

2250. Heidepriem, Nikki, and Celinda C. Lake. "The Winning Edge." *Polling Report* (6 April 1987): 1.

2251. Katzenstein, Mary Fainsod. "Feminism and the Meaning of the Vote." *Signs* 10, no. 1 (Autumn 1984): 4–26.

2252. Kenski, Henry C. "The Gender Factor in a Changing Electorate." In *The Politics of the Gender Gap: The Social Construction of Political Influence,* edited by Carol M. Mueller, 38–60. Women's Policy Studies, 12. Beverly Hill, CA: Sage, 1988.

2253. Klein, Ethel. "The Gender Gap: Different Issues, Different Answers." *The Brookings Review* 3 (Winter 1985): 33–37.

2254. ———. *Gender Politics 1988, Earning the Woman's Vote.* Washington, DC: National Business and Professional Women, 1988.

2255. Lake, Celinda C. "Guns, Butter and Equality: The Women's Vote in 1980." Paper presented at the annual meeting of the Midwest Political Science Association, Milwaukee, 1982.

2256. ———. "Gender Gap Politics: The Democratic Puzzle." *Campaigns and Elections* 16, no. 10 (October–November 1995): 22–23, 69.

2257. Lake, Celinda C., and Nikki Heidepriem. "Whatever Happened to the Gender Gap?" *Campaigns and Elections* 8 (March–April 1988): 37–40.

2258. Mann, Judy. "The Gender Gap from the Reagan Camp." In *Women Leaders in American Politics,* edited by James David Barber and Barbara Kellerman, 350–352. Englewood Cliffs, NJ: Prentice Hall, 1986.

2259. Mansbridge, Jane. "Myth and Reality: The ERA and the Gender Gap in the 1980 Elections." *Public Opinion Quarterly* 49 (1985): 164–178.

2260. Miller, Arthur H. "Gender and the Vote: 1984." In *The Politics of the Gender Gap: The Social Construction of Political Influence,* edited by Carol M. Mueller, 258–282. Women's Policy Studies, 12. Beverly Hills, CA: Sage, 1988.

2261. Miller, Arthur H., and Oksana Malanchuk. "The Gender Gap in the 1982 Elections." Paper presented at the annual meeting of the American Association for Public Opinion Research, 1983.

2262. Monk-Turner, Elizabeth. "Sex and Voting Behavior in the United States of America." *Journal of Social, Political and Economic Studies* 7, no. 4 (1982): 369–376.

2263. Mueller, Carol M., ed. *The Politics of the Gender Gap: The Social Construction of Political Influence.* Beverly Hills, CA: Sage, 1988.

2264. ———. "The Gender Gap and Women's Political Influence." *Annals of the American Academy of Political and Social Science* 515 (May 1991): 23–37.

2265. Norris, Pippa. "The Gender Gap: A Cross-National Trend?" In *The Politics of the Gender Gap: The Social Construction of Political Influence,* edited by Carol M. Mueller, 236–257. Women's Policy Studies, 12. Beverly Hills, CA: Sage, 1988.

2266. "Opinion Roundup: Women and Men, Is a Realignment Under Way?" *Public Opinion* 5, no. 2 (April–May 1982): 21–40.

2267. "A Power at the Polls." *National Business Woman* 69, no. 3 (June–July 1988): 14–22.

2268. Rapoport, Ronald B. "The Sex Gap in Political Persuading: Where the Restructuring Principle Works." *American Journal of Political Science* 25, no. 1 (1981): 32–48.

2269. Rapoport, Ronald B., Walter J. Stone, and Alan I. Abramowitz. "Sex and the Caucus Participant: The Gender Gap and Presidential Nominations." *American Journal of Political Science* 34 (August 1990): 725–740.

2270. Reese, Michael. "Women in Politics: The Gender Gap." *Newsweek*

100, no. 1 November (1982): 26–27, 29–30.

2271. Rice, Stuart D., and Malcolm M. Willey. "A Sex Cleavage in the Presidential Election of 1920." *Journal of the American Statistical Association* 19 (1924): 519–520.

2272. Salinas, Charles Edward. "Gender, Identity, and Voting: The Relationship of Group Membership to Political Behavior." Ph.D. dissertation, University of California, Riverside, 1993.

2273. Sigelman, Lee, and Carol K. Sigelman. "Sexism, Racism, and Ageism in Voting Behavior." *Social Psychological Quarterly* 45, no. 4 (1982): 263–269.

2274. Simpson, Peggy. "What Happened in '84, Did Women Make a Difference?" *Working Woman* 10 (February 1985): 52, 54, 58.

2275. Wirls, Daniel. "Reinterpreting the Gender Gap." *Public Opinion Quarterly* 50 (1986): 316–330.

Women of Color

2276. Lansing, Marjorie. "The Voting Patterns of American Black Women." In *A Portrait of Marginality: The Political Behavior of American Women,* edited by Marianne Githens and Jewell Prestage, 379–394. New York: McKay, 1977.

2277. Logan, Adella Hunt. "Colored Women as Voters." *The Crisis* 4 (September 1912): 242–248. A Woman's Suffrage symposium.

2278. Pickens, William. "The Woman Voter Hits the Color Line." *The Nation* 3 (6 October 1920): 372–373.

2279. Secret, Phillip E., and Susan Welch. "Sex, Race, and Participation: An Analysis of the 1980 and 1984 Elections." *Women and Politics* 9, no. 4 (1989): 57–67.

2280. Welch, Susan, and Lee Sigelman. "A Gender Gap among Hispanics: A Comparison with Blacks and Anglos." *Western Political Quarterly* 45 (1992): 181–199.

Mobilization

2281. Andrews, Lulah T. "Let's Get Out the Vote." *Independent Woman* 13 (September 1932): 223, 240.

2282. Bass, Marie, and Joanne Howes. "Getting Out the Women's Vote." In *The Women's Economic Justice Agenda,* edited by Linda Tarr-Whelan and Lynne Crofton Isensee, 219–222. Washington, DC: National Center for Policy Alternatives, 1987.

2283. Dadourian, Ruth McIntire. "Why Get Out the Vote ?" *The Woman Citizen* 12 (September 1927): 16–17, 41.

2284. Douglas, Helen Gahagan, and Clare Boothe Luce. "Why a Get-Out-The-Vote Campaign." *Independent Woman* 23 (October 1944): 298, 328.

2285. Gidlow, Liette P. "Getting Out the Vote: Gender and Citizenship in the 1920s." Paper presented at the annual meeting of the Western Association of Women Historians, San Marino, CA, 22 May 1994.

2286. Henry, Sherrye. "Why Women Don't Vote for Women (and Why They Should)." *Working Woman* 19 (June 1994): 48–51.

2287. Lewis, Ann F. "A Woman's Place: at the Polls." *Ms.* 16, no. 10 (April 1988): 80.

2288. Mayo, Edith P. "Campaign Appeals to Women." *Journal of American Culture* 3 (Winter 1980): 722–742.

2289. Mead, Margaret. "It's Up to Women to Elect a Good President." *Redbook* 146 (March 1976): 38, 40, 43–44.

2290. Mendelson, Johanna S. R. "The Ballot Box Revolution: The Drive to Register Women." In *The Politics of the Gender Gap: The Social Construction of Political Influence,* edited by Carol M. Mueller, 61–80. Women's Policy Studies, 12. Beverly Hills, CA: Sage, 1988.

2291. Mueller, Carol M. "The Empowerment of Women: Polling and the Women's Voting Bloc." In *The Politics of the Gender Gap: The Social Construction of Political Influence,* edited by Carol M. Mueller, 16–36. Women's Policy Studies, 12. Beverly Hills, CA: Sage, 1988.

2292. Nicholes, S. Grace. "First Aid to New Voters: The Experience of Illinois Made Available for New York Women." *The Survey* 39 (8 December 1917): 275–279.

2293. Smeal, Eleanor. *How and Why Women Will Elect the Next President.* New York: Harper and Row, 1984.

2294. Smith, Susan J. *It's a Man's World Unless Women Vote: Report on Women's Vote Project.* Washington, DC:

The Women's Vote Project, 1984. Joanne Howes, ed.

2295. Stedman, Adelaide. "Peroxide Vote." *Colliers* 66 (28 August 1920): 22–26.

2296. "Use Your Vote in '48." *Independent Woman* 27 (October 1948): 303–304.

2297. Warner, Carolyn. "Coming Together to Make a Difference." *Vital Speeches of the Day* 60 (1 September 1994): 698–701.

2298. Wilson, Louisa. "The Women's Vote Was News in 1944." *Democratic Digest* 21–22, no. 12–1 (December 1944–January 1945): 15, 20–21.

2299. Witt, Evans. "What Republicans Have Learned about Women." *Public Opinion Quarterly* 8 (October-November 1985): 49–52.

2300. Woliver, Laura K. "Feminism at the Grassroots: The Recall of Judge Archio Simonson." *Frontiers* 11, no. 2–3 (1990): 111–119.

2301. Woods, Harriet. "Women May Decide the Presidency in '96, Here's Why." *Working Woman* 20, no. 5 (1995): 26.

Non-Voters

2302. "Are Women Tired of Voting ?" *Colliers* 69 (27 May 1922): 11–12.

2303. Areneson, George E. "Non-Voting in a Typical Ohio Community." *American Political Science Review* 19 (1925): 816–825.

2304. Butler, Sarah Schuyler. "Women Who Do Not Vote." *Scribner's*

Magazine 76 (November 1924): 529–533.

2305. Coolidge, Mary Roberts. "Why They Don't Vote." *The Woman Citizen* 7 (18 November 1922): 16–17.

2306. Daggett, Mabel Potter. "Wanted: Women Voters to Vote." *Good Housekeeping* 79 (July 1924): 40–41, 83–87.

2307. Kent, Frank R. "Women's Faults in Politics." *The Woman Citizen* 11 (March 1927): 23, 46–48.

2308. Lewis, Ann F. "Republican No-Shows at the Ballot Box." *Ms.* 3, no. 6 (1992): 88–89.

2309. Merriam, Charles Edward, and Harold Foote Gosnell. "Disbelief in Woman's Voting." Chap. 5 in *Non-Voting: Causes and Methods of Control,* edited by Charles Edward Merriam and Harold Foote Gosnell, 28–32, 109–122. Chicago: University of Chicago Press, 1924.

2310. Richardson, Anna Steese. "Lost, 14, 000, 000 Women Voters!" *Woman's Home Companion* 55 (October 1928): 43.

2311. Schlesinger, Arthur M., and Eric McKinley Eriksson. "The Vanishing Voter." *The New Republic* 60 (15 October 1924): 162–167.

2312. Shuler, Marjorie "Where Are the Women Voters ?" *Review of Reviews* 69 (1924): 419–422.

2313. Sloan, Elizabeth. "The Story We Didn't Print, Women Who Don't Vote." *McCalls* 114 (November 1986): 12.

2314. Winter, Alice Ames. "To Vote or Not to Vote." *Ladies Home Journal* 41 (October 1924): 21, 155, 157.

Women Voting for Women Candidates

2315. Adams, Mildred. "What the Women's Vote Has Not Done." *The New York Times Magazine* (20 August 1950): VI, 18, 52.

2316. Anthony, Susan B., II. "We Women Throw Away Our Vote." *Saturday Evening Post* 221 (17 July 1948): 23, 119–120.

2317. Arnstein, Walter I. "Votes for Women: Myths and Reality." *History Today* 18 (August 1968): 531–539.

2318. Blair, Emily Newell. "Give Women Time." *The Woman Citizen* 9 (14 June 1924): 16.

2319. Crispell, Diane. "Will Women Vote for Women?" *Working Mother* 17 (October 1992): 21.

2320. "Do Women Vote for Women?" *Public Perspective* 3 (July–August 1992): 98–99.

2321. Gove, Gladys F. "How We Used Our Vote in 1948." *Independent Woman* 27 (March 1948): 89–90.

2322. ———. "How We Used Our Vote in 1948: Women Elected or Appointed to National, State, Town and County Office." *Independent Woman* 28 (March 1949): 89–90.

2323. Richardson, Anna Steese. "Voting for Women." *Woman's Home Companion* 62, no. 6 (June 1935): 33–34.

2324. Smith, Margaret Chase. "No Place for a Woman." *Ladies Home Journal* 68 (February 1952): 50, 83.

2325. Smith, Tom W. "When Do Women Vote for Women?" *Public Perspective* 3 (September–October 1992): 30–31.

2326. Todd, Jane H., and Mrs. Henry Goddard Leach. "How Will You Vote This November?" *Independent Woman* 19 (September 1940): 288–289, 306.

2327. "Votes for Women!" *Life* 49 (15 August 1960): 30.

2328. Williams, Charl Ormond. "Votes for Women." *Independent Woman* 16 (January 1937): 15, 21–23.

2329. "Womanpower at the Polls." *Newsweek* 84 (23 September 1974): 39.

2330. Zipp, John F., and Eric Plutzer. "Gender Differences in Voting for Female Candidates: Evidence from the 1982 Election." *Public Opinion Quarterly* 49 (Summer 1985): 179–197.

Women Voters

Before National Suffrage, 1900–1920

2331. Ackerman, Jessie. *What Women Have Done with the Vote.* New York: W. B. Feakins, 1913.

2332. "Aged Suffrage Victors Cast Their Maiden Votes." *Literary Digest* 58 (13 July 1918): 44–48.

2333. Blackwell, Alice Stone. "Women and the School Vote." *The Woman's Journal* 39 (25 January 1908).

2334. Chomel, Marie Cecile. "Does the Wife Vote Like the Husband?" *Ladies Home Journal* 36 (May 1919): 92.

2335. Creel, George. "What Have Women Done with the Vote?" *Century* 87, no. 5 (March 1914): 663–671.

2336. "Do They Vote Where They Can?" *The Woman Citizen* 2 (1 September 1917): 256.

2337. Edson, Mrs. Charles Farwell (Katherine Phillips). "Actual Operation of Woman's Suffrage in Pacific Coast Cities." *National Municipal Review* 1 (October 1912): 620–629.

2338. Harper, Ida Husted. "Woman Suffrage in Six States." *The Independent* 71 (2 November 1911): 969.

2339. Howells, William Dean. "Civic Equality for Women." *Harper's* 118 (May 1909): 965–968.

2340. Meredith, Ellis. "What It Means to Be an Enfranchised Woman." *Atlantic Monthly* 102 (August 1908): 196–202.

2341. ———. "Do Women Vote?" *National Municipal Review* 3, no. 4 (October 1914): 663–671.

2342. Moore, Elsie Wallace. "The Suffrage Question in the Far West." *Arena* 41 (July 1910): 414–424.

2343. Pugh, Martin D. "Politicians and the Women's Vote, 1914–1918." *History Today* 59 (October 1974): 358–374.

2344. Raine, William MacLeod. "Truth about Women Suffrage." *The Circle* (October 1907): 220.

2345. Stewart, J. A. "Reports from Suffrage States." *Journal of Education* 82 (16 September 1915): 244.

2346. "Success of Woman Suffrage." *The Independent* 73 (8 August 1912): 334–335.

2347. "Votes by Women: A Poll of Survey Subscribers in Equal Franchise States." *The Survey* 35 (23 October 1915): 83–87, 95–96.

2348. "When the Woman Lawyer Votes." *The Woman Citizen* 2 (19 January 1918): 150–151, 157.

2349. "Woman Suffrage in Operation: Symposium." *The Independent* 66 (20 May 1909): 1056–1070.

2350. "Woman Suffrage in the West." *Outlook* 65 (23 June 1900): 430–431.

2351. "The Women's Great Vote." *The Woman's Journal* 31 (17 November 1900): 361.

1920–1943

2352. Andersen, Kristi. "Women and Citizenship in the 1920s." In *Women, Politics and Change,* edited by Louise A. Tilly and Patricia Gurin, 177–198. New York: Russell Sage, 1990.

2353. Barnard, Eunice Fuller. "The Woman Voter Gains Power." *The New York Times Magazine* (12 August 1928): IV, 1–3, 20.

2354. Breckinridge, Sophonisba P. "Women as Voters." Chap. 15 in *Women in the Twentieth Century: A Study of Their Political, Social and Economic Activities,* 245–256. New York: McGraw-Hill, 1933.

2355. Brown, Gertrude Foster. "Are Women Voters Making Good?" *The Woman Citizen* 11, no. 3 (August 1926): 5–7.

2356. Catt, Carrie Chapman. "Woman Suffrage: Only an Episode in an Age-Old Movement." *Current History* 27 (October 1927): 1–6.

2357. Colton, Olive A. "Adventures of a Woman Voter." *The Survey* 60 (1 September 1928): 533–536, 561–565.

2358. Craig, Elisabeth May. "Politics Bloom in the Spring ... !" *Independent Woman* 19 (May 1940): 143, 152.

2359. "Eye Woman Vote." *The Republican Woman of Illinois* 6, no. 3 (October 1928): 6.

2360. Gerould, Katherine F. "Some American Women and the Vote." *Scribner's Magazine* 77 (May 1925): 449–452.

2361. Hornaday, Mary. "A Majority Vote by Women." *Independent Woman* 23 (September 1944): 266–267.

2362. "How Will America's Women Vote?" *Woman's Home Companion* 71 (April 1944): 19.

2363. Kent, Frank R. "How the Machine Handles the Woman Vote." Chap. 26 in *The Great Game of Politics,* edited by Frank R. Kent, 163–167. New York: Doubleday, 1923.

2364. ———. "Don't Worry About the Women." Chap. 25 in *Political Behavior: The Heretofore Unwritten Laws, Customs and Principles of Politics as Practiced in the United States,* edited by Frank Kent, 281–293. New York: William Morrow, 1928.

2365. Lewis, Elizabeth Langhorne. "Woman Voter and Third Party." *Forum* 69 (February 1923): 1247–1251.

2366. Lichtman, Allan J. "Blacks versus Whites and Men versus Women." Chap. 7 in *Prejudice and the Old Politics: The Presidential Election of 1928,* edited by Allan J. Lichtman. Chapel Hill: University of North Carolina Press, 1979.

2367. Low, A. Maurice. "Women in the Election of 1920." *Yale Review* 10 (January 1921): 311–322.

2368. Martin, Anne. "Woman's Vote and Woman's Chains." *Sunset* 48 (April 1922): 12–14.

2369. McLaughlin, Kathleen. "What Women Have Done with the Vote." *The New York Times Magazine* (24 November 1940): VII, 5, 21.

2370. Michelet, Simon. *American Women at the Ballot.* Washington, DC: National Get-Out-The-Vote Club, 1924.

2371. Moyer-Wing, Alice C. "The Vote: Our First Comeback." *Scribner's Magazine* 84 (September 1928): 259–264.

2372. "Much-Surprised City Officials Ousted by Women." *Literary Digest* 67 (4 December 1920): 52–54.

2373. Patterson, Eleanor. "When Women Get Together at the Polls." *Good Housekeeping* 103 (September 1936): 30–31, 155–159.

2374. Rice, Stuart D. "American Women's Ineffective Use of the Vote." *Current California History* 20 (July 1924): 641–647.

2375. Roosevelt, Eleanor. "Women in Politics, What Women Have Done with the Vote." *Good Housekeeping* 110 (March 1940): 45, 48.

2376. Rusk, Jerrold G., and John J. Stucker. "Legal-Institutional Factors and Voting Participation: The Impact of Women's Suffrage on Voter Turnout." In *Political Participation and American Democracy,* edited by William J. Crotly, 113–138. New York: Greenwood, 1991.

2377. Silva, Ruth C. *Rum, Religion, and Votes: 1928 Re-Examined.* University Park: Pennsylvania State University Press, 1962.

2378. Smith, Helena H. "Weighing the Women's Vote." *Outlook* 151 (23 January 1929): 126–129.

2379. "Women's Bloc?" *The Nation* 109 (3 September 1924): 230–233.

2380. Young, Louise M. "Why Do Women Vote the Way They Do?" *Woman's Home Companion* 83 (November 1956): 46–47.

1944–1964

2381. Bennett, Edward M., and Harriet M. Goodwin. "Emotional Aspects of Political Behavior: The Woman Voter." *Genetic Psychology Monographs* 58 (1958): 3–53.

2382. Brown, Nona B. "Women's Vote: The Bigger Half?" *The New York Times Magazine* (21 October 1956): VI, 23, 63–67.

2383. Cole, Margaret. "The Women's Vote: What Has It Achieved?" *Political Quarterly* 33 (January–February–March 1962): 74–83.

2384. Daley, R. J. "The Woman Voter." *Reviewing Stand* (29 June 1952): 1–11.

2385. Eliasberg, Ann Pringle. "How Will Women Vote in November?" *Woman's Home Companion* 81 (August 1954): 9, 115–116.

2386. French, Eleanor Clark. "Key Political Force—The Ladies." *The New York Times Magazine* (11 March 1956): VI, 14, 32, 34.

2387. Harris, Louis. "Newsweek Poll: The Women's Vote." *Newsweek* 64 (21 September 1964): 32.

2388. Hastings, Phillip K. "Hows and Howevers of the Woman Voter." *The New York Times Magazine* (12 June 1960): VI, 14, 80–81.

2389. Kruschke, Earl R. *The Woman Voter: An Analysis Based upon Personal Interviews.* Washington, DC: Public Affairs Press, 1955.

2390. Nelson, Alice D. "First Ladies of the Ballot Box." *American Mercury* 90 (March 1960): 57–58.

2391. "Polls, Propaganda, and Politics: Women in the Election." *The Nation* 159 (26 August 1944): 234.

2392. Priest, Ivy Baker. "Ladies Elected Ike." *American Mercury* 76 (February 1953): 23–28.

2393. Sanders, Marion K. *The Lady and the Vote.* Cambridge: Houghton Mifflin, 1956.

2394. Shalett, Sidney. "Is There a Women's Vote?" *Saturday Evening Post* 233 (17 September 1960): 31, 78–80.

2395. Stanford, Neal. "The Woman's Vote." *Christian Science Monitor Magazine* (16 November 1964): C1.

2396. Thornburgh, Margaret. "Women and Elections." *American Federationist* 62 (March 1955): 16–18.

2397. "Will Women Decide the Election?" *U.S. News and World Report* 48 (7 June 1960): 61–65.

2398. "Women's Vote: How Will It Go?" *McCalls* 91 (March 1964): 70, 72.

1965–1995

2399. Bendyna, Mary E., and Celinda C. Lake. "Gender and Voting in the 1992 Presidential Election." In *The Year of the Woman: Myths and Realities,* edited by Elizabeth Adell Cook, Sue Thomas, and Clyde Wilcox, 237–254. Boulder, CO: Westview Press, 1994.

2400. Costello, Mary. "Women Voters." *Congressional Quarterly Weekly Report* (11 October 1972): 767–784.

2401. "How Women Vote." *Ladies Home Journal* 105 (July 1988): 38.

2402. Kleppner, Paul. "Were Women to Blame? Female Suffrage and Voter Turnout." *Journal of Interdisciplinary History* 12, no. 4 (Spring 1982): 621–643.

2403. Lake, Celinda C. "How Women Voters Will Elect the Next President." *Ms.* 16, no. 10 (April 1988): 76–78.

2404. Peter, Molly Broughton. "Which Presidential Candidate Is the One for You ?" *Glamour* 78 (November 1980): 226.

2405. Sapiro, Virginia. "'You Can Lead a Lady to Vote, but What Will She Do with It? The Problem of a Woman's Bloc Vote." In *Interest Group*

Politics, edited by Allan J. Cigler and Burdett A. Loomis, 221–237. Washington, DC: CQ Press, 1983.

2406. Setlow, Carolyn, and Gloria Steinem. "Why Women Voted for Richard Nixon." *Ms.* 1, no. 9 (March 1973): 66.

2407. Sorenson, Theodore C. "Special Report on the Woman Voter." *Redbook* 130 (April 1968): 61.

2408. Steinem, Gloria. "Exclusive Louis Harris Survey: How Women Live, Vote, Think." *Ms.* 13, no. 1 (13 July 1984): 51–54.

2409. Thomas, Mary. "Elections: Southern Women Hold the Key." *Ms.* 16, no. 8 (February 1988): 22.

2410. "Vote-Getting Makeovers." *Ladies Home Journal* 105 (July 1988): 124–129.

2411. "The Votes Are In, Iowa and New Hampshire Broken Down by Gender." *Ms.* 16, no. 10 (April 1988): 74.

2412. "Will Women Decide the Outcome of the 1984 Election?" *U.S. News and World Report* 95 (12 December 1983): 58–60.

Nations and Tribes

2413. Miller, Bruce G. "Women and Tribal Politics: Is There a Gender Gap in Indian Elections?" *American Indian Quarterly* 18, no. 1 (Winter 1994): 25–41.

In the States

Arizona

2414. Berman, David R. "Gender and Issue Voting: The Policy Effects of Suffrage Expansion in Arizona, 1914–1916." *Social Science Quarterly* 74, no. 4 (1993): 838–850.

Arkansas

2415. "Flanking Drive for Suffrage: Women Vote in Primaries in Arkansas and Texas." *Literary Digest* 57 (11 May 1918): 14.

California

2416. Coolidge, Mary Roberts. "Political Drama in San Francisco." *Harper's Weekly* 61 (27 November 1915): 524.

2417. ———. *What the Women of California Have Done with the Ballot.* San Francisco: League to Enforce Peace, 1916.

2418. "How California Women Voters Made Good." *Review of Reviews* 47 (May 1913): 608–610.

2419. Knaft, James P. "The Fall of Job Harriman's Socialist Party: Violence, Gender and Politics in Los Angeles, 1911." *Southern California Quarterly* 70, no. 1 (1988): 43–68.

2420. Marquis, Neeta. "Woman and the California Primaries." *The Independent* 72 (13 June 1912): 1316–1318.

2421. Paizis, Suzanne. "Frustrated Majority: Consciousness-Raising at the Ballot Box." *California Journal* (March 1974): 80–83.

2422. Smith, Jean M. "The Voting Women of San Diego, 1920." *The Journal of San Diego History* 26, no. 2 (Spring 1980): 133–154.

2423. "Women-Folks Out to Run California." *Literary Digest* 83 (13 December 1924): 53–54.

Colorado

2424. Bradford, Mary C. C. *Equal Suffrage in Colorado from 1908 to 1912.* Denver: Colorado Equal Suffrage Association, 1912.

2425. Creel, George, and Benjamin B. Lindsey. "Measuring Up Equal Suffrage in Colorado." *Delineator* 77 (February 1911): 85–86, 151–152.

2426. Dorr, Rheta Childe. "Women Did It in Colorado." *Hampton* (April 1911): 426–438.

2427. McCracken, Elizabeth. "Woman Suffrage in Colorado." *Outlook* 75 (28 November 1903): 737–744.

2428. Raine, William Macleod. "Woman Suffrage in Colorado." *Chautauquan* 34 (February 1902): 482–484.

2429. Rossignol, J. E. "Colorado: Woman's Suffrage and Municipal Politics." *Annals of the American Academy of Political and Social Science* 18 (November 1901): 552–556.

2430. Sheldon, Lurena. "Bad Woman's Vote." *Overland* 61, no. 2 (February 1913): 165–169.

2431. Slocum, Mary G. "Women in Colorado Under the Suffrage." *Outlook* 75 (26 December 1903): 997–1000.

2432. Sumner, Helen L. *Equal Suffrage: The Results of an Investigation in Colorado.* New York: Harper and Bros., 1909. National report, Collegiate Equal Suffrage League of New York State.

2433. "Woman Suffrage in Colorado Is a Failure ?" *Ladies Home Journal* 28 (1 April 1911): 6.

Idaho

2434. Steunenberg, Frank. "Woman Suffrage in Idaho." *Harper's Bazaar* 33 (26 May 1900): 220–221.

2435. Tyer, Pearl. "Idaho's Twenty Years of Woman Suffrage." *Outlook* 114 (6 September 1916): 33–39.

Illinois

2436. Abbott, Edith. "Are Women a Force for Good Government? An Analysis of the Returns in the Recent Municipal Elections in Chicago." *National Municipal Review* 14, no. 3 (July 1915): 437–448.

2437. ———. "The Woman Voter and the Spoils System in Chicago." *National Municipal Review* 5, no. 3 (July 1916): 460–465.

2438. Buell, Katherine. "How Women Vote." *Harper's Weekly* 58 (25 April 1914): 20–23.

2439. Chenery, William L. "The Protected Sex at the Polls." *Harper's Weekly* 60 (8 May 1915): 439–440.

2440. "Chicago Ladies' Campaign." *Literary Digest* 50 (1 May 1915): 1038.

2441. DePriest, Oscar. "Chicago and Woman Suffrage." *The Crisis* 10 (August 1915): 178–192.

2442. Eckert, Fred W. "The Effect of Woman Suffrage on the Political Situation in the City of Chicago." *Political Science Quarterly* 31 (March 1916): 105–121.

2443. Fairbank, Janet A. "Chicago Women Score One." *The Woman Citizen* 6 (16 July 1921): 19.

2444. Fullerton, Hugh S. "How Women Voted in Chicago." *American Magazine of Civics* 79 (June 1915): 57–58.

2445. Goldstein, Joel. *The Effects of the Adoption of Woman Suffrage: Sex Differences in Voting Behavior—Illinois, 1914–21.* New York: Prager, 1984.

2446. Gosnell, Harold Foote. *Getting Out the Vote.* Chicago: University of Chicago Press, 1927. For women, see pages 81–88, 115–116.

2447. ———. "The Voter's Response." In *Machine Politics: Chicago Model,* 91–125, 145–149, 171–173. Chicago: University of Chicago Press, 1937.

2448. Taylor, Graham. "Women's Voting Significantly Tested in Illinois." *The Survey* 32 (18 April 1914): 69–70.

2449. "Women Vote in Illinois." *Outlook* 106 (7 March 1914): 509–511.

2450. "Women Voters for Hoover." *The Republican Woman of Illinois* 6, no. 2 (September 1928): 7.

2451. "Women's Votes in Illinois." *The Survey* 32 (25 July 1914): 442.

Indiana

2452. Davenport, Walter. "Where Men Go Wrong about Women Voters." *Colliers* 138 (14 September 1956): 32–34, 36.

Louisiana

2453. Rogers, Gayle. "The Shreveport League of Women Voters and the Drive for Permanent Voter Registration in Louisiana." *North Louisiana Historical Association Journal* 24, no. 2–3 (1993): 75–95.

Maine

2454. "Woman's Hand in Maine." *Literary Digest* 66 (25 September 1920): 13–14.

Massachusetts

2455. Blackwell, Alice Stone. "Boston Women's School Vote." *The Woman's Journal* 35 (17 September 1904): 300.

Michigan

2456. Pittenger, Lucille B. "They Got Their Bond." *The Woman Citizen* 7 (18 November 1922): 12, 27.

Minnesota

2457. Groeneman, Sid. "Candidate Sex and Delegate Voting in a Pre-Primary Party Endorsement Election." *Women and Politics* 3, no. 1 (Spring 1983): 39–56.

Mississippi

2458. Prince, Vinton M., Jr. "Will Women Turn the Tide? Mississippi Women and the 1922 United States Senate Race." *Journal of Mississippi History* 42, no. 3 (August 1980): 212–220.

2459. ———. "The Woman Voter and Mississippi Elections in the Early Twenties." *Journal of Mississippi History* 49, no. 2 (May 1987): 105–114.

2460. Shawhan, Dorothy. "Women Behind the Woman Voter." *Journal of Mississippi History* 49 (May 1987): 115–128.

New Jersey

2461. Eck, Carl. "Housewives Jolt Politicians." *National Municipal Review* 38 (September 1949): 377–381.

2462. Kinghoffer, Judith Apter, and Loise Elkin. "The Petticoat Electors: Women Suffrage in New Jersey 1776–1807." *Journal of the Early Republic* 12 (Summer 1991): 159–193.

New York

2463. "Politics and the Woman." *The Woman Citizen* 4 (15 November 1919): 576–578.

North Carolina

2464. Payson, Jane. "Battle Cry of Garbage: Feminine Vote of Charlotte, North Carolina." *The Woman Citizen* 11 (September 1926): 19.

Ohio

2465. Toombs, Elizabeth O., and Katherine Ludington. "Politicians, Take Notice: Columbus, Ohio Women Elected a Mayor." *Good Housekeeping* 70 (March 1920): 149–151, 153, 155, 157, 159–160.

2466. Williams, Brian. "Petticoats in Politics: Cincinnati Women and the 1920 Election." *Cincinnati Historical Society Bulletin* 35, no. 1 (Spring 1977): 43–70.

Oregon

2467. Andersen, Kristi. "Women and the Vote in the 1920s: What Happened in Oregon." *Women and Politics* 14, no. 44 (1994): 43–56.

2468. Lockley, Fred. "Oregon Women in Politics." *Overland* 69 (June 1917): 475–476.

2469. Ogburn, William F., and Inez Goltra. "How Women Vote: A Study of an Election in Portland, Oregon." *Political Science Quarterly* 34, no. 3 (September 1919): 413–433.

Tennessee

2470. Reichard, Gary W. "The Defeat of Governor Roberts." *Tennessee Historical Quarterly* 30, no. 1 (1971): 94–109.

Texas

2471. Marilley, Suzanne M. "Gender Politics: Women Voters and the Texas Primary of 1918." Paper presented at SAWHC, 1990.

Utah

2472. Corev, G. "Utah." *Annals of the American Academy of Political and Social Science* 19 (January 1902): 145–147.

2473. Owen, Erna Von R. "Woman's Vote in Utah." *Harper's Weekly* 58 (2 May 1914): 18.

Washington

2474. "Western Women's View of the Election." *North American Review* 205, no. 1 (January 1917): 155–156.

Wyoming

2475. Roberts, H. H. "Woman Suffrage and Municipal Politics in Wyoming." *Annals of the American Academy of Political and Social Science* 18 (November 1901): 556–558.

2476. "Twenty-Five Years of Woman's Suffrage." *Catholic World* 76 (February 1903): 706.

In the Territories and District

Philippine Islands

2477. Higdon, E. K. "Filipino Women Hold Plebiscite." *Christian Century* 53 (4 November 1936): 1473–1474.

III. Running for Elective Office

General

2478. Belleranti, Shirley W. "An Educated State of Equality." *Westways* 77, no. 5 (1985): 42–45.

2479. "Between the Lines." *Redbook* 154 (April 1980): 34, 40.

2480. Carroll, Susan J. "Women Candidates and Support for Feminist Concerns: The Closet Feminist Syndrome." *Western Political Quarterly* 37 (June 1984): 307–323.

2481. Catt, Carrie Chapman. "Two Routes to Office." *The Woman Citizen* 6 (27 August 1921): 12.

2482. Center for the American Woman and Politics. *Not One of the Boys: A Discussion Guide*. New Brunswick, NJ: Center for the American Woman and Politics, 1985.

2483. CJD. "The Nineteenth Amendment as Affecting the Right of Women to Hold Public Office." *Temple Law Quarterly* 2 (April 1928): 278–279.

2484. Colon, Frank T. "The Elected Woman." *Social Studies* 58, no. 6 (November 1967): 256–261.

2485. Crane, Hattie Elliot. "Woman's Place in Government and Conduct of Society." *Overland Monthly and Out West Magazine* 53 (February 1912): 120–125.

2486. Edstrand, Laurie E., and William A. Eckert. "Impact of Candidates' Sex on Voter Choice." *Western Political Quarterly* 34 (March 1981): 173–184.

2487. Genovese, Michael A. *Women as National Leaders*. Newbury Park, CA: Sage, 1993.

2488. "How Shall We Put Women in Office?" *The Woman Citizen* 7 (18 November 1922): 14.

2489. "How Women Are Doing in Politics." *U.S. News and World Report* 69 (7 September 1970): 23–27.

2490. Hummer, Patricia M. *The Decade of Elusive Promise: Professional Women in the United States, 1920–1930*. Ann Arbor: University of Michigan Research Press, 1979.

2491. Johnson, Marilyn. "Women and Elective Office." *Society* 17 (May–June 1980): 63–70.

2492. Koubek, Richard F. *Politicians: The New Breed*. New York: Newsweek Education Department, 1992.

2493. Maisel, L. Sandy. *From Obscurity to Oblivion*. Knoxville: University of Tennessee Press, 1981.

2494. Martin, Ralph G. "Public Life Needs More Women." *Tomorrow* 10, no. 3 (November 1950): 5–10.

2495. "Meat for the Tiger in Manhattan." *Newsweek* 43 (11 January 1954): 28.

2496. Menon, Lakshmi N. "From Constitutional Recognition to Public Office." *Annals of the American Academy of Political and Social Science* 375 (January 1968): 34–43.

2497. Mueller, Carol M. "Collective Consciousness, Identity Transformation, and the Rise of Women in Public Office in the United States." In *The Women's Movements of the United States and Western Europe: Consciousness, Political Opportunity and Public Policy,* edited by Mary F. Katzenstein and Carol M. Mueller, 89–110. Philadelphia: Temple University Press, 1987.

2498. Rogers, Mary Beth. "Women in Electoral Politics: A Slow Steady Climb." *Social Policy* 23, no. 4 (Summer 1993): 14–21.

2499. Wells, Kate G. "Women in Office." *National* 22 (1905): 133.

2500. Werner, Emmy E., and Louise M. Bachtold. "Personality Characteristics of Women in American Politics." In *Woman and Politics,* edited by Jane S. Jaquette, 75–84. New York: Wiley, 1974.

2501. "Woman's Place." *Atlantic Monthly* 225 (March 1970): 82–156.

2502. "Women Who Help Boss Us." *Literary Digest* 84 (17 January 1925): 38, 40, 42, 44.

2503. "Women's Place Is—In Politics." *Congressional Quarterly Weekly Report* 30 (28 October 1953): 2800.

Recruitment

2504. Briscoe, Jerry B. "Perceptions That Discourage Women Attorneys from Seeking Public Office." *Sex Roles* 21 (1989): 557–567.

2505. Center for the American Woman and Politics. *Women in Public Service: Changing the Opportunity Structure for Women in the Public Sector.* New Brunswick, NJ: Center for the American Woman and Politics, Rutgers University, 1980.

2506. Engel, Margaret. "Wanted: Women to Run for Public Office: Here's What You Need to Consider." *Glamour* 82 (June 1984): 88.

2507. Fahy, Evangeline H. "A Political Challenge in a Presidential Campaign Year." *Independent Woman* 35, no. 8 (August 1956): 8–9, 29.

2508. Fiedler, Maureen. "The Congressional Ambitions of Female Political Elites." In *Women Organizing: An Anthology,* edited by Bernice Cummings and Victoria Schuck, 253–288. Metuchen, NJ: Scarecrow Press, 1979.

2509. Friedan, Betty. "It's Nonsense That There Are No Qualified Women to Run for Office." *McCalls* 98 (September 1971): 52–54.

2510. Hilton, M. Eunice. "If We Want Women in Public Office." *Independent Woman* 27 (March 1948): 83–84, 91.

2511. Keefe, Grace. "To Train Women for Public Affairs, National Business and Professional Women." *Independent Woman* 27 (October 1948): 304.

2512. Kelley, Florence. "Woman Wanted on the Bench." *The Woman Citizen* 7 (21 April 1923): 17.

2513. Lake, Celinda C. *Why Don't More Women Run?* Washington, DC: National Women's Political Caucus, 1994. Survey results, Lake Research, Inc.

2514. Lee, Marcia Manning. "Why Few Women Hold Public Office: Democracy and Sexual Roles." *Political Science Quarterly* 91 (Summer 1976): 297–314.

2515. Mezey, Susan Gluck. "Increasing the Number of Women in Office: Does It Matter?" In *The Year of the Woman: Myths and Realities,* edited by Elizabeth Adell Cook, Sue Thomas, and Clyde Wilcox, 255–270. Boulder, CO: Westview Press, 1994.

2516. Miller, Shari. "Public Affairs Connection." *Working Woman* 6 (August 1981): 87–88, 90.

2517. Mueller, Carol M. "Nurturance and Mastery: Competing Qualifications for Women's Access to High Public Office." In *Women and Politics: Activism, Attitudes and Officeholding,* Vol. 2, edited by Gwen Moore and Glenna Spitze, 211–232. Greenwich, CT: JAI Press, 1986.

2518. National Women's Political Caucus. *Moving More Women into Public Office.* Washington, DC: National Women's Political Caucus, 1995.

2519. Peradotto, Nicole. "Wooing Women." *George* 1 (December 1995): 152–160.

2520. Rosenwasser, Shirley, and Norma Dean. "Gender Role and Political Office." *Psychology of Women Quarterly* 13 (1989): 77–85.

2521. Siddon, Sally Goodyear. *Consider Yourself for Public Office: Guidelines for Women Candidates.* 2d ed. Washington, DC: National Federation of Republican Women, 1981.

2522. Stanwick, Kathy. *Political Women Tell What It Takes.* New Brunswick, NJ: Center for the American Woman and Politics, Rutgers University, 1983.

2523. "Support Women Candidates: What, Me Run for Office?" *Working Mother* 15 (April 1992): 6.

2524. Van Hightower, Nikki R. "The Recruitment of Women for Public Office." *American Politics Quarterly* 5, no. 3 (July 1977): 301–314.

Media

2525. Benze, James G., and Eugene R. Declercq. "Content of Political Television: Spot Ads for Female Candidates." *Journalism Quarterly* 62 (Summer 1985): 278–283.

2526. Haines, Janine. "The Front Page Vs. the Female Pol." *Ms.* 4, no. 4 (January 1993): 84–86.

2527. Kahn, Kim Fridkin, and Edie N. Goldenberg. "Scanty Coverage." *Psychology Today* 25 (July–August 1992): 12.

2528. Kaid, Lynda Lee, Sandra Myers, Val Pipps, and Jan Hunter. "Sex Role Perceptions and Televised Political Advertising: Comparing Male and Female Candidates."

Women and Politics 4 (Winter 1984): 41–54.

2529. Mandel, Ruth. "Women and the Arts of Media Politics." In *Women Leaders in American Politics,* edited by James David Barber and Barbara Kellerman, 261–271. Englewood Cliffs, NJ: Prentice Hall, 1986.

2530. McFeeley, Heather S. "Newspaper Coverage of Female Politicians." Master's thesis, Pont Park College, Pittsburgh, PA, 1994.

2531. Procter, David E., William J. Schenck-Hamlin, and Karen A. Haase. "Exploring the Role of Gender in the Development of Negative Political Advertisements." *Women and Politics* 14, no. 2 (1994): 1–22.

2532. Williams, Leonard. "Political Advertising in the Year of the Woman: Did X Mark the Spot?" In *The Year of the Woman: Myths and Realities,* edited by Elizabeth Adell Cook, Sue Thomas, and Clyde Wilcox, 197–216. Boulder, CO: Westview Press, 1994.

Financing and Political Action Committees

2533. Donovan, Beth. "Women Bring Cash—And Demands." *Congressional Quarterly Weekly Report* 50 (30 May 1992): 1516.

2534. ———. "Women's Campaigns Fueled Mostly by Women's Checks." *Congressional Quarterly Weekly Report* 50 (17 October 1992): 3269–3273.

2535. Eldredge, Marcia. "Political Action Committees, Women Financing Women." *National Business Woman* 73 (Fall 1992): 10–11.

2536. Ferguson, Andrew. "Choice Cuts." *American Spectator* 22 (June 1989): 56.

2537. Hirschmann, Susan. "EMILY's List: Chicks with Checks." *American Spectator* 26, no. 4 (April 1993): 20–23.

2538. Kleeman, Katherine E. *Women's PACs.* New Brunswick, NJ: Center for the American Woman and Politics, Rutgers University, 1983.

2539. "Movers and Shakers: Ellen Malcolm." *Campaigns and Elections* 15, no. 8 (August 1994): 49.

2540. Newman, Jody, Carrie Costantin, Julie Goetz, and Amy Glosser. *Perception and Reality: A Study of Women Candidates and Fundraising.* Washington, DC: Women's Campaign Research Fund, 1985.

2541. Rimmerman, Craig A. "New Kids on the Block: The WISH List and the Gay and Lesbian Victory Fund in the 1992 Elections." In *Risky Business? PAC Decisionmaking in Congressional Election,* edited by Robert Biersack, Paul S. Herrnson, and Clyde Wilcox, 214–223. Armonk, NY: M.E. Sharpe, 1994.

2542. Thomas, Sue. "The National Abortion Rights Action League PAC: Reproductive Choice in the Spotlight." In *Risky Business? PAC Decisionmaking in Congressional Election,* edited by Robert Biersack, Paul S. Herrnson, and Clyde Wilcox, 117–129. Armonk, NY: M.E. Sharpe, 1994.

2543. Wilcox, Clyde, Clifford W. Brown, and Lynda W. Powell. "Sex and the Political Contributor: The Gender Gap among Contributors to

Presidential Candidates in 1988." *Political Research Quarterly* 46, no. 2 (1993): 355–369.

Representation

2544. Abzug, Bella S., and Cynthia Edgar. "Women and Politics: The Struggle for Representation." *Massachusetts Review* 13 (Winter–Spring 1972): 17–24.

2545. Bullock, Charles S., III, and Loch K. Johnson. "Sex and the Second Primary." *Social Science Quarterly* 66 (December 1985): 933–944.

2546. ———. "Myths of the Runoff." In *Runoff Elections in the United States,* edited by Charles S. Bullock III and Loch K. Johnson, 27–78. Chapel Hill: University of North Carolina Press, 1992.

2547. Darcy, Robert. "Electoral Barriers to Women." In *United States Electoral Systems: Their Impact on Women and Minorities,* edited by Wilma Rule and Joseph F. Zimmerman, 221–232. New York: Greenwood Press, 1992.

2548. Darcy, Robert, Susan Welch, and Janet M. Clark. *Women, Elections and Representation.* 2d rev. ed. Lincoln: University of Nebraska Press, 1994 (1987).

2549. De Santis, Victor. "Minority and Gender Representation in American County Legislatures: The Effect of Election Systems." In *United States Electoral Systems: Their Impact on Women and Minorities,* edited by Wilma Rule and Joseph Zimmerman, 143–152. New York: Greenwood Press, 1992.

2550. Duncan, Phil. "How to Make Congress More Representative." *Congressional Quarterly Weekly Report* 49 (26 October 1991): 3166.

2551. ———. "Political Empowerment Strictly by Numbers." *Congressional Quarterly Weekly Report* 50 (4 January 1992): 38.

2552. Herrick, Rebekah, and Susan Welch. "The Impact of At-Large Elections on Representation of Minority Women." In *United States Electoral Systems: Their Impact on Women and Minorities,* edited by Wilma Rule and Joseph Zimmerman, 153–166. New York: Greenwood Press, 1992.

2553. MacManus, Susan A., and Charles S. Bullock III. "Minorities and Women DO Win At-Large." *National Civic Review* 77 (May–June 1988): 231–244.

2554. Perkins, Jerry, and Diane L. Fowlkes. "Opinion Representation Versus Social Representation: Why Women Can't Run as Women and Win." *American Political Science Review* 74 (March 1980): 92–103.

2555. Reingold, Beth. "Concepts of Representation among Female and Male State Legislators." *Legislative Studies Quarterly* 17, no. 4 (November 1992): 509–537.

2556. Rule, Wilma. "Women's Underrepresentation and Electoral Systems." *PS* 27, no. 4 (December 1994): 1689–1692.

2557. Rule, Wilma, and Joseph Francis Zimmerman, eds. *United States Electoral Systems: Their Impact on Women and Minorities.* New York: Greenwood Press, 1992.

2558. ———, eds. *Electoral Systems in Comparative Perspective: Their Impact on Women and Minorities.* New York: Greenwood Press, 1994.

2559. Sainsbury, Diane. "Bringing Women into Elected Office in Sweden and the U.S.: Political Opportunity Structures and Women's Strategies." Paper presented at the annual meeting of the American Political Science Association, Washington, DC, 1991.

2560. Sinclair, Barbara. "Agenda and Alignment Change: The House of Representatives, 1925–1978." In *Congress Reconsidered,* 2d ed., edited by C. Lawrence Dodd and Bruce I. Oppenheimer, 221–245. Washington, DC: CQ Press, 1981.

2561. Volgy, Thomas, John E. Schwarts, and Hildy Gottlieb. "Female Representation and the Quest for Resources: Feminist Activism and Electoral Success." *Social Science Quarterly* 67 (March 1986): 156–168.

2562. Welch, Susan, and Donley Studlar. "Multi-Member Districts and Representation of Women: Evidence from Britain and the United States." *Journal of Politics* 52, no. 2 (May 1990): 391–412.

2563. Zimmerman, Joseph Francis. "Introduction." In *United States Electoral Systems: Their Impact on Women and Minorities,* edited by Wilma Rule and Joseph F. Zimmerman, 3–12. New York: Greenwood Press, 1992.

Women of Color

2564. Baca-Barragan, Polly. "La Chicana in Politics." In *La Chicana: Building for the Future, An Action Plan for the '80s,* edited by National Hispanic University, 21–31. Oakland, CA: National Hispanic University, 1980.

2565. Bryce, Herrington J., and Alan E. Warrick. "Black Women in Elected Offices." *The Black Scholar* 6, no. 2 (October 1974): 17–20.

2566. ———. "Black Women in Electoral Politics." In *A Portrait of Marginality: The Political Behavior of American Women,* edited by Marianne Githens and Jewell Prestage, 395–400. New York: McKay, 1977.

2567. Chisholm, Shirley. "We Have Become Too Plastic." *Glamour* 80 (November 1982): 98, 110.

2568. Darcy, Robert, and Charles D. Hadley. "Black Women in Politics: The Puzzle of Success." *Social Science Quarterly* 69, no. 3 (September 1988): 629–645.

2569. Dumas, Kitty. "The Year of the Black Woman?" *Black Enterprise* 23 (August 1992): 35.

2570. Epstein, Cynthia. "Black and Female: The Double Whamy." *Psychology Today* 7 (1973): 57–99.

2571. Evers, Mrs. Medgar W. "Petunia in an Onion Patch." *Ladies Home Journal* 89 (April 1972): 113, 207, 214.

2572. "First Woman to Be Elected to Assembly." *Sepia* 7 (June 1959): 65.

2573. Horton, Luci. "The Distaff Side of Politics." *Ebony* 28 (December 1973): 48–50, 54.

2574. Malveaux, Julianne. "The Powers That Will Be: Women to Watch in Politics." *Essence* 19 (November 1988): 32.

2575. Natividad, Irene. "Women of Color and the Campaign Trail." In *The American Woman: 1992–1993*, edited by Paula Ries and Anne J. Stone, 127–148. New York: Norton, 1993.

2576. Sierra, Christine Marie. "Surveying the Latina Political Landscape." *Intercambios Femeniles* 2, no. 3 (Fall 1984): 1–24.

2577. "Women in Government: A Slim Past, But a Strong Future." *Ebony* 32 (August 1977): 89–97.

Running Before 1965

2578. "Facing November 4, 1924, a Roll-Call of Women Nominees." *The Woman Citizen* 9 (1 November 1924): 9–10, 28–30.

2579. "Facing toward Washington: A Roll Call of Women Nominees for High Office." *The Woman Citizen* 7 (12 October 1922): 12, 27, 43.

2580. Goldman, Olive Remington. "The Inexperienced Politician: Some Advantages and Handicaps of a Woman Candidate." *American Association of University Women* 41, no. 1 (Fall 1947): 17–19.

2581. Hay, Mary Garrett. "Women as Candidates." *The Woman Citizen* 7 (26 August 1922): 14.

2582. Holly, Hazel. "Some Women Who Won Tell How to Run." *Woman's Home Companion* 82 (July 1955): 18, 48.

2583. Martin, Anne. "Women's Inferiority Complex." *The New Republic* 20 (July 1921): 210.

2584. O'Brien, John C. "Women's Bid for Politics." *The Sign* (January 1959).

2585. Richardson, Anna Steese. "Campaigning with Women Candidates, 1922." *Woman's Home Companion* 49 (November 1922): 4, 80–81.

2586. "Women Candidates." *The Woman's Journal* 15 (November 1930): 5.

2587. "Women Candidates in the Primary Elections." *The Woman Citizen* 7 (26 August 1922): 21–22.

2588. "Women Entries in the Election Races." *The Woman Citizen* 7 (4 November 1922): 12–13, 29–30.

2589. "Women in Politics." *Congressional Quarterly Weekly Report* 15 (20 February 1956): 119–136.

2590. "Women Vs. Men: Three Electoral Battles on America's Western Front." *Literary Digest* 121 (18 April 1936): 10.

2591. Young, Rose. "They Came to Serve—Not to Seek Honors." *The Woman Citizen* 5 (16 October 1920): 542.

Running After 1965

2592. Alexander, Dolores. "It's November—Why Are These Women

Running?" *Working Women* 3 (November 1978): 65–66, 78.

2593. Allen, Cathy. "Women on the Run." *Campaigns and Elections* 16, no. 10 (October–November 1995): 28–29.

2594. Benze, James G., and Eugene R. Declercq. "The Importance of Gender in Congressional and Statewide Elections." *Social Science Quarterly* 66 (December 1985): 954–963.

2595. Carlson, Margaret B. "It's Our Turn." *Time* 136, no. 19 (Fall 1990): 16–18.

2596. Carroll, Susan J. *Women as Candidates in American Politics.* Bloomington: Indiana University Press, 1985.

2597. ———. "The Political Careers of Women Elected Officials: An Assessment and Research Agenda." In *Ambition and Beyond: Career Paths of American Politicians,* edited by Shirley Williams and Edward L. Lascher, Jr., 197–230. Berkeley: Institute of Governmental Studies Press, University of California, 1993.

2598. ———. *Women Candidates in American Politics.* Bloomington: Indiana University Press, 1994.

2599. Carroll, Susan J., and Wendy S. Strimling. *Women's Routes to Elective Office: A Comparison with Men's.* New Brunswick, NJ: Center for the American Woman and Politics, Eagleton Institute for Politics, Rutgers University, 1983.

2600. Chan, Janet. "How Women Candidates Can Win." *McCalls* 105 (August 1978): 65.

2601. Clark, Janet M. "Getting There: Women in Political Office."

Annals of the American Academy of Political and Social Science 515 (May 1991): 63–76.

2602. Clift, Eleanor. "Battle of the Sexes." *Newsweek* 115 (30 April 1990): 20–22.

2603. ———. "Sex Still Matters." *Newsweek* 116 (29 October 1990): 34–35.

2604. ———. "A League of Their Own." *Newsweek* 120 (27 July 1992): 31.

2605. Collins, Gail. "The Year of the Woman." *Ladies Home Journal* 109 (November 1992): 181–185.

2606. Currey, Virginia. "Campaign Theory and Practice —The Gender Variable." In *A Portrait of Marginality: The Political Behavior of American Women,* edited by Marianne Githens and Jewell Prestage, 150–172. New York: McKay, 1977.

2607. Danowitz, Jane. "The Class of '88: Women to Watch." *National Business Woman* 69, no. 3 (June–July 1988): 18–19.

2608. Darcy, Robert, and Sarah Slavin Schramm. "When Women Run against Men." *Public Opinion Quarterly* 41 (Spring 1977): 1–12.

2609. Diamond, Irene. "Exploring the Relationship between Female Candidacies and the Women's Movement." In *Women Organizing: An Anthology,* edited by Bernice Cummings and Victoria Schuck, 241–252. Metuchen, NJ: Scarecrow Press, 1979.

2610. Farenthold, Frances T. "Woman in Politics." *Saturday Evening Post* 246 (March 1974): 14–15.

2611. ———. "Are You Brave Enough to Be in Politics?" *Redbook* 147 (May 1976): 190.

2612. Fulani, Lenora B. *The Making of a Fringe Candidate.* New York: Castillo International Publications, 1992.

2613. Gottlieb, Paul D. "Women's Campaigner Puts Numbers to Work." *National Journal* 20 (1986): 2262.

2614. Hammond, Nancy, and Glenda Belote. "From Deviance to Legitimacy: Women as Political Candidates." *The University of Michigan Papers in Women's Studies* 1 (June 1974): 58–72.

2615. Herrick, Rebekah. "A Reappraisal of the Quality of Women Candidates." *Women and Politics* 15, no. 4 (1995): 25–38.

2616. Kaiser, Charles. "Women on the Verge: Running for the House and Senate." *Vogue* 182 (March 1992): 330–333.

2617. Kathlene, Lyn, and Silvo Lenart. "Who Are the Women Candidates? A Typology of Women Candidates in the 1992 Congressional and State Level Races." Paper presented at the annual meeting of the Midwest Political Science Association, Chicago, 1993.

2618. Kraminer, Wendy. "Crashing the Locker Room." *Atlantic Monthly* 270 (July 1992): 58–67.

2619. Lake, Celinda C. *Campaigning in a Different Voice.* Washington, DC: EMILY's List, 1988. Poll, Greenberg-Lake Analysis Group.

2620. ———. *Winning with Women.* Washington, DC: Greenberg-Lake Associates, 1992. Commissioned by EMILY's List, National Women's Political Caucus, Women's Campaign Fund.

2621. Lamson, Peggy. *Few Are Chosen: American Women in Political Life Today.* Boston: Houghton Mifflin, 1968.

2622. Leeper, Mark. "The Impact of Prejudice on Female Candidates: An Experimental Look at Voter Inference." *American Politics Quarterly* 19 (April 1991): 248–261.

2623. Lewis, Ann F. "Why Winning Won't Be So Easy." *Ms.* 3, no. 2 (September 1992): 85.

2624. Mandel, Ruth. *In the Running: The New Women Candidates.* New Haven: Ticknor and Fields, 1981.

2625. ———. "The Trouble with Women Candidates." *Ms.* 9, no. 11 (May 1981): 76–77.

2626. Marchus, Barbara. "The Year of the Women Candidates." *Ms.* 1, no. 1 (September 1972): 64–69.

2627. Mashek, John W. "A Woman's Place Is on the Ballot in '86." *U.S. News and World Report* 101 (3 November 1986): 21–22.

2628. McLean, Joan Elizabeth. "Strategic Choices: Career Decisions of Elected Women." Ph.D. dissertation, Ohio State University, Columbus, 1994.

2629. Mericle, Margaret, S. Lenart, and K. Heilig. "Women Candidates: Even If All Things Are Equal, Will They Get Elected?" Paper presented at the annual meeting of the Midwest Political Science Association, Chicago, 1989.

2630. Millmore, J. Timothy. "Gender and Political Integration: The Political Aspirations of Women in Partisan Elite Structures." Ph.D. dissertation, Southern Illinois University, Carbondale, 1990.

2631. Moore, Gwen, and Glenna Spitze. *Women and Politics: Activism, Attitudes and Office-holding.* Greenwich, CT: JAI Press, 1986.

2632. National Women's Political Caucus. *Campaigning to Win: A Workbook for Women in Politics.* Washington, DC: National Women's Political Caucus, 1993.

2633. ———. *Facing the 'Religious' Right.* Washington, DC: National Women's Political Caucus, 1993.

2634. "The New Face of Politics." *McCalls* 101 (October 1972): 96–101.

2635. Newman, Jody. *Perception and Reality: A Study Comparing the Success of Men and Women Candidates.* Washington, DC: National Women's Political Caucus, 1994.

2636. Oliver, Janet. "Running and Hoping: Some of Our November Candidates." *Ms.* 3, no. 4 (October 1974): 115–118.

2637. O'Reilly, Jane. "Running for Our Lives." *Glamour* 81 (January 1991): 74, 76.

2638. ———. "Campaign Issues: Women." *Columbia Journalism Review* 31 (November–December 1992): 40–41.

2639. Paizis, Suzanne. *Getting Her Elected: A Political Woman's Handbook.* Sacramento, CA: Creative Editions, 1977.

2640. "Political Careers Appealing to More Women." *National Business Woman* 63, no. 1 (February–March 1982): 5–6.

2641. "Political Women." *National Business Woman* 65 (October–November 1984): 13–16.

2642. Rajoppi, Joanne. *Women in Office: Getting There and Staying There.* Westport, CT: Bergin and Garvey, 1993.

2643. Raymond, Paul B. "The Effects of Candidates' Gender on Electoral Success." Paper presented at the annual meeting of the American Political Science Association, Chicago, 1995.

2644. Rosenberg, Marie Barovic. "The Campaigns and Elections of Congresswomen Edith Green and Julia Butler Hanson." *Politics (Australia)* 24 (May 1989): 42–55.

2645. Rosenberg, Shawn W. "Creating a Political Image: Shaping Appearance and Manipulating the Vote." *Political Behavior* 13, no. 4 (December 1991): 345–367.

2646. "Running for Office." *Ms.* 2, no. 10 (April 1974): 61–68.

2647. Sapers, Jonathan. "Politicking 101." *Working Woman* 19, no. 7 (1994): 14.

2648. Shannon, Salley. "Politics 1992: The Year of the Woman." *Working Mother* 15 (September 1992): 34.

2649. Simpson, Peggy. "Helping Women Win in '84." *Working Woman* 8 (November 1983): 60, 62, 66.

2650. ———. "The Year of the Women." *Working Woman* 11 (October 1986): 90.

2651. Sobkowski, Anna. "See How They Run." *Executive Female* 13 (September–October 1990): 14.

2652. Trafton, Barbara M. *Women Winning: How to Run for Office.* Boston: Harvard Common Press, 1984.

2653. Welch, Susan, and Timothy Bledsoe. "Differences in Campaign Support for Male and Female Candidates." In *Women and Politics: Activism, Attitudes and Officeholding,* edited by Gwen Moore and Glenna Spitze, 233–245. Research in Politics and Society. Vol. 2. Greenwich, CT: JAI Press, 1986.

2654. Witt, Linda, Karen M. Paget, and Glenna Matthews. *Running as a Woman: Gender and Power in American Politics.* New York: Free Press, 1994.

2655. "Women Running for High Office—More Than Ever Before." *U.S. News and World Report* 77 (16 September 1974): 29–30.

2656. Wright, Betsey. "Women Can Win: How to Plan and Run an Effective Campaign." *American Association of University Women* 69 (November 1975): 7–10.

Election Returns, by Year

2657. "Several Women in Legislature." *The Woman's Journal* 45 (14 November 1914): 302.

2658. "Women in State Legislatures." *The Woman Citizen* 3 (7 December 1918): 568–569.

2659. "Women Elected to State Legislatures." *The Woman Citizen* 5 (27 November 1920): 717.

2660. "Pioneers of 1921." *The Woman Citizen* 6 (30 July 1921): 11.

2661. "Woman Legislators." *The Woman Citizen* 5 (8 January 1921): 873.

2662. "How the Women Candidates Fared." *Literary Digest* 75 (25 November 1922): 11.

2663. "Women Who Won." *The Woman Citizen* 7 (18 November 1922): 8–10, 29; (2 December 1922): 10–11, 27.

2664. "Legislators Elected 1922." *The Woman Citizen* 8 (8 September 1923): 23.

2665. "Women Who Won." *The Woman Citizen* 9 (15 November 1924): 10–11, 30; (29 November 1924): 22–23; (13 December 1924): 25; (25 December 1924): 22.

2666. "Some Election Returns." *The Woman Citizen* 10 (December 1925): 33.

2667. "Women Who Won." *The Woman Citizen* 11 (December 1926): 35–36; (January 1927): 35–36; (March 1927): 36.

2668. "Women Who Won." *The Woman Citizen* 12 (December 1927): 35; (January 1928): 35; (March 1928): 36.

2669. Moncure, Dorothy A. "Women in Political Life." *Current History* 29 (January 1929): 639–643.

2670. "More Women Laying Down the Law." *Literary Digest* 100 (19 January 1929): 12.

2671. "Women Elected in 1929." *The Woman's Journal* 14 (December 1929): 30; (February 1930): 31; (April 1930): 30.

2672. "Women Elected." *The Woman's Journal* 15 (December 1930): 5.

2673. Mallon, Winifred. "They Make Legislative History." *Independent Woman* 12 (January 1931): 3, 33–34.

2674. "Women Who Won." *The Woman's Journal* 16 (January 1931): 7, 46–48; (February 1931): 7, 32.

2675. Griffin, Isabel Kinnear. "Democratic Women Victors of 1932." *Democratic Bulletin* 7, no. 12 (December 1932): 12, 28.

2676. National League of Women Voters. *A Survey of Women in Public Office.* Washington, DC: National League of Women Voters, 1937.

2677. "Between You and Me: Election Results from the Feminist Standpoint." *Independent Woman* 17 (December 1938): 369.

2678. Rishel, Virginia. "Women Who Won." *Democratic Digest* 15, no. 12 (December 1938): 10, 28.

2679. "Two Women Secretaries of State." *Independent Woman* 17 (December 1938): 174.

2680. "Women in Public Office." *Commonweal* 29 (13 January 1939): 311.

2681. Arthur, Julietta K. "Who's Who in the Elections: Women in Public Office." *Independent Woman* 19 (December 1940): 479–480, 406.

2682. Bugbee, Emma. "Winners!" *Independent Woman* 21 (December 1942): 357–358, 383.

2683. "Women Who Won." *Democratic Digest* 19, no. 12 (December 1942): 7.

2684. "Women Who Won in the States." *Democratic Digest* 21–22, no. 12–1 (December–January 1944): 10, 11.

2685. "We Still Have a Long Way to Go." *Independent Woman* 29 (December 1950): 374.

2686. "Women in Public Office Tell Us More." *Independent Woman* 29 (November 1950): 341–342.

2687. "More Than Orchid-Bearers." *Time* 60 (24 November 1952): 20–21.

2688. Bardorff, Virginia Roller. "We've Kept the Faith, We've Made New Gains." *Independent Woman* 34 (November 1955): 3–4.

2689. "Now It's Seventeen Women in Congress." *U.S. News and World Report* 45 (12 December 1958): 80.

2690. Burstein, Patricia, and Marlene Cimons. "Women Candidates Who Won." *Ms.* 1, no. 9 (March 1973): 68–71.

2691. "Breakthrough in Politics." *Time* 104 (18 November 1974): 28.

2692. "Some Big Wins for Women." *U.S. News and World Report* 77 (18 November 1974): 32.

2693. "The Year of the Woman." *Newsweek* 84 (4 November 1974): 20–27.

2694. Johnson, Marilyn, and Kathy Stanwick. "Statistical Report: Profile of Women Holding Office, 1975." In *Women in Public Office: A Biographical Directory and Statistical Analysis, 1975,* edited by Marilyn Johnson and Kathy Stanwick, xx-lii. Vol. 1. New York: R. R. Bowker, 1976. Center for the American Woman and Politics, Rutgers University.

2695. "Women in Public Office: How Many Are There?" *Good Housekeeping* 183 (August 1976): 174.

2696. Carroll, Susan J., Marilyn Johnson, Kathy Stanwick, Lynn Korenblit, and Christine Li. "Statistical Report: Profile of Women Holding Office, 1977." In *Women in Public Office: A Biographical Directory and Statistical Analysis.* 2d ed., 1A-68A. Metuchen, NJ: Scarecrow Press, 1978. Compiled by Center for the American Woman and Politics, Rutgers University.

2697. "Score Card of Gains, Losses for Women in Politics." *U.S. News and World Report* 85 (21 August 1978): 70–71.

2698. "Steady Gains for Women and Minorities." *U.S. News and World Report* 85 (18 September 1978): 40–41.

2699. "Women's Work: Election Results." *Time* 112 (20 November 1978): 36.

2700. Mandel, Ruth B. "Who Won? The Women Candidates." *Working Woman* 8 (April 1983): 110–111.

2701. Clark, Janet M. "Women in State and Local Politics: Progress or Stalemate?" *Social Science Quarterly* 21, no. 1 (1984): 1–4.

2702. Wilentz, Amy. "No More Petticoat Politics: Primary Winners." *Time* 128 (22 September 1986): 28–29.

2703. Edmunds, Lavinia. "Women Who Won." *Ms.* 15, no. 7 (January 1987): 29–33.

2704. Schroeder, Patricia, and Olympia Snowe. "Preface." In *The American Woman 1987–88: A Status Report,* edited by Sara E. Rix and Anne J. Stone, 19–24. New York: Norton, 1987.

2705. Kennelly, Barbara B., and Claudine Schneider. "Introduction." In *The American Woman 1988–89: A Status Report,* edited by Sara E. Rix and Anne J. Stone, 27–34. New York: Norton, 1988.

2706. Mandel, Ruth. "The Political Woman." In *The American Woman 1988–89: A Status Report,* edited by Sara E. Rix and Anne J. Stone, 78–122. New York: Norton, 1988.

2707. Reis, Diane. "Election '90: Women Claim Victory in Statewide Races." *National Business Woman* 72 (Winter 1990): 16–17, 30.

2708. Simpson, Peggy. "Election 1990: A Mixed Bag." *Ms.* 2 (January–February 1991): 88–89.

2709. McGurn, William. "The Year of the Women." *National Review* 44, no. 13 (July 1992): 6.

2710. Morris, Celia. "Changing the Rules and the Roles: Five Women in Public Office." In *The American Woman, 1992–93,* edited by Paula Ries and Anne J. Stone, 95–126. New York: Norton, 1992.

2711. Tinman, Danielle. "Election Brings New Faces: Women Make the Difference." *National Business Woman* 73, no. 4 (Winter 1992): 9–12.

2712. Boles, Janet K. "The Year of the Woman—Continued (Or, the Return of the Puritan Ethic?)." Paper presented at the Midwest Political Science Association, Chicago, 1993.

2713. DelliCarpini, Michael X., and Ester R. Fuchs. "The Year of the Woman? Candidates, Voters, and the 1992 Elections." *Political Research Quarterly* 108 (Spring 1993): 29–36.

2714. Cook, Elizabeth Adell, Sue Thomas, and Clyde Wilcox, eds. *The Year of the Woman: Myths and Realities.* Boulder, CO: Westview Press, 1994.

2715. Wilcox, Clyde. "Why Was 1992 the 'Year of the Woman'? Explaining Women's Gains in 1992." In *The Year of the Woman: Myths and Realities,* edited by Elizabeth Adell Cook, Sue Thomas, and Clyde Wilcox, 1–24. Boulder, CO: Westview Press, 1994.

2716. Cook, Elizabeth Adell, and Clyde Wilcox. "The Year of the Woman." In *Democracy's Feast: Elections in America,* edited by Herbert F. Weisberg, 195–219. Chatham, NJ: Chatham House, 1995.

Nations and Tribes

2717. Contreras, Ruth, and Rose Shaw. "Isleta Pueblo's First Woman Governor." *Voces Unidas* 3, no. 2 (1993): 10.

2718. Wallis, Michael. "Hail to the Chief: Wilma Mankiller Is the First Woman to Be Elected Cherokee National Chief." *Philip Morris Magazine* (October 1989): 37–39.

Federal Government

Congress

General

2719. Andersen, Kristi, and Stuart Thorson. "Congressional Turnover and the Election of Women." *Western Political Quarterly* 37 (March 1984): 143–156.

2720. Bernstein, Robert A. "Why Are There So Few Women in the House?" *Western Political Quarterly* 39 (March 1986): 155–164.

2721. Bledsoe, Timothy, and Mary Herring Munro. "Victims of Circumstances: Women in Pursuit of Political Office in America." *American Political Science Review* 84 (March 1990): 213–224.

2722. Engel, Margaret. "Why Not Enough Women Will Be Winning Senate Seats This Year." *Glamour* 82 (May 1984): 238, 240.

2723. Gertzog, Irwin N. "The Matrimonial Connection: The Nomination of Congressmen's Widows for the House of Representatives." *Journal of Politics* 42 (August 1980): 820–833.

2724. Grunwald, Lisa. "If Women Ran America." *Life* 15, no. 1 (June 1992): 36–42.

2725. Kerchten, Dick. "The Reagan Reelection Campaign Hopes 1984 Will Be the Year of the Women." *Na-*

tional Journal 16, no. 22 (2 June 1984): 1082–1085.

2726. Lamson, Peggy. "Three Congresswomen: What Makes Them Run, Martha W. Griffiths, Patsy T. Mink, Margaret M. Heckler." In *Few Are Chosen: American Women in Political Life Today,* 87–126. Boston: Houghton Mifflin, 1968.

2727. Mandel, Ruth, Katherine E. Kleeman, and Lucy Baruch. "No Year of the Woman, Then or Now." *Extensions, A Journal of the Carl Albert Congressional Research and Studies Center* (Spring 1995): 7–10.

2728. Mott, Jonathan D. "Getting Ahead by Holding Ground." *Extensions, A Journal of the Carl Albert Congressional Research and Studies Center* (Spring 1995): 11–14.

2729. National Women's Political Caucus, ed. *NWPC Consultant Roundtable.* Washington, DC: National Women's Political Caucus, 1985.

2730. Thompson, Joan Hulse. "Career Convergence: Election of Women and Men to the House of Representatives, 1916–1975." *Women and Politics* 5 (Spring 1985): 69–90.

2731. "A Woman's Place Is in the House." *National Voter* 22 (March–April 1972): 1–5.

Recruitment

2732. Bullock, Charles S., III, Findley Heys, and Patricia Lee. "Recruitment of Women for Congress: A Research Note." *Western Political Quarterly* 25 (September 1972): 416–423. Reprinted in *A Portrait of Marginality: The Po-*

litical Behavior of American Women, edited by Marianne Githens and Jewell Prestage, 210–220. New York: McKay, 1977.

2733. Gertzog, Irwin N. "Changing Patterns of Female Recruitment to the U.S. House of Representatives." *Legislative Studies Quarterly* 4 (August 1979): 429–445.

2734. Rule, Wilma. "How and Why Do Women's and Men's Congressional Recruitment Patterns Differ?" Paper presented at the annual meeting of the Western Political Science Association, Anaheim, CA, 1987.

Running

2735. Burrell, Barbara C. "The Presence and Performance of Women Candidates in Open Seat Primaries for the U.S. House of Representatives: 1968–1990." *Legislative Studies Quarterly* 17 (November 1992): 493–508.

2736. ———. *A Woman's Place Is in the House: Campaigning for Congress in the Feminist Era.* Ann Arbor: University of Michigan Press, 1994.

2737. Carney, Eliza Newlin. "Weighing In: Women Running for Congress." *National Journal* 24 (13 June 1992): 1399–1403.

2738. Clarke, Ida Clyde. "A Woman for the Senate, Party Affiliation and the Woman Voter." *Century* 112, no. 2 (June 1926): 129–135.

2739. Clift, Eleanor. "The Year of the Smear, Far Right Smears against Congresswomen Running for Reelection." *Newsweek* 124 (11 July 1994): 18–19.

2740. Cooper and Secrest Associates. *Women as Candidates in the 1984 Congressional Elections.* Alexandria, VA: Cooper and Secrest Associates, 1985. Report for the National Women's Political Caucus.

2741. Duke, Lois Lovelace. "Paying Their Dues: Women as Candidates in the U.S. House of Representatives." Paper presented at the annual meeting of the American Political Science Association, Chicago, 1987.

2742. Ehrenhalt, Alan. "The Advantages of the Woman Candidate." *Congressional Quarterly Weekly Report* 42 (24 March 1982): 551.

2743. Falco, Maria J. *'Bigotry': Ethnic, Machine, and Sexual Politics in a Senatorial Election.* Westport, CT: Greenwood Press, 1980.

2744. Finkel, David. "Women on the Verge of a Power Breakthrough." *Washington Post Magazine* (May 1992): 15, 19, 30–34.

2745. Fowler, Linda, and L. Sandy Maisel. "The Changing Supply of Competitive Candidates in House Elections: 1982–1988." Paper presented at the annual meeting of the American Political Science Association, Atlanta, 1989.

2746. Gertzog, Irwin N., and M. Michele Simard. "Women and 'Hopeless' Congressional Candidacies: Nomination Frequency, 1916–1978." *American Politics Quarterly* 9, no. 4 (October 1981): 449–466.

2747. Glover, Keith. "After Years on the Outside, Women … Find They're 'in' as Candidates." *Congressional Quarterly Weekly Report* 50 (2 May 1992): 1178–1179.

2748. Hooper, Jessie Jack, and Anna Dickie Olesen. "Path Finders to the U. S. Senate." *The Woman Citizen* 7 (2 December 1922): 12, 25–26.

2749. Kahn, Kim Fridkin, and Edie N. Goldenberg. "Women Candidates in the News: An Examination of Gender Differences in U.S. Senate Campaign Coverage." *Public Opinion Quarterly* 55 (Summer 1991): 180–199.

2750. Kaplan, Dave. "GOP Looks to Turn the Table on Two Female Freshmen." *Congressional Quarterly Weekly Report* 52 (29 October 1994): 3096–3098.

2751. More, Wendell. "Nun for Congress." *America* 115 (17 December 1966): 797.

2752. "Primaries: Female Candidates, Perot Grab June 2 Spotlight." *Congressional Quarterly Weekly Report* 50 (6 June 1992): 1621–1647.

2753. Rishel, Virginia. "More Women in Government: At Least, More Women Are Candidates for Congressional Office." *American Association of University Women* 42 (October 1948): 21–22.

2754. Rubin, A. J. "Elections Are Looking Like the 'Off Year' of the Woman." *Congressional Quarterly Weekly Report* 52 (15 October 1994): 2972–2974.

2755. Sapiro, Virginia. "If U.S. Senator Baker Were a Woman: An Experimental Study of Candidate Images." *Political Psychology* 3 (1981–82): 61–83.

2756. "There's Room at the Top: Women, Power and Campaigns." *Campaigns and Elections* 8 (May–June 1987): 16–21.

2757. Weston, Marybeth. "Ladies' Day on the Hustings." *The New York Times Magazine* (19 October 1958): VI, 32, 91–95.

2758. "Women Are Running for Congress." *Congressional Quarterly Weekly Report* 18 (4 November 1960): 1831–1832.

2759. "Women Candidates: Many More Predicted for 1974." *Congressional Quarterly Weekly Report* 32 (13 April 1974): 941–944.

2760. "Women in Politics: Leading Candidates in 1970, Their Election Prospects, Past and Present Members." *Congressional Quarterly Weekly Report* 28 (10 July 1970): 1745–1748.

2761. Woodruff, Judy. "Women in the Running." *Harper's Bazaar* 117 (October 1984): 80–88.

Election Returns

2762. Burrell, Barbara C. "Not a Cinderella Story: Success for Women Candidates in 1986." *Campaigns and Elections* 7, no. 5 (January-February 1987): 32–37.

2763. ———. "The Political Opportunity of Women Candidates for the U.S. House of Representatives in 1984." *Women and Politics* 8, no. 1 (Spring 1988): 51–68.

2764. "Campaign '72: Women's Struggle for the Larger Role." *Congressional Quarterly Weekly Report* 30 (22 April 1972): 883–885.

2765. Chaney, Carole, and Barbara Sinclair. "Women and the 1992 House Elections." In *The Year of the Woman: Myths and Realities,* edited by Elizabeth Adell Cook, Sue Thomas, and Clyde Wilcox, 123–140. Boulder, CO: Westview Press, 1994.

2766. "Congress Has Record Number of Women." *Congressional Quarterly Weekly Report* 13 (December 1955): 1310–1311.

2767. Edmunds, Lavinia. "Consolidating Past Gains in the New Congress." *Ms.* 13, no. 9 (March 1985): 95–99.

2768. Gaddie, Ronald Keith, and Charles S. Bullock III. "Congressional Elections and the Year of the Woman." *Social Science Quarterly* 76 (December 1995):749–762.

2769. Gonnerman, Jennifer. "The Femi-Newties." *Village Voice Literary Supplement* 40, no. 5 (31 January 1995): 18–19.

2770. "It Couldn't Happen in Congress Now." *Nation's Business* 25 (February 1937): 18–20.

2771. Katz, Jeffrey L., and Ceci Connolly. "Women, Minorities Rock Records, but Ideology Will Barely Budge." *Congressional Quarterly Weekly Report* 50, no. 44 (7 November 1992): 3557–3564.

2772. Matthews, Glenna. "Women Candidates in the 1990s, Behind the Numbers." *Extensions, A Journal of the Carl Albert Congressional Research and Studies Center* (Spring 1995): 3–6.

2773. McFadden, Judith Nies. "Women's Lib on Capitol Hill." *Progressive* 34 (December 1970): 22–25.

2774. McLaughlin, John. "Women Pols." *National Review* 38, no. 23 (5 December 1986): 24.

2775. "Women Candidates: A Big Increase Over 1972." *Congressional Quarterly Weekly Report* 32 (26 October 1974): 2973–2974.

2776. "Women Candidates: The Voters' Verdict." *U.S. News and World Report* 69 (16 November 1970): 30.

2777. "Women in Politics, Where Do We Stand Now." *National Business Woman* 58, no. 10 (December 1976): 4–6.

Financing and Political Action Committees

2778. Burrell, Barbara C. "Women and Men's Campaigns for the U.S. House of Representatives, 1972–1982: A Finance Gap." *American Politics Quarterly* 13 (July 1985): 251–252.

2779. Nelson, Candice J. "Women's PAC's in the Year of the Woman." In *The Year of the Woman: Myths and Realities,* edited by Elizabeth Adell Cook, Sue Thomas, and Clyde Wilcox, 181–196. Boulder, CO: Westview, 1994.

2780. "Shaking the Money Tree." *Campaigns and Elections* 15, no. 9 (September 1994): 30–131.

2781. Theilmann, John W., and Allen Wilhite. *Discrimination and Congressional Campaign Contributions.* New York: Praeger, 1991.

2782. Uhlaner, Carole Jean, and Kay Lehman Schlozman. "Candidate Gender and Congressional Campaign Receipts." *Journal of Politics* 48 (February 1986): 30–50.

2783. Wilhite, Allen, and John W. Theilmann. "Women, Blacks, and PAC Discrimination." *Social Science Quarterly* 67 (June 1986): 283–298.

Representation

2784. Abzug, Bella S. "Our White, Male, Middle-Class, Middle-Aged Congress." *American Association of University Women* 63 (November 1971): 33–34.

2785. Beckwith, Karen. "Women and Election to National Legislatures: The Effects of Electoral System in France, Italy and the United States." *Rivista Italiana Di Scienza Politica* 20 (1990): 73–103.

2786. Buchanan, Christopher. "Why Aren't There More Women in Congress?" *Congressional Quarterly Weekly Report* 36 (12 August 1978): 2108.

2787. Collins, Gail. "Potty Politics: The Gender Gap." *Working Woman* 18, no. 3 (March 1993): 93.

2788. "50–50 Sex Congress." *Literary Digest* 74 (19 August 1922): 17.

2789. Gersh, Mark. "Shuffling the Deck and Rearranging the Deck Chairs." *Campaigns and Elections* 13, no. 3 (September 1992): 17.

2790. Marchildon, Rudy G. "The 'Persons' Controversy: The Legal Aspects of the Fight for Women Senators." *Atlantis (Canada)* 6 (Spring 1981): 99–113.

2791. Meisol, Patricia. "Women in Politics, Increasing in Numbers, but

Not on the Hill." *National Journal* 10 (July 1968): 1128–1131.

2792. "100 Women in Congress!" *Literary Digest* 82 (23 August 1924): 13.

2793. Paolino, Phillip. "Group-Salient Issues and Group Representation: Support for Women Candidates in the 1992 Senate Elections." *American Journal of Political Science* 39, no. 2 (May 1995): 294–313.

2794. Persons, Georgia A. "Electing Minorities and Women to Congress." In *United States Electoral Systems: Their Impact on Women and Minorities,* edited by Wilma Rule and Joseph F. Zimmerman, 15–30. New York: Greenwood Press, 1992.

2795. Rule, Wilma. "Electoral Systems, Contextual Factors and Women's Opportunity for Election to Parliament in Twenty-Three Democracies." *Western Political Quarterly* 40 (September 1987): 477–498.

2796. ———. "Parliaments of, by, and for the People: Except for Women?" In *Electoral Systems in Comparative Perspective, Their Impact on Women and Minorities,* edited by Wilma Rule and Joseph F. Zimmerman, 15–30. Westport, CT: Greewood Press, 1994.

2797. Rule, Wilma, and Pippa Norris. "Anglo and Minority Women's Underrepresentation in Congress: Is the Electoral System the Culprit?" In *United States Electoral Systems: Their Impact on Women and Minorities,* edited by Wilma Rule and Joseph F. Zimmerman, 55–72. New York: Greenwood Press, 1992.

2798. Shugart, Matthew S. "Minorities Represented and Unrepresented." In *Electoral Systems in Comparative Perspective, Their Impact on Women and Minorities,* edited by Wilma Rule and Joseph F. Zimmerman, 31–44. Westport, CT: Greewood Press, 1994.

2799. Sullivan, Leonor K. "Lack of Leadership in Washington." *Vital Speeches* 23 (1 June 1957): 489–492.

2800. Taagepera, Rein. "Enhancing the Election Prospects of Women and Minorities: Beating the Law of Minority Attrition." In *Electoral Systems in Comparative Perspective, Their Impact on Women and Minorities,* edited by Wilma Rule and Joseph F. Zimmerman, 235–246. Westport, CT: Greenwood Press, 1994.

2801. Tamerius, Karin. "Does Sex Matter? Women Representing Women's Interest in Congress." Paper presented at the annual meeting of the Midwest Political Science Association, Chicago, 1993.

2802. Von Hoffman, Nina. "The Political Woman's Long Hard Climb." *Esquire* 101 (June 1984): 219–222.

2803. Welch, Susan. "Congressional Nomination Procedures and the Representation of Women." *Congress and the Presidency* 16 (Autumn 1989): 121–135.

2804. Williams, Christine. "Women's Electoral Representation: The 1992–94 Congressional Elections." Paper presented at the annual meeting of the American Political Science Association, Chicago, 1995.

2805. Zimmerman, Joseph Francis. "Equity in Representation for

Women and Minorities." In *Electoral Systems in Comparative Perspective, Their Impact on Women and Minorities,* edited by Wilma Rule and Joseph F. Zimmerman, 3–14. Westport, CT: Greenwood Press, 1994.

Congressional Elections in the States

Alabama

2806. "Family Seat." *Time* 30 (30 August 1937): 15.

Arkansas

2807. Deutsch, Hermann B. "Hattie and Huey." *Saturday Evening Post* 205 (15 October 1932): 6–7, 88–90, 92–93.

2808. "First Woman Elected to the United States Senate." *Democratic Digest* 13, no. 5 (May 1936): 8–9.

California

2809. "California Foot Race." *Newsweek* 35 (5 June 1950): 25–26.

2810. DiCamillo, Mark. "How 1992 Truly Became 'The Year of the Woman' in California Politics." Paper presented at the annual meeting of the American Association for Public Opinion Research Conference, Chicago, 1993.

2811. Elving, Ronald D., Ines Pinto Alicea, and Jeffrey L. Katz. "Boxer and Feinstein Victorious in 'Year of the Woman'." *Congressional Quarterly Weekly Report* 50 (6 June 1992): 1621–1631.

2812. Flannery, H. W. "Red Smear in California." *Commonweal* 53 (8 December 1950): 223–225.

2813. Rinehart, Sue Tolleson. "The California Senate Races: A Case Study in the Gendered Paradoxes of Politics." In *The Year of the Woman: Myths and Realities,* edited by Elizabeth Adell Cook, Sue Thomas, and Clyde Wilcox, 25–48. Boulder, CO: Westview, 1994.

2814. Scobie, Ingrid Winther. "Helen Gahagan Douglas and Her 1950 Senate Race with Richard M. Nixon." *Southern California Quarterly* 58 (1976): 113–126.

2815. ———. "Helen Gahagan Douglas: Broadway Star as California Politician." *California History* 66 (December 1987): 242–261.

Connecticut

2816. "Two Connecticut Women Run for Congress." *Democratic Digest* 21, no. 8 (August 1944): 20.

Florida

2817. "A Long Haul for Hawkins (Florida's Senator Paula Hawkins)." *Economist* 296 (24 August 1985): 24.

Georgia

2818. Ethridge, Willie Snow. "The Lady from Georgia." *Good Housekeeping* 76 (January 1923): 27, 122–126.

2819. "Georgia's Black Ballots." *Newsweek* 27 (25 February 1946): 28.

2820. "Good News Down South." *The New Republic* 114 (4 March 1946): 304–305.

2821. "Member Atlanta Club Elected to Congress." *Independent Woman* 25 (March 1946): 44.

2822. "'Mom Is a Congresswoman'." *Ebony* 49, no. 11 (September 1994): 128–130.

2823. Walz, Jay. "Congressman Helen." *The New York Times Magazine* (28 April 1946): VI, 24.

Hawaii

2824. "First Congresswoman from Overseas." *Life* 58 (22 January 1965): 49–50, 52.

Illinois

2825. Adams, Mildred. "Ruth McCormick, Politician and Farmer." *The Woman Citizen* 10 (February 1926): 11.

2826. "Court, Beer and Politics." *The Nation* 130 (23 April 1930): 480.

2827. "First Woman Senator: Does Mrs. McCormick's Candidacy Reflect Those Ideals Which Women Will Be Proud to See Represented?" *Christian Century* 47 (2 April 1929): 425–426.

2828. Jelen, Ted G. "Carol Moseley-Braun: The Insider as Insurgent." In *The Year of the Woman: Myths and Realities,* edited by Elizabeth Adell Cook, Sue Thomas, and Clyde Wilcox, 71–86. Boulder, CO: Westview, 1994.

2829. "Marc Another Hanna." *Colliers* 85 (15 March 1930): 10–11, 56, 59–60.

2830. McCormick, Ruth Hanna. "Candidate for Congressman at Large." *The Republican Woman of Illinois* 5, no. 6 (January 1928): 4.

2831. Miller, Kristie. "Ruth Hanna McCormick and the Senatorial Election of 1930." *Illinois State Historical Journal* 81 (Autumn 1988): 191–210.

2832. "Mrs. McCormick's Trick." *Christian Century* 47 (3 September 1930): 1055–1056.

2833. "Ruth Hanna McCormick." *Time* 11 (23 April 1928): Cover, 12.

Kansas

2834. Bird, John, Jr. "A Campaigner from Kansas." *Independent Woman* 12, no. 1 (January 1933): 49, 70.

Kentucky

2835. "Will It Be Congresswoman Langley?" *Literary Digest* 88 (30 January 1926): 9.

Louisiana

2836. "Lady from Louisiana." *Time* 27 (10 February 1936): 12.

2837. "Third Woman Senator." *Literary Digest* 121 (15 February 1936): 34.

Maine

2838. "A Political First." *National Business Woman* 39 (October 1960): 2.

2839. Sherman, Janann Margaret. "Margaret Chase Smith: The Making of a Senator." Ph.D. dissertation, Rutgers University, 1993.

Maryland

2840. "Katherine Byron Campaigns for Congress." *Democratic Digest* 18, no. 5 (May 1941): 22, 31.

2841. "Maryland Sends Its First Woman to Congress." *Democratic Digest* 18, no. 6 (June 1941): 11, 39.

2842. Mikulski, Barbara. "How We Lost the Election but Won the Campaign." *Ms.* 4, no. 1 (July 1975): 59–61.

2843. Werner, Stella Biddison. "My Dining Room Campaign." *Democratic Digest* 29, no. 1 (January 1952): 6.

Michigan

2844. Romney, Lenore. "Men, Women, and Politics: Lenore Romney Looks Back on Her Unsuccessful Campaign for Senator." *Look* 35 (6 April 1971): 11.

Minnesota

2845. Johnson, Dolores De Bower. "Anna Dickie Olesen, Senate Candidate." In *Women in Minnesota: Selected Biographical Essays,* edited by Barbara Stuhler and Gretchen Kreuter, 226–346. St. Paul: Minnesota Historical Society Press, 1977.

2846. "Out of Andy's Inn." *Time* 71 (19 May 1958): 17–18.

Missouri

2847. Dains, Mary K. "The Congressional Campaign of Luella St. Clair Moss." *Missouri Historical Review* 82, no. 4 (July 1988): 386–407.

2848. "Missouri's Women Candidate." *The Woman Citizen* 7 (7 October 1922): 8, 26.

2849. Moss, Luella St. Clair. "Not 'Outside'." *The Woman Citizen* 7 (13 January 1923): 16.

2850. Sawin, Carol, and Paul Sniderman. "Isolating the Effects of Candidate's Race and Gender in the 1994 Missouri Congressional Elections." Paper presented at the annual meeting of the American Political Science Association, Chicago, 1995.

Montana

2851. Board, John C. "The Lady from Montana." *Montana, The Magazine of Western History* 17 (July 1967): 2–17.

2852. "First Woman Elected to Congress." *Outlook* 114 (22 November 1916): 623–624.

2853. Hardaway, Roger D. "Jeannette Rankin: The Early Years." *North Dakota Quarterly* 48 (Winter 1980): 62–68.

Nebraska

2854. Donovan, Ruth Godfrey. "Lady from the Sandhill." *Independent Woman* 33 (June 1954): 204–206.

2855. "Lady from Nebraska." *Newsweek* 44 (20 December 1954): 20.

Nevada

2856. Anderson, Kathryn. "Practical Political Equality for Women: Anne Martin's Campaigns for the U.S. Senate in Nevada, 1918 and 1920." Ph.D.

dissertation, University of Washington, 1978.

2857. Howard, Anne B. "Anne Martin: Western and National Politics." *Nevada* (1983): 8–14.

2858. ———. *The Long Campaign: A Biography of Anne Martin.* Reno: University of Nevada Press, 1985.

2859. Rannells, W. M. "Woman for Senator." *Public* 21 (19 October 1918): 1308–1310.

New Hampshire

2860. McLane, Susan. "Election Experience Running for Office—The Early Bird." *Ms.* 9, no. 11 (May 1981): 56–58.

New Jersey

2861. Stern, Lynn. "Housewife in Politics." *American Magazine of Civics* 158 (October 1954): 22–25, 118–120.

New Mexico

2862. Cassidy, Mrs. Gerald. "New Mexico Names Her." *The Woman Citizen* 7 (7 October 1922): 8–9.

2863. Hardaway, Roger D. "New Mexico Elects a Congresswoman." *Red River Valley Historical Review* 4 (Fall 1979): 75–89.

2864. Salas, Elizabeth. "Ethnicity, Gender and Issues in the 1922 Campaign by Adeline Otero-Warren for the U.S. House of Representatives." *New Mexico Historical Review* 70 (October 1995): 367–382.

New York

2865. "Case Study U.S. House of Representatives in New York, Sue Kelly." *Campaigns and Elections* 16 (May 1995): 24–29.

2866. "Do Not Overlook These Candidates." *The Woman Citizen* 5 (2 October 1920): 480, 485.

2867. Ferraro, Susan. "What Makes Gerry Run?" *The New York Times Magazine* (22 March 1992): 46–47, 66, 68.

2868. "First Black Woman in the U. S. House of Representatives." *Negro History Bulletin* 33 (May 1970): 128.

2869. Hiss, Toni. "Dilemma in the New 20th Congressional District: Bella Should Be There, So Should Ryan." *The New York Times Magazine* (18 June 1972): 12–13, 53, 56–57, 61–62.

2870. "Izetta Jewel Miller." *Democratic Bulletin* 5, no. 9 (September 1930): 25, 39.

2871. Lockett, Edward B. "FDR's Republican Cousin in Congress." *Colliers* 126 (19 August 1950): 26–27, 40–41.

2872. "Not Women of the Year." *The Nation* 255 (5 October 1992): 345, 347.

2873. Rimmerman, Craig A. "When Women Run against Women: Double Standards and Vitriol in the New York Primary." In *The Year of the Woman: Myths and Realities,* edited by Elizabeth Adell Cook, Sue Thomas, and Clyde Wilcox, 109–122. Boulder, CO: Westview, 1994.

2874. Weis, Jessica McM. "Organizing the Women." In *Politics U.S.A.: A*

Practical Guide to the Winning of Public Office, edited by James Cannon, 171–190. New York: Doubleday, 1960.

Ohio

2875. Cartwright, Marguerite. "Lady Congressman from Ohio." *Negro History Bulletin* 17 (April 1954): 155–156.

2876. Pringle, Henry Fowler, and Katherine Pringle. "He Followed Mom to Congress." *Saturday Evening Post* 226 (15 August 1953): 25.

Oklahoma

2877. "Congresswoman Elected with Want Adds." *Current Opinion* 70 (January 1921): 41–44.

2878. Morgan, Tom P. "Miss Alice of Muskogee." *Ladies Home Journal* 38 (March 1921): 21.

2879. "A Woman Who Got Into Congress Through the Want Ad Column." *Literary Digest* 67 (4 December 1920): 56–58.

Oregon

2880. "Aid to Higher Education: The One That Got Away." *Reporter* 27 (25 October 1962): 28–30.

Pennsylvania

2881. Baer, John M. "The Ultimate Gender Bender." *Lear's* 5, no. 8 (October 1992): 76–79, 116, 119.

2882. "Comstock Rides Again." *The Nation* (5 December 1959): 189–411.

2883. Deber, Raisa B. "The Fault, Dear Brutus: Women as Congression-al Candidates in Pennsylvania." *Journal of Politics* 44, no. 2 (May 1982): 463–479.

2884. Hansen, Susan B. "Lynn Yeakel Versus Arlen Specter in Pennsylvania: Why She Lost." In *The Year of the Woman: Myths and Realities,* edited by Elizabeth Adell Cook, Sue Thomas, and Clyde Wilcox, 87–108. Boulder, CO: Westview, 1994.

2885. "Mrs. Pinchot—Candidate." *The Woman's Journal* 13 (April 1928): 28.

2886. "Women in Congress Now Number Eleven." *Independent Woman* 29 (October 1950): 311.

Rhode Island

2887. Schneider, Claudine. "I Beat the Odds." *Ladies Home Journal* 103 (October 1986): 20, 22.

South Dakota

2888. "In-Between Senators." *Time* 32 (19 December 1938): 10.

Utah

2889. Alicea, Ines Pinto. "Utah: Big Spenders End Up Losers in Primaries for Senate, 2d District Results Set Up the State's First Woman to Woman Congressional Race." *Congressional Quarterly Weekly Report* 50 (12 September 1992): 2739–2740.

2890. "New Faces in Congress." *The New Republic* 120 (24 January 1949): 9.

Virginia

2891. "Shall I Run for Congress?" *Atlantic Monthly* 130 (November 1922): 713–714.

Washington

2892. May, Catherine. "Lady, You Are in Politics." *Successful Farming* 62 (November 1964): 73.

2893. Schroedel, Jean R., and Bruce Snyder. "Patty Murray: The Mom in Tennis Shoes Goes to the Senate." In *The Year of the Woman: Myths and Realities,* edited by Elizabeth Adell Cook, Sue Thomas, and Clyde Wilcox, 49–70. Boulder, CO: Westview, 1994.

West Virginia

2894. Hardin, William H. "Elizabeth Kee: West Virginia's First Woman in Congress." *West Virginia History* 45, no. 1–4 (1984): 109–123.

Wisconsin

2895. Bowen, Edna. "Women Are People." *Democratic Digest* 29, no. 6 (June 1952): 6.

2896. "Elizabeth Hawkes: Candidate for Congress." *Democratic Digest* 21, no. 8 (August 1944): 14.

2897. Graves, Lawrence L. "Two Noteworthy Wisconsin Women: Mrs. Ben Hooper and Ada James." *Wisconsin Magazine of History* 41 (Spring 1958): 176–190.

2898. Smith, James H. "Mrs. Ben Hooper of Oshkosh: Peace Worker and Politician." *Wisconsin Magazine of History* 46, no. 2 (Winter 1962): 124–135.

In the Territories and District

District of Columbia

2899. Whitfield, Tonya. "A Voice—And a Vote—For the District." *National Journal* 25, no. 10 (6 March 1993): 579.

Executive Branch

Presidency

2900. Ade, Ginny. "The Making of a Woman President." *Progressive* 2 (January 1972): 14.

2901. Bird, Caroline. "The Case for a Female President." *New Woman* (April–May 1972): 32–35.

2902. Carpenter, Liz. "Six Women Who Could Be President." *Redbook* 146 (November 1975): 91–93, 132, 134–137.

2903. Cheshire, Herb, and Maxine Cheshire. "Woman for President?" *The New York Times Magazine* (27 May 1956): VI, 60–61.

2904. Clarke, Ida Clyde. "A Woman in the White House: Have We a Presidential Possibility?" *Century* 113 (March 1927): 590–598.

2905. Dusky, Lorraine. "And the First Woman President of the United States Will Be." *McCalls* 117 (September 1990): 88–89. Special issue.

2906. Fine, William M. "Could a Woman Be President?: Why Not?"

Ladies Home Journal 100 (July 1983): 106–108, 175–176.

2907. "For President: A Woman." *Literary Digest* 120 (26 October 1935): 38.

2908. Fryer, Judith. "The Other Victoria: 'The Woodhull' and Her Times." *Old Northwest* 4, no. 3 (1978): 219–240.

2909. "Hey, Look Me Over." *Newsweek* 63 (24 February 1964): 19–20.

2910. Hooton, Earnest. "Woman for President." *Good Housekeeping* 119 (October 1944): 17, 97, 99–100.

2911. "Hormones in the White House." *Time* 96 (10 August 1970): 13.

2912. "If I Were President: Sixteen Famous Women Give Their Program for America." *McCalls* 95 (January 1968): 51–53.

2913. Koepke, Laura A. "Two American Women and Their Candidacies for President of the United States." Master's thesis, University of Southern California, 1985.

2914. Lawrence, David. "Why and Why Not a Woman President?" *U.S. News and World Report* 56 (17 February 1964): 108.

2915. Lesher, Stephan. "Short Unhappy Life of Black Presidential Politics 1972." *The New York Times Magazine* (25 June 1972): 12–13, 15–18.

2916. Lynn, Frank. "Which Woman for the White House?" *50 Plus* 25 (February 1985): 6.

2917. "Madam Candidate." *Time* 83 (7 February 1964): 23.

2918. McGrory, Mary. "Lady in the New England Snow." *America* 110 (22 February 1964): 246.

2919. Morris, Celia. "Waiting for Ms. President." *Harper's Bazaar* 125 (July 1992): 78–88.

2920. Norris, Kathleen. "If I Were President." *Delineator* 114 (January 1929): 9, 50–51.

2921. Sendler, David. "Helen Gurley Brown Predicts: What It Will Be Like When We Elect a Woman President." *Today's Health* 49 (25 December 1971): 26–31.

2922. Shalala, Donna E. "Who Will Be the First Woman President of the United States." *Glamour* 82 (September 1984): 80.

2923. Spain, Jayne Baker. "A Woman Could Be President." *Vital Speeches* 37 (1 April 1971): 357–359.

2924. Steinem, Gloria. "The Ticket That Might Have Been: President Chisholm." *Ms.* 1, no. 7 (January 1973): 72–74.

2925. Summers, Anne, Maureen Dowd, Lorraine Dusky, Jane Ciabattari, and Jody Becker. "Women Who Would Be President." *McCalls* 117 (June 1990): 62–74.

2926. Taylor, Mildred J. "Shall a Woman Be President?" *Christian Science Monitor Magazine* (3 July 1935): 3.

2927. White, Theodore H. "Could a Woman Be President? Not Yet!" *Ladies Home Journal* 100 (July 1983): 106–108, 150–151.

2928. Wieck, Paul R. "On the Chisholm Campaign Trail." *The New*

Republic 165 (4 December 1971): 16–18.

2929. Winner, Julia H. *Belva A. Lockwood.* Lockport, NY: Niagara County Historical Society, 1969.

2930. "A Woman for President? Hurdles in the Path of Margaret Chase Smith." *U.S. News and World Report* 56 (10 February 1964): 34–36.

2931. "Women Who Would Be President." *McCalls* 117 (June 1990): 59–60.

Vice Presidency

2932. Ferraro, Geraldine A. *Ferraro: My Story.* New York: Bantam, 1985.

2933. ———. "The 1984 Campaign and the Women's Movement: Where Do We Go from Here?" In *All American Women, Lines That Divide, Ties That Bind,* edited by Johnnetta B. Cole, 379–382. New York: Free Press, 1986.

2934. ———. *Changing History: Women, Power and Politics.* Wakefield, RI: Moyer Bell, 1993.

2935. Frappallo, Elizabeth. "The Ticket That Might Have Been." *Ms.* 1, no. 7 (January 1973): 74–76.

2936. Gill, Gerald R. "'Win or Lose—We Win': The 1952 Vice Presidential Campaign of Charlotta A. Bass." In *The Afro-American Woman: Struggles and Images,* edited by Sharon Harley and Rosalyn Terborg-Penn, 109–118. Port Washington, NY: Kennikat Press, 1978.

2937. Kunin, Madeleine May. "Woman Vice President for Both Parties in '88." *U.S. News and World Report* 97 (26 November 1984): 33–34.

2938. "Mondale and Women: Courting Disaster." *Economist* 292 (7 July 1984): 20–21.

2939. Northcott, Kaye. "Only a Heartbeat Away: Will the Next Vice President of the United States Be a Woman?" *Mother Jones* 9 (June 1984): 34–40.

2940. "Nothing Like a Dame (W. Mondale's Running Mate)." *Economist* 291 (23 June 1984): 15.

2941. Rosen, Jane. "The Kirkpatrick Factor." *The New York Times Magazine* (28 April 1985): VI, 48–51, 68, 70.

2942. Steinem, Gloria. "A Woman Runs for Vice-President." In *Women Leaders in American Politics,* edited by James David Barber and Barbara Kellerman, 281–293. Englewood Cliffs, NJ: Prentice Hall, 1986.

2943. "Their Hats Were in the Ring." *Independent Woman* 31 (August 1952): 226.

2944. Titchener, Dorothy. "Our Woman for Vice President Campaign." *Independent Woman* 31 (September 1952): 260.

2945. Ward, Cynthia V. "Outstanding Women on the Bush List." *Conservative Digest* 14, no. 6 (1988): 83–90.

2946. "Women in Politics: Mrs. Vice-President?" *Economist* 291 (2 June 1984): 20–21.

State Government

State Legislatures

General

2947. Adams, Linda A. "Changing the Rules." *Journal of State Government* 64, no. 2 (April–June 1991): 60–62.

2948. Cox, Elizabeth M. "Introduction." In *Women State and Territorial Legislators, 1895–1995,* 11–41. Jefferson, NC: McFarland, 1995.

2949. Mannes, Marya. "Channels: Two American Women." *Reporter* 9, no. 9 (24 September 1953): 41.

2950. "The Negro Woman in Politics." *Ebony* 21 (August 1966): 96–100.

2951. Rule, Wilma. "Why More Women Are State Legislators: A Research Note." *Western Political Quarterly* 43 (June 1990): 437–438.

2952. Thompson, Joel A., and Gary F. Moncrief. "Race, Gender and State Legislative Campaign Contributions: A Comparative Analysis." Paper presented at the annual meeting of the Southwestern Political Science Association, San Antonio, March 1991.

Recruitment

2953. Blair, Diane Kincaid, and Ann R. Henry. "The Family Factor in State Legislative Turnover." *Legislative Studies Quarterly* 6 (February 1981): 55–68.

2954. Del Papa, Frankie Sue. "Taking the Risk to Run for Office." *Journal of State Government* 64, no. 2 (April 1991): 55–56.

2955. Mathews, Donald G. "Legislative Recruitment and Legislative Careers." *Legislative Studies Quarterly* 9 (November 1984): 547–585.

2956. Rule, Wilma. "Why Women Don't Run: The Critical Contextual Factors in Women's Legislative Recruitment." *Western Political Quarterly* 34, no. 1 (March 1981): 60–77.

2957. ———. "Why Are More Women State Legislators?" In *Women in Politics: Outsiders or Insiders? A Collection of Readings,* edited by Lois Lovelace Duke, 152–163. Englewood Cliffs, NJ: Prentice Hall, 1993.

2958. Schapiro, Beth Susan. "The Recruitment of Southern State Legislators: A Comparison of Men and Women." Ph.D. dissertation, Emory University, Atlanta, 1979.

2959. "They Do It, You Can Too: Wives and Mothers in Our State Legislatures." *Ladies Home Journal* 73 (April 1956): 70–71.

2960. Welch, Susan. "The Recruitment of Women to Public Office: A Discriminant Analysis." *Western Political Quarterly* 31, no. 3 (September 1978): 372–380.

2961. Williams, Christine. "Women, Law and Politics: Recruitment Patterns in the Fifty States." *Women and Politics* 10, no. 3 (1990): 103–124.

Running

2962. Ambrosius, Margery M., and Susan Welch. "Women and Politics at the Grassroots: Women Candidates for State Office in Three States, 1950–1978." *Social Science Journal* 21, no. 1 (January 1985): 29–42.

2963. Clark, Janet M., Robert Darcy, Susan Welch, and Margery M. Ambrosius. "Women as Legislative Candidates in Six States." In *Political Women: Current Roles in State and Local Government,* edited by Janet A. Flammang, 141–155. Women's Policy Studies. Beverly Hills, CA: Sage, 1984.

2964. Darcy, Robert, Susan Welch, and Janet M. Clark. "Women Candidates in Single- and Multi-Member Districts: American State Legislative Races." *Social Science Quarterly* 66 (December 1985): 945–953.

2965. Dubeck, Paula J., and Marcia Manning Lee. "Women and Access to Political Office: A Comparison of Female and Male State Legislators." *The Sociological Quarterly* 17, no. 1 (Winter 1976): 42–52.

2966. Nechemias, Carol. "Geographic Mobility and Women's Access to State Legislatures." *Western Political Quarterly* 38, no. 1 (March 1985): 119–131.

2967. Welch, Susan, Margery M. Ambrosius, and Janet M. Clark. "The Effect of Candidate Gender on Electoral Outcomes in State Legislative Races." *Western Political Quarterly* 38 (September 1985): 464–475.

Election Returns

2968. Gordon, Dianna. "Republican Women Make Gains." *State Legislatures* 21, no. 2 (February 1995): 15.

2969. Nechemias, Carol. "Women's Success in Capturing State Legislative Seats." Paper presented at the annual meeting of the Midwest Political Science Association, Chicago, April 1985.

2970. ———. "Changes in the Election of Women to U.S. State Legislative Seats." *Legislative Studies Quarterly* 12, no. 1 (February 1987): 125–142.

2971. "Number of Women in State Legislatures Increases Yearly." *State Legislatures* 13, no. 9 (October 1987): 7.

2972. Thaemert, Rita. "Twenty Percent and Climbing: More and More Women Are Being Elected to the Legislatures." *State Legislatures* 20, no. 1 (January 1994): 28–32.

2973. Ulman, Cynthia. *Roster of Women State Legislators.* Washington, DC: National Women's Education Fund, 1979.

Representation

2974. Almquist, Elizabeth M., Ray Darville, and Pat Freudinger. "Women's Share of State Legislative Seats: Political and Social Variables." *Free Inquiry in Creative Sociology* 13 (1985): 165–169.

2975. Calvert, Jerry. "Revolving Doors: Volunteerism in State Legislatures." *State Government* 52 (Autumn 1979): 174–181.

2976. Cox, Elizabeth M. "Redrawing the Lines to Speed Up Equal Representation." *Update* 3, no. No. 1 (Fall 1990): 1–2.

2977. Darcy, Robert. "A Formal Analysis of Legislative Turnover; Women Candidates and Legislative Representation." *American Journal of Political Science* 30 (February 1986): 237–255.

2978. Gross, Debra. "Taking Another Look at Descriptive Representation: The Case of Women Legislators." Paper presented at the annual meeting of the American Political Science Association, Atlanta, 1989.

2979. Hill, David B. "Political Culture and Female Political Representation." *Journal of Politics* 43 (February 1981): 159–168.

2980. Jones, Woodrow, and Albert J. Nelson. "Correlates of Women's Representation in Lower State Legislative Chambers." *Social Behavior and Personality* 1 (1981): 9–15.

2981. Moncrief, Gary F., Joel A. Thompson, and Robert Schulmann. "Gender, Race, and the State Legislature: A Research Note on the Double Disadvantage Hypothesis." *Social Science Journal* 28, no. 4 (October 1991): 481–487.

2982. Sherman, Sharon. "Women Legislators Seek 'Critical Mass'." *State Legislatures* 10 (January 1984): 26–27.

Structural Barriers

2983. Castles, Francis. "Female Legislative Representation and the Electoral System." *Politics (Australia)* 1 (April 1981): 21–26.

2984. Darcy, Robert, Charles D. Hadley, and Jason F. Kirksey. "Election Systems and the Representation of Black Women in American State Legislatures." *Women and Politics* 13, no. 2 (1993): 73–89.

2985. Matland, Richard, and Deborah Dwight Brown. "District Magnitudes Effect on Female Representation in U.S. State Legislatures." *Legislative Studies Quarterly* 17 (November 1992): 469–492.

2986. Moncrief, Gary F., and Joel A. Thompson. "The Move to Limit Terms of Office: Assessing the Consequences for Female State Legislators." Paper presented at the annual meeting of the Western Political Science Association, Seattle, March 1991.

2987. Perry, Pamela Marie. "Proximity and Other Systemic Factors Affecting Women's Social Representation in State Houses of Representatives." Master's thesis, Georgia State University, 1982.

2988. Rule, Wilma. "Multimember Legislative Districts: Minority and Anglo Women's and Men's Recruitment Opportunity." In *United States Electoral Systems: Their Impact on Women and Minorities,* edited by Wilma Rule and Joseph F. Zimmerman, 57–72. New York: Greenwood Press, 1992.

2989. Thompson, Joel A., and Gary F. Moncrief. "The Implications of Term Limits for Women and Minorities: Some Evidence from the States." *Social Science Quarterly* 74 (June 1993): 300–309.

State Executive Branch

2990. Kahn, Kim Fridkin. "The Distorted Mirror: Press Coverage of Women Candidates for Statewide Office." *Journal of Politics* 56 (February 1984): 154–173.

2991. ———. "Does Gender Make a Difference? An Experimental Examination of Sex Stereotype and Press Patterns in Statewide Campaigns." *American Journal of Political Science* 38 (February 1994): 162–195.

2992. Morris, Celia. *Storming the Statehouse: Running for Governor with Ann Richards and Dianne Feinstein.* New York: Charles Scribner's Sons, 1992.

2993. Richards, Ann W. "What's Gender Got to Do with It?" *Redbook* 182 (November 1993): 99.

State Judicial Branch

2994. Martin, Elaine. "The Impact of Candidate's Sex on State Non-Partisan Judicial Campaigns." *Michigan Academician* 18, no. 1 (Winter 1986): 61–72.

2995. Ness, Susan, and Fredrica Wechsler. "Women Judges—Why So Few?" *Graduate Woman* 73 (November–December 1979): 10–12.

In the States

Alabama

2996. "Two Leaders Achieve through Action, Today, Alabama President Announces for State Office." *National Business Woman* 37 (May 1958): 6.

Alaska

2997. "Political Gains Made by Alaska Native Women." *Alaska Native News* (January 1983): 26.

Arizona

2998. Saint-Germain, Michelle A. "Patterns of Legislative Opportunity in Arizona: Sex, Race and Ethnicity." In *United States Electoral Systems: Their Impact on Women and Minorities,* edited by Wilma Rule and Joseph F. Zimmerman, 119–128. New York: Greenwood Press, 1992.

California

2999. Block, A. G. "The Top Six." *California Journal* 19 (July 1988): 280–288.

3000. Chasnoff, Debra. "Ms. Achtenberg (Almost) Goes to Sacramento." *Outlook* 1, no. 4 (Winter 1989): 22–31.

3001. Chen, Edwin. "Rose Bird Runs for Her Life." *The Nation* 242 (18 January 1986): 42–44.

3002. Crawford, Marie Adams. "Political Pioneering in California." *Independent Woman* 32 (February 1953): 44–46, 64.

3003. Knight, Robert H. "Bye Bye Birdie." *National Review* 38 (12 September 1986): 42–44.

3004. Lafferty, Elaine. "Big Political Prizes Elude L.A. Women: Despite Increased Clout." *California Journal* 18 (June 1987): 296–298.

3005. Love, Keith. "Will Dianne Feinstein Play in Pacoima?" *Los Angeles*

Times Magazine (25 February 1990): 11–16, 18, 34–35.

3006. Mills, Kay. "Gloria Molina." *Ms.* 13, no. 7 (January 1985): 80–81, 114.

3007. "The New Gang in California." *Economist* 322 (29 February 1992): 32.

3008. Polos, Nicholas C. "San Diego's 'Portia of the Pacific': California's First Woman Lawyer." *Journal of San Diego History* 2, no. 3 (1980): 185–195.

3009. Roberts, Jerry. *Dianne Feinstein: Never Let Them See You Cry.* San Francisco: HarperCollins West, 1994.

3010. "Women on the Verge?" *California Journal* 23, no. 7 (July 1992): 369.

3011. Zeiger, Richard, and Sherry Bebitch Jeffe. "Women in Politics: Moving In, Yes; Moving Up, Maybe." *California Journal* 19 (January 1988): 7–11.

Colorado

3012. "Colorado Women Win Recognition." *The Woman's Journal* 45 (22 August 1914): 244.

3013. Committee on Promotion of Qualified Women for Elective and Appointive Offices. *See How She Runs.* Pueblo: Colorado Commission on Status of Women, 1972.

3014. Essary, Helen. "Josephine Roche, Candidate for Governor of Colorado." *Democratic Digest* 11, no. 7 (July 1934): 11–12.

3015. Meredith, Ellis. "Women in Colorado Politics." *The Woman's Journal* 36 (1905): 72.

Connecticut

3016. Trester, Joseph B. "Ella Grasso of Connecticut: Running and Winning." *Ms.* 3 (October 1974): 80–82, 122.

3017. Wilson, Gary B. "Women in Politics: Images and Voter Support." Paper presented at the annual meeting of the International Communication Association, Chicago, 1975.

Florida

3018. Morris, Allen. "Florida's First Women Candidates." *Florida Historical Quarterly* 63 (April 1985): 406–422.

3019. Pritchard, Anita. "Changes in Electoral Structure and the Success of Women Candidates: The Case of Florida." *Social Science Quarterly* 73 (March 1992): 62–70. Paper presented at the annual meeting of the American Political Science Association, Atlanta, August, 1989.

3020. ———. "Florida: The Big Electoral Shakeup of 1982." In *United States Electoral Systems: Their Impact on Women and Minorities,* edited by Wilma Rule and Joseph F. Zimmerman, 87–97. New York: Greenwood Press, 1992.

Georgia

3021. Fowlkes, Diane L. "Women in Georgia Electoral Politics: 1970–78." *Social Science Journal* 21 (January 1984): 43–56.

Hawaii

3022. Mezey, Susan Gluck. "Women and Representation; The Case of Hawaii." *Journal of Politics* 40, no. 2 (May 1978): 369–385.

Idaho

3023. "How Five Women Appointed a State Senator." *Democratic Digest* 12, no. 7 (December 1935): 19.

Illinois

3024. "Republican Candidates for State-Wide Office." *The Republican Woman of Illinois* 7, no. 7 (March 1930): 2–8.

Indiana

3025. "Women as State Officers in Indiana." *The Woman's Journal* 39 (8 February 1908): 23.

Iowa

3026. Miller, Judy Ann. "The Representative Is a Lady." *Black Politician* 1 (Fall 1969): 17–18.

Kentucky

3027. Babbage, Bob. *Toward Balance: Women in Politics.* Frankfort, KY: Secretary of State, 1995.

Maryland

3028. Conway, M. Margaret. "Creative Multimember Redistricting and Representation of Women and Minorities in the Maryland Legislature." In *United States Electoral Systems: Their Impact on Women and Minorities,* edited by Wilma Rule and Joseph F. Zimmerman, 99–110. New York: Greenwood Press, 1992.

Massachusetts

3029. Burrell, Barbara C. "The Presence of Women Candidates and the Role of Gender in Campaigns for the State Legislature in an Urban Setting: The Case of Massachusetts." *Women and Politics* 3 (Spring 1990): 85–102.

Michigan

3030. "Black Woman Speaker Pro Tempore of Michigan House, T. P. Hunter." *Jet* 71 (12 January 1987): 22.

Minnesota

3031. Gierzynski, Anthony, and Paulette Budreck. "Women Legislative Caucus and Leadership Campaign Committees." *Women and Politics* 15, no. 2 (1995): 23–36.

3032. "When a Mom Goes into Politics: Mrs. Knutson." *U.S. News and World Report* 45 (5 September 1958): 42–43.

Mississippi

3033. "Elected State Treasure, Evelyn Gandy." *National Business Woman* 39, no. 3 (March 1960): 22.

3034. Johnston, Erle. "First Woman Elected Lieutenant Governor." In *Politics: Mississippi Style,* 246–252. Forest, MS: Lake Harbor, 1993.

3035. "Votes for BEP: Betty Jane Long, Member of Mississippi Legislature." *American Magazine of Civics* 161 (March 1956): 56.

Nebraska

3036. Welch, Susan. *Women Candidates for the Nebraska State Legislature, 1970–1980.* Lincoln: Government Research Institute, University of Nebraska, 1982.

New Hampshire

3037. Hamilton, Ruth M. "It's Better to Have Run and Lost." *Democratic Digest* 18, no. 3 (March 1941): 22, 31.

New Jersey

3038. Beard, Patricia. "Leading Lady." *Town and Country Monthly* 149, no. 5178 (March 1995): 100–105.

New Mexico

3039. Clark, Cal, and Janet M. Clark. "The Growth of Women's Candidacies for Nontraditional Political Offices in New Mexico." *Social Science Journal* 21, no. 1 (January 1984): 57–65.

3040. Jensen, Joan M. "Pioneers in Politics." *El Palacio* 92 (Summer–Fall 1986): 12–19.

3041. Larkin, Anna S. "Between Two Machines." *The Woman Citizen* 10 (November 1925): 13, 36–37.

New York

3042. Shalit, Ruth. "Heavens to Betsy." *New Republic* 21 (7 November 1994): 16–18.

North Carolina

3043. Press, Aric. "A Vote on the Quality of Mercy." *Newsweek* 108 (3 November 1986): 63–64.

North Dakota

3044. Severson, Lynn. "Women in North Dakota Politics." In *Day In, Day Out: Women's Lives in North Dakota,* edited by Bjorn Benson, Elizabeth Hampsten, and Kathryn Sweney, 205–209. Grand Forks: University of North Dakota, 1988.

Ohio

3045. Dean, Rebecca, and Zoe Oxley. "The Representation of Minority Group Interests: Women and African Americans in Ohio." Paper presented at the annual meeting of the American Political Science Association, 1995.

3046. Dickinson, Agnes Bryant. "Judge Allen's Glorious Defeat." *The Woman Citizen* 11 (October 1926): 10–11, 39–40.

3047. Hauser, Elizabeth J. "The Great Achievement." *The Woman Citizen* 7 (30 December 1922): 11–12, 27.

Oklahoma

3048. Darcy, Robert, Margaret Brewer, and Judy Clay. "Women in the Oklahoma Political System: State Legislative Elections." *Social Science Journal* 21 (January 1984): 67–78.

3049. Williams, Nudie. "The Gender Liberation: Black Women as Elected Officials in Oklahoma." In *Women in*

Oklahoma, *A Century of Change*, edited by Melvena K. Thurman, 199–210. Oklahoma City: Oklahoma Historical Society, 1986.

Oregon

3050. Collins, Huntly. "Betty Roberts of Oregon: Running and ... Running." *Ms.* 3, no. 4 (October 1974): 83.

3051. Fadeley, Nancie. "Running for Office—Handbook from the Front Lines." *Ms.* 9, no. 11 (May 1981): 75–76.

Pennsylvania

3052. Gallaher, Sarah M. "Cambria County's Campaign." *The Woman Citizen* 7 (27 January 1923): 12–13, 27.

South Dakota

3053. "Will She Be Governor." *The Woman Citizen* 7 (7 October 1922): 8, 26.

Tennessee

3054. Robertson, Suzanne Craig. "Gearing Up for 1990: Workshop Teaches Women How to Run for Judge." *Tennessee Bar Journal* 24 (March–April 1988): 20–21.

3055. Vial, Rebecca, and W. Calvin Dickinson. "Kate Bradford Stockton." *Tennessee Historical Quarterly* 49 (Fall 1990): 152–160.

3056. Worden, Helen. "Pretty Good Politicians." *Colliers* 125 (14 January 1950): 18–19, 73.

Texas

3057. Catt, Carrie Chapman. "'Ma Ferguson'." *The Woman Citizen* 9 (6 September 1924): 16.

3058. Collins, Gail. "The Unsinkable Meets the Unthinkable." *Working Woman* 20, no. 3 (March 1995): 52–53.

3059. Cunningham, Patricia Ellen. "Too Gallant a Walk: Minnie Fisher Cunningham and Her Race for Governor of Texas in 1944." Master's thesis, University of Texas, Austin, 1985.

3060. ———. "Bonnet in the Ring: Minnie Fisher Cunningham's Campaign for Governor of Texas in 1944." In *Women and Texas History*, edited by Fane Downs and Nancy Baker Jones, 102–115. Austin: Texas State Historical Association, 1993.

3061. Gallaher, Robert S. "Me for Ma, and I Ain't Got a Dern Thing against Pa." *American Heritage* 17 (October 1966): 46–47.

3062. "'Ma' Ferguson of Texas." *Literary Digest* 82 (13 September 1924): 38, 40.

3063. Miller, Lawrence W., and Lillian Noyes. "The Thrill of Victory and the Agony of Defeat: Women Contenders for Seats in the Texas House of Representatives." *Public Service* 6 (September 1978): 1–5.

3064. Richards, Ann W. "Fundraising for Women Candidates: All the Equality You Can Afford." *Journal of State Government* 60, no. 5 (September–October 1987): 216–218.

3065. Stanley, Jeanie R., and Candace Winderl. "Gender Politics in the 1994 Texas Elections." Paper presented at the annual meeting of the American Political Science Association, Chicago, 1995.

3066. Tolleson-Rinehart, Sue, and Jeanie R. Stanley. *Claytie and the Lady: Ann Richards, Gender, and Politics in Texas.* Austin: University of Texas Press, 1994.

Virginia

3067. Hollinger, F. Barnard, ed. *Outside the Magic Circle: The Autobiography of Virginia Foster Durr.* Tuscaloosa: University of Alabama, 1985.

Wisconsin

3068. Youmans, Theodora W. "My Campaign." *The Woman Citizen* 7 (21 October 1922): 26.

Wyoming

3069. Easton, Carol. "Honorable Nellie." *Westways* 68, no. 11 (1976): 22–25, 70–71.

Local Government

General

3070. Antolini, Denise. "Women in Local Government: An Overview." In *Political Women: Current Roles in State and Local Government,* edited by Janet A. Flammang, 23–40. Women's Policy Studies, 8. Beverly Hills, CA: Sage, 1984.

3071. Lee, Marcia Manning. "Toward Understanding Why Few Women Hold Public Office: Factors Affecting the Participation of Women in Local Politics." In *A Portrait of Marginality: The Political Behavior of American Women,* edited by Marianne Githens and Jewell Prestage, 118–138. New York: McKay, 1977.

3072. Lee, Percy Maxim. "Why Not More Women in Public Office?" *National Municipal Review* 43 (October 1954): 307–308.

3073. MacManus, Susan A. "How to Get More Women in Office: The Perspectives of Local Elected Officials." *Urban Affairs Quarterly* 28 (September 1992): 159–170.

3074. McCarty, Kathryn Shane. "Women in Municipal Government, 3,740 Serve as Mayors or on Councils, a 20% Share." *Nation's Cities* 14, no. 36 (16 September 1991).

3075. Merritt, Sharyne. "Winners and Losers: Sex Differences in Municipal Elections." *American Journal of Political Science* 21 (November 1977): 731–744.

3076. Miller, Lawrence W. "Political Recruitment and Electoral Success: A Look at Sex Differences in Municipal Elections." *Social Science Journal* 23, no. 1 (1986): 75–90.

3077. Moore, W. John. "From Dreamers to Doers." *National Journal* 20 (13 February 1988): 372–377.

3078. Stewart, Debra W., ed. *Women in Local Politics.* Metuchen, NJ: Scarecrow Press, 1980.

3079. Welch, Susan, and Albert K. Karnig. "Correlates of Female Office-Holding in City Politics." *Journal of Politics* 41, no. 2 (May 1979): 478–491.

Local Legislatures

3080. Alozie, Nicholas O., and Lynne L. Mangawaro. "Women's Council Representation: Measurement Implication for Public Policy." *Political Research Quarterly* 46, no. 2 (1993): 383–398.

3081. Bellar, Stephanie Lynn. "Cherchez Les Femmes: An Analysis of Gender Based Differences in Recruitment Patterns among City Council Candidates." Ph.D. dissertation, University of Kentucky, 1986.

3082. Brooks, Gary H. "Women on City Councils: National Trends and Mississippi." *Public Administration Survey* 24 (September 1976): 1–5.

3083. Brown, Clyde. "Judgments about the Capabilities of City Councilors and Support for Female Representatives on City Councils." *Social Science Journal* 31, no. 4 (1994): 3555–3573.

3084. Bullock, Charles S., III, and Susan A. MacManus. "Municipal Electoral Structure and the Election of Councilwomen." *Journal of Politics* 53 (February 1991): 75–89.

3085. Center for the American Woman and Politics. *Women and Men on School Boards.* New Brunswick, NJ: Center for the American Woman and Politics, Rutgers University, 1979.

3086. "City Councilwomen: A Different Perspective." *Nation's Cities* 11 (September 1973): 24–31.

3087. Dutton, William H. "The Political Ambitions of Local Legislators: A Comparative Perspective." *Polity* 7 (Summer 1975): 504–522.

3088. "It's 'No Accident' That Men Outnumber Women on School Boards Nine to One." *American School Board Journal* 161, no. 5 (May 1974): 53–55.

3089. MacManus, Susan A. "Women on Southern City Councils: A Decade of Change." *Journal of Political Science* 17 (1989): 32–49.

3090. Merritt, Sharyne. "Recruitment of Women to Suburban City Councils: Higgins v. Chevalier." In *Women in Local Politics,* edited by Debra W. Stewart, 86–105. Metuchen, NJ: Scarecrow Press, 1980.

3091. Morrissey, William. "The Status and Perceptions of Women School Board Members in Indiana." Ph.D. dissertation, Indiana University, Indianapolis, 1972.

3092. Mullins, Carolyn. "The Plight of the Boardwoman: The Female School Board Member Has a Tough Time of It." *American School Board Journal* 159 (February 1972): 27–32.

3093. ———. "If Superintendents Could Pick Their Own School Board Members Here's the Kind They Say They'd Choose." *American School Board Journal* 161 (September 1974): 25–29.

3094. Welch, Susan, and Albert K. Karnig. "Sex and Ethnic Differences in Municipal Representation." *Social*

Science Quarterly 60, no. 3 (December 1979): 465–481.

3095. Well, Kate Gannett. "Women on School Board, September 1905." *North American Review* 272 (1987): 84–85.

Local Executives

3096. Aulette, Judy. "'It's a Fight for Humanity's Sake,' An Interview with Geraldyne Sawyer, First Black 'Woman' Mayor in the South." *Humanity and Society* 11, no. 4 (November 1987): 486–497.

3097. Barker, Stella E. "You Never Know until You Try: Candidate for County Recorder." *Independent Woman* 30 (January 1951): 5.

3098. Bradford, Mary C. C. "Tuning In." *The Woman Citizen* 7 (13 January 1923): 16–17.

3099. Dodd, John Theodore. "Women as Justices of the Peace." *Contemporary* 112 (September 1917): 320.

3100. "An Indian Woman for Sheriff." *Indian's Friend* 42, no. 5 (1930): 4.

3101. Karnig, Albert K., and B. Oliver Walter. "Election of Women to City Councils." *Social Science Quarterly* 56, no. 4 (March 1976): 605–613.

3102. MacManus, Susan A. "Determinants of the Equitably of Female Representation on 243 City Councils." Paper presented at the annual meeting of the American Political Science Association, Chicago, August 1976.

3103. Mayer, Jean. "Let's Put Women in Their Place Like, for Instance, City Hall." *McCalls* 98 (February 1971): 74.

3104. Moyer-Wing, Alice C. "When a Woman Is the Head." *Scribner's Magazine* 81 (June 1927): 589–594.

3105. Saltzstein, Grace Hall. "Female Mayors and Women in Municipal Jobs." *American Journal of Political Science* 30 (February 1986): 140–164.

3106. Stewart, Alva W. "Why, When and How of Women Mayors." *American City* 83 (September 1968): 168, 170.

3107. "Towns Run By Women." *The New York Times Magazine* (27 October 1940): VII, 17.

3108. "Two West Coast Cities Elect Women as Mayors." *American City* 63 (July 1948): 7.

In the States

Alabama

3109. Still, Edward. "Cumulative Voting and Limited Voting in Alabama." In *United States Electoral Systems: Their Impact on Women and Minorities,* edited by Wilma Rule and Joseph F. Zimmerman, 183–196. Westport, CT: Greenwood Press, 1992.

Arkansas

3110. Honeycutt, Tom. "Here Comes Ms. Mayor: Pine Bluff's Two Major Mayoral Candidates Are Women, but That's about All They Have in Common." *Arkansas Times* 11 (October 1984): 75–78.

California

3111. Flammang, Janet A. "Female Officials in the Feminist Capital: The Case of Santa Clara County." *Western Political Quarterly* 38 (March 1985): 94–118.

3112. Fleischman, Arnold, and Lana Stein. "Minority and Female Success in Municipal Runoff Elections." *Social Science Quarterly* 68 (June 1987): 378–388.

3113. "It's a Girl … In the L. A. City Council." *Democratic Digest* 1, no. 2 (September 1953): 49–53.

3114. Lindsey, Estelle. "Running to Win." *Ladies Home Journal* 33 (November 1916): 14–15, 112–113.

Colorado

3115. Meredith, Ellis. "The Denver School Election." *The Woman's Journal* 31 (16 June 1900): 189.

Connecticut

3116. Mezey, Susan Gluck. "The Effects of Sex on Recruitment: Connecticut Local Offices." In *Women in Local Politics*, edited by Debra W. Stewart, 61–85. Metuchen, NJ: Scarecrow Press, 1980.

Florida

3117. MacManus, Susan A. "It's Never Too Late to Run—And Win! The Graying of Women in Local Politics." *National Civic Review* 80 (Summer 1991): 294–311.

3118. MacManus, Susan A., and Charles S. Bullock III. "Electing Women to City Council: A Focus on Small Cities in Florida." In *United States Electoral Systems: Their Impact on Women and Minorities,* edited by Wilma Rule and Joseph F. Zimmerman, 167–182. New York: Greenwood Press, 1992.

3119. "This Mayor Is Sister." *American City* 85 (December 1970): 51.

Illinois

3120. Alter, Sharon Z. "A Woman for Mayor?" *Chicago History* 15, no. 3 (1986): 52–68.

3121. Andreoli, Tom. "Women as Mayors and Village President: From 1% to 15% in Chicago Suburbs." *Illinois Issues* 17 (June 1991): 26–30.

3122. Candeloro, Dominic. "The Chicago School Board Crisis of 1907." *Journal of Illinois State Historical Society* 68, no. 5 (1975): 396–406.

3123. H'Doubler, Mrs. Francis Todd. "Cook County's First Woman Commissioner." *The Woman Citizen* 7 (13 January 1923): 12.

3124. Hickey, Margaret. "Political Babes in the Woods against the Sharp Boys." *Ladies Home Journal* 68 (December 1951): 51, 100.

3125. Penrose, Gertrude. "Party Lines Crossed to Elect BPW Judge in Chicago." *Independent Woman* 33 (February 1954): 51–52.

3126. Sloane, Todd. "Women Poised to Assume Lead Roles." *City and State* 10, no. 2 (18–31 January 1993): 5.

3127. Wendt, Lloyd, and Herman Kogan. "The Challenge of Marion Drake." In *Bosses in Lusty Chicago: The*

Story of Bathhouse John and Rinky Dink, 305–314. Bloomington: Indiana University Press, 1971.

Indiana

3128. Jones, Lisa C. "Evanston Elects Educator." *Ebony* 48 (July 1993): 39, 42.

Kansas

3129. Aley, Marion. "All Around the Town: Mayor Clara Williford of Ellsworth, Kansas." *Independent Woman* 17 (October 1938): 311, 331.

3130. Cooper, Courtney R. "Enter the Mayoress at Hunnewell." *Colliers* 47 (29 July 1911): 20.

3131. "Kansasans Vote Complaining Women into Office." *Literary Digest* 123 (24 April 1937): 7.

Louisiana

3132. Humphreys, Hubert. "Rev. Lula Wardlow: Louisiana's First Elected Woman Mayor." *North Louisiana Historical Association Journal* 18, no. 1 (1987): 2–10.

Massachusetts

3133. Goodman, Ellen. "People: Louise Day Hick—'When They Call Me a Racist, I Don't Listen … '." *Ms.* 4, no. 7 (January 1976): 99–103.

3134. "Why Not Elect a Woman." *The Woman's Journal* 43 (6 January 1912): 1, 3.

Michigan

3135. Ellis, Anne. "An Ordinary Woman in Politics." *Ladies Home Journal* 48 (April 1931): 14–15, 68, 71, 73.

3136. Francis, Martin. "These Women Entered Politics for a Definite Civic Purpose." *American City* 51 (July 1936): 77.

Montana

3137. Manning, Richard D. "How Three Women Took Over Missoula County and the 'Gender Factor' Became an Edge." *Governing* 1, no. 8 (May 1988): 44–50.

New Mexico

3138. Triviz, Rita. "I'll Tell You How I Won." *Ms.* 9, no. 11 (May 1981): 75.

New York

3139. DeCrow, Karen. "Women and Politics." *Mademoiselle* (February 1970): 34, 36, 142.

3140. Weaver, Leon, and Judith Baum. "Proportional Representation on New York City Community School Boards." In *United States Electoral Systems: Their Impact on Women and Minorities,* edited by Wilma Rule and Joseph F. Zimmerman, 197–206. New York: Greenwood Press, 1992.

Ohio

3141. "Ball-Playing Councilwoman, Petite Jean Capers." *Ebony* 6 (November 1950): 48–49.

3142. "Cleveland Gets Out the Vote: Two Negro Women Fight It Out for City Council Job." *Our World* 7 (February 1952): 40–45.

Oregon

3143. "Portland's Cleanup." *Life* 26 (21 March 1949): 40–41.

Pennsylvania

3144. Slaymaker, Samuel R. "Mrs. Frazer's Philadelphia Campaign." *Journal of Lancaster County Historical Society* 73 (September 1969): 185–210.

Texas

3145. Bernstein, Robert A., and Jayne D. Polley. "Race, Class and Support for Female Candidates." *Western Political Quarterly* 28 (December 1975): 733–736.

3146. MacManus, Susan A. "A City's First Female Officeholder: 'Coattails' for Future Female Officeseekers?" *Western Political Quarterly* 35 (March 1981): 88–99.

3147. Tourque, Barbara. "Breaking the Ole Boy Network." *Newsweek* 113 (19 June 1989): 39.

Virginia

3148. LaCoste, Richard. "Petticoat Government Suits This Town." *Independent Woman* 32 (June 1953): 193, 222.

3149. Lemov, Penelope. "Meyera Oberndorf: Being Mayor of a Resort Town Is No Picnic." *Governing* 3 (July 1990): 42–47.

3150. "Virginia Elects All-Woman Slate." *American City* 65 (September 1950): 153.

Washington

3151. Brace, Blanche. "Well ... Why Not a Woman Mayor?" *The Woman Citizen* 11 (September 1926): 8–10, 38.

Wisconsin

3152. Hedlund, Ronald D., Patricia K. Freeman, Keith E. Hamm, and Robert M. Stein. "The Electability of Women Candidates: The Effect of Sex Role Stereotypes." *Journal of Politics* 41, no. 2 (May 1979): 513–524.

In the Territories and District

District of Columbia

3153. Jaffe, Harry. "Running on Empty." *Washingtonian* 27 (January 1992): 50–54.

Puerto Rico

3154. Oliveira, Annette. "Dona Fela: The Great Lady of Puerto Rican Politics." *Americas OAS* 33, no. 1 (1981): 49–53.

IV. Public Institutions

General

Directories

3155. Center for the American Woman and Politics, ed. *Profiles of Women State Legislators, 1995–96.* New Brunswick, NJ: Center for the American Woman and Politics, 1995.

3156. ———, ed. *Women Elected Officials: A Fifty State Resource, 1971 to Present.* New Brunswick, NJ: Center for the American Woman and Politics, 1995.

3157. Chrisman, Sarah B., and Marilyn Johnson. *Women in Public Office: A Biographical Directory and Statistical Analysis.* New York: Bowker, 1976. Compiled by the Center for the American Woman and Politics.

3158. Cox, Elizabeth M. *Women State and Territorial Legislators, 1895–1995.* Jefferson, NC: McFarland, 1995.

3159. Geiger-Parker, Barbara, and Kathy Stanwick, eds. *Directors of Organizations of Women Public Officials.* New Brunswick, NJ: Center for the American Woman and Politics, Rutgers University, 1980.

3160. National Federation of Republican Women. *Leadership 90: Listing of State and Federal Elected Republican Women.* Washington, DC: National Federation of Republican Women, 1990.

3161. National Women's Political Caucus. *National Directory of Women Elected Officials, 1981.* Biennal to present. New York: Philip Morris Companies Inc., 1981.

3162. Republican National Committee, Women's Division. *Women in the Public Service.* Washington, DC: Republican National Committee, 1957.

3163. ———. *Women in the Public Service.* Washington, DC: Republican National Committee, 1959.

3164. ———. *Women in Public Service.* Washington, DC: Republican National Committee, 1969.

3165. ———. *Women in Public Service.* Washington, DC: Republican National Committee, 1971.

3166. Stanwick, Kathy, Marilyn Johnson, Susan J. Carroll, Lynn Korenblit, and Christine Li, eds. *Women in Public Office: A Biographical Directory and Statistical Analysis.* 2d ed. Metuchen, NJ: Scarecrow Press, 1978. Center for the American Woman and Politics, Rutgers University.

Public Officials

3167. Allen, Florence E. "Women in Public Office." *Women Lawyers Journal* 44 (Summer 1958): 12.

3168. American Council of Life Insurance, and National Women's Political Caucus. *Factsheet on Women's Political Progress.* Washington, DC: American Council of Life Insurance, 1989. Biennial to present.

3169. Boneparth, Ellen. "Resources and Constraints on Women in the Policymaking Process: State and Local Arenas." In *Political Women: Current Roles in State and Local Government,* edited by Janet A. Flammang, 277–290. Women's Policy Studies, 8. Beverly Hills, CA: Sage, 1984.

3170. Breckinridge, Sophonisba P. "Women Office Holders." Chap. 18 in *Women in the Twentieth Century: A Study of Their Political, Social and Economic Activities,* 295–346. New York: McGraw-Hill, 1933.

3171. Brown, Dorothy M. "Power in Washington: Networking in the 1920s from Willebrandt to Roosevelt." Paper presented at the New School Conference on Women and Political Change in the 20th Century, New York, 1990.

3172. Buchanan, Angela M. "Women in Politics." *Pepperdine Law Review* 20 (April 1993): 1159–1169.

3173. Carroll, Susan J. "The Personal Is Political: The Intersection of Private Lives and Public Roles among Women and Men in Elective and Appointive Office." *Women and Politics* 9, no. 2 (Summer 1989): 51–67.

3174. Center for the American Woman and Politics, Rutgers University. "Fact Sheets about Women in Elective and Appointive Office." Quarterly since 1977.

3175. ———. *Leaders of Organizations of Women Public Officials: Report from a Conference, June 13–14.* New Brunswick, NJ: Center for the American Woman and Politics, Rutgers University, 1981.

3176. Chauvenet, Beatrice. "Is Politics Woman's Sphere?" *Independent Woman* 15 (April 1934): 109, 122–125.

3177. "Data on Women in Public Office." *Independent Woman* 34 (October 1955): 21.

3178. Doan, Michael. "New Women Politicians." *U.S. News and World Report* 98 (4 March 1985): 76–77.

3179. Doerschuk, Beatrice. "Women in the Public Service: I. Elective Offices." *Independent Woman* 6 (May 1925): 12–14.

3180. Flammang, Janet A., ed. *Political Women: Current Roles in State and Local Government.* Beverly Hills, CA: Sage, 1984.

3181. Fraser, Arvonne S. "Insiders and Outsiders: Women in the Political Arena." In *Women in Washington,* edited by Irene Tinker, 120–139. Beverly Hills, CA: Sage, 1983.

3182. Gruberg, Martin. "From Nowhere to Where? Women in State and Local Politics." *Social Science Journal* 21, no. 1 (January 1984): 5–11.

3183. Hickey, Margaret. "Women Like You and Me in Politics." *Ladies*

Home Journal 68 (February 1952): 18–19, 122.

3184. Jordan, Elizabeth. "Office and the Woman, the New Right and the New Might in the Public Job." *Ladies Home Journal* 38 (June 1921): 25, 101–102.

3185. Kirkpatrick, Jeane. *The New Presidential Elite: Men and Women in National Politics.* New York: Russell Sage, 1976.

3186. Lamson, Peggy. "Two from Connecticut: City Hall and the Capitol Dome, Ann Uccello and Ella T. Grasso." In *Few Are Chosen: American Women in Political Life Today,* 87–126. Boston: Houghton Mifflin, 1968.

3187. Mueller, Carol M. "Feminism and the New Women in Public Office." *Women and Politics* 2, no. 3 (Fall 1982): 7–22.

3188. National Women's Political Caucus. *Don't Miss That Appointment.* Washington, DC: National Women's Political Caucus, 1991.

3189. Roosevelt, Eleanor. "Women in Public Life." In *It's Up to the Women,* by Mrs. Franklin D. Roosevelt, 205–219. New York: Stokes, 1933.

3190. ———. "Women in Politics, Women Public Officials." *Good Housekeeping* 110 (January 1940): 18–19, 150.

3191. Sigelman, Lee. "The Curious Case of Women in State and Local Government." *Social Science Quarterly* 57 (March 1976): 391–604.

3192. Springer, Adele I. "Woman's Role in the Machinery of Govern-

ment." *Vital Speeches* 23 (1 April 1957): 373–376.

3193. Tinker, Irene, ed. *Women in Washington: Advocates for Public Policy.* Women's Policy Studies. 7 vols. Beverly Hills, CA: Sage, 1983.

3194. Van der Vries, Bernice T. "Women in Government." *Women Lawyers Journal* 35 (Winter 1949): 9–11.

3195. "Women Actually in Office." *The Nation* 103 (21 December 1916): 581.

3196. "Women Have Scaled Political Heights Since 1920." *Literary Digest* 117 (3 March 1934): 41.

3197. "Women in Government." *National Business Woman* 36 (March 1957): 14–15, 18.

3198. "Women in Policy-Making Posts." *Independent Woman* 27 (May 1948): 153, 156.

3199. "Women in Power." *Ms.* 16, no. 10 (April 1988): 79.

3200. "Women in Public Life." *American Association of University Women* 49, no. 1 (1955): 12.

3201. "Women in Public Life." *American Association of University Women* 53, no. 1 (1959): 35.

3202. "Women in Public Office." *Independent Woman* 34 (October 1955): 21.

3203. "Women in Public Office Tell Us." *Independent Woman* 29 (July 1950): 217.

3204. "Women in Washington: How Are They Doing?" *Lear's* 6, Special Section (January 1994): 50–59.

3205. "Women Who Are Making Good in Public Office." *Current Opinion* 55 (August 1913): 95–96.

3206. Woodhouse, Chase Going. "The Status of Women." *American Journal of Sociology* 35 (May 1930): 1091–1100.

Public Administration

3207. Bayes, Jane H. *Women and Public Administration: International Perspectives.* New York: Haworth Press, 1992.

3208. Duerst-Lahti, Georgia. "But Women Play the Game Too: Gender Power Dynamics in Administrative Decision Making." Paper presented at the annual meeting of the American Political Science Association, Washington, DC, 1987.

3209. Duerst-Lahti, Georgia, and Cathy Marie Johnson. "Gender, Style and Bureaucracy: Must Women Go Native to Succeed?" Paper presented at the annual meeting of the American Political Science Association, Atlanta, 1989.

3210. Gallas, Nesta M. "A Symposium: Women in the Public Administration." *Public Administration Review* 36 (July–August 1976): 347–389. Special issue.

3211. Hedge, Davd M., and Ronald D. Hedlund. "Women and Public Service Employment: Sex Differences in the Delivery of 'Manpower' Services." *Women and Politics* 4 (Summer 1984): 83–98.

3212. Neuse, Steven M. "Professionalism and Authority: Women in Public Service." *Public Administration Review* 38 (September–October 1978): 436–441.

Women of Color

3213. Alpha Kappa Alpha Sorority. *Negro Women in the Politics.* Vol. 2. Chicago: Alpha Kappa Alpha Sorority, 1969.

3214. Cayer, N. Joseph, and Lee Sigelman. "Minorities and Women in State and Local Government 1973–1975." *Public Administration Review* 40, no. 5 (Spring 1980): 443–450.

3215. Center for the American Woman and Politics. *Women of Color in Elective Office.* New Brunswick, NJ: Center for the American Woman and Politics, Rutgers Institute of Politics, Rutgers University, 1992.

3216. Conyers, James E. "Sex Differences." In *Black Elected Officials in High Government Office,* edited by James E. Conyers, 83–102. New York: Doubleday, 1988.

3217. Cummings, Judith. "Black Women in Public Office." *Black Enterprise* 5 (August 1974): 33–35.

3218. Davis, Marianne W. "Black Women in Local Government." In *Contributions of Black Women to America,* 198–213. Vol. 2. Columbia, SC: Kenday Press, 1982.

3219. ———. "Black Women in National Office." In *Contributions of Black Women to America,* 234–249. Vol. 2. Columbia, SC: Kenday Press, 1982.

3220. ———. "Black Women in State Government." In *Contributions of Black Women to America,* 214–233.

Vol. 2. Columbia SC: Kenday Press, 1982.

3221. Smalley, Hazel C. "Black Women Legislators Answer Questions." *Black Politician* 2 (Summer 1971): 40–44.

Impact

3222. Cantor, Dorothy, Toni Bernay, and Jean Stoess. *Women in Power: The Secrets of Leadership.* New York: Houghton Mifflin, 1992.

3223. Carroll, Susan J. "The Politics of Difference: Women Public Officials as Agents of Change." *Stanford Law and Policy Review* 5 (Spring 1994): 11–20.

3224. Center for the American Woman and Politics. *The Impact of Women in Public Office: An Overview.* New Brunswick, NJ: Center for the American Woman and Politics, 1991.

3225. Dodson, Debra L. *Gender and Policymaking: Studies of Women in Office.* New Brunswick, NJ: Center for the American Woman and Politics, Rutgers University, 1991.

3226. Duerst-Lahti, Georgia, and Rita Mae Kelly. *Gender Power, Leadership, and Governance.* Ann Arbor: University of Michigan, 1995.

3227. Dye, Thomas R., and Julie Strickland. "Women at the Top: A Note on Institutional Leadership." *Social Science Quarterly* 63 (June 1982): 333–341.

3228. George, W. L. "Woman in Politics." *Harper's* 139 (June 1919): 85–92.

3229. "Here's How: Qualified Women in Policy Making Posts." *Independent Woman* 30 (March 1951): 86.

3230. Kirkpatrick, Jeane. *Political Woman.* New York: Basic Books, 1974.

3231. Leader, Shelah Gilbert. "The Policy Impact of Elected Women Officials." In *The Impact of the Electoral Process,* edited by Louis Maisel and Joseph Cooper, 265–285. Beverly Hills, CA: Sage, 1977.

3232. Mandel, Ruth, and Debra L. Dodson. "Do Women Officeholders Make a Difference?" In *The American Woman 1992–1993,* edited by Paula Ries and Anne J. Stone, 149–177. New York: Norton, 1993.

3233. Pore, Renate, and Betty Justice. *Toward the Second Decade: The Impact of the Women's Movement on American Institutions.* Westport, CT: Greenwood Press, 1981.

3234. Stanwick, Kathy, and Katherine E. Kleeman. *Women Make a Difference.* New Brunswick, NJ: Center for the American Woman and Politics, Rutgers University, 1983.

3235. Welch, Susan, and Sue Thomas. "Do Women in Public Office Make a Difference?" In *Gender and Policymaking, Studies of Women in Office,* edited by Debra L. Dodson, 13–20. New Brunswick, NJ: Center for the American Woman and Politics, 1991.

3236. Yoder, Janice D. "Rethinking Tokenism: Looking Beyond Numbers." *Gender and Society* 5 (June 1991): 178–192.

In the Courts

Court Rooms

3237. Bartelme, Mary Margaret. "The Opportunity for Women in Court Administration." *Annals of the American Academy of Political and Social Science* 45 (March 1914): 188–190.

3238. Chesney-Lind, Meda. "Female Offenders: Paternalism Reexamined." In *Women, the Courts and Equality,* edited by Laura L. Crites and Winifred L. Hepperle, 114–139. Beverly Hills, CA: Sage, 1987.

3239. Cook, Beverly Blair, Leslie F. Goldstein, Karen O'Connor, and Susette M. Talarico. *Women in the Judicial Process.* Washington, DC: American Political Science Association, 1988.

3240. Crites, Laura. "Women in the Criminal Court." In *Women in the Courts,* edited by Winifred L. Hepperle and Laura Crites, 176–201. Williamsburg, VA: National Center for State Courts, 1978.

3241. Crites, Laura L., and Winifred L. Hepperle, eds. *Women, the Courts and Equality.* Beverly Hills: Sage, 1987.

3242. Farley, G. M. "Women on Washington Juries." *The Independent* 75 (3 July 1913): 50–52.

3243. Ginsburg, Ruth Bader. "Treatment of Women by the Law: Awakening Consciousness in the Law

Schools." *Valparaiso University Law Review* 5 (1971): 480.

3244. Hepperle, Winifred L. "Female Court Administrators: Stuck at Mid-Level." In *Women, the Courts and Equality,* edited by Laura L. Crites and Winifred L. Hepperle, 175–190. Beverly Hills, CA: Sage, 1987.

3245. Hepperle, Winifred L., and Laura Crites, eds. *Women in the Courts.* Williamsburg VA: National Center for State Courts, 1978.

3246. Hepperle, Winifred L., and Janice L. Hendryx. "Women in Court Administration." In *Women in the Courts,* edited by Winifred L. Hepperle and Laura Crites, 106–113. Williamsburg, , VA: National Center for State Courts, 1978.

3247. Hoffman, Beatrice. "Changes in Domestic Relations Court." In *Women in the Courts,* edited by Winifred L. Hepperle and Laura Crites, 160–175. Williamsburg, VA: National Center for State Courts, 1978.

3248. Mahoney, Anne Rankin. "Sexism in Voir Dire: The Use of Sex Stereotypes in Jury Selection." In *Women in the Courts,* edited by Winifred L. Hepperle and Laura Crites, 114–135. Williamsburg, VA: National Center for State Courts, 1978.

3249. Martin, Elaine. "Judicial Gender and Judicial Choices." In *Gender and Policymaking, Studies of Women in Office,* edited by Debra L. Dodson, 49–62. New Brunswick, NJ: Center for the American Woman and Politics, 1991.

3250. Menkel-Meadow, Carrie. "The Comparative Sociology of Women Lawyers: The 'Feminization of the Legal Profession'." *Osgood Hall Law Journal* 24 (1986): 897.

3251. ———. "Excluded Voices: New Voices in the Legal Profession Making New Voices in the Law." *University of Miami Law Review* 42 (1987): 29.

3252. Nader, Laura, and Jane Collier. "Justice: A Woman Blindfolded?" In *Women in the Courts,* edited by Winifred L. Hepperle and Laura Crites, 202–212. Williamsburg, VA: National Center for State Courts, 1978.

3253. Nagel, Stuart S., and Lenore J. Weitzman. "Women as Litigants." *Hastings Law Journal* 23 (November 1971): 171–198.

3254. O'Connor, Karen. *Women's Organizations' Use of the Courts.* Lexington, MA: Lexington Books, 1980.

3255. O'Connor, Karen, and Lee Epstein. "Beyond Legislative Lobbying: Women's Rights Groups and the Supreme Court." *Judicature* 67, no. 3 (September 1983): 134–143.

3256. Sherry, Suzanna. "Civic Virtue and the Feminine Voice in Constitutional Adjudication." *Virginia Law Review* 72 (April 1986): 543–616.

3257. Weiss, Catherine, and Louise Melling. "The Legal Education of Twenty Women." *Stanford Law Review* 40, no. 5 (May 1988): 1299–1369.

Judges

3258. Abrahamson, Shirley S. "The Woman Has Robes." *Golden Gate University Law Review* 14, no. 3 (Fall 1984): 489–503.

3259. Alozie, Nicholas O. "Distribution of Women and Minority Judges: The Effects of Judicial Selection Methods." *Social Science Quarterly* 71, no. 2 (June 1990): 316–325.

3260. Berkson, Larry. "Women on the Bench: A Brief History." *Judicature* 65, no. 6 (December–January 1982): 286–293.

3261. "Black Women on the Bench: Wielding the Gavel of Change." *Ebony* 38 (February 1983): 110–113.

3262. Brehm, Barbara. "American Women Judges." Master's thesis, Michigan State University, 1974.

3263. Carbon, Susan B. "Women in the Judiciary: An Introduction." *Judicature* 65, no. 6 (December–January 1982): 285–286.

3264. Clepper, P. M. "Oh Wise Young Judge." *Independent Woman* 31 (July 1952): 197.

3265. Cook, Beverly Blair. "Women Judges: A Preface to Their History." *Golden Gate University Law Review* 14 (Fall 1984): 573–610.

3266. ———. "Women Judges in the Opportunity Structure." In *Women, the Courts and Equality,* edited by Laura L. Crites and Winifred L. Hepperle, 143–174. Beverly Hills, CA: Sage, 1987.

3267. Dix, Dorothy. "Case for Women Judges." *Good Housekeeping* 59 (July 1914): 48–51.

3268. Fund for Modern Courts. *The Success of Women and Minorities: The Selection Process.* New York: Fund for Modern Courts, 1985.

3269. Ginsburg, Ruth Bader. "Women as Full Members of the Club: An Evolving American Ideal." *Human Rights* 6 (Fall 1976): 1–21.

3270. Honeyman, R. "Woman of Judgment: Lydia B. Tague." *Sunset* 29 (November 1912): 575–576.

3271. Kirp, David, Marlene Strong Franks, and Mark G. Yudof, eds. *Gender Justice.* Chicago: University of Chicago Press, 1986.

3272. Leive, Cindi. "A New Wave of Women Judges." *Glamour* 93, no. 5 (1995): 106.

3273. "Minority Women Judges." *U.S. News and World Report* 100 (20 January 1986): 10.

3274. Monroe, Anne Shannon. "When Women Sit in Judgment." *Good Housekeeping* 70 (April 1920): 46–47.

3275. Rossman, Lynn C. "Women Judges Unite: A Report from the Founding Convention of the National Association of Women Judges." *Golden Gate University Law Review* 10, no. 3 (Summer 1980): 1237–1265.

3276. "San Francisco BPW's Holding Judgeships." *Independent Woman* 34 (April 1955): 145.

3277. Smith, Susan Moloney. "Diversifying the Judiciary: The Influence of Gender and Race on Judging." *Richmond Law Review* 20 (March 1994): 179–204.

3278. Weller, Sheila. "Taking the Law into Her Own Hands." *Redbook* 179 (June 1992): 94–97.

Jurors

3279. Costantini, Edmond, Michael Mallery, and Diane Yapundich. "Gender and Juror Partiality: Are Women More Likely to Prejudge Guilt?" *Judicature* 67, no. 3 (September 1983): 120–134.

3280. "Eleven Men and One Woman: An Account of an Experience on a Jury." *Outlook* 127 (30 March 1921): 508–509.

3281. Levine, Adeline Gordon, and Claudine Schweber-Koren. "Jury Selection in Erie County: Changing a Sexist System." *Law and Society Review* 11, no. 1 (1976): 43–56.

3282. Mahoney, Anne Rankin. "Women Jurors: Sexism in Jury Selection." In *Women, the Courts, and Equality,* edited by Laura L. Crites and Winifred L. Hepperle, 208–223. Beverly Hills, CA: Sage, 1987.

3283. Moran, Gary, and John Craig Comfort. "Scientific Juror Selection: Sex as a Moderator of Demographic and Personality Predictors of Impaneled Felony Juror Behavior." *Journal of Personality and Social Psychology* 43, no. 5 (November 1982): 1052.

3284. Nagel, Stuart S., and Lenore J. Weitzman. "Sex and the Unbiased Jury." *Judicature* 56, no. 3 (1972): 109–112.

3285. Samuels, Gertrude. "Verdict on Women Jurors." *The New York*

Times Magazine (7 May 1950): VI, 22, 26–29.

3286. Weisbrod, Carol. "Images of the Woman Juror." *Harvard Women's Law Journal* 9 (Spring 1986): 59–82.

Impact

3287. Cook, Beverly Blair. "Will Women Judges Make a Difference in Women's Legal Rights?" In *Women, Power and Political Systems,* edited by Margherita Rendel, 216–239. London: Croon Helm, 1981.

3288. "Different Voices, Different Choices? The Impact of More Women Lawyers and Judges on the Justice System." *Judicature* 74, no. 3 (October––November 1990): 138–148.

3289. Kritzer, Herbert M., and Thomas Uhlman. "Sisterhood in the Courtroom: Sex of the Judge and Defendant in Criminal Case Disposition." *Social Science Journal* 14 (April 1977): 77–89.

3290. Martin, Elaine. "Differences in Men and Women Judges: Perspectives On Gender." *Journal of Political Science* 17 (Spring 1989): 204–209.

3291. ———. "Men and Women on the Bench: Vive La Difference ?" *Judicature* 73, no. 4 (December–January 1990): 204–208.

3292. Minow, Martha. *Making All the Difference: Inclusion, Exclusion and American Law.* Ithaca, NY: Cornell University Press, 1990.

3293. Rhode, Deborah L. "The 'Woman's Point of View'." *Journal of Legal Education* 38, no. 1–2 (March–June 1988): 39–60.

3294. Young, Iris Marion. *Justice and the Politics of Difference.* Princeton, NJ: Princeton University Press, 1990.

Sex Discrimination

3295. Bynum, Victoria. "On the Lowest Ring: Court Control Over Poor White and Free Black Women." *Southern Exposure* 12, no. 6 (1984): 40–44.

3296. Davidson, Kenneth M., Ruth Bader Ginsburg, and Herma Hill Kay. *Sex Based Discrimination: Text, Cases and Materials.* St. Paul, MN: West Publishing Co., 1974.

3297. Harrison, Cynthia E. "Politics and Law." In *The Women's Annual,* 4th ed., edited by Sarah Pritchard, 145–166. Boston: G. K. Hall, 1984.

3298. Lefcourt, Carol. *Women and the Law.* 2d ed. New York: Clark Boardman, Ltd., 1987.

3299. Nagel, Stuart S., and John Hagan. "Gender and Crime: Offense Patterns and Criminal Court Crime Sanctions." *Crime and Justice Annual Review of Research* 4 (1983): 91–144.

3300. Nagel, Stuart S., and Lenore J. Weitzman. "Double Standard of American Justice." *Society* 9, no. 5 (1972): 18–25.

3301. Rhode, Deborah L. "Justice, Gender, and the Justices." In *Women, The Courts and Equality,* edited by Laura L. Crites and Winifred L. Hepperle, 13–34. Beverly Hills, CA: Sage, 1987.

3302. Schafran, Lynn Hecht. "Educating the Judiciary about Gender Bias: National Judicial Education Program to Promote Equality for Women and Men in the Courts and the New Jersey Supreme Court Task Force on Women in the Courts." *Women's Rights Law Reporter* 9 (1986): 109.

3303. ———. "Practicing Law in a Sexist Society." In *Women, the Courts and Equality*, edited by Laura L. Crites and Winifred L. Hepperle, 191–207. Beverly Hills, CA: Sage, 1987.

3304. Schneider, Elizabeth. "Equal Rights to Trial for Women: Sex Bias in the Law of Self-Defense." *Harvard Civil Rights–Civil Liberties Law Review* 15 (Winter 1980): 623–647.

3305. Tong, Rosemarie. *Women, Sex and the Law.* Totowa, NJ: Rowman and Allenheld, 1984.

3306. Weiss, Penny. "Legal Anti-Feminisms: Judicial Rationales for Differential Treatment of the Sexes." Paper presented at the annual meeting of the American Political Science Association, Washington, DC, 1988.

3307. Wikler, Norma J. "Educating Judges about Gender Bias in the Courts." In *Women, The Courts and Equaltiy*, edited by Laura L. Crites and Winifred L. Hepperle, 227–245. Beverly Hills, CA: Sage, 1987.

3308. Williams, Wendy W. "The Equality Crisis: Some Reflections on Culture, Courts and Feminism." *Women's Rights Law Reporter* 7, no. 3 (Spring 1982): 175–200.

Nations and Tribes

3309. Ariffin, Connie. "Relearning to Trust Ourselves: An Interview with Chief Wilma Mankiller." *Women of Power* 7 (Summer 1987): 38–40, 72–74.

3310. Barnett, Franklin. *Viola Jimulla: The Indian Chieftess.* Prescott, AZ: Prescott Yavapai Indians, 1968.

3311. Brown, Rusty. "Verna Williamson." *Ms.* 16, no. 1–2 (July–August 1987): 102, 104.

3312. Foreman, Carolyn Thomas. *Indian Woman Chiefs.* Muskogee, OK: Hoffman, 1954. Reprint. Washington, DC: Zengers, 1976.

3313. "In the News, Georgia C. George." *Native Peoples* 6, no. 2 (Winter 1993): 78.

3314. Jumper, Betty Mae. … *and with the Wagon Came God's Word.* Hollywood, FL: Seminole Tribe, 1980.

3315. Mankiller, Wilma, and Michael Wallis. *Mankiller, A Chief and Her People.* New York: St. Martin's Press, 1993.

3316. McCoy, Melanie. "Gender or Ethnicity: What Makes a Difference? A Study of Women Tribal Leaders." *Women and Politics* 12, no. 2 (1992): 57–68.

3317. Mozee, Yvonne. "Esther Wunnicke: Top Female Fed in the North." *Alaskan Woman Magazine* (February–March 1978): 59.

3318. Nelson, Mary Caroll. *Annie Wauneka.* Minneapolis, MN: Dillon, 1972.

3319. Roderick, Libby. "Native Women: A Voice in State Government." *Alaska Native News* (February 1984): 24.

3320. "Seri Indian Women Rule." *Indian's Friend* 33 (1920): 2.

3321. Waldowski, Paula. "Alice Brown Davis: A Leader of Her People." *Chronicles of Oklahoma* 58, no. 4 (1980–81): 455–463.

3322. Wallace, Michelle. "Wilma Mankiller: Principal Chief of the Cherokee Nation." *Ms.* 16, no. 7 (January 1988): 68–69.

3323. Whittemore, Hank. "She Leads a Nation." *Parade Magazine* (18 August 1991): 4–5.

3324. Witt, Shirley Hill. "An Interview with Dr. Annie Dodge Wauneka." *Frontiers* 6, no. 3 (Fall 1981): 64–67.

Federal Government

Congress

History

3325. Engelbarts, Rudolf. *Women in the United States Congress, 1917–1972.* Littleton, CO: Libraries Unlimited, 1974.

3326. Gehlen, Frieda L. "Women Members of Congress: A Distinctive Role." In *A Portrait of Marginality: The Political Behavior of American Women,* edited by Marianne Githens and Jewell Prestage, 304–319. New York: McKay, 1977.

3327. Ingersoll, Fern S. "Why Can't a (Congress)Woman Be More Like a Man? Interviewing Former Congresswomen." *The Maryland Historian* 13, no. 2 (Fall–Winter 1982): 17–22.

3328. Lee, Essie. *Women in Congress.* New York: Julian Messner, 1979.

3329. Morin, Isobel V. *Women of the United States Congress.* Minneapolis, MN: Oliver Press, 1994.

3330. Paxton, Annabel. *Women in Congress.* Richmond, VA: The Dietz Press, 1945.

3331. Randolph, Laura B. "'The True Pioneers of the Women's Movement'." *Ebony* 46, no. 10 (August 1991): 96–102.

3332. Tolchin, Susan. *Women in Congress: 1917–1976.* Washington, DC: Government Printing Office, 1976.

3333. Werner, Emmy E. "Women in Congress, 1917–1964." *Western Political Quarterly* 19 (March 1966): 16–30.

Organizations

3334. "Congressional Caucus for Women's Issues." *Ms.* 13, no. 9 (March 1985): 96.

3335. Rix, Sara E. "Congressional Caucus on Women's Issues." In *American Woman, 1988–89,* edited by Sara E. Rix, 310–332. New York: Norton, 1988.

3336. ———. "The Congressional Caucus for Women's Issues in the 101st Congress." In *American Woman, 1990–91,* edited by Sara E. Rix, 325–348. New York: Norton, 1990.

3337. Swanson, K. C. "The Old Order Is Changing." *National Journal* 27, no. 8 (25 February 1995): 493.

3338. Thompson, Joan Hulse. "The Congressional Caucus for Women's Issues: One-Hundred and Thirty Feminist in the House." Paper presented at the annual meeting of the

Midwest Political Science Association, Chicago, 1984.

3339. ———. "Lobbying in the House: The Congressional Caucus for Women's Issues Versus the Insurance Industry." Paper presented at the annual meeting of the Midwest Political Science Association, Chicago, 1985.

3340. Thompson, Joan Hulse, and Robert Thompson. "The 1980 Caucuses: A Case Study of Representation." *Southeastern Political Review* (Fall 1983).

Impact

3341. Center for the American Woman and Politics. *Voices, Views, Votes: The Impact of Women in the 103d Congress.* New Brunswick, NJ: Center for the American Woman and Politics, 1995.

3342. Connolly, Ceci. "A Political Novelty No More, Women Test Endurance." *Congressional Quarterly Weekly Report* 52 (7 May 1994): 1139–1141.

3343. Frankovic, Kathleen A. "Sex and Voting in the U.S. House of Representatives: 1961–1975." *American Politics Quarterly* 5, no. 3 (July 1977): 315–330.

3344. Gehlen, Frieda L. "Women in Congress: Their Power and Influence in a Man's World." *Transaction* 6, no. 11 (October 1969): 35–40.

3345. Gertzog, Irwin N. *Congressional Women: Their Recruitment, Treatment, and Behavior,* 2d rev. ed. New York: Praeger, 1995 (1984).

3346. Grier, Ruth. "In the House: Women and Environmental Politics." *Women and Environments* 13 (Winter–Spring 1991): 42–43.

3347. Guigin, Linda C. "The Impact of Political Structure on the Political Power of Women: A Comparison of Britain and the United States." *Women and Politics* 6 (1986): 37–55.

3348. Hook, Janet. "Women Remain on Periphery Despite Electoral Gains." *Congressional Quarterly Weekly Report* 51 (9 October 1993): 2707–2709.

3349. Kincaid, Diane D. "Over His Dead Body: A Positive Perspective on Widows in the U.S. Congress." *Western Political Quarterly* 31, no. 1 (March 1978): 96–104.

3350. Meredith, Ellis. "What Six Congresswomen Could Do." *Democratic Digest* 12, no. 6 (June 1935): 7, 27.

3351. Miller, Karen Czarnecki. "Will These Women Clean House? GOP Freshman Lawmakers Back Congressional Reform." *Policy Review* 72 (Spring 1995): 77–80.

3352. Pincus, Ann. "How the Women in Congress Use Their Power." *Redbook* 150, no. 5 (March 1978): 114–115, 178, 184, 186, 188.

3353. Plattner, Andy. "Varied Legislative Styles, Philosophies Found among Congress' 23 Women." *Congressional Quarterly Weekly Report* 41 (April 1993): 784–785.

3354. Reid, Inez Smith. "How Powerful Is Powerful? The Women's Movement and the Four Black Congresswomen." In *Women Organizing: An Anthology,* edited by Bernice Cummings and Victoria Schuck, 25–46. Metuchen, NJ: Scarecrow Press, 1979.

3355. Rosenthal, Cindy Simon. "Once They Get There: The Role of Gender in Legislative Careers." *Extensions, A Journal of the Carl Albert Congressional Research and Studies Center* (Spring 1995): 15–17.

3356. Rosin, Hanna. "Invasion of the Church Ladies." *The New Republic* 212, no. 17 (24 April 1995): 20–27.

3357. Smith, Ethel M. "What a Congresswoman Has Done for Working Women." *The Woman Citizen* 2 (21 July 1917): 136.

3358. Steinem, Gloria. "Life after Backlash: Our Women in Washington." *Ms.* 3, no. 4 (January–February 1993): 28–32.

3359. Welch, Susan. "Are Women More Liberal Than Men in the U.S. Congress?" *Legislative Studies Quarterly* 11 (February 1985): 125–134.

3360. "Woman's Dilemma—Home or Politics: Getting Elected Is Just One Problem for Office-Holding Wife." *U.S. News and World Report* 44 (23 May 1958): 68–70.

3361. "Women in Congress Speak Out." *Good Housekeeping* 185 (November 1977): 26, 127.

Staff

3362. Cheers, D. Michael. "The Lady in Charge." *Ebony* 41, no. 12 (October 1986): 117–122.

3363. Davidson, Sara. "The Girls on the Bandwagon: Political Girls on Capitol Hill." *McCalls* 97 (August 1970): 42–43, 80–82.

3364. Deming, Angus. "Women of Washington: Congressional Staffers." *Newsweek* 87 (14 June 1976): 28.

3365. Johannes, John R. "Women as Congressional Staffers: Does It Make a Difference?" *Women and Politics* 4 (Summer 1984): 69–81.

3366. "Pro Who Sits at Holling's Side, Senate Communications Sub-Committee's Mary Jo Manning." *Broadcasting* 93 (15 August 1977): 65.

3367. "Washington, DC: Great Jobs in the Fast Lane." *Harper's Bazaar* 121 (November 1987): 46, 48, 243.

Members

3368. Anderson, George. "Women in Congress." *Commonweal* 9 (March 1929): 532–534.

3369. Bingham, Clara. "The Women on the Hill." *Vogue* 183 (August 1993): 264–269.

3370. Boyd, Lucille N. "Salute to Our Congresswomen." *Independent Woman* 30 (March 1951): 70.

3371. Caraway, Hattie Wyatt. "Women in Congress." *State Government* 10, no. 10 (October 1937): 203–204.

3372. Cullinan, Kathleen. "Women in the Senate." *Southern Exposure* 12 (February 1984): 37–38.

3373. Davis, Maxine. "Five Democratic Women." *Ladies Home Journal* 50 (May 1933): 114, 117.

3374. "Democratic Women in the Seventy-ninth Congress." *Democratic Digest* 21–22, no. 12–1 (December 1944–January 1945): 6–7.

3375. "Eight Ladies of Congress." *Review of Reviews* 79 (April 1929): 118–121.

3376. Gilfond, Duff. "Gentlewomen of the House." *American Mercury* 18 (October 1929): 151–160.

3377. Hard, Anne. "Three Ruths in Congress." *Ladies Home Journal* 46 (March 1929): 13.

3378. Holbrooke, Blythe. "Over 40 Powerhouses." *Harper's Bazaar* 115 (September 1982): 102, 106, 108.

3379. Holcomb, Morrigene. *Women in the United States Congress.* Washington, DC: Library of Congress, Congressional Research Service, 1975.

3380. Kaiser, Charles. "Women of the Year." *Vogue* 183 (February 1993): 132–133.

3381. Keyes, Frances Parkinson. "A Congressional Record." *Delineator* 113 (September 1928): 24, 103–105.

3382. Kohn, Walter S. G. *Women in National Legislatures: A Comparative Study of Six Countries.* New York: Praeger, 1980.

3383. "Liberating Capitol Hill." *Newsweek* 85 (21 April 1975): 47.

3384. Longworth, Alice Roosevelt. "What Are the Women Up To?" *Ladies Home Journal* 51 (March 1934): 9, 120–122.

3385. McQuatters, Geneva F. "Ladies Be Seated." *Independent Woman* 28 (January 1949): 2–4.

3386. ———. "Women in the 82nd Congress." *Independent Woman* 30 (January 1951): 2–4.

3387. Northrop, Ann, and Nancy Haberman. "The Freshwomen in Congress." *Ms.* 7, no. 7 (January 1979): 58, 70, 93.

3388. Phillips, B. J. "Recognizing the Gentleladies of the Judiciary Committee." *Ms.* 3, no. 5 (November 1974): 70–74.

3389. Porter, Amy. "Ladies in Congress." *Colliers* 112 (28 August 1943): 22–23.

3390. Randolph, Laura B. "Sisters in the House." *Ebony* 49, no. 11 (September 1994): 20.

3391. Riordan, Teresa, and Sue Kirchhoff. "Women on the Hill: Can They Make a Difference?" *Ms.* 5 (January–February 1995): 85–90.

3392. Roberts, Cokie. "Seven Women Who Could Change Your Life." *McCalls* 121, no. 11 (August 1994): 102–105.

3393. "Salute to Women in the 87th Congress." *National Business Woman* 40 (January 1961): 4–5, 29.

3394. "Salute to the Women of the 89th Congress." *National Business Woman* 44 (January 1965): 25–28.

3395. Schoonmaker, Nancy M. "Where Does She Stand; Woman's Progress and Position in Politics." *Century* 113 (January 1927): 354–360.

3396. Temple, Majorie L. "Women in the 83rd Congress." *Independent Woman* (February 1953): 32–34, 59.

3397. "Ten New Standouts in Congress." *Working Woman* 18, no. 4 (April 1993): 14–15.

3398. "Tribute to Our Women in Congress." *Independent Woman* 34 (February 1955): 48–50.

3399. "Twelve Women Serve in the 90th Congress." *National Business Woman* 46 (January 1967): 2, 14.

3400. Van Helden, Morrigene. *Freshman Women Members of the 93rd Congress.* Washington, DC: Library of Congress, Congressional Research Service, 1973.

3401. Wait, Marianne. "Women of the House." *Ladies Home Journal* 108 (November 1991): 180–182, 184.

3402. Weddington, Sarah. "Five New Female Faces in the House." *Glamour* 81 (March 1983): 142.

3403. Whicker, Marcia Lynn, Malcolm Jewell, and Lois Lovelace Duke. "Women in Congress." In *Women in Politics: Outsiders or Insiders? A Collection of Readings,* edited by Lois Lovelace Duke, 136–151. Englewood Cliffs, NJ: Prentice Hall, 1993.

3404. "Women in Congress." *National Education Association Journal* 38 (April 1949): 283.

3405. "Women in Legislative Halls." *Literary Digest* 121 (25 January 1936): 29.

3406. "Women in the 84th Congress." *Independent Woman* 34 (January 1955): 20–23, 38.

3407. "The Women of the 89th Congress." *National Business Woman* 44 (January 1965): 25–28.

Executive Branch

Cabinet

3408. Blankenhorn, Mary D. "The First Woman in the Cabinet." *Independent Woman* 14 (April 1933): 123–124.

3409. Chunko, Mary T. "Call Her Madam Secretary." *Humanities* 8 (May–June 1987): 22–23.

3410. Clift, Eleanor. "Clinton's Cabinet: Beyond White Men." *Newsweek* 120 (21 December 1992): 37.

3411. Cobble, Dorothy Sue. "A Self-Possessed Woman: A View of FDR's Secretary of Labor, Madame Perkins." *Labor History* 29, no. 2 (1988): 225–229.

3412. Crawford, Ann Fears, and Crystal Sasse Ragsdale. "Mrs. Secretary, Oveta Culp Hobby." In *Women in Texas,* 272–283. Austin, TX: State House Press, 1992.

3413. Dole, Bob, Elizabeth H. Dole, and Richard Norton Smith. *The Doles: Unlimited Partners.* New York: Simon and Schuster, 1988.

3414. Feaver, Douglas B. "Secretary of Transportation Elizabeth Dole: First Madame President ?" In *Women Leaders in American Politics,* edited by James David Barber and Barbara Kellerman, 345–349. Englewood Cliffs, NJ: Prentice Hall, 1986.

3415. Glick, Daniel. "Hazel O'Leary Had Better Be Tough." *Working Woman* 19 (December 1994): 42–47.

3416. Lamson, Peggy. "Juanita Kreps: Secretary of Commerce." In *In the Vanguard, Six American Women in*

Public Life, 37–68. Boston: Houghton Mifflin, 1979.

3417. Lawson, Don. *Frances Perkins, First Lady of the Cabinet.* London: Abelard-Schuman, 1966.

3418. Martin, George Madden. *Madam Secretary: Frances Perkins, A Biography of America's First Woman Cabinet Member.* New York: Houghton Mifflin, 1976.

3419. Martin, Janet M. "The Recruitment of Women to Cabinet and Subcabinet Posts." *Western Political Quarterly* 42, no. 1 (March 1989): 161–172.

3420. Mohr, Lillian Holmen. *Frances Perkins, That Woman in FDR's Cabinet!* Great Barrington, MA: North River Press, 1979.

3421. "Mr. President: These Women Belong in Your Cabinet." *Ms.* 5, no. 7 (January 1977): 91–94.

3422. Mulford, Carolyn. *Elizabeth Dole, Public Servant.* Hillside, NJ: Enslow, 1992.

3423. Nye, Peter. "Conversation with Patricia Robert Harris." *Nation's Cities* 15, no. 8 (August 1977): 10–13.

3424. Perkins, Frances. "Eight Years as Madame Secretary." *Fortune* 24 (September 1941): 76–79, 94, 96, 99.

3425. Ross, Irwin. "Carla Hills Gives the Woman's Touch a Brand New Meaning." *Fortune* 92 (December 1975): 120–123.

3426. Sheed, Wilfrid. *Clare Boothe Luce.* New York: Dutton, 1982.

3427. Stolberg, Benjamin. "Madame Secretary: A Study in Bewilderment." *Saturday Evening Post* 213 (27 July 1940): 9–11, 63, 65–66, 68.

3428. Symons, Joanne L. "Women Cabinet Members in the Spotlight." *Executive Female* 17 (March–April 1994): 52.

3429. Tolleson-Rinehart, Sue. "Madam Secretary: The Careers of Women in the U.S. Cabinet, 1932–1988." Paper presented at the annual meeting of the Southern Political Science Association, Charlotte, NC, 1988.

3430. "Why Not a Woman in the Cabinet?" *Picture Review* 30 (February 1929): 1.

3431. Wingert, Pat. "Nannygate II: A Women's Backlash?" *Newsweek* 121 (15 February 1993): 20–21.

Appointees

3432. Alexander, Ruth Ann. "Elaine Goodale Eastman and the Failure of the Feminist Protestant Ethic." *Great Plains Quarterly* 8, no. 2 (Spring 1988): 89–101.

3433. Anderson, Mary. *Women at Work, The Autobiography of Mary Anderson as Told to Mary N. Winslow.* Westport, CT: Greenwood Press, 1951.

3434. "Appointed to Policy Making Post." *Independent Woman* 29 (December 1950): 370.

3435. "Attacking the Old Boy Network, Appointments of the Carter Administration." *Time* 109 (28 March 1977): 16–17.

3436. Babyak, Blythe. "All the President's Women." *The New York Times Magazine* (22 January 1978): VI, 10–11.

3437. Baeder, Lydia C. "Assistant United States District Attorney." *Independent Woman* 7, no. 6 (December 1923): 7.

3438. Barnes, Fred. "Politics." *Vogue* 179, no. 6 (1989): 144.

3439. Bethune, Mary McLeod. "My Secret Talks with FDR." *Ebony* 5 (April 1949): 42–51.

3440. Blair, Emily Newell. "First Aides to Uncle Sam." *Independent Woman* 17 (September 1938): 276–277, 294.

3441. Boehm, Randolph H. "Mary Grace Quackenbos and the Federal Campaign against Peonage: The Case of Sunnyside Plantation." *Arkansas Historical Quarterly* 150, no. 1 (1991): 40–59.

3442. Boyd, James. "Following the Rules with Dita and Dick." *Washington Monthly* 4, no. 5 (1972): 5–26.

3443. Brown, Dorothy M. *Mabel Walker Willebrandt: A Study of Power, Loyalty and Law.* Knoxville: University of Tennessee Press, 1984.

3444. Carlson, Margaret B. "As State Department Spokesperson, Margaret Tutwiler Has Won Even the Press's Respect." *Vogue* 170 (October 1989): 276, 278.

3445. Carpenter, Theresa. "Making the World Safe for Children." *Redbook* 182 (April 1994): 124–127, 136.

3446. Carroll, Susan J. "Women Appointed to the Carter Administration: More or Less Qualified ?" *Polity* 18 (Summer 1986): 696–706.

3447. ———. "New Strategies to Bring More Women into Office: Organized Efforts to Increase the Number of Women Appointed to Recent Presidential Administrations in the United States." Paper presented at the Vater Staat Und Seine Frauen, Technical University of Berlin, November 14–20, 1988.

3448. Carroll, Susan J., and Barbara Geiger-Parker. *Women Appointed to the Carter Administration: A Comparison with Men.* New Brunswick, NJ: Center for the American Woman and Politics, Eagleton Institute for Politics, Rutgers University, 1983.

3449. Cates, John M., Jr. "An Interview with Margaret Mead on the Woman Diplomat." *Foreign Service Journal* 46 (February 1969): 16.

3450. Chambers, Marcia. "Sua Sponte." *National Law Journal* 15, no. 20 (18 January 1993): 17–18.

3451. Chan, Janet. "44 Qualified Women for the Cabinet and Supreme Court." *McCalls* 104 (November 1976): 37–38.

3452. Chord, Lillian A. "Guardian of Our Gold." *Independent Woman* 32 (July 1953): 231–232.

3453. Clarke, Ida Clyde. "Feminism and the New Technique, Strike for High Places." *Century* 119 (April 1929): 753.

3454. Clingerman, Frances F. "Heads the Distaff Side of the Nation's Farm Program." *Independent Woman* 33 (February 1954): 45, 79.

3455. Cook, C. Clyde. "A Portia of the West, Mabel Walker Willebrandt." *Sunset* 59 (July 1927): 43, 63.

3456. Curtis, Isabel Gordon. "The Housekeeper-at-Large: The People and the Problems She Meets." *Good Housekeeping* 50 (1910): 477.

3457. Detzer, Karl. "Little Anna Goes to Washington." *Independent Woman* 30 (January 1951): 8–10, 30–31.

3458. Doerschuk, Beatrice. "Women in the Public Service: II. Appointive Offices." *Independent Woman* 6 (June 1925): 7–9.

3459. Dunn, Arthur. "A Portia in the Federal Court." *Sunset Magazine* 34 (February 1915): 334–337.

3460. Edmunds, Lavinia. "Betrayed by Reagan's Women's Policy, Barbara Honegger's Real Story." *Ms.* 12, no. 5 (November 1983): 86, 88–92.

3461. Ehrlich, Henry. "State Department's Poetic Powerhouse: Kate Loucheim." *Look* 31 (17 October 1967): 118.

3462. Gatov, Elizabeth Rudel. *Grassroots Party Organizer to Treasure of the United States.* Berkeley: University of California, 1978. The Bancroft Library Oral History Interview.

3463. George, Elsie. "The Woman Appointees of the Franklin Delano Roosevelt and Truman Administration." Ph.D. dissertation, American University, Washington, DC, 1972.

3464. Gould, Beatrice B. "Appointments for Women." *Ladies Home Journal* 78 (January 1961): 64.

3465. Hackett, Catherine I. "Bessie Brueggeman, Politician." *The Woman Citizen* 8 (9 February 1924): 9, 28–29.

3466. Haynes, Karima A. "The Prosecutor Is a Lady." *Ebony* 49 (June 1994): 44–46, 48, 50.

3467. Himelstein, Linda. "Putting the Collar on White-Collar Crime." *Business Week* (27 June 1994): 64–66.

3468. Hinshaw, Augusta W. "The Tax Lady." *The Woman's Journal* 16 (April 1931): 20–21, 30.

3469. Hitt, Patricia. *Precinct Worker to Assistant Secretary of HEW.* Berkeley: University of California, 1980. The Bancroft Library Oral History Interview.

3470. Holt, Rockham. *Mary McCleod Bethune.* Garden City, NJ: Doubleday, 1964.

3471. "If Your Job Is 'Ladylike' Watch Out for Mrs. Richards." *Literary Digest* 57 (4 May 1918): 53–54, 57.

3472. Jensen, Joan M. "Annette Abbott Adams, Politician." *Pacific Historical Review* 35, no. 2 (May 1966): 185–201.

3473. Keesling, Karen, and Suzanne Cavanagh. *Women Presidential Appointees Serving or Having Served in Full-Time Positions Requiring Senate Confirmation 1912–1977.* Washington, DC: Congressional Research Service of the Library of Congress. Report No. 78–73G, March 23, 1978.

3474. "Kennedy Administration to Have Record Number of Negro Women." *Jet* 19 (22 December 1960): 14–15.

3475. Ladd-Taylor, Mary Madeleine, and Molly Taylor. "Hull House Goes to Washington: Women and the Children's Bureau." In *Gender, Class, Race* *and Reform in the Progressive Era,* edited by Noralee Frankel and Nancy S. Dye, 110–126. Lexington: University Press of Kentucky, 1991.

3476. Lisagor, Peter, and Marguerite Higgins. "L.B.J.'S Hunt for Womanpower." *Saturday Evening Post* 237 (27 June 1964): 86–87.

3477. "Marion Harron Appointed to Board of Tax Appeals." *Democratic Digest* 13, no. 9 (September 1936): 14.

3478. Martin, Janet M. "An Examination of Executive Branch Appointments in the Reagan Administration by Background and Gender." *Western Political Quarterly* 44, no. 1 (March 1991): 173–184.

3479. McGlen, Nancy E., and Meredith Reid Sarkees. "Leadership Styles of Women in Foreign Policy." Paper presented at the annual meeting of the American Political Science Association, San Francisco, 1990.

3480. McQuatters, Geneva F. "Lady with Our Money." *Independent Woman* 28 (November 1949): 325–349.

3481. "More BPW's in Policy Making Posts." *Independent Woman* 33 (June 1954): 202–203.

3482. "Mr. Roosevelt's New Deal for Women." *Literary Digest* 115 (15 April 1933): 22, 24.

3483. "Mrs. Secretary." *Time* 56 (20 November 1950): 23.

3484. "New Head for Women's Bureau Takes Office." *Independent Woman* 33 (January 1954): 3.

3485. "New Women's Bureau Director." *National Business Woman* 40 (February 1961): 5.

3486. "One Woman and a Good Many Diplomats." *The Woman Citizen* 4 (14 February 1920): 864–865.

3487. "The Only Woman Collector of Customs." *Sunset* 58 (January 1927): 45.

3488. Parker, Jacqueline K., and Edward M. Carpenter. "Julia Lathrop and the Children's Bureau: The Emergence of an Institution." *Social Service Review* 55, no. 1 (1981): 60–77.

3489. Poole, Isiah J. "New Yield at Agriculture, Jean S. Wallace." *Black Enterprise* 10 (November 1979): 49–50.

3490. ———. "Hot Seat at OMB." *Black Enterprise* 10 (May 1980): 23.

3491. "Presenting the New Director of the Mutual Security Refugee Program." *Independent Woman* 32 (June 1953): 189.

3492. Priest, Ivy Baker. *Green Grows Ivy.* New York: McGraw-Hill, 1958.

3493. Randolph, Laura B. "Black Women in the White House." *Ebony* 45, no. 12 (October 1990): 76–81.

3494. "Reagan's Women." *The New Republic* 185 (October 1981): 5–6.

3495. "Republican Postmistress of East Westmoreland Loses Job to New Democratic Appointee." *Life* 26 (23 May 1949): 63.

3496. Rockefeller, Sharon Percy. "Rockefeller Reflects on 10-Year CPB Tenure." *Broadcasting* 112 (23 March 1987): 142–143.

3497. Ross, B. Joyce. "Mary McLeod Bethune and the National Youth Administration: A Case Study of Power

Relationships in the Black Cabinet of Franklin D. Roosevelt." *Journal of Negro History* 60, no. 1 (1975): 1–28. Reprinted in *Black Women in United States History*, Vol. 4, edited by Darlene Clark Hines, 1020–1050. New York: Carlson, 1990.

3498. Rubin, Marilyn Marks. "Women in ASPA: The Fifty Year Climb toward Equality." *Public Administration Review* 50 (April 1990): 277–287.

3499. Saavedra-Vela, Pilar. "Linda Chavez: Commentary by a Political Professional." *Agenda* 8, no. 1 (1977): 34–36.

3500. Schwindt, Helen Dimos. "All the President's Women." *Ms.* 6, no. 7 (January 1978): 50–54, 91–92.

3501. "She's the Only Woman Delegate to Buenos Aires Conference." *Democratic Digest* 13, no. 12 (December 1936): 5, 13–14.

3502. Shofner, Jerrell H. "Mary Grace Quackenbos, A Visitor Florida Did Not Want." *Florida Historical Quarterly* 58, no. 3 (1980): 273–290.

3503. Smith, Elaine M. "Mary McLeod Bethune and the National Youth Administration." In *Black Women in United States History*, Vol. 4, edited by Darlene Clark Hines, 1092–1122. New York: Carlson, 1990.

3504. Swain, Martha H. "Ellen S. Woodward: The Gentlewoman as Federal Administrator." *Furman Studies* 26 (December 1980): 92–101.

3505. ———. "Eleanor Roosevelt and Ellen Woodward: A Partnership for Women's Work." In *Without Precedent*, edited by Joan Hoff-Wilson, 135–152. Bloomington: Indiana University Press, 1984.

3506. ———. *Ellen S. Woodward: New Deal Advocate for Women.* Jackson: University of Mississippi, 1995.

3507. "Trialog on Office Holders." *Independent Woman* 17 (January 1938): 17–18, 31.

3508. "Truman Appoints Mrs. Georgia Neese Clark, Treasurer of United States." *Life* 26 (27 June 1949): 65–67.

3509. Weddington, Sarah. "Carter Women: Where Will They Go Now?" *Glamour* 79 (April 1981): 106, 110.

3510. Welch, Mary Scott. "Donna Quixote." *Look* 15 (17 July 1951): 76.

3511. "What Women Do in Politics: C. B. Williams and Kate Loucheim." *U.S. News and World Report* 45 (12 December 1958): 72–79.

3512. White, Ruth Beeler. "Young Lady with a Big Job." *Independent Woman* 28 (June 1949): 179–180.

3513. Whiteman, Marjorie M. "Mrs. Franklin D. Roosevelt and the Human Rights Commission." *American Journal of International Law* 62, no. 4 (1968): 918–921.

3514. Willebrandt, Mabel Walker. "Half or Whole-Hearted Prohibition?" *The Woman Citizen* 8 (23 February 1924): 16–17.

3515. Williams, J. R. "Dorothy Deemer Houghton: A Memoir." *Palimpsest* 54, no. 3 (1973): 24–30.

3516. Winter, Alice Ames. "First Lady in the Law, Mrs. Mabel Walker Willebrandt." *Ladies Home Journal* 42 (June 1925): 39.

3517. Wolper, Gregg. "Woodrow Wilson's New Diplomacy: Vira Whitehouse in Switzerland, 1918." *Prologue* 24, no. 3 (1992): 227–239.

3518. "Women at the San Francisco Conference." *Democratic Digest* 22, no. 5 (May 1945): 16.

3519. "Women in Government." *U.S. News and World Report* 72 (17 January 1972): 62–69.

3520. Yanowitch, Murray. "Protecting the Consumer: Carol Foreman." *Challenge* 20 (September 1977): 24–28.

Ambassadors and Ministers

3521. Black, Shirley Temple. "Telling It Like It Is." *National Business Woman* 51, no. 4 (May 1970): 8.

3522. Douglas, Helen Gahagan. *The Eleanor Roosevelt We Remember.* New York: Hill and Wang, 1963.

3523. Forbes, Malcolm S., Jr. "The Democrats' Dazzling Diplomat, Pamela Harriman." *Forbes* 155, no. 9 (24 April 1995): 24.

3524. Hatch, Alden. *Ambassador Extraordinary: Claire Boothe Luce.* New York: Henry Holt, 1956.

3525. Lash, Joseph. *Eleanor: The Years Alone.* New York: Norton, 1972.

3526. ———. *A World of Love: Eleanor Roosevelt and Her Friends, 1943–1962.* Garden City, NJ: Doubleday, 1984.

3527. McQuatters, Geneva F. "Representing U.S.—An American Family." *Independent Woman* 29 (January 1950): 2–4.

3528. Mesta, Perle, and Robert Conn. *Perle: My Story.* New York: McGraw Hill, 1960.

3529. Morin, Ann Miller. "Do Women Make Better Ambassadors ?" *Foreign Service Journal* 71 (December 1994): 26–30.

3530. "New Minister to Denmark." *Newsweek* 1 (15 April 1933): 18–19.

3531. "Our Woman in Denmark, Katherine Elkus White." *National Business Woman* 46 (February 1967): 4–8, 14.

3532. "Patricia Harris, Our Lady in Luxembourg." *Sepia* 14 (December 1965): 18–22.

3533. Roosevelt, Eleanor. *The Autobiography of Eleanor Roosevelt.* New York: Harper and Row, 1961.

3534. "Ruth Bryan Owen, Our First Woman Diplomat." *Christian Century* 50 (26 April 1933): 549–550.

3535. Shadegg, Stephen C. *Clare Boothe Luce.* New York: Simon and Schuster, 1970.

3536. "Stateswoman's Shin." *Time* 28 (5 October 1936): 16.

Commissions

3537. Berry, Mary Frances. "Taming the Civil Rights Commission." *The Nation* 240 (2 February 1985): 106–108.

3538. Drew, Ellizabeth. "On Giving Oneself a Hotfoot: Government by Commission." *Atlantic Monthly* 221 (May 1968): 45–49.

3539. East, Catherine. "Newer Commissions." In *Women in Washington,* edited by Irene Tinker, 35–36. Beverly Hills, CA: Sage, 1983.

3540. "Frieda Miller Heads Women's Bureau." *Democratic Digest* 21, no. 6–7 (June–July 1944): 31.

3541. Lamson, Peggy. "Eleanor Holmes Norton Reforms the Equal Employment Opportunity Commission." In *Women Leaders in American Politics,* edited by James David Barber and Barbara Kellerman, 340–342. Englewood Cliffs, NJ: Prentice Hall, 1986.

3542. Mead, Margaret, and Frances Balgley Kaplan, eds. *American Women, the Report of the President's Commission on the Status of Women and Other Publications of the Commission.* New York: Charles Scribner's Sons, 1965.

3543. Peterson, Esther. "The Kennedy Commission." In *Women in Washington: Advocates for Public Policy,* edited by Irene Tinker, 21–34. Beverly Hills, CA: Sage, 1983.

3544. Rigby, Cora. "'The Diplomatic Corps'." *The Woman Citizen* 9 (2 May 1925): 12–13.

3545. Weisenberger, Carol A. "Women of the FCC: Activists or Tokens?" *Business and Economic History* 21 (1992): 192–198.

3546. "Woman Is Given High Office." *The Woman's Journal* 48 (19 May 1917): 115.

3547. "Woman to Serve on Commission." *The Woman's Journal* 48 (13 January 1917): 7.

East Wing

3548. Anthony, Carl Sferrazza, ed. *First Ladies: The Saga of the Presidents' Wives and Their Power.* Vol. 1, 1789–1961; Vol. 2, 1961–1990. 2 vols. New York: William Morrow, 1990.

3549. Black, Allida M. "Championing a Champion: Eleanor Roosevelt and the Marian Anderson 'Freedom Concert'." *Presidential Studies Quarterly* 20, no. 4 (1990): 719–736.

3550. Bush, Barbara. *Barbara Bush: A Memoir.* New York: Charles Scribner's Sons, 1994.

3551. Carpenter, Liz. *Ruffles and Flourishes: The Warm Tender Story of a Simple Girl Who Found Adventure in the White House.* Garden City, NY: Doubleday, 1970.

3552. ———. "Catching Up with the Johnson Women." *Good Housekeeping* 208 (January 1989): 88–91.

3553. Carter, Roslynn. *First Lady from Plains.* Chapel Hill: University of North Carolina Press, 1984.

3554. Dunlay, Leslie W. *Our Vice Presidents and Second Ladies.* Metuchen, NJ: Scarecrow Press, 1988.

3555. Eisenhower, Julie Nixon. *Pat Nixon: The Untold Story.* New York: Simon and Schuster, 1986.

3556. Ford, Betty, and Chris Chase. *The Times of My Life.* New York: Harper and Row, 1978.

3557. Griffin, Isabel Kinnear. "Mrs. Roosevelt's Press Conferences." *Democratic Bulletin* 8, no. 5 (May 1933): 8–9.

3558. Hard, Anne. "Mrs. Hoover: Friendly Impressions." *The Woman Citizen* 11 (October 1926): 14–15, 41.

3559. "Hillary Clinton, Trail-Blazer." *Economist* 325 (5 December 1992): 325–330.

3560. Hoff-Wilson, Joan, and Marjorie Lightman, eds. *Without Precedent: The Life and Career of Eleanor Roosevelt.* Bloomington: Indiana University Press, 1984.

3561. Jamieson, Kathleen Hall. "Hillary Clinton as Rorschach." In *Beyond the Double Bind: Women and Leadership,* 22–52. New York: Oxford University Press, 1995.

3562. Jensen, Faye Lind. "An Awesome Responsibility: Rosalyn Carter as First Lady." *Presidential Studies Quarterly* 20, no. 4 (1990): 769–775.

3563. Johnson, Claudia A. "Mrs. Lyndon Baines Johnson's Challenge to Women." *Saturday Evening Post* 237 (27 June 1964): 88–89.

3564. Johnson, Lady Bird. *A White House Diary.* New York: Dell, 1970.

3565. Lash, Joseph. *Eleanor and Franklin.* New York: Norton, 1971.

3566. Mayo, Edith P., and Denise D. Meringolo. *First Ladies, Political Role and Public Image.* Washington, DC: Smithsonian Institute, 1995.

3567. Phifer, Gregg. "Edith Bolling Wilson: Gatekeeper Extraordinary." *Speech Monographs* 38 (November 1971): 277–289.

3568. Reagan, Maureen. *First Father, First Daughter: A Memoir.* Boston: Little, Brown, 1989.

3569. Reagan, Nancy. *My Turn: The Memoirs of Nancy Reagan.* New York: Random House, 1989.

3570. Rizzo, Sergio. "Presidential Wives: The Unacknowledged Legislators of the Race." *Journal of American Culture* 14 (Winter 1991): 23–27.

3571. Ross, Ishbel. *Grace Coolidge and Her Era: The Story of a President's Wife.* New York: Dodd Mead, 1962.

3572. Seeber, Frances M. "Eleanor Roosevelt and Women in the New Deal: A Network of Friends." *Presidential Studies Quarterly* 20, no. 4 (1990): 707–717.

3573. Smith, Gene. "Mrs. Woodrow Wilson." In *When the Cheering Stopped: The Last Years of Woodrow Wilson,* 89–190. New York: Morrow, 1964.

3574. Tobin, Lessa E. "Betty Ford as First Lady: A Woman for Women." *Presidential Studies Quarterly* 20, no. 4 (1990): 761–767.

3575. Truman, Margaret. *First Ladies.* New York: Random House, 1995.

3576. Winfield, Betty Houchin. "The Legacy of Eleanor Roosevelt." *Presidential Studies Quarterly* 20, no. 4 (Fall 1990): 699–706.

White House

3577. Cadden, Vivian. "Midge Costanza: One Door from the Oval Office." *Ms.* 6, no. 7 (January 1978): 48–51, 75, 77–78.

3578. Costa, Maryanne Sugarman, and Diane Reis. "Keeping the Public Pulse for the President." *National Business Woman* 70, no. 3 (Fall 1989): 16, 26.

3579. Crawford, Ann Fears, and Crystal Sasse Ragsdale. "Adviser to the President, Sarah Ragle Weddington." In *Women in Texas*, 332–343. Austin, TX: State House Press, 1992.

3580. Dole, Elizabeth H. "My Side, Assistant to the President for Public Liaison." *Working Woman* 6 (May 1981): 154, 156.

3581. Lamson, Peggy. "Presidential Appointment: Esther Peterson." In *Few Are Chosen: American Women in Political Life Today*, 61–86. Boston: Houghton Mifflin, 1968.

3582. "New First in the White House." *Independent Woman* 31 (November 1952): 327.

3583. Noonan, Peggy. *What I Saw at the Revolution: A Political Life in the Reagan Era.* New York: Ballantine, 1990.

3584. Simpson, Peggy. "Faith Whittlesey: Presidential Assistant." *Working Woman* 8 (October 1993): 132–135.

3585. Stern, Lynn. "Sarah Weddington: Advocate with Clout." *Working Woman* 5 (February 1981): 35–37.

3586. "Third Black Woman Named to Key White House Slot." *Jet* 85, no. 13 (31 January 1994): 8.

3587. "Wexler Fills the Vacuum." *Time* 113 (5 February 1979): 10–11.

3588. Wood, Susan. "The Weddington Way." *Washington Post Magazine* (11 February 1979): 6–11.

Civil Service

3589. Adler, Nancy J. "Women in Management Worldwide." In *Women in Management Worldwide.* Armonk, NY: M. E. Sharpe, 1988.

3590. Bayes, Jane H. "Women in Public Administration in the United States." *Women and Politics* 11, no. 3 (1991): 85–109.

3591. Crook, Dorothy D. "Representing American Women." *Independent Woman* 25 (February 1946): 37–39, 59.

3592. Duerst-Lahti, Georgia, and Cathy Marie Johnson. "Gender and Style in Bureaucracy." *Women and Politics* 10, no. 4 (1990): 67–120.

3593. Gove, Gladys F. "High Profile Public Women on the Job." *Independent Woman* 22 (July 1943): 200–201.

3594. ———. "More Specialists in Personnel, Civilian." *Independent Woman* 30 (March 1951): 58–60, 80.

3595. ———. "Specialists in Personnel, Military." *Independent Woman* 30 (February 1951): 34–36, 54.

3596. Greenbie, Marjorie Barstow. "Women Work with Uncle Sam." *Independent Woman* 21 (March 1942): 74–76, 86.

3597. Hale, Mary M., and Rita Mae Kelly, eds. *Gender, Bureaucracy and Democracy: Careers and Equal Opportunity in the Public Sector.* New York: Greenwood Press, 1989.

3598. Lepper, Mary M. "A Study of Career Structures of Federal Executives: A Focus on Women." In *Woman and Politics*, edited by Jane S. Jaquette, 109–130. New York: Wiley, 1974.

3599. Mallon, Winifred. "Women in Our Foreign Service." *Independent*

Woman 10 (September 1929): 387–388.

3600. McGlen, Nancy E., and Meredith Reid Sarkees. "The Unseen Influence of Women in the State and Defense Departments." In *Gender and Policymaking, Studies of Women in Office,* edited by Debra L. Dodson, 81–92. New Brunswick, NJ: Center for the American Woman and Politics, 1991.

3601. Mead, Margaret. "Women in National Service." *Teachers College Record* 73, no. 1 (1971): 59–63.

3602. Mellon, Winifred. "Uncle Sam and the Ladies." *Independent Woman* 11 (September 1930): 355, 397–398.

3603. Pardon, Carolyn. "The Foreign Service Wife and Diplomacy in the 70's." *Foreign Service Journal* 48 (1971): 34–35.

3604. "Progress Report on Women in Government Policy Making Posts." *Independent Woman* 33 (January 1954): 4.

3605. Saint, Avis Marion. "Women in the Public Service: General Survey." *Public Personnel Studies* 8, no. 4 (1930): 46–54.

3606. Smith, Nancy Kegan. "Archivist's Perspective: Women and the White House: A Look at Women's Papers in the Johnson Library." *Prologue* 18 (Summer 1986): 123–129.

3607. "Top Women Bureaucrats Talk about Jobs, Bias and Their Changing Roles." *U.S. News and World Report* 83 (5 September 1977): 38–40.

3608. Vission, Andre. "Watchdog of the State Department." *Independent*

Woman 30 (August 1951): 225–226, 234.

3609. Weidner, Bethany. "Women in Public Power." *Public Power* 43 (September–October 1985): 12–13, 15, 17–18.

Judicial Branch

Judges

3610. Abernathy, Maureen Howard. "Women Judges in the United States Courts." *Women Lawyers Journal* 55, no. 1 (Winter 1969): 56–58.

3611. Adams, Mildred. "First on a Federal Bench: Kathryn Sellers, Juvenile Court." *The Woman Citizen* 9 (4 April 1925): 12, 24–25. Reprinted in *Literary Digest* (9 May 1925): 46.

3612. Allen, Florence E. *To Do Justly.* Forest Grove, OR: International School Book Service, 1965.

3613. Allread, Opal Howard. "Sarah T. Hughes: A Case Study in Judicial Decision-Making." Ph.D. dissertation, University of Oklahoma, Norman, 1987.

3614. Arledge, Paula C., and Edward V. Heck. "A Freshman Justice Confronts the Constitution: Justice O'Connor and the First Amendment." *Western Political Quarterly* 43, no. 3 (1992): 761–772.

3615. Behuniak-Long, Susan. "Justice Sandra Day O'Connor and the Power of Maternal Legal Thinking." *Review of Politics* 54, no. 3 (Summer 1992): 417–444.

3616. Brenner, Maurice. "Judge Motley's Verdict." *New Yorker* 70 (16 May 1994): 65–71.

3617. Cedarbaum, Miriam Goldman. "Women and the Federal Bench." *Boston University Law Review* 73 (January 1993): 39–45.

3618. Eastland, Terry. "Mainstream Radical." *American Spectator* 26 (November 1993): 66–67.

3619. ———. "Shameless in Seattle." *American Spectator* 27 (July 1994): 57–58.

3620. Farrell, Rita Katz, and Andrea Rothman. "Helen Balick's Bailiwick Is a Backwater No More." *Business Week* (30 November 1994): 82.

3621. Gottschall, Jin. "Carter's Judicial Appointments: The Influence of Affirmative Action and Merit Selection on Voting on the U.S. Courts of Appeals." *Judicature* 67, no. 4 (October 1983): 165–173.

3622. "Justice Cline to the United States Customs Court." *Women Lawyers Journal* 16 (July 1928): 2.

3623. "Lady of Law: Burnita Matthews." *Good Housekeeping* 147 (July 1958): 14.

3624. Marshall, Constance. "Lady Sits in Judgment: Interview with Genevieve R. Cline." *The Woman's Journal* 13 (September 1928): 17, 42–44.

3625. Martin, Elaine. "Women on the Federal Bench: A Comparative Profile." *Judicature* 65, no. 6 (December–January 1982): 306–313.

3626. ———. "Gender and Judicial Selection: A Comparison of the Rea-

gan and Carter Administrations." *Judicature* 71, no. 3 (October–November 1987): 136–142.

3627. More, Richter H., Jr. "Justice Sandra Day O'Connor: Law and Order Justice?" *International Social Science Journal* 63, no. 4 (1988): 147–157.

3628. O'Connor, Karen, and Jeffrey A. Segal. "Justice Sandra Day O'Connor and the Supreme Court's Reaction to Its First Female Member." *Women and Politics* 10, no. 2 (1990): 95–104.

3629. Politzer, Anita. "Her Honor, The Judge, Burnita Shelton Matthews, U.S. District Court for the District of Columbia." *Independent Woman* 30 (January 1951): 11–12, 31.

3630. Rowe, Lily Lykes. "Judge Kathryn Sellers: The First Woman Appointed to the Federal Judiciary." *Ladies Home Journal* 37 (January 1920): 45, 138.

Appointment Process

3631. Carpenter, Liz. "What's Wrong with This Picture ?" *Redbook* 151 (October 1979): 27, 178, 180, 182, 184–185.

3632. Cohodas, Nadine. "First Woman to Serve: Senate Confirms O'Connor as Supreme Court Justice." *Congressional Quarterly Weekly Report* 39 (26 September 1981): 1831.

3633. Cook, Beverly Blair. "The First Woman Candidate for the Supreme Court—Florence E. Allen." In *Supreme Court Historical Society Yearbook 1981*, 19–35. Washington, DC:

Supreme Court Historical Society, 1981.

3634. ———. "Women as Supreme Court Candidates: from Florence Allen to Sandra Day O'Connor." *Judicature* 65, no. 6 (December–January 1982): 314–326.

3635. ———. "The Path to the Bench: Ambitions and Attitudes of Women in the Law." *Trial* 19 (August 1983): 48–56.

3636. Lawrence, David. "Should a Woman Be on the Supreme Court ?" *U.S. News and World Report* 71 (25 October 1971): 104.

3637. Matthews, Burnita Shelton. *Pathfinder in the Legal Aspects of Women.* Berkeley: University of California, 1975. Interview for Suffragists Oral History Project, The Bancroft Library Oral History Program.

3638. Palley, Marian Lief, and Howard A. Palley. "The Thomas Appointment: Defeats and Victories for Women." *PS* 25, no. 3 (September 1992): 473–476.

3639. Slotnick, Elliot C. "Gender, Affirmative Action, and Recruitment to the Federal Bench." *Golden Gate University Law Review* 14 (Fall 1984): 519–571.

3640. Tolchin, Susan. "The Exclusion of Women from the Judicial Process." *Signs* 2, no. 4 (1977): 877–887.

Congress, in the States

Alabama

3641. "Alabama Likes 'Miss Dixie' Its New Senator." *Democratic Digest* 14, no. 10 (October 1937): 15.

Arizona

3642. Gordon, Mildred Nixon. "Representing Arizona." *Independent Woman* 12, no.11 (November 1933): 367, 391.

3643. Morrison, Betty. "Isabella Greenway: Arizona's First Congresswoman." Master's thesis, Arizona State University, Tempe, 1973.

Arkansas

3644. Caraway, Hattie Wyatt. "Women's Opportunity in Congress." *Democratic Digest* 14, no. 1 (January 1937): 5.

3645. ———. *Silent Hattie Speaks: The Personal Journal of Senator Hattie Caraway.* Westport, CT: Greenwood Press, 1979.

3646. Creel, George. "Woman Who Holds Her Tongue." *Colliers* 100 (18 September 1937): 22, 55.

3647. "Last of the First." *Time* 44 (7 August 1944): 19.

3648. "Representative Pearl Peden Oldfield." *Democratic Bulletin* 4, no. 4 (April 1929): 10.

California

3649. Boxer, Barbara, and Nicole Boxer. *Strangers in the Senate: Politics and the New Revolution of Women in*

America. Washington, DC: National Press Books, 1994.

3650. Douglas, Helen Gahagan. *A Full Life.* Garden City, NY: Doubleday, 1982.

3651. ———. *Interviews with Helen Gahagan Douglas, Congresswoman, Actress, and Opera Singer, and 25 Colleagues.* Berkeley: University of California, 1983. The Bancroft Library Oral History Interview.

3652. Elliot, Jeffrey M. "The Congressional Black Caucus: An Interview with Yvonne Brathwaite Burke." *Negro History Bulletin* 40, no. 1 (1977): 650–652.

3653. "How I Conceive the Congresswoman's Role During the Next Two Years." *Free World* 8 (November 1944): 425–427.

3654. Ickes, Harold L. "Helen Douglas and Tobey." *The New Republic* 123 (16 October 1950): 18.

3655. Keyes, Frances Parkinson. "Lady from California." *Delineator* 118 (February 1931): 14, 40, 64, 67–68.

3656. Maddux, Edith Walker. "New Congresswoman." *The Woman Citizen* 9 (7 March 1925): 10.

3657. Scobie, Ingrid Winther. "Helen Gahagan Douglas and the Roosevelt Connection." In *Without Precedent: The Life and Career of Eleanor Roosevelt,* edited by Joan Hoff-Wilson and Marjorie Lightman, 153–176. Bloomington: Indiana University Press, 1984.

3658. ———. *Center Stage: A Biography of Helen Gahagan Douglas.* New York: Oxford University Press, 1992.

Colorado

3659. Schroeder, Patricia. *Champion of the Great American Family.* New York: Random House, 1989.

Connecticut

3660. "Good Governor and Fighting Lady." *Time* 48 (26 August 1946): 19–20.

3661. Jarin, Ken, and James Burkhardt. *Ella T. Grasso, Democratic Representative from Connecticut.* Washington, DC: Grossman Publishers, 1972. Ralph Nader Congress Project, Citizens Look at Congress.

3662. Luce, Clare Boothe. "Victory Is a Woman." *Woman's Home Companion* 70 (November 1943): 34, 121–122.

3663. McKee, Mary Julians. "Congresswoman Clare Boothe Luce: Her Rhetoric against Communism." Ph.D. dissertation, University of Illinois, Urbana-Champaign, 1962.

3664. Potomacus. "Connecticut's Clare." *The New Republic* 109 (19 July 1943): 72–74.

3665. Woodhouse, Chase Going. *Oral History Interview, Former Member of Congress Association.* Interviews conducted by Betty G. Seaver and Morton J. Tenzer, Oral History Project, University of Connecticut for the Modern Congress in American History Project. Washington, DC: Manuscript Division, Library of Congress, 1979.

Florida

3666. Kalter, J. "New Career at 50? She Got Elected to Congress." *New Choices for Retirement Living* 33 (December 1993): 72–75.

3667. Owen, Ruth Bryan. "Woman in the House." *Woman's Home Companion* 58 (November 1931): 11–12.

3668. ———. "My Daughter and Politics." *Woman's Home Companion* 60 (October 1933): 27, 30.

Georgia

3669. "First Woman Senator." *Outlook* 132 (18 October 1922): 272–274.

3670. "The First Woman Senator." *Literary Digest* 75 (21 October 1922): 14–15.

3671. Floyd, Josephine Bonem. "Rebecca Latimer Felton: Political Independent." *Georgia Historical Quarterly* 30 (March 1946): 14–34.

3672. Hirsch, Eleanor. "Grandma Felton and the U.S. Senate." *Mankind* 4 (1974): 53–57.

Hawaii

3673. Davidson, Sue. *Jeannette Rankin and Patsy Takemoto Mink: A Heart in Politics.* Seattle, WA: Seal Press, 1994.

3674. Farrington, Elizabeth P. *Oral History Interview, Former Member of Congress Association.* Recorded by Michaelyn P. Chou for the Modern Congress in American History Project. Washington, DC: Manuscript Division, Library of Congress, 1978.

3675. Gates, Nancy S. *Patsy T. Mink, Democratic Representative from Hawaii.* Washington, DC: Grossman, 1972.

3676. Mink, Patsy T. *Oral History Interview, Former Member of Congress Association.* Recorded by Fern S. Ingersoll for the Modern Congress in American History Project. Washington, DC: Manuscript Division, Library of Congress, 1979.

3677. Russell, Anne. "Patsy Takemoto Mink: Political Women." Ph.D. dissertation, University of Hawaii, Honolulu, 1977.

Idaho

3678. Shelton, Isabelle. "Her Gracie Is Also Called Hell's Belle." *Democratic Digest* 1, no. 1 (August 1953): 73–75.

Illinois

3679. Braun, Carol Mosley. "Statement on the Extension of the Patent of the Insignia of the United Daughters of the Confederacy." *Vital Issues* 14, no. 1–2 (1992): 20–27.

3680. Church, Marguerite Still. *Oral History Interview, Former Member of Congress Association.* Recorded by Fern S. Ingersoll for the Modern Congress in American History Project. Washington, DC: Manuscript Division, Library of Congress, 1978.

3681. Dean, David, and Martha Dean. "Moma Went to Congress and Then to Jail." *American History Illustrated* 12, no. 7 (1977): 37–43.

3682. Douglas, Emily Taft. *Oral History Interview, Former Member of Congress*

Association. Recorded by Fern S. Ingersoll for the Modern Congress in American History Project. Washington, DC: Manuscript Division, Library of Congress, 1978.

3683. Huck, Winifred Sprague Mason. "What Happened to Me in Congress." *Woman's Home Companion* 50 (July 1923): 4, 100.

3684. Kennedy, David M. "Among Friends: Lynn Martin, Jerry Lewis, and the Race for the Chair of the House Republican Conference." In *Gender and Public Policy, Cases and Comments,* edited by Kenneth Winston and Mary Jo Bane, 367–383. Boulder, CO: Westview Press, 1993.

3685. Keyes, Frances Parkinson. "Mark Hanna's Little Girl." *Delineator* 117 (October 1930): 14, 54, 57–58, 60, 63.

3686. Miller, Kristie. *Ruth Hanna McCormick: A Life in Politics, 1880–1944.* Albuquerque: University of New Mexico Press, 1992.

3687. "Salute to Three Freshmen." *National Business Woman* 38 (February 1959): 12.

3688. "She Snoops to Conquer." *Literary Digest* 106 (20 September 1930): 5–7.

Indiana

3689. Catlin, Robert A. "Organizational Effectiveness and Black Political Participation: The Case of Katie Hall." *Phylon* 46 (September 1985): 179–192.

3690. Jenkes, Virginia Ellis. "Ladies and Legislation." *Democratic Bulletin* 8, no. 5 (May 1933): 12–13, 27.

3691. ———. "What American Women Expect from Congress." *Democratic Digest* 14, no. 1 (January 1937): 8, 31.

3692. Rishel, Virginia. "A Hoosier Congresswoman at Home and Abroad." *Democratic Digest* 14, no. 11 (November 1937): 14, 39.

Kansas

3693. Richter, Linda K. "Nancy Landon Kassebaum: From School Board to Senate." In *Women Leaders in Contemporary U.S. Politics,* edited by Frank P. Leveness and Jane P. Sweeney, 77–90. Boulder, CO: Lynne Rienner, 1987.

Kentucky

3694. "Kentucky's First Congresswoman." *Literary Digest* 90 (21 August 1926): 14–15.

Louisiana

3695. Boggs, Lindy. *Washington through a Purple Veil: Memoirs of a Southern Woman.* New York: Harcourt Brace, 1994.

3696. Clifford, Geraldine J. "Lindy Boggs Quits Congress." *People's Weekly* 34 (13 August 1990): 57–58.

3697. "Elaine Edwards." *Newsweek* 80 (14 August 1972): 40.

Maine

3698. Cook, Gay, and Dale Pullen. *Margaret Chase Smith, Republican Senator from Maine.* Washington, DC: Grossman Publishers, 1972. Ralph Nader Congress Project, Citizens Look at Congress.

3699. Fleming, Alice M. *The Senator from Maine: Margaret Chase Smith.* New York: Thomas Y. Crowell, 1969.

3700. Graham, Frank. *Margaret Chase Smith: Woman of Courage.* New York: John Day, 1964.

3701. Ickes, Harold L. "And Woman Shall Lead Them." *The New Republic* 122 (19 January 1950): 16.

3702. Smith, Margaret Chase. *Declaration of Conscience.* New York: Doubleday, 1972.

Maryland

3703. LeVeness, Frank P., and Jane P. Sweeney. "Barbara Mikulski: Representing the Neighborhood." In *Women Leaders in Contemporary U.S. Politics,* edited by Frank P. LeVeness and Jane P. Sweeney, 105–116. Boulder, CO: Lynne Rienner, 1987.

3704. Seifer, Nancy. "Barbara Mikulski and the Blue-Collar Women." *Ms.* 2, no. 5 (November 1973): 70–74.

3705. "Widow's Might." *Time* 37 (23 June 1941): 16.

Massachusetts

3706. Belonzi, Arthur A. "Margaret M. Heckler: Student Legislator to Ambassador." In *Women Leaders in Contemporary U.S. Politics,* edited by Frank P.

LeVeness and Jane P. Sweeney, 53–64. Boulder, CO: Lynne Rienner, 1987.

3707. "Breeze That Whispered Louise." *National Review* 22 (6 October 1970): 1038.

3708. Kuriansky, Joan. *Louise Day Hicks, Democratic Representative from Massachusetts.* Washington, DC: Grossman Publishers, 1972. Ralph Nader Congress Project, Citizens Look at Congress.

3709. Lyness, Jack. *Margaret M. Heckler, Republican Representative from Massachusetts.* Washington, DC: Grossman Publishers, 1972. Ralph Nader Congress Project, Citizens Look at Congress.

Michigan

3710. Abramson, Marcia. *Martha W. Griffiths, Democratic Representative from Michigan.* Washington, DC: Grossman Publishers, 1972. Ralph Nader Congress Project, Citizens Look at Congress.

3711. George, Emily R. S. M. *Martha W. Griffiths.* Washington, DC: University Press of America, 1982.

3712. Griffiths, Martha W. "Life without a Newspaper." *U.S. News and World Report* 52 (11 June 1962): 106.

3713. ———. "The Outlook for Legislation Affecting Women." *National Business Woman* 50 (October 1969): 9–10.

3714. ———. *Oral History Interview, Former Member of Congress Association.* Recorded by Emily George and Fern S. Ingersoll for the Modern Congress in American History Project. Washington, DC: Manuscript Division, Library of Congress, 1979.

3715. "Martha Griffiths: Graceful Feminist." *Time* 96 (24 August 1970): 10–11.

Minnesota

3716. "After Reunion with Andy, Coya Still Has a Bone to Pick." *Life* 45 (8 December 1958): 34–35.

3717. Bailey, F. "Meet the Farm Woman's Congresswoman." *Better Farming* 125 (March 1955): 116–117.

3718. Beito, Gretchen Urnes. *Coya Come Home: A Congresswoman's Journey.* Los Angeles: Pomegranate Press, 1990.

3719. "Senator Muriel: Following in a Tradition." *U.S. News and World Report* 84 (6 February 1978): 50.

Missouri

3720. Sussman, Robert. *Leonor K. Sullivan, Democratic Representative from Missouri.* Washington, DC: Grossman Publishers, 1972. Ralph Nader Congress Project, Citizens Look at Congress.

Montana

3721. "Jeannette Rankin Addresses 3,000." *The Woman's Journal* 48 (10 March 1917): 55–56.

3722. Giles, Kevin S. *Flight of the Dove: The Story of Jeannette Rankin.* Beaverton, OR: Touchstone, 1980.

3723. Harris, Ted Carlton. "Jeannette Rankin in Georgia." *Georgia Historical Quarterly* 58, no. 1 (Spring 1974): 55–78.

3724. ———. *Jeannette Rankin: Suffragist, First Woman Elected to Congress, and Pacifist.* New York: Arno, 1982.

3725. Josephson, Hannah. *Jeannette Rankin: First Lady in Congress.* Indianapolis: Bobbs-Merrill, 1974.

3726. "Political Power in the Hands of a Woman." *The Survey* 38 (21 July 1917): 357.

3727. Rankin, Jeannette. *Activist for World Peace, Women's Rights, and Democratic Government.* Berkeley: University of California, 1974. Interview by Amelia Fry for the Suffragists Oral History Project, The Bancroft Library Oral History Program.

3728. Wilhelm, Donald. "Lady from Missoula." *The Independent* 90 (2 April 1917): 25.

3729. Wilson, Joan Hoff. "Jeannette Rankin and American Foreign Policy: Her Lifework as a Pacifist." *Montana, The Magazine of Western History* 30, no. 2 (1980): 38–53.

3730. ———. "'Peace Is a Woman's Job': Jeannette Rankin and American Foreign Policy: The Origins of Her Pacifism." *Montana, The Magazine of Western History* 30, no. 1 (1980). 28–41.

New Jersey

3731. Fenwick, Millicent. *Speaking Up.* New York: Harper and Row, 1982.

3732. "Lady Blocks the Pork Barrel." *Life* 61 (23 September 1966): 6.

3733. Lynch, D. T. "Her Honor, the Mayor of Washington." *Literary Digest* 119 (30 March 1935): 24.

3734. Mitchell, Gary. "Women Standing for Women: The Early Political Career of Mary T. Norton." *New Jersey History* 96, no. 1–2 (Spring–Summer 1978): 27–42.

3735. Norton, Mary T. "Women in Congress Should Raise Voice against War." *Democratic Digest* 14, no. 1 (January 1937): 7.

New York

3736. Abzug, Bella S. *Bella!* New York: Saturday Review Press, 1972.

3737. "Bella. " *Newsweek* 76 (5 October 1970): 28–29.

3738. Brownmiller, Susan. *Shirley Chisholm.* Garden City, NY: Doubleday, 1970.

3739. Canning, Hazel. "She Represents New York." *Independent Woman* 14 (December 1934): 375, 402.

3740. Chisholm, Shirley. *Unbought and Unbossed.* New York: Houghton Mifflin, 1970.

3741. ———. *The Good Fight.* New York: Harper and Row, 1973.

3742. "Congresswoman." *Vital Speeches* 1 (11 March 1935): 381–383.

3743. Faber, Doris. *Bella Abzug.* New York: Lothrop, Lee and Shepard, 1976.

3744. "First Black Woman on Capitol Hill." *Ebony* 24 (February 1969): 58–59.

3745. Haskins, James. *Fighting Shirley Chisholm.* New York: Dial, 1975.

3746. Hicks, Nancy. *The Honorable Shirley Chisholm: Congresswoman from Brooklyn.* New York: Lion Press, 1971.

3747. Kelly, Edna Flannery. *Oral History Interview, Former Member of Congress Association.* Recorded by Charles T. Morrissey for the Modern Congress in American History Project. Washington, DC: Manuscript Division, Library of Congress, 1976.

3748. Kuriansky, Joan, and Catherine Smith. *Shirley Chisholm, Democratic Representative from New York.* Washington, DC: Grossman Publishers, 1972. Ralph Nader Congress Project, Citizens Look at Congress.

3749. "Lady of the House." *Outlook* 152 (3 July 1929): 377.

3750. Lamson, Peggy. "Elizabeth Holtzman and the Impeachment of Richard Nixon." In *Women Leaders in American Politics,* edited by James David Barber and Barbara Kellerman, 307–312. Englewood Cliffs, NJ: Prentice Hall, 1986.

3751. Marshall, Marguerite Mooers. "Ask Your Congressman." *Colliers* 88 (18 July 1931): 29, 41–42.

3752. St. George, Katharine Prince Collier. *Oral History Interview, Former Member of Congress Association.* Recorded by Fern S. Ingersoll for the Modern Congress in American History Project. Washington, DC: Manuscript Division, Library of Congress, 1979.

3753. Scheader, Catherine. *Shirley Chisholm: Teacher and Congresswoman.* Hillside, NJ: Enslow, 1990.

3754. Weinberg, Nancy, and Pauline Jennings. *Bella S. Abzug, Democratic Representative from New York.* Washington, DC: Grossman Publishers, 1972. Ralph Nader Congress Project, Citizens Look at Congress.

Ohio

3755. Batdorff, Virginia R. "Hard Work: She Likes It." *Independent Woman* 32 (December 1953): 441–442.

3756. Loth, David. *A Long Way Forward: The Biography of Congresswoman F. P. Bolton.* New York: Longman, 1957.

Oklahoma

3757. Foreman, Grant. "The Honorable Alice M. Robertson." *Chronicles of Oklahoma* 10 (March–December 1932): 13–15.

3758. James, Louise Boyd. "Alice Mary Robertson: Anti-Feminist Congresswoman." *Chronicles of Oklahoma* 55, no. 4 (Winter 1977–78): 454–461.

3759. Marshall, Marguerite Mooers. "Woman's Place in Politics." *Woman's Home Companion* 48 (October 1921): 15.

3760. Mazumdar, Maitreyi. "Alice's Restaurant: Expanding a Woman's Sphere." *Chronicles of Oklahoma* 70, no. 3 (1992): 302–325.

3761. Morris, Cheryl Haun. "Alice M. Robertson: Friend or Foe of the American Soldier?" *Journal of the West* 12, no. 2 (April 1973): 307–316.

3762. Spaulding, Joe Powerll. "The Life of Alice Mary Robertson." Ph.D. dissertation, University of Oklahoma, Norman, 1959.

3763. Stanley, Ruth Moore. "Alice M. Robertson, Oklahoma's First Congresswoman." *Chronicles of Oklahoma* 45 (Autumn 1967): 259–289.

Oregon

3764. Cahn, Robert. "Madam Senator from Oregon." *Saturday Evening Post* 234 (7 January 1961): 24–25, 80–82.

3765. Dreifus, Claudia. "Women in Politics: An Interview with Edith Green." *Social Policy* 2 (January–February 1972): 16–22.

3766. Green, Edith. "School Busing: Are We Hurting the People We Want to Help?" *U.S. News and World Report* 67 (18 August 1969): 72–73.

3767. ———. *Oral History Interview, Former Member of Congress Association.* Recorded by Shirley Tanzer for the Modern Congress in American History Project. Washington, DC: Manuscript Division, Library of Congress, 1980.

3768. Honeyman, Nan Wood. "Government Needs Viewpoint of Both Men and Women." *Democratic Digest* 14, no. 1 (January 1937): 6.

3769. Hunt, John Clark. "Westways Women: Maurine, Margarine and Cigarettes." *Westways* 67, no. 11 (1975): 46–50.

3770. "Interview with Representative Edith Green." *Urban Review* 4, no. 1 (1969): 3–8.

3771. Neuberger, Maurine. *Oral History Interview, Former Member of Congress Association.* Recorded by Shirley Tanzer for the Modern Congress in

American History Project. Washington, DC: Manuscript Division, Library of Congress, 1979.

3772. "Smoke Screen: Tobacco and the Public Welfare." *PTA Magazine* 58 (May 1964): 10–11.

3773. Wides, Louise. *Edith Green, Democratic Representative from Oregon.* Washington, DC: Grossman Publishers, 1972.

Pennsylvania

3774. Margolies-Mezvinsky, Marjorie. *A Woman's Place: The Freshmen Women Who Changed the Face of Congress.* New York: Crown, 1994.

South Dakota

3775. Kinyon, Jeannette. *The Incredible Gladys Pyle.* Vermillion, SD: Dakota Press, 1985.

Texas

3776. Bryant, Ira B. *Barbara Charline Jordan: From the Ghetto to the Capitol.* Houston, TX: D. Armstrong, 1977.

3777. Haskins, James. *Barbara Jordan.* New York: Dial, 1977.

3778. Jarboe, Jan. "Sitting Pretty." *Texas Monthly* 22, no. 8 (August 1994): 80–83.

3779. Jordan, Barbara, and Shelby Hearon. *Barbara Jordan: A Self-Portrait.* New York: Doubleday, 1979.

3780. "Texas 30th District: Eddie Bernice Johnson." *Congressional Quarterly Weekly Report* 51, no. 3 (16 January 1993): 139.

3781. Thompson, Wayner N. "Barbara Jordan's Keynote Address: The Juxtaposition of Contradictory Values." *Southern Speech Communication Journal* 44, no. 3 (1979): 223–232.

Utah

3782. Bosone, Reva Beck. *Oral History Interview, Former Member of Congress Association.* Recorded by Charles T. Morrissey and Fern S. Ingersoll for the Modern Congress in American History Project. Washington, DC: Manuscript Division, Library of Congress, 1978.

3783. Kosova, Weston, and Martha Brant. "Scandal, Politics, Love, Money." *Newsweek* 125 (27 November 1995): 38.

Washington

3784. Bedell, Catherine May. *Oral History Interview, Former Member of Congress Association.* Recorded by Fern S. Ingersoll for the Modern Congress in American History Project. Washington, DC: Manuscript Division, Library of Congress, 1979.

3785. Darmstader, Ruth. *Julia Butler Hansen, Democratic Representative from Washington.* Washington, DC: Grossman Publishers, 1972. Ralph Nader Congress Project, Citizens Look at Congress.

3786. Hansen, Julia Butler. *Oral History Interview, Former Member of Congress Association.* Recorded by Shirley Tanzer for the Modern Congress in American History Project. Washington, DC: Manuscript Division, Library of Congress, 1979.

3787. May, Catherine Dean. "Every Man Should Have His Say." *Vital Speeches* 31 (1 August 1965): 622–624.

3788. ———. "The Outlook for the Advancement of Women." *National Business Woman* 50 (October 1969): 11–13.

3789. Rosenberg, Marie Barovic. "Women in Politics: A Comparative Study of Congresswomen Edith Green and Julia Butler Hansen." Ph.D. dissertation, University of Washington, Seattle, 1973.

State Government

Legislatures

Impact

3790. Berkman, Michael B., and Robert E. O'Connor. "Do Women Legislators Matter? Female Legislators and State Abortion Policy." *American Politics Quarterly* 21 (January 1993): 102–124.

3791. Carroll, Susan J. "Taking the Lead." *Journal of State Government* 64, no. 2 (April–June 1991): 43–45.

3792. Carroll, Susan J., and Etta Taylor. "Gender Differences in Policy Priorities of U.S. State Legislators." Paper presented at the annual meeting of the American Political Science Association, Atlanta, 1989.

3793. Center for the American Woman and Politics. *Women State Legislators: Report from a Conference, May 18–21, 1972.* New Brunswick, NJ: Center for the American Woman and Politics, Rutgers University, 1974.

3794. ———. *Women State Legislators: Report from a Conference, June 17–29, 1982.* New Brunswick, NJ: Center for the American Woman and Politics, Rutgers University, 1983.

3795. ———. "Women as State Policymakers." *Journal of State Government* 60, no. 5 (September–October 1987): 199–234. Special edition.

3796. Cohen, Naomi K. "Shaking Off Legislative Typecasting." *Journal of State Government* 64, no. 2 (April–June 1991): 57–59.

3797. Diamond, Irene. *Sex Roles in the State House.* New Haven, CT: Yale University Press, 1977.

3798. Dodson, Debra L. "A Comparison of the Impact of Women and Men's Attitudes on Their Legislative Behavior: Is What They Say What They do?" Paper presented at the annual meeting of the American Political Science Association, Atlanta, 1989.

3799. Dodson, Debra L., and Susan J. Carroll. *Reshaping the Agenda: Women in State Legislatures.* New Brunswick, NJ: Center for the American Woman and Politics, Rutgers University, 1991.

3800. Dolan, Kathleen, and Lynne E. Ford. "Women in the State Legislatures: Feminist Identity and Legislative Behaviors." *American Politics Quarterly* 23, no. 1 (January 1995): 96–108.

3801. Feagans, Janet. "Female Political Elites: Case Studies of Female Legislators." Ph.D. dissertation,

Howard University, Washington, DC, 1972.

3802. Garcia, F. Chris, Christine Marie Sierra, and Margaret Maier Murdock. "The Politics of Women and Ethnic Minorities." In *Politics and Public Policy in the Contemporary American West,* edited by Clive S. Thomas, 195–230. Albuquerque: University of New Mexico Press, 1991.

3803. Githens, Marianne. "Women and State Politics: An Assessment." In *Political Women: Current Roles in State and Local Government,* edited by Janet A. Flammang, 41–64. Beverly Hills, CA: Sage, 1984. Women's Policy Studies.

3804. Githens, Marianne, and Jewell Prestage. "Women State Legislators: Styles and Priorities." *Policy Studies Journal* 7, no. 2 (Winter 1978): 264–270.

3805. Gluck, Hazel Frank. "The Difference." *Journal of State Government* 60, no. 5 (September–October 1987): 223–226.

3806. Gurwitt, Rob. "Legislatures: The Faces of Change: New Political Maps and a New Cast of Characters Make 1993 a Year of Upheaval in the States." *Governing* 6 (Fall 1993): 28–32.

3807. Handberg, Roger, Jr., and Wanda Lowery. "Women State Legislators, Lobbyists, and the Equal Rights Amendment." *Women's Law Forum* 9 (1978–79): 609–616.

3808. ———. "Women State Legislators and Support for the Equal Rights Amendment." *Social Science Journal* 17, no. 1 (1980): 65–71.

3809. Havens, Catherine M., and Lynne M. Healy. "Do Women Make a Difference?" *Journal of State Government* 64, no. 2 (April–June 1991): 63–67.

3810. Hawks, Joanne V., and Mary Carolyn Ellis. "A Challenge to Racism and Sexism: Black Women in Southern Legislatures, 1965–1986." *Sage* V, no. 2 (1988): 4–8.

3811. ———. "Heirs of the Southern Progressive Tradition: Women in Southern Legislatures in the 1920s." In *Southern Women,* edited by Caroline Matheny Dillman, 81–92. Washington, DC: Hemisphere, 1988.

3812. Hawks, Joanne V., and Carolyn Ellis Staton. "On the Eve of Transition: Women in Southern Legislatures, 1946–1968." In *Women in Politics: Outsiders or Insiders?: A Collection of Readings,* edited by Lois Lovelace Duke, 97–106. Englewood Cliffs, NJ: Prentice Hall, 1993.

3813. Hill, David B. "Women State Legislators and Party Voting on the ERA." *Social Science Quarterly* 64, no. 2 (June 1983): 318–326.

3814. ———. "Female State Senators as Cue Givers: ERA Roll-Call Voting, 1972–1979." In *Political Women: Current Roles in State and Local Government,* edited by Janet A. Flammang, 177–190. Women's Policy Studies, 8. Beverly Hills, CA: Sage, 1984.

3815. Hunter, Teola P. "A Different View of Progress—Minority Women in Politics." *Journal of State Government* 64, no. 2 (April–June 1991): 48–52.

3816. Kleeman, Katherine E. "Women in State Government: Looking

Back, Looking Ahead." *Journal of State Government* 60, no. 5 (1987): 199–203.

3817. Knoll, Catherine Baker. "Using the Powers of Office." *Journal of State Government* 64, no. 2 (April–June 1991): 53–54.

3818. Maggenti-Milano, M. E. "The National Women's Political Caucus: It's Role as a Reference Group for the Women State Legislators." Ph.D. dissertation, Pennsylvania State University, 1977.

3819. McClure, Mary. "Leaders among Equals." *Journal of State Government* 60, no. 5 (September–October 1987): 219–222.

3820. Mueller, Carol M. "Women's Organizational Strategies in State Legislatures." In *Political Women: Current Roles in State and Local Government,* edited by Janet A. Flammang, 156–176. Women's Policy Studies, 8. Beverly Hills, CA: Sage, 1984.

3821. ———. "Consensus without Unity." *Journal of State Government* 60, no. 5 (September–October 1987): 230–234.

3822. Poeter, Emma R. *History of the National Order of Women Legislators: Founded in Washington, D. C. in 1938.* Las Vegas, NV: Hanes-Thomas Printers, 1981.

3823. Reingold, Beth. "Representing Women: A Comparison of Female and Male Legislators in California and Arizona." Paper presented at the annual meeting of the American Political Science Association, San Francisco, 1990.

3824. Richardson, Lilliard E. "Gender Differences in Constituency Services among State Legislators." *Political Research Quarterly* 48, no. 1 (1995): 169–179.

3825. Strimling, Wendy S. *Elected Women Organize Statewide Associations.* New Brunswick, NJ: Center for the American Woman and Politics, Rutgers University, 1986.

3826. Thomas, Sue. "The Impact of Women on State Legislative Policies." *Journal of Politics* 53, no. 4 (November 1991): 958–976.

3827. ———. "The Effects of Race and Gender on Constituency Service." *Western Political Quarterly* 45 (March 1992): 169–180.

3828. ———. *How Women Legislate.* New York: Oxford University Press, 1994.

3829. ———. "Women in State Legislatures: One Step at a Time." In *The Year of the Woman: Myths and Realities,* edited by Elizabeth Adell Cook, Sue Thomas, and Clyde Wilcox. Boulder, CO: Westview Press, 1994.

3830. Thomas, Sue, and Susan Welch. "The Impact of Gender on Activities and Priorities of State Legislators: Legislative Styles and Policy Priorities." *Western Political Quarterly* 44, no. 2 (June 1991): 445–456.

Leadership

3831. Blair, Diane D., and Jeanie R. Stanley. "Personal Relationships and Legislative Power: Male and Female Perceptions." *Legislative Studies Quarterly* 16 (November 1991): 495–507.

3832. Carroll, Susan J., and Etta Taylor. "Gender Differences in the Committee Assignments of State Legislators: Preferences or Discrimination?" Paper presented at the annual meeting of the American Political Science Association, Atlanta, 1989.

3833. Center for the American Woman and Politics. *Women in Legislative Leadership: Report from a Conference, November 14–17.* New Brunswick, NJ: Center for the American Woman and Politics, Rutgers University, 1986.

3834. Jewell, Malcolm, and Marcia Lynn Whicker. "The Feminization of Leadership in State Legislatures." *PS* 26, no. 4 (December 1993): 705–712.

3835. Kathlene, Lyn. "Power and Influence in State Legislative Policymaking: The Interaction of Gender and Position in Committee Hearing Debates." *American Political Science Review* 88 (September 1994): 560–576.

3836. King, Rex Daphne. "Women Politicians: Influences on Development of Leadership and Self-Esteem." Ph.D. dissertation, University of California, Los Angeles, 1993.

3837. Knapp, Elaine S. "A Woman's Place Is in the Capitol." *State Government* 27 (September 1984): 4–9.

3838. Kolb, Deborah M., and Gloria G. Coolidge. "Her Place at the Table." *Journal of State Government* 64, no. 2 (April–June 1991): 68–75.

3839. Mandel, Ruth. "Women and Political Leadership: The Road Ahead." *State Legislatures* 8, no. 1 (January 1982): 30–31.

3840. "National Black Caucus of State Legislators Elects Female President." *Jet* 86 (9 May 1994): 46.

3841. Nelson, Albert J. *Emerging Influentials in State Legislatures: Women, Blacks and Hispanics.* New York: Praeger, 1991.

3842. Pierce, Neil R. "Women Legislators Aim for Power Slots." *Public Administration Times* 5 (15 July 1982): 2.

3843. Rosenthal, Alan. "Where Do You Sit? Where a Lawmaker Sits in a Legislative Chamber Affects His or Her Standing on the Floor." *State Legislatures* 10 (March 1984): 22–24.

3844. Thomas, Sue. "How Women Legislate: Exercising Agenda Leadership in the Nineties." *Woman of Power: A Magazine of Feminism, Spirituality, and Politics* 24 (1995): 83.

Members

3845. Almquist, Elizabeth M., and Dana Dunn. "Women in State Legislatures, 1970–1985." Paper presented at the annual meeting of the American Political Science Association, Chicago, 1987.

3846. "Black Women State Legislators." *Ebony* 39 (May 1984): 107–108.

3847. Caraway, Hattie Wyatt. "Women in State Capitols." *State Government* 10 (October 1929): 213–215.

3848. Carroll, Kathleen M. "The Age Difference between Men and Women Politicians." *Social Science Quarterly* 64, no. 2 (June 1983): 332–339.

3849. Freeman, Patricia K., and William Lyons. "Female Legislators: Is There a New Type of Woman in Office?" In *Changing Patterns in Legislative Careers,* edited by Gary F. Moncrief and Joel A. Thompson, 59–70. Ann Arbor: University of Michigan Press, 1992.

3850. Hawks, Joanne V., and Mary Carolyn Ellis. "Women Legislators in the Lower South: South Carolina, Georgia, Alabama, and Mississippi, 1922–1984." *Southern Anthropological Society Proceedings, Women in the South* 22 (1989): 110–121.

3851. "An Interview with State Senators Polly Baca-Baragan (Colorado) and Lena Guerrero (Texas)." *National Hispanic Journal* 1, no. 2 (1982): 8–11.

3852. Marcy, Mary B. "'Anticipate the Best Women': Female Elected Officials in the Great Plains." Ph.D. dissertation, University of Oxford, Trinity College, 1991.

3853. Martin, Marion E. "Women in State Capitols." *State Government* 10 (October 1937): 212–213.

3854. Prestage, Jewell. "Black Women State Legislators: A Profile." In *A Portrait of Marginality: The Political Behavior of American Women,* edited by Marianne Githens and Jewell Prestage, 401–418. New York: McKay, 1977.

3855. Rishel, Virginia. "Legislative Housekeepers, Their Records Prove Their Worth." Parts I–III. *Democratic Digest* 15 (July 1938): 18–19, 28; (August 1938): 19, 34; (October 1938): 14–15, 42.

3856. Robinson, Louise. "Women Lawmakers on the Move." *Ebony* 27 (October 1972): 48–56.

3857. Stoper, Emily. "Wife and Politician: Role Strain among Women in Public Office." In *A Portrait of Marginality: The Political Behavior of American Women,* edited by Marianne Githens and Jewell Prestage, 320–338. New York: McKay, 1977.

3858. Van der Vries, Bernice T. "Women in Government." *State Government* 21 (June 1948): 127–128, 134.

3859. Werner, Emmy E. "Women in State Legislatures." *Western Political Quarterly* 21 (March 1968): 372–380.

3860. "When Women Are in Politics." *The Woman Citizen* 4 (20 March 1920): 1009.

3861. "Women, A New Force in Politics." *The Woman Citizen* 4 (21 February 1920): 899.

3862. "Women in Politics: Negro Women Hold Ten Positions as State Legislators and City Councilors." *Ebony* 11 (August 1956): 81–84.

3863. "Women in State and Local Politics." *Social Science Journal* 21, no. 1 (January 1984): 1–107.

3864. "Women in State Politics." *Journal of State Government* 64, no. 2 (April–June 1991). Special issue.

3865. "Women Who Make State Laws: Distaff Politicos Hold 17 State Legislative Posts." *Ebony* 22 (September 1967): 27–34.

Executives

3866. Carroll, Susan J. "The Recruitment of Women for Cabinet Level Posts in State Government: A Social

Control Perspective." *Social Science Journal* 21, no. 1 (January 1984): 91–207.

3867. ———. "Women in State Cabinets: Status and Prospects." *Journal of State Government* 60, no. 5 (September–October 1987): 204–208.

3868. Carroll, Susan J., Barbara Geiger-Parker, and Wendy S. Strimling. *Women Appointed to State Government: A Comparison with All State Appointees.* New Brunswick, NJ: Center for the American Woman and Politics, Rutgers University, 1983.

3869. Charters, Jean. "Entering the Public Service." *State Government* 10, no. 10 (October 1937): 209–211.

3870. Duerst-Lahti, Georgia. "Organizational Ethos and Women's Power Capacity: Perceived and Formal Structure in State Administrative Organizations." Paper presented at the annual meeting of the American Political Science Association, Washington, DC, 1986.

3871. Guy, Mary E., ed. *Women and Men of the States: Public Administrators at the State Level.* Armonk, NY: M. E. Sharpe, 1992.

3872. Lenroot, Katharine F. "Women in Public Office." *State Government* 10, no. 10 (October 1937): 205–206.

3873. Reilly, Loretta. "Careers Unlimited." *National Business Woman* 36 (March 1957): 28–29.

3874. Rosenberg, Rina. "Representing Women at the State and Local Levels: Commissions on the Status of Women." In *Women, Power and Policy,* edited by Ellen Boneparth, 38–46. New York: Pergamon Press, 1982.

3875. Stanwick, Kathy, and Marilyn Johnson. *Women Appointed to State Boards and Commissions.* New Brunswick, NJ: Center for the American Woman and Politics, Rutgers University, 1976.

3876. Tillet, Rebecca, and Lucia Giudice. *The Appointment of Women: A Survey of Governors' Cabinets, 1985–1989.* Washington, DC: National Women's Political Caucus, Leadership Development, Education and Research Fund, 1989.

Judiciary

3877. Allen, David W. "The Behavior of Women State Supreme Court Justices: Are They Tokens or Outsiders." *The Justice System Journal* 12, no. 2 (1987): 232–245.

3878. Allen, David W., and Diane E. Wall. "Role Orientations and Women State Supreme Court Justices, Women on the Bench: A Different Voice?" *Judicature* 77, no. 3 (November–December 1993): 156–166.

3879. Alpha Kappa Alpha Sorority. *Negro Women in the Judiciary.* Vol. 1. Chicago: Alpha Kappa Alpha Sorority, 1969.

3880. Boles, Janet K. "Tough but Caring: Elected Women and Criminal Justice Policy." Paper presented at the annual meeting of the American Political Science Association, Chicago, 1995.

3881. Carbon, Susan B., Pauline Houlden, and Larry Berkson. "Women on the State Bench: Their Characteristics and Attitudes about Judicial

Selection." *Judicature* 65, no. 6 (December–January 1982): 294–305.

3882. Cook, Beverly Blair. "Women Judges: The End of Tokenism." In *Women in the Courts,* edited by Winifred L. Hepperle and Laura Crites, 84–105. Williamsburg, VA: National Center for State Courts, 1978.

3883. ———. "Women in the State Bench: Correlates of Access." In *Political Women: Current Roles in State and Local Government,* edited by Janet A. Flammang, 191–218. Women's Policy Studies, 8. Beverly Hills, CA: Sage, 1984.

3884. Eastland, Terry. "Daughtrey, Shanahan, Barkett and Gertner." *American Spectator* 26 (December 1993): 63–64.

3885. Macauley, W. A., Anne W. Rowland, and C. K. Rowland. "Female Representation on State Grand Juries: A Case Study with Application of Minority Representation Standards." *Women and Politics* 2, no. 3 (Fall 1982): 23–32.

3886. Martin, Elaine. "State Court Political Opportunity Structures: Implications for the Representation of Women." Paper presented at the annual meeting of the American Political Science Association, Washington, DC, 1988.

3887. ———. "Views from the State Bench: Gender Roles and Judicial Roles." In *Women in Politics: Outsiders or Insiders? A Collection of Readings,* edited by Lois Lovelace Duke, 177–184. Englewood Cliffs, NJ: Prentice Hall, 1993.

3888. McCarrick, Earlean M. "Women and the Criminal Justice System." In *Women and Public Policy,* edited by M. Margaret Conway, 169–192. Washington, DC: CQ Press, 1995.

3889. Oliver, Myrna. "The Female in the Trial Court." In *Women in the Courts,* edited by Winifred L. Hepperle and Laura Crites, 1–20. Williamsburg, VA: National Center for State Courts, 1978.

3890. Roberts, Marily McCoy, and David Rhein, eds. *Women in the Judiciary: A Symposium for Women Judges.* Williamsburg, VA: National Center for State Courts, 1983.

3891. Runge, Emily Foote. "Women in the Juvenile Court." *Annals of the American Academy of Political and Social Science* 56 (November 1914): 88–92.

In the States

Alabama

3892. Hawks, Joanne V. "A Select Few: Alabama's Women Legislators 1922–1983." *Alabama Review* 38, no. 3 (July 1985): 175–201.

3893. ———. "Stepping Out of the Shadows, Women in the Alabama Legislature, 1922–1990." In *Stepping Out of the Shadow, 1819–1990,* edited by Mary Martha Thomas, 154–173. Tuscaloosa: University of Alabama Press, 1995.

3894. "Pa and Ma Wallace as a Dynasty." *Life* 60 (11 March 1966): 4.

Alaska

3895. Foster, Scott. "Secretary Keeps Senate Secrets." *We Alaskans Magazine* (20 January 1984): 1–4.

3896. Woodman, Betzi. "Kay Wallis, Carrier of the Arrow." *Alaska Native News* (August 1984): 34.

Arizona

3897. "Arizona's Men Legislators." *The Woman Citizen* 3 (27 July 1918): 175.

3898. "BPW Member: from Secretary to Governor." *National Business Woman* 69, no. 5 (October–November 1988): 41.

3899. Jones, Kay F. "Ana Frohmiller: Watchdog of the Arizona Treasury." *Journal of Arizona History* 25 (Winter 1982): 349–368.

3900. Kelly, Rita Mae, ed. *Women and the Arizona Political Process.* Lanham, MD: University Press of America, 1987. Womens Studies Program.

3901. Kelly, Rita Mae, Michelle A. Saint-Germain, and Jody D. Horn. "Female Public Officials: A Different Voice?" *Annals of the American Academy of Political and Social Science* 515 (May 1991): 77–87.

3902. Leeper, Gertrude Bryan. "Lady in the Legislature." *Forum* 88 (July 1932): 54–59.

3903. Munds, Frances Willard. "My Work as a Woman Senator." *The Woman's Journal* 46 (24 April 1915): 134.

3904. Robinson, Geriod. "Arizona's Mothers of Law." *Overland* 67 (February 1916): 158–161.

3905. Saint-Germain, Michelle A. "Does Their Difference Make a Difference? The Impact of Elected Women on Public Policy in Arizona." *Social Science Quarterly* 70, no. 4 (December 1989): 956–968.

Arkansas

3906. Dorough, Jefferson M. "The First Woman Legislator in Arkansas: A Tribute to Miss Erle Chambers." *Pulaski County Historical Review* 32 (Summer 1984): 32–34.

3907. Stanley, Jeanie R., and Diane D. Blair. "Gender Differences in Legislative Effectiveness: The Impact of the Legislative Environment." In *Gender and Policymaking, Studies of Women in Office,* edited by Debra L. Dodson, 115–130. New Brunswick, NJ: Center for the American Woman and Politics, 1991.

California

3908. Adams, Mildred. "California's Able Five." *The Woman Citizen* 8 (22 September 1923): 10.

3909. Bayes, Jane H. "Do Female Managers in Public Bureaucracies Manage with a Different Voice? Studies of Bureaucracies in the United States and the State of California." Paper presented at the annual meeting of the American Political Science Association, Chicago, September 1987.

3910. Bird, Rose. "No Room for Error: The Problems Facing Women and Minorities on the Bench." *Judges Journal* 19 (Spring 1980): 5–8.

3911. Bornfield, Ethel L. "Mrs. Elizabeth Hughes, Butte County's Only Woman Legislator." *Diggins* 22, no. 3–4 (Fall–Winter 1978): 35–70.

3912. Braitman, Jacqueline R. "A California Stateswoman: The Public Career of Katherine Philips Edson." *Current California History* 65 (June 1986): 92–95.

3913. Burke, Yvonne Braithwaite. *New Arenas of Black Influence.* Los Angeles: University of California, 1982. Interview by Steven D. Edgington for the UCLA Oral History Program.

3914. "California Women's Caucus Blasts White Senator." *Jet* 69 (7 October 1969): 6.

3915. Christmas, Faith. "Touch of Brown." *Black Enterprise* 11 (August 1980): 31–32.

3916. Cook, Beverly Blair. "Moral Authority and Gender Difference: Georgia Bullock and the Los Angeles Women's Court." *Judicature* 77 (November–December 1993): 144–156.

3917. Davis, Pauline. *California Assemblywoman, 1952–1976.* Berkeley: University of California, 1986. The Bancroft Library Oral History Interview.

3918. Dobbin, Muriel. "As Voters Try to Overrule a Top Judge." *U.S. News and World Report* 99 (2 December 1985): 71.

3919. Eu, March Fong. *High Achieving Nonconformist in Local and State Government.* Berkeley: University of California, 1977. The Bancroft Library Oral History Interview.

3920. Fuller, Jean Wood. *Organizing Women: Careers in Volunteer Politics and Government Administration.* Berkeley: University of California, 1977. The Bancroft Library Oral History Interview.

3921. Heller, Elinor Raas. *A Volunteer Career in Politics, in Higher Education, and on Governing Boards.* Berkeley: University of California, 1984. The Bancroft Library Oral History Interview.

3922. Hundley, Norris C. "Katherine Philips Edson and the Fight for the California Minimum Wage, 1912–1913." *Pacific Historical Review* 29 (1960): 271–285.

3923. "In Sacramento, They Call the High-Ranking Women in the Brown Administration the 'Old Girls' Network'." *California Journal* 11 (January 1980): 37–39.

3924. MacFarlane, Peter Clark. "Katherine Philips Edson, a California Stateslady." *Colliers* 52, no. 7 (1 November 1913): 5–6, 29–31.

3925. Medsger, Betty. *Framed: The New Right Attack on Chief Justice Rose Bird and the Courts.* New York: Pilgrim, 1983.

3926. Mills, Kay. "Maxine Waters: The Sassy Legislator Who Knows There's More Than One Way to Make a Political Statement." *Governing* 1, no. 6 (March 1988): 26–33.

3927. Molina, Gloria. *Oral History Interview with Gloria Molina.* Berkeley: University of California, 1990. The

Bancroft Library Oral History Interview.

3928. Morris, Ann. "Women Fare Well on Appointment to the Judiciary." *California Journal* (May 1973): 160–161.

3929. Press, Aric. "Bird Hunting in California." *Newsweek* 106 (9 December 1985): 30, 35.

3930. Sankary, Wanda. *From Sod House to State House.* Berkeley, CA: University of California, 1979. The Bancroft Library Oral History Interview.

3931. Schultz, Vera. *Ideals and Realities in State and Local Government.* Berkeley: University of California, 1977. The Bancroft Library Oral History Interview.

3932. Schwartz, Mortimer D., Susan L. Brandt, and Patience Milrod. "Clara Shortridge Foltz: Pioneer in the Law." *Hastings Law Journal* 27 (January 1976): 548.

3933. Streshinsky, Shirley. "A Woman's Suicide." *Glamour* 93 (October 1995): 288–289.

3934. Takash, Paule Cruz. "Breaking Barriers to Representation: Chicana-Latina Elected Officials in California." *Urban Anthropology and Studies of Cultural Systems and World Economic Development* 22 (Fall–Winter 1993): 325–360.

3935. Thomas, Sue. "Voting Patterns in the California Assembly: The Role of Gender." *Women and Politics* 9, no. 4 (1990): 43–56.

Colorado

3936. Cannon, Helen. "First Ladies of Colorado." *Colorado Magazine* 39 (July 1962): 179–184.

3937. Cox, Elizabeth M. "The Three Who Came First." *State Legislatures* 20, no. 11 (November 1994): 12–19.

3938. Dean, Katie. "Nancy Dick: Colorado's New Lt. Governor." *Denver Post Empire Magazine* (31 December 1978): 16–17.

3939. Kathlene, Lyn. "Gender, Public Policy, and the Legislative Process: Delineating the Gendered Perspectives and Outcomes of Policymaking in the 1989 Colorado State House." Ph.D. dissertation, University of Colorado, 1991.

3940. Kathlene, Lyn, Susan E. Clarke, and Barbara A. Fox. "Ways Women Politicians Are Making a Difference." In *Gender and Policymaking: Studies of Women in Office,* edited by Debra L. Dodson, 31–38. New Brunswick, NJ: Center for the American Woman and Politics, 1991.

3941. Klein, Alexander. "The Woman with the Fighting Heat." *Independent Woman* 33 (February 1954): 55–56.

3942. Kreutz, Martha Hill, and Claire Nagle. "Diary of a Freshman Legislator." *Colorado Business Magazine* 20, no. 6 (June 1993): 1–18.

3943. Lafferty, Alma V. "Being a Woman Legislator in Colorado." *Delineator* 74 (September 1909): 204, 250–251.

3944. "Mrs. Helen L. Grenfell." *The Woman's Journal* 42 (1 April 1911): 104.

3945. "Mrs. Lafferty's Bill Went Through." *The Woman's Journal* 41 (2 July 1910): 107.

3946. Orr, Gertrude. "Colorado's Prime Minister." *Harper's Weekly* 60 (6 March 1915): 227.

3947. Reeve, Phoebe. "Colorado Women Legislators." *The Modern World* 7, no. 4 (April 1907): 210–211. Reprinted in *The Woman's Journal* (11 May 1907): 73–74.

3948. Robinson, Helen Ring. "Agnes Riddle, Dairywoman-Legislator." *Good Housekeeping* 55, no. 2 (August 1912): 168–172.

3949. ———. "On Being a Woman Senator." *The Independent* 78 (April 1914): 130–132.

3950. Smith, Eudochia Bell. *They Ask Me Why.* Denver, CO: World Press, 1945.

3951. "A Woman Legislator." *The Woman's Journal* 41 (8 April 1910): 300.

Connecticut

3952. Busiewicz, Susan. "Governor Ella Grasso of Connecticut." In *Women Leaders in American Politics,* edited by James David Barber and Barbara Kellerman, 47–55. Englewood Cliffs, NJ: Prentice Hall, 1986.

3953. Carroll, Kathleen M. "A Study on the Age Difference between Men and Women State Legislators." Master's thesis, University of Connecticut, 1979.

3954. Fazzio, Gilda. "The Political Impact of Women State Legislators: The Case of Connecticut." Ph.D. dissertation, New York University, 1984.

3955. Havens, Catherine M., and Lynne M. Healy. "Cabinet-Level Appointees in Connecticut: Women Making a Difference." In *Gender and Policymaking, Studies of Women in Office,* edited by Debra L. Dodson, 21–30. New Brunswick, NJ: Center for the American Woman and Politics, 1991.

Florida

3956. Carver, Joan S. "Women in Florida." *Journal of Politics* 41, no. 3 (August 1979): 941–955. Reprinted in *Florida's Politics and Government,* 2d ed., edited by Dauer Manning, 294–308. Gainesville: University Press of Florida, 1984.

3957. Good, Maya. "Paula Hawkins." *Working Woman* 7 (September 1982): 76–79.

3958. Hawks, Joanne V., and Mary Carolyn Ellis. "Creating a Different Pattern; Florida's Women Legislators 1928–1986." *Florida Historical Quarterly* 66 (July 1987): 68–83.

3959. Morphonios, Ellen, and Linda Marx. "Crime and Punishment: A View from a Broad." *People's Weekly* 32 (3 July 1989): 79–80, 82.

3960. Morris, Allen. *A Changing Pattern: Women in the State Legislature.* Tallahassee: Florida House of Representatives, 1987.

Georgia

3961. Jones, Leslie Ellen. "The Relationship between Home Styles and Legislative Styles and Its Implication for Representation: A Comparison of Women and Men in a Southern State Legislature." Ph.D. dissertation, Georgia State University, 1990.

3962. "Jurist Born to the Bench, Phyllis Kravitch." *Southern Living* 13 (April 1978): 145.

3963. Mullins, Sharon Mitchell. "The Public Career of Grace Towns Hamilton: A Citizen Too Busy to Hate." Ph.D. dissertation, Emory University, Atlanta, 1976.

3964. Salter, Dari Giles. "Essence Woman, Assemblywoman Mable Thomas." *Essence* 17 (August 1986): 42.

3965. Wantuck, Karen E. "Georgia on Her Mind, Cathey Steinberg." *Working Woman* 6 (October 1981): 62–63.

Hawaii

3966. Gething, Judith Dean. "The Educational and Civic Leadership of Elsie Wilcox, 1920–1932." *Hawaiian Journal of History* 16 (1982): 184–202.

3967. King, Jean. *Interview with Jean King*, 1975. Interviewed by P. Hooper and D. Boylan for the John A. Burns Oral History Project.

3968. Mezey, Susan Gluck. "Does Sex Make a Difference? A Case Study of Women in Politics." *Western Political Quarterly* 31, no. 4 (1981): 492–501.

3969. Otaguro, Janice. "Unsung Heroines." *Honolulu* (March 1990): 48–54.

Idaho

3970. Cox, Elizabeth M. "'Women Will Have a Hand in Such Matters from Now On', Idaho's First Women Lawmakers." *Idaho Yesterdays* 38 (Fall 1994): 2–9.

3971. D'Easum, Dick. *Dowager of Discipline: The Life of Dean of Women Permeal French.* Moscow: University Press of Idaho, 1981.

3972. Lisle, Charles J. "School-Mistress of the Lands." *Sunset* 34, no. 4 (April 1915): 742–744.

3973. Swank, Gladys Rae. *Ladies of the House (and Senate), History of Idaho Women Legislators.* Sune St. Hood, ID: Privately published, 1978.

Illinois

3974. Catania, Susan. *Interview for Oral History Collection.* Urbana: University of Illinois, 1972–1980. Politics and Government.

3975. Dawson, Frances. *Interview for Oral History Collection.* Urbana: University of Illinois, 1972–1980. Politics and Government.

3976. Everson, David H. "The Effect of the 'Cutback' on the Representation of Women and Minorities in the Illinois General Assembly." In *United States Electoral Systems: Their Impact on Women and Minorities,* edited by Wilma Rule and Joseph F. Zimmerman, 111–118. New York: Greenwood Press, 1992.

3977. "First to Hold a Cabinet Post." *Independent Woman* 32 (April 1953): 138.

3978. Harmon, Sandra D. "Florence Kelley in Illinois." *Journal of Illinois State Historical Society* 74, no. 3 (1981): 162–178.

3979. Netsch, Dawn. *Interview for Oral History Collection.* Urbana: University of Illinois, 1972–1980. Politics and Government.

3980. Saperstein, Esther. *Interview for Oral History Collection.* Urbana: University of Illinois, 1972–1980. Politics and Government.

3981. Van der Vries, Bernice T. "Housekeeping in the Legislature." *State Government* 10, no. 10 (October 1937): 207–209. Issue dedicated to women in public life.

3982. ———. *Interview for Oral History Collection.* Urbana: University of Illinois, 1972–1980. Politics and Government.

3983. Willard, Debbie. "Women in State Government: Why So Few at the Top?" *Illinois Issues* 11 (August–September 1985): 39–42.

3984. Willer, Anne. *Interview for Oral History Collection.* Urbana: University of Illinois, 1972–1980. Politics and Government.

3985. "Woman Gets Manpower Post in Illinois." *Jet* 39 (11 February 1971): 11.

Indiana

3986. "Indiana's Coed Legislator." *Life* 26 (28 February 1949): 101–102, 104.

3987. Walsh, Justine E. "Women Legislators, 1931–1986." Chap. 10 in *The Centennial History of the General Assembly, 1916–1978,* 370–371, 578–584, Appendix Q. Indianapolis: Select Committee on the Centennial History of the Indiana General Assembly and the Indiana Historical Bureau, 1987.

Iowa

3988. Jordan, David W. "Those Formidable Females—Iowa's Early Women Votegetters." *The Iowan* 31, no. 2 (Winter 1982): 46–52.

3989. King, Elizabeth G. "Women in Iowa Legislative Politics." In *A Portrait of Marginality: The Political Behavior of American Women,* edited by Marianne Githens and Jewell Prestage, 284–303. New York: McKay, 1977.

3990. Lex, Louise. "The Feminist Movement: It's Impact on Women in State Legislatures." Ph.D. dissertation, Iowa State University, Ames, 1977.

3991. Noun, Louise R. "Roxanne Conlin." In *More Strong Minded Women,* 118–133. Ames: Iowa State University Press, 1992.

3992. Schenken, Suzanne O'Dea. *Legislators and Politicians: Iowa's Women Lawmakers.* Ames: Iowa State University Press, 1995.

Kansas

3993. "Kansas Woman Making Mark in State Legislature." *Democratic Digest* 18, no. 7–8 (July–August 1941): 37.

3994. Richardson, Anna Steese. "Mrs. MacMurphy—'Official Snooper'." *Pictorial Review* 12, no. 5 (February 1911): 6–7.

3995. Sharistanian, Janet. *Gender, Ideology and Action: Historical Perspectives on Women's Public Lives.* Westport, CT: Greenwood Press, 1986.

Kentucky

3996. Campbell, Lindsay. *Kentucky Women Legislators, 1922–1996, Biographical Sketches.* Frankfort: Kentucky Commission on Women, 1995.

3997. Cromwell, Emma Guy. *Woman in Politics.* Louisville, KY: Standard Printing Co., 1939.

3998. Hawkesworth, Mary E. "The Quest for Equality: Women in Kentucky Politics." In *Kentucky: Government and Politics,* edited by Joel Goldstein, 236–258. Bloomington, IN: College Town Press, 1984.

3999. "Janice Martin Installed as First Black Woman Judge in Kentucky." *Jet* 83 (1 February 1993): 18.

4000. Powers, Georgia Davis. *I Shared the Dream: The Pride, Passion and Politics of the First Black Woman Senator from Kentucky.* Far Hills, NJ: New Horizon Press, 1995.

Louisiana

4001. Johnson, Louise. "Beatrice H. Moore, Pioneer Caddo Parish Woman Legislator, 1940–1944." *North Louisiana Historical Association Journal* 17, no. 4 (1986): 137–146.

4002. ———. *Women of the Louisiana Legislature.* Farmerville, LA: Greenbay, 1986.

Maine

4003. Marston, Doris Ricker. "Maine's Commissioner of Labor." *Independent Woman* 31 (January 1952): 5–6.

4004. Martin, Marion E. "Fair Play in Maine: Down East Women Legislators Given Equal Footing." *State Government* 10 (October 1937): 212–213.

Maryland

4005. Calcott, Doris Gay. "Responsibility Is the Word She Lives By." *Independent Woman* 34 (March 1955): 95, 116.

4006. Githens, Marianne. "Spectators, Agitators, or Lawmakers: Women in State Legislatures." In *A Portrait of Marginality: The Political Behavior of American Women,* edited by Marianne Githens and Jewell Prestage, 196–209. New York: Longman, 1977.

4007. Kretman, Kathy Postel, and Gregory G. Lebel. *Claiming A Voice: Women Legislators of Maryland.* Annapolis: Maryland Women's Legislative Caucus, 1991.

4008. Meredith, Ellis. "What Can One Woman Do?" *Democratic Bulletin* 8, no. 5 (May 1933): 18, 28.

Massachusetts

4009. Barrows, Mary Livermore. "How Do Women Fit into Politics." *The Republican Woman of Illinois* 6, no. 8 (April 1929): 9.

4010. Cannon, Joan Bartczak, and Mary Ann Marusich-Smith. "Political

Marriages: When the Wife Is the Politician." *Women and Politics* 6 (Fall 1986): 57–64.

4011. Dalton, Cornelius, John Wirkkala, and Anne Thomas. "Women." In *Leading the Way: A History of the Massachusetts General Court 1629–1980,* 239–245. Boston: Secretary of State, 1984.

4012. Nies, Judith. "Elaine Noble: Not Just Another Gay Legislator." *Ms.* 4, no. 2 (August 1975): 58–61, 108.

4013. "Two First Judges." *The Woman's Journal* 16 (January 1931): 5–6.

Michigan

4014. Berman, Maxine. *The Only Boobs in the House Are Men.* Troy, MI: Momentum Books, 1994.

4015. Blakely, Mary Kay. "The Nuns' Revolt: Sister Agnes Mary Mansour: Her Vow to the People." *Ms.* 12, no. 3 (September 1983): 54–56, 102–103.

4016. Brown, Mary C. *Women in the Michigan Legislature 1921–1994.* Lansing: House of Representatives, Michigan Legislative Council, 1994.

4017. Cartwright, Allison S. "Jessie P. Slaton: A Renaissance Woman." *Michigan History* 73, no. 5 (1989): 20–23.

4018. "Controversial Appointment, Sister Agnes Mary Mansour." *Christian Century* 100 (23 March 1983): 266–267.

4019. Elliott, Daisy. "Black Power in State Government." *Ebony* 27 (April 1972): 94–103.

4020. Kohlmeier, Louis M. "Justice Report: Detroit's Cornelia Kennedy Is Top Supreme Court Possibility." *National Journal* 7 (10 May 1975): 690–691.

4021. Kotsis, Chrysanthe A., and Carol J. Karr. "Comments from Six Michigan Women Judges." *Michigan Bar Journal* 63, no. 6 (June 1984): 490–495.

4022. Silver, Diane. "A Comparison of Coverage of Male and Female Officials in Michigan." *Journalism Quarterly* 63, no. 1 (1986): 144–149.

Minnesota

4023. Aldrich, Darragh. *Lady in Law: A Biography of Mabeth Hurd Paige.* Chicago: Ralph Fletcher Seymour, 1950.

4024. Fraser, Arvonne S., and Sue E. Holbert. "Women in the Minnesota Legislature, 1923–1977." In *Women in Minnesota: Selected Biographical Essays,* edited by Barbara Stuhler and Gretchen Kreuter, 347–378. St. Paul: Minnesota Historical Society, 1977.

4025. Kreuter, Gretchen, and Rhoda R. Gilman. "Women in Minnesota's History." In *Minnesota Legislative Manual, 1975–76,* 18. St. Paul: Minnesota Legislature, 1976.

Mississippi

4026. Hawks, Joanne V. "Like Mother, Like Daughter: Nellie Nugent Somerville and Lucy Somerville Howorth." *Journal of Mississippi History* 45, no. 2 (May 1983): 116–123.

4027. Hawks, Joanne V., Mary Carolyn Ellis, and J. Byron Morris. "Women in the Mississippi Legislature." *Journal of Mississippi History* 33, no. 4 (November 1981): 266–292.

4028. Kearney, Belle. *A Slaveholder's Daughter.* New York: Negro University Press, 1969. Reprint.

4029. Muirhead, Jean Denman. *An Oral History with Jean Muirhead.* Hattiesburg: University of Southern Mississippi, 1990. Interview for the Mississippi Oral History Program of the University of Southern Mississippi.

4030. Payne, Jacqueline P., Joanne V. Hawks, Mary Carolyn Ellis, and J. Byron Morris. *Women of the Mississippi Legislature 1922–1980.* Jackson: Mississippi Library Commission, 1980.

4031. Vaughan, Donal S. "Women in Mississippi Government." *Public Administration Survey* 9 (May 1962): 1–4.

Missouri

4032. Calloway, DeVerne. "The Missouri Experience." *Focus* 9 (1973): 20–21.

4033. Dains, Mary K. "Women Pioneers in the Missouri Legislature." *Missouri Historical Review* 85, no. 1 (October 1990): 40–52.

4034. ———. "Forty Years in the House: A Composite of Missouri Women Legislators." *Missouri Historical Review* 87, no. 2 (January 1993): 150–167.

4035. O'Connor, Candance. *Missouri Women in Political Life, 1972–1993.* Jefferson City, MO: Secretary of State, 1993. Reprinted from the *Official Manual of the State of Missouri, 1993–94.* Jefferson City, MO: Secretary of State, 1993.

4036. Tokarz, Karen L. "Pioneers in the Legal Profession: The History of Women State Court Judges in Missouri." *St. Louis Bar Journal* 35, no.4 (Spring 1989): 34–42.

Montana

4037. Bridenstine, Ellenore M. "My Years as Montana's First Woman State Senator." *Montana, The Magazine of Western History* 39 (Winter 1989): 54–58.

4038. Tascher, Harold. *Maggie and Montana: The Story of Maggie Smith Hathaway.* New York: Exposition Press, 1954.

4039. Tobias, Carl. "The Gender Gap on the Montana State Bench." *Montana Law Review* 54 (Winter 1993): 125–128.

4040. "Women Sponsor Many Bills in Montana." *The Woman's Journal* 48 (12 May 1917): 109–110.

Nebraska

4041. Bemis, Doris Ella. "A Comparison of the Women Nebraska Legislators with Other States." Master's thesis, University of Nebraska, Lincoln, 1930.

4042. Nebraska Commission on the Status of Women, ed. *Nebraska Women in History: Women Senators from 1925–1981.* Lincoln: Nebraska Commission on the State of Women, 1981.

Nevada

4043. Bennett, Dana R. "Leading Ladies." *Nevada* 55, no. 2 (April 1995): 18–20, 74–75, 77.

4044. Glass, Mary Ellen. "Nevada's Lady Lawmakers: Women in the Nevada Legislature." *Nevada Public Affairs Report* XIV, no. 1 (October 1975): 1–17.

4045. Patterson, Edna B. "Kate St. Clair: One of Nevada's Great Women." *Northeastern Nevada Historical Society Quarterly* 92, no. 4 (1992): 136–143.

4046. Winckler, Karen. "Nevada's First Woman Justice: Justice Miriam Shearing." *Nevada Lawyer* 1 (April 1993): 11–12.

New Hampshire

4047. Anderson, Leon W. *New Hampshire Women Legislators 1921 to 1971.* Concord: The Evans Printing Company, 1971.

4048. "From Farm to Forum: Miss Jessie Doe." *The Woman Citizen* 5 (15 January 1921): 891.

4049. Hickey, Margaret. "Women in Politics: New Hampshire Legislators." *Ladies Home Journal* 68 (November 1951): 25, 222.

4050. Yantis, Mrs. A. S. "Mother-At-Law." *The Woman Citizen* 9 (20 September 1924): 11.

New Jersey

4051. McCormick, Katheryne C., and Richard P. McCormick. *Equality Deferred, Women Candidates for the New Jersey Assembly 1920–1993.* New Brunswick, NJ: Center for the American Woman and Politics, Eagleton Institute of Politics, Rutgers University, 1994.

4052. "Mrs. Van Ness as an Answer to Miss Hauser." *The Woman Citizen* 5 (5 March 1921): 1045–1046.

4053. "New Jersey's Nine Assemblywomen." *Charm* (March 1927): 16–18, 84.

4054. Roberts, Steven V. "A Poster Daughter for GOP Diversity." *U.S. News and World Report* 118, no. 5 (6 February 1995): 10–11.

4055. Stanwick, Kathy. *Getting Women Appointed, New Jersey's Bipartisan Coalition.* New Brunswick, NJ: Center for the American Woman and Politics, Rutgers University, 1984.

New Mexico

4056. Coe, Louise Holland. *Lady and the Law Books: Sixteen Years First and Only Woman Member of the New Mexico Senate.* Albuquerque: Modern Press, 1981.

4057. Schackel, Sandra. *Social Housekeepers: Women Shaping Public Policy in New Mexico, 1920–1940.* Albuquerque: University of New Mexico Press, 1992.

4058. "A Woman Governor in New Mexico." *Sunset* 53 (October 1924): 24–25.

New York

4059. "Assemblywoman Proposes Bill for Women's Rights." *Jet* 4 (9 April 1971): 8.

4060. Burstein, Karen. "Notes from a Political Career." In *Women Organizing—An Anthology,* edited by Bernice Cummings and Victoria Schuck, 49–60. Metuchen, NJ: Scarecrow Press, 1979.

4061. Dreifus, Claudia. "I Hope I'm Not a Token: New York's Commissioner of Human Rights." *McCalls* 99 (October 1971): 51.

4062. Giambanco, Jacqueline. "Long Island's On-The-Move Legislator, Barbara Patton." *Working Woman* 11 (February 1986): 91–92, 94.

4063. Hepburn, D. "Politics Is Her Business: Mrs. Bessie Buchanan Excels as New York's First Negro Assemblywoman." *Sepia* 8 (October 1960): 32–35.

4064. Knapp, Florence E. S. "A Woman Politician and Proud of It." *Ladies Home Journal* 44 (May 1927): 37.

4065. Lilly, Mary M. "The Log of a Woman Legislator." *The Woman Citizen* 4 (7 June 1919): 9.

4066. "Mrs. Buchanan Goes to Albany: For New York's First Negro Woman Legislator." *Our World* 10 (May 1955): 50–53.

4067. Prindle, Janice, and John Boynton Priestley. "Women Legislators: A Paradox of Power, Ten Women in the New York State Legislature." *Empire State Report* 2 (January 1976): 3–7.

4068. Rockefeller, Nelson A. "Women and Government." *Women Lawyers Journal* 54, no. 2 (Spring 1968): 6–8, 11.

4069. Spencer, Gary. "Carmen Beauchamp Ciparick Named to Court of Appeals: Supreme Court Justice Is First Hispanic Nominee." *New York Law Journal* 210 (2 December 1993): 1.

4070. Wandersee, Winifred. "Frances Perkins Meets Tammany Hall: The Co-Adaptation of Machine Politics and Social Reform: 1910–1916." Paper presented at the Conference on Women and Political Change in the 20th Century, New School for Social Research, New York, April 1990.

4071. Weinstein, Helene E., ed. *Lawmakers: Biographical Sketches of the Women of the New York State Legislature, 1918–1988.* Albany: New York State Library, 1989.

4072. "The Women in the New York Governor's Cabinet." *Democratic Digest* 14, no. 6 (June 1937): 10.

North Carolina

4073. Bartlett, Marie. "My Life as a Judge." *Good Housekeeping* 212 (February 1991): 50, 52–53.

4074. McLeod, Harriet H. "Women in the North Carolina General Assembly." Master's thesis, University of North Carolina, Chapel Hill, 1980.

4075. Parrish, Rebecca Mixson. "Women in North Carolina Politics: A Study of Women Legislators' and Women's Political Groups' Influence in the State." Master's thesis, University of North Carolina, Chapel Hill, 1994.

4076. Stewart, Debra W. "Public Policy and Decision Processes: The Impact of Women's Policy Issues on Decision Making in the North Carolina Legislature." Ph.D. dissertation, University of North Carolina, Chapel Hill, 1975.

North Dakota

4077. Hanson, Nancy Edmonds. "Aloha Eagles: First Elected in 1966, She's Now Dean of Fargo Legislative Delegation After 9 House Sessions." *Howard Binford's Guide* 15, no. 10 (April 1983): 36, 40, 46–47.

4078. ———. "Tish Kelly: Fargo Housewife Is Only Second Woman to Be Elected Speaker of North Dakota House." *Howard Binford's Guide* 15, no. 10 (April 1983): 24–27, 32.

4079. Rathke, Ann. *Lady, If You Go into Politics: North Dakota's Women Legislators 1923–1989.* Bismarck, ND: Sweetgrass Communications, 1991.

4080. Rice, Hazel F. "A Memo from Memory: Working with the North Dakota Workmen's Compensation Bureau, 1919–1922." *North Dakota History* 46, no. 2 (1979): 22–29.

4081. "Two Eminent Homemakers." *Democratic Digest* 17, no. 1 (January 1940): 17.

Ohio

4082. Jones, Olga Anna. "Ohio's Pioneer Six." *The Woman Citizen* 8 (1 December 1923): 9, 27.

4083. Lee, Annabel. "Her Honor, Judge Allen." *Independent Woman* 18 (December 1939): 385, 399–400.

4084. Tuve, Jeanette, E. *First Lady of the Law.* Lanham, MD: University Press of America, 1984.

Oklahoma

4085. Barnard, Kate. "Working for the Friendless." *The Independent* 63 (28 November 1970): 1308.

4086. Barnard, Kate, and Julia Short. "Stump Ashby Saves the Day." *Journal of the West* 12, no. 2 (April 1973): 296–306.

4087. Bryant, Keith L., Jr. "Kate Barnard, Organized Labor and Social Justice in Oklahoma During the Progressive Era." *Journal of Social History* 35, no. 2 (May 1969): 145–164.

4088. Crawford, Suzanne Jones, and Lynn R. Musslewhite. "Progressive Reform and Oklahoma Democrats: Kate Barnard Versus Bill Murray." *The Historian* 53 (Spring 1991): 473–488.

4089. Crockett, Bernice Norman. "'No Job for a Woman'." *Chronicles of Oklahoma* 61, no. 2 (Summer 1983): 148–167.

4090. Darcy, Robert. "Why So Few Women in Public Office? A Look at Oklahoma Politics." In *Southwest Cultural Festival: 1982,* edited by Gordon Weaver, 21–30. Stillwater: Oklahoma University Press, 1982.

4091. Hougen, Harvey R. "Kate Barnard and the Kansas Penitentiary Scandal, 1908–1909." *Journal of the West* 17, no. 1 (1978): 9–18.

4092. Kirksey, Jason F., and David E. Wright. "Black Women in State Legislatures: The View from Oklahoma."

Oklahoma Politics 1 (October 1992): 67–79.

Oregon

4093. Katz, Vera. "Women Chart New Legislative Course." *Journal of State Government* 60, no. 5 (September–October 1987): 213–215.

4094. Neuberger, Maurine. "Footnotes on Politics by a Lady Legislator." *The New York Times Magazine* (27 May 1951): VIII, 18.

4095. Neuberger, Richard L. "My Wife Succeeds at Politics, Too." *Coronet* 33 (November 1952): 36–38.

4096. ———. *Adventures in Politics.* New York: Oxford University Press, 1954.

4097. Paulus, Norma. "Women Find Political Power in Unity." *Journal of State Government* 60, no. 5 (September–October 1987): 227–229.

4098. Thompson, Leah Illidge. "Lady on the Bench: Mary Jane Spurin." *Sunset* 60 (January 1928): 48.

4099. Waldron, Sue. "Yeomanettes: Jackson County's Blue Star Daughters and Marian B. Towne, Oregon's First Woman Legislator." *Table Rock Sentinel Magazine* 10, no. 2 (March–April 1977): 2–10.

4100. Zink, Laurie Ann. "Women in the Oregon Political Elite 1960–1990." Ph.D. dissertation, University of Oregon, 1993.

Pennsylvania

4101. "A Career of Firsts." *Ebony* 44 (February 1989): 77–78, 80.

4102. "Commissioner of Public Welfare of the State of Pennsylvania." *Medical Woman's Journal* 30 (September 1923): 274.

4103. Featherman, Sandra A. "Representing Women and Blacks in Pennsylvania: The Impacts of Demography, Culture, and Structure." In *United States Electoral Systems: Their Impact on Women and Minorities,* edited by Wilma Rule and Joseph F. Zimmerman, 73–86. New York: Greenwood Press, 1992.

4104. Hubbs, Harriet L. "Pennsylvania's Eight: Her Women Legislators Met the Test." *The Woman Citizen* 8 (3 November 1923): 7–8, 26.

4105. ———. "Pennsylvania's Welfare Woman: Dr. Ellen C. Potter—Who She Is and What She Does." *The Woman Citizen* 8 (29 December 1923): 9, 30.

4106. Jensen, Rita Henley. "A Day in Court." *Ms.* 5 (September–October 1994): 48–49.

4107. "People's Portia in Pennsylvania, Anmne X. Alpern, Attorney General." *National Business Woman* 39, no. 1 (January 1960): 12–13.

4108. "Philadelphia's Lady Judge." *Ebony* 15 (March 1960): 97–98, 100.

4109. Yulick, Carol Blake, and Robert L. Cable. *Women in the Pennsylvania Legislature, 1921–1984.* Harrisburg, PA: Legislative Reference Bureau, 1984.

Rhode Island

4110. Adler, Emily Stier, and J. Stanley Lemons. "The Independent Woman: Rhode Island's First Woman Legislator." *Rhode Island Historical Journal* 49, no. 1 (1991): 2–11.

4111. ———. *The Elect: Rhode Island's Women Legislators 1922–1990.* Providence: League of Rhode Island Historical Societies, 1990.

4112. Violet, Arlene. *Convictions: My Journey from the Convent to the Courtroom.* New York: Random House, 1988

4113. "A Woman Legislator's Ideas." *Democratic Bulletin* 4, no. 4 (April 1929): 22–23.

South Carolina

4114. Burkett, Tracy Lynn. "The Political Networks of South Carolina State Legislators." Master's thesis, University of South Carolina, 1993.

4115. Hawks, Joanne V., and Mary Carolyn Ellis. "Ladies in the Gentleman's Club: South Carolina Women Legislators 1928–1984." *Proceedings of the South Carolina Historical Association* (1986): 17–32.

4116. "South Carolina Representative Juanita White Elected to Committee Post." *Jet* 72 (24 August 1987): 24.

Texas

4117. Aldave, Barbara Bader. "Women in the Law in Texas: The Stories of Three Pioneers." *St. Mary's*

Law Journal 25 (Summer 1983): 289–301.

4118. Almquist, Elizabeth M. "Professions and Politics: The Status of Women in Texas and the Other Forty Nine States." Paper presented at the annual meeting of the American Political Science Association, Chicago, 1987.

4119. Boles, Janet K. "The Texas Woman in Politics: Role Model or Mirage?" *Social Science Journal* 21, no. 1 (January 1984): 79–90.

4120. Coleman, Suzanne. "The Politics of Participation: The Emergent Journey of Frances Farenthold." Master's thesis, University of Texas, Arlington, 1973.

4121. Cottrell, Debbie Mauldin. *Pioneer Woman Educator: The Progressive Spirit of Annie Webb Blanton.* The Centennial Series of the Association of Former Students, 48. College Station: Texas A & M University, 1993.

4122. Dow, Bonnie J., and Mari Boor Tonn. "'Feminine Style' and Political Judgment in the Rhetoric of Ann Richards." *The Quarterly Journal of Speech* 79 (August 1993): 286–302.

4123. Harris, Walter L. "Margie E. Neal: First Woman Senator in Texas." *East Texas Historical Journal* 11 (Spring 1973): 40–50.

4124. Ivins, Molly. "The Women Who Run Texas." *McCalls* 17 (August 1990): 98–101, 121, 123.

4125. Moses, Carolyn H. "Miss Sally, Texas' District Judge." *Independent Woman* 17 (April 1938): 107, 118–119.

4126. "The Most Influential Black Woman in Texas, Secretary of State M. McDaniel." *Ebony* 40 (September 1985): 60–65.

4127. Nelle, Quida Ferguson. *The Fergusons of Texas or Two Governors for the Price of One: A Biography of James Edward and His Wife, Miriam Armanda Ferguson.* San Antonio, TX: The Naylor Co., 1946.

4128. Paulissen, Maisie. "Pardon Me, Governor Ferguson." In *Legendary Ladies of Texas,* edited by Francis Edward Abernathy, 145–161. Denton: University of North Texas, 1994.

4129. Saavedra-Vela, Pilar. "Irma Rangel—Breaking Down Barriers in Texas, Interview." *Agenda* 8, no. 1 (1978): 34–36.

4130. Scott, Mary M. "Annie Webb Blanton: First Lady of Texas Education." Ph.D. dissertation, Texas A & M University, 1992.

4131. Strickland, Kristi Throne. "Sarah Tilghman Hughes: Activist for Women's Causes." Master's thesis, Tarleton State University, 1989.

Utah

4132. Arrington, Harriet Horne. "Alice Merrill Horne, Art Promoter and Early Utah Legislator." *Utah Historical Quarterly* 58, no. 3 (Summer 1990): 261–276.

4133. Brooks, Juanita, and Janet G. Butler. "Utah's Peace Advocate, The 'Mormona': Elsie Furer Musser." *Utah Historical Quarterly* 46, no. 2 (Spring 1978): 151–166.

4134. Clopton, Beverly B. *Her Honor, The Judge: The Story of Reva Beck Bosone.* Ames: Iowa State University Press, 1980.

4135. Lubomudrov, Carol Ann. "A Woman State School Superintendent: Whatever Happened to Mrs. McVicker?" *Utah Historical Quarterly* 49, no. 3 (1981): 254–261.

4136. White, Beverly, and Delila M. Abbott. *Women Legislators in Utah 1896–1993.* Salt Lake City, UT: Governor's Commission for Women and Families, 1993.

4137. White, Jean Bickmore. "Gentle Persuaders Utah's First Women Legislators." *Utah Historical Quarterly* 38 (Winter 1970): 31–49.

Vermont

4138. Aronson, Linda C. "The Political Socialization, Legislative Participation and Productivity of Women Legislators in Vermont." Master's thesis, University of Vermont, 1985.

4139. Bailey, Consuelo Northrop. *Leaves before the Wind: The Autobiography of Vermont's Own Daughter, Consuelo Northrop Bailey.* Burlington, CT: Little Press, 1976.

4140. Briggs, Marion L. "Mrs. Speaker of the House." *Independent Woman* 32 (June 1953): 201, 223.

4141. Drown, Susan E., Margaret Hammond, and Mildred Hayden. *History of the Vermont Branch of OWLS, 1936–1973.* Montpelier: Vermont Organization of Women Legislators (OWLS), 1973.

4142. Kroger, Althea Przybylo. "Women State Legislators." Master's thesis, University of Vermont, 1985.

4143. Kunin, Madeleine May. "Lessons from One Woman's Career." *Journal of State Government* 60, no. 5 (September–October 1987): 209–212.

4144. ———. "Speech." *Ladies Home Journal* 106 (November 1989): 62.

4145. ———. *Living a Political Life.* New York: Knopf, 1994.

4146. ———. "Living a Political Life." *University of West Los Angeles Law Review Annual* 25 (1994): 401–403.

4147. "Vermont Ladies Are Taking Over: Members of Legislature." *Life* 34 (6 April 1953): 21–23.

Virginia

4148. Crater, Flora, Muriel Smith, and Anne Donley. "A Roll Call of Women Legislators in the Virginia General Assembly, 1924–1988." In *Almanac of Virginia Politics,* 6th ed. and supplement, 36–40. Falls Church, VA: The Woman Activist Fund, Inc., 1988.

4149. Treadway, Sandra Gioia. "Sarah Lee Fain: Norfolk's First Woman Legislator." *Virginia Cavalcade* 30 (Winter 1981): 124–133.

4150. "Whatever Happened to Dr. Jean L. Harris ?" *Ebony* 37 (November 1981): 108, 110.

Washington

4151. Cater, Linda. "Stories to Be Told: Political Women and the Femi-nist Movement." Master's thesis, Eastern Washington University, 1987.

4152. Coe, Earl. *Washington Women in State Government.* Olympia: Washington Secretary of State, 1952.

4153. Elected Washington Women. *Political Pioneers, The Women Lawmakers.* Olympia: Elected Washington Women, 1983.

4154. Gooding, Barbara. "Women in the Washington State Legislature 1913–1983." Master's thesis, Evergreen State College, Olympia, 1983.

Wyoming

4155. Donaldson, Lee. "The First Woman Governor." *The Woman Citizen* 11, no. 6 (November 1926): 7–9, 48–49.

4156. Ross, Nellie Tayloe. "The Lady Governor." Parts I–III. *Good Housekeeping* 85 (August 1927): 30–31, 118–124; (September 1927): 36–37, 206–208, 211–218; (October 1927): 72–73, 180–189, 192–195.

4157. Scharff, Virginia. "Feminism, Femininity, and Power: Nellie Tayloe Ross and the Woman Politician's Dilemma." *Frontiers* 15, no. 3 (1995): 87–106.

4158. "Woman Leads Reform in Wyoming: Representative Anna B. Miller." *The Woman's Journal* 44 (9 August 1913): 249.

In the Territories

Puerto Rico

4159. Fonfrias, Ernesto Juan. *La Mujer en La Politica de Puerto Rico.* Hato Rey, PR: Master Typesetting and Word Processing, 1984.

Virgin Islands

4160. Collins, John. "Women Legislators." In *History of the Legislature of the United States Virgin Islands,* 46–49. St. Croix: Legislature of the Virgin Islands, 1984.

Local Government

Legislatures

4161. Beck, Susan Abrams. "Rethinking Municipal Governance: Gender Distinctions on Local Councils." In *Gender and Policymaking, Studies of Women in Office,* edited by Debra L. Dodson, 103–114. New Brunswick, NJ: Center for the American Woman and Politics, 1991.

4162. Dyer, Louise. "The American School Board Member and His—and Her—Era of Fierce New Independence." *American School Board Journal* 160 (July 1973): 17–20.

4163. Karnig, Albert K., and Susan Welch. "Sex and Ethnic Differences in Municipal Representation." *Social Science Quarterly* 60 (December 1979): 465–481.

4164. MacManus, Susan A., and Charles S. Bullock III. "Women on Southern City Councils: Does Struc-ture Matter?" In *Women in Politics: Outsiders or Insiders? A Collection of Readings,* edited by Lois Lovelace Duke, 107–122. Englewood Cliffs, NJ: Prentice Hall, 1993.

4165. Malvik, Patti. "Women Elected Share Lessons Learned, Challenges Faced." *Nation's Cities* 17, no. 50 (19 December 1994): 5.

4166. Merritt, Sharyne. "Sex Differences in Role Behavior and Policy Orientations of Suburban Office-holders: The Effect of Women's Employment." In *Women in Local Politics,* edited by Debra W. Stewart, 115–129. Metuchen, NJ: Scarecrow Press, 1980.

4167. Wilson, Mary, and Mary Frances Gordon. "Women in Municipal Government, Address by National League of Cities President Carolyn Long Banks." *Nation Cities Weekly* 18, no. 49 (18 December 1995): 10.

Executives

General

4168. Campbell, Jane. "Women Holding Office." *National Municipal Review* 3 (January 1914): 145–148.

4169. ———. "Women in Office." *National Municipal Review* 4 (April 1915): 211–216.

4170. Knowles, R. S. F. "Place of Women in Local Government." *Municipal Journal* (3 May 1968): 1072–1073.

4171. Malone, James. "Minorities, Women and Young People in Local Government." *Public Management* 55 (May 1973): 16–17.

4172. National League of Cities. *Women in Municipal Government.* Washington, DC: National League of Cities, 1974.

4173. Shaul, Marnie S. "The Status of Women in Local Governments: An International Assessment." *Public Administration Review* 42 (November–December 1982): 491–500.

4174. Welch, Susan, Albert K. Karnig, and Richard A. Eribes. "Correlates of Women's Employment in Local Governments." *Urban Affairs Quarterly* 18 (June 1983): 551–564.

Mayors

4175. Adams, Mildred. "What Are Women Mayors Doing?" *American City* 26 (4 June 1922): 543–544.

4176. Chenault, Julie. "Her Honor, The Mayor." *Essence* 14 (July 1983): 14.

4177. "In More Big Cities, It's 'Her Honor the Mayor'." *U.S. News and World Report* 87 (16 July 1979): 52–54.

4178. Jennings, Jeanette. "Black Women Mayors: Reflections on Race and Gender." In *Gender and Policymaking, Studies of Women in Office,* edited by Debra L. Dodson, 73–80. New Brunswick, NJ: Center for the American Woman and Politics, 1991.

4179. Rinehart, Sue Tolleson. "Do Women Leaders Make a Difference ? Substance, Style and Perceptions." In *Gender and Policymaking, Studies of Women in Office,* edited by Debra L. Dodson, 93–102. New Brunswick, NJ: Center for the American Woman and Politics, 1991.

4180. Smith, Wallace. "The Birth of Petticoat Government." *American History Illustrated* 19, no. 3 (May 1984): 50–55.

4181. Watts, Patti. "Votes of Confidence for Two First-Time Mayors." *Executive Female* 13 (March–April 1990): 6–7.

Commissions

4182. Stewart, Debra W. "Commissions on the Status of Women and Building a Local Policy Agenda." In *Women in Local Politics,* edited by Debra W. Stewart, 198–214. Metuchen, NJ: Scarecrow Press, 1980.

4183. ———. "Organizational Role Orientations on Female-Dominant Commissions: Focus on Staff-Commissioner Interaction." In *Women in Local Politics,* edited by Debra W. Stewart, 149–176. Metuchen, NJ: Scarecrow Press, 1980.

4184. ———. *The Women's Movement in Community Politics in the U.S.: The Role of Local Commissions on the Status of Women.* New York: Pergamon Press, 1980.

Managers

4185. Burns, Ruth Ann. "Breaking Down the Barriers: Women in Urban Management." *Signs* 5, no. 3 (Spring 1980): S231-S237. Supplement.

4186. ———. "Women in Municipal Management." *Urban Data Service Report* 12, no. 2 (February 1980): 1–12.

4187. Center for the American Woman and Politics. *Women in Municipal Management: Choice, Challenge and*

Change. New Brunswick, NJ: Center for the American Woman and Politics, 1980.

4188. Mohr, Judith. "Why Not More Women City Managers?" *Public Management* 55 (1973): 13–15.

4189. Pastor, J. "Hispanic Female in City Management." *Public Management* 62 (October 1980): 20–22.

4190. Scanlan, Mary. "Women in Local Government Management." *Public Management* 61 (May 1979): 17–18.

4191. Stewart, Alva W. "Women in City Management." *Municipal South* 10 (January 1963): 20–22.

4192. ———. "Feminine City Managers." *American City* 79 (May 1964): 154, 156.

4193. "Women in Public Administration." In *Public Administration, the State of the Discipline,* edited by Naomi B. Lynn and Aaron Wildavsky, 203–227. Chatham, NJ: Chatham House Publishers, 1990.

4194. Wood, Barbara. "Profile: A Woman's Place: In City Hall." *Public Manager* 76 (May 1994): 26–27.

School Superintendents and Boards

4195. Bers, Trudy Haffrom. "Local Political Elites: Men and Women on Boards of Education." *Western Political Quarterly* 31, no. 3 (September 1978): 381–391.

4196. Cordier, Mary Hurlbut. "Prairie School Women, Mid-1850s to 1920s, in Iowa, Kansas, and Nebras-

ka." *Great Plains Quarterly* 8, no. 2 (Spring 1988): 102–119.

4197. Doing, Laura T. "Women on School Boards: Nine Winners Tell How They Play the Game." *American School Board Journal* 160 (March 1973): 34–40.

4198. "Superwomen of Public Education: Black Women Superintendents." *Ebony* 38 (June 1983): 88, 90, 92, 94.

Law Enforcement

4199. Ott, E. Marlies. "Effect of the Male-Female Ratio at Work: Policewomen and Male Nurses." *Psychology of Women Quarterly* 13, no. 1 (March 1989): 41–57.

4200. Segrave, Kerry. *Policewomen: A History.* Jefferson, NC: McFarland, 1995.

4201. "Western Women as Police Officers." *The Survey* 29 (21 December 1912): 345–347.

Judiciary

4202. Cook, Beverly Blair. "Political Culture and Selection of Women Judges in Trial Courts." In *Women in Local Politics,* edited by Debra W. Stewart, 42–60. Metuchen, NJ: Scarecrow Press, 1980.

4203. ———. "Women Judges and Public Policy in Sex Integration." In *Women in Local Politics,* edited by Debra W. Stewart, 130–148. Metuchen, NJ: Scarecrow Press, 1980.

4204. ———. "The Personality and Procreative Behavior of Trial Judges:

A Biocultural Perspective." *International Political Science Review* 3 (1982): 51–70.

4205. Gruhl, John, Cassia Spohn, and Susan Welch. "Women as Policymakers: The Case of Trial Judges." *American Journal of Political Science* 25 (May 1981): 308–323.

4206. Murphy, Fanny B. "Careers Unlimited." *National Business Woman* 36, no. 5 (May 1957): 28–29.

4207. Popkin, Zelda. "Should Women 'Man' Our Juvenile Courts?" *Independent Woman* 16 (April 1937): 310–11, 328–331.

4208. Schutt, Russell K., and Dade Donnefer. "Detention Decisions in Juvenile Cases: JINS, JDS, and Gender." *Law and Society Review* 22, no. 3 (1988): 509–520.

In the States

Alabama

4209. Reid, E. E. "Ladies Run Clerk's Office in 91 Cities." *Alabama Review* (September 1954): 7–9.

Alaska

4210. Mozee, Yvonne. "Myrtle Johnson of Nome: Femme Extraordinaire." *Alaskan Woman Magazine* (December–January 1977): 30.

4211. Richardson, Jeff. "Dee Olin: Mayor of Ruby." *Alaska Journal* 9, no. 2 (1979): 11–15.

4212. Woodman, Betzi. "Woman Mayor for Haines." *The Alaska Magazine* (Winter 1950): 21.

4213. ———. "Frontier Mayor Fights for Economic Fitness." *Alaskan Woman Magazine* (April 1982): 27.

Arizona

4214. Kyte, Elinor C. "A Tough Job for a Gentle Lady." *Journal of Arizona History* 25, no. 4 (1984): 385–398.

4215. "Women to Watch: Political Firebird Vice Mayor Mary Wilcox of Phoenix, Arizona, Remembers the 1960s and Looks to the 1990s." *Hispanic Business* 10, no. 12 (1988): 83.

Arkansas

4216. Poe, Peggy. "Only Women Rule in Winslow, Arkansas." *American City* 36 (February 1927): 222.

4217. Winn, Robert G. "Winslows Petticoat Government, 1925–27." *Washington County Flashback (AR)* 28 (August 1978): 33–36.

California

4218. Bonfante, Jordan. "Lady Power in the Sunbelt, Maureen F. O'Connor, Helen Copley, Joan Kroc in San Diego." *Time* 135 (19 March 1990): 21.

4219. Braun, Stephen. "The Trouble with Terrigno." *Los Angeles Times Magazine* 2 (1 June 1986): 17–21, 29–31.

4220. Collins-Jarvis, Lori A. "Gender Representation in an Electronic City Hall: Female Adoption of Santa Monica's PEN System." *Journal of Broadcasting and Electronic Media* 37 (Winter 1993): 49–65.

4221. Fukuda, Kimiko A. "Chinese American and Japanese American Women in California Public School Administration." Ph.D. dissertation, University of Southern California, Los Angeles, 1984.

4222. Horton, Luci. "Her Honor the Mayor." *Ebony* 28 (September 1973): 104–112.

4223. Huckle, Patricia. *Employment of Women in Local Government.* Los Angeles, CA: Center for Urban Affairs, University of Southern California, 1972. Working Paper No. 2.

4224. Joseph, Nadine. "Mayor Dianne Feinstein." *Present Tense* 11, no. 1 (1983): 47–49.

4225. League of Women Voters, ed. *The San Francisco Board and Commissions.* San Francisco: League of Women Voters, 1981.

4226. May, Bernice Hubbard. *A Native Daughter's Leadership in Public Affairs.* Berkeley: University of California, 1976. The Bancroft Library Oral History Interview.

4227. Nowicki, Ron. "San Francisco Politics: The Feinstein Era." *North American Review* 268 (December 1983): 24–28.

4228. Odem, Mary. "Single Mothers, Delinquent Daughters, and the Juvenile Court in Early Twentieth Century Los Angeles." *Journal of Social History* 25, no. 1 (1992): 27–43.

4229. Place, Estella M. "Woman Judge: G.P. Bullock of the Woman's Court of Los Angeles." *Sunset* 61 (July 1928): 46.

4230. "Political Power in Pasadena." *Ebony* 36 (August 1982): 113–115.

4231. Porter, Julia. *Dedicated Democrat and City Planner, 1941–1975.* Berkeley: University of California, 1977. The Bancroft Library Oral History Interview.

4232. Saint, Avis Marion. "Women in the Public Service: The City of Berkeley." *Public Personnel Studies* 8, no. 7 (1930): 104–107.

4233. ———. "Women in the Public Service: The City of Oakland." *Public Personnel Studies* 8, no. 8 (1930): 119–122.

4234. Wiener, Rosaland. "How a Woman Member of a City Council Sees Her Job." *American City* 69 (April 1954): 119.

4235. "Women with Clout in City Government." *Ebony* 39 (October 1984): 88–93.

4236. Wyman, Rosalind. *'It's a Girl:' Three Terms on the Los Angeles City Council, 1953–1965: Three Decades in the Democratic Party, 1948–1979.* Berkeley: University of California, 1979. The Bancroft Library Oral History Interview.

Colorado

4237. "The Lady on the Bench: Linda M. Lee." *Sunset* 53 (December 1924): 29–30.

Connecticut

4238. Marshall, Marilyn. "Carrie Saxon Perry: More Than a Pretty Hat." *Ebony* 43, no. 6 (April 1988): 60–64.

4239. Mezey, Susan Gluck. "Support for Women's Rights Policy: An Analysis of Local Politicians." *American Political Quarterly* 6, no. 4 (1978): 485–497.

4240. ———. "Perceptions of Women's Roles on Local Council in Connecticut." In *Women in Local Politics,* edited by Debra W. Stewart, 177–197. Metuchen, NJ: Scarecrow Press, 1980.

Florida

4241. Bailey, Bernadine. "Homemaker for City Commissioner." *Independent Woman* 28 (November 1949): 325, 349.

4242. Walch, Barbara Hunter. "Sallye B. Mathis and Mary L. Singleton: Black Pioneers on the Jacksonville, Florida, City Council." Master's thesis, University of Florida, 1988.

Georgia

4243. Fowlkes, Diane L. "Conceptions of the 'Political': White Activists in Atlanta." In *Political Women: Current Roles in State and Local Government,* edited by Janet A. Flammang, 66–86. Women's Policy Studies, 8. Beverly Hills, CA: Sage, 1984.

Hawaii

4244. "Hawaii's Top Woman Politician." *Ebony* 18 (April 1963): 51–52, 54, 56.

Idaho

4245. Jones, Carrie Maude. "Women as County Treasurers in Idaho." *Independent Woman* 5, no. 5 (May 1924): 7, 13.

Illinois

4246. Alson, Peter. "The Unlikely Tamer of Lyons." *Life* 12 (November 1989): 29–30.

4247. Beck, Melinda, and Frank Maier. "Sisterhood at City Hall." *Newsweek* 93 (16 April 1979): 48.

4248. Byrne, Jane. *My Chicago.* New York: Norton, 1992.

4249. "Chicago's Jane Byrne Et Al Prove the Old Male Mayor Ain't What He Used to Be." *People's Weekly* 11 (19 March 1979): 28–33.

4250. Daggett, Mabel Potter. "A Lady, A Scholar and A Diplomat: Dr. Ella Flagg." *Delineator* 77 (March 1911): 177, 248.

4251. FitzGerald, Kathleen. *Brass, Jane Byrne, and the Pursuit of Power.* Chicago: Contemporary Books, 1981.

4252. Greenbaum, Betsy. "The Court of 'Another Chance'." *The Woman Citizen* 12 (August 1927): 12–14.

4253. Kennedy, Eugene. "Mayor Jane Byrne of Chicago." In *Women Leaders in American Politics,* edited by James David Barber and Barbara Kellerman, 56–65. Englewood Cliffs, NJ: Prentice Hall, 1986.

4254. "Sharon Gist Gilliam: The Woman in Charge of Chicago's $3.8 Billion Budget." *Ebony* 42 (March 1987): 31–32.

4255. Smith, Joan K. "Progressive School Administration: Ella Flagg Young and the Chicago Schools,

1905–1915." *Journal of Illinois State Historical Society* 73, no. 1 (1980): 27–44.

4256. Stribling, T. S. "Mary Bartelme, Friend in Court." *The Woman Citizen* 8 (17 November 1923): 9–10.

4257. Williams, Dennis A. "How Love Lost in Chicago." *Newsweek* 104 (6 August 1984): 71.

4258. "Women Make Good Supervisors." *The Republican Woman of Illinois* 6, no. 9 (May 1929): 8.

Iowa

4259. Hickle, Evelyn Myers. "Ruth Iowa Jones Myers, 1887–1974: Rural Iowa Educator." *Annals of Iowa* 45, no. 3 (1980): 196–211.

4260. Hovelson, Jack. "Profile: Terri Lea Schroeder, City Manager, Iowa Falls, Iowa." *Public Management* 66 (December 1984): 20–22.

4261. Shultz, Gladys Denny. "Mrs. Morris, Councilwoman." *The Woman Citizen* 9 (21 March 1925): 10, 26.

Kansas

4262. Brunner, Carolyn Cryss J. "By Power Defined: Women in the Superintendency." Ph.D. dissertation, University of Kansas, Lawrence, 1994.

4263. "First Woman Mayor in United States Reaches 100." *American City* 75 (May 1960): 23.

4264. Fussman, H. Louise. "Can a Woman Do a Mayor's Job?" *American City* 37 (November 1927): 603–604.

4265. Gehring, Lorraine A. "Women Officeholders in Kansas, 1872–1912."

Kansas History 9 (Summer 1986): 48–57.

Maryland

4266. "Judge Fanny B. Murphy." *National Business Woman* 36 (May 1957): 28.

Massachusetts

4267. "Lady Selectman." *Ebony* 14 (September 1959): 35–36, 38.

Michigan

4268. "In Michigan Women Are People." *The Woman Citizen* 5 (8 January 1921): 865.

4269. Robb, Jessie. "Royal Oak Has Woman Commissioner." *Independent Woman* 5, no. 2 (February 1924): 7.

Minnesota

4270. Anderson, Mary. *Mary Anderson Oral History Interview.* Chisholm, MN: Iron Range Research Center, 1988. Interview for the Women in Politics and the Women of the Iron Range Projects.

4271. Brooks, Gladys. "Politics ... A Family Enterprise." *American Association of University Women* 46, no. 2 (January 1953): 88–90.

4272. Gault, Lillian Cox. "What Are Women Mayors Doing? A Reply." *American City* 27 (August 1922): 121.

4273. Prebich, Elizabeth. *Liz Prebich Oral History Interview.* Chisholm, MN: Iron Range Research Center, 1990. Interview for the Women in Politics Project.

4274. Taylor, Kimberly. "Minneapolis: Among the Nation's Best Secrets." *Black Enterprise* 24 (May 1994): 58–59.

4275. Waldock, Donna Rae. "Personal Characteristics, Leadership Definitions and Temperament Types of Female County Commissioners and State Legislators in Minnesota." Master's thesis, Mankato State University, 1986.

Mississippi

4276. "Lady Mayor of Mayersville, Unita Blackwell." *Ebony* 33 (December 1977): 53–58.

Nebraska

4277. "Deputy Municipal Attorney." *National Business Woman* 36 (September 1957): 26.

4278. "No 'Yes Woman', Mayor Arabelle Hanna." *National Business Woman* 37 (August 1958): 22–23.

New Jersey

4279. "Appointment as Judges." *Independent Woman* 25 (September 1946): 288.

4280. "Her Honor the Mayor." *Democratic Digest* 27 (December–January 1950–1951): 14.

4281. Johnson, Marilyn, and Kathy Stanwick. "Local Officeholding and the Community: The Case of Women on New Jersey's School Boards." In *Women Organizing: An Anthology,* edited by Bernice Cummings and Victoria Schuck, 49–60. Metuchen, NJ: Scarecrow Press, 1979.

4282. Women Serving as Mayors or Governing Body Members in New Jersey's Local Governments." *New Jersey Municipalities* 51 (June 1974): 12–13.

New Mexico

4283. "Petticoat Rule in New Mexico." *Life* 28 (29 May 1950): 24–25.

New York

4284. Adams, Mildred. "Judging around the World." *The Woman Citizen* 8 (11 August 1923): 9.

4285. Berrol, Selma. "When Uptown Met Downtown: Julia Richman's Work in the Jewish Community of New York, 1880–1912." *American Jewish History* 70, no. 1 (1980): 35–51.

4286. Norris, Jean H. "Judging Women." *Woman's Home Companion* 48 (August 1921): 23.

4287. Rodden, Donna. *An Interview with Donna Rodden.* Oral History Tapes. Oswego, NY: State University College, 1974.

4288. Seely, Nancy, and Gail Greco. "New York's Women Mayors Speak Out but Few Show Signs of Moving Up." *Empire State Report* 12 (June 1986): 57–58, 60, 62–63.

4289. Shull, Adda M. "A Chronic 'Trail Blazer'." *Independent Woman* 5, no. 5 (August 1924): 11, 18.

4290. White, Kate. "Talking with Carol Bellamy." *Glamour* 76 (November 1978): 151–154, 156.

North Carolina

4291. Bliss, Peggy Ann. "Lady Is a Straight-Shooter, I. Cannon, Mayor of Raleigh." *Retired Living* 18 (June 1978): 40–41.

4292. Blount, Jackie Marie. "Women and the Superintendency, 1900–1990: 'Destined to Rule the Schools of Every City … '." Ph.D. dissertation, University of North Carolina, Chapel Hill, 1993.

North Dakota

4293. Geelan, Agnes. *Agnes Geelan, Mayor of Enderlin, North Dakota.* Bismarck: University of North Dakota, 1970. Interview for the Camp Depression Project.

4294. Richardson, Anna Steese. "Holding Office on Main Street: Municipal Housekeeping as the Women Are Actually Doing It in North Dakota." *Woman's Home Companion* 49 (October 1922): 21–22.

Ohio

4295. "How Other Women Do It." *The Republican Woman of Illinois* 8, no. 4 (November 1930): 4.

4296. Huus, Randolph O. "Cleveland Women in Government and Allied Fields." *National Municipal Review* 19 (February 1930): 88–92.

4297. White, Clarice F. "Judge Mary." *The Woman's Journal* 14 (October 1929): 24–25.

Oregon

4298. Hickey, Margaret. "When a Woman Runs the Town." *Ladies Home Journal* 69 (January 1952): 49, 105–107.

4299. Lee, Dorothy McCullough. "What I Have Learned as Mayor." *American Association of University Women* 46, no. 3 (March 1953): 143–145.

4300. Myers, Gloria E. *A Municipal Mother: Portland's Lola Greene Baldwin, America's First Policewoman.* Corvallis: Oregon State University, 1995.

4301. Pitzer, Paul C. "Dorothy McCullough Lee: The Successes and Failures of 'Dottie-Do-Good'." *Oregon Historical Quarterly* 91 (Spring 1990): 5–42.

4302. Vincent, Fred. W. "Running a Town Like a Home: Umatilla, Oregon." *Sunset* 46 (January 1921): 36–37.

4303. Wallace, Shelley Burtner. "Umatilla's 'Petticoat Government', 1916–1920." *Oregon Historical Quarterly* 88 (Winter 1987): 385–402.

Pennsylvania

4304. Bregman, Lillian. "Her Honor, the Mayor, Sandra Shenfeld." *American Home* 80 (January 1977): 6, 68.

4305. Hamlin, Dora Jane. "Her Honor Bops the Hoodlums." 59 (9 July 1965): 74–82.

4306. "Philadelphia's Tough Lady Judge." *Sepia* 14 (October 1965): 8–10, 12, 14–15.

4307. Smith, Marion. "Women in Pennsylvania Local Government." *Pennsylvanian* (May 1976): 6–8.

4308. Stout, Kate. "Shaking Up the System: Black Woman School Superintendent Clayton." *Working Woman* 9 (April 1984): 114–118.

Tennessee

4309. "Municipal Mother: Interview with Camille Kelley." *The Woman's Journal* 13 (November 1928): 19.

4310. Van Ark, Carroll. "Women Rule a Cumberland Town." *Colliers* 110 (7 November 1942): 58–59.

4311. York, Mary. "A Municipal Mother." *The Woman's Journal* 13 (November 1928): 19.

Texas

4312. Barrett, Kathy. "A New Breed of Women Mayor, The Real Politik of Kathy Whitmire." *Ms.* 11, no. 1–2 (July–August 1982): 177–178.

4313. Belkin, Lisa. "'Lace Over Steel': The Women Mayors of Texas." *The New York Times Magazine* (20 March 1988): VI, 41, 59–60, 81–82, 92.

4314. Dubose, Louis. "Texas Mayor Fights the Klan." *Progressive* 57 (April 1993): 15.

4315. Ivins, Molly. "Kathy Whitmire." *Working Woman* 12 (March 1987): 120–122.

4316. Shapiro, Walter. "Reforming Our Image of a Chief." *Time* 136 (26 November 1990): 80–82.

4317. Weber, Dick. "Beaumont's City Manager." *Independent Woman* 33 (October 1954): 378–379.

Utah

4318. King, Anna H. "A Town Run by Women." *The Woman's Journal* 45 (28 February 1914): 65, 70.

Virginia

4319. Lockett, Edward B. "She-Town." *Colliers* 126 (4 November 1950): 20–21, 76.

4320. "Petticoat Rule Scores Again, Washington, Virginia." *Life* 29 (18 September 1950): 48–49.

4321. Wilkinson, Sandra. "Women in Government: The Role of Women as Members of Local Governing Bodies." *Virginia Town and City* (April 1974): 18–19.

4322. "Women Run the Town of Clintwood, Virginia." *American Magazine of Civics* 147 (March 1949): 93.

Washington

4323. Dunbar, Marie Rose. "Even the Men She Sentences Learn to Like Judge Kerr." *American Magazine of Civics* 104 (September 1927): 71.

4324. Haarsager, Sandra. *Bertha Knight Landes of Seattle, Big-City Mayor.* Norman: University of Oklahoma Press, 1994.

4325. "Her Honor the Mayor: A. B. Smith of Olympia, Washington." *Good Housekeeping* 145 (November 1957): 14.

4326. Landes, Bertha K. "Does Politics Make Women Crooked?" *Colliers* 83 (16 March 1929): 24, 36, 38.

4327. Pieroth, Doris Hinson. "Bertha Knight Landes: The Woman Who Was Mayor." *Pacific Northwest Quarterly* 75 (July 1984): 117–127.

4328. Stewart, Anne Bigony. "Seattle Justices of the Peace." *The Woman Citizen* 3 (21 December 1918): 617.

4329. "The Temporary Lady Mayor Who Fired Seattle's Chief of Police." *Literary Digest* 82 (9 August 1924): 42–45.

4330. "Woman Judge on Seattle Bench." *The Woman's Journal* 47 (8 January 1916): 10.

4331. "World's Foremost Woman Mayors." *American City* 38 (January 1928): 111.

Wisconsin

4332. Boles, Jane K. "Advancing the Women's Agenda within Local Legislatures: The Role of Female Elected Officials." In *Gender and Policymaking, Studies of Women in Office,* edited by Debra L. Dodson, 39–48. New Brunswick, NJ: Center for the American Woman and Politics, 1991.

4333. "Milwaukee's First Lady Councilman." *Ebony* 13 (June 1958): 40–42.

4334. "More Than Four Hundred Women Hold Municipal Office in Wisconsin." *American City* 31 (August 1924): 155.

4335. Mowry, Duane. "Women as School Officers." *Arena* 24 (August 1900): 198–206.

Wyoming

4336. Bell, Tom. "Pioneer Profiles: Mrs. Mary Mason." *Wind River Mountaineer* 8, no. 2–3 (1992): 2, 40–46.

In the Territories and District

District of Columbia

4337. Cummins, Ken. "Prattfall." *The New Republic* 208, no. 6 (8 February 1993): 14–16.

4338. "An Interview with Clara Sears Taylor: Rent Commissioner of Washington." *Independent Woman* 2, no. 1 (December 1920): 8–9.

4339. "An Interview with Mabel Throop Boardman: Commissioner of Washington." *Independent Woman* 2, no. 1 (January 1921): 15–16.

4340. "Judge Jean Norris." *Women Lawyers Journal* 9 (February 1920): 12.

4341. "Miss Jones, Recorder of Deeds." *Democratic Digest* 12, no. 10 (October 1935): 25.

4342. Randolph, Laura B. "Mayor Sharon P. Kelly On: Her Marriage … Her Mission and … Her Mid-Life Transformation." *Ebony* 47 (February 1992): 27–28, 31, 34.

Puerto Rico

4343. LaCossitt, Henry. "The Mayor Wears Flowers in Her Hair." *Saturday Evening Post* 226 (22 May 1954): 38–39.

Political Parties

General

4344. Avery, Patricia. "For Women, A Slow Climb Up the Political Ladder." *U.S. News and World Report* 97 (8 October 1984): 76–78.

4345. Baer, Denise L. "Men and Women in Political Parties: A Comparison of Partisan Elites and Party Identifiers." Ph.D. dissertation, Southern Illinois University, 1983.

4346. ———. "Political Parties: The Missing Variable in Women and Politics Research." *Political Research Quarterly* (1993): 547–576.

4347. Boyd, Mary Sumner. "Parties and Primaries," Parts I and II. *The Woman Citizen* 3 (20 July 1918): 149, 158; (27 July 1918): 169, 178.

4348. Burrell, Barbara C. "Party Politics and Gender in the U.S." In *Gender and Political Parties,* edited by Joni Lovenduski and Pippa Norris, 291–308. Thousand Oaks, CA: Sage, 1994.

4349. Clarke, Harold G., and Allan Kornberg. "Moving Up the Political Escalator: Women Party Officials in the United States and Canada." *Journal of Politics* 41 (May 1979): 442–477.

4350. Costain, Anne N. "Strategy and Tactics of the Women's Movement in the United States: The Role of Political Parties." In *The Women's Movements of the United States and Western Europe: Consciousness, Political Opportunity and Public Policy,* edited by Mary F. Katzenstein and Carol M. Mueller, 196–214. Philadelphia: Temple University Press, 1987.

4351. "Democratic and Republican Women Working for Suffrage Amendment." *The Woman Citizen* 2 (5 January 1918): 108–109.

4352. Dodson, Debra L. "Are Parties Gender-Neutral?" Paper presented at the annual meeting of the Midwest Political Science Association, Chicago, 1989.

4353. Flanagan, Maureen A. "Chicago Women and Party Politics, 1914–1932." Paper presented at the annual meeting of the American Political Science Association, Chicago, 1995.

4354. Fowlkes, Diane L., Jerry Perkins, and Sue Tolleson Rinehart. "Gender Roles and Party Roles." *American Political Science Review* 73 (September 1979): 772–780.

4355. Freudenberger, Ruby Westlake. "Why Outside?" *The Woman Citizen* 7 (18 November 1922): 17.

4356. Harvey, Anna L. "Women, Party, and Policy: A Rational Choice Approach." Paper presented at the annual meeting of the American Political Science Association, Chicago, 1995.

4357. Jennings, M. Kent. "Women in Party Politics." In *Women, Politics and Change,* edited by Louise A. Tilly and Patricia Gurin, 221–249. New York: Russell Sage, 1990.

4358. Jennings, M. Kent, and Norman Thomas. "Men and Women in Party Elites: Social Roles and Political Resources." *Midwest Journal of Political*

Science 12 (November 1968): 469–492.

4359. Kerr, Barbara Wendell. "Don't Kid the Women." *Woman's Home Companion* 83 (October 1956): 4, 6.

4360. Ladd, Everett Carll. "Gender and Party ID." *Public Perspective* 3 (July–August 1992): 27–28.

4361. Lovenduski, Joni, and Pippa Norris. *Gender and Party Politics.* New York: Sage, 1993.

4362. Patrick, Mary. "Now Is the Time for All Good Women to Come to the Aid of Their Party, Country." *Woman's Home Companion* 71 (May 1944): 4, 16.

4363. Ranney, Austin. *Curing the Mischiefs of Faction: Party Reform in America.* Berkeley: University of California Press, 1975.

4364. Ray, P. Orman. "Woman Suffrage and Party Organization Before 1920." In *An Introduction to Political Parties and Practical Politics,* 184–185. New York: Charles Scribner's Sons, 1924 (1913).

4365. Sabato, Larry. "Parties, PACs, and Independent Groups." In *The American Elections of 1982,* edited by Thomas E. Mann and Norman J. Ornstein, 72–110. Washington, DC: American Enterprise Institute, 1983.

4366. Sanders, Marion K. "Women in Politics." *Harper's Weekly* 211 (August 1955): 20–22, 56–64.

4367. Sapiro, Virginia, and Barbara G. Farah. "New Pride and Old Prejudice: Political Ambition and Role Orientations among Female Partisan

Elites." *Women and Politics* 1, no. 1 (Spring 1980): 13–36.

4368. Segal, Phyllis N. "Women and Political Parties: The Legal Dimension of Discrimination." Unpublished paper inserted in *Congressional Record,* 6 April 1971, Vol. 117, 9896–9897 by Rep. Martha Griffith, D-MI.

4369. Upton, Harriet Taylor. "The Machine and the Woman." *Ladies Home Journal* 39 (October 1922): 13, 159.

4370. Westwood, Jean M. "The Political Status of Women—1974." *Wisconsin Academy Review* 20 (1974): 2.

4371. "What Women Do in Politics: Interviews with the Two Women Leaders of the Republican and Democratic Parties." *U.S. News and World Report* 45 (12 September 1958): 72–79.

History

4372. Adams, Elmer C., and Warren Dunham Foster. "J. Ellen Foster." In *Heroines of Modern Progress,* 245–279. New York: Sturgis and Walton, 1913.

4373. Biersack, Robert, and Paul S. Herrnson. "Political Parties and the Year of the Woman." In *The Year of the Woman: Myths and Realities,* edited by Elizabeth Adell Cook, Sue Thomas, and Clyde Wilcox, 161–180. Boulder, CO: Westview Press, 1994.

4374. Blair, Emily Newell. "Women in the Political Parties." *Annals of the American Academy of Political and Social Science* 143 (May 1929): 217–229.

4375. Breckinridge, Sophonisba P. "Women and Party Organization Activities." Chap. 17 in *Women in the Twentieth Century: A Study of Their Political, Social and Economic Activities,* 275–294. New York: McGraw-Hill, 1933.

4376. Fisher, Marguerite J. "Women in the Political Parties." *Annals of the American Academy of Political and Social Science* 251 (May 1947): 87–93.

4377. Grove, A. "Ideals of a Woman's Party." *Fortnightly* 89 (April 1908): 634–644.

4378. Harriman, Florence J. *From Pinafores to Politics.* New York: Henry Holt, 1923.

4379. Merriam, Charles Edward, and Harold Foote Gosnell. *The American Party System.* New York: Macmillan, 1940, 25–33, 139–141.

4380. Ostrogorski, Moisei I. *Democracy and the Party System in the United States: A Study in Extra Constitutional Government.* New York: MacMillan, 1902, 170–174.

4381. Taylor, Paul. "The Entrance of Women in Party Politics: 1920–1940." Ph.D. dissertation, Harvard University, 1966.

Fifty-Fifty Plan

4382. Dewson, Mary W. "'Why Build on Sand?' Says Congressman Moran." *Democratic Bulletin* 11, no. 4 (April 1934): 11.

4383. "50–50 Works in New York." *The Republican Woman of Illinois* 8, no. 8 (April 1931): 7.

4384. Meredith, Ellis. "Again—And Yet Again—Organize, Fifty-Fifty." *Democratic Digest* 11, no. 5 (May 1934): 10, 12.

4385. "South Dakota and Oregon Pass Bill for 50–50 Representation of Women and Men on Party Committees." *Democratic Digest* 14, no. 3 (March 1937): 9.

4386. "What Do We Mean When We Say 50–50?" *The Republican Woman of Illinois* 8, no. 7 (February 1931): 3.

4387. White, Sue S. "Fifty Fifty." *Democratic Bulletin* 8, no. 2 (February 1933): 20, 29.

4388. ———. "Organized Women Succeed." *Democratic Bulletin* 8, no. 11 (November 1933): 13.

4389. "Women Must Be Given Equal Representation with Men on All Party Committees." *Democratic Digest* 14, no. 2 (February 1937): 5.

Women's Partisan Clubs

4390. Baer, Denise L. "National Democratic Women's Club." In *Political Parties and Elections in the United States: An Encyclopedia,* edited by L. Sandy Maisel, 682–683. New York: Garland, 1991.

4391. ———. "National Federation of Republican Women." In *Political Parties and Elections in the United States: An Encyclopedia,* edited by L. Sandy Maisel, 683–684. New York: Garland, 1991.

4392. Baer, Denise L., and Lisa Young. "The National Federation of Republican Women: Female Auxiliary or Feminist Force?" Paper presented at the annual meeting of the American Political Science Association, Chicago, 1995.

4393. Blair, Emily Newell. "Why Clubs for Women?" *Forum* 77 (March 1927): 354–363.

4394. Bradford, Mary C. C. "Oldest Political Club of Women in America." *Fortnightly Bulletin* 1, no. 27 (27 October 1923): 1.

4395. Caleca, Linda. "Women in Politics: Not Skirting the Issues: Democratic Women." *Saturday Evening Post* 252 (March 1980): 27, 32, 113, 124.

4396. Chittenden, Alice Hill. "A National Club for Republican Women." *The Republican Woman* 5, no. 5 (October 1927): 1–2.

4397. Davis, Adalyn. *The Women's National Democratic Club: The Place Where Democrats Meet.* Washington, DC: Women's National Democratic Club, 1992.

4398. Ferris, William H. "The Value and Need of Political Organization among Colored Women." *The Political Recorder* 1, no. 3 (May 1925): 4–5.

4399. Hobbs, Mrs. Franklin Warren. "Women's Republican Club of Massachusetts." *The Republican Woman* 5, no. 6 (November 1927): 1.

4400. "Inaugural Visitors Given Reception by Political Clubs." *The Political Recorder* 1, no. 2 (April 1925): 4–5.

4401. Le Van, Wilma Sinclair. "Republican Women of Ohio Organize." *The Republican Woman* 5, no. 7 (January 1928): 4, 10.

4402. Lippincott, Mrs. A. Haines. "The New Jersey Women's Republican Club." *The Republican Woman* 5, no. 8 (February 1928): 7.

4403. McCormick, Mrs. Medill. "The Reason for Women's Republican Clubs." *The Republican Woman* 1, no. 2 (January 1924): 3.

4404. ———. "The Women's Roosevelt Republican Club." *The Republican Woman* 6, no. 2 (May 1928): 2.

4405. Meredith, Ellis. "The Party Organization and the Club." *Democratic Bulletin* 8, no. 6 (June 1933): 19, 30.

4406. ———. "Still Harping on Organization." *Democratic Bulletin* 8, no. 7 (July 1933): 7, 15.

4407. Miller, Holly G. "Women in Politics: Not Skirting the Issues: Republican Women." *Saturday Evening Post* 252 (March 1980): 26, 28, 30.

4408. Nardin, Mrs. William Thompson. "Republican Woman's Club of St. Louis." *The Republican Woman* 6, no. 1 (March 1928): 6.

4409. "A Political Club for Women Only." *Good Housekeeping* 146 (February 1958): 131–132.

4410. Ray, P. Orman. "Seventh Ward Women's Republican Organization in Chicago." In *An Introduction to Political Parties and Practical Politics,* 3d ed., 185–186. New York: Charles Scribner's Sons, 1924 (1917).

4411. "The Republican Women's Club." *The Woman Citizen* 8 (23 March 1924): 22.

4412. Smith, Margaret Griggs. "What a Political Club Can Do For You." *Independent Woman* 33 (February 1954): 57–58.

4413. Stone, Edith. "Do Women Like Politics? Ask Hawaii." *The Woman Citizen* 7 (15 July 1922): 11, 16.

Organizations

National

4414. Bass, Mrs. George. "Democratic Party: Its Record and Its Appeal to Women." *Woman's Home Companion* 46 (November 1919): 11.

4415. Bone, Hugh Alvin. *Party Committees and National Politics.* Seattle: University of Washington Press, 1958. 52–57, 107–111.

4416. Cotter, Cornelius P., and Bernard C. Hennessy. *Politics Without Power—The National Party Committees.* New York: Atherton Press, 1964, 149–154.

4417. "Emily Newell Blair." *Independent Woman* 15 (March 1935): 1–2.

4418. Heffelfinger, Elizabeth Bradley. *Oral History Interview with Elizabeth Bradley Heffelfinger.* Chisholm, MN: Iron Range Research Center, 1978. Interview by James E. Fogerty for the Women in Politics Project.

4419. Miller, Vivian. "Women in Politics: The American National Committeewomen." In *Research on Women in Politics,* Vol. 2. Towson, MD: Goucher College Library, 1977.

4420. "Present Organization: National Committee and Woman Heads." *Congressional Digest* 9 (October 1930): 238–239.

4421. Reagan, Ronald. "Republican Women's Leadership Forum." *Weekly Compilation of Presidential Documents* 19 (5 September 1983): 1175–1179.

4422. ———. "Republican Women Officials." *Weekly Compilation of Presidential Documents* 20 (January 1984): 31–35.

4423. "Sharon Pratt Dixon: Rising to the Top in the DNC." *Focus* 14, no. 4 (April 1986): 3.

4424. "To Wear Mantle of India Edwards: Mrs. Walter Loucheim." *Independent Woman* 32 (November 1953): 40.

4425. Tone, Mary Hutchison. "Mary Louise Smith, a Republican with All the Right Stuff." *The Iowan* 32 (Spring 1984): 18–22, 52.

4426. Ware, Susan. *Partner and I: Molly Dewson, Feminism, and New Deal Politics.* New Haven, CT: Yale University Press, 1987.

4427. Wolfe, Carolyn. *Educating for Citizenship: A Career in Community Affairs and the Democratic Party, 1906–1976.* Berkeley: University of California, 1978. The Bancroft Library Oral History Interview.

State

4428. Allen, Germfread. "Party Girl." *Ladies Home Journal* 79 (November 1962): 68–69.

4429. Anderson, Eleanor. "She Gets Her Way: Introducing Representative Norton, the First Woman State Chairman." *Today Magazine* 2, no. 19 (1 September 1934): 5.

4430. Braitman, Jacqueline R. "Elizabeth Snyder and the Role of Women in the Postwar Resurgence of California's Democratic Party." *Pacific Historical Review* 65 (May 1993): 197–220.

4431. Burrell, Barbara C. "Women's Political Leadership and the State of the Parties." In *The State of the Parties: The Changing Role of Contemporary American Parties,* edited by Daniel M. Shea and John C. Green, 165–174. Lanham, MD: Rowman and Littlefield, 1994.

4432. Claggett, William, and John Van Winger. "Conversion and Recruitment in Boston during the New Deal Realignment: A Preliminary Comparison of Men and Women." Paper presented at the annual meeting of the Southern Political Science Association, Atlanta, 1990.

4433. Clark, Janet M. "Political Ambition among Men and Women State Party Leaders: Testing the Countersocialization Perspective." *American Political Quarterly* 17, no. 2 (April 1989): 194–207.

4434. Conian, Timothy, Ann Martio, and Robert Dilger. "State Parties in the 1980s: Adaptation, Resurgence and Continuing Constraints." *Intergovernmental Perspective* 10 (1984): 6–13.

4435. Constantine, Edmond, and Kenneth H. Craik. "Women as Politicians: The Social Background, Personality, and Political Careers of Female Party Leaders." In *A Portrait of Marginality: The Political Behavior of American Women,* edited by Marianne Githens and Jewell Prestage, 221–240. New York: McKay, 1977. (First printed in *Journal of Social Issues,* 28 (1972): 217–236.)

4436. Costantini, Edmond, and Julie Davis Bell. "Women in Political Parties: Gender Differences in Motivations among California Party Activists." In *Political Women: Current Roles in State and Local Government,* edited by Janet A. Flammang, 114–138. Women's Policy Studies, 8. Beverly Hills, CA: Sage, 1984.

4437. Darcy, Robert, Charles D. Hadley, and Janet M. Clark. "The Changing Roles of Women in Southern State Party Politics." In *Political Parties in the Southern States: Party Activists in Partisan Coalitions,* edited by Tod A. Baker, Charles D. Hadley, Robert P. Steed, and Laurence W. Moreland, 88–102. New York: Praeger, 1990.

4438. Fowlkes, Diane L. "Ambitious Political Woman: Countersocializaton and Political Party Context." *Women and Politics* 4 (Winter 1984): 5–32.

4439. Fowlkes, Diane L., Jerry Perkins, and Sue Tolleson Rinehart. "Women in Southern Party Politics: Roles, Activities and Futures." In *Party Politics in the South,* edited by Tod A. Baker, Laurence W. Moreland, and Robert P. Steed, 214–231. New York: Praeger, 1980.

4440. Gordon, Felice Dosik. "After Winning: The New Jersey Suffragists in the Political Parties, 1920–1930." *New Jersey History* 101, no. 3 (1983): 12–35.

4441. Kyle, Patricia A. "Political Sex-Role Distinctions: Motivations, Recruitment and Demography of Women Party Elites in North Carolina." Ph.D. dissertation, Georgetown University, Washington, DC, 1973.

4442. Myers, Helen Linder. *Oral History Interview with Helen Linder Myers.* The Claremont Graduate School and the California State Archives State Government Oral History Program, 1990. Interview for California Women and Public Policymaking Oral History Program.

4443. Pratt, Mrs. John T. "Plea for Party Partisanship." *The Woman Citizen* 10 (March 1926): 23.

4444. Snyder, Elizabeth. *California's First Woman State Party Chairman.* Berkeley: University of California, 1977. The Bancroft Library Oral History Interview.

Local

4445. Baker, Tod A., Robert P. Steed, and Laurence W. Moreland. "Gender and Race among Democratic Party Activists in Two Southern States." *Social Science Quarterly* 65 (December 1984): 1088–1091.

4446. Bowman, Lewis, and G. R. Boynton. "Recruitment Patterns among Local Party Officials: A Model and Some Preliminary Findings in Selected Locales." *American Political Science Review* 54 (June 1960): 667–677.

4447. " 'Committeewomen' and County 'Chairwomen' in the New Politics." *Literary Digest* 65 (29 May 1920): 68–70.

4448. Hays, Samuel P. "Political Parties and the Community-Society Continuum." In *The American Party Sys-*

tems, edited by William Nisbet Chambers and Walter Dean Burnham. New York: Oxford, 1967.

4449. Kelley, Anne E., William E. Hulbary, and Lewis Bowman. "Gender, Party and Political Ideology: The Case of Mid-Elite Party Activists in Florida." *Journal of Political Science* 17 (1989): 6–18.

4450. Margolis, Diane Tothbard. "The Invisible Hands: Sex Roles and the Division of Labor in Two Local Political Parties." *Social Problems* 25, no. 3 (February 1979): 314–324. Reprinted in *Women in Local Politics,* by Debra W. Stewart, 22–41. Metuchen, NJ: Scarecrow Press, 1980.

4451. McDonald, Jean Graves, and Vicky Howell Pierson. "Female County Party Leaders and the Perception of Discrimination: A Test of the Male Conspiracy Theory." *Social Science Journal* 21 (January 1984): 13–20.

4452. Porter, Mary Cornelia, and Ann B. Matasar. "The Role and Status of Women in the Daley Organization." In *Woman and Politics,* edited by Jane S. Jaquette, 85–108. New York: Wiley, 1974.

4453. Van Assendelft, Laura, and Karen O'Connor. "Background Motivations and Interests: A Comparison of Male and Female Local Party Activities." *Women and Politics* 14, no. 3 (1994): 77–92.

4454. "Women Sachems in Tammany's Wigwam." *The New York Times Magazine* (8 June 1919): VII, 910.

Conventions

General

4455. Addams, Jane. "Why I Seconded Roosevelt's Nomination." *The Woman's Journal* 35 (17 August 1912).

4456. ———. "My Experiences as a Progressive Delegate." *McClure* 40 (November 1912): 12–14.

4457. Baer, Denise L., and David A. Bositis. "Party Reform or Social Change? A Comparison of Men and Women at Nominating Conventions and County Seats." Paper presented at the annual meeting of the American Political Science Association, New Orleans, 1985.

4458. Blair, Emily Newell. "Women at the Conventions." *Current History* (*New York Times Magazine*) 13 (20 October 1920): 26–28.

4459. ———. "On to the Conventions." *The Woman Citizen* 8 (19 April 1924): 20–21.

4460. Carroll, Susan J. "Women's Rights and Political Parties: Issue Development, the 1972 Conventions, and the National Women's Political Caucus." Master's thesis, Indiana University, 1975.

4461. Cimons, Marlene. "Who's Picking the Next President? Your Convention Delegate! But Who's Picking Her?" *Ms.* 7, no. 7 (January 1980): 69–70.

4462. Cottin, Jonathan. "Comparing Slates in Illinois: Differing Quotas for Women Delegates." *National Journal* (25 March 1972): 506–509.

4463. Donaldson, Alice. "Women Emerge as Political Speakers." *Speech Monographs* 18 (March 1951): 54–61.

4464. "The First Woman's Platform." *The Woman Citizen* 4 (15 May 1920): 1254.

4465. Fisher, Marguerite J. "If Women Only Voted, Top Men in Number by Thousands Gain Influence in Party Organizations." *Christian Science Monitor Magazine* (30 October 1948): 2.

4466. Fisher, Marguerite J., and Betty Whitehead. "Women's Participation in National Party Nominating Conventions: 1892–1914." *American Political Science Review* 38 (October 1944): 896–903.

4467. Flynn, Sharon, and R. Ellen Boddie. "Go Where the Power Is, Women National Convention Delegates." *Working Woman* 5 (January 1980): 47–50.

4468. Freeman, Jo. "The Women's Movement and the 1984 Democratic and Republican Conventions." *Off Our Backs* (February 1985): 11–13, 20. Reprinted in *Women Leaders in American Politics,* edited by James David Barber and Barbara Kellerman, 236–245. Englewood Cliffs, NJ: Prentice Hall, 1986.

4469. ———. "Feminism Vs. Family Values: Women at the 1992 Democratic and Republican Conventions." *Off Our Backs* 23, no. 1 (January 1995): 2–3, 10–17. Abridged in *Different Roles, Different Voices: Women and Politics in the United States and Europe,* 70–83. New York: HarperCollins,

1995; and in *Political Science and Politics,* 26, no. 1 (March 1993): 21–28.

4470. Friedan, Betty. "On the Conventions." *Mademoiselle* (October 1968): 22, 24, 220.

4471. Goldman, David, and Richard Baid. "Women Delegates." In *The Politics of National Nominating Conventions.* Washington, DC: Brookings Institution, 1960.

4472. Hickey, Margaret. "Women Organizing for Action." *Ladies Home Journal* 69 (September 1952): 25, 162.

4473. Jennings, M. Kent, and Barbara G. Farah. "Social Roles and Party Resources: An Over-Time Study of Men and Women in Party Elites." *American Journal of Political Science* 25, no. 3 (August 1981): 462–482.

4474. Kirkpatrick, Jeane. "Representation in the American National Conventions: The Case of 1972." *British Journal of Political Science* 5 (July 1975): 265–322.

4475. Komisar, Lucy. "Conventions, the Campaigns: Women Come into Their Own." *The Nation* 223 (18 September 1976): 230–233.

4476. "Legislative Victory at Both Conventions." *Independent Woman* 33 (October 1954): 7, 28.

4477. Lynn, Naomi B., and Cornelia Butler Flora. "Societal Punishment and Aspects of Female Political Participation: 1972 National Convention Delegates." In *A Portrait of Marginality: The Political Behavior of American Women,* edited by Marianne Githens and Jewell Prestage, 139–149. New York: McKay, 1977.

4478. McLaughlin, M. "Women's Planks in the Party Platforms." " *McCalls* 103 (June 1976): 36.

4479. Michelet, Simon. *Women Delegates at National Conventions.* Washington, DC: National Get-Out-The-Vote Club, 1928.

4480. Pierce, Ponchitta. "What Do Women Want at the Conventions?" *McCalls* 99 (July 1972): 42.

4481. "Two Utah Women in Politics." *The Woman's Journal* 31 (23 June 1900): 196.

4482. "Women and Parties: With the Democrats, with the Republicans." *The Woman Citizen* 4 (17 January 1920): 721–722.

4483. "Women in Politics." *The Woman Citizen* 5 (19 June 1920): 88.

Democratic

4484. Bass, Mrs. George. "Political History Made in 1920." *Democratic Digest* 13, no. 7 (July 1936): 15.

4485. Bennetts, Leslie. "How Women Took Charge at the Democratic Convention." *Ms.* 9, no. 5 (November 1980): 58–59, 63–65.

4486. Blair, Emily Newell. "Get Ready for 1924." *The Woman Citizen* 8 (11 August 1923): 16–17.

4487. ———. "Democratic Women Pass the Test." *Democratic Digest* 13, no. 7 (July 1936): 11.

4488. Clement, Ellis Meredith. "Women at Past National Conventions." *Democratic Digest* 13, no. 7 (July 1936): 28–29.

4489. "Colorado's Woman Delegate." *The Woman's Journal* 39 (July 1908): 112.

4490. Democratic National Committee, ed. *Mandate for Reform: A Report of the Commission on Party Structure and Delegate Selection to the Democratic National Committee.* Washington, DC: Democratic National Committee, 1970.

4491. ———. *Commission on Delegate Selection and Party Structure, Democrats All.* Washington, DC: Democratic National Committee, 1973.

4492. "Democratic Women at New York." *The Woman Citizen* 9 (14 June 1924): 2.

4493. "The Democrats in the Garden." *The Woman Citizen* 9 (12 July 1924): 7–9, 24–25.

4494. "Equal Number of Men and Women Appointed National Vice-Chairmen." *Democratic Digest* 13, no. 8 (August 1936): 8–9.

4495. "Eve's Operatives: Women Delegates of the Democratic Convention." *Time* 100 (24 July 1972): 25–26.

4496. Freeman, Jo. "Something DID Happen at the Democratic Convention." *Ms.* 5, no. 4 (October 1976): 113–115.

4497. ———. "Feminist Coalition Faces Down the Carter Campaign." *In These Times* 33, no. 4 (27 August 1980): 2.

4498. ———. "Women at the 1988 Democratic Convention." *Off Our Backs* 18, no. 9 (October 1988): 4–5. Reprinted in *PS: Political Science and Politics,* 21, no. 4 (Fall 1988): 875–881.

4499. Friedan, Betty. "Our Party." *The New Republic* 207 (5 October 1992): 16, 18, 20.

4500. Hickey, Margaret. "Delegate in a Draft." *Ladies Home Journal* 69 (November 1952): 54–55, 114–115.

4501. Leeds, Isabelle R. "Women at the Democratic Convention." *Mademoiselle* (November 1972): 84, 92, 94.

4502. Lewis, Ann F. "Looking toward the Democratic Convention." *National Business Woman* 69, no. 3 (June–July 1988): 16, 22.

4503. Locke, Mamie E. "Is This America? Fannie Lou Hamer and the Mississippi Freedom Democratic Party." In *Women in the Civil Rights Movement: Trailblazers and Torchbearers,* edited by Vicki L. Crawford, Jacqueline Anne Rouse, and Barbara Wood, 27–38. New York: Carlson, 1990.

4504. Lyle, Adrienne. "The Woman Bloc at the Democratic Convention." *Democratic Digest* 13, no. 7 (July 1936): 21–23.

4505. McGrath, Wilma E., and John W. Soule. "Rocking the Cradle or Rocking the Boat: Women at the 1972 Democratic National Convention." *Social Science Quarterly* 55, no. 1 (June 1974): 141–150.

4506. National Women's Political Caucus. *Democratic Women Are Wonderful: A History of Women at Democratic National Conventions.* Washington, DC: National Women's Political Caucus, 1980.

4507. "New Jersey Women Hold State Rally." *Democratic Digest* 17, no.

10–11 (October–November 1940): 42–43.

4508. Ross, Nellie Tayloe. "Women and the Democratic National Convention." *Democratic Bulletin* 7 (July 1932): 18–19, 48–49.

4509. Sullivan, Denis G., Jefrey L. Pressman, Benjamin I. Page, and F. Christopher Arterton, eds. *Explorations in Convention Decision Making: The Democratic Party in the 1970s.* San Francisco, CA: W. H. Freeman, 1976.

4510. Sullivan, Denis G., Jefrey L. Pressman, Benjamin I. Page, and John J. Lyons. *The Politics of Representation: The Democratic Convention of 1972.* New York: St. Martin's Press, 1974.

4511. White, Sue S. "Women in Democratic Convention." *Democratic Bulletin* 7, no. 8 (August 1932): 21, 27.

4512. "Woman and the Democrat's Convention." *The Woman Citizen* 5 (3 July 1920): 126.

4513. "Women Continue Gains at 1944 Convention." *Democratic Digest* 21, no. 8 (August 1944): 9–11.

4514. "Women Have Big Convention Roles." *Democratic Digest* 8, no. 7 (July 1960): 20, 23.

4515. "Women in the National Democratic Convention." *Progress* 7, no. 8 (August 1908): 2.

4516. "Women's Role in 1952 Convention." *Democratic Digest* 29, no. 8–9 (August–September 1952): 12.

Republican

4517. Blakey, George T. "Esther Griffin White: An Awakener of Hoosier Potential." *Indiana Magazine of History* 84, no. 3 (September 1990): 281–309.

4518. Freeman, Jo. "The Republican Convention, What's Half Elephant, Half Woman and All Establishment?" *Majority Report* (4 September 1976): 6–7.

4519. ———. "Republican Politics—Let's Make a Deal." *Ms.* 5, no. 5 (November 1976): 19–20.

4520. ———. "Republicans: Feminists Avoid a Direct Showdown." *In These Times* 4, no. 32 (30 July 1980): 5.

4521. ———. "Feminist Activities at the 1988 Republican Convention." *Off Our Backs* 18, no. 10 (November 1988): 10–11, 14. Reprinted in *PS: Political Science and Politics,* 22, no. 11 (March 1989): 39–46.

4522. Hickey, Margaret. "From Kitchen to Convention." *Ladies Home Journal* 69 (October 1952): 74–75, 108, 110–222.

4523. "How to Deradicalize: Republican National Convention." *Time* 100 (4 September 1972): 17–18.

4524. "An Idaho Delegate." *The Woman's Journal* 35 (25 June 1904): 204.

4525. Kanner, Melinda. "Sex, Sexuality and the Quest for Power: A Feminist Analysis of the 1988 Republican Presidential Campaign Discourse." Paper presented at the annual meeting of the American Political Science Association, Atlanta, 1989.

4526. Knobe, Bertha Damaris. "The Suffragist and the G.O.P." *Harper's Weekly* 52 (4 July 1908): 16.

4527. Lewis, Ann F. "Advice for the Trenches, Republican Women Convention Delegates." *Ms.* 17, no. 3 (September 1988): 66.

4528. McCormick, Ruth Hanna. "United Effort Will Bring Recognition." *The Republican Woman of Illinois* 6, no. 11 (July 1928): 7.

4529. Metcalf, Henry Harrison. "New Hampshire Women." *Granite Monthly* 59 (June 1927): 161–170.

4530. Morris, Celia. "The Revolt of the Republican Women." *Vogue* 182, no. 8 (August 1992): 232–235, 294–295.

4531. Republican National Committee. *Delegate and Organizations Committee, The Delegate Selection Procedures for the Republican Party II: Progress Report of the DO Committee.* Washington, DC: Republican National Committee, 1971.

4532. "Republican Women Take a Hand." *The Woman's Journal* 31 (23 June 1900): 199.

4533. Rosenfeld, Megan. "Insurgents in Pearls." *Lear's* 5 (August 1992): 57–59, 87–88.

4534. Simpson, Peggy. "Games Republicans Play." *Ms.* 17, no. 1 (July 1988): 42–45.

4535. Stone, Anne J. "What to Expect at the Republican Convention." *National Business Woman* 69, no. 3 (June–July 1988): 17, 22.

4536. "Utah's Woman Alternate." *The Woman's Journal* 31 (30 June 1900): 201.

4537. "Women as Spectators and Participants." *The Republican Woman of Illinois* 6, no. 11 (July 1928): 4.

4538. "Women at the Republican Convention." *The Woman Citizen* 5 (12 June 1920): 41.

4539. "Women in National Republican Convention." *The Woman's Journal* 35 (9 July 1904): 224.

4540. "Women in National Republican Politics." *Progress* 7, no. 7 (July 1908): 1.

Parties

Democratic

4541. Abzug, Bella S., Phyllis Seal, and Miriam Kelber. "Women in the Democratic Party: A Review of Affirmative Action." *Human Rights Law Review* 6 (Spring 1974): 3–24. Columbia University.

4542. Bass, Elizabeth. "Advance of Democratic Women." *Democratic Digest* 17, no. 2 (February 1940): 17, 39. Part I (1916–1920) of 5-part article.

4543. Battiata, Mary. "Stag Party." *Harper's* 267 (September 1983): 27–28.

4544. Blair, Emily Newell. "How the Democratic Party Has Organized Women." In *Democratic Campaign Book,* edited by Democratic National Committee, 89–102. Washington, DC: Democratic National Committee, 1922.

4545. ———. "How the Democratic Party Has Organized Women." *Fortnightly Bulletin* 1, no. 17 (9 June 1923): 1.

4546. ———. "Fooling the Women." In *Women's Democratic Campaign Manual,* edited by Women's Division, 131–133. Washington, DC: Democratic National Committee, 1924.

4547. ———. "The Congress and the Country." *The Woman Citizen* 11 (September 1926): 20, 40.

4548. ———. "The Case for the Opposition." *The Woman's Journal* 13 (April 1928): 9.

4549. ———. "Putting Women into Politics." *The Woman's Journal* 16 (March 1931): 14–15, 29.

4550. ———. "Advance of Democratic Women." *Democratic Digest* 17, no. 4 (April 1940): 15, 38. Part 3 (1922–1928) of 5-part article.

4551. Burke, Susan. "Women's Role in Politics." *National Business Woman* 53, no. 4 (April 1972): 8.

4552. Burrell, Barbara C. "John Bailey's Legacy: Political Parties and Women's Candidacies for Public Office." In *Women in Politics: Outsiders or Insiders? A Collection of Readings,* edited by Lois Lovelace Duke, 123–134. Englewood Cliffs, NJ: Prentice Hall, 1993.

4553. Coffin, Tris. "India Edwards: Queen-Maker of Washington." *Coronet* 29 (April 1951): 124–128.

4554. Congressional Wives Forum. *History of Democratic Women.* Washington, DC: Democratic National Committee, 1960.

4555. Daly, Michael. "The Lady and the Pol." *The New York Magazine* 16 (25 July 1983): 16–17.

4556. "Democracy and Women." In *The Democratic Text Book,* edited by Democratic National Committee, 436–451. Washington, DC: Democratic National Committee, 1920.

4557. Democratic National Committee. *Women's Democratic Campaign Manual.* Edited by Marion Glass Bannister. Washington, DC: Democratic National Committee and Democratic Congressional Committee, 1924.

4558. "Democratic Party's Recognition of Negro Women." *Color* 11 (January 1957): 14–15.

4559. Denning, Carolyn Luckett. "The Louisville Democratic Party: Political Times of 'Miss Lennie' McLaughlin." Master's thesis, University of Louisville, 1981.

4560. Dewson, Mary W. "Advance of Democratic Women." *Democratic Digest* 17, no. 6–7 (June–July 1940): 61, 90–91. Part 5 (1928–1938) of 5-part article.

4561. Edelman, Anne S. "A Housewife's Discovery, Politics Is Exhilarating." *Democratic Digest* 4 (March 1956): 50–55.

4562. Edwards, India. *Pulling No Punches: Memoirs of a Woman in Politics.* New York: G.P. Putnam's Sons, 1977.

4563. Hard, Anne. "'Politician'— Emily Newell Blair." *The Woman Citizen* 10 (April 1926): 15–16, 40, 42.

4564. Howe, Louis McHenry. "Women's Ways in Politics." *Woman's Home*

Companion 62, no. 6 (June 1935): 9–10.

4565. Hurst, Fannie. "Politics … And Woman-Power." *Democratic Digest* 23, no. 8 (August 1946): 8–9, 22.

4566. Kerr, Barbara Wendell. "Opening a Window in the Smoke-Filled Room: New York County Democratic Women's Workshop." *Reporter* 14 (12 January 1956): 22–25.

4567. Keyes, Frances Parkinson. "American Woman and the Democratic Party." *Delineator* 113 (November 1928): 17, 86, 89, 90, 95.

4568. Kiplinger, Leslie J. "How to Increase Male Membership." *Democratic Bulletin* 4, no. 10 (October 1929): 26–27, 33.

4569. Kitayama, Kimiko Fujii. *Nisei Leader in Democratic Politics and Civic Affairs.* Berkeley, CA: University of California, 1979. The Bancroft Library Oral History Interview.

4570. Kizenkavich, Marian. *Oral History Interview with Marian Kizenkavich.* Chisholm, MN: Iron Range Research Center, 1987. Interview for the Women of the Iron Range Project.

4571. Louchheim, Katie. *By the Political Sea.* Garden City, NY: Doubleday, 1970.

4572. Meredith, Ellis. "The Democratic Party in National Politics in the 20th Century." In *The Woman Citizen: A General Handbook of Civics with Special Consideration of Women's Citizenship,* edited by Mary Sumner Boyd, 189–195. New York: Frederick A. Stokes, 1918.

4573. Morgan, Georgia Cook. "India Edwards: Distaff Politician of the Truman Era." *Missouri Historical Review* 78 (April 1984): 293–310.

4574. Morrow, Elise, and Sylvia Brooks. "The Lady Who Told Off the President." *Saturday Evening Post* 224 (7 July 1951): 28, 108–110.

4575. "New Jersey Frauds Denied." *Americana* 6 (June 1911): 621–622.

4576. Rishel, Virginia. "Women in Politics—1940 Style." Parts I–III. *Democratic Digest* 17, no. 8 (August 1940): 28–29; (September 1940): 24, 35; (October 1940): 34–35.

4577. Robb, Inez. "Democrats' Golden Girl: Marietta Peabody Tree." *Saturday Evening Post* 233 (22 October 1960): 36–37, 88, 90.

4578. Roosevelt, Mrs. Franklin D. "Women's Political Responsibility." *Democratic Bulletin* 7, no. 1 (January 1932): 12.

4579. Ross, Nellie Tayloe. "A Call to Service, an Appeal to Democratic Women." *Democratic Bulletin* 4, no. 11 (November 1929): 20–21.

4580. ———. "G.O.P. Notable for Disregard of Women." *Democratic Bulletin* 5, no. 10 (October 1930): 10–11, 38.

4581. ———. "Woman Power of the Democratic Party." *Democratic Bulletin* 6, no. 3 (March 1931): 10–11, 27.

4582. ———. "Women Important in Politics." *Democratic Bulletin* 6, no. 7 (July 1931): 12–13, 19.

4583. ———. "Advance of Democratic Women." *Democratic Digest* 17, no. 5 (May 1940): 13, 37. Part 4 (1928–1936) of 5-part article.

4584. Schlesinger, Arthur M., Jr. "The Democratic Party." *Woman's Home Companion* 75 (October 1948): 34–35, 41–42.

4585. Shafer, Byron. "The Re-creation of Reform: The Women's Caucus and Demographic Representation." In *The Quiet Revolution: The Struggle for the Democratic Party and the Shaping of Post-Reform Politics,* 460–491. New York: Russell Sage Foundation, 1983.

4586. Shirpser, Clara. *One Woman's Role in Democratic Party Politics: Nation, State, and Local, 1950–1973.* Berkeley: University of California, 1975. The Bancroft Library Oral History interview.

4587. Sirgo, Henry B. "Women, Blacks and the New Deal." *Women and Politics* 14, no. 3 (1994): 57–76.

4588. Warschaw, Carmen. *A Southern California Perspective on Democratic Party Politics.* Berkeley: University of California, 1983. The Bancroft Library Oral History Interview.

4589. White, Sue S. "Women in the Democratic Party, County Organization Plans." *Democratic Bulletin* 7 (September 1932): 26, 31.

4590. Williams, Charl Ormond. "Advance of Democratic Women." *Democratic Digest* 17, no. 2 (February 1940): 15, 38. Part 2 (1919–1920) of 5-part article.

4591. "Women in the Democratic Party: Equal Rank with Men Accorded Them in Organization and Councils." In *Democratic Campaign Book,* edited by Democratic National Committee, 273–280. Washington, DC: Democratic National Committee, 1924.

4592. "Women's Political Progress: The First Woman Democratic State Chairman." *Democratic Bulletin* 11, no. 7 (July 1934): 8.

Republican

4593. "The American Home: Record of the Republican Party in Behalf of Childhood, Womanhood and the Home." In *Republican Campaign Text Book,* edited by Republican National Committee, 355–371. Washington, DC: Republican National Committee, 1928.

4594. Armstrong, Anne. "Women's Role in Politics." *National Business Woman* 53, no. 5 (May 1972): 8.

4595. Benedict, Marjorie. *Developing a Place for Women in the Republican Party.* Berkeley: University of California, 1984. The Bancroft Library Oral History Interview.

4596. Boswell, Helen Varick. "Republicans in National Politics." In *The Woman Citizen: A General Handbook of Civics with Special Consideration of Women's Citizenship,* edited by Mary Sumner Boyd, 196–201. New York: Frederick A. Stokes, 1918.

4597. Butler, Sarah Schuyler. "I Am Not Disappointed in Women in Politics." *The Woman's Journal* 16 (April 1931): 14, 39.

4598. Catt, Carrie Chapman. "Their First Convention." *The Woman Citizen* 3 (27 July 1918): 168–169.

4599. Coolidge, Calvin. "A Tribute to the Women of America." *The Woman Citizen* 9 (6 September 1924): 11.

4600. Davis, Maxine. "Cutting the Political Pie." *Woman's Home Companion* 59 (September 1932): 16, 77.

4601. English, Mae A., ed. *Our Government: Ten Units of Study for Republican Study Clubs: Republican Woman's Federation of California.* Los Angeles: Gem, 1926.

4602. "Every Door of Opportunity." *The Woman Citizen* 3 (4 January 1919): 656.

4603. Furlow, John W. "Cornelia Bryce Pinchot: Feminism in the Post-Suffrage Era." *Pennsylvania History* 43 (October 1976): 329–346.

4604. Gaines, Irene M. "Colored Women's Republican Clubs." *The Republican Woman of Illinois* 7, no. 3 (October 1929): 5.

4605. Gann, Dolly Curtis. "The Republican Party Will Come Back and Women Can Have a Part in the Work." *The Republican Woman* 9, no. 3 (December 1932): 5, 8.

4606. Good, Josephine L. *Republican Womanpower: The History of Women in Republican National Conventions and Women in the Republican National Committee.* Washington, DC: Women's Division, Republican National Committee, 1963.

4607. Harvey, Anna L. "Uncertain Victory: The Electoral Incorporation of Women into the Republican Party, 1920–1928." Paper presented at the annual meeting of the American Political Science Association, Chicago, 1992.

4608. "Heads State Women on National Committee." *The Republican Woman of Illinois* 6, no. 11 (July 1928): 5.

4609. Helmes, Winifred Gertrude. *Republican Women of Maryland, 1920–1980.* Salisbury, MD: Privately published, 1983.

4610. Hert, Mrs. Alvin T. "Ten Reasons for Being a Republican." *The Woman's Journal* 13 (April 1928): 8.

4611. Hickey, Margaret. "Girl in the Back Room." *Ladies Home Journal* 68 (May 1952): 54, 204–207.

4612. Hosmer, Lucile. *A Conservative Republican in the Mainstream of Party Politics.* Berkeley: University of California, 1983. The Bancroft Library Oral History Interview.

4613. "How Clubs Conducted Local Campaigns." *The Republican Woman of Illinois* 5, no. 9 (May 1928): 3–5.

4614. Huber, Caroline M. *As I See Politics.* Philadelphia: G. S. Ferguson, 1954.

4615. "Illinois Woman on Republican State Committee." *The Women's Voice* 1 (June 1939): 5, 24.

4616. Keyes, Frances Parkinson. "American Woman and the Republican Party." *Delineator* 114 (October 1928): 21, 102, 104.

4617. Lawton, Maria C. "New York Women Make Record, State Republican Committee Finds Colored Women Respond to Representative Leadership." *The Women's Voice* 1, no. 2 (June 1939): 11, 21.

4618. Liebschutz, Sarah F. "Republican Women and the Future of the Republican Party." In *Women Organizing: An Anthology,* edited by Bernice Cummings and Victoria Schuck, 304–318. Metuchen, NJ: Scarecrow Press, 1979.

4619. Lippincott, Mrs. A. Haines. "Independence within the Party." *The Republican Woman* 1, no. 1 (March 1924): 6.

4620. Livermore, Henrietta. "Women's Place in Political Parties." *The Republican Woman of Illinois* 5, no. 5 (December 1927): 1.

4621. MacHenry, Mrs. W. Scott. "Young Republican Women of Pennsylvania." *The Republican Woman* 9, no. 3 (June 1931): 8.

4622. Maloney, Russell. "Women, Republican." *New Yorker* 16 (5 October 1940): 36, 40.

4623. Martin, Marion E. "Minorities in Politics." *The Women's Voice* 1, no. 2 (June 1939): 4–5.

4624. McMurran, Kristin. "Reagan Is Shortchanging Women Says G.O.P. Feminist Kathy Wilson." *People's Weekly* 20 (1 August 1983): 93–94.

4625. Mott, David C. "Judith Ellen Foster." *Annals of Iowa* 19, no. 2 (October 1933): 126–138.

4626. Mundy, Alicia. "It Happened One Night." *Campaigns and Elections* 13, no. 4 (November 1992): 17–18.

4627. National Federation of Republican Women. *National Federation of Republican Women: Fifty Years of Leadership, 1938–1988.* Washington, DC: National Federation of Republican Women, 1987.

4628. National Women's Political Caucus. *Republican Women Are Wonder-* ful: A History of Women at Republican National Conventions. Washington, DC: National Women's Political Caucus, 1980.

4629. Pohle, Kirsten Kim Loutzenhiser. "Party Talk: Considerations of Gender in a Regional Republican Context." Ph.D. dissertation, St. Louis University, 1995.

4630. Republican National Committee. "Highlights of Women and the Republican Party." In *Highlights of Republican Leadership.* Washington, DC: Republican National Committee, 1984. A briefing book prepared by the research department of the communications division and the Office of the Co-Chairman.

4631. Republican National Committee, Women's Division. *Win with Womanpower.* Washington, DC: Republican National Committee, 1962.

4632. Runyon, Alfred Damon. "Woman Boss of Denver: Mrs. Anna Scott." *Harper's Weekly* 52 (26 December 1908): 8–9.

4633. Savage, Courtenay. "Women as Citizens: Harriet Taylor Upton." *The Woman Citizen* 8 (31 May 1924): 18–19.

4634. Schlesinger, Arthur M., Jr. "The Republican Party." *Woman's Home Companion* 75 (September 1948): 36–38, 126.

4635. Simpson, Peggy. "Why They'd Rather Fight Than Switch." *Ms.* 17, no. 5 (November 1988): 92–95.

4636. Stewart, Mary. "The New Politics." *Good Housekeeping* 71 (5 July–August 1920): 19–20.

4637. "Why Colored Women Should Support the Republican Party." *The Women's Voice* 1, no. 1 (May 1939): 15–19.

4638. Williams, Clare B. *The History of the Founding and Development of the National Federation of Republican Women.* Washington, DC: Republican National Committee, 1962.

4639. Wise, Ora. "Women in Politics." *The Women's Voice* 1 (5 September 1939): 16–17.

4640. "Women and the Republican Party." In *Republican Campaign Text Book,* edited by Republican National Committee, 292–298. Washington, DC: Republican National Committee, 1924.

4641. "Women in National Republican Politics." *Progress* 9, no. 7 (July 1908): 1.

4642. "Women to Help Run the G.O.P." *Literary Digest* 78, no. 1 (14 July 1923): 15.

4643. Yost, Lenna Lowe. "A Word from Republican National Headquarters." *The Republican Woman of Illinois* 8, no. 7 (February 1931): 5.

4644. Yost, Mrs. Ellis A. "The Next Ten Years." *The Republican Woman* 8, no. 7 (January 1931): 1, 6.

4645. ———. "An Interpretation of Politics." *The Republican Woman* 9, no. 5 (January 1932): 8, 17.

4646. ———. "Republican Women Contributing to Party Strength." *The Republican Woman* 12, no. 2 (May 1934): 4.

Other Parties

4647. Allen, Davis. "Social Workers and the Progressive Party, 1912–1916." *American Historical Review* 69, no. 3 (1964): 671–688.

4648. Baker, Ellen R. "Women Working for the Cooperative Commonwealth: Populists and Socialists Address the Woman Question, 1890–1914." Master's thesis, University of Wisconsin, Madison, 1992.

4649. Basen, Neil K. "Kate Richards O'Hare: The 'First Lady' of American Socialism, 1901–1917." *Labor History* 21 (Spring 1980): 165–169.

4650. Baxandall, Rosalyn. "Pioneer and Aunt Tom: Elizabeth Gurley Flynn's Feminism." *Rethinking Marxism* 1, no. 1 (1988): 74–85.

4651. Block, Anita C. "Aims of the Socialist Party." In *The Woman Citizen: A General Handbook of Civics with Special Consideration of Women's Citizenship,* edited by Mary Sumner Boyd, 202–208. New York: Frederick A. Stokes, 1918.

4652. Blumberg, Dorothy Rose. "Mary Elizabeth Lease, Populist Orator: A Profile." *Kansas History* 1, no. 1 (1978): 1–15.

4653. Buhle, Mari Jo. "Women and the Socialist Party, 1901–1914." In *From Feminism to Liberation Women,* edited by Edith Altbach, 65–86. Cambridge, MA: Schenkman, 1971.

4654. ———. *Women and American Socialism, 1870–1920.* Urbana: University of Illinois, 1983.

4655. Colvin, Mamie W. "A Party of Principle, the Prohibition Party." In

The Woman Citizen: A General Handbook of Civics with Special Consideration of Women's Citizenship, edited by Mary Sumner Boyd, 209–214. New York: Frederick A. Stokes, 1918.

4656. Costigan, Mabel Cory. "Why Women Support the Progressive Ticket." *The Woman Citizen* 9 (6 September 1924): 12.

4657. Faue, Elizabeth. "Women, Family, and Politics: Farmer-Labor Women and Social Policy in the Great Depression." In *Women, Politics and Change,* edited by Louise A. Tilly and Patricia Gurin, 436–456. New York: Sage, 1990.

4658. Gustafson, Melanie. "Partisan Women: Gender, Politics and the Progressive Party of 1912." Ph.D. dissertation, New York University, 1993.

4659. Hyde, Florence Slown. "The National Party—A New Voice in American Politics." In *The Woman Citizen: A General Handbook of Civics with Special Consideration of Women's Citizenship,* edited by Mary Sumner Boyd, 220–224. New York: Frederick A. Stokes, 1918.

4660. McCormick, LaRue. *Activist in the Radical Movement, 1930–1960: The International Labor Defense and the Communist Party.* Berkeley: University of California, 1980. The Bancroft Library Oral History Interview.

4661. Miller, Sally M. "Other Socialists: Native-Born and Immigrant Women in the Socialist Party of America, 1901–1917." *Labor History* 24 (Winter 1983): 84–102.

4662. Nielsen, Kim E. "'We All Leaguers by Our House': Women, Suffrage, and Red-Baiting in the National Nonpartisan League." *Journal of Women's History* 6, no. 1 (Spring 1995): 31–49.

4663. Potter, Adella. "The Anti-Saloon League—A Non-Partisan Political Party." In *The Woman Citizen: A General Handbook of Civics with Special Consideration of Women's Citizenship,* edited by Mary Sumner Boyd, 215–219. New York: Frederick A. Stokes, 1918.

4664. Ratliff, Beulah A. "The Cream Lady." *The New Republic* 28 (26 October 1921): 240–242.

4665. Shaffer, Robert. "Women and the Communist Party, USA, 1920–1940." *Socialist Review* 45 (May–June 1979): 73–118.

4666. Sillito, John R. "Women and the Socialist Party in Utah, 1900–1920." *Utah Historical Quarterly* 49 (Summer 1981): 220–238.

4667. Starr, Karen. "Fighting for a Future: Farm Women of the Nonpartisan League." *Minnesota History* 48 (Summer 1983): 255–262.

4668. Stiller, Richard. *Queen of Populists: The Story of Mary Elizabeth Lease.* New York: Dell, 1970.

4669. Wagner, Mary Jo. "Farms, Families, and Reform: Women in the Farmers' Alliance and Populist Party." Ph.D. dissertation, University of Oregon, 1986.

4670. "Women Leaders of the Progressives." *The Woman Citizen* 9 (6 September 1924): 4.

4671. Zickefoose, Sandra. "Women and the Socialist Party of America,

1900–1915." *University of California, Los Angeles, Historical Journal* 1 (1980): 26–41.

Impact

4672. Baer, Denise L., and John S. Jackson. "Are Women Really More 'Amateur' in Politics Than Men?" *Women and Politics* 5, no. 2–3 (Summer–Fall 1985): 79–92.

4673. Barnard, Eunice Fuller. "Madame Arrives in Politics." *North American Review* 226, no. 5 (November 1928): 551–556.

4674. ———. "Women Who Wield Political Power." *The New York Times Magazine* (2 September 1928): VI, 6–7, 23.

4675. Berelson, Bernard, and Paul F. Lazarsfeld. "Women: A Major Problem for the P.A.C." *Public Opinion Quarterly* 9 (1945): 79–82.

4676. Blair, Emily Newell. "What Is Nonpartisanship?" *The Woman Citizen* 9 (7 March 1925): 15.

4677. ———. "Boring from Within." *The Woman Citizen* 12 (July 1927): 49–50.

4678. Catt, Carrie Chapman. "Party Clean-Ups Are the Crying Need." *The Woman's Journal* 16 (31 April 1931): 15, 30.

4679. Clark, Janet M. "Party Leaders and Women's Entry into the Political Elites." Paper presented at Southwestern PSA, Fort Worth, April 1979.

4680. Costain, Anne N. "After Reagan: New Party Attitudes toward Gender." *Annals of the American Academy of Political and Social Science* 515 (May 1991): 114–125.

4681. Dobyns, Winifred Starr. "The Lady and the Tiger." *The Woman Citizen* 11 (January 1927): 20–21.

4682. Dougherty, Page H. "It's a Man's Game, But Woman Is Learning." *The New York Times Magazine* (3 November 1946): VI, 17, 54, 56.

4683. Ducas, Dorothy. "All for the Party, The Truth Is That Politicians Use Women to Get the Votes, But Keep the Spoils for Themselves." *Delineator* 129 (October 1936): 10–11, 50.

4684. Egan, Eleanor Franklin. "Women in Politics to the Aid of Their Party." *Saturday Evening Post* 192 (22 May 1920): 12–13, 185–186, 189–190.

4685. Frazer, Elizabeth. "This Thing Called Party Loyalty." *Good Housekeeping* 74 (May 1922): 37, 176–179.

4686. Freeman, Jo. "Whom You Know versus Whom You Represent: Feminist Influence in the Democratic and Republican Parties." In *The Women's Movements of the United States and Western Europe: Consciousness, Political Opportunity and Public Policy,* edited by Mary F. Katzenstein and Carol M. Mueller, 215–246. Philadelphia: Temple University Press, 1987.

4687. Green, Elizabeth. "I Resign from Female Politics." *The New Republic* 42 (22 April 1925): 234–235.

4688. Hay, Mary Garrett, and Mrs. George Bass. "In Which of the Two Big Parties Will You Enroll?" *Woman's Home Companion* 46 (November 1919): 10–11.

4689. Higginbotham, Evelyn Brooks. "In Politics to Stay: Black Women Leaders and Party Politics in the 1920s." In *Women, Politics and Change,* edited by Louise A. Tilly and Patricia Gurin, 199–220. New York: Russell Sage, 1990.

4690. Lape, Esther Everett. "New Woman Voter and the Grand Old Parties." *Ladies Home Journal* 37 (May 1920): 39, 86, 88.

4691. Loomis, Alice Bell. "Why Political Parties." *The Woman Citizen* 4 (29 May 1920): 1319.

4692. McCormick, Anne O'Hare. "Enter Women, The New Boss of Politics." *The New York Times Magazine* (21 October 1928): V, 3, 22.

4693. Moskowitz, Belle L. "Junior Politics and Politicians." *Saturday Evening Post* 203 (6 September 1930): 6–7, 149–150.

4694. "Politics and the Woman." *The Woman Citizen* 3 (28 December 1918): 628.

4695. Pratt, Ruth. "Lady or the Tiger." *Ladies Home Journal* 45 (May 1928): 8.

4696. Rogers, Edith Nourse. "Women's New Place in Politics." *Nation's Business* 18 (August 1930): 39–41, 120, 124.

4697. Roosevelt, Mrs. Franklin D. "Women Must Learn to Play the Game as Men Do." *Redbook* 1, no. 6 (April 1928): 78–79, 141–142.

4698. Ross, John Gordon. "Ladies in Politics: The Gentle Experiment." *Forum and Century* 96 (November 1936): 209–215.

4699. Samuels, Gertrude. "Really a Man's World, Politics." *The New York Times Magazine* (15 October 1950): VI, 17, 51–53.

4700. Silverberg, Helene Norma. "Political Organization and the Origin of Political Identity: The Emergence and Containment of Gender in American Politics, 1960–1984." Ph.D. dissertation, Cornell University, 1988.

4701. "Suffragists First." *The Woman Citizen* 4, no. 21 (13 December 1919): 557.

4702. Sykes, Patricia L., and Julianna S. Gonen. "The Semi-Sovereign Sex: U.S. Parties as Obstacles to the Women's Movement." Paper presented at the annual meeting of the Midwest Political Science Association, Chicago, 1991.

4703. Upton, Harriet Taylor. "Wade In." *The Woman Citizen* 6 (16 July 1921): 17.

4704. "When You Get into the Parties." *The Woman Citizen* 5 (7 August 1920): 249.

4705. "Why I Joined My Party." *The Woman Citizen* 4 (14 February 1920): 541, 569; and (21 February 1920): 594–595.

4706. "Woman Suffragists and Party Politics." *The New Republic* 9 (9 December 1916): 138–140.

4707. Young, Rose. "Party Affiliation for Women." *The Woman Citizen* 5 (20 November 1920): 678.

V. Public Policy

General

4708. Bernard, Jessie. *Women and the Public Interest: An Essay in Policy and Protest.* Chicago: Aldine-Atherton, 1971.

4709. Blair, Diane D., and Robert L. Savage. "Dimensions of Responsiveness to Women's Policies in the Fifty States." *Women and Politics* 4 (Summer 1984): 49–68.

4710. Boneparth, Ellen, ed. *Women, Power and Policy.* New York: Pergamon, 1982. Revised edition, 1989.

4711. Boneparth, Ellen, and Emily Stoper, eds. *Women, Power, and Policy: Toward the Year 2000.* 2d ed. New York: Pergamon Press, 1989.

4712. Clark, Cal, Janet M. Clark, and Jose Z. Garcia. "Policy Impacts on Hispanics and Women: A State Case Study." In *Race, Sex and Policy Problems,* edited by Marian Lief Palley and Michael B. Preston. Lexington, MA: Lexington Books, 1979.

4713. Conway, M. Margaret, David W. Ahern, and Gertrude A. Steuernagel, eds. *Women and Public Policy: A Revolution in Progress.* Washington, DC: CQ Press, 1995.

4714. Costain, Anne N., and W. Douglas Costain. "Movements and Gatekeepers: Congressional Response to Women's Movement Issues, 1900–1982." *Congress and the Presidents* 12 (Spring 1985): 21–42.

4715. Erie, Steven. "Women, Reagan and the New Class War." Paper presented at the annual meeting of the American Political Science Association, Chicago, September 1983.

4716. Freeman, Jo. "Protest and Policy: Women Make Waves." In *Prospects: An Annual of American Cultural Studies,* edited by Jack Salzman, 595–610. New York: Burt Franklin, 1979.

4717. ———. "Women and Public Policy: An Overview." In *Women, Power and Policy,* edited by Ellen Boneparth, 47–67. New York: Pergamon Press, 1982.

4718. ———. "Women, Law and Public Policy." In *Women: A Feminist Perspective,* 3d ed., edited by Jo Freeman, 381–401. Palo Alto, CA: Mayfield Publishing, 1984.

4719. Garcia, Jose Z., Cal Clark, and Janet M. Clark. "Policy Impacts on Chicanos and Women: A State Case Study." *Policy Studies Journal* 7, no. 2 (Winter 1978): 251–257.

4720. Gelb, Joyce, and Marian Lief Palley, eds. *Women and Public Policies.* 2d ed. Princeton: Princeton University Press, 1987 (1982).

4721. "Gender Politics and Public Policies." *Social Research* 58 (Fall 1991): 621–705.

4722. Goldman, Josephine. "Legislative Gains for Women in 1912." *The Survey* 28 (13 April 1912): 95–96.

4723. Greene, Mrs. Frederick Stuart, and Mildred Adams. "What Women Want and What They Get." *The Woman's Journal* 16 (July 1931): 8–9, 36–38.

4724. Griffiths, Martha W. "Women and Legislation." In *Voices of the New Feminism,* edited by Mary Lou Thompson, 103–114. Boston: Beacon Press, 1970.

4725. Harrison, Cynthia E. "A New Frontier for Women: The Public Policy of the Kennedy Administration." *Journal of American History* 67 (December 1980): 630–646. Reprinted and revised in *Our American Sisters,* 4th ed., edited by Jean Friedman and Williams Shade, 493–514. Washington, DC: D. C. Heath, 1982.

4726. ———. "Prelude to Feminism: Women's Organizations, the Federal Government, and the Rise of the Women's Movement, 1942–1968." Ph.D. dissertation, Columbia University, 1982.

4727. ———. "Stalemate: Federal Legislation for Women in the Truman Era." In *Harry S. Truman: The Man from Independence,* edited by William F. Levantrosser, 217–232. New York: Greenwood, 1986.

4728. ———. *On Account of Sex: The Politics of Women's Issues, 1945–1968.* Los Angeles: University of California Press, 1988.

4729. Kanowitz, Leo. "Sex-Based Discrimination in American Law I: Law and the Single Girl." *St. Louis University Law Journal* 11 (1967): 293.

4730. Kelber, Miriam. "Carter and Women: The Record." *The Nation* 230, no. 20 (24 May 1980): 609, 624–628.

4731. "Legislative Gains Must Be Protected, Expanded." *National Business Woman* 63, no. 1 (February–March 1982): 4–6.

4732. Lenz, Elinor, and Barbara G. Myerhoff. *The Feminization of America: How Women's Values Are Changing Our Public and Private Lives.* New York: St. Martin's Press, 1985.

4733. Mattei, Laura Winsky. "The Weight of Women's Testimony in Congressional Hearings: The Souter Confirmation." Paper presented at the annual meeting of the American Political Science Association, Chicago, 1995.

4734. McQuatters, Geneva F. "One Hundred Years of Women in Legislation." *Independent Woman* 27 (July 1948): 211–212.

4735. Mueller, Carol M. "Continuity and Change in Women's Political Agenda." In *The Politics of the Gender Gap: The Social Construction of Political Influence,* edited by Carol M. Mueller, 1988. Women's Policy Studies, 12. Beverly Hills, CA: Sage Publications, 1988.

4736. Murphy, Irene. *Public Policy on the Status of Women.* Lexington, MA: Lexington Books, 1973.

4737. Nelson, Lin. "Promise Her Everything: The Nuclear Power Industry's Agenda for Women." *Feminist Studies* 10 (Summer 1984): 291–314.

4738. Palley, Marian Lief, and Michael B. Preston, eds. *Race, Sex and Policy Problems.* Lexington, MA.: Lexington Books, 1979.

4739. Presidential Task Force on Women's Rights and Responsibilities. *Simple Justice: Report of the Presidential Task Force on Women's Rights and Responsibilities.* Washington, DC: Presidential Task Force on Women's Rights and Responsibilities, 1969.

4740. President's Task Force on Legal Equity for Women. *Survey of the Reagan Administration Accomplishments on Behalf of Women.* Washington, DC: President's Task Force on Legal Equity for Women, 1984.

4741. Schumaker, Paul, and Nancy Elizabeth Burns. "Gender Cleavages and the Resolution of Local Policy Issues." *American Journal of Political Science* 32, no. 4 (1988): 1070–1095.

4742. Segers, Mary C. "Equality, Public Policy and Relevant Sex Differences." *Polity* 11 (Spring 1979): 319–339.

4743. Stetson, Dorothy McBride. *Women's Rights in the U.S.A.: Policy Debates and Gender Roles.* Pacific Grove, CA: Brooks-Cole, 1991.

4744. Tangri, Sandra, and Georgia Strasburg. "Can Research on Women Be More Effective in Shaping Policy?" *Psychology of Women Quarterly* 3 (Summer 1979): 321–343.

4745. Truman, Harry S. "Moral Force of Women." *Vital Speeches* 14 (15 October 1947): 23–24.

4746. Welch, Susan, and Levitt Gottlieb. "Women and Public Policy: A Comparative Analysis." In *Race, Sex and Policy Problems,* edited by Marian Lief Palley and Michael B. Preston, 193–206. Lexington, MA: Lexington Books, 1979.

4747. Winston, Kenneth, and Mary Jo Bane, eds. *Gender and Public Policy, Cases and Comments.* Boulder, CO: Westview, 1993.

4748. Wood, Stephen B. *Constitutional Politics in the Progressive Era.* Chicago: University of Chicago Press, 1968.

Assessments

4749. Costain, Anne N. *Inviting Women's Rebellion: A Political Process Interpretation of the Women's Movement.* Baltimore: Johns Hopkins University, 1992.

4750. Haber, Barbara, ed. *The Women's Annual — The Year in Review 1982–83.* Boston: G.K. Hall, 1983.

4751. Hopkins, William D. "Reagan Administration Efforts to Eliminate Sex Bias in Federal Law: A Critical Assessment." *Journal of Law and Politics* (Winter 1986): 71–102.

4752. Kreps, Juanita Morris. "Introduction." In *American Woman, 1987–88,* edited by Sara E. Rix and Anne J. Stone, 24–32. New York: Norton, 1987.

4753. "Legislation for Women … Then and Now." *Independent Woman* 23 (July 1944): 212–213, 229.

4754. Rix, Sara E., ed. *The American Woman 1987–88: A Report in Depth.* New York: Norton, 1987.

4755. ——, ed. *The American Woman, 1990–91: A Status Report.* New York: Norton, 1990.

Issues

Affirmative Action

4756. Cohn, Bob, Bill Turgue, Martha Brant, and Leslie Kaufman-Rosen. "What About Women?" *Newsweek* 125, no. 13 (27 March 1995): 22–25.

4757. Gearhart, Dona. "Women Coal Miners, The Orchard Valley Mine, and the Efficacy of Affirmative Action." *Journal of the Western Slope* 7 (Spring 1992).

4758. Johnson, Roberta Ann. "Affirmative Action as a Woman's Issue." In *Women in Politics: Outsiders or Insiders? A Collection of Readings,* edited by Lois Lovelace Duke, 236–250. Englewood Cliffs, NJ: Prentice Hall, 1989.

4759. Leonard, Jonathan S. "Women and Affirmative Action." *Journal of Economic Perspectives* 31, no. 1 (1989): 61–75.

4760. Orlans, Harold, and June O'Neill. "Affirmative Action Revisited." *Annals of the American Academy of Political and Social Science* 523 (September 1992): 100–220.

4761. Slack, James D. "Affirmative Action and City Managers; Attitudes toward Recruitment of Women." *Public Administration Review* 47, no. 2 (1987): 199–206.

Aging

4762. Datan, Nancy. "The Lost Cause: The Aging Woman in American Feminism." In *Toward the Second Decade: The Impact of the Women's Movement on American Institutions,* edited by Renate Pore and Betty Justice, 119–125. Westport, CT: Greenwood Press, 1981.

4763. Gould, Ketayun. "A Minority-Feminist Perspective on Women and Aging." In *Women as They Age: Challenge, Opportunity and Triumph,* edited by J. Dianne Garner and Susan O. Mercer, 195–216. New York: Haworth Press, 1989.

4764. Hessel, Dieter. *Maggie Kuhn on Aging, a Dialogue.* Philadelphia: Westminster, 1977.

4765. Jackson, Jacquelyn J. "The Plight of Older Black Women in the United States." *The Black Scholar* 7, no. 7 (1976): 47–54.

4766. Jones, Ann. "Political Importance of the Older Women." In *No Longer Young: The Older Woman in America, Work Group Reports,* edited by Institute of Gerontology, 27–30. Ann Arbor: University of Michigan, 1974.

4767. Jorgensen, Lou Ann B. "Women and Aging: Perspectives on Public and Social Policy." In *Women as They Age: Challenge, Opportunity and Triumph,* edited by J. Dianne Garner and Susan O. Mercer, 291–316. New York: Haworth Press, 1989.

4768. Sommers, Tish. "A Free-Lance Agitator Confronts the Establishment." In *The New Old: Struggling for Decent Aging,* edited by Ronald Gross, Beatrice Gross, and Sylvia Sideman, 231–240. Garden City, NY: Anchor, 1978.

Citizenship

4769. Abbott, Grace. "After Suffrage—Citizenship." *The Survey* 44 (1 September 1920): 655–657.

4770. Belmont, Alva E. "Are Women Really Citizens?" *Good Housekeeping* 93 (September 1931): 99, 132, 135.

4771. Cable, John L. "The Citizenship of American Women Since 1830." *Atlantic Monthly* 145 (May 1930): 649–653.

4772. ———. "Woman's Victory for Full Citizenship." *Current History* 34 (June 1931): 395–397.

4773. "Equal Nationality Rights for Women." *The New Republic* 77 (27 December 1933): 179–180.

4774. Harrison, Gladys. "A Married Woman's Nationality." *The Woman's Journal* 15 (March 1930): 10–12, 39.

4775. Mettler, Suzanne. "Dual Citizenship: Gender, the State and the New Deal." Ph.D. dissertation, Cornell University, 1994.

4776. Sapiro, Virginia. "Women, Citizenship, and Nationality: Immigration and Naturalization Policies in the United States." *Politics and Society* 13, no. 1 (1984): 1–26.

4777. Wold, Emma. "Alien Women Vs. The Immigration Bureau." *The Survey* 59 (15 November 1927): 217–219.

Crime

4778. Kelley, Camille. "Have We Won Equal Rights in Crime? No." *Independent Woman* 14 (November 1933): 365, 384–386.

4779. Meikle, Theresa. "Have We Won Equal Rights in Crime? Yes." *Independent Woman* 14 (November 1933): 364, 381–382.

4780. Moulds, Elizabeth Fry. "Women's Crime, Women's Justice." In *Women, Power and Policy,* edited by Ellen Boneparth, 205–234. New York: Pergamon Press, 1982.

4781. Schweber-Koven, Claudine, and Clarice Feinman. "Criminal Justice Politics and Women: The Aftermath of Legally Mandated Change." *Women and Politics* 4 (Fall 1984): 1–133.

4782. Snider, Laureen. "The Potential of the Criminal Justice System to Promote Feminist Concerns." *Studies in Law, Politics and Society* 10 (1990): 143–172.

Economics and Budget

4783. Burke, Yvonne Braithwaite. "Economic Strength is What Counts." In *Women Organizing: An Anthology,* edited by Bernice Cummings and Victoria Schuck, 210–220. Metuchen, NJ: Scarecrow Press, 1979.

4784. Conway, M. Margaret. "Discrimination and the Law: The Equal Credit Opportunity Act." In *Race, Sex and Policy Problems,* edited by Marian

Lief Palley and Michael Preston, 75–85. Lexington, MA: D.C. Heath, 1979.

4785. Costain, Anne N. "Lobbying for Equal Credit." In *Women Organizing: An Anthology,* edited by Bernice Cummings and Victoria Schuck, 82–110. Metuchen, NJ: The Scarecrow Press, 1979.

4786. Elliot, Patricia. "Women: Their Changing Status and Income Tax Law." *The Woman CPA* (May 1972): 5–8.

4787. Froomkin, Daniel. "'Easy Vote' on Insurance Gender Gap Turns Out to Be a Tough Call." *National Journal* 15, no. 30 (23 July 1983): 1545–1549.

4788. Gelb, Joyce, and Marian Lief Palley. "Women and Interest Group Politics: A Case Study of the Equal Credit Opportunity Act." *American Politics Quarterly* 5, no. 4 (July 1977): 331–352.

4789. Hutchinson, Emilie J. "The Economic Problems of Women." *Annals of the American Academy of Political and Social Science* 143 (May 1929): 132–136.

4790. Kreps, Juanita Morris. *Women and the American Economy: A Look to the 1980s.* Englewood Cliffs, NJ: Prentice Hall, 1976.

4791. "Lady of the House Looks Into Taxes." *Business Week* (23 May 1964): 28–29.

4792. Merrill, Flora. "Mrs. Franklin D. Roosevelts' Opinion on What Tariff Bill Means in the Home." *Democratic Bulletin* 4, no. 10 (October 1929): 10–11, 31.

4793. Norton, Mary T. "Women and the Tariff." *Democratic Bulletin* 4, no. 9 (September 1929): 12–13, 38.

4794. Polikoff, Nancy D. "Legislative Solutions to Sex Discrimination in Credit." *Women's Rights Law Reporter* 2, no. 2 (December 1974): 26–33.

4795. Rix, Sara E. "The Reagan Years: Budgetary Backlash." In *Women, Power and Policy: Toward the Year 2000,* 2d ed., edited by Ellen Boneparth and Emily Stoper, 66–88. New York: Pergamon Press, 1989.

4796. Sassoon, Anne Showstack, ed. *Women and the State: The Shifting Boundaries of Public and Private.* Boston: Unwin Hyman, 1987.

4797. Tarr-Whelan, Linda. *The Women's Economic Justice Agenda: Ideas for the States.* Washington, DC: National Center for Policy Alternatives, 1994.

4798. Tarr-Whelan, Linda, and Lynne Crofton Isensee, eds. *The Women's Economic Justice Agenda.* Washington, DC: National Center for Policy Alternatives, 1987.

4799. Tobias, Sheila. "Towards a Feminist Analysis of Defense Spending." *Frontiers* 8, no. 2 (1985): 65–68.

4800. Weed, Helena H. "New Deal That Women Want." *Current History* 41 (November 1934): 179–183.

Education

4801. Arnot, Madeleine. *Race and Gender: Equal Opportunities Policies in Education.* New York: Pergamon Press, 1985.

4802. Carter, Patricia A. "'Completely Discouraged': Women Teachers' Resistance in the Bureau of Indian Affairs Schools, 1900–1910." *Frontiers* 15, no. 3 (1995): 53–86.

4803. Conway, M. Margaret. "Title IX and the Battle over Implementation." In *Women and Public Policy,* 26–30. Washington, DC: CQ Press, 1995.

4804. Costain, Anne N. "Eliminating Sex Discrimination in Education: Lobbying for Implementation of Title IX." *Policy Studies Journal* 7, no. 2 (Winter 1978): 189–195.

4805. Craig, Arlene Fong, Theresa Cusick, and Leslie R. Wolfe. "Toward Educational Equity: An Overview of the Law." In *Women and the Law,* 2d ed., edited by Carol Lefcourt. New York: Clark Boardman, 1987.

4806. Fishel, Andrew, and Janice Pottker, eds. *National Politics and Sex Discrimination in Education.* Lexington, MA: Lexington Books, 1977.

4807. Millsap, Mary Ann. "Sex Equity in Education." In *Women in Washington,* edited by Irene Tinker, 79–89. Beverly Hills, CA: Sage, 1983.

4808. Millsap, Mary Ann, and Holly Knox. "Sex Discrimination and Bureaucratic Politics: The U.S. Office of Education's Task Force on Women's Education." In *National Politics and Sex Discrimination in Education,* edited by Andrew Fishel and Janice Pottker, 49–66. Lexington, MA: D. C. Heath, 1977.

4809. Millsap, Mary Ann, and Leslie R. Wolfe. "A Feminist Perspective in Law and Practice: The Women's Educational Equity Act." In Vol. 8 of *Readings on Equal Education,* edited by Margarete Barnett and Charlene Harrington, 125–444. New York: AMS Press, 1985.

4810. Pinderhughes, Dianne M. "Black Women and National Educational Policy." *Journal of Negro Education* 51, no. 3 (1982): 301–308.

4811. Sandler, Bernice. "A Little Help from Our Government: WEAL and Contract Compliance." In *Academic Women on the Move,* edited by Alice Rossi and Anne Calderwood, 439–462. New York: Russell Sage Foundation, 1973.

4812. Scott, Ann London. "The Half-Eaten Apple: A Look at Sex Discrimination in the University." *Reporter* (14 May 1970): 1.

4813. Simmons, Judy. "She Helped to Pluck the E out of HEW." *Black Enterprise* 10: (February 1980): 75–76, 78.

4814. Verheyden-Hilliard, Mary Ellen. "Education, Girls, and Power." In *Toward the Second Decade: The Impact of the Women's Movement on American Institutions,* edited by Betty Justice and Renate Pore, 129–139. Westport, CT: Greenwood Press, 1981.

4815. Wirtenberg, Jeana. "A Case Study of Title IX Implementation: Some Unexpected Effects." Paper presented at the annual meeting of the American Political Science Association, Washington, DC, 1979.

Employment

General

4816. Blair, Emily Newell. "Woman's Hand in the New Deal." *Independent Woman* 14 (November 1933): 363, 390.

4817. Bose, Christine, and Glenna Spitze, eds. *Ingredients in Women's Employment Policy.* Albany: State University of New York Press, 1987.

4818. Freeman, Jo. "Full Employment: Toward Economic Equality for Women." In *Women in the Economy: Policies and Strategies for Change,* edited by Ann Beaudry and Kim Yonkers. Washington, DC: Institute for Policy Studies, 1978. Conference report, Cleveland, OH, May 12–13, 1978.

4819. "From the Women: What about Our Job Rights?" *U.S. News and World Report* 61 (14 July 1966): 61–62.

4820. Greenwald, Maurine Weiner. *Women, War and Work: The Impact of World War I on Women Workers in the United States.* Westport, CT: Greenwood Press, 1980.

4821. Harlan, Sharon L., and Ronnie J. Steinberg. *Job Training for Women: The Promise and Limits of Public Policies.* Philadelphia: Temple University Press, 1989.

4822. Hilton, Kathleen C. "'Both in the Field, Each with a Plow': Race and Gender in USDA Policy, 1907–1929." In *Hidden Histories of Women in the New South,* edited by Virginia Bernhard, Betty Brandon, Elizabeth Fox-Genovese, and Theda Perdue, 114–133. Columbia: University of Missouri Press, 1994.

4823. May, Martha. "The Historical Problem of the Family Wage: The Ford Motor Company and the Five Dollar Day." *Feminist Studies* 8, no. 2 (Summer 1982): 399–424. Reprinted in *Unequal Sisters: A Multicultural Reader in U.S. Women's History,* edited by Ellen DuBois and Vicki L. Ruiz. New York: Routledge, 1990.

4824. Morrison, Ann M., Randall P. White, and Ellen Van Velsor. *Breaking the Glass Ceiling.* 2d ed. Reading, MA: Addison-Wesley, 1992 (1989).

4825. Mussey, Henry Raymond. "Law and a Living for Women." *Survey Graphic* 61 (1 November 1928): 156–158, 194–195.

4826. Neuse, Steven M. "Sex Employment Patterns in State Government." *State Government* 52, no. 2 (Spring 1979): 52–57.

4827. Rhode, Deborah L. "Perspectives on Professional Women." *Stanford Law Review* 40 (1988): 1163.

4828. Simmons, Adele, Anne E. Freedman, Margaret Dunkle, and Francine Blau, eds. *Exploitation from 9 to 5: Report of the Twentieth Century Fund Task Force on Women and Employment.* Lexington, MA: Lexington Books, 1975.

4829. Steinberg, Ronnie J. *Equal Employment Policy for Women: Strategies for Implementation in the United States, Canada, and Western Europe.* Philadelphia: Temple University Press, 1980.

4830. Steinberg-Ratner, Ronnie. *Wages and Hours: Labor and Reform in Twentieth-Century America.* New

Brunswick, NJ: Rutgers University Press, 1982.

4831. Stoper, Emily. "Alternative Work Patterns and the Double Life." In *Women, Power and Policy: Toward the Year 2000,* 2d ed., edited by Ellen Boneparth and Emily Stoper, 93–112. New York: Pergamon Press, 1988.

4832. Taub, Nadine. "A Public Policy of Private Caring." *The Nation* 242, no. 21 (31 May 1986): 756–758.

4833. "What Uncle Sam Does Not Do for Women in Industry." *The New Republic* 7 (29 July 1916): 324–326.

4834. Woollacott, Angela, and Miriam Cooke. *Gendering War Talk.* Princeton, NJ: Princeton University, 1993.

4835. Zelman, Patricia G. *Women, Work and National Policy: The Kennedy-Johnson Years.* Ann Arbor, MI: UMI Research Press, 1980.

Comparable Worth

4836. Aaron, Henry, and Cameran M. Lougy. *The Comparable Worth Controversy.* Washington, DC: Brookings Institution, 1986.

4837. Acker, Joan. *Doing Comparable Worth: Gender, Class and Pay Equity.* Philadelphia: Temple University Press, 1989.

4838. Blum, Linda. *Between Feminism and Labor: The Significance of the Comparable Worth Movement.* Berkeley: University of California Press, 1991.

4839. California Commission on the Status of Women. *Pay Inequities for Women: Comparable Worth and Other So-*

lutions. Sacramento, CA: California Commission on the Status of Women, 1983.

4840. "Comparable Worth." *National Business Woman* 63, no. 1 (February–March 1982): 7–9.

4841. Evans, Sara M., and Barbara Evans. *Wage Justice: Comparable Worth and the Paradox of Technocratic Reform.* Chicago: University of Chicago Press, 1989.

4842. Evans, Sara M., and Barbara J. Nelson. "Comparable Worth: The Paradox of Technocratic Reform." *Feminist Studies* 15, no. 1 (Winter 1989): 171–190.

4843. Ferraro, Geraldine A. "Who Will Fight for the Worth of Women's Work?" *Vital Speeches* 49 (15 November 1982): 70–73.

4844. Flammang, Janet A. "Women Made a Difference: Comparable Worth in San Jose." In *The Women's Movements of the United States and Western Europe: Consciousness, Political Opportunity and Public Policy,* edited by Mary F. Katzenstein and Carol M. Mueller, 290–312. Philadelphia: Temple University Press, 1987.

4845. Flick, Rachel. "Undermining the Women's Movement—The Comparable Worth Debate: Can Equality Be Measured by Money." *Human Rights* 12, no. 2 (Fall 1984): 26–29, 51–53.

4846. Hutchison, Kay Bailey, and Barbara Mikulski. "With Liberty, Justice and IRA Equity for All." *Insight on the News* 11, no. 11 (13 March 1995): 35–36.

4847. Hunter, Frances. *Equal Pay for Comparable Worth: The Working Women's Issue of the Eighties.* New York: Praeger, 1986.

4848. Johansen, Elaine. *Comparable Worth: The Myth and the Movement.* Boulder, CO: Westview Press, 1986.

4849. Kahn, Wendy, and Joy Ann Grune. "Pay Equity: Beyond Equal Pay for Equal Work." In *Women, Power and Policy,* edited by Ellen Boneparth, 75–89. New York: Pergamon Press, 1982.

4850. Kelly, Rita Mae, and Jane H. Bayes. *Comparable Worth, Pay Equity, and Public Policy.* Westport, CT: Greenwood Press, 1988.

4851. King, Kathleen, and Anne F. Hoffman. "Comparable Worth: A Trade Union Issue." *Women's Rights Law Reporter* 8 (Winter 1984): 95–107.

4852. Lavin, Maud. "Waging War on Wages, Eleanor Holmes Norton." *New Woman* 25, no. 2 (1995): 126–129.

4853. Mann, Pamela. "Pay Equity in the Courts: Myth v. Reality." *Women's Rights Law Reporter* (Winter 1984): 7–16.

4854. Nelson, Barbara J., and Sara M. Evans. "Feminist, Union Leaders, and Democrats: The Passage of Comparable Worth Laws." In *Gender and Public Policy, Cases and Comments,* edited by Kenneth Winston and Mary Jo Bane, 199–207. Boulder, CO: Westview Press, 1993.

4855. Remick, Helen, ed. *Comparable Worth and Wage Discrimination: Technical Possibilities and Political Realities.* Philadelphia: Temple University Press, 1984.

4856. Schribner, Sylvia. "Interview: Comparable Worth in the Forties: Reflections by Sylvia Schribner." *Women's Rights Law Reporter* 8 (Winter 1984): 105–107.

4857. Spiegel, Fredelle Zaiman. *Women's Wages, Women's Worth: Politics, Religion, and Equity.* New York: Continuum, 1994.

4858. Steinberg-Ratner, Ronnie. *The Politics and Practice of Pay Equity.* Philadelphia: Temple University Press, 1996.

4859. Vladek, Judith. "Women in the Workplace: Comparable Worth." *Fordham Law Review* 52 (1984): 1110–1119.

Equal Pay

4860. Blumrosen, Ruth. "Update: Wage Discrimination Revisited." *Women's Rights Law Reporter* (Winter 1984): 109–131.

4861. Buck, Dorothy Pifer. "Colorado's Women Go After Equal Pay." *Independent Woman* 33 (September 1954): 330–332, 357.

4862. ———. "How Colorado Won Equal Pay." *Independent Woman* 34 (June 1955): 3–5, 35.

4863. Chateauvetrte, Melinda, Winn Newman, and Chris Owens. "Pay Equity." In *The Women's Economic Justice Agenda,* edited by Linda Tarr-Whelan and Lynne Crofton Isensee, 141–146. Washington, DC: National Center for Policy Alternatives, 1987.

4864. Doherty, Robert. "Tempest on the Hudson: The Struggle for Equal Pay for Equal Work in the New York City Public Schools, 1907–1911." *Harvard Educational Quarterly* 19 (Winter 1979): 413–439.

4865. "The Governors View Equal Pay." *National Business Woman* 36 (July 1957): 18–19.

4866. Lander, Byron G. "The Making of Missouri's Equal Pay Law and the Legislative Process." *Missouri Historical Review* 77, no. 3 (April 1983): 310–327.

4867. Simchak, Morag MacLeod. "Equal Pay in the United States." *International Labor Review* 103, no. 6 (June 1971): 541–557.

4868. Tanabe, Patricia White. "Views of Women's Work in Public Policy in the U.S: Social Security and Equal Pay Legislatiom, 1935–1967." Ph.D. dissertation, Bryn Mawr, 1973.

4869. Vertz, Laura L. "Pay Inequalities between Women and Men in State and Local Government." *Women and Politics* 7 (Summer 1987): 43–57.

4870. Vladek, Judith. "The Equal Pay Act of 1963." In *Proceedings of the 18th New York University Conference on Labor,* 381–399. Albany, NY: Bender, 1966.

Married Women and Mothers

4871. Boris, Eileen. "Mothers Are Not Workers: Homework Regulation and the Construction of Motherhood, 1948–1953." In *Contested Terrains: Constructions of Mothering,* edited by Evelyn Nakano Gloenn, Grace Chang, and Linda Rennie Forcey, 161–180. New York: Routledge, 1993.

4872. ———. *Home to Work: Motherhood and the Politics of Industrial Homework in the US.* New York: Cambridge University Press, 1994.

4873. Conner, Valerie J. "'The Mothers of the Race' in World War I: The National War Labor Board and Women in Industry." *Labor History* 21, no. 1 (1980): 31–54.

4874. Crosby, Faye J. *Juggling: The Unexpected Advantage of Balancing Career and Home for Women and Their Families.* New York: Free Press, 1991.

4875. Daniels, Cynthia R. "There's No Place Like Home: The Politics of Home-Based Work." *Dollars and Sense* (December 1986): 16–18.

4876. Ehrenreich, Barbara, and Deirdre English. "Blowing the Whistle on the 'Mommy Track'." *Ms.* 18, no. 1–2 (July–August 1989): 56–58.

4877. Ehrlich, Elizabeth. "The Mommy Track." *Business Week* (20 March 1989): 126–134.

4878. Frug, Mary Jo. "Securing Job Equality for Women: Labor Market Hostility to Working Mothers." *Boston University Law Review* 59 (1979): 55.

4879. Giraldo, Zaida Irene. *Public Policy and the Family: Wives and Mothers in the Work Force.* Lexington, MA: Lexington Books, 1980.

4880. Greenwald, Maurine Weiner. "Working-Class Feminism and the Family Wage Ideal: The Seattle Debate on Married Women's Right to

Work, 1914–1920." *Journal of American History* 76 (June 1989): 118–149.

4881. Harris, Diane. "Maternity Leave Yours, Maternity Leave Hers." *Working Woman* 16 (August 1991): 56–59.

4882. Huckle, Patricia. "The Womb Factor: Policy on Pregnancy and the Employment of Women." In *Women, Power and Policy: Toward the Year 2000,* 2d ed., edited by Ellen Boneparth and Emily Stoper, 131–148. New York: Pergamon Press, 1988.

4883. Kirschten, Dick. "Earning Bread at Home: The Labor Department's Move to Lift Bans on Working at Home Arouses Some Modern Worries." *National Journal* 21 (11 February 1989): 332–336.

4884. Lawson, Annette, and Deborah L. Rhode, eds. *The Politics of Pregnancy.* New Haven, CT: Yale University Press, 1993.

4885. Pedersen, Sharon. "Married Women and the Right to Teach in St. Louis, 1941–1948." *Missouri Historical Review* 81, no. 2 (January 1987): 141–158.

4886. Radigan, Anne L. *Concept and Compromise: The Evolution of Family Leave Legislation in the U.S. Congress.* Washington, DC: Women's Research and Educational Institute, 1988.

4887. Scharf, Lois. *To Work and to Wed: Female Employment, Feminism and the Great Depression.* Westport, CT: Greenwood Press, 1980.

4888. Schroeder, Patricia. "Parental Leave." In *Gender and Public Policy, Cases and Comments,* edited by Kenneth Winston and Mary Jo Bane,

228–246. Boulder, CO: Westview Press, 1993.

4889. Shallcross, Ruth. *Should Married Women Work?* New York: Public Affairs Committee, 1940.

4890. Siegel, Revar. "Employment Equality under the Pregnancy Discrimination Act of 1978." *Yale Law Journal* 94, no. 4 (March 1985): 929–956.

4891. Smith, Mary Phlegar. "Legal and Administrative Restrictions Affecting the Rights of Married Women to Work." *Annals of the American Academy of Political and Social Science* 143 (November 1929): 255–264.

4892. Taub, Nadine. "From Parental Leaves to Nurturing Leaves." *New York University Review of Law and Social Change* 13 (1984–85): 381.

4893. Thompson, Joan Hulse. "The Family and Medical Leave Act: A Policy for Families." In *Women in Politics: Outsiders Or Insiders? A Collection of Readings,* edited by Lois Lovelace Duke, 212–226. Englewood Cliffs, NJ: Prentice Hall, 1993.

4894. Williams, Wendy W. "Equality's Riddle: Pregnancy and the Equal Treatment–Special Treatment Debate." *New York University Review of Law and Social Change* 13 (1984–5): 325.

Minimum Wage

4895. Cohen, Harry. "Minimum Wage Legislation and the Adkins Case." *New York University Law Review* 2 (1925): 48.

4896. "The Cost of a $4.95 'Bargain'." *Literary Digest* 115 (18 February 1933): 20.

4897. Morris, Victor P. *Oregons' Experience with Minimum Wage Legislation.* New York: Columbia University Press, 1930.

4898. National Consumers' League. *The Supreme Court and Minimum Wage Legislation.* New York: New Republic, 1925.

4899. Tripp, Joseph F. "Toward an Efficient and Moral Society: Washington State Minimum-Wage Law, 1913–1925." *Pacific Northwest Quarterly* 67 (July 1976): 97–112.

4900. Zimmerman, Joan G. "The Jurisprudence of Equality: The Women's Minimum Wage, the First Equal Rights Amendment and *Adkins v. Children's Hospital,* 1905–1923." *Journal of American History* 78, no. 1 (1991): 188–225.

Protective Legislation

4901. Baer, Judith A. *The Chains of Protection: The Judicial Response to Women's Labor Legislation.* Westport, CT: Greenwood Press, 1978.

4902. Baker, Elizabeth F.. *Protective Labor Legislation.* New York: Columbia University Press, 1925.

4903. ———. "At the Crossroads in the Legal Protection of Women in Industry." *Annals of the American Academy of Political and Social Science* 143 (May 1929): 265–279.

4904. Breen, Nancy J. "Shedding Light on Women's Consequences of Protective Legislation." Ph.D. disser-tation, New School for Social Research, 1989.

4905. Erickson, Nancy S. "Historical Background of 'Protective' Labor Legislation: *Muller v. Oregon.*" In Vol. 2 of *Women and the Law: The Social Historical Perspective,* edited by D. Kelly Weisberg, 155–186. Chicago: Schenkman, 1982.

4906. ———. "*Muller V. Oregon* Reconsidered: The Origins of a Sex-Based Doctrine of Liberty of Contract." *Labor History* 30 (Spring 1989): 228–520.

4907. Esbeck, Carl H. "Employment Practices and Sex Discrimination: Judicial Extension of Beneficial Female Protective Labor Laws." *Cornell University Law Review* 59 (1973): 133.

4908. Goldmark, Josephine C. "Working Women and the Laws: A Record of Neglect." *Annals of the American Academy of Political and Social Science* 28 (September 1906): 261–276.

4909. Hill, Ann Corrine. "Protection of Women Workers and the Courts: A Legal Case History." *Feminist Studies* 5 (Summer 1979): 247–273.

4910. Matthews, Burnita Shelton. "Phases of Restrictive Labor Legislation for Women." *Equal Rights* (1 May 1926): 93.

4911. Muncy, Robyn. "The State and the Woman Worker: Struggles over Protective Legislation." Paper presented at the Ninth Berkshire Conference on the History of Women, Vassar College, June 1993.

4912. Perkins, Frances, and Elizabeth F. Baker. "Do Women in Industry Need Special Protection?" *The Survey* 55 (15 February 1926): 529–532.

4913. Steinberg, Ronnie J. "The Paradox of Protection: Maximum Hours Legislation in the United States." *International Labor Review* 119, no. 2 (March–April 1980): 185–198.

4914. Winslow, Mary N. "The Effects of Labor Legislation on Women's Work." *Annals of the American Academy of Political and Social Science* 143 (May 1929): 280–285.

4915. Wright, Michael J. "Reproductive Hazards and 'Protective' Discrimination." *Feminist Studies* 5, no. 2 (Summer 1979): 302–309.

4916. Younger, Maud. "NRA and Protective Laws for Women." *Literary Digest* 117 (2 June 1934): 27.

Title VII

4917. Brauer, Carl M. "Women Activists, Southern Conservatives, and the Prohibition of Sex Discrimination in Title VII of the 1964 Civil Rights Act." *Journal of Southern History* 49 (February 1983): 37–57.

4918. Cooper, Sandi E. "Women's History Goes to Trial: *EEOC v. Sears, Roebuck and Company.*" In *Gender and Public Policy, Cases and Comments,* edited by Kenneth Winston and Mary Jo Bane, 173–198. Boulder, CO: Westview Press, 1993.

4919. Deitch, Cynthia. "Gender, Race and Class Politics and the Inclusion of Women in Title VII of the 1964 Civil Rights Act." *Gender and Society* 7, no. 2 (June 1993): 183–203.

4920. Freeman, Jo. "How Sex Got into Title VII: Persistent Opportunism as a Maker of Public Policy." *Law and Inequality: A Journal of Theory and Practice* (March 1991): 163–184.

4921. Hardy, Richard J., and Donald J. McCrone. "The Impact of the Civil Rights Act of 1964 on Women." *Policy Studies Journal* 7, no. 2 (Winter 1978): 241–243.

4922. Murray, Pauli, and Mary O. Eastwood. "Jane Crow and the Law: Sex Discrimination and Title VII." *George Washington Law Review* 34 (December 1965): 232–256.

4923. Robinson, Donald Allen. "Two Movements in Pursuit of Equal Employment Opportunity." *Signs* 4 (Spring 1979): 413–433.

4924. Winston, Judith A. "Mirror, Mirror on the Wall; Title VII, Section 1981, and the Intersection of Race and Gender in the Civil Rights Act of 1990." *California Law Review* 79 (1991): 775–805.

Equal Opportunity

4925. Burstein, Paul. *Discrimination, Jobs, and Politics: The Struggle for Equal Employment Opportunity in the United States since the New Deal.* Chicago: University of Chicago Press, 1985.

4926. "Compromise Civil Rights Bill Passed." In *Congressional Quarterly Almanac,* 1992 ed., 251–261. Washington, DC: Congressional Quarterly, 1991.

4927. Haskell, Thomas, and Sanford Levinson. "Academic Freedom and Expert Witnessing: Historians and the Sears Case." *Texas Law Review* 66 (June 1988): 1629–1659.

4928. Henderson, Lenneal J. "The Impact of the Equal Employment Opportunity Act of 1972 on Employment Opportunities for Women and Minorities in Municipal Government." *Policy Studies Journal* 7, no. 2 (Winter 1978): 235–239.

4929. Hernandez, Aileen C. "E.E.O.C. and the Women's Movement 1965–1975." Paper presented at the Symposium on the Tenth Anniversary of the Equal Employment Opportunity Commission, Rutgers University Law School, November 1975.

4930. Kessler-Harris, Alice. "*Equal Employment Opportunity Commission v. Sears, Roebuck and Company,* A Personal Account." In *Unequal Sisters: A Multicultural Reader in U.S. Women's History,* edited by Ellen DuBois and Vicki L. Ruiz, 432–446. New York: Routledge, 1990.

4931. Martin, William. "Equal Employment Opportunities and Government Contracting: Three Theories for Obtaining Judicial Review of Executive Order 11246 Determinations." *Wisconsin Law Review* 197, no. 1 (1972): 133–152.

4932. Milkman, Ruth. "Women's History and the Sears Case." *Feminist Studies* 12, no. 2 (Summer 1986): 375–400.

4933. ———. *Gender at Work: The Dynamics of Job Segregation by Sex during World War II.* Urbana: University of Illinois Press, 1987.

4934. Steinberg-Ratner, Ronnie. "The Unsubtle Revolution: Women, the State and Equal Employment." In *The Feminization of the Labor Force,* edited by Jane Jansen et al., 189–213. New York: Oxford University Press, 1988.

4935. Zelman, Patricia G. "Development of Equal Employment Opportunity for Women as a National Policy, 1960–1967." Ph.D. dissertation, Ohio State University, 1980.

Equal Rights

General

4936. Boyd, Mary Sumner. "Wanted: Equality." *Good Housekeeping* 72, no. 3 (March 1921): 18–19, 147.

4937. Bruton, Margaret Perry. "Present-Day Thinking on the Woman Question: Equal Rights Amendment and Alternative Resolution." *Annals of the American Academy of Political and Social Science* 251 (May 1947): 10–13.

4938. Costain, Anne N., and Steven Majstorovic. "Congress, Social Movements and Public Opinion: Multiple Origins of Women's Rights Legislation." *Political Research Quarterly* 47 (March 1994): 111–135.

4939. DeHart, Jane Sherron. "Equality Challenged: Equal Rights and Sexual Difference." *Journal of Policy History* 6 (1994): 40–72.

4940. Freeman, Jo. "The Political Impact of the ERA." In *Impact ERA: Limitations and Possibilities,* edited by California Commission on the State of Women, 58–70. Millbrae, CA: Les

Femmes Publishing, 1976. Equal Rights Amendment Project.

4941. Griffiths, Martha W. "The Law Must Reflect the New Image of Women." *Hastings Law Journal* 23 (November 1971): 1–14.

4942. League of Women Voters. *A Survey of the Legal Status of Women in the Forty–Eight States.* Washington, DC: National League of Women Voters, 1924.

4943. Matthews, Burnita Shelton. "Report of Legislative Work from 1921 to 1929." *Equal Rights* (4 January 1930): 379–381.

4944. Smith, Ethel M. *Toward Equal Rights for Men and Women.* Washington, DC: Committee on the Legal Status of Women, National League of Women Voters, 1929.

4945. Swain, Martha H. "Organized Women in Mississippi: The Clash over Legal Disabilities in the 1920s." *Southern Studies* 23, no. 1 (Spring 1984): 91–102.

4946. Warrington, Carina C. *What Has Been Done to Remove Legal Discrimination.* New York: League of Women Voters, 1922. *Pamphlets in American History,* Microfilm No. W061.

4947. Wold, Emma. "Equal Rights in the Legislatures of 1925." *Equal Rights* (24 October 1925): 295.

4948. Women's Research Center for Boston. *Who Rules Massachusetts Women.* Boston: Women's Research Center for Boston, 1972.

State ERA

4949. Altschuler, Bruce E. "State ERAs: What Have They Done?" *State Government* 56, no. 4 (1983): 134–137.

4950. Bensen, Clark H., and Frank M. Bryan. "Strengthening Democratic Control: Vermont's 1986 Election in Historical Perspective." *Vermont History* 56, no. 4 (1988): 213–229.

4951. Gale, Zona. "What Women Won in Wisconsin." *The Nation* 115 (23 August 1922): 184–185.

4952. Kanowitz, Leo. "The New Mexico Equal Rights Amendment: Introduction and Overview." *New Mexico Law Review* 3, no. 1 (January 1973): 1–10.

4953. Putnam, Mabel Raef. *The Winning of the First Bill of Rights for American Women.* Milwaukee: Frank Putnam, 1924.

4954. Rivera, S. Patricia. "Suffrage for Military Wives: North Carolina Woman Challenges Archaic Rule." *Ms.* 9, no. 1 (July 1980): 25.

4955. Sanders, Marion K. "Requiem for ERA: Defeat in New York and New Jersey." *The New Republic* 173 (29 November 1975): 20–21.

4956. Search, Mabel. "Women's Rights in Wisconsin." *Marquette Law Review* 6 (1922): 164–169.

Family

General

4957. Berry, Mary Frances. *The Politics of Parenthood: Child Care, Women's*

Rights, and the Myth of the Good Mother. New York: Viking, 1993.

4958. Boris, Eileen. "The Power of Motherhood: Black and White Activist Women Redefine the 'Political'." *Yale Journal of Law and Feminism* 2 (Fall 1989): 25–49.

4959. Diamond, Irene, and Mary Lyndon Shanley, eds. *Families, Politics and Public Policy.* New York: Longman, 1983.

4960. Eisenstein, Zillah. "State, Patriarchal Family and Working Mothers." In *Families, Politics and Public Policy,* edited by Irene Diamond, 41–58. New York: Longman, 1983.

4961. Geiger, Shirley M. "African-American Single Mothers: Public Perceptions and Public Policies." In Vol. 2 of *Black Women in America,* edited by Kim Marie Vaz, 244–260. Thousand Oaks, CA: Sage, 1995.

4962. Mondale, Walter F. "Government Policy, Stress, and the Family." *Journal of Home Economics* 68, no. 5 (November 1976): 11–15.

4963. Okin, Susan Moller. *Justice, Gender and the Family.* New York: Basic Books, 1989.

4964. Schroeder, Patricia. "Toward a National Family Policy." *American Psychologist* 44, no. 11 (November 1989): 1410–1413.

4965. Steiner, Gilbert Y. *The Futility of Family Policy.* Washington, DC: Brookings Institution, 1981.

Law

4966. Burt, Robert A. "The Constitution of the Family." *Supreme Court Review* (1979): 329–395.

4967. Freed, Doris Jonas, and Timothy B. Walker. "Family Law in the Fifty States: An Overview." *Family Law Quarterly* 18 (1985): 369–471; 22 (1989): 367–525; 24 (1991): 309–405.

4968. Kanowitz, Leo. "Sex-Based Discrimination in American Law I: Law and the Married Woman." *St. Louis University Law Journal* 11 (1967): 293.

4969. Kay, Herma Hill. "Equality and Difference: The Case of Pregnancy." *Berkeley Women's Law Journal* 1 (1986): 34.

4970. Mason, Mary Ann. "Motherhood v. Equal Treatment." *Journal of Family Law* 29, no. 1 (1990–91): 1–50.

4971. Olsen, Frances. "The Family and the Market: A Study of Ideology and Legal Reform." *Harvard Law Review* 96 (1983): 1497.

4972. ———. "The Politics of Family Law." *Law and Inequality: A Journal of Theory and Practice* (February 1984): 1–20.

4973. Redden, Kenneth R. *Federal Regulation of the Family.* Charlottesville, VA: Michie Co., 1982.

4974. Welch, Susan, Sue Thomas, and Margery M. Ambrosius. "Politics of Family Policy." In *Politics in the American States,* 6th ed., edited by Virginia Gray and Herbert Jacob, 549–587. Washington, DC: CQ Press, 1995.

Marriage and Divorce

4975. Bouton, Katherine. "Women and Divorce: How the New Law Works against Them." *The New York Magazine* 17 (8 October 1984): 34–41.

4976. Fineman, Martha L. "Implementing Equality: Ideology, Contradiction and Social Change: A Study of Rhetoric and Results in the Regulation of the Consequences of Divorce." *Wisconsin Law Review* (1983): 789.

4977. ———. *The Illusion of Equality: The Rhetoric and Reality of Divorce Reform.* Chicago: University of Chicago Press, 1991.

4978. Freed, Doris Jonas, and Henry H. Foster, Jr. "Divorce in the Fifty States: An Overview." *Family Law Quarterly* 14 (Winter 1985): 229–283.

4979. Glendon, Mary Ann. "Modern Marriage Law and Its Underlying Assumption: The New Marriage and the New Property." *Family Law Quarterly* (Winter 1980): 441–460.

4980. Jacob, Herbert. "Women and Divorce Reform." In *Women, Politics and Change,* edited by Louise A. Tilly and Patricia Gurin, 482–502. New York: Russell Sage, 1990.

4981. Kay, Herma Hill. "Equality and Difference: A Perspective on No-Faulty Divorce and Its Aftermath." *University of Cinncinnati Law Review* 56 (1987): 1–90.

4982. Krom, Howard A. "California's Divorce Law Reform: An Historical Analysis." *Pacific Law Journal* 1 (1970): 156–181.

4983. Molinoff, Daniel D. "Men's Rights Groups Fight to Change Divorce Laws." *Parade Magazine* (3 April 1977): 14.

4984. O'Neill, William L. "Divorce in the Progressive Era." *American Quarterly* 17, no. 1 (Summer 1965): 203–217.

4985. Stoper, Emily, and Ellen Boneparth. "Divorce and the Transition to the Single-Parent Family." In *Women, Power and Policy: Toward the Year 2000,* 2d ed., edited by Ellen Boneparth and Emily Stoper, 206–220. New York: Pergamon Press, 1988.

4986. Weitzman, Lenore J. "Legal Regulation of Marriage: Tradition and Change." *California Law Review* 62 (July–September 1974): 1169.

4987. ———. *The Divorce Revolution: The Unexpected Social and Economic Consequences for Women and Children in America.* New York: Free Press, 1985.

4988. ———. "Judicial Perceptions and Perceptions of Judges: The Divorce Law Revolution in Practice." In *Women, the Courts and Equality,* edited by Laura L. Crites and Winifred L. Hepperle, 74–113. Beverly Hills, CA: Sage, 1987.

4989. Weitzman, Lenore J., and Ruth B. Dixon. "The Alimony Myth: Does No-Fault Divorce Make a Difference?" *Family Law Quarterly* 14 (Fall 1980): 141–185.

Child Care

4990. Boles, Janet K. "The Politics of Child Care." *Social Service Review* 54, no. 3 (1980): 344–362.

4991. Dratch, Howard. "The Politics of Childcare in the 1940's." *Science and Society* 38 (Summer 1974): 167–204.

4992. Edelman, Marian Wright. "A Child Care Agenda for the 1990's." *Focus* 16, no. 11–12 (November–December 1988): 4–5.

4993. Ellis, Katherine. "The Politics of Day Care." In *Female Liberation,* edited by Roberta Salper, 219–227. New York: Knopf, 1972.

4994. Ellis, Katherine, and Rosalind Pollack Petchesky. "Children of the Corporate Dream: An Analysis of Day Care as a Political Issue under Capitalism." *Socialist Revolution* 2 (November–December 1972): 8–28.

4995. Lang, Frances. "Women in Congress, Legislative Proposals and Public Policy." *Ramparts Magazine* 9 (May 1971): 10, 12.

4996. Nelson, Margaret K. "A Critical Analysis of the Act for Better Child Care Services." *Women and Politics* 12, no. 3 (Fall 1992): 1–26.

4997. Norgren, Jill. "Child Care." In *Women: A Feminist Perspective,* 4th ed., edited by Jo Freeman, 176–194. Mountain View, CA: Mayfield, 1989.

4998. ———. "In Search of a National Child-Care Policy." In *Women, Power and Policy: Toward the Year 2000,* 2d ed., edited by Ellen Boneparth and Emily Stoper, 124–142. New York: Pergamon, 1989.

4999. Roth, William. "The Politics of Daycare." *Society* 19, no. 2 (1982): 62–69.

5000. Schroeder, Patricia, and Nancy D. Reder. "Ensuring Quality, Affordable Child Care: Mobilizing for Action." *Pediatrics* 91, no. 1 (January 1993): 244–247.

Child Custody

5001. Arendell, Terry. *Mothers and Divorce.* Berkeley: University of California Press, 1986.

5002. Chesler, Phyllis. *Mothers on Trial: The Battle for Children and Custody.* New York: McGraw-Hill, 1986.

5003. Costin, Lela B. "Women and Physicians—The 1930 White House Conference on Children." *Social Work* 28 (April–May 1983): 38–51.

5004. Folberg, Jay. "Joint Custody Law—The Second Wave." *Journal of Family Law* 23 (1984–85): 1–55.

5005. Garfinkel, Irwin, and Sara S. McLanahan, eds. *Single Mothers and Their Children.* Washington, DC: Urban Institute Press, 1986.

5006. Gibson, John D. "Childbearing and Childrearing: Feminists and Reform." *Virginia Law Review* 73, no. 6 (September 1987): 1145–1182.

5007. Hunter, Nan D. "Child Support Law and Policy: The Systematic Imposition of Costs on Women." *Harvard Women's Law Journal* 6 (Spring 1983): 1–27.

5008. Lemon, Nancy K. "Joint Custody as a Statutory Presumption: California's New Civil Codes 4600 and 4600.5." *Golden Gate University Law Review* 11 (Spring 1981).

5009. Polikoff, Nancy D. "Why Are Mothers Losing: A Brief Analysis of Criteria Used in Child Custody Determinations." *Women's Rights Law Reporter* 7 (Spring 1982): 235–244.

5010. Robinson, Holly. "Joint Custody: Constitutional Imperatives." *University of Cincinnati Law Review* 21 (August 1983): 641–685.

5011. Roth, Allen. "The Tender Years Presumption in Child Custody Disputes." *Journal of Family Law* 15 (April 1977): 423–462.

5012. Schulman, Joanne, and Valerie Pitt. "Second Thoughts on Joint Child Custody: Analysis of Legislation and Its Implications for Women and Children." *Golden Gate University Law Review* 12 (Summer 1982): 538–577.

5013. Smart, Carol, and Selma Sevenhuijsen, eds. *Child Custody and the Politics of Gender.* London: Routledge, 1989.

5014. Uviller, Rena K. "Fathers' Rights and Feminism: The Maternal Presumption Revisited." *Harvard Women's Law Journal* 1, no. 1 (Spring 1978): 107–130.

5015. Williams, Gwyneth I. "The Politics of Joint Custody." Ph.D. dissertation, Princeton University, Princeton, 1989

Foreign Policy

5016. Crapol, Edward P., ed. *Women and American Foreign Policy: Lobbyists, Critics, and Insiders.* Wilmington, DE: SR Books, 1992.

5017. Howes, Ruth, and Michael Stevenson. *Women and the Use of Military Force.* Boulder, CO: Lynne Rienner, 1993.

5018. Jeffreys-Jones, Rhodri. *Changing Differences: Women and the Shaping of American Foreign Policy, 1917–1994.* New Brunswick, NJ: Rutgers University, 1995.

5019. Marshall, George. "Secretary of State Marshall to Women of America." *Woman's Home Companion* 74 (November 1947): 36.

5020. Papachristou, Judith. "American Women and Foreign Policy, 1898–1905: Exploring Gender in Diplomatic History." *Diplomatic History* 14 (Fall 1990): 493–509.

5021. Roosevelt, Mrs. Franklin D. "Women in World Affairs." *Independent Woman* 27 (July 1948): 198.

5022. Sealander, Judith. "In the Shadow of Good Neighbor Diplomacy: The Women's Bureau and Latin America." *Prologue* 11, no. 4 (1979): 236–250.

5023. Staudt, Kathleen A. "Bureaucratic Resistance to Women's Programs: The Case of Women in Development." In *Women, Power and Policy,* edited by Ellen Boneparth, 263–295. New York: Pergamon Press, 1982.

5024. Wilcox, Clyde, David Fite, and Marc Genest. "Gender Differences in Foreign Policy Attitudes: A Longitudinal Analysis." *American Politics Quarterly* 18 (1990): 492–512.

Health

5025. Belle, Dolores. "Poverty and Women's Health." *American Psychologist* 45, no. 3 (1990): 385–389.

5026. Chaney, Betty Norwood. "Black Women's Health Conference." *Southern Changes* 5, no. 5 (1983): 18–20.

5027. Clift, Eleanor. "Goodbye to White Male Privilege: Women Challenge Health Care Research." *On the Issues* (Winter 1991): 7–9.

5028. Conway, M. Margaret. "Contemporary Women's Health Issues and the Policy-making Process." In *Women and Public Policy,* 43–55. Washington, DC: CQ Press, 1995.

5029. Dreifus, Claudia, ed. *Seizing Our Bodies: The Politics of Women's Health.* New York: Vintage, 1977.

5030. Fee, Elizabeth, and Nancy Krieger, eds. *Women's Health, Politics, and Power: Essays on Sex, Gender, Medicine, and Public Health.* Amityville, NY: Baywood, 1994.

5031. Ickovics, Jeanette Rose, and E. Epel. "Women's Health Research Policy and Practice." *IRB, A Review of Human Subjects Research* 15, no. 4 (1993): 1–7.

5032. Kiely, Kathy. "The Coming Fight Over Women's Health in the Proposed National Health Plan." *Working Woman* 18 (December 1993): 13.

5033. Moses-Zinkes. "In Health Reform, Promotion of Women's Health Needs Is Critical." *APA Monitor* 24, no. 9 (September 1933): 33.

5034. Randall, Donna M. "Women in Toxic Work Environments: A Case Study and Examination of Policy Impact." In *Women and Work,* 259–281. New York: Sage, 1985.

5035. Ratcliff, Kathryn Strother, ed. *Healing Technology: Feminist Perspectives.* Ann Arbor: University of Michigan Press, 1989.

5036. Rochman, Susan. "Breast Cancer Politics." *Progressive* 55 (November 1991): 12.

5037. Tahul, Susan, and Dana Hotra. *An Assessment of the NIH Women's Health Initiative.* Washington, DC: Institute of Medicine, 1993.

5038. Walker, Lenore E., ed. *Women and Mental Health Policy.* Beverly Hills, CA: Sage, 1985.

5039. Weissman, Gloria. "Women and AIDS." In *The American Woman 1987–88: A Status Report,* edited by Sara E. Rix and Anne J. Stone, 286–291. New York: Norton, 1987.

5040. Williams, Louise A. "Toxic Exposure in the Workplace: Balancing Job Opportunity with Reproductive Health." In *Women, Power and Policy: Toward the Year 2000,* 2d ed., edited by Ellen Boneparth and Emily Stoper, 113–132. New York: Pergamon Press, 1988.

Law

5041. Alumbaugh, Steve, and C. K. Rowland. "The Links between Platform-Based Appointment Criteria and Trial Judges' Abortion Judgments." *Judicature* 74, no. 3 (October–November 1990): 153–162.

5042. Baer, Judith A. *Women in American Law: The Struggle toward Equality from the New Deal to the Present.* New York: Holmes and Meier, 1991.

5043. Berger, Caruthers Gholson. "Equal Pay, Equal Employment Opportunity and Equal Enforcement of the Law for Women." *Valparaiso Law Review* 5, no. 2 (Spring 1971): 326–373.

5044. Brown, Jennifer K. "The 19th Amendment and Women's Equality." *Yale Law Journal* 102, no. 8 (June 1993): 2175–2204.

5045. Cook, Beverly Blair. "Sex Roles and the Burger Court." *American Politics Quarterly* 5, no. 3 (July 1977): 353–394.

5046. ———. "The Burger Court and Women's Rights 1971–1977." In *Women in the Courts,* edited by Winifred L. Hepperle and Laura Crites, 47–83. Williamsburg, VA: National Center for State Courts, 1978.

5047. Crozier, Blanche. "Constitutionality of Discrimination Based on Sex." *Boston University Law Review* 15 (1935): 723–755.

5048. Daly, Kathleen. "Discrimination in the Federal Courts: Family, Gender, and the Problems of Equal Treatment." *Social Forces* 66, no. 1 (1987): 152–175.

5049. DeCrow, Karen. *Sexist Justice.* New York: Random House, 1974.

5050. Eastwood, Mary O. "Feminism and the Law." In *Women: A Feminist Perspective,* 2d ed., edited by Jo Freeman, 385–404. Palo Alto, CA: Mayfield, 1979 (1975).

5051. Ellis, Mary Carolyn. "The Decline and Near Fall of Statutory Sexism in Mississippi." *Mississippi Law Journal* 51 (June–September 1980): 191–234.

5052. Erickson, Nancy S. "Women and the Supreme Court: Anatomy Is Destiny." *Brooklyn Law Review* 41 (Fall 1974): 209–282.

5053. Freedman, Anne E. "Sex Equality, Sex Differences, and the Supreme Court." *Yale Law Journal* (May 1983): 913–968.

5054. Freeman, Jo. "The Legal Revolution." In *Women: A Feminist Perspective,* 4th ed., edited by Jo Freeman, 371–394. Mountain View, CA: Mayfield, 1989. Reprinted in *Views of Women's Lives in Western Tradition,* edited by Frances Richardson Keller, 635–679. Lewiston, NY: Edwin Mellen Press, 1990.

5055. ———. "From Protection to Equal Opportunity: The Revolution in Women's Legal Status." In *Women, Politics and Change,* edited by Louise A. Tilly and Patricia Gurin, 457–481. New York: Russell Sage, 1990.

5056. ———. "The Revolution for Women in Law and Public Policy." In *Women: A Feminist Perspective,* 5th ed., edited by Jo Freeman, 365–404. Mountain View, CA: Mayfield, 1995.

5057. Ginsburg, Ruth Bader. "Women, Men, and the Constitution: Key Supreme Court Rulings." In

Women in the Courts, edited by Winifred L. Hepperle and Laura Crites, 21–46. Williamsburg, VA: National Center for State Courts, 1978.

5058. ———. "The Burger Court's Grapplings with Sex Discrimination." In *The Burger Court: The Counter-Revolution That Wasn't,* edited by V. Blasi, 132–156. New Haven, CT: Yale University Press, 1983.

5059. Goldstein, Leslie F. "The Politics of the Burger Court toward Women." *Policy Studies Journal* 7 (Winter 1978): 213–218.

5060. Hargis, Donald E. "Women's Rights in California, 1949." *Southern California Historical Quarterly* 37 (December 1955): 320–335.

5061. Hoff-Wilson, Joan. "The Unfinished Revolution: Changing Legal Status of U.S. Women." *Signs* 13, no. 1 (Autumn 1987): 7–36.

5062. Kanowitz, Leo. "Constitutional Aspects of Sex-Based Discrimination in American Law." *Nebraska Law Review* 48, no. 1 (November 1968): 131–182.

5063. ———. *Women and the Law: The Unfinished Revolution.* Albuquerque: University of New Mexico Press, 1969.

5064. Lindgren, J. Ralph, and Nadine Taub. *The Law of Sex Discrimination.* St. Paul, MN: West Publishing, 1988.

5065. Lynn, Naomi B., ed. *Women, Politics and the Constitution.* New York: Haworth Press, 1990.

5066. Matsuda, Mari J. "The West and the Legal Status of Women: Ex-

planations of the Frontier Feminism." *Journal of the West* 24, no. 1 (1985): 47–56.

5067. Mezey, Susan Gluck. *In Pursuit of Equality, Women, Public Policy and the Federal Courts.* New York: St. Martin's Press, 1992.

5068. O'Connor, Karen. "Sex and the Supreme Court." *Social Science Quarterly* 64 (1983): 327–331.

5069. Paul, Alice. "Towards Equality: A Study of the Legal Position of Women in the United States." D.C.L. dissertation, American University, School of Law, Washington, DC, 1928.

5070. Porter, Mary Cornelia. "Androgyny and the Supreme Court." *Women and Politics* 1 (Winter 1980–1981): 23–38.

5071. Rhode, Deborah L. *Justice and Gender: Sex Discrimination and the Law.* Cambridge: Harvard University Press, 1989.

5072. Rock, Andrea. "Unequal Justice." *Ladies' Home Journal* 112, no. 4 (April 1995): 106–112

5073. Ross, Susan Deller, Isabelle Katz Pinzler, Deborah A. Ellis, and Kary L. Moss, eds. *The Rights of Women: The Basic ACLU Guide to Women's Rights.* 3d ed. Carbondale: Southern Illinois University, 1993.

5074. Sachs, Albie, and Joan Hoff-Wilson. *Sexism and the Law: A Study of Male Beliefs and Legal Bias in Britain and the United States.* New York: Free Press, 1978.

5075. Sassower, Doris L. "Women and the Judiciary: Undoing 'The Law of the Creator'." *Case and Comment* 85 (January–February 1975): 30–38.

5076. Segal, Jeffrey A., and Cheryl D. Reedy. "The Supreme Court and Sex Discrimination: The Role of the Solicitor General." *Western Political Quarterly* 41 (September 1988): 553–568.

5077. Simpson, Peggy. "Politics and Law." In *Women's Annual, 1980–81,* edited by Barbara Haber, 144–176. Boston: G. K. Hall, 1981.

5078. Stidham, Ronald. "Women's Rights before the Federal District Courts, 1971–1977." *American Politics Quarterly* 11 (April 1983): 205–218.

5079. Strum, Philippa. "The Supreme Court and Sexual Equality: A Case Study of Factors Affecting Judicial Policy-Making." *Policy Studies Journal* 4, no. 2 (1975): 146–150.

5080. Walker, Thomas G., and Deborah J. Barrow. "The Diversification of the Federal Bench: Policy and Process Ramifications." *Journal of Politics* 47 (May 1985): 596–617.

5081. Wildman, Stephanie M. "The Legitimation of Sex Discrimination: A Critical Response to Supreme Court Jurisprudence." *Oregon Law Review* 63 (1984): 265–307.

Military

5082. Binkin, Martin, and Shirley J. Bach. *Women and the Military.* Washington, DC: Brookings Institution, 1977.

5083. Bolton, Frances Payne. "Women Should Be Drafted." *American Magazine of Civics* 147 (June 1949): 47.

5084. Hartmann, Susan M. "Women in the Military Service." In *Clio Was A Woman: Studies in the History of American Women,* edited by Mabel E. Deutrich and Virginia C. Purdy, 196. Washington, DC: Howard University, 1980.

5085. Hine, Darlene Clark. "Mabel K. Staupers and the Integration of Black Nurses into the Armed Forces." In *Black Women in United States History,* edited by Darlene Clark Hine, 630–648. New York: Carlson, 1990.

5086. Johnson, Jesse, ed. *Black Women in the Armed Forces, 1943–1974.* Hampton, VA: Johnson, 1974.

5087. Jones, Kathleen B. "Dividing the Ranks: Women and the Draft." *Women and Politics* 4 (Winter 1984): 75–87.

5088. Rapoport, Daniel. "Women in the Military—The Barriers to Full Equality—Carter's Plan to Include Women in the Draft—And Congress's Violent Opposition to It—Demonstrates Continuing Ambivalence toward Women in Uniform." *National Journal* 7 (April 1980): 565–567.

5089. Sherman, Janann Margaret. "'They Either Need These Women or They Do Not': Margaret Chase Smith and the Fight for Regular Status for Women in the Military." *Journal of Military History* 54, no. 1 (1990): 47–78.

5090. Steihm, Judith H. "Women, Men, and Military Service: Is Protection Necessarily a Racket?" In *Women, Power and Policy,* edited by Ellen

Boneparth, 282–295. New York: Pergamon Press, 1982.

5091. Treadwell, Mattie E. *The Women's Army Corps, The United States Army in World War II.* Vol. VIII. Washington, DC: Department of the Army, 1954.

5092. Wilcox, Clyde. "Race, Sex, and Support for Women in the Military." *Social Science Quarterly* 73, no. 2 (June 1992): 310–323.

Pornography

5093. Bessner, Sue. "Antiobscenity: A Comparison of the Legal and Feminist Perspectives." In *Women, Policy and Power,* edited by Ellen Boneparth, 167–183. New York: Pergamon Press, 1982.

5094. Brill, Alida. "Freedom, Fantasy, Foes and Feminism: The Debate around Pornography." In *Women Politics and Changes,* edited by Louise A. Tilly and Patricia Gurin, 503–529. New York: Russell Sage, 1990.

5095. Downs, Donald Alexander. *The New Politics of Pornography.* Chicago: University of Chicago Press, 1989.

5096. Dworkin, Andrea. *Pornography: Men Possessing Women.* New York: E. P. Dutton, 1979.

5097. ———. "Against the Male Flood: Censorship, Pornography, and Equality." In *Feminist Jurisprudence,* edited by Patricia Smith, 449–466. New York: Oxford University Press, 1993.

5098. Lederer, Laura, ed. *Take Back the Night: Women on Pornography.* New York: William Morrow, 1980.

5099. Russo, Ann Marie. "The Feminist Pornography Debates: Civil Rights and Civil Liberties." Ph.D. dissertation, University of Illinois, Urbana-Champaign, 1990.

5100. Vance, Carol S. "Negotiating Sex and Gender in the Attorney General's Commission on Pornography." In *Uncertain Terms,* edited by Faye Ginsburg and Anna Tsing, 118–134. Boston: Beacon, 1990.

5101. Wolgast, Elizabeth. "Pornography and the Tyranny of the Majority." In *Feminist Jurisprudence,* edited by Patricia Smith, 431–448. New York: Oxford University Press, 1993.

Prostitution

5102. Decker, John F. *Prostitution: Regulation and Control.* Littleton, CO: Rothman, 1979.

5103. Jones, James B., Jr. "Municipal Vice: The Management of Prostitution; Tennessee's Urban Experience: Chattanooga and Knoxville, 1838–1917." *Tennessee Historical Quarterly* 50 (Summer 1991): 110–122.

5104. Klausner, Patricia Robin. "The Politics of Massage Parlor Prostitution: The International Traffic in Women for Prostitution in New York City, 1970–Present." Ph.D. dissertation, University of Delaware, Wilmington, 1987.

5105. Leab, Daniel J. "Women and the Mann Act." *American Studies* (*Germany*) 21, no. 1 (1976): 55–65.

5106. Lubove, Roy. "The Progressives and the Prostitute." *The Historian* 24 (May 1962): 308–330.

5107. Millett, Kate. *The Prostitution Papers.* New York: Avon, 1973.

5108. Pivar, David J. "Cleansing the Nation, the War on Prostitution, 1917–1921." *Prologue* 12, no. 1(1980): 29–40.

5109. Walkowitz, Judith. "The Politics of Prostitution." *Signs* 6 (Autumn 1980): 123–135.

Public Accommodations

5110. Burns, Michael M. "The Exclusion of Women from Influential Men's Clubs: The Inner Sanctum and the Myth of Full Equality." *Harvard Civil Rights–Civil Liberties Law Review* 18 (Summer 1983): 321.

5111. Finlay, Paula J. "Prying Open the Clubhouse Door: Defining the 'Distinctly Private' Club after *New York State Club Association v. City of New York.*" *Washington University Law Quarterly* 68 (Spring 1990): 371.

5112. Kelley, M. Page. "*Roberts v. United States Jaycees:* How Much Help for Women?" *Harvard Women's Law Journal* 8 (Spring 1985): 215–230.

5113. Leiferman, Cynthia A. "Private Clubs: A Sanctuary for Discrimination?" *Baylor Law Review* 40 (Winter 1988): 71.

5114. McGovern, Kimberly S. "Case Comments: 'Board of Directors of Rotary International v. Rotary Club of Duarte: Prying Open the Doors of the All-Male Club'." *Harvard Women's Law Journal* 11 (Spring 1988): 117–145.

5115. McKenna, Lois M. "Note: Freedom of Association or Gender Discrimination? *New York State Club Association v. City of New York.*" *American University Law Review* 38 (1 April 1989): 1061.

5116. Starr, Roger. "Men's Clubs, Women's Rights." *The Public Interest* 89 (1987): 57–70.

Reproductive Rights

General

5117. Appelton, Susan Frelich. "The Abortion-Funding Cases and Population Control: An Imaginary Lawsuit and Some Reflections on the Uncertain Limits of Reproductive Privacy." In *The Law of Politics and Abortion,* edited by Carl E. Schneider and Maris A. Vinovskis, 122–157. Lexington, MA: D. C. Heath, 1980.

5118. Brown, Wendy. "Reproductive Freedom and the Right to Privacy: Paradox for Feminists." In *Families, Politics and Public Policy,* edited by Irene Diamond, 322–338. New York: Longman, 1983.

5119. Cisler, Lucinda. "A Major Battle Is Over–But the War Is Not." *Feminist Studies* 1, no. 2 (Fall 1972): 121–131.

5120. Cohen, Sherrill, and Nadine Taub, eds. *Reproductive Laws for the 1990s.* Clifton, NJ: Humana Press, 1989. Women's Rights Litigation Clinic, Rutgers Law School.

5121. Nsiah-Jefferson, Laurie. "Reproductive Laws, Women of Color, and Low-Income Women." In *Feminist Jurisprudence,* edited by Patricia Smith, 332–334. New York: Oxford University Press, 1993.

5122. O'Brien, Mary. *The Politics of Reproduction.* Boston: Routledge and Kegan Paul, 1981.

5123. Sapiro, Virginia, ed. *Women, Biology and Public Policy.* Beverly Hills, CA: Sage, 1985.

5124. Wattleton, Faye. "Preserving Reproductive Freedom: Implications for Black Americans in the Next Decade." *Vital Issues* 2 (1992): 25–26.

States

5125. Carney, Eliza Newlin. "Abortion Rights Test: Maryland Voters Will Decide." *National Journal* 24 (10 October 1992): 2304–2307.

5126. Center for the American Woman and Politics. *Election 1989: The Abortion Issue in New Jersey and Virginia.* New Brunswick, NJ: Center for the American Woman and Politics, 1990.

5127. Day, Christine L. "State Legislative Voting Patterns on Abortion Restriction in Louisiana." *Women and Politics* 14, no. 2 (1994): 45–63.

5128. Nossiff, Rosemary Alise. "Abortion Policy in New York and Pennsylvania, 1965–1972: Machine Politics, Pennsylvania Catholic Conference, Reform Democrats, Feminism." Ph.D. dissertation, Cornell University, 1994.

5129. Reagan, Leslie J. "'About to Meet Her Maker': Women, Doctors, Dying Declarations, and the States' Investigation of Abortion, Chicago, 1867–1940." *Journal of American History* 77, no. 4 (1991): 1240–1264.

5130. Simms, Madeleine. "Abortion Politics in New York." *New Scientist* 57 (1 February 1973): 252–253.

Birth Control

5131. Dennett, Mary Ware. *Birth Control Laws.* New York: Graton Press, 1926.

5132. Dienes, C. Thomas. *Law, Politics and Birth Control.* Urbana: University of Illinois Press, 1972.

5133. Gordon, Linda. "The Politics of Population: Birth Control and the Eugenics Movement." *Radical America* 8 (1974): 661–698.

5134. Joffe, Carol. *The Regulation of Sexuality: Experiences of Family Planning Workers.* Philadelphia: Temple University Press, 1986.

5135. Kennedy, David. *Birth Control in America.* New Haven, CT: Yale University Press, 1970.

5136. Leung, Marianne. "'Better Babies': Birth Control in Arkansas during the 1930s." In *Hidden Histories of Women in the New South,* edited by Virginia Bernhard, Elizabeth Fox-Genovese, and Theda Perdue, 52–70. Columbia: University of Missouri Press, 1994.

5137. McCann, Carole R. *Birth Control Politics in the United States, 1916–1945.* Ithaca, NY: Cornell University, 1994.

5138. Reed, James. *Birth Control and American Society: From Private Vice to Public Virtue.* Princeton, NJ: Princeton University Press, 1978.

5139. "Should Legal Barriers against Birth Control Be Removed." *Congressional Digest* 10 (April 1931): 106–107.

5140. Simmons, Mrs. C. B. "For a Better Breed." *The Woman Citizen* 7 (21 April 1923): 17.

5141. Smith, Mary. "Birth Control and Negro Woman." *Ebony* 23 (March 1968): 29–32, 34, 36–37.

Abortion

5142. Ball, Donald W. "An Abortion Clinic Ethnography." *Social Problems* 14 (1967): 293–301.

5143. Blanchard, Dallas A. *The Gideon Project: Religious Violence and Abortion in America Today.* Gainesville: University Press of Florida, 1993.

5144. Center for the American Woman and Politics. *Abortion Politics in State Elections: Comparisons Across States, 1989–90.* New Brunswick, NJ: Center for the American Woman and Politics, 1991.

5145. Cisler, Lucinda. "On Abortion and Abortion Law, Abortion Law Repeal (Sort Of): A Warning to Women." In *Notes from the Second Year: Women's Liberation—the Major Writings of the Radical Feminists,* 89–93. New York: Radical Feminism, 1970.

5146. Dice, Dr. Lee R. "When Abortion Is Justified." *The Nation* 200, no. 8 (22 February 1965): 189–191.

5147. Friedman, Lawrence M., Roger H. Davidson, G. Calvin Mackenzie, John E. Jackson, Maris A. Vinovskis, and Cynthia E. Harrison, eds. *The Abortion Dispute and the American System.* Washington, DC: Brookings Institution, 1983.

5148. Frohock, Fred M. *Abortion: A Case Study in Law and Morals.* Westport, CT: Greenwood Press, 1983.

5149. Ginsburg, Faye D. *Contested Lives: The Abortion Debate in an American Community,* Berkeley: University of California Press, 1990.

5150. Ginsburg, Ruth Bader. "Some Thoughts on Autonomy and Equality in Relation to *Roe vs. Wade.*" *North Carolina Law Review* 63 (1985): 375.

5151. Keynes, Edward, and Randall K. Miller. *The Court vs. Congress, Abortion, Busing and Prayer.* Durham, NC: Duke University Press, 1989.

5152. Legge, Jerome S., Jr. "Abortion as a Policy Issue: Attitudes of the Mass Public." *Women and Politics* 7 (Spring 1987): 63–82.

5153. McDonagh, Eileen Lorenzi. "From Pro-Choice to Pro-Consent in the Abortion Debate: Reframing Women's Reproductive Rights." In Vol. 14 of *Studies in Law, Politics and Society,* edited by Susan S. Silbey and Austin Sarat, 245–290. Greenwich, CT: JAI Press, 1994.

5154. Mohr, James C. *Abortion in America: The Origins and Evolution of National Policy, 1800–1900.* New York: Oxford University Press, 1979.

5155. Moore, Emily C. "Abortion and Public Policy: What Are the Issues?" *New York Law Forum* 17 (1971): 411–436.

5156. Morehouse, Lawrence. "Parental Consent and a Minor's Right to an Abortion: An Analysis of the Florida Supreme Court's Controversial Ruling." *Comparative State Politics* 13 (April 1992): 11–22.

5157. Morgan, Richard Gregory. "*Roe v. Wade* and the Lesson of the Pre-Roe Case Law." In *The Law and Politics of Abortion,* edited by Carl E. Schneider and Maris A. Vinovskis, 184–205. Lexington, MA: D. C. Heath, 1980.

5158. Palley, Howard A. "Abortion Policy: Ideology, Political Cleavage and the Political Process." *Policy Studies Journal* 7, no. 2 (Winter 1978): 224–233.

5159. Petchesky, Rosalind Pollack. *Abortion and Woman's Choice: The State, Sexuality, and Reproductive Freedom.* Rev. ed. Boston: Northeastern University Press, 1990.

5160. Regan, Donald H. "Rewriting *Roe v. Wade.*" In *The Law and Politics of Abortion,* edited by Carl E. Schneider and Maris A. Vinovskis, 1–80. Lexington, MA: D. C. Heath, 1980.

5161. Rhode, Deborah L. "Reproductive Freedom." In *Feminist Jurisprudence,* edited by Patricia Smith, 305–334. New York: Oxford University Press, 1993.

5162. Rubin, Eva R. *Abortion, Politics, and the Courts: Roe v. Wade and Its Aftermath.* Westport, CT: Greenwood Press, 1982.

5163. Sachdev, Paul, ed. *Perspectives on Abortion.* Metuchen, NJ: Scarecrow Press, 1985.

5164. Sarvis, Betty, and Human Rodman. *The Abortion Controversy.* New York: Columbia University Press, 1973.

5165. Solinger, Rickie. "'A Complete Disaster': Abortion and the Politics of Hospital Abortion Committee, 1950–70." *Feminist Studies* 19 (Summer 1993): 241–268.

5166. Steiner, Gilbert Y., ed. *The Abortion Dispute and the American System.* Washington, DC: Brookings Institution, 1983.

5167. Strickland, Ruth Ann, and Marcia Lynn Whicker. "Banning Abortion: An Analysis of Senate Votes on a Bimodal Issue." *Women and Politics* 6 (Spring 1986): 41–56.

5168. Tatalovich, Raymond, and Byron W. Daynes. *The Politics of Abortion: A Study of Community Conflict in Public Policy Making.* New York: Praeger, 1981.

5169. Uslaner, Eric M. "Public Support for Pro-Choice Abortion Policies in the Nation and States: Changes and Stability after the Roe and Doe Decisions." In *The Law and Politics of Abortion,* edited by Carl E. Schneider and Maris A. Vinovskis, 206–223. Lexington, MA: D. C. Heath, 1980.

5170. Vinovskis, Maris A. "The Politics of Abortion in the House of Representatives in 1976." In *The Law and Politics of Abortion,* edited by Carl E. Schneider and Maris A. Vinovskis, 224–261. Lexington, MA: D. C. Heath, 1980.

5171. Wattleton, Faye. "Teenage Pregnancies and the Recriminalization of Abortions." *American Journal of Public Health* 80, no. 3 (March 1990): 269–270.

5172. Weddington, Sarah. *A Question of Choice.* New York: Grosset-Putnam, 1992.

5173. Yishai, Yael. "Public Ideas and Public Policy: Abortion Politics in Four Democracies (Comparison of Israel, Ireland, Sweden and the United States)." *Comparative Politics* 25 (January 1993): 207–228.

Fetal Rights

5174. Daniels, Cynthia R. *At Women's Expense: State Power and the Politics of Fetal Rights.* Cambridge: Harvard University Press, 1993.

5175. Johnson, Dawn E. "The Creation of Fetal Rights: Conflicts with Women's Constitutional Rights to Liberty, Privacy and Equal Protection." *Yale Law Journal* (January 1986): 599–625.

5176. King, Patricia. "The Juridical Status of the Fetus: A Proposal for Legal Protection of the Unborn." In *The Law and Politics of Abortion,* edited by Carl E. Schneider and Maris A. Vinovskis, 81–121. Lexington, MA: D. C. Heath, 1980.

5177. Merrick, Janna C., and Robert H. Blank. *The Politics of Pregnancy: Policy Dilemmas in the Maternal-Fetal Relationship.* New York: Haworth Press, 1994.

5178. Pollitt, Katha. "Fetal Rights: A New Assault on Feminism." *The Nation* 250, no. 12 (26 March 1990): 409–418.

Workplace Hazards

5179. Bayer, Ronald. "Reproductive Hazards in the Workplace: Bearing the Burden of Fetal Risk." *Milbank Memorial Fund Quarterly Health and Safety* 60 (Fall 1982): 633–656.

5180. Bertin, Joan E. "Reproduction, Women and the Workplace: Legal Issues." *Occupational Medicine: State of the Art Reviews* 1 (July–September 1986): 497–507.

5181. Buss, Emily. "Getting Beyond Discrimination: A Regulatory Solution to the Problem of Fetal Hazard in the Workplace." *Yale Law Journal* 95 (January 1986): 577–598.

5182. Goldhaber, Marilyn K., Michael Polen, and Robert A. Hiatt. "The Risk of Miscarriage and Birth Defects among Women Who Use Video Display Terminals during Pregnancy." *American Journal of Industrial Medicine* 13 (1988): 695–706.

5183. Mattson, Lynn. "The Pregnancy Amendment: Fetal Rights and the Workplace." *Case and Comment* 86 (November–December 1981): 33–41.

5184. Terry, Jane. "Conflict of Interest: Protection of Women from Reproductive Hazards in the Workplace." *Industrial and Labor Relations Forum* 15 (January 1981): 43–55.

5185. Timko, Patricia. "Exploring the Limits of Legal Duty: A Union's Responsibilities with Respect to Fetal Protection Policies." *Harvard Journal* on *Legislation* 23 (Winter 1986): 159–210.

5186. Williams, Wendy W. "Firing the Woman to Protect the Fetus: The Reconciliation of Fetal Protection with Equal Employment Opportunity Goals under Title VII." *Georgetown Law Journal* 69 (1981): 641.

The Future

5187. Baruch, Elaine Hoffman. *Embryos, Ethics, and Women's Rights: Exploring the New Reproductive Technologies.* New York: Haworth Press, 1988.

5188. Diamond, Irene. "Medical Science and the Transformation of Motherhood: The Promise of Reproductive Technologies." In *Women, Power and Policy: Toward the Year 2000,* 2d ed., edited by Ellen Boneparth and Emily Stoper, 149–154. New York: Pergamon, 1988.

5189. Rothman, Barbara Katz. *The Tentative Pregnancy: Prenatal Diagnosis and the Future of Motherhood.* New York: Viking, 1986.

Sex Discrimination

5190. Abel, Emily. "Collective Protest and the Meritocracy: Faculty Women and Sex Discrimination Lawsuits." *Feminist Studies* 7, no. 3 (1981): 505–538.

5191. Abramson, Joan. *Old Boys, New Women: The Politics of Sex Discrimination.* New York: Praeger, 1979.

5192. Babcock, Barbara A., Anne E. Freedman, Eleanor Holmes Norton, and Susan Deller Ross, eds. *Sex Dis-*

crimination and the Law: Causes and Remedies. Boston: Little, Brown, 1975.

5193. Bamberger, Ruth. "Sex at Risk in Insurance Classifications? The Supreme Court as Shaper of Public Policy." In *Women in Politics: Outsiders or Insiders? A Collection of Readings,* edited by Lois Lovelace Duke, 227–235. Englewood Cliffs, NJ: Prentice Hall, 1993.

5194. Brown, Williams H. "Sex Discrimination: It Isn't Funny, It Is Illegal, and the Battle Has Just Begun." *Good Government* 88 (Winter 1971): 18–21.

5195. Conway, M. Margaret. "Anti-Discrimination Law and the Problems of Policy Implementation." In *The Analysis of Policy Impact,* edited by John G. Grumm and Stephen L. Wasby, 35–42. Lexington, MA: Lexington Books, 1981.

5196. Freeman, Jo. "The Legal Basis of the Sexual Caste System." *Valparaiso University Law Review* 5, no. 2 (Spring 1971): 203–236.

5197. Ginsburg, Ruth Bader. "Women's Right to Full Participation in Shaping Society's Course: An Evolving Constitutional Precept." In *Toward the Second Decade: The Impact of the Women's Movement on American Institutions,* edited by Betty Justice and Renate Pore, 171–188. Westport, CT: Greenwood Press, 1984.

5198. Graebner, William. "'Uncle Sam Just Loves the Ladies': Sex Discrimination in the Federal Government, 1917." *Labor History* 21, no. 1 (1917): 75–85.

5199. Jamieson, Kathleen Hall. *The Double Bind, Sex Discrimination against Women.* New York: Oxford University Press, 1995.

5200. Kanowitz, Leo. "Benign Sex Discrimination: Its Troubles and Their Cure." *Hastings Law Journal* 31 (1980): 1379–1429.

5201. Lichtman, Judith L., and Carol Baekey. "DeJure Sex Discrimination." In *Toward the Second Decade: The Impact of the Women's Movement on American Institutions,* edited by Betty Justice and Renate Pore, 149–161. Westport, CT: Greenwood, 1981.

5202. Purcell, Susan Kaufman. "Ideology and the Law: Sexism and Supreme Court Decisions." In *Women in Politics,* edited by Jane S. Jaquette, 131–154. New York: Wiley, 1974.

5203. Ringler, Susan Moss. "Sex Equality: Not for Women Only." *Catholic University of America Law Review* 29 (1980): 427–460.

5204. Schmid, Gunter, and Renate Wertzel, eds. *Sex Discrimination and Equal Opportunity.* New York: St. Martin's Press, 1984.

5205. Toufexis, Anastasia. "Now for a Woman's Point of View: Feminist Scholars Challenge Male Bias in the U. S. Legal System." *Time* 1 (17 April 1989): 51–52.

Sexual Harassment

5206. Bravo, Ellen, and Ellen Cassedy. *The 9 to 5 Guide to Combating Sexual Harassment: Candid Advice from 9 to 5, the National Association of Working Women.* New York: Wiley, 1992.

5207. Chan, Anja Angelica. *Women and Sexual Harassment: A Guide to the Legal Protections of Title VII and the Hostile Environment Claim.* New York: Haworth Press, 1993.

5208. Chrisman, Robert, Robert L. Allen, and Gloria T. Hull, eds. *Court of Appeal: The Black Community Speaks Out on Racial and Sexual Politics of Thomas v. Hill.* New York: Ballantine Books, 1992.

5209. Clark, Charles S. "Sexual Harassment." *Congressional Quarterly Researcher* 1, no. 13 (9 August 1991): 537–559.

5210. Cohen, Lloyd R. "Sexual Harassment and the Law." *Society* 28, no. 4 (1991): 8–31.

5211. Lewis, Ann F. "New Club Rules." *Ms.* 17, no. 9 (May 1989): 78–79.

5212. MacKinnon, Catharine A. *Sexual Harassment of Working Women: A Case of Sex Discrimination.* New Haven, CT: Yale University Press, 1979.

5213. ———. "Sexual Harassment: Its First Decade in Court." In *Feminist Jurisprudence,* edited by Patricia Smith, 145–157. New York: Oxford University Press, 1993.

5214. McIntyre, Douglas I., and James C. Renick. "Sexual Harassment and the States as Policy-Makers and Employers." *State Government* 56, no. 4 (1983): 128–133.

5215. Morris, Celia. *Bearing Witness, Sexual Harassment and Beyond—Everywoman's Story.* New York: Little, Brown, 1994.

Social Welfare

5216. Baker, S. Josephine. "The First Year of the Sheppard-Towner Act." *The Survey* 52 (15 April 1924): 89–91.

5217. Bohrer, Florence Fifer. "Pay-Rolls and Public Welfare." *The Republican Woman of Illinois* 6, no. 8 (April 1929): 9.

5218. Brenner, Johanna, and Barbara Laslett. "Gender, Social Reproduction and Women's Self-Organization: Considering the U.S. Welfare State." *Gender and Society* 5 (September 1991): 311–333.

5219. Chepaitis, Joseph Benedict. "The First Federal Social Welfare Measure: The Sheppard-Towner Maternity and Infancy Act, 1918–1932." Ph.D. dissertation, Georgetown University, Washington, DC, 1968.

5220. Eric, Steven P., and Martin Rein. "Women and the Welfare State." In *The Politics of the Gender Gap: The Social Construction of Political Influence,* edited by Carol M. Mueller, 173–191. Women's Policy Studies, 12. Beverly Hills, CA: Sage, 1988.

5221. Eric, Steven P., Martin Rein, and Barbara Wiget. "Women and the Reagan Revolution: Thermidor for the Social Welfare Economy." In *Families, Politics and Public Policy,* edited by Irene Diamond, 94–119. New York: Longman, 1983.

5222. Folbre, Nancy. "The Pauperization of Motherhood; Patriarchy and Public Policy in the United States." In *Families and Work,* edited by Naomi Gerstel and Harriet Engel Gross, 491–511. Philadelphia: Temple University Press, 1987.

5223. Gelpi, Barbara C., Nancy C. M. Hartsock, Clare C. Novak, and Myra H. Strober, eds. *Women and Poverty.* Chicago: University of Chicago Press, 1986.

5224. Gimenez, Martha E. "The Feminism of Poverty: Myth or Reality?" *Social Justice* 17, no. 3 (1990): 43–69.

5225. Gordon, Linda, ed. *Women, the State, and Welfare.* Madison: University of Wisconsin Press, 1990.

5226. ———. "Social Insurance and Public Assistance: The Influence of Gender in Welfare Thought in the United States, 1890–1935." *American Historical Review* 97, no. 1 (February 1992): 19–54.

5227. Howard, Christopher. "Sowing the Seed of 'Welfare': The Transformation of Mothers' Pensions, 1900–1940." *Journal of Policy History* 4, no. 2 (1992): 188–227.

5228. Iglitzin, Lynne B. "A Case Study in Patriarchal Politics: Women on Welfare." *American Behavioral Scientist* 17, no. 4 (March–April 1974): 487–506. Reprinted in *A Portrait of Marginality: The Political Behavior of American Women,* edited by Marianne Githens and Jewell Prestage, 96–112. New York: McKay, 1977.

5229. Joe, Tom, and Cheryl Rogers. *By the Few for the Few: The Reagan Welfare Legacy.* Lexington, MA: Lexington Books, 1985.

5230. Keefe, David E. "Governor Reagan, Welfare Reform, and AFDC

Fertility." *Social Service Review* 57, no. 2 (1983): 234–253.

5231. Kemp, Alice Abel. "Poverty and Welfare for Women." In *Women: A Feminist Perspective,* 5th ed., edited by Jo Freeman, 458–480. Mountain View, CA: Mayfield, 1995.

5232. Koven, Seth, and Sonya Michel. "Womanly Duties: Maternalist Politics and the Origins of Welfare States in France, Germany, Great Britain, and the United States, 1880–1920." *American Historical Review* 95 (October 1990): 1076–1114.

5233. ———, eds. *Mothers of a New World: Maternalist Politics and the Origins of Welfare States.* New York: Routledge, 1993.

5234. Law, Sylvia A. "Women, Work, Welfare and the Preservation of Patriarchy." *University of Pennsylvania Law Review* 131 (1983): 1249.

5235. Lincoln, Richard, Brigette Doering-Bradley, Barbara L. Linhdeim, and Maureen A. Cotterill. "The Court, the Congress and the President: Turning Back the Clock on the Pregnant Poor." *Family Planning Perspectives* 9 (September–October 1977): 207.

5236. Martin, Anne. "An Everlasting Benefit." *Good Housekeeping* 70 (February 1920): 20–21, 144–148.

5237. McLanahan, Sara S. "Family Structure and the Reproduction of Poverty." *American Journal of Sociology* 90, no. 4 (1985): 873–901.

5238. McLanahan, Sara S., and Irwin Garfinkel. "Single Mothers, the Underclass, Social Policy." *Annals of the*

American Academy of Political and Social Science 501 (January 1989): 92–104.

5239. Miller, Dorothy. *Women and Social Welfare: A Feminist Analysis.* Westport, CT: Praeger, 1990.

5240. Naples, Nancy A. "'Women against Poverty', Community Workers in Anti-Poverty Programs, 1964–1984." Ph.D. dissertation, City University of New York, 1989.

5241. Nelson, Barbara J. "The Gender, Race and Class Origins of Early Welfare Policy and the Welfare State: A Comparison of Workmen's Compensation and Mother's Aid." In *Women, Politics and Change,* edited by Louise A. Tilly and Patricia Gurin, 413–435. New York: Russell Sage, 1990.

5242. Owen, Ruth Bryan. "Ruth Bryan Owen, M.C. Proposes a Department of Home and Child." *The Woman's Journal* 16 (February 1931): 8–9, 37–39.

5243. Pollitt, Katha. "Subject to Debate, Failure of Women to Speak Out against Welfare Reform." *The Nation* 261 (4 December 1995): 697.

5244. Rainwater, Lee, and William L. Yancey, eds. *The Moynihan Report and the Politics of Controversy.* Cambridge, MA: MIT Press, 1967.

5245. Rose, Nancy E. "Gender, Race, and the Welfare State Government Work Programs from the 1930s to the Present." *Feminist Studies* 19 (Summer 1993): 319–342.

5246. Sapiro, Virginia. "The Gender Bias of American Social Policy." *Political Science Quarterly* 101 (1986): 221–238.

5247. Schaffer, Diane M. "The Feminization of Poverty: Prospects for an International Feminist Agenda." In *Women, Power and Policy: Toward the Year 2000,* 2d ed., edited by Ellen Boneparth and Emily Stoper, 223–246. New York: Pergamon Press, 1988.

5248. Skocpol, Theda. *Protecting Soldiers and Mothers: The Political Origins of Social Policy in the United States.* Cambridge: Harvard University Press, 1992.

5249. Stoper, Emily. "Raising the Next Generation: Who Shall Pay?" In *Women, Power and Policy: Toward the Year 2000,* 2d ed., edited by Ellen Boneparth and Emily Stoper, 190–205. New York: Pergamon Press, 1988.

5250. Sumner, Helen L. "What the Federal Government Has Done for Mothers." *American Association of University Women* 11, no. 1 (September 1917): 17.

5251. Van Den Bergh, Nan, and Lynne B. Cooper, eds. *Feminist Visions of Social Work.* Silver Springs, MD: National Association of Social Work, 1986.

5252. Vezzosi, Elisabetta. "From Roosevelt to Roosevelt: Women's Welfare and Maternity Policies in the United States, 1901–1935." *Storia Nordamericana (Italy)* 5, no. 2 (1988): 95–104.

5253. Willebrandt, Mabel Walker. *The Inside of Prohibition.* Indianapolis, IN: Bobbs-Merrill, 1929.

5254. Zopf, Paul E., Jr. *American Women in Poverty.* Westport, CT: Greenwood Press, 1989.

Urban and Housing

5255. Birch, Eugenie Ladner. "Woman-Made America: The Case of Early Public Housing Policy." *Journal of the American Institute of Planners* 2, no. 1 (1978): 52–56.

5256. Diamond, Irene. "Women and Housing: The Limitations of Liberal Reform." In *Women, Power and Policy,* edited by Ellen Boneparth, 109–120. New York: Pergamon Press, 1982.

5257. Freeman, Jo. "Women and Urban Policy." *Signs* 5, no. 3 (Spring 1980): 4–21.

5258. Thorpe, Dagmar. "Native American Women Win Historic Rights Case." *Ms.* 12, no. 6 (December 1983): 17.

Violence Against Women

General

5259. Andler, Judy, and Gail Sullivan. "The Price of Government Funding." *Aegis: Magazine on Ending Violence Against Women* (1980): 10–15.

5260. Bush, Diane Mitsch. "Women's Movements and State Policy Reform Aimed at Domestic Violence against Women: A Comparison of the Consequences of Movement Mobilizations in the U.S. and India." *Gender and Society* 6, no. 4 (December 1992): 587–608.

5261. Crites, Laura L. "Wife Abuse: The Judicial Record." In *Women, the Courts and Equality,* edited by Laura L. Crites and Winifred L. Hepperle, 38–53. Beverly Hills, CA: Sage, 1987.

5262. Davis, Angela Yvonne. *Violence against Women and the Ongoing Challenge to Racism.* New York: Kitchen Table, 1985.

5263. Dobash, R. Emerson, and Russell P. Dobash. *Women, Violence and Social Change.* New York: Routledge, 1992.

5264. Gardener, Carol B. "Access Information: Public Lies and Private Peril." *Social Problems* 35, no. 4 (1988): 384–397.

5265. Gelles, Richard J. *Family Violence.* Beverly Hills, CA: Sage, 1979.

5266. Gordon, Linda. "Family Violence, Feminism, and Social Control." In *Unequal Sisters: A Multicultural Reader in U.S. Women's History,* edited by Ellen DuBois and Vicki L. Ruiz, 141–156. New York: Routledge, 1990.

5267. Guberman, Connie, and Margie Wolfe. *No Safe Place: Violence against Women and Children.* Toronto: The Women's Press, 1985.

5268. Hanmer, Jalna, and Mary Maynard. *Women, Violence and Social Control.* Atlantic Highlands, NJ: Humanities Press, 1987.

5269. Landes, Alison B., Mark A. Siegel, and Carol D. Foster. *Domestic Violence: No Longer Behind the Curtains.* Wylie, TX: Information Plus, 1993.

5270. Pahl, Jan, ed. *Private Violence and Public Policy.* London: Routledge and Kegan Paul, 1985.

5271. Pleck, Elizabeth. *Domestic Tyranny: The Making of American Social Policy against Family Violence from Colonial Times to the Present.* New York: Oxford University Press, 1987.

5272. Stanko, Elizabeth. *Intimate Intrusions: Women's Experience of Male Violence.* London: Routledge and Kegan Paul, 1985.

5273. Sullivan, Gail. "Funny Things Happen on Our Way to Revolution." *Aegis: Magazine on Ending Violence Against Women* 34 (1982): 12–32.

Battered Women

5274. Davis, Nanette J. "Shelters for Battered Women: Social Policy Response to Interpersonal Violence." *Social Science Journal* 25, no. 4 (1988): 401–419.

5275. Ferguson, Kathy. "Negotiating Trouble in a Battered Women's Shelter." *Urban Life* 12, no. 3 (1983): 287–306.

5276. Ferraro, Kathleen. "Processing Battered Women." *Journal of Family Issues* 2, no. 4 (1981): 415–438.

5277. Findlen, Barbara. "In Search of a Nonviolent Past, American Indian Women and Family Violence." *Ms.* 2, no. 2 (September–October 1990): 46.

5278. Gee, Pauline W. "Ensuring Police Protection for Battered Women: The *Scott v. Hart* Suit." *Signs* 8, no.3 (Spring 1983): 554–567.

5279. Grau, Janice. "Restraining Orders for Battered Women: Issues of Access and Efficacy." *Women and Politics* 4 (Fall 1984): 13–28.

5280. Morgan, Patricia. "From Battered Wife to Program Client: The

State's Shaping of Social Problems." *Kapialistate* 9 (1981): 17–39.

5281. Murray, Susan B. "The Unhappy Marriage of Theory and Practice: An Analysis of a Battered Women's Shelter." *National Women's Studies Association Journal* 1, no. 1 (1988): 75–92.

5282. Rodriguez, Noelie Maria. "Transcending Bureaucracy: Feminist Politics at a Shelter for Battered Women." *Gender and Society* 2, no. 2 (June 1988): 214–227.

5283. Waits, Kathleen. "The Criminal Justice System's Response to Battering: Understanding the Problem, Forging the Solutions." In *Feminist Jurisprudence,* edited by Patricia Smith, 188–210. New York: Oxford University Press, 1993.

5284. Weiner, Merle H. "From Dollars to Sense: A Critique of Government Funding for the Battered Women's Shelter Movement." *Journal of Law and Inequality* 9, no. 2 (March 1991): 185–277.

5285. Wexler, Sandra. "Battered Women and Public Policy." In *Women, Power and Policy,* edited by Ellen Boneparth, 184–204. New York: Pergamon, 1982.

5286. Wharton, Carol. "Establishing Shelters for Battered Women: Local Manifestations of a Social Movement." *Qualitative Sociology* 10, no. 2 (1987): 146–163.

5287. Wurr, Anne. "The Case of a Battered Women's Shelter: Community Responses to Violence against Women." In *Political Women: Current Roles in State and Local Government,* edited by Janet A. Flammang, 221–241. Beverly Hill, CA: Sage, 1984.

Legislation

5288. Buzawa, Eva Schlesinger, and Carl G. Buzawa. *Domestic Violence: The Changing Criminal Justice Response.* Westport, CT: Auburn House, 1992.

5289. Caringella-MacDonald, Susan. "Sexual Assault Prosecution: An Examination of Model Rape Legislation in Michigan." *Women and Politics* 4 (Fall 1984): 65–82.

5290. Estrich, Susan. "Rape." In *Feminist Jurisprudence,* edited by Patricia Smith, 158–187. New York: Oxford University Press, 1993.

5291. Lafree, Gary D. "Jurors' Responses to Victims' Behavior and Legal Issues in Sexual Assault Trials." *Social Problems* 32 (1985): 389.

5292. Lengyl, Linda. "Survey of Domestic Violence Legislation." *Legal Reference Services Quarterly* 10, no. 1–2 (1990): 59–82.

5293. MacManus, Susan A., and Nikki R. Van Hightower. "Limits of State Constitutional Guarantees: Lessons from Efforts to Implement Domestic Violence Policies." *Public Administration Review* 49 (May–June 1989): 269–277.

5294. Quarm, Daisy, and Martin D. Schwartz. "Domestic Violence in Criminal Court: An Examination of New Legislation in Ohio." *Women and Politics* 4 (Fall 1984): 29–46.

Rape

5295. Brownmiller, Susan. *Against Our Will: Men, Women and Rape.* New York: Bantam, 1976.

5296. Harvey, Mary R. *Exemplary Rape Crisis Programs: A Cross-Site Analysis and Case Studies.* Washington, DC: National Center for the Prevention and Control of Rape, U.S. GPO, 1985.

5297. Loh, Wallace D. "Q: What Has Reform of Rape Legislation Wrought? A: Truth in Criminal Labeling." *Journal of Social Issues* 37, no. 4 (1981): 28–52.

5298. MacKellar, Jean Scott. *Rape: The Bait and the Trap.* New York: Crown Publishers, 1975.

5299. Matthews, Nancy. "Feminist Clashes with the State: Tactical Choices by State-funded Rape Crisis Centers." In *Feminist Organizations: Harvest of the New Women's Movement,* edited by Myra Marx Ferree and Patricia Yancey Martin, 291–305. Philadelphia: Temple University, 1995.

5300. Olsen, Frances. "Statutory Rape: A Feminist Critique of Rights Analysis." *Texas Law Review* 63 (1984): 387.

5301. Russell, Diane. *The Politics of Rape: The Victim's Perspective.* New York: Stein & Day, 1974.

5302. ———. *Rape in Marriage.* New York: Macmillan, 1982.

5303. Schwendinger, Julia R., and Herman Schwendinger. *Rape and Inequality.* Newbury Park, CA: Sage, 1983.

5304. Spencer, Cassie C. "Sexual Assault: The Second Victimization." In *Women, the Courts, and Equality,* edited by Laura L. Crites and Winifred L. Hepperle, 54–73. Beverly Hills, CA: Sage Publications, 1987.

5305. Tyson, Gretchel Hathaway. "The Effect of Women's Advocacy Groups on Legislative Changes in the United States with Specific Emphasis on Marital Rape Legislation in Pennsylvania and New York." Ph.D. dissertation, University of Pittsburgh, 1993.

5306. Weiner, R. D. "Shifting the Communication Burden; A Meaningful Consent Standard in Rape." *Harvard Women's Law Journal* 6 (1983): 143–161.

5307. Wriggins, Jennifer. "Rape, Racism, and the Law." *Harvard Women's Law Journal* 8 (Spring 1985): 103–141.

Programs, Commissions, and Bureaus

5308. Chapman, Jane Roberts. "Policy Centers: An Essential Resource." In *Women in Washington,* edited by Irene Tinker, 177–190. Beverly Hills, CA: Sage, 1983.

5309. Koontz, Elizabeth Duncan. "Women's Bureau Looks to the Future." *Monthly Labor Review* 93 (June 1970): 3–9.

5310. Markoff, Helen S. "The Federal Women's Program." *Public Administration Review* 32 (March–April 1972): 144–151.

5311. Morton, Marian J. "'Go and Sin No More': Maternity Homes in Cleveland, 1869–1936." *Ohio History* 93 (June–August 1984): 117–146.

5312. Sealander, Judith. *As Minority Becomes Majority: Federal Reaction to the Phenomenon of Women in the Workforce, 1920–1963.* Westport, CT: Greenwood, 1983.

5313. Staudt, A. Kathleen, and Jane S. Jaquette. "Women's Programs, Bureaucratic Resistance and Feminist Organizations." In *Women, Power and Policy: Toward the Year 2000,* 2d ed., edited by Ellen Boneparth and Emily Stoper, 263–281. New York: Pergamon Press, 1988.

5314. Stewart, Debra W. "Institutionalization of Female Participation at the Local Level: Commissions on the Status of Women and Agenda-Building." *Women and Politics* 1, no. 1 (Spring 1980): 37–64.

5315. Wunder, Suzanne A. "Woman's Bureau Celebrates 25th Anniversary." *Independent Woman* 22 (July 1943): 200, 217.

VI. Attitudes and Opinions

General

5316. Claggett, William. "The Life Cycle and Generational Models of the Development of Partisanship: A Test Based on the Delayed Enfranchisement of Women." *Social Science Quarterly* 60 (1980): 643–650.

5317. ———. "Life Cycle Model of Partisanship Development: An Analysis of Aggregate Electoral Instability Following the Enfranchisement of Women." *American Political Quarterly* 10, no. 2 (1982): 219–230.

5318. Friedan, Betty, and Midge Decter. "Are Women Different Today?" *Public Opinion* 5 (April–May 1982): 20, 41.

5319. Gallup, George. "Women in America." *The Gallup Poll Index* 128 (March 1976): 7.

5320. Gallup, George, and Evan Hill. "The American Woman." *Saturday Evening Post* 235 (22 December 1962): 15–32.

5321. Gilbert, Dennis A. "Women." In *Compendium of American Public Opinion,* 387–411. Facts on File, 1988.

5322. Harris, Louis. *Virginia Slims American Women's Opinion Poll: A Survey of the Attitudes of Women on Their Role in Politics and the Economy.* New York: Louis Harris and Associates, 1972.

5323. March, James G. "Husband-Wife Interaction over Political Issues." *Public Opinion Quarterly* 17 (Winter 1953–1954): 461–570.

5324. McLaughlin, Kathleen. "Women's Impact on Public Opinion." *Annals of the American Academy of Political and Social Science* 251 (May 1947): 104–112.

5325. Niemi, Richard G., Roman B. Hedges, and M. Kent Jennings. "The Similarity of Husbands and Wives Political Views." *American Politics Quarterly* 5, no. 2 (April 1977): 133–148.

5326. Pierce, John C., William P. Avery, and Addison Carey. "Sex Differences in Black Political Beliefs and Behavior." *American Journal of Political Science* (May 1973): 422–430.

5327. Schapiro, Beth S. "It's a Man's World: (Unless You Know the Right Questions to Ask)." *Campaigns and Elections* 13, no. 1 (June 1992): 52–54.

5328. Shabad, Goldie, and Kristi Andersen. "Candidate Evaluations by Men and Women." *Public Opinion Quarterly* 43 (Spring 1979): 18–35. Reprinted in *Women and the Public Sphere: A Critique of Sociology and Politics,* edited by Janet Siltanen and Michelle Stanworth. New York: St. Martin's Press, 1984.

5329. Soule, John W., and Wilma E. McGrath. "A Comparative Study of Male-Female Political Attitudes at Citizen and Elite Levels." In *A Portrait of Marginality: The Political Behavior of American Women,* edited by Marianne Githens and Jewell Prestage, 178–195. New York: McKay, 1977.

5330. "Women in the Poll, A Triumphant Test." *Literary Digest* 113 (9 April 1932): 7–9.

Toward Women

Political Women

5331. Alexander, Deborah, and Kristi Andersen. "Gender as a Factor in the Attribution of Leadership Traits." *Political Research Quarterly* 46 (September 1993): 527–545.

5332. Bennett, Linda L. M., and Stephen E. Bennett. "Changing Views about Gender Equality in Politics: Gradual Change and Lingering Doubts." In *Women in Politics: Outsiders or Insiders? A Collection of Readings,* edited by Lois Lovelace Duke, 46–56. Englewood Cliffs, NJ: Prentice Hall, 1993.

5333. Bird, A. T. "Women in Politics—Changing Perceptions." *Journal of the Association for the Study of Perceptions* 10 (1975): 1–9.

5334. Boles, Janet K., and H. Durio. "Social Stereotyping of Males and Females in Elected Office: The Implications of an Attitudinal Study." Paper presented at the annual meeting of the Midwest Political Science Association, Chicago, 1980.

5335. Bonafede, Dom. "Political Woman and Superwoman: Sex Stereotyping of Females in Elected Office." Paper presented at the annual meeting of the Midwest Political Science Association, Cincinnati, 1981.

5336. Burrell, Barbara C. "Public Opinion and Hillary Clinton as First Lady." Paper presented at the annual meeting of the American Political Science Association, Chicago, 1995.

5337. Cook, Elizabeth Adell. "Voter Responses to Women Senate Candidates." In *The Year of the Woman: Myths and Realities,* edited by Elizabeth Adell Cook, Sue Thomas, and Clyde Wilcox, 217–236. Boulder, CO: Westview Press, 1994.

5338. Deutchman, Iva Ellen. "Ungendered but Equal: Male Attitudes toward Women in State Legislatures." *Polity* 24 (Spring 1992): 417–432.

5339. Erskine, Hazel. "The Polls: Women's Role from Roosevelt to the Present." *Public Opinion Quarterly* 35 (Summer 1971): 275–290.

5340. Gallup, George. "Women in Politics." *The Gallup Poll Index* 228–229 (August–September 1984): 2–16.

5341. Hershey, Marjorie Random. "The Politics of Androgyny? Sex Roles and Attitudes toward Women in Politics." *American Politics Quarterly* 5, no. 3 (July 1977): 261–287.

5342. ———. "Support for Political Women: The Effects of Race, Sex, and Sexual Roles." In *The Electorate Reconsidered,* edited by Joch C. Pierce and John L. Sullivan: 177–198. Beverly Hills, CA: Sage, 1980.

5343. Howard, George E. "Changing Ideas and Status of the Family and the Public Activities of Women." *Annals of the American Academy of Political and Social Science* 56 (November 1914): 27–37.

5344. Kelly, Rita Mae, and Kimberly Fisher. "An Assessment of Articles about Women in the 'Top 15' Political Science Journals." *PS* 26 (September 1993): 544–558.

5345. Main, Eleanor C., Gerard S. Gryski, and Beth S. Schapiro. "Different Perspectives: Southern State Legislators' Attitudes about Women in Politics." *Social Science Journal* 21, no. 1 (January 1984): 21–28.

5346. Mend, Michael R., Toni Bell, and Lawrence Bath. "Dynamics of Attitude Formation Regarding Women in Politics." *Experimental Study of Politics* 5 (1976): 25–39.

5347. Patrick, Catherine. "Attitudes about Women Executives in Government Positions." *Journal of Social Psychology* 19 (February 1944): 3–34.

5348. Shilvock, A. R., and Gerald J. Schnepp. "Women in Politics: Catholic Collegiate Attitudes." *Social Order* 3 (October 1953): 361–366.

5349. Tate, Katherine. "Invisible Woman, Black Opinion on the Thomas-Hill Controversy." *The American Prospect* 8 (Winter 1992): 74–81.

5350. Turner, Barbara F., and Castellano B. Turner. "The Political Implications of Social Stereotyping of Women and Men among Black and White College Students." *Sociology and Social Research* 58 (1974): 155–162.

5351. Welch, Susan, and Lee Sigelman. "Changes in Public Attitudes toward Women in Politics." *Social Science Quarterly* 63 (June 1982): 312–321.

5352. Wells, Audrey Siess, and Eleanor Cutri Smeal. "Women's Attitudes toward Women in Politics: A Survey of Urban Registered Voters and Party Committeewomen." In *Woman and Politics,* edited by Jane S. Jaquette, 54–72. New York: Wiley, 1974.

5353. "What America Thinks of Votes for Women." *Literary Digest* 51 (October 1915): 753–756, 800–813.

Women Candidates

5354. Ferree, Myra Marx. "A Woman for President? Changing Responses, 1958–1972." *Public Opinion Quarterly* 38 (Fall 1974): 390–399.

5355. Frankovic, Kathleen A. "The Ferraro Factor: The Women's Movement, the Polls, and the Press." In *The Politics of the Gender Gap: The Social Construction of Political Influence,* edited by Carol M. Mueller, 102–123. Women's Policy Studies, 12. Beverly Hills, CA: Sage, 1988.

5356. Geis, Florence L. "Why Not a Woman for President? The Psychology of Sex Role Expectation." In *The Role of Women in Politics,* edited by Mae R. Carter. Newark: University of Delaware, Division of Continuing Education, 1964.

5357. Gitelson, Idy B., and Alan R. Gitelson. "Adolescent Attitudes toward Male and Female Political Candidates: An Experimental Design." *Women and Politics* 1, no. 4 (Winter 1980–1981): 53–64.

5358. Huddy, Leonie, and Nayda Terkildsen. "The Consequences of Gender Stereotypes for Women Candidates at Different Levels and Types of Office." *Political Research Quarterly* 46 (September 1993): 503–525.

5359. Rosenwasser, Shirley, Robyn Rogers, Sheila Fling, Kayla Silver-Pickens, and John Butemeyer. "Attitudes toward Women and Men in Politics: Perceived Male and Female Candidate Competencies and Participant Personality Characteristics." *Political Psychology* 8 (1987): 191–200.

5360. Rosenwasser, Shirley, and Jana Scale. "Attitudes toward a Hypothetical Male or Female Presidential Candidate—A Research Note." *Political Psychology* 9 (1988): 591–598.

5361. Schreiber, Eugene M. "Education and Change in American Opinions on a Woman for President." *Public Opinion Quarterly* 42, no. 2 (Summer 1978): 171–182.

5362. Sigelman, Carol K., Dan B. Thomas, and Lee Sigelman. "Gender, Physical Attractiveness, and Electability: An Experimental Investigation of Voter Biases." *Journal of Applied Social Psychology* 16, no. 2 (1986): 229–248.

5363. Sigelman, Lee, Carol K. Sigelman, and Christopher Fowler. "A Bird of a Different Feather? An Experimental Investigation of Physical Attractiveness and the Electability of Female Candidates." *Social Psychological Quarterly* 50 (March 1987): 32–43.

5364. Sigelman, Lee, and Susan Welch. "Race, Gender and Opinion toward Black and Female Presidential Candidates." *Public Opinion Quarterly* 48 (Summer 1984): 467–475.

5365. Wells, Audrey Siess. "Female Attitudes toward Women in Politics: The Propensity to Support Women." Ph.D. dissertation, University of Florida, Gainesville, 1972.

Views of Women

General

5366. Deutchman, Iva Ellen, and Sandra Prince-Embury. "Political Ideology of Pro- and Anti-ERA Women." *Women and Politics* 2, no. 1–2 (Spring–Summer 1982): 39–56.

5367. Dimierei, Thomas, and Carol M. Mueller. "The Structure of Belief Systems among Contending ERA Activists." *Social Forces* 60 (1982): 657–673.

5368. Newsome, Chevelle A. "The Subjective Identification of Women: Citizens to Political Representatives." Ph.D. dissertation, University of Oklahoma, 1994.

5369. Tedin, Kent L. "If the Equal Rights Amendment Becomes Law: Perceptions of Consequences among Female Activists and Masses." Paper presented at the annual meeting of the Midwest Political Science Association, Chicago, 1980.

5370. Tedin, Kent L., David W. Brady, Mary E. Buxton, Barbara M. Gorman, and Judy L. Thompson. "Social Background and Political Differences between Pro- and Anti-ERA

Activists." *American Politics Quarterly* 5, no. 3 (July 1977): 395–408.

5371. "Women and Politics: Poll Results." *Redbook* 151 (November 1979): 37.

Political Women

5372. Andersen, Kristi, and Elizabeth Adell Cook. "Women, Work and Political Attitudes." *American Journal of Political Science* 29, no. 3 (1985): 606–625.

5373. Chen, Diana. "A Study of Political Attitudes of Chinese and Puerto Rican Women." *International Journal of Group Tensions* 11, no. 1–4 (1981): 59–80.

5374. Cook, Elizabeth Adell. "Measuring Feminist Consciousness." *Women and Politics* 9 (1989): 71–88.

5375. ———. "Feminist Consciousness and Candidate Preference among American Women: 1972–1988." Paper presented at the annual meeting of the Southern Political Science Association, Tampa, 1990.

5376. Costantini, Edmond. "Political Women and Political Ambition: Closing the Gender Gap." *American Journal of Political Science* 34 (August 1990): 741–770.

5377. Farah, Barbara G. "Climbing the Political Ladder: The Aspirations and Expectations of Partisan Elites." In *New Research on Women and Sex Roles at the University of Michigan,* edited by Dorothy G. McGuigan, 238–250. Ann Arbor: University of Michigan Center for the Continuing Education of Women, 1977.

5378. Freedman, Estelle B. "The New Woman: Changing Views of Women in the 1920s." *The Journal of American History* 61, no. 2 (September 1974): 372–393.

5379. Ghaffaradli-Doty, Paricher, and Earl R. Carlson. "Consistency in Attitude and Behavior of Women with a Liberated Attitude toward the Rights and Roles of Women." *Sex Roles* 5, no. 4 (August 1979): 395–404.

5380. Holsti, Ole R., and James N. Rosenau. "The Foreign Policy Beliefs of Women in Leadership Positions." *Journal of Politics* 43 (May 1981): 326–347. Reprinted in *Women, Policy and Politics,* edited by Ellen Boneparth, 238–262. New York: Pergamon, 1982.

5381. Kruschke, Earl R. "Female Politicals and Apoliticals: Some Measurements and Comparisons." Ph.D. dissertation, University of Wisconsin, 1963.

5382. McWilliams, Nancy. "Contemporary Feminism, Consciousness-Raising, and Changing Views of the Political." In *Woman and Politics,* edited by Jane S. Jaquette, 157–170. New York: Wiley, 1974.

5383. Poole, Keith T. "Political Woman: Gender Indifference." *Public Opinion Quarterly* 8 (August–September 1985): 54–57.

5384. Poole, Keith T., and L. Harmon Zeigler. *Women, Public Opinion, and Politics: The Changing Political Attitudes of American Women.* New York: Longman, 1985.

5385. Steihm, Judith H., ed. *Women's Views of the Political World of Men.* Dobbs Ferry, NY: Transnational, 1984.

5386. Tilton, Elizabeth. "What Women Want." *Current History* 17 (November 1922): 282–287.

5387. Welch, Susan. "Support among Women for the Issues of the Women's Movement." *The Sociological Quarterly* 16, no. 2 (Spring 1975): 215–227.

Participation

5388. Fulenwider, Claire Knoche. "Feminist Ideology and the Political Attitudes and Participation of White and Minority Women." *Western Political Quarterly* 34, no. 1 (March 1981): 17–30.

5389. Hansen, Susan B., Linda M. Franz, and Margaret Netemeyer-Mays. "Women's Political Participation and Policy Preferences." *Social Science Quarterly* 56, no. 4 (March 1976): 576–540.

5390. Hershey, Marjorie Randon, and John L. Sulivan. "Sex Role Attitudes, Identities and Political Ideology." *Sex Roles* 3 (February 1977): 36–57.

5391. Hofstetter, C. Richard, and William Schultze. "Some Observations about Participation and Attitudes among Single Parent Women: Inferences Concerning Political Translation." *Women and Politics* 9, no. 1 (1989): 83–105.

5392. Kruschke, Earl R. "Level of Optimism as Related to Female Polit-ical Behavior." *Social Science Journal* 41, no. 2 (April 1966): 67–75.

5393. McMiller, Darryl L. "The Effects of Economic Circumstances and Attitudes on Black Women's Political Opinions and Participation." Paper presented at the annual meeting of the American Political Science Association, Chicago, 1995.

5394. Merritt, Sharyne. "Sex Roles and Political Ambition." *Sex Roles* 8 (September 1982): 1025–1036.

5395. Sapiro, Virginia. "Private Costs of Public Commitments or Public Costs of Private Commitments: Family Roles Versus Political Ambition." *American Journal of Political Science* 26 (May 1982): 265–279.

5396. Stewart, Abigail J., and Sharon Gold-Steinberg. "Midlife Women's Political Consciousness: Case Studies of Psychosocial Development and Political Commitment." *Psychology of Women Quarterly* 14 (December 1990): 543–566.

5397. Tingsten, Herbert. "Electoral Participation and Political Attitude of Women." Chap. 1 in *Political Behavior: Studies in Election Statistics,* edited by Herbert Tingsten, 30–33. Totowa, NJ: Bedminster Press, 1937.

5398. Wuthnow, Robert, and William Lehrman. "Religion: Inhibitor or Facilitator of Political Involvement among Women?" In *Women, Politics and Change,* edited by Louise A. Tilly and Patricia Gurin, 300–322. New York: Sage, 1990.

Gender Gap

5399. Aiegler, Harmon, and Keith Pole. "Political Woman: Gender in Difference." *Public Opinion* (August–September 1985): 55.

5400. Burrell, Barbara C. "Sex Differences in Political Ambition among Elites: Examination of Some Assumptions and Findings." Paper presented at the annual meeting of the American Political Science Association, Washington, DC, 1980.

5401. Carroll, Susan J. "Political Elites and Sex Differences in Political Ambition: A Reconsideration." *Journal of Politics* 47 (November 1985): 1231–1243.

5402. Deitch, Cynthia. "Sex Differences in Support for Government Spending." In *The Politics of the Gender Gap: The Social Construction of Political Influence*, edited by Carol M. Mueller, 192–216. Women's Policy Studies, 12. Beverly Hills, CA: Sage, 1988.

5403. Goertzel, Ted George. "The Gender Gap: Sex, Family, Income and Political Opinions in the Early 1980's." *Journal of Political and Military Sociology* 11, no. 2 (Fall 1983): 209–222.

5404. Greenstein, Fred. "Sex-Related Political Differences in Childhood." *Journal of Politics* 23 (May 1961): 353–371.

5405. Jennings, M. Kent. "Gender Roles and Inequalities in Political Participation: Results from an Eight-Nation Study." *Western Political Quarterly* 36 (September 1983): 364–385.

5406. Lake, Celinda C., and Vicent J. Breglio. "Different Voices, Different Views: The Politics of Gender." In *The American Woman: 1992–1993*, edited by Paula Ries and Anne J. Stone, 178–201. New York: Norton, 1993.

5407. McLoughlin, Merrill, Tracy L. Shryer, Erica E. Goode, and Kathleen McAuliffe. "Attitude in Politics and Management, the 'Gender Gap' Is Real." *U.S. News and World Report* 105 (8 August 1988): 56–57.

5408. Moley, Raymond. "What Every Woman Should Know: No Political Distinctions between Men and Women." *Newsweek* 24 (14 August 1944): 100.

5409. Nechemias, Carol. "Plenary Panelists Analyze Gender Differences in Politics." *PS* 16 (Fall 1983): 733–737.

5410. Somma, Mark. "The Gender Gap and Attitudes towards Economic Development Strategies among Midwestern Adults." *Women and Politics* 12, no. 2 (1992): 41–57.

5411. Tedin, Kent L., David W. Brady, and Arnold Vedlitz. "Sex Differences in Political Attitudes: The Case for Situational Factors." *Journal of Politics* 39 (May 1977): 448–456.

5412. Wassenberg, Pinky, Kay G. Wolsborn, Paul R. Hagner, and John C. Pierce. "Gender Differences in Political Conceptualization, 1956–1980." *American Political Science Quarterly* 11, no. 2 (April 1983): 181–204.

5413. Wilcox, Clyde, and Dee Alsop. "Group Differences in Early Support for Military Action in the Gulf: The Effects of Gender, Generation, and Ethnicity." *American Politics Quarterly* 21 (1993): 343–359.

Women's Issues

5414. Blake, Judith. "Abortion and Public Opinion: The 1960–1970 Decade." *Public Opinion and Science* 171 (February 1971): 540–549.

5415. Gallup, George. "Majority Feels Reagan Administration Deals Fairly with Women and Blacks." *Gallup Report* (May 1983): 3–15.

5416. Granberg, Donald, and Beth Wellman Granberg. "Social Bases of Support and Opposition to Legalized Abortion." In *Perspectives on Abortion,* edited by Paul Sachdev, 191–204. Metuchen, NJ: Scarecrow Press, 1985.

5417. Jackson, John E., and Maris A. Vinovskis. "Public Opinion, Elections and the Single Issue." In *The Abortion Dispute and the American System,* edited by Gilbert Y. Steiner, 64–81. Washington, DC: Brookings, 1983.

5418. Marshall, Susan E. "Equity Issues and Black-White Differences in Women's ERA Support." *Social Science Quarterly* 71, no. 2 (June 1990): 298–314.

5419. Schramm, Sarah Slavin. "Women's Educational Equity: Favorable Student Response." *Policy Studies Journal* 7, no. 2 (Winter 1978): 243–250.

5420. Shapiro, Robert V., and Harpreet Mahajan. "Gender Differ-

ences in Policy Preferences: A Summary of Trends from the 1960s to the 1980s." *Public Opinion Quarterly* 50 (Spring 1986): 42–61.

5421. Smith, Tom W. "The Polls: Gender and Attitudes Toward Violence." *Public Opinion Quarterly* 48 (Spring 1984): 384–396.

5422. Tedrow, Lucky M., and E. R. Mahoney. "Trends in Attitudes Toward Abortion: 1972–1976." *Public Opinion Quarterly* 43 (Summer 1979): 181–189.

5423. Volgy, Thomas. "Dimensions of Support for Women's Issues: The Salience of Sex-Roles." Paper presented at the annual meeting of the American Political Science Association, Washington, DC, 1979.

5424. Wilcox, Clyde. "Race Differences in Abortion Attitudes: Some Additional Evidence." *Public Opinion Quarterly* 54 (1990): 248–255.

Political Socialization

5425. Dauphinais, Pat Dewey, Steven E. Barkan, and Steven F. Cohn. "Predictors of Rank-and-File Feminist Activism: Evidence from the 1983 General Social Survey." *Social Problems* 39, no. 4 (1992): 332–344.

5426. Feltner, Paula, and Leneen Goldie. "Impact of Socialization and Personality on the Female Voter: Speculations Tested with 1964 Presidential Data." *Western Political Quarterly* 27, no. 4 (1974): 680–692.

5427. Flora, Cornelia Butler, and Naomi B. Lynn. "Women and Political Socialization: Considerations of the Impact of Motherhood." In *Woman and Politics,* edited by Jane S. Jaquette, 37–53. New York: Wiley, 1974.

5428. Hess, Robert D., and Judith V. Torney. "The Influence of Sex Role Orientation." In *The Development of Political Attitudes in Children,* edited by Robert D. Hess and Judith V. Torney, 173–194. Chicago: Aldine, 1967.

5429. Iglitzin, Lynne B. "The Making of Apolitical Woman: Femininity and Sex-Stereotyping in Girls." In *Women in Politics,* edited by Jane Jaquette, 25–36. New York: Wiley, 1974.

5430. Jelen, Ted G. "The Effects of Gender Role Stereotypes on Political Attitudes." *Social Science Journal* 25 (1988): 353–365.

5431. Kelly, Rita Mae, ed. *Gender and Socialization to Power and Politics.* New York: Haworth Press, 1986.

5432. Kelly, Rita Mae, and Mary Boutilier. "Political Efficacy and Women." In *The Making of Political Women, A Study of Socialization and Role Conflict,* edited by Rita Mae Kelly and Mary Boutilier, 49–84. Chicago: Nelson-Hall, 1978.

5433. ———, eds. *The Making of Political Woman: A Study of Socialization and Role Conflict.* Chicago: Nelson-Hall, 1978.

5434. Kronenfeld, Jennie Jacobs, and Marcia Lynn Whicker. "Feminist Movements and Changes in Sex Roles: The Influence of Technology." *Sociological Focus* 19, no. 1 (January 1986): 47–60.

5435. Lewis, Kathryn, and Margaret Bierly. "Toward a Profile of the Female Voter: Sex Differences in Perceived Physical Attractiveness and Competence of Political Candidates." *Sex Roles* 22 (1990): 1–11.

5436. Lynn, Naomi B. "Motherhood and Political Participation: The Changing Sense of Self." *Journal of Political and Military Sociology* 1, no. 1 (Spring 1973): 91–102.

5437. McGlen, Nancy E. "The Impact of Parenthood on Political Participation." *Western Political Quarterly* 33, no. 3 (1980): 297–313.

5438. Orum, Anthony M., Roberta S. Cohen, Sherri Grasmucy, and Amy W. Orum. "Sex, Socialization, and Politics." In *A Portrait of Marginality: The Political Behavior of American Women,* edited by Marianne Githens and Jewell Prestage, 17–37. New York: McKay, 1977.

5439. Perkins, Jerry. "Political Ambition among Black and White Women: An Intergender Test of the Socialization Model." *Women and Politics* 6 (1986): 27–40.

5440. Ridington, Jilliam. "The Transition Process: A Feminist Environment as Reconstitutive Milieu." *Victimology: An International Journal* 2, no. 3, 4 (1977): 563–575.

5441. Sapiro, Virginia. *The Political Integration of Women: Role, Socialization and Politics.* Urbana: University of Illinois, 1983.

5442. Thompson, Joan Hulse. "Role Perceptions of Women in the Ninety-Fourth Congress, 1975–76." *Political*

Science Quarterly 95, no. 1 (Spring 1980): 71–81.

5443. Whicker, Marcia Lynn, and Jennie Jacobs Kronenfeld. *Sex Role Changes: Technology, Politics, and Policy.* New York: Praeger, 1986.

5444. Wilcox, Clyde. "Race, Gender Role Attitudes and Support for Feminism." *Western Political Quarterly* 43 (March 1990): 113–123.

VII. Political Theory

General

5445. Boals, Kay. "Review Essay: Political Science." *Signs* 1 (1975): 161–174.

5446. Bonder, Gloria. "The Study of Politics from the Standpoint of Women." *International Social Science Journal* 35 (1983): 569–583.

5447. Chafetz, Janet Saltzman. *Gender Equity: An Integrated Theory of Stability and Change.* Newbury Park, CA: Sage, 1990.

5448. Cott, Nancy F. "What's in a Name? The Limits of 'Social Feminism'—Or Expanding the Vocabulary of Women's History." *Journal of American History* 76 (1989): 809–829.

5449. DuBois, Ellen Carol, Mari Jo Buhle, Temma Kaplan, Gerda Lerner, and Carroll Smith-Rosenberg. "Politics and Culture in Women's History: A Symposium." *Feminist Studies* 6, no. 1 (1980): 26–64.

5450. Ehrenreich, Barbara. "Sorry Sister, This Is Not the Revolution." *Time* 136 (Fall 1990): 15. Special issue on women.

5451. Fox-Genovese, Elizabeth. *Feminism without Illusions: A Critique of Individualism.* Chapel Hill: University of North Carolina, 1991.

5452. Fraser, Nancy. *Unruly Practices: Power, Discourses, and Gender in Contemporary Social Theory.* Minneapolis: University of Minnesota Press, 1989.

5453. Getliln, J. Osh, and Heidi Evans. "Sex and Politics." *The Quill* 80 (March 1992): 16–17.

5454. Hansen, Karen V., and Ilene J. Philipson, eds. *Women, Class and the Feminist Imagination.* Philadelphia: Temple University Press, 1990.

5455. Hewitt, Nancy A. "Beyond the Search for Sisterhood: American Women's History in the 1980s." *Social History* 10, no. 3 (October 1985): 299–321.

5456. Jaquette, Jane S. "Political Science." *Signs* 2 (1976): 147–164.

5457. Jones, Kathleen B., and Anna G. Jonasdottir. *The Political Interests of Gender: Developing Theory and Research with a Feminist Face.* London: Sage, 1988.

5458. Kelly, Rita Mae, Linda M. Williams, and Kimberly Fisher. "Women and Politics: An Assessment of Its Role within the Discipline of Political Science." *Women and Politics* 14, no. 4 (1994): 3–18.

5459. Keohane, Nannerl O. "Speaking from Silence: Women and the Science of Politics." *Soundings* 64, no. 4 (1981): 422–436.

5460. Lerner, Gerda. *The Majority Finds Its Past, Placing Women in History.* New York: Oxford University Press, 1979.

5461. Roberts, Helen, ed. *Doing Feminist Research.* London: Routledge and Kegan Paul, 1981.

5462. Rosenberg, Rosalind. "The Academic Prison: The New View of American Women." *Women of America: A History,* edited by Carol Ruth Berkin and Mary Beth Norton, 318–341. Boston: Houghton Mifflin, 1979.

5463. Stimpson, Catherine E. *Women's Studies in the United States.* New York: Ford Foundation, 1986.

Feminism

5464. Alcoff, Linda. "Cultural Feminism Versus Post-Structuralism: The Identity Crisis in Feminist Theory." *Signs* 13 (Winter 1988): 405–436.

5465. Ashe, Marie, and Naomi R. Cahn. "Child Abuse: A Problem for Feminist Theory." *Texas Journal of Women and the Law* (Winter 1992): 75–112. Symposium on new perspectives on women and violence.

5466. Austin, Regina. "Sapphire Bound!" In *Feminist Jurisprudence,* edited by Patricia Smith, 575–593. New York: Oxford University Press, 1993.

5467. Barry, Kathleen. "Feminist Theory: The Meaning of Women's Liberation." In *The Woman's Annual—The Year in Review, 1982–83,* edited by Barbara Haber, 55–78. Boston: G. K. Hall, 1983.

5468. Billington, Rosamund. "Ideology and Feminism: Why the Suffragettes Were 'Wild Women'." *Women's Studies* 5, no. 6 (1982): 663–674.

5469. Black, Naomi. *Social Feminism.* Ithaca, NY: Cornell University, 1989.

5470. Boles, Janet K. "American Feminism: New Issues for a Mature Movement." *Annals of the American Academy of Political and Social Science* 515 (May 1991): 8–9. Special issue.

5471. ———. "Form Follows Function: The Evolution of Feminist Strategies." *Annals of the American Academy of Political and Social Science* 515 (May 1991): 38–49.

5472. Brenner, Johanna. "Feminist Political Discourses: Radical Versus Liberal Approaches to the Feminization of Poverty and Comparable Worth." *Gender and Society* 1 (December 1987): 447–465.

5473. Bryson, Valerie. *Feminist Political Theory.* New York: Paragon House, 1992.

5474. *Building Feminist Theory: Essays from Quest, A Feminist Quarterly.* New York: Longman, 1981.

5475. Bulkin, Elly, Minnie Bruce Pratt, and Barbara Smith. *Yours in Struggle: Three Feminist Perspectives on Anti-Semitism and Racism.* Brooklyn, NY: Long Haul Press, 1984.

5476. Bunch, Charlotte. *Passionate Politics: Feminist Theory in Action.* New York: St. Martin's Press, 1987.

5477. Chafe, William H. *Women and Equality: Changing Patterns in American Culture.* New York: Oxford University Press, 1977.

5478. Donovan, Josephine. *Feminist Theory: The Intellectual Traditions of American Feminism.* New York: Unger, 1985.

5479. Eisenstein, Hester. *Contemporary Feminist Thought.* Boston: G.K. Hall, 1983.

5480. Eisenstein, Zillah. *The Radical Future of Liberal Feminism,* rev. ed. New York: Longman, 1993 (1986, 1981).

5481. ———. *Feminism and Sexual Equality: Crisis in Liberal America.* New York: Monthly Review Press, 1984.

5482. Epstein, Barbara. "Feminist Spirituality and Magical Politics." In *Political Protest and Cultural Revolution,* edited by Barbara Epstein, 157–194. Berkeley: University of California, 1991.

5483. Estrich, Susan. *Real Rape.* Cambridge: Harvard University, 1987.

5484. Evans, Judith, ed. *Feminism and Political Theory.* London: Sage, 1986.

5485. Farganis, Sondra. *The Social Reconstruction of the Feminine Character.* Totowa, NJ: Rowman and Littlefield, 1986.

5486. "Feminism in the Law: Theory, Practice and Criticism." *University of Chicago Legal Forum* 1989 (1989). Special issue.

5487. Ferguson, Kathy. *The Man Question: Visions of Subjectivity in Feminist Theory.* Berkeley, CA: University of California, 1993.

5488. Flammang, Janet A. "Feminist Theory: The Question of Power." In *Current Perspective in Social Theory,* edited by S. C. McNall, 37–38. Greenwich, CT: JAI Press, 1983.

5489. Freeman, Bonnie Cook. "Power Patriarchy and 'Political Primitives'." In *Beyond Intellectual Sexism,* edited by Joan I. Roberts, 251. New York: McKay, 1976.

5490. Frye, Marilyn. *The Politics of Reality: Essays in Feminist Theory.* Trumansburg, NY: Crossing Press, 1983.

5491. ———. "Do You Have to Be a Lesbian to Be a Feminist?" *Off Our Backs* (August–September 1990): 21–23.

5492. Fulenwider, Claire Knoche. *Feminism in American Politics: A Study of Ideological Influence.* New York: Praeger, 1980.

5493. Gelb, Joyce. *Feminism and Politics: A Comparative Perspective.* Berkeley: University of California, 1989.

5494. Gould, Carol C. "Feminism and Democratic Community Revisited." In *Democratic Community,* edited by Ira Shapiro, 396–413. NOMOS, Vol. XXXV. New York: New York University Press, 1993.

5495. Hawkesworth, Mary E. *Beyond Oppression: Feminist Theory and Political Strategy.* New York: Continuum, 1990.

5496. ———. "Knowers, Knowing, Known Feminist Theory and Claims of Truth." *Signs* 14, no. 3 (1989): 533–557.

5497. ———. *Beyond Oppression: Feminist Theory and Political Strategy.* New York: Continuum, 1990.

5498. Hooks, Bell. *Feminist Theory: From Margin to Center.* Boston: South End Press, 1984.

5499. Jones, Kathleen B. "Citizenship in a Woman-Friendly Polity." *Signs* 15 (Summer 1990): 781–812.

5500. MacKinnon, Catharine A. "The Male Ideology of Privacy: Feminist Perspective on the Right to Abortion." *Radical America* 17, no. 4 (1983): 23–38.

5501. ———. *Feminism Unmodified.* Cambridge: Harvard University Press, 1987.

5502. ———. "Toward Feminist Jurisprudence." In *Feminist Jurisprudence,* edited by Patricia Smith, 610–620. New York: Oxford University Press, 1993.

5503. Macy, John. "Equality of Woman with Men: A Myth, a Challenge to Feminism." *Harper's Weekly* 153 (November 1926): 705–713.

5504. Miles, Angela. *Feminism Radicals in the 1980s.* Quebec, Canada: Culture Texts, 1985.

5505. Minow, Martha. "Feminist Reason: Getting It and Losing It." *Journal of Legal Education* 38 (1988): 47.

5506. O'Neill, William L. "Feminism as a Radical Ideology." In *Dissent: Explorations in the History of American Radicalism,* edited by Alfred F. Young, 273–300. DeKalb: North Illinois University Press, 1968.

5507. Pateman, Carole. *The Disorder of Women: Democracy, Feminism and Political Theory.* Oxford: Polity Press, 1980.

5508. Radin, Margaret Jane. "The Pragmatist and the Feminist." In *Feminist Jurisprudence,* edited by Patricia Smith, 531–558. New York: Oxford University Press, 1993.

5509. Rakow, Lana. *Women Making Meaning.* New York: Routledge, 1992.

5510. Rhode, Deborah L. "Feminist Critical Theories." In *Feminist Jurisprudence,* edited by Patricia Smith, 594–609. New York: Oxford University Press, 1993.

5511. Rosenberg, Rosalind. *Beyond Separate Spheres: Intellectual Roots of Modern Feminism.* New Haven, CT: Yale University Press, 1982.

5512. Shanley, Mary Lyndon, and Carole Pateman, eds. *Feminist Theory and Interpretations.* Oxford: Polity Press, 1991.

5513. Spelman, Elizabeth V. *Inessential Woman: Problems of Exclusion in Feminist Thought.* Boston: Beacon Press, 1988.

5514. Stacey, Judith. "The New Conservative Feminism." *Feminist Studies* 9, no. 3 (Fall 1983): 559–583.

5515. Stoper, Emily, and Roberta Ann Johnson. "The Weaker Sex and the Better Half: The Idea of Women's Moral Superiority in the American Feminist Movement." *Polity* 10 (Winter 1977): 192–217.

5516. Sunstein, Cass R. *Feminism and Political Theory.* Chicago: University of Chicago Press, 1990.

5517. Wilcox, Clyde, and Elizabeth Adell Cook. "Evangelical Women and Feminism: Some Additional Evidence." *Women and Politics* 9, no. 2 (1989): 27–50.

5518. Williams, Joan C. "Deconstructing Gender." In *Feminist Jurisprudence,* edited by Patricia Smith, 493–530. New York: Oxford University Press, 1993.

5519. Willis, Ellen. "Radical Feminism and Feminist Radicalism." In *The '60s without Apology,* edited by Sohnya Sayres, Aners Stephanson, Stanley Aronowitz, and Fredric Jameson, 91–118. Minneapolis: University of Minnesota, 1984.

5520. "Women's Law Forum." *Golden Gate Law Review* 20 (1990). Special Issue.

Women of Color

5521. Anzaldua, Gloria. *Making Face, Making Soul, Haciendo Caras: Creative and Critical Perspectives by Women of Color.* San Francisco: Aunt Lute, 1990.

5522. Aptheker, Bettina. *Woman's Legacy: Essays on Race, Sex and Class in American History.* Amherst: University of Massachusetts, 1982.

5523. Collins, Patricia Hill. "Learning from the Outsider within: The Sociological Significance of Black Feminist Thought." *Social Problems* 33 (December 1986): 514–543.

5524. ———. "The Social Construction of Black Feminist Thought." *Signs* 14, no. 4 (1989): 745–773.

5525. ———. *Black Feminist Thought: Knowledge, Consciousness and the Politics of Empowerment.* Boston: Unwin Hyman, 1991.

5526. Dill, Bonnie Thornton. "Race, Class and Gender: Prospects for an All-Inclusive Sisterhood." *Feminist Studies* 9 (1983): 131–150. Reprinted in *Black Women in United States History,* edited by Darlene Clark Hine, 121–140. Brooklyn, NY: Carlson, 1990.

5527. Guy-Sheftall, Beverly. *Words of Fire: An Anthology of African-American Feminist Thought.* New York: The New Press, 1995.

5528. Higginbotham, Evelyn Brooks. "African-American Women's History and the Metalanguage of Race." *Signs* 17 (Winter 1995): 251–274. Reprinted in *"We Specialize in the Wholly Impossible": A Reader in Black Women's History,* edited by Darlene Clark Hine, Wilma King, and Linda Reed, 3–24. Brooklyn, NY: Carlson; 1995.

5529. Hooks, Bell. "Black Women: Shaping Feminist Theory." In *Words of Fire: An Anthology of African-American Feminist Thought,* edited by Beverly Guy-Sheftall, 269–282. New York: The New Press, 1995.

5530. Hull, Gloria T., Patricia Bell Scott, and Barbara Smith, eds. *All the Women Are White, All the Blacks Are Men, But Some of Us Are Brave: Black Women's Studies.* Old Westbury, NY: The Feminist Press, 1982.

5531. King, Deborah K. "Multiple Jeopardy, Multiple Consciousness: The Context of a Black Feminist Ideology." In *Black Women in America: Social Science Perspectives,* edited by

Micheline R. Malston, Elisabeth Mudimbe-Boyi, Jean F. O'Barr, and Mary Wyer, 265–296. Chicago: University of Chicago Press, 1988. Reprinted in *Black Women in United States History*, edited by Darlene Clark Hine, 331–362. Brooklyn, NY: Carlson, 1990.

5532. King, Mae C. "The Politics of Sexual Stereotypes." *The Black Scholar* 46–7 (March–April 1973): 12–23. Reprinted in *A Portrait of Marginality: The Political Behavior of American Women,* edited by Marianne Githens and Jewell Prestage, 346–365. New York: McKay, 1977.

5533. Lewis, Diane K. "A Response to Inequality: Black Women, Racism and Sexism." *Signs* 3, no. 2 (1977): 339–361. Reprinted in Vol. 9 of *Black Women in United States History,* edited by Darlene Clark Hine, 383–406. Brooklyn, NY: Carlson, 1990.

5534. Lourde, Audre. *Sister Outsider.* Trumansburg, NY: Crossing Press, 1984.

5535. Marable, Manning. "Groundings with My Sisters: Patriarchy and the Exploitation of Black Women." In Vol. 9 of *Black Women in United States History,* edited by Darlene Clark Hine, 406–446. Brooklyn, NY: Carlson, 1990.

5536. Morrison, Toni, ed. *Race–ing Justice, En–gendering Power: Essays on Anita Hill, Clarence Thomas, and the Construction of Social Reality.* New York: Pantheon, 1992.

5537. Omolade, Barbara. "Black Women and Feminism." In *The Future of Difference,* edited by Zillah Eisenstein and A. Jardine, 247–257.

Metuchen, NJ: Rutgers University Press, 1980.

5538. Smitherman, Geneva, ed. *African American Women Speak Out on Anita Hill–Clarence Thomas.* Detroit, MI: Wayne State University, 1995.

5539. Swerdlow, Amy, and Hannah Lessinger, eds. *Race, Class and Sex, the Dynamics of Control.* Boston: G. K. Hall, 1983.

5540. White, Carol Wayne. "Toward an Afra-American Feminism." In *Women: A Feminist Perspective,* 5th ed., edited by Jo Freeman, 529–545. Mountain View, CA: Mayfield, 1995.

5541. White, E. Francis. "Listening to the Voices of Black Feminism." *Radical America* 2, no. 3 (March–June 1984): 9.

5542. Winkler, Karen J. "The Rise of Black Feminist Thought." *Chronicle of Higher Education* 40, no. 30 (March 1994): 12–17.

Mothers

5543. Alpert, Jane. "Mother Right: A Feminist Theory." *Ms.* 2, no. 2 (August 1973): 90–92.

5544. Bay, Christian. "Gentleness and Politics: The Case for Motherhood Reconsidered." *Politics (Australia)* 10, no. 2 (1975): 125–137.

5545. Boling, Patricia. "The Democratic Potential of Mothering." *Political Theory* 19 (November 1991): 606–625.

5546. Dietz, Mary G. "Citizenship with a Feminist Face: The Problem with Maternal Thinking." *Political Theory* 13, no. 3 (1985): 19–37.

5547. Finley, Lucinda. "Transcending Equality Theory: A Way Out of the Maternity and the Workplace Debate." *Columbia University Law Review* 86 (1986): 1118.

5548. Rendall, Jane. "Feminism and Republicanism: American Motherhood." *History Today* 34 (December 1984): 28–33.

5549. Rothman, Barbara Katz. *Recreating Motherhood: Ideology and Technology in a Patriarchal Society.* New York: Norton, 1989.

5550. Ruddick, Sara. *Maternal Thinking: Toward a Politics of Peace.* Boston: Beacon, 1989.

5551. Trebilcot, Joyce. *Mothering Essays in Feminist Theory.* Totowa, NJ: Rowman and Allanheld, 1983.

Women's Movement

5552. Buechler, Steven M. "Conceptualizing Radicalism and Transformation in Social Movements: The Case of the Woman Suffrage Movement." *Perspective on Social Problems* 2 (1982): 105–118.

5553. Campbell, Karlyn Kohrs. "The Rhetoric of Women's Liberation: An Oxymoron." *Quarterly Journal of Speech* 59 (February 1973): 74–86.

5554. Carroll, Susan J. "Gender Politics and the Socializing Impact of the Women's Movement." In *Political Learning in Adulthood: A Sourcebook of Theory and Research,* edited by Rober-

ta S. Sigel, 306–339. Chicago: University of Chicago Press, 1989.

5555. Freeman, Jo. "Crises and Conflicts in Social Movement Organizations." *Chrysalis: A Magazine of Women's Culture* 5 (1978): 43–51.

5556. Gelb, Joyce. "Social Movement 'Success': A Comparative Analysis of Feminism in the United States and the United Kingdom." In *The Women's Movements of the United States and Western Europe: Consciousness, Political Opportunity and Public Policy,* edited by Mary F. Katzenstein and Carol M. Mueller, 267–289. Philadelphia: Temple University Press, 1987.

5557. Huber, Joan. "Toward a Sociotechnological Theory of the Women's Movement." *Social Problems* 23, no. 2 (April 1976): 371–385.

5558. Klein, Ethel. "The Diffusion of Consciousness in the United States and Western Europe." In *The Women's Movements of the United States and Western Europe: Consciousness, Political Opportunity and Public Policy,* edited by Mary F. Katzenstein and Carol M. Mueller, 23–43. Philadelphia: Temple University Press, 1987.

5559. Levine, T. Z. "Ideas of Revolution in the Women's Movement." *American Behavioral Scientist* 20 (March–April 1977): 535–566.

5560. Mansbridge, Jane. "What Is the Feminist Movement ?" In *Feminist Organizations: Harvest of the New Women's Movement,* edited by Myra Marx Ferree and Patricia Yancey Martin, 27–34. Philadelphia: Temple University Press, 1995.

5561. McGlen, Nancy E., and Karen O'Connor. "An Analysis of the U.S. Women's Rights Movements: Rights as a Public Good." *Women and Politics* 1, no. 1 (Spring 1980): 65–86.

5562. Morris, Monica B. "The Public Definition of a Social Movement: Women's Liberation." *Sociology and Social Research* 57, no. 4 (July 1973): 526–543.

5563. Rosenfeld, Rachael A., and Kathryn B. Ward. "The Contemporary U.S. Women's Movement: An Empirical Example of Competition Theory." *Sociological Forum* 6, no. 3 (September 1991): 471–500.

5564. Samuels, Catherine. *Evolution of the Women's Movement: 1971–1974.* New York: Women's Action Alliance, 1975.

5565. Simon, Rita J., and Gloria Danziger. *Women's Movements in America.* New York: Praeger, 1991.

Organizations

5566. Ferguson, Kathy. *The Feminist Case against Bureaucracy.* Philadelphia: Temple University Press, 1984.

5567. Freeman, Jo. "The Tyranny of Structurelessness." *Berkeley Journal of Sociology* 17 (1972–73): 151–165. Reprinted in *Women in Politics,* edited by Jane Jaquette, 202–214. New York: John Wiley and Sons, 1974. Revised version published in *Ms.* (July 1973): 76.

5568. Gould, Meredith "When Women Create Organizations: The Ideological Imperatives of Femi-

nism." In *The International Yearbook of Organization Studies,* edited by David Dunkerley and Graeme Salaman, 237–252. London: Routledge and Kegan Paul, 1979.

5569. Mansbridge, Jane. "Feminism and Democratic Community." In *Democratic Community,* edited by Ira Shapiro, 339–395. NOMOS, Vol. XXXV. New York: New York University Press, 1993.

5570. Martin, Patricia Yancey. "Rethinking Feminist Organizations." *Gender and Society* 4, no. 2 (June 1990): 182–206.

5571. Mueller, Carol M. "The Organizational Basis of Conflict in Contemporary Feminism." In *Feminist Organizations: Harvest of the New Women's Movement,* edited by Myra Marx Ferree and Patricia Yancey Martin, 263–276. Philadelphia: Temple University Press, 1995.

5572. Sears, David O., and Leonie Huddy. "On the Origins of Political Disunity among Women." In *Women, Politics and Change,* edited by Louise A. Tilly and Patricia Gurin, 249–277. New York: Russell Sage, 1990.

5573. Sirianni, Carmen. "Learning Pluralism: Democracy and Diversity in Feminist Organizations." In *Democratic Community,* edited by Ira Shapiro, 283–312. NOMOS, Vol. XXXV. New York: New York University Press, 1993.

5574. Staggenborg, Suzanne. "Stability and Innovation in the Women's Movement: A Comparison of Two Movement Organizations." *Social Problems* 36, no. 1 (1989): 75–92.

Political Women

5575. Beard, Mary R. *American Women through Women's Eyes.* New York: Macmillan, 1933.

5576. Benenson, Robert. "Women and Politics." *Editorial Research Reports* (17 September 1982): 695–716.

5577. Bookman, Ann, and Sandra Morgen, eds. *Women and the Politics of Empowerment.* Philadelphia: Temple University Press, 1988.

5578. Carter, Mae R. *The Role of Women in Politics.* Newark: University of Delaware, Division of Continuing Education, 1974.

5579. Clatterbaugh, Kenneth. *Men, Contemporary Perspectives on Masculinity: Men, Women and Politics in Modern Society.* Boulder, CO: Westview Press, 1990.

5580. Coole, Diana. *Women in Political Theory: From Ancient Misogyny to Contemporary Feminism.* Boulder, CO: Lynn Rienner, 1988.

5581. Deutchman, Iva Ellen. "Feminist Theory and the Politics of Empowerment." In *Women in Politics: Outsiders or Insiders? A Collection of Readings,* edited by Lois Lovelace Duke, 3–15. Englewood Cliffs, NJ: Prentice Hall, 1993.

5582. Elshtain, Jean Bethke. *Public Man, Private Woman.* Princeton, NJ: Princeton University Press, 1981.

5583. Fowlkes, Diane L. *White Political Women, Paths from Privilege to Empowerment.* Knoxville: University of Tennessee Press, 1992.

5584. Gay, Kathlyn. *The New Power of Women in Politics.* Hillside, NJ: Enslow, 1994.

5585. Githens, Marianne, Pippa Norris, and Joni Lovenduski, eds. *Women and Politics.* New York: HarperCollins College, 1994.

5586. Hartsock, Nancy C. M. "Feminism, Power, and Change: A Theoretical Analysis." In *Women Organizing: An Anthology,* edited by Bernice Cummings and Victoria Schuck, 2–24. Metuchen, NJ: Scarecrow, 1979.

5587. Jaquette, Jane S., and Kathleen A. Staudt. "Two Conferences about Women and Politics." *Signs* 13 (Winter 1988): 372–376.

5588. Kelly, Rita Mae, and Jayne Burgess. "Gender and the Meaning of Power and Politics." *Women and Politics* 9, no. 1 (Winter 1989): 47–82.

5589. Marshner, Connaught C. *The New Traditional Woman.* Washington, DC: Free Congress Research and Education Foundation, 1982.

5590. McGerr, Michael E. "Political Style and Women's Power, 1830–1930." *Journal of American History* 77, no. 3 (December 1990): 864–885.

5591. Palley, Marian Lief. "Women and the Study of Public Policy." *Policy Studies Journal* 4 (Spring 1976): 288–296.

5592. Scott, Anne Firor, ed. *The American Woman: Who Was She?* Englewood Cliffs, NJ: Prentice Hall, 1971.

5593. ———. *What Is Happening to American Women.* Atlanta: Southern Newspaper Publishers Association, 1971.

5594. Shanley, Mary Lyndon. *Women's Rights, Feminism, and Politics in the United States.* Washington, DC: American Political Science Association, 1988.

5595. Shanley, Mary Lyndon, and Victoria Schuck. "In Search of Political Woman." *Social Science Quarterly* 55 (1975): 632–644.

5596. Stamm, Lisa, and Carol D. Ryff, eds. *Social Power and Influence of Women.* Boulder, CO: Westview Press, 1984.

5597. Stucker, John J. "Women's Political Role." *Current History* 70 (May 1976): 211–232.

5598. Verba, Sidney. "Women in American Politics." In *Women, Politics and Change,* edited by Louise A. Tilly and Patricia Gurin, 555–572. New York: Sage, 1990.

Socialist Feminism

5599. Eisenstein, Zillah. *Capitalist Patriarchy and the Case for Socialist Feminism.* New York: Monthly Review, 1979.

5600. Fraser, Nancy. "Struggle over Needs: Outline of a Socialist-Feminist Critical Theory of Late-Capitalist Political Culture." In *Women, the State and Welfare,* edited by Linda Gordon, 199–225. Madison: University of Wisconsin Press, 1990.

5601. Gordon, Linda. "Malthusianism, Socialism, and Feminism in the United States." *History of European Ideas* 4, no. 2 (1983): 203–214.

Law

5602. Baer, Judith A. "Nasty Law or Nice Ladies? Jurisprudence, Feminism, and Gender Difference." *Women and Politics* 11, no. 1 (1991): 1–31.

5603. ———. "Women's Rights and the Limits of Constitutional Doctrine." *Western Political Quarterly* 44, no. 4 (1991): 821–852.

5604. Baron, Ava. "Feminist Legal Strategies: The Powers of Difference." In *Analyzing Gender,* edited by Beth B. Hess and Myra Marx Ferree, 474–503. Newberry Park, CA: Sage, 1987.

5605. Bartlett, Katharine T. *Gender and Law.* New York: Little Brown, 1991.

5606. Bartlett, Katharine T., and Rosanne Kennedy. *Feminist Legal Theory: Readings in Law and Gender.* Boulder, CO: Westview Press, 1991.

5607. Becker, Nancy, Cynthia Grant Bowman, and Morrison Torrey, eds. *Cases and Materials on Feminist Jurisprudence: Taking Women Seriously.* St. Paul, MN: West Publishing Co., 1994.

5608. Bender, Leslie. "A Lawyer's Primer on Feminist Theory and Tort." *Journal of Legal Education* 38, no. 42 (March–June 1988): 3–38.

5609. Carleton, Francis Joseph. "Sex Discrimination Law and Women in the Workplace: A Feminist Analysis of Legal Ideology." Ph.D. dissertation, Indiana University, 1991.

5610. Cook, Beverly Blair. "Ghosts and Giants in Judicial Politics." *PS* 27 (March 1994): 78–84.

5611. Daly, Kathleen. "Reflections on Feminist Legal Thought." *Social Justice* 17, no. 3 (1990): 7–24.

5612. ———. *Gender, Crime, and Punishment.* New Haven, CT: Yale University Press, 1994.

5613. Eisenstein, Zillah. *The Female Body and the Law.* Berkeley: University of California, 1989.

5614. Estrich, Susan, and Virginia Kerr. "Sexual Justice." In *Our Endangered Rights,* edited by Norman Dorsen, 98–133. New York: Pantheon Books, 1984.

5615. Fenberg, Matilda. "Blame Coke and Blackstone." *Women Lawyers Journal* 34, no. 2 (Spring 1948): 7–10, 42.

5616. Fineman, Martha L., and Nancy Sweet Tomadsen, eds. *At the Boundaries of Law: Feminism and Legal Theory.* New York: Routledge, 1990.

5617. Frug, Mary Jo. *Postmodern Feminism.* New York: Routledge, 1992.

5618. Getman, Julius G. "The Emerging Constitutional Principle of Sexual Equality." *Supreme Court Review* (1972): 157–180.

5619. Ginsburg, Ruth Bader. "Gender and the Constitution." *University of Cincinnati Law Review* 44, no. 1 (1975): 1–42.

5620. Goldstein, Leslie Friedman, ed. *Feminist Jurisprudence: The Difference Debate.* Lanham, MD: Rowman and Littlefield, 1992.

5621. Graycar, Regina, and Jenny Morgan. *The Hidden Gender of Law.* Annandale, New South Wales: Federation Press, 1990.

5622. MacKinnon, Catharine A. "Feminism, Marxism, Method, and the State: Toward Feminist Jurisprudence." *Signs* 7, no. 3 (1982): 515–544.

5623. Mezey, Susan Gluck. "When Should Differences Make a Difference: A New Approach to the Constitutionality of Gender-Based Laws." *Women and Politics* 10, no. 2 (1990): 105–119.

5624. Rabkin, Peggy A. *Fathers to Daughters: The Legal Foundations of Female Emancipation.* Westport, CT: Greenwood Press, 1980.

5625. Scales, Ann M. "Toward a Feminist Jurisprudence." *Indiana Law Journal* 56, no. 3 (1981): 375–444.

5626. ———. "The Emergence of Feminist Jurisprudence: An Essay." *Yale Law Review* 95 (June 1986): 1373–1403.

5627. ———. "Militarism, Male Dominance and Law: Feminist Jurisprudence as Oxymoron?" *Harvard Women's Law Journal* 12 (Spring 1989): 25–73.

5628. Schneider, Elizabeth. "The Dialectic of Rights and Liberties: Perspectives from the Women's Movement." *New York University Law Review* 61 (October 1986): 589–652.

5629. Shanley, Mary Lyndon. "Individualism, Marriage and the Liberal State: Beyond the Equal Rights Amendment." In *Women Organizing: An Anthology,* edited by Bernice Cummings and Victoria Schuck, 363–388. Metuchen, NJ: Scarecrow, 1979.

5630. Smith, Patricia, ed. *Feminist Jurisprudence.* New York: Oxford University Press, 1993.

5631. Weisberg, D. Kelly. *Feminist Legal Theory: Foundations.* Philadelphia: Temple University Press, 1993.

5632. West, Robin. "Jurisprudence and Gender." *University of Chicago Law Review* 55 (Winter 1988): 1–72.

5633. Williams, Wendy W. "Deconstructing Gender." *Michigan Law Review* 87 (1989): 797.

5634. Wishik, Heather R. "To Question Everything: The Inquiries of Feminist Jurisprudence." *Berkeley Women's Law Journal* 1 (Fall 1985): 64–77.

The State

5635. Boris, Eileen. "The Racialized Gendered State: Constructions of Citizenship in the United States." *Social Politics* 2 (Summer 1995): 160–180.

5636. Boris, Eileen, and Peter Bardaglio. "The Transformation of Patriarchy: The Historic Role of the State." In *Families, Politics and Public Policy,* edited by Irene Diamond, 70–93. New York: Longman, 1983.

5637. Diamond, Irene, and Nancy C. M. Hartsock. "Beyond Interest in Politics: A Comment on Virginia Sapiro's 'When Are Interests Interesting?', The Problem of Political Representation of Women." *American Political Science Review* 75 (September 1981): 717–721.

5638. Kendrigan, Mary Lous. *Political Equality in a Democratic Society.* Westport, CT: Greenwood Press, 1984.

5639. MacKinnon, Catharine A. *Toward a Feminist Theory of the State.* Cambridge: Harvard University Press, 1989.

5640. Morgen, Sandra. "Two Faces of the State: Women, Social Control and Empowerment." In *Uncertain Terms,* edited by Faye Ginsburg and Anna Tsing, 169–182. Boston: Beacon, 1990.

5641. Nelson, Barbara J., and Kathryn A. Carver. "Many Voices but Few Vehicles: The Consequences for Women of Weak Political Infrastructure in the United States." In *Women and Politics World Wide,* edited by Barbara J. Nelson and Najma Chowdhury, 737–757. New Haven, CT: Yale University Press, 1994.

5642. Phillips, Anne. *Engendering Democracy.* University Park: Pennsylvania State University, 1991.

5643. Rosenthal, Cindy Simon. "The Role of Gender in Descriptive Representation." *Political Research Quarterly* 48, no. 3 (September 1995): 599–612.

5644. Sapiro, Virginia. "Research Frontier Essay: When Are Interests Interesting? The Problem of Political Representation of Women." *American Political Science Review* 75 (September 1981): 701–716.

5645. Schramm, Sarah Slavin. "Women and Representation: Self-government and Role Change." *Western Political Quarterly* 34 (March 1981): 46–59.

Difference

5646. Brown, Elsa Barkley. "What Has Happened Here: The Politics of Difference in Women's History and Feminist Politics." *Feminist Studies* 18, no. 2 (Summer 1991): 295–312. Reprinted in *"We Specialize in the Wholly Impossible": A Reader in Black Women's History,* edited by Darlene Clark Hine, Wilma King, and Linda Reed, 39–56. Brooklyn, NY: Carlson, 1995.

5647. Eisenstein, Hester, and Alice Jardine, eds. *The Future of Difference.* New Brunswick, NJ: Rutgers University Press, 1980.

5648. Gordon, Linda. "On Difference." *Genders* 10 (Spring 1991): 91–111.

5649. Scott, Joan W. "Deconstructing Equality-Versus-Difference: Or the Uses of Post-Structuralist Theory for Feminism." *Feminist Studies* 14 (Spring 1988): 33–50.

5650. Tronto, Joan C. "Beyond Gender Difference to a Theory of Care." *Signs* 12, no. 4 (1987): 644–663.

Postmodern Feminism

5651. Flax, Jane. "Postmodernism and Gender Relations in Feminist Theory." *Signs* 12, no. 4 (1987): 621–643.

5652. Hekman, Susan. *Gender and Knowledge: Elements of a Postmodern Feminism.* Boston: Northeastern University Press, 1990.

5653. Mann, Patricia. *Micro Politics: Agency in a Post Feminist Era.* Minneapolis: University of Minnesota, 1994.

VIII. Reference

General

5654. Anderson, Ellen. *Guide to Women's Organizations.* Washington, DC: Public Affairs Press, 1950.

5655. Capek, Mary Ellen. *A Women's Thesaurus.* New York: Harper and Row, 1987.

5656. Darcy, Robert. "Women and Politics Data Bases." *Women and Politics* 3 (Spring 1983): 75–81.

5657. Franck, Irene M., and David Brownstone. *The Woman's Desk Reference.* New York: Viking, 1993.

5658. Frost-Knappman, Elizabeth, ed. *The ABC-CLIO Companion to Women's Progress in America.* Santa Barbara, CA: ABC-CLIO, 1994.

5659. Gager, Nancy, ed. *Women's Rights Almanac 1974.* Bethesda, MD: Elizabeth Cady Stanton, 1974.

5660. Gibson, Anne, and Timothy Fast, eds. *The Women's Atlas of the United States.* New York: Facts on File, 1986.

5661. Humm, Maggie. *The Dictionary of Feminist Theory.* Columbus: Ohio State, 1990.

5662. Lynn, Naomi B., Ann B. Matasar, and Marie Barovic Rosenberg, eds. *Research Guide in Women's Studies.* Morristown, NJ: General Learning Press, 1974.

5663. McCullough, Joan. *First of All: Significant 'Firsts' by American Women.* New York: Holt, Rinehart and Winston, 1980.

5664. McPhee, Carol, and Ann FitzGerald, eds. *Feminist Quotations: Voices of Rebels, Reformers, and Visionaries.* New York: Thomas Y. Crowell, 1979.

5665. The National Council for Research on Women, ed. *NWO, A Directory of National Women's Organizations.* Washington, DC: The National Council for Research on Women, 1992.

5666. ———, ed. *WIP, A Directory of Work-In-Progress and Recent Publications.* New York: The National Council for Research on Women, 1992.

5667. *National Women of Color Organization.* New York: Ford Foundation, 1991.

5668. Partnow, Elaine. *The Quotable Women, 1800–1981.* New York: Facts on File, 1982.

5669. Schneider, Dorothy, and Carl J. Schneider, eds. *The ABC-CLIO Companion to Women in the Workplace.* Santa Barbara, CA: ABC-CLIO, 1993.

5670. Slee, Amruta. "A Guide to Women's Direct-Action Groups."

Harper's Bazaar 125 (November 1992): 165–167.

5671. Williamson, Jane, Diane Winston, and Wanda Wooten. *Women's Action Almanac.* New York: William Morrow, 1979.

5672. Zophy, Angela Howard, ed. *Handbook of American Women's History.* New York: Garland, 1990.

Bibliography

5673. Alonso, Harriet Hyman, and Melanie Gustafson. "Bibliography on the History of U.S. Women in Movements for Peace." *Women's Studies Quarterly* 12 (Summer 1984): 46–50.

5674. Ausman, Jon M. *Published Works on Women and Politics.* Monticello, IL: Vance Bibliographies, 1979.

5675. Ballou, Patricia K. *Women, A Biliography of Bibliographies.* Boston: G. K. Hall, 1980.

5676. Borenstein, Audrey, ed. *Older Women in 20th Century America.* New York: Garland, 1982.

5677. Cantor, Aviva. *The Jewish Woman, 1900–1980: A Bibliography.* 2d ed. Fresh Meadows, NY: Biblio Press, 1982.

5678. Carroll, Bernice. "Political Science Part I: American Politics and Political Behavior." *Signs* 5 (Winter 1979): 289–306. Review essay.

5679. ———. "Political Science Part II: International, Comparative, and Feminist Radicals." *Signs* 5 (Spring 1980): 449–458. Review essay.

5680. Carroll, Susan J., and Adrienne Scerbak. *Women Candidates and Their Campaigns: A Bibliography.* New Brunswick, NJ: Center for the American Woman and Politics, Rutgers University, 1985.

5681. Carter, Sarah, and Maureen Richie. *Women's Studies: A Guide to Information Sources.* Jefferson, NC: McFarland, 1990.

5682. Center for Research on Women, ed. *Women of Color and Southern Women: A Bibliography of Social Science Research.* Memphis, TN: Memphis State University, 1988.

5683. Center for the American Woman and Politics. *Women and Politics: A Selected Bibliography, 1965–1974.* New Brunswick, NJ: Center for the American Woman and Politics, Rutgers University, 1974.

5684. ———. *Voluntary Participation among Women in the United States: A Selected Bibliography, 1950–1976.* New Brunswick, NJ: Center for the American Woman and Politics, Rutgers University, 1976.

5685. ———. *The Political Participation of Women in the United States: A Selected Bibliography, 1950–1976.* New Brunswick, NJ: Center for the American Woman and Politics, Rutgers University, 1977.

5686. Een, JoAnn Delores, and Marie Barovic Rosenberg. *Women and Society, Citations 3601 to 6000: An Annotated Bibliography.* Beverly Hills, CA: Sage, 1978.

5687. Ellison, Charles E. *Women and Citizen Participation: A Selected Bibliog-*

raphy. Monticello, IL: Vance Bibliographies, 1981.

5688. Equal Rights Amendment Project, ed. *The Equal Rights Amendment: A Bibliographic Study.* Westport, CT: Greenwood, 1976.

5689. Feinberg, Renee. *Women, Education, and Employment: A Bibliography of Periodical Citations, Pamphlets, Newspapers, and Government Documents, 1970–1980.* Hamden, CT: Library Professional Publications, 1982.

5690. ———. *The Equal Rights Amendment: An Annotated Bibliography of the Issues, 1976–1985.* Westport, CT: Greenwood Press, 1986.

5691. ———. *The Feminization of Poverty in the United States: A Select Annotated Bibliography of the Issue, 1978–1989.* New York: Garland, 1990.

5692. Fischer, Gayle Veronica. *Journal of Women's History Guide to Periodical Literature.* Bloomington: Indiana University Press, 1992.

5693. ———. "The Seventy-Fifth Anniversary of Woman Suffrage in the United States: A Bibliographic Essay." *Journal of Women's History* 7, no. 3 (Fall 1995): 172–199.

5694. Fitch, Nancy Elizabeth. *Women in Politics: The U.S. and Abroad: A Selected Annotated Bibliography, 1970–October 1980.* Public Administration Series. Monticello, IL: Vance Bibliographies, 1982.

5695. Fuller, Kathryn Wagnild, and Gayle Veronica Fischer. "Edited Collections of Primary Sources in United States Women's History: An Annotated Bibliography." *Journal of Women's*

History 7, no. 4 (Winter 1995): 206–229.

5696. Ginsburg, Ruth Bader. "The Progression of Women in the Law: A Bibliography." *Valparaiso University Law Review* 28 (Summer 1994): 1181–1182.

5697. Harrison, Cynthia E., ed. *Women in American History: A Bibliography.* Clio Bibliography, 5. Vol. 1. Santa Barbara, CA: ABC-CLIO, 1979.

5698. Hayler, Barbara. "Abortion." *Signs* 5 (Winter 1979): 307–324. Review essay.

5699. Herman, Kali, ed. *Women in Particular: An Index to American Women.* Phoenix, AZ: Oryx Press, 1984.

5700. Husted, Deborah. *Women and Urban America: A Selected and Multidisciplinary Bibliography of Materials Published Since 1960.* Monticello, IL: Vance Bibliographies, 1988.

5701. Karuss, Wilma Rule. "Political Implications of Gender Roles: A Review of the Literature." *American Political Science Review, 68* (December 1974): 1706–1723.

5702. Kirkpatrick, Meredith. *Women in the Public Service: A Selective Bibliography.* Bibliography, No. 1465. Monticello, IL: Council of Planning Librarians, 1978.

5703. Krichmar, Albert. *The Women's Rights Movement in the United States 1848–1970: A Bibliography and Source Book.* Metuchen, NJ: Scarecrow Press, 1972.

5704. ———. *The Women's Movement in the Seventies: An English-Language*

Bibliography. Metuchen, NJ: Scarecrow Press, 1977.

5705. Lepper, Mary M. "Women in Bureaucracy." *Women and Politics* 1, no. 4 (Winter 1980–81): 65–75.

5706. Lerner, Gerda. *Bibliography in the History of American Women.* 2d rev. ed. Philadelphia: Sarah Lawrence, 1975.

5707. Lerner, Gerda, and Marie Anne Laberge. *Women Are History: A Bibliography in the History of American Women.* 4th ed. Madison: University of Wisconsin, 1986.

5708. Levenson, Rosaline. *Women in Government and Politics: A Bibliography of American and Foreign Sources.* Monticello, IL: Council of Planning Librarians, 1973.

5709. Levitt, Morris. *Women's Role in American Politics.* Monticello, IL: Council of Planning Librarians, 1973. Exchange Bibliography 446.

5710. ———. *Dissertations in Political Science on Women.* Monticello, IL: Vance Bibliographies, 1982.

5711. Manning, Beverly. *Index to American Women Speakers, 1828–1978.* Metuchen, NJ: Scarecrow Press, 1978.

5712. ———. *We Shall Be Heard: An Index to Speeches by American Women, 1978 to 1985.* Metuchen, NJ: Scarecrow Press, 1988.

5713. Miller, Anita, and Hazel Greenberg. *The Equal Rights Amendment: A Bibliographic Study.* Westport, CT: Greenwood, 1976.

5714. Mumford, Laura Stempel. *Women's Issues, An Annotated Bibliography.* Englewood Cliffs, NJ: Sale Press, 1989.

5715. Nelson, Barbara J. *American Women and Politics: A Selected Bibliography and Resource Guide.* New York: Garland, 1984.

5716. Phelps, Edith M. "Equal Rights Amendment." *University Debaters Annual* 1926–1927 (1927): 369–413.

5717. Pierce, Patrick A. "Gender Role and Political Culture: The Electoral Connection." *Women and Politics* 9, no. 1 (1989): 21–46.

5718. Pritchard, Sarah M. *How to Find Sources of Information on Women and Women's Issues in the Library of Congress.* Washington, DC: Library of Congress, 1981.

5719. Rhodes, Carolyn H., ed. *First Person Female American: A Selected and Annotated Bibliography of the Autobiographies of American Women Living After 1950.* Vol. 2. Troy, NY: Whitson Publishing, 1980.

5720. Rosenberg, Marie Barovic, and Len V. Bergstrom. *Women and Society: A Critical Review of the Literature with a Selected Annotated Bibliography.* Beverly Hills, CA: Sage, 1975.

5721. Sapiro, Virginia. *A Guide to Published Works on Women and Politics II.* Ann Arbor: University of Michgan, Institute for Social Research, Center for Political Studies, 1975.

5722. Schramm, Sarah Slavin. "Women in the American Political System: A Selected Bibliography." *Women and Politics* 1, no. 1 (Spring 1980): 87–102.

5723. Seller, Maxine Schwartz, ed. *Immigrant Women.* 2d ed. Albany, NY: New York Press, 1994. Part: Political Activism.

5724. Sklar, Kathryn Kish, ed. *Women in American History: A Bibliography.* Clio Bibliography, 20. Vol. 2. Santa Barbara, CA: ABC-CLIO, 1985.

5725. Soltow, Martha Jane, and Mark K. Wery. *American Women and the Labor Movement, 1825–1974: An Annotated Bibliography.* Metuchen, NJ: Scarecrow Press, 1976.

5726. Stanwick, Kathy, and Christine Li. *The Political Participation of Women in the United States: A Selected Bibliography, 1950–1976.* Metuchen, NJ: Scarecrow Press, 1977. Center for the American Women and Politics, Rutgers University.

5727. Staudt, Kathleen A. "Women's Issues in 198 Academic Journals: An Annotated Bibliography." *Women and Politics* 3 (Spring 1983): 57–83.

5728. Stewart, Alva W. *Women in American State and Local Government: A Bibliographic Survey.* Monticello, IL: Vance Bibliographies, 1983.

5729. Terris, Virginia R. *Woman in America: A Guide to Information Sources.* American Studies Information Guide. Detroit, MI: Gale Research Company, 1980.

5730. Unitarian Universalist Women's Heritage Society, ed. *Compendium of Resources.* 4th ed. Medford, MA: Unitarian Universalist Women's Heritage Society, 1995.

5731. Vaux, Rina. *Guide to Women's History Resources in Delaware Valley Area.* Philadelphia: University of Pennsylvania Press, 1983.

5732. Weis, Ina J. *Women in Politics: A Bibliography.* Monticello, IL: Vance Bibliographies, 1979.

5733. Wilson, Carolyn R. *Violence against Women: Causes and Prevention: A Literature Search and Annotated Bibliography.* 2d ed. Rockville, MD: National Clearinghouse on Domestic Violence, 1980.

5734. Young, Louise M. "The American Woman at Mid Century: A Bibliographic Essay." *American Review* 2 (December 1961): 121–138.

Bibliography: Women of Color

5735. Bataille, Gretchen M. "Bibliography on Native American Women." *Concerns: The Newsletter of the Modern Language Association's Women's Caucus* 10, no. 2 (1980): 61–27.

5736. Cole, Johnetta B. "Black Women in America, An Annotated Bibliography." *The Black Scholar* 3 (December 1971): 42–53.

5737. Davis, Lenwood G. *Black Women in Cities: 1872–1972.* Monticello, IL: Council of Planning Librarians, 1972.

5738. ———, ed. *The Black Woman in American Society: A Selected Annotated Bibliography.* Boston: G. K. Hall, 1975.

5739. *Directory of Significant 20th Century American Minority Women.* Nashville, TN: Fisk University, 1983.

5740. Green, Rayna. *Native American Women: A Bibliography*. Wichita Falls, TX: Ohoyo Resource Center, 1981.

5741. Hardy, Gayle J. *American Women Civil Rights Activist: Biobibliographies of 68 Leaders, 1825–1992*. Jefferson, NC: McFarland, 1992.

5742. *Native American Women: A Biographical Dictionary*. New York: Garland, 1993.

5743. Sierra, Christine Marie, and Adaljiza Sosa-Riddell. "Chicanas as Political Actors: Rare Literature Complex Practice." *National Political Science Review* 4 (1994): 297–317.

5744. Sims-Wood, Janet L. *The Progress of Afro-American Women: A Selected Bibliography and Resource Guide*. Westport, CT: Greenwood, 1980.

5745. Spradling, Mary Mace, ed. *In Black and White*. 3d ed. Vol. 1–2. Detroit, MI: Gale Research, 1980.

5746. Timberlake, Andrea, Lynn Weber Cannon, Rebecca F. Guy, and Elizabeth Higginbotham, eds. *Women of Color and Southern Women: A Bibliography of Social Science Research, 1975 to 1988*. Memphis, TN: Center for Women of Color, Memphis State University, 1988. Annual Supplement, 1989, 1990, 1991–92, 1993.

Biography

5747. Adams, Elmer C., and Warren Dunham Foster. *Heroines of Modern Progress*. New York: Macmillan, 1913.

5748. Berkson, Larry, and Donna Vandenberg. *National Roster of Women Judges*. Chicago: American Judicature Society, 1980.

5749. *Biographical Directory of the American Congress, 1774–1971*. Washington, DC: Government Printing Office, 1971.

5750. Bowman, Kathleen. *New Women in Politics*. Mankato, MN: Creative Education, 1976.

5751. Bradford, Gamaliel. *Portraits of American Women*. Boston: Houghton Mifflin, 1919.

5752. Calkin, Homer L. *Women in American Foreign Affairs*. Washington, DC: Department of State, 1977.

5753. Cameron, Mabel W., ed. *Biographical Cyclopedia of American Women*. New York: Halvard, 1924; Vol. 2, Erma C. Lee, ed., New York: Franklin W. Lee, 1925; Vol. 3, Erma C. Lee and Henry C. Wiley, eds., New York: Williams-Wiley, 1928. Vols. 1–3 published by Gale Research, Detroit, MI, 1974.

5754. Campbell, Karlyn Kohrs. *Women Public Speakers in the United States, 1800–1925: A Biocritical Sourcebook*. Westport, CT: Greenwood Press, 1993.

5755. ———. *Women Public Speakers in the United States, 1925–1993: A Biocritical Sourcebook*. Westport, CT: Greenwood Press, 1994.

5756. Chamberlin, Hope. *A Minority of Members: Women in the U.S. Congress*. New York: Praeger, 1973.

5757. Conway, Jill K., ed. *Written by Herself: Autobiographies of American Women: An Anthology*. New York: Vintage, 1992.

5758. Fireside, Bryna J. *Is There a Woman in the House—or Senate?* Morton Grove, IL: A. Whitman, 1994.

5759. Frost-Knappman, Elizabeth. *Women's Suffrage in America: An Eyewitness History.* New York: Facts on File, 1992.

5760. Golemba, Beverly E. *Lesser Known Women: A Biographical Dictionary.* Boulder, CO: Lynne Rienner, 1992.

5761. *Good Housekeeping Woman's Almanac.* New York: Newspaper Enterprise Association, 1977.

5762. Hagan, John, and Fiona Kay. *Gender in Practice: A Study of Lawyers Lives.* New York: Oxford University Press, 1995.

5763. Hilli, Melvin G., and Peter d'A. Jones, eds. *Dictionary of American Mayors, 1820–1980, Biography of Big City Mayors.* Westport, CT: Greenwood, 1981.

5764. Howes, Durward, ed. *American Women: The Standardized Biographical Dictionary of Notable Women, 1939–1940.* Vol. 3. Los Angeles, CA: American Publications, 1939. Reprint. Teaneck, NJ: Zephyrus, 1974.

5765. Ireland, Norma Olin. *Index to Women of the World from Ancient to Modern Times.* Westwood, MA: F. W. Faxc, 1970.

5766. James, Edward T., Janet Wilson James, and Paul S. Boyer. *Notable American Women, 1607–1950: A Biographical Dictionary.* 3 vols. Cambridge: Harvard University Press, 1971.

5767. Kaptur, Marcy. *Women of Congress: A Twentieth-Century Odyssey.* Washington, DC: Congressional Quarterly: 1996.

5768. Kostman, Samuel. *Twentieth Century Women of Achievement.* New York: Richard Rosen Press, 1976.

5769. Leavitt, Judith A. *American Women Managers and Administrators: A Selective Biographical Dictionary of Twentieth-Century Leaders in Business, Education, and Government.* Westport, CT: Greenwood, 1985.

5770. Lee, E. C. *Biographical Cyclopedia of American Women.* Vol. 2. New York: Franklin W. Lee, 1925.

5771. Leonard, John William, ed. *Woman's Who's Who of America: A Biographical Dictionary of Contemporary Women in the United States and Canada, 1914–15.* New York: American Commonwealth, 1914. Republished 1976.

5772. LeVeness, Frank P., and Jane P. Sweeney, eds. *Women Leaders in Contemporary U.S. Politics.* Boulder, CO: Lynne Rienner, 1987.

5773. Loventhal, Milton. *Autobiographies of Women, 1946–1970: A Bibliography.* San Jose, CA: San Jose State College Library, 1972.

5774. McHenry, Robert, ed. *Famous American Women: A Biographical Dictionary from Colonial Times to the Present.* New York: Dover, 1983.

5775. National Women's Political Caucus. *National Directory of Women Elected Officials.* New York: Philip Morris Inc., 1981. Biennial, odd years, to present.

5776. Outstanding Young Women of America, ed. *Outstanding Young*

Women of America. Washington, DC: Outstanding Young Women of America, 1966. Annual, 1966 to present.

5777. Ross, Ishbel. *Ladies of the Press.* New York: Harpers, 1936.

5778. ———. *Sons of Adam, Daughters of Eve.* New York: Harper and Row, 1967.

5779. Sicherman, Barbara, and Carol Hurd Green, eds. *Notable American Women, The Modern Period: A Biographical Dictionary.* Cambridge: Harvard University Press, 1980.

5780. Sobel, Robert, ed. *Biographical Dictionary of the United States Executive Branch, 1774–1977.* Westport, CT: Greenwood, 1977.

5781. Sobel, Robert, and John Raimo, eds. *Biographical Dictionary of the Governors of the United States.* 4 vols. Westport, CT: Meckler, 1978.

5782. Stineman, Esther. *American Political Women: Contemporary and Historical Profiles.* Littleton, CO: Libraries Unlimited, 1980.

5783. Stoneburner, Carol, and John Stoneburner, eds. *The Influence of Quaker Women on American History, Biographical Studies.* Lewiston, ME: Edwin Mellen Press, 1986.

5784. Thais, Paul A., and Edmund Lee Henshaw, eds. *Who's Who in American Politics.* Vol. 1. New York: Bowker, 1967. Biennal, 1967 to present.

5785. Thomas, Dorothy. *Women Lawyers in the United States.* New York: Scarecrow Press, 1957.

5786. Tuttle, Lisa. *Encyclopedia of Feminism.* New York: Facts on File, 1986.

5787. Uglow, Jennifer S., ed. *The Continuum Dictionary of Women's Biography.* New York: Continuum, 1989.

5788. Westherford, Doris, ed. *American Women's History.* Englewood Cliffs, NJ: Prentice Hall, 1994.

5789. Who's Who of American Women, ed. *Who's Who of American Women: A Biographical Dictionary of Notable Living American Women.* Chicago: Marquis, 1958. Biennial, 1958 to present.

5790. Williard, Frances L., and Mark K. Livermore. *Women of the Century.* 2 vols. Buffalo, NY: Charles W. Moulton, 1893.

Biography: Women of Color

5791. Brawley, Benjamin. *Women of Achievement within the Fireside Schools.* Chicago: Woman's American Baptist Home Missionary Society, 1919.

5792. Dannett, Sylvia G. L. *Profiles of Negro Womanhood.* Yonkers, NY: Educational Heritage, 1964.

5793. DeLeon, Olga. *Outstanding American Women of Mexican Descent.* Austin: University of Texas, Center for Public School Ethnic Studies, 1973.

5794. Hill, Ruth Edmonds, ed. *The Black Women Oral History Project.* 9 vols. Westport, CT: Meckler, 1991.

5795. Hine, Darlene Clark, Elsa Barkley Brown, and Rosalyn Terborg-Penn, eds. *Black Women in America: An Historical Encyclopedia.* 2 vols. Brooklyn, NY: Carlson, 1993.

5796. Joint Center for Political and Economic Studies. *Black Elected Officials: A National Register.* Washington, DC: Joint Center for Political and Economic Studies, 1971. Biennial, 1971 to present.

5797. National Association of Latino Elected Officials, ed. *Latino Elected Officials.* Washington, DC: National Association of Latino Elected Officials, 1985. Biennial, 1985 to present.

5798. Salem, Dorothy C., ed. *African American Women: A Biographical Dictionary.* New York: Garland, 1993.

5799. Smith, Jessie Carney, ed. *Notable Black American Women.* Detroit, MI: Gale Research, 1992.

Guides to Collections

5800. Batts, Grover, and Thelma Queen, eds. *The Breckinridge Family, A Register of Its Papers in the Library of Congress.* Washington, DC: Manuscript Division, Library of Congress, 1980. Revised 1982, 1984, 1988, 1995.

5801. *The Blackwell Family, Carrie Chapman Catt, and the National American Woman Suffrage Association.* Rev. ed. Washington, DC: Manuscript Division, Library of Congress, 1985.

5802. Blair, Karen J. *The History of American Women's Voluntary Organizations, 1810–1960, A Guide to Sources.* Boston: G.K. Hall, 1989.

5803. Boehm, Randolph H., ed. *A Guide to the Microfilm Edition of Women's Studies Manuscript Collections from the Schlesinger Library, Radcliffe*

College. Bethesda, MD: University Publications of America, 1993.

5804. Bogenschneider, Duane R., ed. *The Gerritsen Collection of Women's History, 1543–1945.* 2 vols. Sanford, NC: Microfilming Corporation of America, 1983.

5805. Bryan, Mary Lynn McCree, ed. *The Jane Addams Papers.* Chicago: University Microfilms International, 1985.

5806. Buhle, Mari Jo. *Women and the American Left: A Guide to Sources.* Boston: G.K. Hall, 1983.

5807. *Catalogs of the Sophia Smith Collection, Women's History Archive, Smith College, Northampton, Massachusetts.* 7 vols. Boston: G. K. Hall, 1975.

5808. *Catalogue of the Library of the International Archives for the Women's Movement, Amsterdam.* 4 vols. Boston: G. K. Hall, 1980.

5809. Darcy, Robert, and Cheryl Handley. "Women and Politics Data Bases: The Roper Center: The Machine Readable Archives Division of the National Archives and Records Service." *Women and Politics* 2, no. 1–2 (Spring–Summer 1982): 115–120.

5810. Haggerty, Donald L., ed. *National Woman's Party Papers: The Suffrage Years, 1913–1920, A Guide to the Microfilm Edition.* Sanford, NC: Microfilming Corporation of America, 1981.

5811. *HERSTORY Microfilm Collection.* Berkeley, CA: Women's History Library, 1971. Supplements: Set I, Set II, 1976.

5812. Hildenbrand, Suzanne, ed. *Women's Collections, Libraries, Archives, and Consciousness.* Vol. 3. New York: Haworth Press, 1985.

5813. Hinding, Andrea, ed. *Women's History Sources: A Guide to Archives and Manuscript Collections in the United States.* 2 vols. New York: Bowker, 1979.

5814. Holland, Patricia G., and Ann D. Gordon, eds. *The Papers of Elizabeth Cady Stanton and Susan B. Anthony, Guide and Index to the Microfilm Edition.* Wilmington, DE: Scholarly Resources, Inc., 1992.

5815. James, Edward T., Robin Miller Jacoby, and Nancy Schrom, eds. *Papers of the Women's Trade Union League and Its Principal Leaders.* Woodbridge, CT: Research Publications for the Schlesinger Library, Radcliffe College, 1981. Guide to microfilm.

5816. Jimerson, Randall C., Francis X. Blouis, and Charles A. Osetts, eds. *Guide to the Microfilm Edition of Temperance and Prohibition Papers.* Ann Arbor: University of Michigan, 1977.

5817. *The Manuscript Inventories and the Catalogs of Manuscripts, Books and Periodicals of the Arthur and Elizabeth Schlesinger Library on the History of Women in America.* 2d rev. and enl. ed. 10 vols. Boston: G. K. Hall, 1984.

5818. Mikusko, M. Brady. *Preliminary Sourcebok of Oral Histories of Trade Union and Working Women in the United States.* Ann Arbor: Institute of Labor and Industrial Relations, University of Michigan, Wayne State University, 1981.

5819. "The Papers of the Women Who Have Served in Congress." *Extensions, A Journal of the Carl Albert Congressional Research and Studies Center* (Spring 1995): 18–20. Special Issue, Women in the United States Congress.

5820. Pardo, Thomas C. *The National Woman's Party Papers, 1913–1974: A Guide to the Microfilm Edition.* Sanford, NC: Microfilm Corporation of America, 1979.

5821. Pritchard, Sarah M. *Women's Studies Resources in Microform at the Library of Congress.* Washington, DC: Library of Congress, 1985.

5822. ———. "Resources for the Study of Women at the Library of Congress." *Special Collections* 3, no. 3–4 (Spring–Summer 1986): 13–36.

5823. Rossi, Alice S., ed. *The Feminist Papers: From Adams to de Beauvoir.* New York: Columbia University Press, 1973.

5824. Scott, Anne Firor, and Randolph H. Boehm, eds. *Women's Studies Manuscript Collections from the Schlesinger Library, Radcliffe College: Series 2, Women in National Politics.* Bethesda, MD: University Publications of America, 1993.

5825. Shane, Martha P. *Papers of Emily Greene Balch, 1875–1961: Guide to the Scholarly Resources Microfilm Edition.* Wilmington, DE: Scholarly Resources, Inc., 1988.

5826. Tingley, Elizabeth, and Donald F. Tingley, eds. *Women and Feminism in American History, A Guide to Informational Sources.* Detroit, MI: Gale Research, 1992.

5827. Women's History Research Center. *Guide to the Microfilm Edition of* the Women's Law Library of the Women's History Research Center: Women and Law. Berkeley, CA: The Center, 1975.

Documents

5828. Cott, Nancy F., ed. *Root of Bitterness: Documents of the Social History of American Women*. 2d ed. Boston: Northeastern University, 1986.

5829. Huls, Mary Ellen. *U.S. Government Documents on Women, 1890–1990*. Westport, CT: Greenwood Press, 1994.

5830. Kerber, Linda K., and Jane DeHart Mathews, eds. *Women's America: Refocusing the Past*. New York: Oxford University Press, 1982.

5831. Langley, Winston E., and Vivian C. Fox, eds. *Women's Rights in the United States, A Documentary History*. Westport, CT: Greenwood Press, 1994.

5832. Lerner, Gerda. *The Female Experience: An American Documentary*. Indianapolis: Bobbs-Merrill, 1977.

5833. Martin, Wendy, ed. *The American Sisterhood: Writings of the Feminist Movement from Colonial Times to the Present*. Part II: Political, Legal, and Economic Questions. New York: Harper and Row, 1972.

5834. Papachristou, Judith, ed. *Women Together: A History in Documents of the Women's Movement in the United States*. New York: Knopf, 1976.

5835. Ruether, Rosemary Radford, and Rosemary Skinner Keller, eds. *Women and Religion in America, A Doc-*

umentary History. Vol. 3, 1900–1965. San Francisco, CA: Harper and Row, 1986.

Nations and Tribes

5836. Anderson, Owana, ed. *Ohoyo One Thousand: A Resource Guide of American Indian–Alaska Native Women*. Wichita Falls, TX: Ohoyo Resource Center, 1982.

5837. Bataille, Gretchen M., and Kathleen M. Sands. *American Indian Women: A Guide to Research*. New York: Garland, 1991.

5838. Farley, Ronnie. *Women of the Native Struggle: Portraits and Testimony of Native American Women*. New York: Random House, 1994.

5839. Green, Rayna. *Native American Women: A Contextual Bibliography*. Bloomington: Indiana University Press, 1983.

5840. Gridley, Marion Eleanor. *American Indian Women*. New York: Hawthorn, 1974.

5841. International Indian Treaty Council, ed. *Native American Women*. New York: United Nations, 1975.

5842. Koehler, Lyle. "Native Women of the Americas: A Bibliography." *Frontiers* 6, no. 3 (1981): 73–101.

In the Regions

North

5843. Howe, Julia Ward, ed. *Representative Women of New England.* Boston: New England Historical Publishing Co., 1904.

5844. *Who's Who in New Jersey: A Biographical Dictionary of Leading Living Men and Women of the States of New Jersey, Pennsylvania, Delaware, Maryland, and West Virginia.* Chicago: A.N. Marquis Co., 1939.

5845. Zambrana, Ruth E., and Nilsa M. Burgos, eds. *Directory of Latina Women on the Northeast Coast and Puerto Rico.* Bronx, NY: Hispanic Research Center, 1981.

South

5846. Beaird, Miriam G. *Notable Women of the Southwest: A Pictorial Biographical Encyclopedia of the Leading Women of Texas, New Mexico, Oklahoma and Arizona.* Dallas, TX: William T. Tardy, 1938.

West

5847. Armitage, Susan, Helen Bannar, Katherine G. Morrissey, and Vicki L. Ruiz, eds. *Women in the West: A Guide to Manuscript Sources.* New York: Garland, 1991.

5848. Binheim, Max, and Charles A. Elvin, eds. *Women of the West: A Series of Biographical Sketches of Living Eminent Women in the Eleven Western States of the United States of America.* Los Angeles, CA: Publishers Press, 1928.

5849. Reiter, Joan Swallow. *The Old West: The Women.* Alexandria, VA: Time-Life Books, 1978.

In the States

Alaska

5850. Atwood, Evangeline, and Robert N. deArmond, eds. *Who's Who in Alaska Politics: A Biographical Dictionary of Alaska Political Personalities, 1884–1974.* Portland, OR: Binford and Mort for the Alaska Historical Commission, 1977.

5851. Breslford, Ginna. *Profiles in Change: Names, Notes and Quotes for Alaskan Women.* Juneau: Alaska Commission on the Status of Women, 1983.

5852. Graham, Roberta. *A Sense of History: A Reference Guide to Alaska's Women, 1896–1985.* Studies in History, 179. Juneau: Alaska Historical Commission, 1985.

Arizona

5853. Crowe, Rosalie, and Diane Tod. *Arizona Women's Hall of Fame.* Phoenix: Arizona Historical Society, 1985.

5854. *Men and Women of Arizona, Past and Present.* Phoenix, AZ: Pioneer Publishing Co., 1940.

California

5855. Donovan, Lynn, and Joan Hoff-Wilson. "Women's History: A

Listing of West Coast Archival and Manuscript Sources." *California Historical Society Quarterly* 55 (Spring–Summer 1976): 74–83, 170–184.

5856. *Who's Who among the Women of California.* San Francisco, CA: Security Publishing Co., 1922.

Colorado

5857. Bluemel, Elinor. *One Hundred Years of Colorado Women.* Denver: Colorado Imprints, 1973.

5858. Goldstein, Marcia T., and Rebecca A. Hunt. "From Suffrage to Centennial: A Research Guide to Colorado and National Women's Suffrage Sources." *Colorado Heritage* (Spring 1993): 40–48.

5859. Semple, James Alexander. *Representative Women of Colorado.* Denver: The Williamson-Haffner Co., 1911.

5860. Whistler, Nancy, ed. *Colorado Oral History Guide.* Denver: Denver Public Library, 1980.

Florida

5861. Blackman, Lucy W. *The Women of Florida: The Biographies.* Vol. 2. n.c.: Southern Historical Publishing, 1940.

5862. Cozens, Eloise N. *Florida Women of Distinction.* n.c.: College Publishing Co., 1956.

Georgia

5863. American Association of University Women, ed. *Georgia Women: A Celebration.* Atlanta: Atlanta Branch, 1976.

5864. Georgia Department of Archives and History, ed. *Georgia Women of 1926.* Atlanta: Georgia Department of Archives and History, 1926.

5865. Nevin, James B. *Prominent Women of Georgia.* Atlanta: National Biographical Publishers, 1929.

Hawaii

5866. Peterson, Barbara B. *Notable Women of Hawaii.* Honolulu: University of Hawaii, 1984.

Idaho

5867. Penson-Ward, Betty. *Who's Who of Idaho Women in the Past.* Boise: Idaho Commission on Women's Programs, 1981.

Illinois

5868. Wheeler, Adade Mitchell, and Marge Wortman. *The Roads They Made: Women in Illinois History.* Chicago: C. H. Kerr Publishing Co., 1977.

Indiana

5869. Boruff, Blanche Foster, ed. *Women of Indiana.* Indianapolis: Indiana Women's Biography Association, 1941.

Iowa

5870. Hanft, Ethel W., and Paula J. Manley, eds. *Outstanding Iowa Women, Past and Present*. Muscatine, IA: River Bend Publishing, 1980.

Kansas

5871. Garner, Ann L. *Kansas Women*. Lawrence: Kansas Key Press, 1986.

Kentucky

5872. Irvin, Helen D. *Women in Kentucky*. Lexington: University of Kentucky Press, 1979.

Maryland

5873. Helmes, Winifred Gertrude, ed. *Notable Maryland Women*. Cambridge, MD: Tidewater Publishers, 1977.

Michigan

5874. Harley, Rachel Brett, and Betty MacDowell. *Michigan Women Firsts and Founders*. Lansing: Michigan Women's Studies Association, 1992.

Minnesota

5875. Foster, Mary D. *Who's Who among Minnesota Women*. n.c.: Mary D. Foster, 1924.

5876. Palmquist, Bonnie Beatson. "Women in Minnesota History." *Minnesota History* 45 (1977): 187–191.

5877. Stuhler, Barbara, and Gretchen Kreuter, eds. *Women of Minnesota: Selected Biographical Essays*. St. Paul: Minnesota Historical Society, 1977.

Mississippi

5878. Hawks, Joanne V. *A Guide to Women's Sources in Mississippi Repositories*. Jackson: Society of Mississippi Archivists, 1993.

Missouri

5879. Bishop, Beverly D., and Deborah W. Bolas, eds. *In Her Own Write: Women's History Resources in the Library and Archives of the Missouri Historical Society*. Columbia: Missouri Historical Society, 1983.

5880. Dains, Mary K. "Missouri Women in Historical Writing." *Missouri Historical Review* 83, no. 4 (July 1989): 417–428.

5881. ———, ed. *Show Me Missouri Women: Selected Biographies*. A Missouri Women's History Project of American Association of University Women. Kirksville, MO: Thomas Jefferson University Press, 1989.

5882. Johnson, Anna A. *Notable Women of St. Louis*. St. Louis, MO: Anna A. Johnson, 1914.

New Jersey

5883. Steiner-Scott, Elizabeth, and Elizabeth Pearce Wagle, eds. *New Jersey Women, 1770–1970*. Rutherford,

NJ: Fairleigh Dickinson University Press, 1978.

5884. The Women's Project of New Jersey, Inc., ed. *Past and Promise, Lives of New Jersey Women.* Metuchen, NJ: Scarecrow Press, 1990.

New York

5885. New York State Library. *Women in Government: Selected Sources from the Collections of the New York State Library: A Bibliography.* Albany: University of the State of New York, 1992.

North Carolina

5886. Rani, Jennifer, ed. *Notable North Carolina Women.* Winston-Salem, NC: Bandit Books, 1992.

5887. Scott, Marda, and Elizabeth Power. *The Woman's Collection at the University of North Carolina at Greensboro: A Checklist of Holdings.* Greensboro, NC: Walter Clinton Jackson Library, 1975.

5888. Thompson, Catherine E. *A Selective Guide to Women-Related Records in the North Carolina State Archives.* Raleigh: North Carolina Division of Archives and History, 1977.

North Dakota

5889. Stutenroth, Stella M., ed. *Daughters of Docatah.* Mitchell, SD: Educator Supply Co., 1942.

Oregon

5890. Leasher, Evelyn M. *Oregon Women: A Bio-Bibliography.* Corvallis: Oregon State University Press, 1980.

Pennsylvania

5891. American Association of University Women, ed. *Our Hidden Heritage: Pennsylvania Women in History.* Washington, DC: American Association of University Women, 1983.

5892. Biddle, Gertrude, ed. *Notable Women of Pennsylvania.* Philadelphia: University of Pennsylvania Press, 1942.

South Carolina

5893. Bodie, Idella. *South Carolina Women.* Orangeburg, SC: Sandlapper, 1991.

South Dakota

5894. South Dakota Commission on the Status of Women. *South Dakota Women, 1850–1919: A Bibliography.* Pierre: South Dakota Commission on the Status of Women, 1975.

Tennessee

5895. Cornwell, Ilene J. *A Bicentennial Tribute to the Women of Tennessee, 1776–1996.* Nashville: Tennessee Historical Society, 1996.

5896. Yellin, Carol Lynn, and Wilma Dykeman, eds. *Tennessee Women, Past* *and Present.* Nashville, TN: Brunner, 1977.

Texas

5897. Crawford, Ann Fears, and Crystal Sasse Ragsdale. *Women in Texas: Their Lives, Their Experiences, Their Accomplishments.* Rev ed. Austin, TX: State House Press, 1992.

5898. Farrell, Mary D., and Elizabeth Silverthorne. *First Ladies of Texas: The First One Hundred Years, 1836–1936.* Belton, TX: Stillhouse Hollow, 1976.

5899. Fernea, Elizabeth E., Marilyn P. Duncan, Sarah Weddington, Jane Hickie, and Deanna Fitzgerald, eds. *Texas Women in Politics.* Austin, TX: Foundation for Women's Resources, Inc., 1977.

5900. McAdams, Ira May. *Texas Women of Distinction.* Austin, TX: McAdams Publications, 1962.

5901. Moreland, Sinclair. *The Texas Women's Hall of Fame.* Austin, TX: Biographical Press, 1917.

5902. Smith, Nancy Kegan. "Private Reflections on a Public Life: The Papers of Lady Bird Johnson at the Lyndon Baines Johnson Library." *Presidential Studies Quarterly* 20, no. 4 (1990): 737–744.

5903. Texas Federation of Women's Clubs, ed. *Who's Who of the Womanhood of Texas, 1923–1924.* Fort Worth, TX: Stafford-London, 1924.

5904. Winegarten, Ruthe, ed. *Bibliography: Texas Women's History Project.* Austin: Texas Foundation for Women's Resources, 1980.

5905. ———, ed. *Governor Ann Richards and Other Texas Women, A Pictorial History: from Indians to Astronauts.* Austin, TX: Eakin Press, 1986.

Vermont

5906. Pepe, Faith L. "Toward a History of Women in Vermont: An Essay and Bibliography." *Vermont History* 45 (Spring 1977): 69–101.

Virginia

5907. Lebsock, Suzanne. *Virginia Women, 1600–1945: 'A Share of Honour'.* Richmond: Virginia State Library, 1987.

5908. Treadway, Sandra Gioia. "New Directions in Virginia Women's History." *Virginia Magazine of History and Biography* 100, no. 1 (January 1992): 5–28.

West Virginia

5909. *West Virginia Women.* West Virginia Heritage Encyclopedia, Supplemental Series. Vol. 25. Richwood, WV: Jim Constock, 1974.

Wisconsin

5910. Bletzinger, Andrea, and Anne Short, eds. *Wisconsin Women: A Gifted Heritage.* Milwaukee, WI: American Association of University Women, 1982.

5911. Danky, James P., and Eleanor McKey, eds. *Women's History: Resources at the State Historical Society of Wiscon-*

sin. Madison: The State Historical Society of Wisconsin, 1982.

5912. Parker, Linda. "Wisconsin Women: A Biliographic Checklist." In *Wisconsin Women: A Gifted Heritage: A Project of the American Association of University Women,* edited by Andrea Bletzinger and Anne Short, 303–304. Milwaukee, WI: American Association of University Women, 1982.

Wyoming

5913. Beach, Cora May. *Women of Wyoming.* Casper: W. E. Boyer and Co., 1927.

In the Territories and District

Puerto Rico

5914. Torres, Lola Kruger. *Enciciopedia Grandes Mujeres De Puerto Rico.* Puerto Rico: Amallo Bros. Printing, 1975.

5915. Votaw, Carmen Delgado. *Puerto Rican Women.* Washington, DC: National Conference of Puerto Rican Women, 1995.

Author Index

Author Index

Grau, Janice, 5279
Graves, Lawrence L., 577, 2897
Gray, Virginia, 1523
Graycar, Regina, 5621
Greco, Gail, 4288
Green, Carol Hurd, 5779
Green, Edith, 3766, 3767
Green, Elizabeth, 4687
Green, Elna C., 1455, 1456
Green, Raynal, 188, 887, 888, 1189, 5740, 5839
Greenbaum, Betsy, 4252
Greenberg, Hazel, 5713
Greenbie, Marjorie Barstow, 3596
Greene, Christina, 818
Greene, Dana, 245
Greene, Mrs. Frederick Stuart, 1608, 4723
Greenstein, Fred, 5404
Greenwald, Maurine Weiner, 4820, 4880
Grenfell, Helen L., 1713
Gridley, Marion Eleanor, 5840
Grier, Ruth, 3346
Griffin, Isabel Kinnear, 2675, 3557
Griffith, Elizabeth, 97
Griffiths, Martha W., 3712, 3713, 3714, 4724, 4941
Grimes, Alan P., 271
Grimes, Ann, 1691
Grimke, Francis J., 137
Grinnell, Katherine, 2001
Groeneman, Sid, 2457
Gross, Debra, 2978
Grossholtz, Jean, 1806
Grove, A., 4377
Gruberg, Martin, 1557, 3182
Gruenebaum, Jane, 1769
Gruening, Martha, 138
Gruhl, John, 4205
Grune, Joy Ann, 4849
Grunwald, Lisa, 2724
Gryski, Gerard S., 5345
Guberman, Connie, 5267
Guethlein, Carol, 364
Guigin, Linda C., 3347
Guiterman, A., 1609
Guiterrez, Armando, 1877
Gullett, Gayle, 2051, 2052
Gurin, Patricia, 1799
Gurovitz, Judy, 98
Gurwitt, Rob, 3806
Guseiler, Mert, 1153
Gustafson, Melanie, 4658, 5673
Guy, Mary E., 3871
Guy, Rebecca F., 5746
Guyol, Mary Ann, 1944
Guy-Sheftall, Beverly, 5527

H., Pamela, 1258
Haarsager, Sandra, 4324
Haase, Karen A., 2531
Haber, Barbara, 4750
Haberman, Nancy, 3387

Hackett, Catherine I., 1714, 1994, 3465
Hadley, Charles D., 2568, 2984, 4437
Hagan, John, 3299, 5762
Hagan, Martha Ann, 1457
Haggerty, Donald L., 5810
Hagner, Paul R., 5412
Haines, Janine, 2526
Hairston, Julie, 1502
Hale, Mary M., 3597
Hall, Florence Howe, 99, 433
Hall, Jacquelyn Dowd, 673, 674
Hall, Robert F., 591
Halliday, E. M., 211
Hallowell, Ann, 2015
Halsey, Theresa, 892
Hamick, Joann, 2249
Hamilton, Alice, 687
Hamilton, Ruth M., 3037
Hamlin, Dora Jane, 4305
Hamm, Keith E., 3152
Hammel, Lisa, 1118
Hammond, Margaret, 4141
Hammond, Nancy, 2614
Hamos, Julie E., 1715
Handberg, Jr., Roger, 982, 3807, 3808
Handley, Cheryl, 5809
Haney, Eleanor Humes, 1107
Hanft, Ethel W., 5870
Hanger, Frances Marion Harrow, 2044
Hanhn, Harlan, 1770
Hanmer, Jalna, 5268
Hansen, Julia Butler, 3786
Hansen, Karen V., 1134, 5454
Hansen, Susan B., 2884, 5389
Hanson, Nancy Edmonds, 4077, 4078
Hard, Anne, 3377, 3558, 4563
Hardaway, Roger D., 2853, 2863
Harder, Ida Husted, 426
Harder, Sarah, 1207
Hardesty, Carolyn, 1579
Hardin, William H., 2894
Hardy, Gayle J., 5741
Hardy, Richard J., 4921
Hardy-Fanta, Carol, 2123
Hareven, Tamara K., 629
Hargis, Donald E., 5060
Harlan, Sharon L., 4821
Harley, Rachel Brett, 5874
Harley, Sharon, 755, 839, 2204
Harmon, Sandra D., 3978
Harper, Ida Husted, 116, 172, 212, 254, 504, 556, 561, 2016, 2338
Harper, Marieta L., 1868
Harriman, Alice Stratton, 2141
Harriman, Florence J. (Mrs. J. Borden), 1855, 1906, 4378
Harris, Adrienne, 1379
Harris, Corra, 1834
Harris, Diane, 4881

Harris, Katherine, 1414
Harris, Louis, 2387, 5322
Harris, Ted Carlton, 3723, 3724
Harris, Walter L., 4123
Harrison, Beppie, 1790
Harrison, Beverly Wildung, 1286
Harrison, Cynthia E., 1208, 1231, 3297, 4725, 4726, 4727, 4728, 5147, 5697
Harrison, Gladys, 4774
Hart, Vivien, 678
Hartmann, Susan M., 1027, 1028, 1436, 5084
Hartsock, Nancy C. M., 5223, 5586, 5637
Harvey, Anna L., 1580, 4356, 4607
Harvey, George, 1458
Harvey, Mary R., 5296
Haselmayer, Louis A., 353
Haskell, Thomas, 4927
Haskins, James, 3745, 3777
Hastings, Phillip K., 2388
Hatch, Alden, 3524
Hauptman, Laurence M., 889, 890
Hauser, Elizabeth J., 3047
Havemeyer, Louisine, 181
Havens, Catherine M., 3809, 3955
Hawkesworth, Mary E., 3998, 5495, 5496, 5497
Hawks, Joanne V., 3810, 3811, 3812, 3850, 3892, 3893, 3958, 4026, 4027, 4030, 4115, 5878
Hay, Mary Garrett, 1856, 2581, 4688
Hay, Melba Porter, 2111
Hayden, Casey, 819
Hayden, Mildred, 4141
Hayler, Barbara, 5698
Haynes, Karima A., 3466
Hays, Samuel P., 4448
Hayward, Mary Smith, 416
H'Doubler, Mrs. Francis Todd, 3123
Healy, Lynne M., 3809, 3955
Hearon, Shelby, 3779
Heath, Mrs. Juhan, 669
Hebard, Grace Raymond, 587
Heck, Edward V., 3614
Hedblom, Milda K. W., 1771
Hedge, David M., 3211
Hedges, Roman B., 1817, 5325
Hedlund, Ronald D., 3152, 3211
Heffelfinger, Elizabeth Bradley, 4418
Hefner, Loretta L., 1716
Heidepriem, Nikki, 2236, 2250, 2257
Height, Dorothy, 1953
Heilig, K., 2629
Hekman, Susan, 5652
Heller, Elinor Raas, 3921
Helmes, Winifred Gertrude, 957, 4609, 5873

Mandel, Ruth B., 1781, 1922, 2221, 2529, 2624, 2625, 2700, 2706, 2727, 3232, 3839
Mandle, Joan, 1078
Mangawaro, Lynne L., 3080
Mankiller, Wilma, 3315
Manley, Paula J., 5870
Mann, Judy, 2258
Mann, Pamela, 4853
Mann, Patricia, 5653
Mannes, Marya, 2949
Manning, Beverly, 5711, 5712
Manning, Richard D., 3137
Mano, D. Keith, 1121
Mansbridge, Jane, 983, 984, 1012, 1013, 2259, 5560, 5569
Marable, Manning, 5535
Marcella, Andre, 467
March, James G., 5323
Marchildon, Rudy G., 2790
Marchus, Barbara, 2626
Marcy, Mary B., 3852
Margolies Mezvinsky, Marjorie, 3774
Margolis, Diane Tothbard, 1923, 1924, 4450
Marilley, Suzanne M., 61, 62, 532, 1014, 2471
Mark, Mrs. O. H. 420
Markoff, Helen S., 5310
Markson, Stephen L., 1508
Marquez, Benjamin, 762
Marquis, Neeta, 2420
Marshall, Constance, 3624
Marshall, George, 5019
Marshall, Marguerite Mooers, 3751, 3759
Marshall, Marilyn, 4238
Marshall, Susan E., 1471, 1529, 1530, 1531, 1532, 5418
Marshall, Thelma E., 1160
Marshner, Connaught C., 5589
Marston, Doris Ricker, 4003
Martelet, Penny, 1440
Marti, Donald B., 2020, 2131
Martin, Anne, 942, 943, 2368, 2583, 5236
Martin, Cora A., 1322
Martin, Elaine, 2994, 3249, 3290, 3291, 3625, 3626, 3886, 3887
Martin, George Madden, 1722, 3418
Martin, I. T., 1472
Martin, Janet M., 3419, 3478
Martin, Joanna, 1232
Martin, Marion E., 3853, 4004, 4623
Martin, Patricia Yancey, 1112, 1113, 5570
Martin, Ralph G., 2494
Martin, Wendy, 5833
Martin, William, 4931
Martio, Ann, 4434
Marusich Smith, Mary Ann, 4010
Marx, Linda, 3959

Masel-Walters, Lynne, 226, 227
Mashek, John W., 2627
Mason, Karen Malinda, 2094
Mason, Mary Ann, 4970
Massachusetts State Federation of Womens Clubs, 2125
Massey, Mary Elizabeth, 32
Matasar, Ann B., 4452, 5662
Mather, Anne, 1233
Mathes, Valerie Sherer, 1897
Mathews, Donald G., 916, 985, 1490, 2955
Mathews, Glenna, 33
Mathews, Jane, 454
Mathews, Jane DeHart, 908, 916, 985, 1202, 1490, 1540, 4939, 5830
Mathews, Shaler, 34
Matlak, Carol, 2222
Matland, Richard, 2985
Matsuda, Mari J., 5066
Mattei, Laura Winsky, 4733
Matthews, Burnita Shelton, 3637, 4910, 4943
Matthews, Glenna, 1559, 2654, 2772
Matthews, Mark D., 844
Matthews, Nancy A., 1330, 5299
Matthews, Shailer, 187
Matthews, Tracye, 845
Mattison, Georgia, 1723
Mattson, Lynn, 5183
Mauel, Frances, 1033
May, Bernice Hubbard, 4226
May, Catherine Dean, 2892, 3787, 3788
May, Martha, 4823
Mayer, Jane, 1626
Mayer, Jean, 3103
Maynard, Mary, 5268
Mayo, Edith P., 917, 2288, 3566
Mayo, Mara, 1473
Mazumdar, Maitreyi, 3760
McAdams, Ira May, 5900
McArthur, Judith N., 533, 534, 665, 2177
McAuliffe, Kathleen, 5407
McBride, Genevieve G., 579, 580
McCallum, Jane Y., 535, 536, 2178
McCann, Carole R., 5137
McCarrick, Earlean M., 3888
McCarthy, Kathleen D., 1959
McCarty, Kathryn Shane, 3074
McClintock, Laura V., 896
McClure, Mary, 3819
McComas, Alice Moore, 301
McCormick, Anne Ohare, 4692
McCormick, Katheryne C., 4051
McCormick, Larue, 4660
McCormick, Richard P., 4051
McCormick, Ruth Hanna (Mrs. Medill), 2830, 4403, 4404, 4528, 4529
McCourt, Kathleen, 728
McCoy, Melanie, 3316

McCracken, Elizabeth, 1960, 2427
McCreesh, Carolyn D., 799
McCrone, Donald J., 4921
McCullough, Joan, 5663
McCune, Shirley, 1915
McDonagh, Eileen Lorenzi, 63, 64, 65, 1782, 1816, 5153
McDonald, David Kevin, 455
McDonald, Jean Graves, 4451
McDowell, Madeline, 366
McDowell, Margaret B., 1079
McFadden, Grace Jordan, 846
McFadden, Judith Nies, 2773
McFarland, Charles, 214
McFarland, Charles K., 666
McFeeley, Heather S., 2530
McGerr, Michael E., 5590
McGlashan, Zena Beth, 729
McGlen, Nancy E., 35, 1783, 3479, 3600, 5437, 5561
McGoldrick, Neale, 241
McGovern, James R., 978
McGovern, Kimberly S., 5114
McGowan, Josephine, 1586
McGranery, Regina, 1681
McGrath, Wilma E., 4505, 5329
McGraw, Mrs. J. W., 342
McGrory, Mary, 2918
McGuinness, Kate, 1382
McGurn, William, 2709
McHenry, Robert, 5774
McIntyre, Douglas I., 5214
McKee, Mary Julians, 3663
McKee, Jr., Oliver, 1587
McKeegan, Michele, 1509
McKenna, Lois M., 5115
McKenzie, Edna B., 498
McKey, Eleanor, 5911
McLanahan, Sara S., 5005, 5237, 5238
McLane, Susan, 2860
McLaughlin, John, 2774
McLaughlin, Kathleen, 2369, 5324
McLaughlin, M., 1984, 4478
McLean, Hulda Hoover, 2055
McLean, Joan Elizabeth, 2628
McLendon, Mary Latimer, 326, 327
McLeod, Harriet H., 4074
McLoughlin, Merrill, 5407
McMiller, Darryl L., 5393
McMullen, Frances Drewry, 1419, 1935
McMurran, Kristin, 1122, 4624
McNeal, Margaret, 436
McPhee, Carol, 5664
McQuatters, Geneva F., 3385, 3386, 3480, 3527, 4734
McQuillen, Jacinta, 2009
McWilliams, Nancy, 5382
Mead, Margaret, 1784, 1785, 2289, 3542, 3601
Medsger, Betty, 3925
Meikle, Theresa, 4779

Author Index

Meisol, Patricia, 2791
Melcher, Dale, 800
Mellecker, Alsatia, 352
Melling, Louise, 3257
Mellon, Winifred, 3602
Melosh, Barbara, 571, 1724
Melville, Margarita B., 877
Melville, Mildred McClellan, 2064
Menchken, Henry Louis, 36
Mend, Michael R., 5346
Mendelson, Johanna S. R., 2290
Menkel-Meadow, Carrie, 3250, 3251
Menon, Lakshmi N., 2496
Merchant, Carolyn, 1341
Meredith, Ellis. *See* Clement, Ellis Meredith
Meredith, Emily, 308
Meredith, Mary Louise, 399
Mericle, Margaret, 2629
Meringolo, Denise D., 3566
Meriwether, Lida A., 521
Merk, Lois Bannister, 385, 2126
Merriam, Charles Edward, 2095, 2309, 4379
Merrick, Janna C., 5177
Merrill, Flora, 4792
Merritt, Sharyne, 3075, 3090, 4166, 5394
Merton, Andrew H., 1510
Mesta, Perle, 3528
Metcalf, Henry Harrison, 4529
Mettler, Suzanne, 4775
Meyer, Howard N., 986
Meyerowitz, Joanne, 1034
Mezey, Susan Gluck, 2515, 3022, 3116, 3968, 4239, 4240, 5067, 5623
Michel, Sonya, 5232, 5233
Michelet, Simon, 2370, 4479
Mikulski, Barbara, 2842, 4846
Mikusko, M. Brady, 5818
Miles, Angela, 5504
Milk, Leslie, 2031
Milkman, Ruth, 801, 4932, 4933
Miller, Anita, 5713
Miller, Arthur H., 2260, 2261
Miller, Bruce G., 2413
Miller, Dorothy, 5239
Miller, Holly G., 1985, 4407
Miller, Judy Ann, 3026
Miller, Karen Czarnecki, 3351
Miller, Kathleen Atkinson, 675
Miller, Kristie, 2831, 3686
Miller, Lawrence W., 3063, 3076
Miller, Liselen M., 1898
Miller, Lorna Clancy, 2021
Miller, Randall K., 5151
Miller, Sally M., 4661
Miller, Shari, 2516
Miller, Vivian, 4419
Miller, Warren E., 2211
Millett, Kate, 5107
Millmore, J. Timothy, 2630
Mills, Kay, 847, 3006, 3926

Mills, Trudy, 2041
Millsap, Mary Ann, 4807, 4808, 4809
Milrod, Patience, 3932
Mink, Patsy T., 3676
Minnis, Myra S., 1925, 1926
Minow, Martha, 3292, 5505
Mitchell, Gary, 3734
Mohr, James C., 5154
Mohr, Judith, 4188
Mohr, Lillian Holmen, 3420
Moley, Raymond, 5408
Molina, Gloria, 3927
Molinoff, Daniel D., 4983
Moncrief, Gary F., 2952, 2981, 2986, 2989
Moncure, Dorothy A., 2669
Mondale, Walter F., 4962
Monkturner, Elizabeth, 2262
Monoson, S. Sara, 1612
Monroe, Anne Shannon, 3274
Monroy, Dugleas, 763
Montgomery, James, 109
Moody, Anne, 848
Moody, Howard, 1275
Moore, Dorothea, 2056, 2057
Moore, Elsie Wallace, 2342
Moore, Emily C., 5155
Moore, Gwen, 2631
Moore, Laura, 549
Moore, Madeline, 2193
Moore, W. John, 3077
Mora, Magdalena, 878
Moraga, Cherrie, 1145
Moran, Barbara K., 1092
Moran, Gary, 3283
Moran, Kevin J., 813
More, Jr., Richter H., 3627
More, Wendell, 2751
Morehouse, Lawrence, 5156
Moreland, Laurence W., 4445
Moreland, Sinclair, 5901
Morgan, David, 161
Morgan, Georgia Cook, 4573
Morgan, Jenny, 5621
Morgan, Patricia, 5280
Morgan, Richard Gregory, 5157
Morgan, Robin, 1095, 1108
Morgan, Tom P., 2878
Morgen, Sandra, 1344, 1345, 1346, 1347, 2022, 5577, 5640
Morgenthau, Jr., Mrs. Henry, 1676
Morin, Ann Miller, 3529
Morin, Isobel V., 3329
Morphonios, Ellen, 3959
Morris, Allen, 3018, 3960
Morris, Ann, 3928
Morris, Celia, 2710, 2919, 2992, 4530, 5215
Morris, Cheryl Haun, 3761
Morris, J. Byron, 4027, 4030
Morris, Monia Cook, 405
Morris, Monica B., 1234, 5562

Morris, Robert C., 589
Morris, Terry, 1899
Morris, Victor P., 4897
Morrison, Ann M., 4824
Morrison, Betty, 3643
Morrison, Glenda Eileen, 1662
Morrison, Mary Foulke, 66
Morrison, Toni, 1161, 5536
Morrissey, Katherine G., 5847
Morrissey, William, 3091
Morrow, Elise, 4574
Morton, Marian J., 1420, 5311
Moses, Carolyn H., 4125
Moses, Wilson Jeremiah, 1135
Moses-Zinkes, 5033
Moskowitz, Belle L., 4693
Mosmiller, Thomas, 234
Moss, Kary L., 5073
Moss, Luella St. Clair, 2849
Motley, Constance Baker, 1004
Mott, David C., 4625
Mott, Jonathan D., 2728
Moulds, Elizabeth Fry, 4780
Mowry, Duane, 4335
Moyer-Wing, Alice C., 2371, 3104
Moynihan, Ruth Barnes, 275, 490
Mozee, Yvonne, 3317, 4210
Mueller, Carol M., 849, 987, 1212, 2263, 2264, 2291, 2497, 2517, 3187, 3820, 3821, 4735, 5367, 5571
Mueller, Ruth Caston, 1954
Mughan, Anthony, 1690
Muihead, Jean Denman, 4029
Mulford, Carolyn, 3422
Mullinax, Ira D., 476
Mullins, Carolyn, 3092, 3093
Mullins, Sharon Mitchell, 3963
Mumford, Laura Stempel, 5714
Muncy, Robyn, 614, 4911
Munds, Frances Willard, 286, 3903
Mundy, Alicia, 4626
Munro, Mary Herring, 2721
Munro, Petra, 2096
Muntz, Leonora Ferguson, 2081
Murdock, Margaret Maier, 3802
Murolo, Priscilla, 719
Murphy, Cliona, 67
Murphy, Fanny B., 4206
Murphy, Irene, 4736
Murray, Pauli, 949, 1109, 1162, 4922
Murray, Susan B., 5281
Murrell, Ethel Ernest, 918
Muskie, Jane, 1694
Mussey, Henry Raymond, 4825
Musslewhite, Lynn R., 4088
Myerhoff, Barbara G., 4732
Myers, Gloria E., 4300
Myers, Helen Linder, 4442
Myers, Sandra, 2528
Myron, Nancy, 1262

Nader, Laura, 3252

Subject Index

Alexander, Ruth Ann, 2167
Allen, Florence E., 1565, 1998, 3046, 3047, 3167, 3612, 3633, 4083, 4084
Allison, Ida B., 140
Alpern, Anne X., 4107
Alpha Kappa Alpha, 1979
Alpha Suffrage Club, 148, 339
Ambassadors, 3521, 3523–3527, 3529, 3531, 3532, 3576, 3706, 4378, 4594
American Association of University Women, 957, 1929–1931
  and Equal Rights Amendment campaign, 919, 966
  in Georgia, 5863
  in Maine, 2116, 2117
  in Missouri, 5881
  in Pennsylvania, 5891
  in Wisconsin, 5910
American Civil Liberties Union, 1749, 5073
American Indian Movement, 882, 896
Ames, Blanche, 384
Ames, Jessie Daniel, 674
Anderson, Elizabeth Preston, 634
Anderson, Eugenie, 3527
Anderson, Marian, 3549
Anderson, Mary, 647, 3433, 4270
Anderson, Sarah Elizabeth N., 4137
Androgyny, 5070, 5341
Anthony, Susan B., 1, 2, 23, 50, 80, 89, 100, 113
  collection guide, 5814
Anti-Saloon League, 4663
Appointments
  Cabinet, 3429–3431
  federal history of, 3473
  President Bush, 3422, 3444, 3493, 3578
  President Carter, 3317, 3416, 3421, 3423, 3462, 3489, 3490, 3500, 3509, 3520, 3577, 3579, 3585, 3587, 3588, 3621, 3626
  President Clinton, 3410, 3415, 3428, 3523, 3586
  President Eisenhower, 3412, 3426, 3452, 3454, 3481, 3484, 3491, 3524, 3535, 3604
  President Ford, 3425, 3426
  President Hoover, 3468
  President Johnson, 3461, 3476, 3531, 3581
  President Kennedy, 3464, 3474, 3485, 4571
  President Nixon, 3426, 3519, 3784
  President Reagan, 3422, 3426, 3478, 3494, 3499, 3580, 3583, 3584, 3626, 3706
  President Roosevelt (Franklin D.), 3408, 3411, 3420, 3424, 3439, 3482, 3505, 3506, 3507, 4378
  President Taft, 620
  President Truman, 3434, 3457, 3483, 3495, 3508, 3527, 3528, 4553, 4562, 4573
  President Wilson, 3465, 3486, 3517, 3544, 3546, 4378
  public office, 2481
  recruitment, 3188
Arizona
  auxiliary organizations, 2041
  biography, 5846, 5853, 5854
  Congressional Union, 287
  fundamentalism, 1538
  governor, 3898
  legislature, 2998, 3823, 3897, 3900–3905
  local government, 3094
  Native Americans, 3318, 3324
  school superintendents, 2297, 4214
  state treasurer, 3899
  strike, 798, 2041
  suffrage, 285, 286, 2414
  Supreme Court justice, 3627
  U.S. Congress, 3642, 3643
  voting, 2414
  women's clubs, 2042

Arkansas
  birth control, 5136
  city government, 3110, 4216, 4217
  civil rights, 825
  Equal Rights Amendment, 995
  participation, 2043
  prison, 3441
  legislature, 3906, 3907
  suffrage, 288–291, 2415
  U.S. Congress, 2808, 3644–3648
  women's clubs, 2044
Armstrong, Anne, 4594
Asian Americans
  acculturation, 869
  Asian Pacific, 870
  biography, 5791
  California, 4235
  Chinese, 1174, 4221
  feminism and, 1169–1174
  Hawaii, 1169, 1875
  Japanese, 4221
  judge, 4106
  lesbians, 1258
  liberation, 867
  Nisei Leader, 4569
  and prisons, 868
  and sexism, 871
  state legislatures and, 3676, 3677, 3967
  and the U.S. Congress, 2824, 2911, 3673, 3675–3677
Asian Women United of California, 1168
Association of Southern Women for the Prevention of Lynching, 672, 673, 675
Association Opposed to Woman Suffrage, 1452
Austin, Mary, 1336
Axtell, Frances C., 3546, 3547

Baca-Barragan, Polly, 2564, 3851
Bagley, Mrs. F. P., 606
Bailey, Consuelo Northrop, 4139, 4140, 4147
Bailey, John, 4552
Baird-Olson, Karren, 882
Baker, Ella, 849, 853
Baker, Howard, 2755
Balch, Emily Greene, 5825
Baldwin, Lola Green, 4300
Balick, Helen, 3620
Banks, Carolyn Long, 4167
Bannister, Marion Glass, 4557
Baptists, 139, 250, 995
Barkley v. Pool, 417
Barnard, Kate, 4085–4088, 4091
Barr, Daisy Douglas, 2101
Barrows, Mary Livermore, 4009
Bartelme, Mary, 4256
Bartlett, Marie, 4073
Bass, Charlotta A., 2936
Bass, Elizabeth, 4414, 4484, 4542, 4688
Bass, Mrs. George. *See* Bass, Elizabeth
Bates, Daisy, 825
Bathouse John, 3127
Battered women, 1324–1335, 5274–5287
  and the courts, 5261, 5279, 5283
  movement, 1325, 1332, 1333, 1335
  Native American, 5277
  public policy, 1324, 1328, 1331
Bedell, Catherine May, 2892, 3687, 3784, 3787
Bellamy, Carol, 4290
Belmont, Alva E., 96, 104, 173, 4770
Belmont, Mrs. O. H. P., 934
Berman, Maxine, 4014
Berry, Mary Frances, 904, 3537
Bethune, Mary McCleod, 3439, 3470, 3503
Beveridge, Albert J., 208

411